Effective Digital Marketing for Improving Society Behavior Toward DEI and SDGs

Inês Veiga Pereira
Accounting and Business School, Polytechnic of Porto, Portugal

Paulo Botelho Pires
Centre for Organizational and Social Studies, Polytechnic of Porto, Portugal

José Duarte Santos
Accounting and Business School, Polytechnic of Porto, Portugal

A volume in the Advances in Marketing, Customer Relationship Management, and E-Services (AMCRMES) Book Series

IGI Global
PUBLISHER of TIMELY KNOWLEDGE

Published in the United States of America by
IGI Global
Business Science Reference (an imprint of IGI Global)
701 E. Chocolate Avenue
Hershey PA, USA 17033
Tel: 717-533-8845
Fax: 717-533-8661
E-mail: cust@igi-global.com
Web site: http://www.igi-global.com

Library of Congress Cataloging-in-Publication Data

Names: Pereira, Inês Veiga, 1977- editor. | Pires, Paulo, 1967- editor. | Santos, José Duarte, 1966- editor.
Title: Effective digital marketing for improving society behavior toward DEI and SDGs / edited by: Inês Veiga Pereira, Paulo Botelho Pires, and José Duarte Santos.
Description: Hershey, PA : Business Science Reference, [2024] | Includes bibliographical references and index. | Summary: "This book offers readers a wide range of knowledge areas, including corporate social responsibility, marginalized communities, and sustainability index, providing the necessary skills to understand and apply different digital marketing and communication strategies. Aimed at a diverse audience, including management and marketing academics, digital marketing managers and consultants, social marketers, NPOs managers, and brand communication managers, this book serves as an essential guide for anyone seeking to develop effective digital marketing and communication strategies that promote DEI and contribute to achieving SDGs. By providing practical guidance on non-profit marketing, storytelling for DEI, and sustainability, the book helps organizations measure their impact, contributing to improved society behavior towards DEI and SDGs"-- Provided by publisher.
Identifiers: LCCN 2023025880 (print) | LCCN 2023025881 (ebook) | ISBN 9781668489840 (hardcover) | ISBN 9781668489857 (paperback) | ISBN 9781668489864 (ebook)
Subjects: LCSH: Social responsibility of business. | Internet marketing--Social aspects. | Business communication.
Classification: LCC HD60 .E336 2024 (print) | LCC HD60 (ebook) | DDC 658.8/72--dc23/eng/20230628
LC record available at https://lccn.loc.gov/2023025880
LC ebook record available at https://lccn.loc.gov/2023025881

This book is published in the IGI Global book series Advances in Marketing, Customer Relationship Management, and E-Services (AMCRMES) (ISSN: 2327-5502; eISSN: 2327-5529)

British Cataloguing in Publication Data
A Cataloguing in Publication record for this book is available from the British Library.

For electronic access to this publication, please contact: eresources@igi-global.com.

Advances in Marketing, Customer Relationship Management, and E-Services (AMCRMES) Book Series

Eldon Y. Li
National Chengchi University, Taiwan & California Polytechnic State University, USA

ISSN:2327-5502
EISSN:2327-5529

Mission

Business processes, services, and communications are important factors in the management of good customer relationship, which is the foundation of any well organized business. Technology continues to play a vital role in the organization and automation of business processes for marketing, sales, and customer service. These features aid in the attraction of new clients and maintaining existing relationships.

The Advances in Marketing, Customer Relationship Management, and E-Services (AMCRMES) Book Series addresses success factors for customer relationship management, marketing, and electronic services and its performance outcomes. This collection of reference source covers aspects of consumer behavior and marketing business strategies aiming towards researchers, scholars, and practitioners in the fields of marketing management.

Coverage

- Legal Considerations in E-Marketing
- Customer Retention
- E-Service Innovation
- Mobile CRM
- Telemarketing
- CRM in financial services
- CRM and customer trust
- Mobile Services
- Electronic Services
- B2B marketing

IGI Global is currently accepting manuscripts for publication within this series. To submit a proposal for a volume in this series, please contact our Acquisition Editors at Acquisitions@igi-global.com or visit: http://www.igi-global.com/publish/.

The Advances in Marketing, Customer Relationship Management, and E-Services (AMCRMES) Book Series (ISSN 2327-5502) is published by IGI Global, 701 E. Chocolate Avenue, Hershey, PA 17033-1240, USA, www.igi-global.com. This series is composed of titles available for purchase individually; each title is edited to be contextually exclusive from any other title within the series. For pricing and ordering information please visit http://www.igi-global.com/book-series/advances-marketing-customer-relationship-management/37150. Postmaster: Send all address changes to above address.

Titles in this Series

For a list of additional titles in this series, please visit: www.igi-global.com/book-series

The Rise of Blockchain Applications in Customer Experience
Mohammed Majeed (Tamale Technical University, Ghana) Kwame Simpe Ofori (International University of Grand Bassam, Cote D'Ivoire) George Kofi Amoako (Ghana Communication Technology University, Ghana) Abdul-Raheed Alolo (Tamale Technical University, Ghana) and Gideon Awini (Business School, University of Ghana, hana)
Business Science Reference • © 2024 • 300pp • H/C (ISBN: 9781668476499) • US $250.00

Sustainable Marketing, Branding, and Reputation Management Strategies for a Greener Future
Reason Masengu (Middle East College, Oman) Stanilas Bigirimana (Africa University, Zimbabwe) Option Takunda Chiwaridzo (University of Science and Technology, Beijing, China) Ruzive Bensson (Modern College of Business and Science, Oman) and Christina Blossom (Middle East College,Oman)
Business Science Reference • © 2023 • 670pp • H/C (ISBN: 9798369300190) • US $250.00

Origin and Branding in International Market Entry Processes
Carlos Francisco e Silva (Universidade Europeia, Portugal)
Business Science Reference • © 2023 • 298pp • H/C (ISBN: 9781668466131) • US $250.00

The Role of Brands in an Era of Over-Information
Ricardo Fontes Correia (Polytechnic Institute of Bragança, Portugal) Dominyka Venciūtė (ISM University of Management and Economics, Lithuania) and Bruno Miguel Sousa (Polytechnic Institute of Cávado and Ave, Portugal)
Business Science Reference • © 2023 • 257pp • H/C (ISBN: 9781668483510) • US $250.00

Influences of Social Media on Consumer Decision-Making Processes in the Food and Grocery Industry
Theodore Tarnanidis (International Hellenic University, Greece) Maro Vlachopoulou (University of Macedonia, Greece) and Jason Papathanasiou (University of Macedonia, Greece)
Business Science Reference • © 2023 • 317pp • H/C (ISBN: 9781668488683) • US $250.00

Contemporary Approaches of Digital Marketing and the Role of Machine Intelligence
Afzal Sayed Munna (University of Sunderland in London, UK) Md Sadeque Imam Shaikh (University of Wales Trinity Saint David, UK) and Baha Uddin Kazi (Humber Institute of Technology and Advanced Learning, Canada)
Business Science Reference • © 2023 • 260pp • H/C (ISBN: 9781668477359) • US $250.00

Social Media and Online Consumer Decision Making in the Fashion Industry
Theodore Tarnanidis (International Hellenic University, Greece) Evridiki Papachristou (International Hellenic University, Greece) Michail Karypidis (International Hellenic University, Greece) and Vasileios Ismyrlis (Hellenic Open University, Greece & Hellenic Statistical Authority, Greece)
Business Science Reference • © 2023 • 393pp • H/C (ISBN: 9781668487532) • US $250.00

IGI Global
PUBLISHER of TIMELY KNOWLEDGE

701 East Chocolate Avenue, Hershey, PA 17033, USA
Tel: 717-533-8845 x100 • Fax: 717-533-8661
E-Mail: cust@igi-global.com • www.igi-global.com

Table of Contents

Detailed Table of Contents

Not-for-profit organisations (NPOs) are active participants in the global efforts of making the world a better place for all. The fluctuating political climate and shrinking space for civil society in many countries worldwide, coupled with the disruptions caused by the Covid-19 pandemic, have heightened fundraising woes for NPOs, making it hard for them to financially sustain their missions. Through an extensive literature review, the chapter aimed at demonstrating how NPOs can leverage the power of digital marketing to build and maintain sustainable organisations to continue providing vital impactful services. It covers the importance and the types of digital marketing strategies for NPOs. The chapter established that digital marketing has emerged as a cost-effective way through which NPOs can expand their missions and promote DEI in society.

The use of social media in health is emerging as a means of bringing the various actors together with several benefits. In the specific case of cancer disease, these tools can help patients to improve their psychological well-being and their outcomes. As cancer is the cause of a quarter of deaths in Portugal, it is a pressing issue to understand which tools and information both patients and health professionals find most useful to build effective health social media. It was observed that there is a latent need for an oncology social environment, allowing greater well-being for patients and strengthening their relationship with health professionals and institutions, constituting an asset to the services provided. This chapter fills a gap in the bibliography by bringing together the views of both patients and health professionals from several areas, in close collaboration with the Francisco Gentil Portuguese Oncology Institute of Porto, E.P.E.

Deeba Hasan, Indian Institute of Technology, Madras, India
T. J. Kamalanabhan, Indian Institute of Technology, Madras, India

Rapidly proliferating organizational digital marketing communications (DMC) can adversely affect employees and, in turn, organizational success. Past research indicates that perceived organizational support (POS) engenders employee attitudinal and behavioral outcomes that warrant organizational success. However, studies evaluating the effects of POS on DMC employees are lacking. This study conducted an integrative literature review on POS to increase understanding related to it, determine how POS leads to DMC success, and facilitate organizational contribution towards SDGs 3, 8, and 16. Sixty-three papers were reviewed to conduct a qualitative thematic template analysis that identified significant themes of POS. The psychology of reciprocity was determined to engender DMC success. The mechanisms through which POS facilitates SDGs 3, 8, and 16 were illustrated. A conceptual framework is proposed delineating the pathway from POS to outcomes, including enablers, barriers, mediators, moderators, and boundary conditions. Future studies could identify more factors operating in this pathway.

Marcia Siqueira Costa Marques, Grupo Design e Convergencia, Brazil

This chapter provides a comprehensive examination of the multifaceted implications of diversity and inclusion within business and societal contexts. This elucidates the economic, image, and meaning dimensions of diversity and inclusion, highlighting their potential to foster social progress, enhance reputation, and improve financial performance. The chapter further delves into the challenges faced by organizations in implementing these initiatives, such as resistance to change, lack of diversity in leadership, and the need for greater accountability. Future directions for enhancing the effectiveness of diversity and inclusion efforts were also explored. This chapter aims to provide a deeper understanding of these concepts, emphasizing their critical role in the current globalized and interconnected world.

Ascensão Maria Martins Braga, University Polytechnic of Guarda, Portugal
Paulo Alexandre Vieira, University Polytechnic of Guarda, Portugal

One of the most important concerns of companies is engagement with stakeholders. One of the main ways of engaging is using gamification. To create engagement is the principal aim of a gamification system. In this work, and from literature, the authors survey how it has gamified the relationship between companies and stakeholders. The aim is to gather data to create a dataset for training an artificial neural network model. Among the artificial intelligence (AI) models, this kind of model has been the one that has been shown to increase human analytical capacity and is responsible for the emergence of generative AI. The final aim of this work is to create a generative AI that enables the design gamification system to create engagement between stakeholders and companies in the more diverse areas. This AI will be used as a service in a platform as a service (PaaS), where companies can get the best way to engage the stakeholders.

Every year, 1.3 billion pieces of food are wasted, which impacts the circular economy's (CE) effective transition, and greater knowledge of the consumer's opinion and valorisation of food waste has positive consequences on food safety, the environment and sustainable consumption. There are different platforms and apps for improving food waste behaviour, some linked to social concerns and others trying to achieve circular economy goals. This study aims to analyse the influence drivers of users' motivation to use these food waste technologies in Portugal. It follows a qualitative approach to fully understand the user's motivation and link to their social and environmental concerns. Results revealed that most of the interviewees who used these platforms/apps were driven by economic influences and had environmental concerns. Identifying the users' drivers of influence on food waste and reflecting on the consequences for businesses and their marketing strategies on positioning and communication was possible, so promoting behaviour to facilitate the social dimension of the CE transition.

Based on a conceptual discussion, this chapter focused on current consumer behavior, with a special emphasis on its relationship with sustainability, and on the recent sustainable practices of companies. Through the analysis of these two pillars, this narrative review aimed to frame sustainability and emphasize the greenwashing processes that take place in this context. To this end, some reasons why sustainability has been a major subject of debate in recent decades and also evidence on consumer behavior about this discussion were pointed out. The role of companies was also outlined – through corporate social responsibility practices – bridging the issue of greenwashing. As a negative aspect associated with sustainability, greenwashing was observed in depth, with a special focus on the digital environment, and in the context of marketing and influence.

Preface

Dear Readers,

In a world driven by progress and innovation, the pursuit of Diversity, Equity, and Inclusion (DEI) and the realization of the United Nations Sustainable Development Goals (SDGs) have become defining challenges for societies and organizations alike. As editors of *Effective Digital Marketing for Improving Society Behavior Toward DEI and SDGs*, we are delighted to present this comprehensive reference book, offering insights and strategies that can empower you to make a meaningful impact on these vital global initiatives.

Diversity, equity, and inclusion are not merely buzzwords; they are central to building a just and sustainable future. As the world evolves, so too does the importance of digital communications in advancing these goals. The capacity of digital marketing to bridge gaps and amplify messages has become a powerful tool for both for-profit and non-profit organizations. It is within these digital realms that the promise of equity and the pursuit of SDGs find their footing.

In the digital landscape, organizations face multifaceted challenges. They must define their primary objectives, identify how to align with one or more SDGs, determine the most effective means of engaging their target audiences, and measure the impact of their strategies on company performance. These complexities underscore the need for an interdisciplinary approach that integrates diverse knowledge areas, experiences, and best practices.

This book aspires to encompass the full spectrum of expertise required to navigate the world of digital marketing and communication, with a laser focus on diversity, equity, and inclusion. Our mission is to furnish you, the reader, with the knowledge and skills to comprehend, apply, and innovate with the myriad concepts, techniques, and tools that underpin digital marketing and communication strategies, all in service of promoting positive social behavior toward DEI and SDGs.

Our target audience is as diverse as the challenges themselves. Whether you are a management or marketing academic looking to delve into new ideas, a researcher seeking to keep pace with evolving concepts and methodologies, a digital marketing manager or consultant navigating the complex terrain of corporate social responsibility, or a non-profit organization leader or brand communication manager driven to harness the power of storytelling and creativity, this book is designed with your needs in mind.

The array of topics covered within this volume reflects the interplay of digital marketing and communication with DEI and SDGs. From business communication to circular economy, corporate social responsibility to non-profit marketing, and from sustainability to the art of storytelling, each chapter is a piece in the larger puzzle of societal change. The chapters interconnect, forming a tapestry of insights and strategies to help you navigate this ever-evolving landscape.

In Chapter 1, the authors dive into the challenges that non-profit organizations (NPOs) face in a world of fluctuating political climates and fundraising woes. They explore how NPOs can employ digital marketing to build sustainable organizations, ensuring they can continue to provide vital services and promote diversity, equity, and inclusion (DEI) within society. Through an extensive literature review, this chapter uncovers the importance and types of digital marketing strategies tailored to the unique needs of NPOs. The authors emphasize that digital marketing offers a cost-effective means for NPOs to expand their missions and foster DEI.

Chapter 2 delves into the world of health and social media, with a specific focus on cancer patients. It examines the potential benefits of using social media tools to enhance the psychological well-being and outcomes of individuals battling cancer. By exploring the views of both patients and health professionals, in collaboration with the Portuguese Oncology Institute of Porto, the authors shed light on the need for a dedicated oncology social environment. This chapter fills a critical gap in the literature by providing insights into the tools and information that can empower patients and strengthen their relationship with healthcare professionals.

Chapter 3 explores the world of lifestyle applications from a user perspective, shedding light on the reasons behind non-usage. Drawing from focus group interviews with students, the authors identify favored applications and the significant factors influencing user preferences. They also delve into the effects of these applications on physical and mental health and highlight the barriers that lead to non-usage. This chapter contributes valuable insights into the changing landscape of health practices and mobile device usage, offering a unique perspective on the field of service literature.

The authors of Chapter 4 delve into the world of social media marketing for non-profit organizations (NPOs). In a qualitative approach, they conduct an integrative literature review from 2013 to 2021, aiming to elucidate the state of the art in the use of social media marketing for NPOs. They seek to identify the most successful social media tools for NPOs in securing donors and meeting fundraising goals. Through their work, they aim to bridge the gap between academic knowledge and practical application in the realm of social media marketing for NPOs.

Chapter 5 embarks on an analysis of the main Search Engine Optimization (SEO) metrics of significant social marketing associations worldwide. The authors introduce research objectives, offer theoretical systematization, detail their methodology, and provide empirical evidence to answer research questions. Furthermore, they discuss the practical implications, while acknowledging the limitations and suggesting future research directions. This chapter highlights the importance of improving the online visibility of social marketing associations in an age of social media marketing.

In Chapter 6, the authors explore the concept of transmedia storytelling and its profound impact on building understanding and attitudes towards the United Nations Sustainable Development Goals (SDGs). Transmedia storytelling is a method employed by entertainment franchises, as well as in marketing and education. The authors discuss the foundations of transmedia storytelling and how it can be harnessed to promote awareness and action regarding SDGs.

Chapter 7 shines a light on the crucial intersection of digital marketing and Diversity, Equity, and Inclusion (DEI). The authors emphasize the significance of incorporating DEI principles into digital marketing campaigns, content creation, and overall marketing strategies. By doing so, organizations can strengthen their online presence and build meaningful connections with diverse audiences. This chapter underscores the strategic advantage of embracing DEI in digital marketing, both as a moral imperative and a means to unlock new opportunities.

Chapter 8 investigates consumer perceptions of brand-associated controversy in marketing. It delves into the role of subjectivity in shaping consumer behavior and cognitive processing in comprehending information. Through an experimental study, the authors explore the interaction between brand presence and controversial topics, shedding light on how consumers associate branded content with irritation. This chapter offers valuable insights into the complexities of marketing in a world where consumer perceptions are shaped by cognitive processes and cultural backgrounds.

Chapter 9 takes an integrative approach to examine the effects of perceived organizational support (POS) on employees engaged in digital marketing communications. The authors conduct a qualitative thematic analysis to identify significant themes of POS and illustrate the mechanisms through which POS leads to digital marketing communication success. The chapter provides a conceptual framework for understanding the pathway from POS to outcomes and highlights the enablers, barriers, mediators, and moderators in this context. Additionally, it explores the contributions of POS to achieving Sustainable Development Goals (SDGs) 3, 8, and 16.

Chapter 10 provides an in-depth examination of the multifaceted implications of diversity and inclusion within business and societal contexts. It explores the economic, image, and meaning dimensions of diversity and inclusion and their potential to foster social progress, enhance reputation, and improve financial performance. The chapter also highlights the challenges organizations face in implementing these initiatives, such as resistance to change and the lack of diversity in leadership. It offers insights into future directions for enhancing the effectiveness of diversity and inclusion efforts.

Chapter 11 focuses on the use of gamification to engage stakeholders, a key concern for companies. The authors examine how gamification can foster engagement and its applications in diverse areas. The ultimate goal is to create a generative AI that facilitates the design of gamification systems for engagement between stakeholders and companies. This chapter takes a forward-looking approach, recognizing the potential of AI and gamification to shape the future of stakeholder-company interactions.

In Chapter 12, the authors explore the influence drivers behind users' motivation to engage with food waste technologies. With a qualitative approach, they uncover the motivations of users and the role of economic influences and environmental concerns in driving engagement with platforms and apps designed to combat food waste. This chapter provides insights into the social and environmental dimensions of the circular economy transition, offering valuable input for businesses and their marketing strategies.

Chapter 13 takes a conceptual discussion approach, focusing on consumer behavior in the context of sustainability and recent sustainable practices of companies. It delves into the reasons why sustainability has become a major topic of debate and the role of companies in shaping sustainability through Corporate Social Responsibility practices. The chapter also explores the issue of greenwashing in the digital marketing landscape, emphasizing the relationship between marketing and influence in this context.

Chapter 14 evaluates and compares the approaches of European and Slovak cities to city branding, with a specific focus on the utilization of digital marketing communication tools. Through questionnaire surveys and an examination of the branding process in Amsterdam, the authors provide insights into the current approaches to urban branding in various cities. This chapter highlights the importance of city branding as a systematic and targeted process aimed at shaping a city's positive image and promoting it on the market.

We extend our gratitude to the contributors who have shared their expertise and experience to make this book a reality. We also thank our readers for your commitment to making the world a better place. The knowledge within these pages can be the catalyst for meaningful change, one step at a time.

Inês Veiga Pereira
Accounting and Business School, Polytechnic of Porto, Portugal

Paulo Botelho Pires
Centre for Organizational and Social Studies, Polytechnic of Porto, Portugal

José Duarte Santos
Accounting and Business School, Polytechnic of Porto, Portugal

Chapter 1
Digital Marketing for NPOs

Edward Mudzimba
https://orcid.org/0000-0002-6278-2605
Midlands State University, Zimbabwe

Fainos Chokera
https://orcid.org/0000-0002-1270-7682
Midlands State University, Zimbabwe

Mercy Dube
https://orcid.org/0000-0003-0429-8441
Midlands State University, Zimbabwe

ABSTRACT

Not-for-profit organisations (NPOs) are active participants in the global efforts of making the world a better place for all. The fluctuating political climate and shrinking space for civil society in many countries worldwide, coupled with the disruptions caused by the Covid-19 pandemic, have heightened fundraising woes for NPOs, making it hard for them to financially sustain their missions. Through an extensive literature review, the chapter aimed at demonstrating how NPOs can leverage the power of digital marketing to build and maintain sustainable organisations to continue providing vital impactful services. It covers the importance and the types of digital marketing strategies for NPOs. The chapter established that digital marketing has emerged as a cost-effective way through which NPOs can expand their missions and promote DEI in society.

1. INTRODUCTION

The tremendous developments in Information and Communication Technologies (ICTs) have significantly altered how business is conducted across the broad spectrum of industries. Due to the disruptive nature of technology in recent years Musingwini et al., (2023) opined that the world is witnessing a variety of new ways of doing things we could not have imagined a few decades ago. One such business practice which has significantly been disrupted by the changes in technology is the field of marketing.

DOI: 10.4018/978-1-6684-8984-0.ch001

The incorporation of ICTs and or the Internet in marketing has given birth to the field of digital marketing, a term that emerged three decades ago and has now become an established practice. To date, digital marketing tools have transformed how organizations engage with their stakeholders, allowing them to become active participants in organizational activities (Seo &Vu, 2020; Wang & Kim, 2017). Marketing is the heart of a successful company in every field including the non-commercial sector (Maxim, 2016). We, therefore, argue in this chapter that there is a myriad of benefits that NPOs stand to benefit from through the adoption of digital marketing tools. This is because marketing to NPOs has both social and economic benefits as it aids in addressing a wide range of society's problems which includes the need to promote diversity, equality, and inclusion.

Using an extensive literature review, the authors explored a wide range of refereed journals and articles in the fields of digital marketing and NPOs. The study revealed that NPOs have a myriad of digital marketing strategies at their disposal that they can utilize to enhance their brand visibility and attract more followers who can support their causes. It also emerged in the study that, for effective implementation of digital marketing campaigns, NPOs must generate relevant content resonating with their causes and consistently feed it across all their digital marketing channels. The study concluded that digital marketing, a concept that has been widely used by commercial entities, can also change the fortunes of non-commercial entities like NPOs by strengthening and cementing constituent relationships.

The chapter starts by providing a historical background on the digital marketing concept and its importance to NPOs. The authors then proceeded to examine the various digital marketing strategies that NPOs can use to promote their missions across different constituencies and the challenges they face in implementing these strategies. A discussion and reflection section follows, which seeks to synthesise the major issues that emerged from the review. The chapter ends with a section on recommendations and a conclusion section.

2. BACKGROUND, HISTORY, AND CONTEXT

Digital marketing is a term that came in the 1990s. It is often used interchangeably with online marketing, internet marketing, or web marketing. It is however important to note that online marketing and digital marketing in not the same thing, digital marketing is broader and encompasses online marketing (Desai, 2019; Uma &Simran, 2021). Digital marketing represents the marketing of products and services using digital technologies mainly the internet but also includes display advertising, mobile phones, and other digital platforms. It extends beyond the Internet to incorporate channels that do not require the use of the Internet like short message services (SMS), and electronic or interactive billboards to promote products and services. It remains difficult to credit a single person to the emergence of digital marketing as several people played a part in what it is today. However, others believe that Guglielmo Marconi who invented the radio was the first digital marketer, and another notable figure was Ray Tomlison because he was the first person to send an email in 1971. Figure 1 provides a preview of major historical developments which summarizes the evolution of digital marketing to what it is today.

As shown in Figure 1, the origin of digital marketing can be traced to the early 1970s when the first email and the first cell phone were developed in 1971 and 1973 respectively. While the term digital marketing was popularized in the 1990s the way it was conducted was by far different to what we are witnessing nowadays. The major reason for this emanated from the fact that it relied on Web 1.0 and during this time there were no real communities. Additionally, the content posted was not as captivating as

Figure 1. The evolution of digital marketing
Source: https://www.mediaocean.com/digital-marketing-guide/overview-history

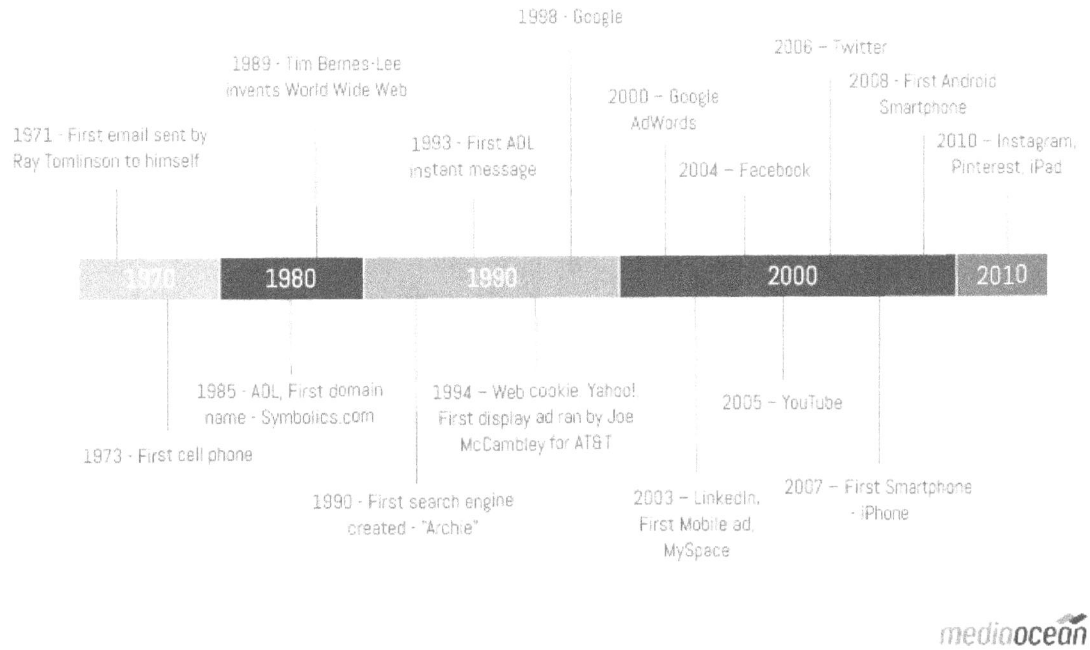

we now see today but rather static with limited interaction opportunities. Notable digital marketing was not until 1993 when the first clickable banner was launched and HotWired bought some of the banner ads for their advertising campaign. Before this around 1991 however, a network protocol called Gopher had already launched the first search engine. It is important to note also that search engines however as we know them today according to Kingsnorth (2016) emanated from the first web crawler (called WebCrawler) which can into existence in 1994. In the year 2000, the internet bubble burst and a majority of small search engines were wiped out of the market by the giants. This was an era when Google had just been launched in 1998 and Yahoo and Microsoft had just launched their search engines Yahoo web search and MSN respectively. This era significantly transformed the digital marketing landscape and witnessed its first steep surge, which came after search engine traffic had already witnessed a growth of 6.4 billion in a single month. The majority of social media platforms emerged in 2003. The first social network platform launched was MySpace in 2003, followed by Facebook in 2004, YouTube came in 2005, and Twitter in 2006. The emergence of social network sites presented tremendous opportunities for marketers to promote their offerings. Smartphones particularly the iPhone and the Android came in the years 2007 and 2008 respectively and together with social media, these devices have significantly altered the marketing landscape allowing corporates fast and cheap access to their target markets.

To date, digital marketing is a broad area and comes in several forms like content marketing, e-commerce, data-driven marketing, search engine optimization, search engine marketing, influencer marketing, social media marketing, email marketing, display advertising, social media optimization, e-books, games, optical disks, SMS, MMS, call back and on-hold mobile rings (Desai, 2019). We therefore argue that the adoption of these tools by NPOs will go a long way in ensuring the continued provision of vital services in society.

Not-for-profit organizations (NPOs) are those organizations that are not driven by profit but by dedication to a given cause. They are created to serve the public good in some way and do not distribute profits to their owners, but profits are used for furthering the advancement of the organization. They are usually created to champion religious, charitable, scientific, literary, or educational purposes (Hanna, 2022) and they include universities, art museums, religious congregations, hospitals, environmental groups, community development organizations, political parties, social clubs, labor unions and others (Boris & Steuerle, 1999).

NPOs have historically played a pivotal role in trying to resolve the challenges and inequalities within communities across the world. They play a significant role in advocating for the rights of the marginalized (Chikwanda, 2020). They work to make the world a better place for all. It can thus be added that the pursuit of the various causes by NPOs to a larger extent promotes diversity, equality, and inclusion (DEI) across societies worldwide. Of special concern, however, is the fact that these vital organizations have not been spared by the disruption that was caused by the Covid-19 pandemic. In one report conducted by Charities Aid Foundation of America among 544 NPOs in 93 countries, it emerged that NPOs were largely impacted by the Covid -19 pandemic negatively through reduced contributions, disrupting contact with donors and beneficiaries, affecting staffing, operations, and supply chains (Cafamerica.org, 2020). Similarly, Epic-Africa surveyed 1 015 civil society organizations from 44 African countries about the impact of Covid-19. The results of the survey showed that 56% of NPOs experienced funding losses, while 66% had expected financial loss within the next three to six months. A total of 69% said they had reduced or ceased operations (Epic-Africa and African NGOs, 2020.

Apart from the above, the current fluctuating political climate and shrinking space for civil society in many countries worldwide have heightened fundraising woes for NPOs making it hard for them to financially sustain their missions. In countries such as Zimbabwe, Mali, and Uganda for instance legal barriers have been erected barring NPOs from pursuing their missions (Biryabarema, 2022; Kouyate, 2022; Ndangana, 2022). Equality and inclusion are at stake not only in communities but even within the structures of NPOs, with some countries like Afghanistan going to the extent of banning women from working for foreign NPOs (Farzan et al., 2022). On top of the above challenges, past studies have shown that many NPOs lack the strategies to build and maintain a sustainable organization to continue providing vital impactful services (Chikwanda, 2022). We thus argue in this chapter that while long ago promotional campaigns could succeed by incorporating digital activities as add-ons to traditional marketing activities, nowadays the ongoing digital transformation is now calling upon marketing practitioners to re-think and design clear and targeted digital strategies to enable their brands to remain relevant on the market. The next subsection looks at the importance of digital marketing to NPOs.

3. THE IMPORTANCE OF DIGITAL MARKETING TO NPOS

It has been established that leaders of NPOs are increasingly under pressure to prove and assure their constituencies that they have effective and efficient measures in place to achieve their missions and goals (Murray, 2005). Many authors among them Pinto et al. (2019), Srivastava (2018) as well as Judhay and Yallatti, (2018) concur on the fact that the adoption of digital marketing strategies by NPOs promotes efficiency in the sense that it can cheaply and easily target multiple stakeholders and has instant analytics to assess whether the marketing efforts were effective or not. Apart from promoting efficiency and enabling impact assessment of a marketing program, digital marketing strategies are crucial to NPOs as they promote engagement leading to the establishment of strong relationships with key stakeholders (Appel et al., 2020; Wang & Kim, 2017). In similar fashion Seo and Vu (2020), pointed out that digital marketing practices particularly the personalization and tailoring of messages could result in the building of strong relationships between NPOs and their key stakeholders. Equally important is the fact that digital marketing promotes instant dialogue by providing a two-way communication where NPO executives can receive and give feedback to key stakeholders (Pinto et al., 2019; Srivastava. 2018) which results in the building of strong relationships. The above authors thus agree with the fact that digital marketing leads to the establishment of quality relationships between NPOs and their stakeholders.

The need for a quality relationship with stakeholders was also emphasized by Waters (2008), who asserts that donors hold NPOs in high regard as far as the values of transparency and accountability are concerned, a fact that underscores the need for NPO leaders to spend much of their time cultivating strong relationships with existing and potential donors. On the issue of donations, it has been established that a significant chunk of NPO funds come from donations, and without donors, the ability of NPOs to run programs to support their missions would be nearly impossible (Mitchell & Calabrese, 2019; Shin, 2019). Furthermore, Xu and Saxton (2019) clarified the above arguing that to attain the demands of their mission, NPOs rely on stakeholders' donation of time, money, and other resources. Many authors among them Milde and Yawson (2017), Bala and Verma (2018) as well as Istvacic et al. (2017) concur on the notion that digital marketing affords NPO executives a cost-effective way of growing and maintaining a donor base. In particular, Milde and Yawson (2017), emphasizes that through digital marketing NPO executives can share their missions and goals with donors cheaply regardless of their location. More so, Zuzana and Dagmar (2021) argue that digital marketing can be used to provide the various ways in which stakeholders and partners can support an NPO's mission. Apart from the above the important role of digital marketing in attracting donations was also emphasized by Quevedo and Quevedo-Prince (2019) who argued that while NPO executives do not have control over stakeholders' disposable income they can at least impact stakeholders' knowledge of their missions and goals, which can go a long way in influencing future intention to donate. Apart from the above, digital marketing can also be utilized by NPOs to recruit volunteers, board members, and other supporters (Zuzana & Dagmar, 2021). Given the above benefits which can accrue to NPOs through implementing digital marketing strategies, the next subsection looks at the various digital marketing strategies which can be adopted by NPOs.

4. DIGITAL MARKETING STRATEGIES FOR NPOS

There are quite several digital marketing strategies which can be utilized by companies. In this subsection, the authors provide the common digital marketing strategies that NPOs may utilize to promote their missions. These include social media marketing, email marketing, content marketing, search engine optimization, and website marketing.

4.1. Social-Media Marketing Strategies for NPOs

Social media platforms have brought enormous opportunities for firms across the broad spectrum of industries in both developed and developing nations. With their unique capabilities, these platforms have significantly transformed the marketing field. One example of an NPO that effectively uses social media is the World Wildlife Fund (WWF). The WWF uses social media to raise awareness about environmental issues and encourage action. Through the power of social media, WWF has a strong presence on Facebook, Twitter, and Instagram, and this allows for creating content that is tailored to each platform. For example, WWF created a Facebook post that encourages communities to reduce plastic use by using reusable bags. They also created an Instagram post that showcases the beauty of nature and encourages people to protect it.

4.1.1. Understanding Social Media Marketing

Deepa and Deshmukh (2013) opined that social media marketing involves strategies that business leaders use to participate in networks of online people. Furthermore, Kirby and Marsden (2006), define social media marketing as representing all marketing techniques that are deployed online to stimulate users to talk positively about a brand, a company, a product, or a service. From the above it can be noted that the concept of social media marketing is in simple terms, marketing through social media platforms. Social media marketing strategies have been heralded as one of the main pillars for successfully operating a business in the 21st century (Felix et al., 2017). Similarly, Millaet al. (2018) have suggested that social media will remain the main form of communication for NPOs future. The reasons for the adoption of social media by NPOs include enhancing cost efficiency and increasing marketing orientation (Water et al., 2017; Zor et., 2011). Furthermore, the usage of these platforms has also been motivated by the need to enhance stakeholder engagement (Ihm, 2015)

4.1.2. Benefits of Social Media Marketing to NPOs

Many authors have suggested a wide range of benefits that tend to accrue to NPOs which have included social media marketing among their digital marketing portfolios. According to Soboleva et al. (2017) one of the major benefits of social media marketing is that it enhances the overall efficiency of the marketing programme. This is true if one considers the fact that through social media platforms, NPO management is offered an opportunity to engage in a dialogue with key stakeholders, which promotes stakeholder engagement and reinforcement of existing relationships (Ihm, 2015). More so, authors such as Fink et al. (2020) as well as Milla et al. (2018) have singled out the usage of communication platforms like YouTube, WhatsApp, Instagram, and Facebook by NPOs as offering enormous efficiency, reach and intimacy. Likewise, the Twitter platform has also been acknowledged as a useful instrument in cementing relationships between NPOs and their corporate partners (Soboleva et al., 2017). More broadly Namisango et al. (2019), alleges that stakeholder engagement through social media platforms by NPOs promotes information exchange, co-creation, innovation, community building, collective action, reputation, and legitimacy. Idealware (2012), cautioned that if an NPO has not yet established its presence on social media in this era, it is missing a great deal of support and potential revenue, for the greater part of the world's population is now connected to social media supporting causes they identify with and the people they like. From the above, it can be established that the marketing of NPOs through social media presence has enormous benefits.

Apart from the above benefits, some authors have identified challenges that have been associated with the usage of social media marketing by NPOs. Campbell et al. (2014) noted issues such as institutional policies, client confidentiality, and inappropriateness of target audiences among the major shortfalls of social media marketing. Other obvious hindrances to social media marketing efforts by NPOs could emanate from infrastructural issues such as the availability of electricity, the internet, and the high cost of smart devices. Some of the factors may negatively largely impact the efforts of NPOs to reach their targets in developing economies, thus impacting efforts to promote inclusion, equity, and diversity globally.

4.1.3. Key Success Factors for Social Media Marketing for NPOs

For the successful implementation of a social media marketing campaign, several issues have been identified as key. One of the major factors which have been identified as a key determinant of a successful social media campaign is the establishment of a social media policy. According to Idealware (2012), a social media policy is vital to the success of a social media marketing campaign as it frees the staff to think more strategically by guiding what should and should not be done when interacting and posting on social media platforms. Furthermore, Kanter and Paine (2012) highlighted that the crafting of a social media strategy will go a long way in aiding the attainment of NPO goals as it guarantees the transmission of clear and consistent messages to stakeholders. Apart from the establishment of a social media policy, the selection of appropriate platforms has also been identified as vital for the success of a social media marketing campaign. Many authors among them, Lovejoy and Saxton, 2012 as well as Burton and Daellenbach (2017) concurred on the notion that the success of a social media campaign strategy by NPOs hinges on the ability of the managers to selection of relevant platforms to use for the campaign. It can thus be necessary for NPOs to research the preferred platforms for their stakeholders.

Apart from the above factors, the quality of communication has also been cited as a key determinant of a successful social media campaign (Carboni & Maxwell, 2015). Quality is largely in terms of the nature of information sent by NPOs to stakeholders. In this regard, Zuzana and Dagmar (2020) suggested that NPOs need to constantly update their social media accounts with relevant content in all formats like videos, pictures, and audio. Furthermore, these authors revealed that NPOs can also share reports on their activities and thank donors and volunteers for the support they render to the organization. In the same way, Idealware (2012) opined that the content shared must be worth sharing and NPOs must use tactics like storytelling, humor, and urgency to grab the attention of stakeholders. In a similar fashion Chary (2014) argued that NPO leaders need to create content that attracts and inspires the audience to share information with others. In sharing information NPO leadership must be careful and share information that they own or have sought permission from the owners, so as not to be found wanting on matters of intellectual property. In general, on social media, there is a lot of posting personal information like names, health matters, pictures, private contact numbers, and personal songs without contacting the owners which can expose a company to lawsuits. Apart from the above NPOs need to utilise different channels, multimodal streaming of communication can help NPOs to create a close bond with their partners and they also stand to benefit from the cross-channel and echo channel effect. According to Kanter and Paine (2012) for NPOs to reap the rewards of using different social media platforms the messages relayed on each platform must be unified, integrated, and interchangeable. What is posted on Facebook for instance must not contradict what has been sent on twitter. Furthermore, for effective utilization of social media for digital marketing, Idealware (2012) highlighted that NPOs need also to assign specific individuals for monitoring and tracking of questions and relevant comments and mentions. While this task nowadays can be attained through utilizing social listening and other analytics tools it remains important to know who can and who cannot do what of organizational social media pages.

4.2. Content Marketing Strategies for NPOs

Not-for-profit organizations (NPOs) have the same goal as any other business: to reach and engage their target audience (Musikavanhu et al., 2022). However, unlike their for-profit counterparts, NPOs may face unique challenges when it comes to content marketing. They need to create compelling content that resonates with their target audience while also fulfilling their mission and purpose. In this subsection, the authors will define content marketing and explore the various content marketing strategies for not-for-profit organizations. We will also discuss the importance of storytelling and the benefits of video content. Additionally, we will provide tips for creating a content marketing plan that aligns with an NPO's goals and objectives.

4.2.1. Understanding Content Marketing

Content marketing is a term used to refer to a method of marketing that includes creating and sharing online content that does not only promote a brand but more importantly designed to encourage its audience to visit a brand's website (Baker, 2022). In other words, content marketing is about the development and distribution of relevant, useful content – blogs, newsletters, white papers, social media posts, emails, and videos among others to current and potential customers. In support to the above, Muller and Christandl (2019) opine that content marketing engages customers at the appropriate point of buying as it converts customers into beneficial business outcomes. Perhaps, a vivid definition of content marketing for NPOs comes from Yodelpop (2021) who describes content marketing for NPOs as involving creating and distributing valuable, relevant, and consistent content in an endeavour to attract and retain a clearly defined audience and ultimately to drive that audience to take action that advances the organization's vision. Perhaps a more suitable definition of content marketing for NPOs comes from Baglioni et al. (2017) and Choto et al. (2020) who opine that NGOs do not exist to make a profit but rather to add value to society through their positive impactful activities. Elsewhere, as given by Rose (2016), content marketing involves several steps that include (1) content planning, (2) content creation, (3) asset development, (4) shareability and viral marketing, (5) content promotion, (6) repurposing and (7) ongoing measurement. Generally, content marketing is about brand awareness which is increased through various strategies including storytelling and information sharing.

4.2.2. The Importance of Storytelling

Storytelling is a powerful tool for any organization, but it can be especially impactful for not-for-profit organizations. Sharing stories of impact and success can help donors and supporters feel connected to the cause, which can encourage them to give and get involved (Miller, 2013). When crafting a storytelling strategy, it is essential to focus on the emotional impact of your work. Share stories of individuals or communities that have been positively impacted by your organization's efforts. Use descriptive language and imagery to create a vivid picture of the difference your organization is making. One effective storytelling strategy is to use a "before and after" approach. For example, sharing a story of someone who was struggling before they received help from an organization and how their life has improved since then. In his book, Miller (2013), storytelling using a "before and after" approach can be especially impactful for organizations that work in areas like healthcare, education, or poverty relief.

4.2.3. The Benefits of Video Content

Video content is becoming increasingly popular in the world of content marketing and for a good reason. As is already known, videos can be incredibly engaging and can convey complex information quickly and effectively (Baker, 2022). For not-for-profit organizations, video content can be especially impactful. For example, one effective video content strategy is to create short, impactful videos that highlight the impact of the organization's work. One example of an NPO that effectively uses video content is the American Red Cross. The American Red Cross uses video content to share the impact of their work and encourage donations. For example, they created a video that tells the story of a woman named Deidre who was helped by the American Red Cross after a house fire. In the video content strategy, NPOs should use emotional storytelling to create a powerful message and encourage donations (Baker, 2022). The videos should be emotionally engaging, using storytelling techniques to create a powerful message. Additionally, NPOs can create explainer videos that provide an overview of the organization's mission and purpose. Live streaming is another powerful technique for not-for-profit organizations as it allows organizations to connect with their audience in real-time, creating a sense of community and connection. Besides, live streaming events or fundraisers provides behind-the-scenes access to the organization's work as well as hosting Q&A sessions with your team (Schrage et al., 2019)

4.2.4. Creating a Content Marketing Plan

To make the most of content marketing, not-for-profit organizations need to create a strategic plan (Schrage et al., 2019). This plan should align with your organization's goals and objectives, focusing on the key messages and themes that are most important to the NPO's mission. When creating the organization's content marketing plan, it is advisable to start by (1) defining the target audience (2) specifying the target audience and decide on the content that resonates with them, (3) considering the platforms that will be used to reach the audience, (4) deciding on the social media platforms that are most effective, as well as (5) making the most of content marketing (du Plessis, 2017). One example of an NPO that effectively creates a content marketing plan is the National Park Foundation (NPF). The NPF creates a content marketing plan that aligns well with its goals and objectives. For example, NPF created a social media campaign that encourages people to visit national parks and share their experiences on social media using the hashtag #FindYourPark. This campaign aligns with the NPF's goal of encouraging people to connect with and support national parks.

4.3. Search Engine Optimization (SEO) for NPOs

According to Google's Search Engine Optimization Starter Guide (2013), SEO is a series of modifications, and techniques that make it easier for search engines to crawl, index, and understand the content of a website. Search engine optimization (SEO) is an essential aspect of digital marketing for not-for-profit organizations. With the growing number of organizations vying for attention online, it is crucial for non-profit organizations to adopt effective SEO strategies to increase their online visibility, attract more traffic to their websites, and ultimately drive more donations and support for their causes. In this chapter, we will provide an overview of SEO for not-for-profit organizations, including the key factors that influence search rankings, best practices for optimizing content and website structure, and tips for measuring SEO success. We will also examine case studies of successful SEO strategies employed by non-profit organizations and the impact they have had on their overall mission.

Non-profit organizations rely heavily on donations and support from the public to achieve their mission. In today's digital age, having a strong online presence is critical to reaching a wider audience and generating support. SEO is a key tool for achieving this goal. By optimizing their website and content for search engines, non-profit organizations can increase their visibility in search results, attract more traffic to their site, and ultimately drive more donations and support for their cause (Iqbal et al., 2022). Research has shown that most online experiences begin with a search engine, making SEO a vital component of any non-profit organization's digital marketing strategy (Cho et al., 2014). According to a survey by the Nonprofit Technology Network, 93% of non-profit organizations have a website, but only 27% of them have a documented SEO strategy in place (NTEN, 2019). This highlights the need for non-profit organizations to prioritize SEO in their digital marketing efforts.

4.3.1. Best Practices for SEO Optimization

To improve their search rankings and increase their online visibility, non-profit organizations should adopt best practices for SEO optimization. These practices include:

- Conducting keyword research: non-profit organizations should identify the keywords and phrases that their target audience is searching for and incorporate them into their website content.
- Creating high-quality content: non-profit organizations should create high-quality, relevant content that provides value to the user and incorporates their target keywords.
- Optimizing website structure: non-profit organizations should ensure that their website has a clear navigation structure and a logical hierarchy of pages.
- Building high-quality backlinks: non-profit organizations should aim to build high-quality links from reputable websites in their industry.
- Optimizing for mobile devices: non-profit organizations should ensure that their website is mobile-friendly and optimized for mobile devices (Iqbal et al., 2022).

4.3.2. Measuring SEO Success

Measuring the success of search engine optimization (SEO) efforts is critical to determining the effectiveness of a non-profit organization's digital marketing strategy (Iqbal et al., 2022). In this section, we will discuss key metrics that non-profit organizations should track to measure their SEO success and provide examples of how successful organizations have leveraged these metrics to improve their online visibility and drive more support for their cause.

- **Organic Traffic**

One of the most important metrics to track for SEO success is organic traffic. Organic traffic refers to the number of visitors that come to a website through search engine results, without any paid advertising (Khan & Mahmood, 2018; Younan et al., 2020). This metric is a strong indicator of how well a non-profit organization's SEO efforts are performing, as it reflects the number of people finding the website through search engines. To track organic traffic, non-profit organizations can use tools such as

Google Analytics or Moz to monitor the number of visitors coming to their website from search engines over time. By analyzing this data, organizations can identify trends and patterns in their website traffic and adjust their SEO strategy accordingly.

- **Keyword Rankings**

Keyword rankings are another important metric for measuring SEO success. Keyword rankings as given by Khan and Mahmood (2018) refer to how well a website ranks in search results for specific keywords and phrases related to the non-profit organization's mission and cause. To track keyword rankings, non-profit organizations can use tools such as SEMrush or Ahrefs to monitor their website's search engine rankings for specific keywords over time. As NPOs track keyword rankings, they can identify opportunities to improve their rankings for specific keywords and phrases and adjust their SEO strategy accordingly (Khan & Mahmood, 2018).

- **Conversion Rate**

Conversion rate refers to the percentage of website visitors who take a specific action, such as donating or signing up for a newsletter. Measuring conversion rate is critical for non-profit organizations, as it reflects how well their website is converting visitors into supporters and donors. To track conversion rates, non-profit organizations can use tools such as Google Analytics or Crazy Egg to monitor the number of visitors who take specific actions on their website over time. By analyzing this data, organizations can identify areas of their website that are performing well and areas that may need improvement to increase conversion rates.

- **Backlink Quality and Quantity**

Backlinks refer to links from other websites that point to a non-profit organization's website. High-quality backlinks from reputable websites can significantly improve a website's search engine rankings and increase its online visibility (Younan et al., 2020). By tracking backlink quality and quantity, non-profit organizations can use tools such as Ahrefs or Majestic to monitor the number and quality of backlinks pointing to their website over time. As indicated in their study, Younan et al. (2020), by analyzing the data, organizations can identify opportunities to improve their backlink profile and adjust their SEO strategy accordingly.

4.3.3. Examples of Successful SEO Metrics for Not-for-Profit Organizations

Several successful non-profit organizations have leveraged SEO metrics to increase their online visibility and drive more support for their cause. For example:

- The American Red Cross increased their organic traffic by 20% through a targeted SEO campaign focused on improving its website's content and backlink profile.
- Charity: Water improved their conversion rate by 64% by optimizing their website's design and navigation to make it easier for visitors to donate.

- World Wildlife Fund (WWF) improved their keyword rankings for key phrases related to their mission by implementing a targeted content marketing strategy focused on creating high-quality, informative content.

4.4. Email Marketing Strategies for Non-Profit Organizations

Email marketing is an essential tool for non-profit organizations to engage with supporters, communicate their mission, and drive donations (Rosnerovan & Hraskova, 2022). In this chapter, we outlined effective email marketing strategies for non-profit organizations, with global examples and insights from cited scholars.

4.4.1. Segment Your Audience

Segmenting your email list is critical to delivering personalized and relevant content to the organization's target audience (Rosnerova & Hraskova, 2022). According to a study by Mailchimp, segmented campaigns can result in a 14.31% higher open rate than non-segmented campaigns. By segmenting the audience, non-profit organizations can segment their email lists based on several criteria, including past donations, geographic location, or engagement with previous email campaigns. For example, charity: water segments their email list based on donors and non-donors, allowing them to send targeted campaigns to each segment.

4.4.2. Use Personalization

Personalization is another essential aspect of effective email marketing for non-profit organizations. By including the recipient's name or other personal details, non-profit organizations can increase open rates and engagement with their emails. According to a study by Experian, personalized emails have a 29% higher open rate and 41% higher click-through rate than non-personalized emails. Non-profit organizations can also use personalization to thank supporters for their past donations or encourage them to take specific actions, such as signing a petition or attending an event (Rosnerova, & Hraskova, 2022)

4.4.3. Include a Clear Call-to-Action (CTA)

Including a clear call-to-action (CTA) in email, campaigns are critical to driving donations and engagement with your organization's mission (Holliman & Rowley, 2014). The CTA should be prominent, easy to find, and clearly communicate the action you want the recipient to take. For example, Amnesty International includes a clear CTA in its email campaigns, encouraging supporters to sign petitions or donate to specific campaigns. They also use urgency and emotional appeals to encourage supporters to act quickly.

4.4.4. Use Storytelling

Non-profit organizations can use storytelling to engage supporters and communicate their mission effectively. By sharing stories of individuals or communities that have benefited from their programs, non-profit organizations can demonstrate the impact of their work and inspire supporters to take action

(Jones-Smith, 2021). For example, charity: water uses storytelling to communicate the impact of their work in providing clean water to communities around the world. They share stories of individuals who have been impacted by their work and use these stories to encourage supporters to make donations and support their mission.

4.4.5. Seek Permission

Effective implementation of an email marketing strategy by NPOs requires that permission is sought from stakeholders allowing the NPOs to send them messages. It's not appropriate for NPOs to send Spam messages to potential supporters of their causes. This practice does not only damage the reputation of the NPOs but may result in the closure of both the email and the website of the concerned NPO. Permission can be granted through availing a variety of opt-in points be it offline or online. More importantly, opt-out options must also be availed in a few clicks which demonstrates that the organization respects the time of its supporters.

4.4.6. Test and Optimise

Testing and optimizing email campaigns are critical to improving their effectiveness and driving more donations and engagement. Non-profit organizations can test different subject lines, CTAs, and content to identify what resonates best with their audience and improve their email marketing strategy over time. According to a study by HubSpot (2022), companies that test their email campaigns see a 20% increase in open rates and a 70% increase in click-through rates. Non-profit organizations can also use tools such as Mailchimp or Constant Contact to track metrics such as open rates, click-through rates, and conversion rates to measure the effectiveness of their email campaigns. Examples of Successful Email Marketing Strategies for Non-Profit Organizations include but are not limited to "leverage personal connections you' audience", "subscribe to the newsletters, "Donate now", "Commit to regular sends", and "Refer a friend" e.t.c (Jones-Smith, 202; Rosnerova & Hraskova, 2022).

Several successful non-profit organizations have leveraged email marketing strategies to engage with supporters and drive donations (Crotty & Ljubownikow, 2019). For example, charity: water uses storytelling and personalization to engage supporters and drive donations. NPOs send personalized emails to donors and use stories of individuals impacted by their work to encourage support. As can be seen on Amnesty International urgency and emotional appeals are used to encourage supporters to act quickly. In addition, Amnesty International also include clear CTAs in their emails and uses storytelling to communicate the impact of their work. Movember uses humor and storytelling to engage supporters and raise awareness of men's health issues. They use creative email campaigns and social media to encourage supporters to grow mustaches and fundraise for their cause.

4.5. Website Marketing Strategies for NPOs

A Website is a very vital component of all digital marketing efforts of an NPO. It is the epicenter of all online marketing activities. For an NPO a website derives its significance largely from the fact that it is the home space for all the digital marketing content about an NPO. Maxim (2016) alleges that the website is now mandatory for every NPO. In a similar fashion Huang and Ku (2016) asserts that websites are the nucleus of the brand image of an organization. It thus becomes imperative for NPO leadership to give thorough consideration in the designing of a good website cable of linking their organization to the outside world and portraying a good brand image. A poorly designed website sends wrong signals to key stakeholders and Wymer et al. (2006) stress that a professionally designed website reflects the level of professionalism of an NPO.

The main purpose of the website by NPOs is largely to communicate with relevant stakeholders. Many authors among them Rosnerova and Hraskova (2021); Wyner et al. (2006), as well as Jones-Smith (2021), agree on the notion that for the website of NPOs to effectively fulfill their role as communication tools information posted must be current and always updated. More importantly, the website must be able to facilitate dialogue with visitors. Visitors on the website must be able to ask questions and receive feedback timeously. Seelig et al. (2019) allege that websites that facilitate two-way communication between NPO leadership and donors result in the creation of strong relationships with the donor community as they feel part and parcel of the NPO. By being given opportunities to ask questions and receive feedback Donors feel obliged to support the missions of NPOs. Besides the above NPOs need also to utilize their websites to demonstrate financial accountability to their stakeholders, particularly their donors. Waters (2008) proposes that a website of an NPOs must be able to communicate relevant information tailor-made to all stakeholders and most importantly the message must be in line with the mission of the NPO. To Donors, the author opines that NPOs can share their audited financial statements which would go a long way in demonstrating a high level of accountability (Seelig et al., 2019).

On top of the above some others (Jones-Smith, 2021; Levenshus, 2010; Maxim, 2006) seem to be inclined towards the idea that for an NPO to derive maximum benefits from websites as a marketing tool, the site must meet certain standards aesthetically pleasing. Firstly, it must be easy to navigate to enable stakeholders to access the information quickly and easily they want. In addition to the above the site must not have error messages which imply that the design of the website must be up to standard. Furthermore, the website must be free from broken links. Another strategy that can lead to enhanced NPO digital visibility involves linking the website with NPO's social media platforms. This can be made possible by directing website visitors through links like-' Like us on Facebook', 'Follow us on Twitter', ' Email us on …' etc. The other strategy is to provide an appropriate call to action. According to DeMint and Sproule (2014), information on the website must not be ambiguous and whoever is mandated with the task to update the site must provide clear messages which will enable visitors to know what they are expected to do to help. There must be easy-to-understand instruction and if it's money that is needed it must be clear.

From the above, it can thus be established that a website is a key component of the digital marketing campaign an NPO and NPO executives must try to ensure that it communicates an appropriate brand image. Apart from the above strategies of enhancing the website's effectiveness in NPOs' digital campaigns, the performance of the website must be measured. This would enable NPO executives to know whether the site is fulfilling its mandate and whether the resources invested in it are yielding any returns. As stakeholders visit the site, they leave a lot of digital footprints which if harnessed by NPOs can go a long way in enhancing knowledge about stakeholder preferences which can aid in crafting tailor-made services. This can be attained by installing third-party applications like heat maps and eye-tracking devices or even collecting stakeholder intelligence through cookies. NPOS must be above to gather stakeholder intelligence data such as the number of visits, devices used to log, location of visitors, and areas visited among other data.

5. CHALLENGES FACED BY NPOS IN IMPLEMENTING DIGITAL MARKETING

Digital marketing has emerged as a powerful tool for businesses to reach their target audience and generate revenue. However, non-profit organizations (NPOs) have struggled to adopt digital marketing strategies effectively due to several challenges. There are several challenges faced by NPOs in adopting digital marketing and some of them will be discussed below:

Limited resources are one of the major challenges for the adoption of digital marketing by NPOs. NPOs often operate on limited budgets, and digital marketing requires significant resources such as skilled staff, technology, and budget allocation. According to a study by Light et al . (2020), smaller NPOs face significant challenges in implementing digital marketing strategies due to their limited resources.

Another challenge faced by NPOs is the lack of expertise. NPOs may not have access to digital marketing expertise and may not have the technical knowledge or skills required to implement digital marketing campaigns. A study by Wang et al. (2020) found that the lack of digital marketing knowledge among NPOs was a significant barrier to their adoption of digital marketing.

Fuentes and Jimenez (2017) assert that NPOs have a challenge in measuring the success of digital marketing campaigns. Unlike businesses that can measure success through revenue, NPOs need to measure success through other metrics such as engagements, donations, and awareness. This makes it challenging for NPOs to evaluate the effectiveness of their digital marketing campaigns.

NPOs must adhere to ethical guidelines, and this can limit their use of certain digital marketing techniques such as targeted advertising. This becomes a challenge because NPOs need to balance their marketing objectives with ethical considerations, and they may find it challenging to navigate this balance. NPOs must maintain a high level of authenticity and trustworthiness in their online communications. This can be a challenge in a digital landscape where misinformation and fake news are common.

NPOs may struggle to reach their target audience through digital marketing as they may not have the same reach as larger organizations. NPOs may find it challenging to cut through the noise of digital marketing which is dominated by commercial organizations (Singh, 2017). The online space is crowded and NPOs must compete for attention with a wide range of other organizations and content creators. This can make it difficult to stand out and engage with potential supports (Zahay & Griffin, 2019).

6. DISCUSSION AND REFLECTION

From the above, it can be established that digital marketing has now become an integral part of NPOs' marketing program. At very low-cost NPOs can reach out to a wide pool of potential supporters who can help them in sustaining their missions. Additionally, Digital marketing strategies help them to build a good reputation in society and to their stakeholders and be able to differentiate themselves from others offering similar programs. We have established that digital marketing strategies such as website marketing, search engine optimization, email marketing, content marketing, and social media marketing while they are commonly utilized by commercial entities are equally useful to non-commercial entities like NPOs. Figure 2 summarizes some of the major issues that emerged from the review of variety of sources regarding digital marketing strategies for NPOs.

As can be noted from Figure 2, the study established a variety of issues in so far as harnessing digital marketing strategies for the effective promotion of NPOs. As far as website marketing strategies go, we established that the website is the heart or the epicenter of all digital marketing content for an NPO

Figure 2. Digital marketing strategies for NPOs

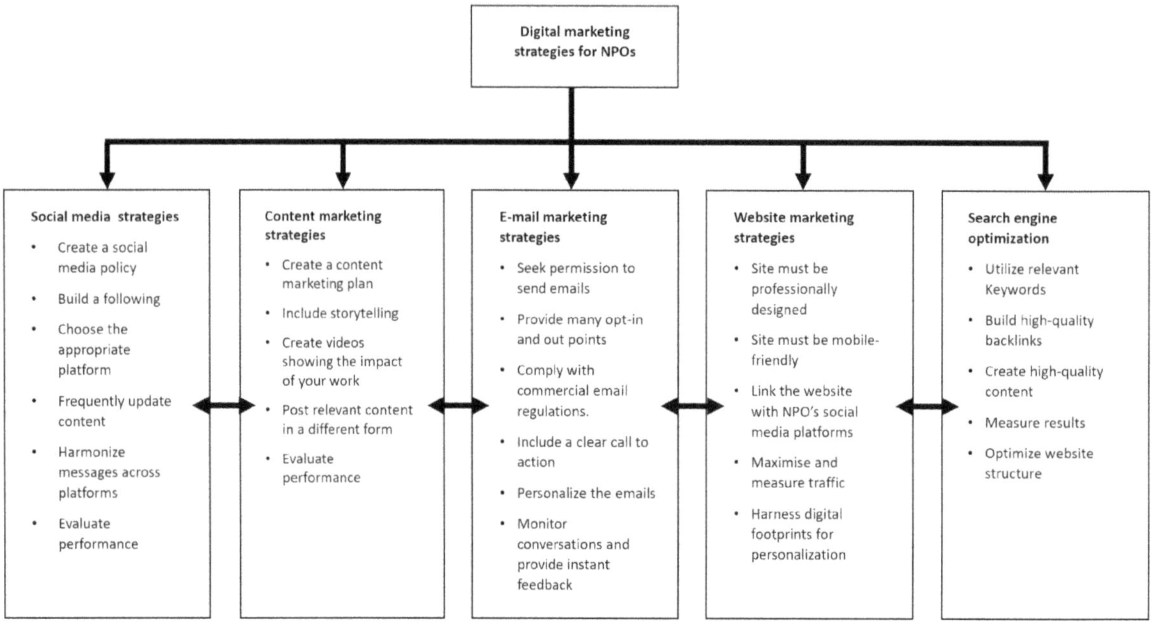

(Huang & Ku, 2016; Maxim 2016). This underscores the need to ensure that the website is designed in line with the best standards and that those mandated to administer its content must be skilled and of high integrity. Notable design features underscored by many authors include being easy to navigate, mobile-friendly, free from error messages and broken links, and facilitating dialogue with key stakeholders. Furthermore, the other key issue that emerged is that the website must be linked to all other digital marketing platforms being utilized by an NPO. In other words, it must be an opt-in point for the NPOs' email marketing campaign and must also have links like 'like us on Facebook or follow us on Twitter…', directing website visitors to an NPO's social media platforms. We have also established a variety of issues as far as the utilization of the social media marketing strategy by NPOs. Some authors were inclined to the idea that for NPOs to gain from the usage of social media, it is imperative to provide a social media policy (Idealware 2012; Kanter & Paine 2012). We also believe that such a policy would indeed be vital, as it would guide not only resource allocation but also task distribution. Such a policy would spell out the 'dos and don'ts' when interacting with stakeholders on social media. In addition to the above, we have also established that the utilization of appropriate platforms and building a following are pivotal for the success of a social media strategy by NPOs (Burton & Daellenbach 2017; Lovejoy & Saxton, 2012). It would amount to a waste of Donor funds for NPOs to pursue social media strategies when their platforms do not have any meaningful full-time following. NPOs must create engaging and captivating content to lure potential supporters to their social media handles. We have further noted that valuable content does not only lure supporters to the social media platforms of NPOs but would also enhance NPOs' brand visibility on search engines. In simpler terms, we noted that content is key in all digital marketing endeavors. All the strategies highlighted thrive only when relevant content has been created.

Apart from the above, the study also revealed that email marketing campaigns are an integral component of an NPO's digital marketing efforts. Direct emails from an NPO build and strengthen constituent relationships. We have established that key considerations for successfully implementing an email marketing strategy for NPOs include seeking permission to send messages, personalizing messages, and providing many opt-in and opt-out points, among others (McPheat, 2011). The above will go a long way toward establishing trust between an NPO and its stakeholders. It's important to highlight that this trust is vital since NPOs derive much of their funding from donations from well-wishers. Last but not least, we established that the implementation of digital marketing strategies by NPOs is just one part of the equation; measuring the success of these efforts is critical for non-profit organizations to ensure that they are effectively reaching their target audience and driving more support for their cause.

7. RECOMMENDATIONS

It is our humble submission that given the multiplicity of digital marketing platforms which NPOs can utilize, there is a need for efforts to be made on ensuring consistency and uniformity in the messages sent to stakeholders. We, therefore, implore NPO executives to ensure the establishment of a digital marketing policy that spells out who must do what, how, where, and when. On top of harmonization of messages across digital platforms, we also recommend that such messages must be in tandem with the NPO mission, vision, and brand image. More importantly, we urge digital marketers of NPOs to observe privacy and confidentiality issues, respect intellectual property rights and desist from publishing unverified content. The above does not only expose the organization to a lawsuit but tarnishes the brand image which may negatively impact NPO's integrity in the eyes of Donors. Furthermore, digital marketing strategies offered in this chapter are not exhaustive and neither do we recommend their adoption in a one size fits all approach. Rather, we implore NPO executives to apply tools that reflect what is obtained in their local environments as far as ICT infrastructure and developments are concerned. We also recommend that all the platforms must be integrated such that visitors on one platform can easily find ways to get to the other platforms of the same organization.

To sum it all up and also not take anything from the above-highlighted issues, we propose a content-centered digital marketing campaign for NPOs. We submit that under this campaign framework, NPOs should first create relevant and high-quality content that resonates with their missions and causes. Such content may revolve around testimonies of their work, the showcasing of previous outreaches and events held, or any other content that can lure potential supporters to their cause. The content must be in all forms to appeal to all stakeholders, including the disadvantaged members of our society. This content must then be fed to all the digital channels in line with established policies. In this proposed framework, we underscore the establishment of standard operating procedures (SOPs) for each digital channel, which must be aligned to the NPO's marketing procedures and regulations. In a nutshell, our framework for the digital marketing strategies for NPOs must not be divorced from the entire marketing plan of an NPO. In other words, the proposed framework of strategies must speak to the earlier and later segments of an NPO's marketing plan, which are the marketing objectives and the marketing tactics.

8. CONCLUSION

Digital marketing is a concept that continues to evolve in line with the changes in ICTs. Its history has been a fascinating one which may date back to the year 1971when the first email was sent. To date, it has thus evolved to become an integral part of the marketing campaign of not only commercial entities but also non-commercial entities like NPOs. NPOs stand to benefit immensely through utilization of digital marketing strategies like email marketing, content marketing, website marketing, search engine optimization as well as social media marketing. Implementation of digital marketing by NPOs however has its fair share of challenges. Much of the challenges stem from the fact that NPOs rely upon donor funding to sustain their mission and in many instances have less finances to fund their digital marketing campaign. Limited budgets mean that they cannot hire experts to run their platforms and, in some instances, may not afford the required devices. However, with more ICT innovations expected to emerge, the future of digital marketing to NPOs very bright, and its popularity among these organization will increase. Our chapter is in tandem with the major goal of the book which is to allow readers to understand and apply the different concepts, techniques, and tools to implement digital marketing and communication strategies to improve society's behavior towards diversity, equity, and inclusion. We argue in the chapter that NPOs important players in the promotion of diversity, equality, and inclusion and need to be capacitated by cost-effective strategies like digital marketing to ensure the continued provision of their impactful services. The chapter relied more on secondary data sources, we recommend future studies to explore the application of digital marketing strategies in different contexts using empirical cases, for instance, comparative studies between developed and developing countries.

REFERENCES

Appel, G., Grewal, L., Hadi, R., & Stephen, A. T. (2020). The future of social media inmarketing. *Journal of the Academy of Marketing Science*, *48*(1), 79–95. doi:10.100711747-019-00695-1 PMID:32431463

Baglioni, S., de Pieri, B., & Tallarico, T. (2017). Surplus Food Recovery and Food Aid: The Pivotal Role of Non-profit Organisations. *Insights From Italy and Germany. Voluntas*, *28*(5), 2032–2052. doi:10.100711266-016-9746-8

Baker, K. (2022) *The Ultimate Guide to Content Marketing*. HubSpot. https://blog.hubspot.com/marketing/content-marketing

Bala, M., & Verma, D. (2018). A Critical review of Digital Marketing. *International Journal of Mnanagement. IT& Engineering*, *8*(10), 321–329.

Boris, E. T., & Steuerle, C. E. (1999). *Nonprofits and government: Collaboration and conflict*. Urban Institute Press.

Brooks, M. (2022). *Why your Non-Profit should invest in Search Engine Optimisation*. HubSpot. https://blog.hubspot.com/marketing/nonprofit-seo

Carboni, J. L., & Maxwell, S. P. (2015). Effective social media engagement for nonprofits: What matters? *Journal of Public and Nonprofit Affairs*, *1*(1), 18–28. doi:10.20899/jpna.1.1.18-28

Chary, S. R. K. (2014). Social media marketing: The paradigm shift in internationalmarketing. *IOSR Journal of Business and Management*, *16*(9), 11–13. doi:10.9790/487X-16921113

Chikwanda, H. K. (2020). Challenges and Strategies in NPOs' Operations during Covid-19 Pandemic. In *Proceedings of the 2nd African International Conference on Industrial Engineering and Operations Management*, Harare, Zimbabwe.

Choto, P., Iwu, C. G., & Tengeh, R. K. (2020). Non-Profit Organisations and Socio-Economic Development in South Africa: A literature analysis. *Humanities & Social Sciences Reviews*, *8*(2), 689–600. doi:10.18510/hssr.2020.8267

Crotty, J. L., & Jubownikow, S. (2019). Restrictive Institutions and Critical Resources:Non-Profit Organisations and Volunteer Resources in the Russian Federation. *Europe-Asia Studies*, *72*(1), 99–116. doi:10.1080/09668136.2019.1686462

Deepa, N., & Deshmukh, S. (2013). Social media marketing: The next generation of business engagement. *International Journal of Management Research and Reviews*, *3*, 2461–2468.

Desai, V. (2019). Digital Marketing: *A Review.* [ijtsrd]. *International Journal of Trend in Scientific Research and Development*, (Special Issue), 196–200. doi:10.31142/ijtsrd23100

du Plessis, C. (2017). The role of content marketing in social media content communities. *South African Journal of Information Management*, *19*(1), 1–7. doi:10.4102ajim.v19i1.866

Felix, R., Rauschnabel, P. A., & Hinsch, C. (2017). Elements of strategic social media marketing: A holistic framework. *Journal of Business Research*, *70*, 118–126. doi:10.1016/j.jbusres.2016.05.001

Fink, M., Koller, M., Gartner, J., Floh, A., & Harms, R. (2020). Effective entrepreneurial marketing on Facebook–A longitudinal study. *Journal of Business Research*, *113*, 149–157. doi:10.1016/j.jbusres.2018.10.005

Fuentes, C., & Jimenez, M. (2017). Challenges and Opportunities for non-profit organisations in the digital era. *Social Responsibility Journal*, *13*(4), 833–849.

Gruber, T., & Schlegelmilch, B. B. (2017). Digital transformation of nonprofit organisations: A research agenda. *Journal of Business Research*, *70*, 322–326.

Hanna, T. K. 2022. What is a non-profit organisation. *Tech Target.* https://www.techtarget.com/

Heaslip, E. (2023) Non-profit vs. Not for profit vs For-profit: What is the difference? *US Chamber.* https://www.uschamber.com/co/start/startegy/

Holliman, G., & Rowley, J. (2014). Business to business digital content marketing: Marketers' perceptions of best practice. *Journal of Research in Interactive Marketing*, *8*(4), 269–293. doi:10.1108/JRIM-02-2014-0013

Huang, S. L., & Ku, H. H. (2016). Brand image management for nonprofit organizations: Exploring the relationship between websites, brand images and donations. *Journal of Electronic Commerce Research*, *17*(1), 80–97.

Idealware. (2012). *Notprofit social media policybook.* Wordpress. https://www.sustainingplaces.files-wordpress.com/2012/10/

Ihm, J. (2015). Network measures to evaluate stakeholder engagement with nonprofit organizations on social networking sites. *Public Relations Review*, *41*(4), 501–503. doi:10.1016/j.pubrev.2015.06.018

Iqbal, M., Khalid, M. N., Manzoor, A., Abid, M. M., & Shakh, N. A. (2022). Search Engine optimisation: A study of key factors in achieving in achieving a better search result page (SERP) position. *Sukkur IBA Journal of Computing and Mathematical Science*, *6*(1), 1–15. doi:10.30537jcms.v6i1.924

Ištvanić, M., Crnjac Milić, D., & Krpić, Z. (2017). Digital marketing in the business environment. *International Journal of Electrical and Computer Engineering Systems*, *8*(2), 67–75. doi:10.32985/ijeces.8.2.4

Jadhav, V. S., & Yallatti, R. M. (2018). A critical study on digital marketing with reference to different components of digital marketing. *International Journal of Trend in Scientific Research and Development*, (Special Issue), 231–233. doi:10.31142/ijtsrd18711

Jones-Smith, V. (2021). *Nonprofifit Leaders' Digital Marketing Strategies to Secure and Sustain Donors* [Doctoral dissertation, Walden university].

Khan, M. N. A., & Mahmood, A. (2018). A distinctive approach to obtain higher page rank through search engine optimization. *sādhanā, 43*(3), 43.

Kirby, J., & Marsden, P. (2006). *Connected Marketing: The Viral, Buzz and Word of Mouth Revolution*. Elsevier.

Knater, B., & Paine, K. D. (2012). *Measuring the networked NPO. Using data to change the world.* John Wiley and Sons.

Levenshus, A. (2010). Online relationship management in a presidential campaign: A case study of the Obama campaign's management of its internet-integrated 177 grassroots effort. *Journal of Public Relations Research*, *22*(3), 313–335. doi:10.1080/10627261003614419

Lovejoy, K., & Saxton, G. D. (2012). Information, community, and action: How non-profit organizations use social media. *Journal of Computer-Mediated Communication*, *17*(3), 337–353. doi:10.1111/j.1083-6101.2012.01576.x

Macedo, I. M., & Pinho, J. C. (2006). The relationship between resource dependence and market orientation. *European Journal of Marketing*, *40*(5/6), 533–553. doi:10.1108/03090560610657822

Maxim, E. (2016). *Planning strategic marketing for non-profit organizations case study* [Bachelor's Thesis, Laurea university of applied sciences].

Milde, K., & Yawson, R. M. (2017). Strategies for social media use in nonprofits. *Journal of Management Policy and Practice*, *18*(1), 19–27.

Milla, A. C., Mataruna-Dos-Santos, L. J., & Ristic, M. R. (2018). Adopting social media for nonprofits as a main marketing tool: Analysis of a youth non-profit organization. *International Journal of Applied Business and Economic Research*, *22*(2), 741–752.

Mitchell, G. E., & Calabrese, T. D. (2019). Proverbs of nonprofit financial management. *American Review of Public Administration*, *49*(6), 649–661. doi:10.1177/0275074018770458

Müller, J., & Christandl, F. (2019). Content is king – But who is the king of kings? The effect of content marketing, sponsored content & user-generated content on brand responses. *Computers in Human Behavior*, *96*, 46–55. doi:10.1016/j.chb.2019.02.006

Musikavanhu, T. B., Asoba, S. N., & Mefi, N. P. (2022). Content Marketing strategies for Non-governmental organisations in a developing nation. *International Journal of Scientific Research*, *78*(4), 17–24. doi:10.5281/zenodo.7269280

Musungwini, S., Gavai, P. V., Munyoro, B., & Chare, A. (2023). Emerging ICT Technologies for Agriculture, Training, and Capacity Building for Farmers in Developing Countries. *Advances in Environmental Engineering and Green Technologies*, (January), 12–30. doi:10.4018/978-1-6684-6413-7.ch002

Namisango, F., Kang, K., & Rehman, J. (2019). What do we know about social media in nonprofits? A review. In *Pacific Asia conference on information systems*. AIS e-library.

Pinto, L., Loureiro, S. M. C., Rita, P., & Sarmento, E. M. (2019). Fostering online relationships with brands through websites and social media brand pages. *Journal of Promotion Management*, *25*(3), 379–393. doi:10.1080/10496491.2019.1557817

Quevedo, F. J., & Quevedo-Prince, A. K. (2019). A predictive model for the US non-profit market; a macro to a micro perspective. *Advanced Journal of Social Science*, *5*(1), 1–9. doi:10.21467/ajss.5.1.1-9

Rose, R. (2016). *The 2017 Content Marketing Framework: 5 Building Blocks for Profitable, Scalable Operations*. Content Marketing Institute. https://contentmarketinginstitute.com/2016/10/contentmarketing-framework-profitable/

Rosnerova, Z., & Hraskova, D. (2021). The Application and Importance of Marketing and its Tools in the Conditions of Non-profit Organizations on a Global Scale. In *SHS Web of Conferences* (Vol. 92, p. 02055). EDP Sciences. 10.1051hsconf/20219202055

Schrage, R., Hubert, M., & Linzmajer, M. (2019) Content is king? The effectiveness of message content, personalization, and location in mobile in-store advertising. In *Proceedings of the Annual Hawaii International Conference on System Sciences* (pp. 1373–1382). Scholar Space. 10.24251/HICSS.2019.167

Seelig, M. I., Millette, D., Zhou, C., & Huang, J. (2019). A new culture of advocacy: An exploratory analysis of social activism on the web and social media. *Atlantic Journal of Communication*, *27*(1), 15–29. doi:10.1080/15456870.2019.1540418

Seo, H., & Vu, H. T. (2020). Transnational nonprofits' social media use: A survey ofcommunications professionals and an analysis of organizational characteristics. *Nonprofit and Voluntary Sector Quarterly*, *49*(4), 849–870. doi:10.1177/0899764020908340

Shin, N. (2019). The impact of the web and social media on the performance of non-profit organizations. *Journal of International Technology and Information Management*, *27*(4), 17–35. doi:10.58729/1941-6679.1386

Singh, S. (2017). Challenges of digital marketing for non-profit organisations. *International Journal of Social Sciences and Economic Research*, *2*(11), 5303–5311.

Soboleva, A., Burton, S., Daellenbach, K., & Basil, D. Z. (2017). Tweets for tots: Using Twitter to promote a charity and its supporters. *Journal of Consumer Marketing*, *34*(6), 515–523. doi:10.1108/JCM-03-2017-2123

Srivastava, J., Saks, J., Weed, A. J., & Atkins, A. (2018). Engaging audiences on social media: Identifying relationships between message factors and user engagement on the American Cancer Society's Facebook page. *Telematics and Informatics*, *35*(7), 1832–1844. doi:10.1016/j.tele.2018.05.011

Wang, Y., Ki, E.-J., & Kim, Y. (2017). Exploring the perceptual and behavioral outcomes of public engagement on mobile phones and social media. *International Journal of Strategic Communication*, *11*(2), 133–147. doi:10.1080/1553118X.2017.1280497

Waters, R. D. (2008). Applying relationship management theory to the fundraising process for individual donors. *Journal of Communication Management (London)*, *12*(1), 73–87. doi:10.1108/13632540810854244

Waters, R. D., Burnett, E., Lamm, A., & Lucas, J. (2009). Engaging stakeholders through social media: How nonprofit organizations are using Facebook. *Public Relations Review*, *35*(2), 102–106. doi:10.1016/j.pubrev.2009.01.006

Werthner, H., & Ricci, F. (2018). Digitalisation challenges and opportunities for nonprofit organisations. *Nonprofit Management & Leadership*, *28*(1), 5–18.

Wymer, W., Knowles, P., & Gomes, R. (2006). *Non-profit Marketing – Marketing Management for Charitable and Nongovernmental Organizations*. Sage Publications.

Xu, W., & Saxton, G. D. (2019). Does stakeholder engagement pay off on social media? A social capital perspective. *Nonprofit and Voluntary Sector Quarterly*, *48*(1), 28–49. doi:10.1177/0899764018791267

Yalcin, N., & Kose, U. (2011). What is search engine Optimisation: SEO. *Procedia: Social and Behavioral Sciences*, *9*, 487–493. doi:10.1016/j.sbspro.2010.12.185

Younan, M., Houssein, E. H., Elhoseny, M., & Ali, A. A. (2020). Challenges and recommended technologies for the industrial internet of things: A comprehensive review. *Measurement*, *151*, 107198. doi:10.1016/j.measurement.2019.107198

Zahay, D., & Griffin, A. (2019). Digital Marketing for nonprofits: Challenges and opportunities. *Journal of Nonprofit & Public Sector Marketing*, *31*(1), 1–14.

Zorn, T. E., Flanagin, A. J., & Shoham, M. D. (2011). Institutional and non-institutional influences on information and communication technology adoption and use among non-profit organizations. *Human Communication Research*, *37*(2), 1–33. doi:10.1111/j.1468-2958.2010.01387.x

Zuzana, R., & Dagmar, H. (2021). The Application and Importance of Marketingand its Tools in the Conditions of Non-profit Organizations on a Global Scale. In SHS web of Conferences 92. doi:10.1051hsconf/20219202055

ADDITIONAL READING

Bataoui, S., & Boch, E. (2023). The Role of Socially Rich Photos in Generating Favourable Donation Behaviour on Charity Websites. *Journal of Retailing and Consumer Services*, *74*, 103–439. doi:10.1016/j.jretconser.2023.103429

Convio. (2010). *Basics of Email Marketing for Non-profits: Using Email Communications to Build and Strengthen Constituent Relationships*. Convio. https://www.convio.com

Dimitrios, B., Loannis, R., Angelos, N., & Nikolaos, T. (2023). Digital Marketing: The Case of Digital Marketing Strategies on Luxurious Hotels. *Electronic Commerce Research and Applications*, *219*, 688–696.

Hou, T., Hou, K., Wang, X., & Lou, X. (2021). Why I Gave Money to Unknown People? An Investigation of Online Donation and Forwarding Intention. *Electronic Commerce Research and Applications*, *47*, 101055. doi:10.1016/j.elerap.2021.101055

Kenza, B., Ounacer, S., & Mohamed, A. (2023). A Conceptual Framework Using Big Data Analytics for Effective Email Marketing. *Procedia Computer Science*, *220*, 1044–1050. doi:10.1016/j.procs.2023.03.146

KEY TERMS AND DEFINATIONS

Call-to-Action: Any prompt designed to encourage the targeted audiences to take a desired action.

Content Marketing: Creation and distribution of relevant content for marketing purposes.

Email Marketing: The act of sending emails to potential and current customers for marketing purposes.

Search Engine Optimization: Is the process by which marketers attempt to get more visibility for their website in search engines.

Social Media Marketing: All marketing techniques which can be deployed on social media in an effort to promote a company, product or a service.

Spam: Unsolicited and or bulk commercial emails often sent to several customers at once. **Personalization:** Utilizing consumer data to provide personal experiences to customers.

Website Marketing: Utilization of a company's website in promoting a company, product, or service.

Chapter 2
Intra-Hospital Virtual Communities and Well-Being of Cancer Patients:
Impact of Features on Healthcare Relationships

Ricardo Jorge Silva
https://orcid.org/0009-0003-1301-8613
School of Economics and Management, University of Porto, Portugal

Paulo Botelho Pires
https://orcid.org/0000-0003-3786-6783
CEOS.PP, ISCAP, Polytechnic of Porto, Portugal

Catarina Delgado
https://orcid.org/0000-0002-1494-0517
School of Economics and Management, University of Porto, Portugal

José Duarte Santos
https://orcid.org/0000-0001-5815-4983
CEOS.PP, ISCAP, Polytechnic of Porto, Portugal

ABSTRACT

The use of social media in health is emerging as a means of bringing the various actors together with several benefits. In the specific case of cancer disease, these tools can help patients to improve their psychological well-being and their outcomes. As cancer is the cause of a quarter of deaths in Portugal, it is a pressing issue to understand which tools and information both patients and health professionals find most useful to build effective health social media. It was observed that there is a latent need for an oncology social environment, allowing greater well-being for patients and strengthening their relationship with health professionals and institutions, constituting an asset to the services provided. This chapter fills a gap in the bibliography by bringing together the views of both patients and health professionals from several areas, in close collaboration with the Francisco Gentil Portuguese Oncology Institute of Porto, E.P.E.

DOI: 10.4018/978-1-6684-8984-0.ch002

1. INTRODUCTION

According to the 2018 Portugal's Health Portrait, prepared by the Ministry of Health, cancer is the second leading cause of death in Portugal, accounting for about 25% of deaths that year.

Cancer is a life-threatening disease, and it is not always easy for the patient to maintain confidence and positive thinking about the outcome of their condition. However, as Erfani et al. (2017) highlight, a patient's optimism and the social support they receive are critical to their psychological well-being which, in turn, contributes positively to the likelihood of surviving the cancer (Chida & Steptoe, 2008).

The use of social media in health emerges as a means of bringing the various actors together with several benefits. For example, the use of social media allows patients to get more information about their disease and the treatment that they are undergoing (Al-Muhtadi et al., 2019), as well as interact with other patients and share experiences, knowledge, and advice (Gupta et al., 2020; Johansson et al., 2021). In addition to this, social media can impact the relationship with healthcare professionals, opening doors to greater personalization of care, and strengthening the doctor-patient relationship (Rajkomar et al., 2019). This last point became quite visible as the pandemic progressed, namely in the Facebook social network groups aimed at clarifying doubts about the disease caused by the SARS-COV2 virus. In these groups, health professionals played a pivotal role, acting as sensitizers and reassurers for the thousands of group members (Furstrand et al., 2021). However, the use of social media is not without risk (Benetoli et al., 2018; Eysenbach, 2003; Johansson et al., 2021; Schweizer et al., 2006) and its structure should be suitable for the users' needs (Fu et al., 2020).

Thus, this chapter aims to clarify the functionalities and characteristics seen as most relevant, by patients and by health professionals, of an oncology virtual community, which leads to forming the research question of this chapter: "What are the functionalities of virtual communities and their most important features to support cancer patients and what kind of information do health professionals consider important and want to obtain in virtual communities?".

By bringing health professionals' views on these platforms into the study, this chapter bridges a gap in the literature (Johansson et al., 2021). Data were collected in close collaboration with the Francisco Gentil Portuguese Oncology Institute of Porto, E.P.E. (hereinafter IPO Porto), using a mixed methodology, with patients and health professionals of this institution. Since it was carried out within an health institution and with its support, data collection followed a rigorous assessment process, namely by the Data Protection Officer and the Ethics Committee for Health, with a favorable opinion from them and the Board of Directors of IPO Porto.

The provision of this social medium by the healthcare institution, especially with the features and information most sought after by users, could be a further asset to the health service provided (Li et al., 2018). This is an important factor in the evaluation of health services in Portugal (pp 43-47 of the Standards Manual for Health Care Facilities/Hospital Centers) and one of the areas of action of the Portuguese National Strategy for Quality in Health, placing the patient at the center of the service provided, as a customer of the institution.

2. BACKGROUND

2.1. Social Media

According to Obar and Wildman (2015), the terms social media and social networks are confused in the literature. These authors define the term social media as Web 2.0-based applications in which user-generated content is vital to their operation. To use these services, users must create a profile specific to that platform. These platforms also facilitate the development of online connections by allowing the user to connect his profile to that of other users.

Similarly, Kaplan and Haenlein (2010) define social media as a group of Web 2.0-based applications that enable the creation and sharing of user-generated content. Hlavac (2014) proposed a classificatory model of various types of social media, dividing them into a pyramid, depending on how the audience conversion evolves from superficiality to specific topics, as shown in Figure 1.

Hlavac (2014) states that there are three types of strategies for social media which are (i) engagement, (ii) conversion, and (iii) integration. The engagement strategy aims to create a social dimension in the intended markets. The conversion strategy seeks to progressively lead the consumer to the end of the funnel, i.e., to convert, and, finally, the integration strategy aims at creating a virtual community, with a mission.

Figure 1. Social media pyramid
Source: Adapted from Hlavac (2014).

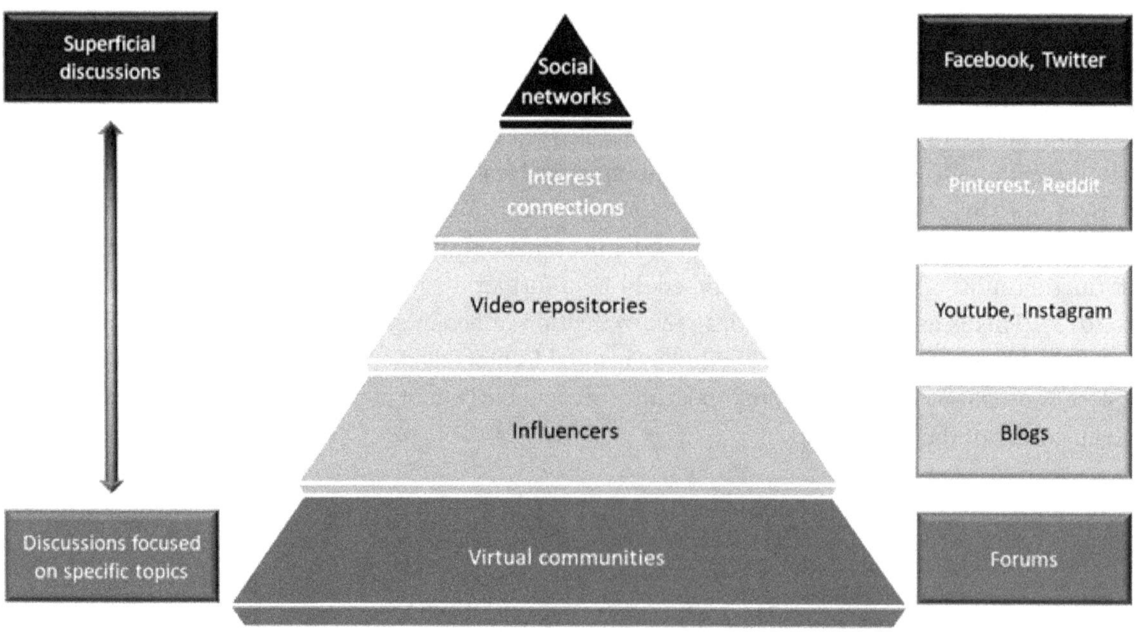

2.2. Social Networks

Kaplan and Haenlein (2010) define social networks as applications that allow users to connect by creating profiles with personal information and exchanging instant messages with each other. The authors also mention that profiles can include information such as photos, videos, and audio, among others. This definition is shared, with some nuances, by the Organization for Economic Cooperation and Development (OECD, 2007) and by Boyd and Ellison (2007). OECD (2007) mentions that some social networks may be dedicated to a specific topic, and Boyd and Ellison (2007) mention that profiles may be public or semi-public and allow consultation of the list of connections established by users.

Later, Kane et al. (2014) presented a more complete definition, presenting social networks with four essential characteristics: (i) users have a unique profile that is built by themselves, members of their network, and the platform; (ii) users can access and protect the digital content through various mechanisms; (iii) users can form and browse a list of other users with whom they share a relational connection; (iv) users can view and browse their connections and the connections of others on the platform. The authors also add that these networks are no longer only *web-based* since a large part of them already have applications for use on other devices, such as smartphones, a view also shared by Kietzmann et al. (2011) for the generality of social media.

2.3. Virtual Communities

According to the classificatory model proposed by Hlavac (2014), the major difference between social networks and virtual communities is the superficiality with which issues are addressed on social networks, compared to the depth with which topics are addressed in virtual communities. These communities are divided, in turn, into two major groups: communities of interest and communities originated by events. Both have distinct characteristics and objectives, as shown in Table 1.

Hlavac (2014) also provides the conceptual model for the integration strategy that can be applied to virtual communities, as shown in Figure 2.

For the author, there are some assumptions to be observed for the community to be successful, namely: (i) the management of the community is carried out by some of its members; (ii) the entry of

Table 1. Types of virtual communities

Communities of interests	Event-driven communities
Subjects people like They want the influencers' opinion They want to relate to others who share the same interests Intrinsic Motivation Levels of motivation vary May have professional or personal interests	Occurrence of a life-altering event They want guidance from the experts The relationship has a beginning and an end Intrinsic and extrinsic motivation Evolution in the stage of life or by the occurrence of an event The needs will vary along the route/event
Stable communities with regular members The website must have up-to-date and recent content "Listening" to members' interests and adapting the content strategy Seeking relationships with other members and getting expert opinions to learn	Stable communities with temporary members Members have a well-defined goal or problem they want to achieve or solve They only seek expert opinions that give them the answers they seek They are looking for information that will provide them with the pursuit to reach their goal or the resolution of their problem

Source: Adapted from Hlavac (2014).

Figure 2. Conceptual model of the integration strategy applied to virtual communities
Source: Adapted from Hlavac (2014).

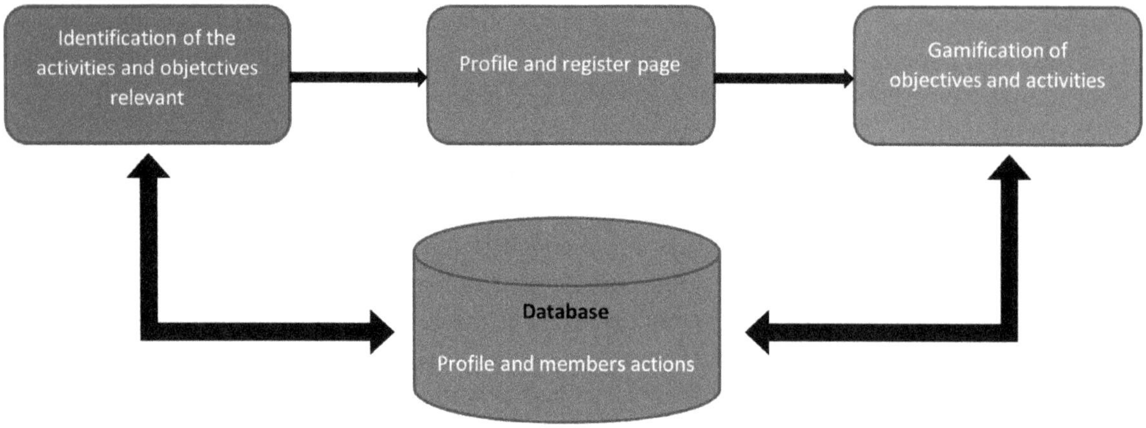

members must meet requirements; (iii) there must be a social structure; (iv) the community must have the necessary tools to support its activities and goals.

The first action is to identify the relevant activities and goals for the community, which then determine the production of content and requirements. The registration and profile page are mandatory, and it is advisable to implement gamification mechanisms for the activities and objectives. The author further highlights that the motivation to participate breaks down into:

- Elevation of member status: more privileges over other members; public recognition; assign new roles.
- Differentiating access: prior access to new launches and novelties; privileged access to product managers; access to pre-launches.
- Power: moderator roles in community forums or events; co-creation of new features in the community; moderately managing the community.
- Rewards: monetary; products; services; upgrades; extensions; invitations to events.

Other authors present a definition for virtual communities, such as Dholakia et al. (2004) who present them as groups of consumers, of various sizes, who meet and interact online in pursuit of a personal or common goal. Also, Gupta and Schapira (2018) define virtual communities as platforms dedicated to hosting the interaction of users with a common goal, specifically defining the oncology virtual communities as groups of people, with an interest in the topic, who communicate with each other through the platform or instant messaging.

Cancer is an event of great physical and psychological impact on the patient's life, which implies a change in his dynamics and does not allow predicting the end of this event in time-space, due to the uncertainty of the evolution of the disease, its response to treatments and possible future relapses (Leimeister et al., 2005). For this reason, and attending to the characteristics described by Hlavac (2014), we propose that:

RP1: The most suitable type of social media will be an event-driven virtual community.

2.4. Social Media in Health Care

The use of social media in healthcare, according to Al-Muhtadi et al. (2019) has great results, with many people using these networks to search and research information related to health problems, which justifies the growing importance of these platforms in this area.

Li et al. (2018) state that the use of social media allows patients to save time and improve the quality of healthcare services provided, allowing patient questions and doubts to be more easily answered, as well as enabling appointment scheduling and facilitating patient follow-up during treatment and post-treatment. Healthcare institutions can, on these platforms, place content beyond the traditional text, such as images and videos, increasing their comprehension and accessibility.

The features and functionalities of these social media should be thoughtful and appropriate for the users, as information overload, links, and tools can lead to user withdrawal from participating in this medium (Fu et al., 2020). Still in the health context, Gupta et al. (2020); Johansson et al. (2021) conclude that the main uses attributed, respectively, to social networks and virtual communities by patients are the search for information about the disease and its treatment, the search for experiences of other patients, the connection to a support group with a similar disease and the search for emotional support, thus complementing traditional health care.

Eysenbach (2003) states that virtual communities are the social environment with the greatest contribution to cancer patients. The author warns that the use of these communities may have a negative impact on the patient, although most cancer patients will benefit from their use. Also in this line of thought, Schweizer et al. (2006) conclude that virtual communities can help cancer patients cope with their situation, and function as a platform where patients can interact with each other, share experiences and information, and form online relationships, although they are not without risks, such as sharing misleading or malicious information or social isolation. The authors further conclude that the adoption of these communities is not related to patient demographics, but rather to the reasons for habitual internet use and the risks and benefits perceived by the user.

Gupta and Schapira (2018) and Johansson et al. (2021) conclude that the impact of virtual communities is equivocal and that while their use has numerous advantages for some patients, it may be harmful to others, highlighting the need for structured and rigorous clinical trials on this impact. That said, we formulate the following research propositions:

RP2: Patients consider that the existence of a virtual community would be an added value to the service provided by IPO Porto.

RP3: Patients feel that having a virtual community would have benefits for their emotional well-being.

2.5. Impact on the Doctor-Patient Relationship

Rajkomar et al. (2019) believe that the collection and analysis of health-related data will change the delivery of that care by enriching the doctor-patient relationship with the knowledge gained from data analysis, making that relationship the cornerstone of healthcare delivery. Benetoli et al. (2018) conclude that patients consider the impact of social media use on their relationship with health professionals to be positive, feeling more involved in the decision and care they receive, although a large proportion of patients report health professional opposition to social media use, which may be due to the potential for access to incorrect information, misuse of the media, and even disavowal of the health professional's knowledge and position.

One of the negative points reported by Johansson et al. (2021) is the pressure on health professionals to be always available to answer patients' questions on social media. However, in a study of physicians' activity on social media during the Covid-19 pandemic, Furstrand et al. (2021) concluded that the voluntary participation of health professionals in groups about this disease has been a major factor and has contributed to the clarification and sense of calm and confidence among the inquirers. This participation may indicate a greater openness of health professionals and an opportunity to use this type of tools in the health sector. That said, we formulate that:

RP4: A virtual community will improve the doctor-patient relationship.

2.6. Structure

The tools proposed for this virtual community will be presented in this subchapter, although there is no established taxonomy for them (Hlavac, 2014). To facilitate the organization of the content, the honeycomb model proposed by Kietzmann et al. (2011) will serve as a guide, being grouped with various descriptions of other authors.

Kietzmann et al. (2011) point out that not all blocks have to be present on each platform, and that, as a rule, each platform focuses on a mix between only some of the blocks. In the end, other features that are expected to impact these platforms will also be presented.

2.6.1. Profile

This tool is present in almost all definitions of social networks and social media and Boyd and Ellison (2007) even consider it to be the backbone of social networks. These authors present profiles as visible personal pages where one can see a list of that user's connections within the network. These profiles are generally built with the user's personal data, such as age, location, a short personal presentation, and a profile picture, and some social networks allow the user to customize and enhance the appearance of his profile with multimedia content (videos, animations, etc.) or applications.

Kietzmann et al. (2011) present this tool in the functional block "Identity". These authors consider that profiles include personal data such as name, age, gender, and other information that characterize the user. They also consider that this identity is central in many social environments and that, therefore, it should be thought carefully, especially in what concerns privacy. The authors also say that the identity of the user may vary depending on the purpose of the platform that is used, i.e., the identity created on LinkedIn may be different from the one created on Facebook.

In their definition of a social network, Kane et al. (2014) mention that profiles can represent a person, company, or group, and can be built by the user himself, by other users, and by the platform. Kane et al. (2014) also point to a negative side of this tool, which has to do with privacy. This negative side will be greater the more faithfully the profile represents the user's life and the greater the exposure and recording of data by the platform.

Kietzmann et al. (2011) state that it is important to define a balance between the disclosure of identity on the social network and the privacy of users, otherwise, undesirable behaviors and offenses may occur on these platforms, such as *cyberbullying*. This risk is also assumed by Baccarella et al. (2018) who, based on the model proposed by Kietzmann et al. (2011), present the negative side for each functional block of this model arguing, for the "Identity" block, that the sharing of personal data for the construction of profiles and the behavior that the user has on the social network lead to privacy and security risks. Given the described functionality, the following research proposition is formulated:

RP5: Patients want the 'Profiles' feature.

2.6.2. Private Messages and Comments

According to Boyd and Ellison (2007) and Kaplan and Haenlein (2010), one of the possibilities of social networks is the exchange of instant messages between users. Kietzmann et al. (2011), in their model, present a block entitled "Conversations", which refers to the reason for communication between users. According to the authors, many social media are designed to facilitate communication between users, which can occur for a variety of purposes, such as professional or passionate. Similar to other tools, private messaging also has potential downsides, with Baccarella et al. (2018) warning that interactions between users, facilitated by private messages, may occur in an unwanted way and lead to situations of threats and cyberbullying. It is thus proposed that:

RP6: Patients want the 'Messages' and 'Comments' features.

2.6.3. Connections

One of the aspects common to the various definitions of social networks and social media presented here is the existence of connections between users' profiles. The characteristics of these links will have an impact on user behavior, acting as repressors or promoters of certain types of attitudes, and allowing various types of interaction between users (Kane et al., 2014). Kietzmann et al. (2011) present a functional block called "Relationships" that seeks to explain how users can list themselves, mutually or not, as friends or fans. These connections will largely dictate how information flows within the social network. The authors state that the greater the number of connections a user has, the more likely they are to become an influencer, due to their large reach.

According to Boyd and Ellison (2007), these connections can take on different names, adapted by social networks and by the type of connection: unilateral or bilateral. A unilateral connection is a connection that requires only the willingness of one user to connect with another. A bilateral connection requires the agreement of both parties to establish such a connection. Kane et al. (2014) refer to this characteristic as connection symmetry, defining it as the need for reciprocity to form connections. To these authors a symmetric connection requires the acceptance of both parties, and an asymmetric connection requires only the willingness of one user to follow another (such as Twitter followers), admitting the joint existence of these two types of connection in the same social network. According to these authors, in a social network with symmetrical connections, users may be more willing to share certain types of personal information.

Kane et al. (2014) further define some more characteristics of these connections, such as degree, affection, and strength. The degree of connection represents the number of connections a user can maintain. Affection has to do with whether the users in the connection like each other. The strength of the connection has to do with the frequency and depth of the connection between users, and the authors argue that this strength should be used to organize the information presented to the user. According to Baccarella et al. (2018), there is a negative point mainly related to the possibility of stimulating online harassment, violent attitudes, and invasion of privacy. It is thus formulated that:

RP7: Patients want the 'Connections' feature.

2.6.4. Share

The functional block "Sharing" of the model proposed by Kietzmann et al. (2011) refers to all content that circulates between users. For the authors, the term "social" often implies the existence of content exchange between users. However, in some cases, the socialization experienced on the platform has to do with the social object: that which is shared, and which can take the form of images, videos, and careers, among others, thus uniting users. It is important for the platform to understand what social object unites users and to identify new social objects that are of common interest.

The information shared can have different levels of privacy defined by the user, implying the content that he will share and the scope and range that it will have (Kane et al., 2014). Like all tools, this one also has its downsides. Kietzmann et al. (2011) warn about the importance of defining the limits of shared content to avoid offensive content sharing and violations of property rights. Similarly, Baccarella et al. (2018) alerted to the abusive sharing of content, which may even be fake news. It is then formulated:

RP8: Patients want the 'Share' feature.

2.6.5. Presence

The model block proposed by Kietzmann et al. (2011) entitled "Presence" intends to reflect to what extent users of social media are aware of the availability and/or location of others. This knowledge of users' availability and location can be used negatively, by monitoring them without authorization, posing problems with privacy protection and even with the safety of the users themselves (Baccarella et al., 2018). Thus, we propose that:

RP9: Patients want the 'Presence' feature.

2.6.6. Reputation

The "Reputation" block refers to the identification of the positioning of users and their content in a social environment. If the sharing of information is important in a platform, it should develop metrics that allow it to monitor and understand this positioning, such as likes, views, ratings, or others (Kietzmann et al., 2011). The recognition of user participation is one of the reasons given by Hlavac (2014) for users to join and participate in virtual communities. In this block, Baccarella et al. (2018) warn in particular about the risk of destroying a user's reputation by posting content, which may be false, circulating the faster the more scandalous it is. That said, we propose that:

RP10: Patients want the 'Reputation' feature.

2.6.7. Groups

The last functional block of the model by Kietzmann et al. (2011) intends to reflect on the possibility of users creating groups on a platform. These groups can have different levels of restriction (groups open to all users, restricted or secret). As for the formation of these groups, Baccarella et al. (2018) reiterate that these can enhance prejudice towards those who do not belong to the group and can lead to polarization and radicalization of users' positions and beliefs, similar to political populism. We, therefore, propose that:

RP11: Patients want the 'Groups' feature.

2.6.8. Participants

In the context of social media in health services, Li et al. (2018) distinguish two groups of participants, with different roles in seeking and contributing content: patients and health professionals. As for the former, the authors mention that, as content contributors, they mainly share information about their knowledge of health care, their experiences, symptoms, and evaluations of products, medicines, and professionals who assisted them. On the information-seeking side, they use social media mainly for information, through search tools and their links.

Healthcare professionals, where doctors, nurses, volunteers, and others are included, contribute content on social media when answering questions and queries posed by patients and communicating with them, and exchanging information with other professionals. Thus, they seek content on social media to get information and create knowledge, to train, and to network. Gupta and Schapira (2018) argue that users in oncology virtual communities ask and answer questions from other users and contribute to the creation of resources in that space. Users of virtual communities seeking information will only find communities useful if other users are willing to share that information (Dholakia et al., 2004).

2.6.9. Collecting Data on the Disease

2.6.9.1. Importance of Data Collection

The collection of data, with the proper guarantee of security and privacy, will allow the creation of significant databases and take advantage of the benefits of Big Data, which, combined with artificial intelligence, will allow the discovery of new patterns and correlations between previously unknown variables, enabling better prevention, early diagnosis of diseases, more effective management of hospital resources and, consequently, higher quality of life for patients (Aceto et al., 2020; Laurenza et al., 2018; Papa et al., 2020; Topol, 2019; Wallace et al., 2020). The advantages of these processes extend to physicians, thanks to better decision support, and to the healthcare system itself, with reduced medical errors, costs, and improved processes (Rajkomar et al., 2019; Topol, 2019).

2.6.9.2. Types of Data to be Collected

Servan-Schreiber (2009) establishes four key pillars that impact health and cancer: diet, psychological state, physical activity, and the surrounding environment (such as air quality or the presence of toxins in water). Regarding diet, several studies have found foods and substances that can help prevent cancer and others that can harm health, increasing the risk of cancer (Anand et al., 2008; McGlynn et al., 2021; Molina et al., 2008; Pantuck et al., 2006; Song et al., 2015).

As for the psychological part, certain personalities with negative traces are related to higher cancer incidence and lower disease survival rates (Chida et al., 2008; Lutgendorf & Sood, 2011) as social and emotional support and optimism towards the disease contribute to higher cancer survival rates (Chida & Steptoe, 2008).

As physical activity plays an important role in the prevention and treatment of cancer disease (Anand et al., 2008; Garcia & Thomson, 2014; Molina et al., 2008), the presence of pollution in the environment, exposure to UV radiation, radioactive elements, and carcinogens substances increases the risk of several diseases, cancer included (Anand et al., 2008; Molina et al., 2008).

In addition, Patel and Kondratov (2021) highlight the importance of chronotherapy, i.e., the matching of traditional cancer treatment with the circadian cycle, which may contribute to better tumor responses to treatments and symptom relief from traditional treatments. Instead, circadian cycle disturbances (which can occur with eating at irregular times or sleeping in overly bright environments) can lead to uncontrolled tumor cell growth.

2.6.9.3. Means of Data Collection

All this data can be reported manually, by the patient himself, or automatically, through wearable technology, leveraging the functionalities of the Internet of Things (Papa et al., 2020). Similarly, they can be reported individually or through questionnaires. These questionnaires, well accepted by the oncology and medical population (Gold et al., 2020) can measure specific behaviors, such as fruit and vegetable consumption (Wallace et al., 2020), assess the patient's degree of anxiety and depression, physical status, pain, among others, providing an overview of the patient's condition (Gold et al., 2020). Therefore, and considering all the information presented throughout this point we propose that:

RP12: Patients want a digital diary.

2.7. Privacy

Social media users have a great concern about defending their privacy (Dey et al., 2019; Kane et al., 2014; Li et al., 2018). To do so, some users choose to use nicknames as an alternative to the real name (Kietzmann et al., 2011), as a way to ensure the authenticity of the profile without jeopardizing the user's privacy (Kane et al., 2014).

Al-Muhtadi et al. (2019) proposed a categorization of personal data into four levels of privacy and a series of measures, for social networks aimed at health, to ensure the security and privacy of users and their data. Thus, among others, the authors suggest that the social network must ensure that users will remain unidentifiable, even in cases of improper access to the network. They also suggest that profiles should be kept private by default and that there should be a clear definition of permissions for each user according to their role on the network. Furthermore, only the network administrators can authorize the creation of a new profile. We thus propose that:

RP13: Patients want to control the privacy of their information.

RP14: Access to the community should be restricted to IPO Porto patients and health professionals.

3. METHODOLOGY

This study followed a double methodology, considering the objectives and available literature.

On one hand, there is little literature about the specific information that physicians/researchers are interested in collecting from a virtual community. Considering that the purpose of interviews is to explore a topic and ensure a broader thematic scope (Britten, 1995; Dicicco-Bloom & Crabtree, 2006), there were interviewed 10 health professionals from IPO Porto, with a mean professional time of 19 years. It followed both convenience and referral sampling (per colleagues) approaches, ideal for recruiting participants whose reach is more difficult, like health professionals during the pandemic time and its recovery (Robinson, 2013). The interviews had a mean duration of 14 minutes and 24 seconds.

On the other hand, considering the relevant literature on virtual community tools and the lack of literature on its most desired characteristics, it was followed a mixed methodology questionnaires approach, with qualitative and quantitative answers. This method allows for testing the stipulated research hypotheses and to approach a significantly larger sample, while assuming an exploratory character (Evans & Mathur, 2005; Malhotra & Birks, 2003).

The questionnaires were applied to IPO Porto's patients that were undergoing chemotherapy there, following a non-random sampling by convenience method. There was a total of 83 questionnaires applied, 11 of which were considered invalid due to withdrawal. The valid questionnaires had an average completeness rate of 90%, implying that not all the questions were answered.

Breast, colorectal, and lung cancers and lymphomas, and leukemias represent 60% of the sample. 72% of the respondents said they were social media users and 82% were 41 or more years old.

4. ANALYSIS OF THE COLLECTED DATA

4.1. Interview Analysis (Qualitative Method)

When asked about what type of information health professionals wanted to collect, all of them said that patients' clinical information, physical activity, and emotions were relevant to their daily work and to assess patients' global health. Only diet wasn't relevant to all of them, but it was shown very relevant to nutritionists.

The reference to the need to adapt the information to the specialty, pathology, and patient was observed in 80% of the interviews. This is important, as one of the professionals said, to "not overwhelm the consultation with information.". Some excerpts about this topic can be seen in Table 2.

4.1.1. Clinical Information

Regarding patients' clinical information, data on vital signs, such as blood pressure, glucose, and temperature were the most mentioned (6 interviews), followed by anthropometric data, especially weight and its evolution (2 interviews). Also in two interviews, data regarding the level of pain were mentioned. In Table 3 are some excerpts from the interviews.

4.1.2. Information on Physical Activity

Like the clinical information, the collection of information on physical activity met with the consensus of all the professionals interviewed, although the type of data mentioned varied. Half of the interviews mentioned the collection of data on the type of activity performed can help to understand the patient's

Table 2. Excerpts from the interviews about the adaptation of information

Interview	Excerpts taken from the interviews
E1	"I would only suggest that the information be available as needed by the specialty"
E7	"All this has to be adjusted according to the condition of the patient at that time, because he goes through various phases, depending on the treatment, and even the patient himself"

Table 3. Excerpts from the interviews about clinical information

Interview	Excerpts taken from the interviews
E1	" (...) in some pathologies we must watch the blood pressure because of side effects to drugs"
E3	"In our data collection we take into account weight, height, weight history, that is, when did the patient start losing weight (...)"
E7	"For example, if the patient does a hypothermia, a hypertension or a hypotension."
E8	"For example, the blood pressure and diabetes, even because the patient may feel bad (...) and we have a faster way of consulting that data"
E10	"A fever, vomiting, pain, (...) a fall or an episode of epistaxis (a bleeding from the nose)"

functional status and limitations, the impact of the disease and the treatment, and to achieve a better patient follow-up (see Table 4).

4.1.3. Information on Emotions

This was the type of information in which the professionals interviewed showed the most enthusiasm. Despite the importance attributed, most professionals were unable to define concrete data to collect. However, the psychology professional highlighted the usefulness of this information, especially when acting as a triage of patients: "If not within a psychological intervention work plan, what would make more sense is to use the platform, possibly, as an identification of people who are moving towards the orange or red line, who are at levels of intensity or nature of what they are feeling that already leads to guessing a framework of greater suffering, who need help, and that could eventually help identify them" (E2).

From the analysis of the remaining interviews, it was possible to see that the main objective of the professionals, with the collection of this type of data, is to have an understanding of the general condition of the patient, as can be read in Table 5.

4.1.4. Diet Information

As mentioned before, this was the category of information with the least interest. However, the main goal of health professionals in obtaining this information is the follow-up of the general patient's condition, as well as monitoring the adequacy of eating habits. Also on this point, it was possible to observe the need to adapt the information to the pathology and stage of the disease, as can be seen in Table 6.

Table 4. Excerpts from the interviews about the information on physical activity

Interview	Excerpts taken from the interviews
E1	"The physical exercise part may be more useful to us, mainly because of the impact it can have even on the prognosis of the cancer disease."
E2	"For example, if the person does a moderate-intensity activity, like a half-hour walk, it's important, because that also helps us understand the person's state and helps improve the patient's mental health."
E3	"Imagine a patient who was used to running x kilometers a day and suddenly doesn't have that capacity due to the disease (…). So, to try to understand how the disease influenced the physical part."
E9	"I think patients are very afraid to know what they can do, they always have that fear of knowing how far they can go or not, what kind of activity they can do or not (...) to know if they are adequate training or not"

Table 5. Excerpts from the interviews about the information related to emotions

Interview	Excerpts taken from the interviews
E2	**"A questionnaire on whether the person can sleep, on indicators that tell us if the person may be well or not (...) the use of the *Distress* thermometer. (...)"**
E3	"we usually refer to this in the clinical diary, for example, that the patient is sad with his clinical situation or that he is more satisfied, the treatments going well, the patient emotionally more balanced."
E4	"I think it's important (...) because it would be an easy way for them, to fill out questionnaires"
E6	"It is undeniably important to know how the patients are feeling, even to know to what extent they can be receptive to certain therapeutic or surgical interventions".
E9	"I even think that in these (cancer) patients it ends up being the most important parameter (...) and maybe many don't even talk, they don't want to worry the family, others also don't have a family to support them, and we notice here that many times when they are alone with us they get it off their chest".

Table 6. Excerpts from the interviews about food information

Interview	Excerpts taken from the interviews
E3	"The number of meals, what they consist of, quality and quantity, whether you are a patient who also takes nutritional supplements or not."
E6	"That could be something useful for us to understand the patient's potential and whether they are recovering well."
E7	"Yes, there are treatments that imply certain care with food, there are things that are allowed, there are others that are completely forbidden, (...) but you could go along if this platform existed."
E9	"If you're a digestive cancer patient, in terms of nutrition it's critical because a lot of them run out of stomach and then they do a lot of supplements."

4.1.5. Other Information Mentioned

In addition to the areas addressed above, other types of information were mentioned throughout the interviews. Patient Reported Outcomes Measures (PROMs), quality of life questionnaires as well as data regarding the patient's sexuality were the most mentioned, as can be seen in Table 7.

Table 7. Excerpts from the interviews regarding other information

Interview	Excerpts taken from the interviews
E1	"The *PROMs* and I think that's fundamental and very important"; "The onco-sexuality part, in those diseases that have more impact on breast, prostate cancer..."
E2	"Other questionnaires for emotional disturbances, (...) prescription monitoring, (...) a journal in the cognitive therapy line or the thoughts and behaviors line"
E4	"Micturition diaries (...) and PROMs, because it would be easy, probably with a greater compliance by the patient"
E5	"Micturition pattern questionnaires, namely the IPSS (International Prostate Symptom Score), erectile dysfunction questionnaires"
E6	"Urinary quality of life questionnaires like IPSS or the IEF which is a measure of sexual dysfunction (...) and also the general quality of life questionnaires"; "Patient's costs with the treatments they do (travel, how much they spend on medication) and geography"

4.1.6. Impact on Decision-Making and Follow-Up

When asked whether the collection of the data mentioned could impact and assist in decision-making and patient follow-up, all the professionals interviewed agreed. The most prominent points of this potential impact are the adaptation of treatment to the patient's current status, the updating of the patient's status in real-time and outside the institution, the early detection and action on problems, and also the involvement of the patient in his treatment (see Table 8).

4.1.7. Impact on Pattern Detection and Cancer Knowledge

When asked whether collecting and storing data in a database could help detect patterns and increase knowledge about cancer, only one professional was skeptical. The aspects mentioned by the professionals, have to do mainly with the detection of patterns between patients' behaviors and the treatments they are undergoing, as well as the appropriateness of the treatment, the evaluation of the evolution of patient satisfaction, and the creation of knowledge based on this data. Some excerpts are transcripts in Table 9.

4.1.8. Impact on Patient Well-Being and Care

When asked whether the collection of the information addressed above could impact patient well-being and the quality of care provided, the professionals were unanimous in agreeing, although most professionals did not justify or explain their reasons for agreeing, making it difficult to draw specific conclusions (see Table 10).

4.1.9. Other Aspects

Regarding the availability to participate, answer simple questions, and contribute with cancer information, all professionals expressed interest and availability. It is noteworthy, however, that half of the professionals reported not having working hours available to participate (see Table 11). All the professionals interviewed agreed that the creation of a virtual community, with the particularity of data collection,

Table 8. Excerpts from the interviews regarding the impact on decision-making and follow-up

Interview	Excerpts taken from the interviews
E2	"The question of people being able to put their data, even in behavioral terms, to enhance the process of the consultations, that seems very useful to me (...) and then putting that data together in a database, which can help us in future questions, that seems interesting to me. To directly help patients with that data and create an interesting data pool to help understand the disease."
E3	"The more involved you are in your condition and your health, your treatments, the easier it is for you to tolerate some treatments"
E6	"I advocate that we should integrate our diary, have some classical records and summaries of what we want, but with well-founded and quantified measurement units for many variables. And it would be excellent because that gives us more real measures and allows us to make better decisions in terms of benefit to the patient."
E7	"Yes, even in earlier decision-making. At this moment we only have contact when the patient comes here (…). If there is this network, in which the patient can permanently tell us what his changes are, and what he is feeling earlier, we can intervene. And it would prevent the whole situation from progressing to more complicated situations."

Table 9. Excerpts from the interviews regarding the impact on pattern detection and cancer knowledge

Interview	Excerpts taken from the interviews
E4	"In the follow-up sometimes of prostate cancers, for example, of localized symptoms, if there was a record of the onset of symptoms, type of pain or even in bladder tumors the record of urinary symptoms (frequency, incontinence or even blood in the urine), it could anticipate even the performance of tests that would already be scheduled and even in the follow-up."
E5	"It can. I consider it and I think it makes sense, even from an internal audit perspective of the service itself to know, in terms of quality, how the service is evolving, if the patients are satisfied or not, if the quality of life of the patients is satisfactory."
E6	" I have a lot of doubt that through these databases you create the information about the direct relationship between exercise, or the way you urinate, and the tumor. What it does allow is the extraction of information used for the creation of science, i.e., we can see various correlations, between patients who survive chemotherapy or surgery better with the amount of exercise they did before those interventions and after. We can relate urinary symptoms and the before and after results. These kinds of units of measurement create scientific added value, no doubt. Direct correlation with cancer prevention and cancer progression is more difficult, but they can... once a person had those data well compiled, well defined, and aggregated by a journal, it was much easier. In databases, it is much easier to go from there to scientific work that validates theories of any kind, for example, something that works better or worse, whether the patient's previous conditions are very important or not important for that treatment to work well. From the moment we had the measurement instrument in a database, we can do a lot of science based on that, yes."

Table 10. Excerpts from the interviews regarding the impact on patient well-being and care

Interview	Excerpts taken from the interviews
E2	"Yes. If it was in articulation with consultation yes, because we can evaluate to intervene."
E3	"By having tighter *feedback* from the patient, we may be able to see sometimes when we're not acting and maybe we need to act. That can also give us that insight into the background."
E9	"Yes. If nothing else, they also feel more supported by having a support network that they can always turn to."

could be a factor of proximity between the professionals, the patient, and the hosting health institution. Throughout the interviews, some additional comments and observations were made spontaneously.

Among the ideas mentioned is the potential that, from the perspective of health professionals, this community may have on patients, namely through the sharing of experiences and contact with other similar people, although this is not a risk-free relationship. To reduce this risk, the need to have a team dedicated entirely to the community was mentioned, to be able to control interaction between patients and, eventually, block users whose behavior is inappropriate. Such a team, dedicated to the community, was also invoked to make up for the professionals' lack of time available for communication with patients. Setting tight rules for the community was another topic that was spontaneously brought up.

4.2. Analysis of the Questionnaires (Mixed Method)

Data collection with the patients was done mostly through the application of paper questionnaires, causing some non-responses to some items. The item with the most non-responses had 57 out of 66 possible answers. The statistics were made using SPSS software.

4.2.1. Analysis of the RPs

Considering **RP1** ("The most suitable type of social medium is an event-driven virtual community"), it may be concluded that most respondents want a social environment dedicated exclusively to cancer

Table 11. Excerpts from the interviews with other important information

Interview	Excerpts taken from the interviews
E1	"Sometimes people, either because they come accompanied or because they don't want to say face to face (data about their sexuality) ... maybe they could feel a little more at ease through these platforms, which is also important because it ends up affecting the psychological part and the part of the relationship and quality of life."
E2	"It had to be an IPO system because of data protection."; "So, for this to work, in my opinion, there had a team dedicated to this, otherwise I don't recommend having something like this, because it can be very risky"; "to have strict rules of operation and people to monitor and, perhaps, make more of a kind of rooms, like sub-communities by disease, and that could eventually talk to each other, always with many rules and very regulated, very monitored".
E4	"I think it can help to bond with other patients who have been through the same thing. I think that's where there's a lot of value. We make little use of support groups and patient communities and I think that that, for patient support, could be an important tool. So that they can even sometimes come up with coping strategies and understand what's going on and talk to someone who will have gone through the same thing. They sometimes ask, 'But how does it stay, how doesn't it stay' and we say, but I think they would be more satisfied if they happened to talk to someone who had been through the same thing."
E5	"From the perspective of an internal IPO social network, maybe it would also be interesting for the patients themselves to share experiences, so that new patients, who come to the IPO, can understand how other patients have been treated and what they've been through, how they are doing now, sharing experiences.
E6	"I think those kinds of communities are good for improvement and for the patient to feel more confident about the treatments and the institution that instituted them, and that's always a plus."
E7	"It has to be a community that serves also for us to monitor and weed out the profile of those who are there and want to destabilize. Because if it's really what it's created for, I think it's an asset."
E10	"But in terms of his home, that's where there might be a gap because we don't know unless he comes here to the consultation and tells us (...) something like that at that level would be super interesting"

disease (n=61; mean=3.87, p=0.000). However, their participation does not end with the cure of the disease, and most intend to continue using the social environment (n=60; mean=2.39; p=0.000). When tested if the diagnosis could be a triggering event for their participation in this environment, there is statistical neutrality towards the statement (n=59; mean=3.28; p=0.055). Considering this, it is not possible to conclude on the rejection or non-rejection of RP1 and it is suggested that future studies focus on this classification, to assess which type of social environment is more appropriate.

For **RP2** ("Patients consider that the existence of a virtual community would be an added value to the service provided by IPO Porto."), it can be concluded that most respondents perceive this community as an asset to the IPO Porto' service (n=63; mean=4.03; p=0.000).

It was possible to conclude that participation in this community will help patients feel better (n=60; mean=3.97; p=0.000) and cope with the disease (n=61; mean=3.95; p=0.000). Also, questioned patients want that cancer survivors (n=64; mean=4.06; p=0.000) and current cancer patients (n=62; mean=4.02; p=0.000) share their experience with them. They also want to share their experience with cancer with other patients (n=63; mean=4.02; p=0.000). Patients reported that they will feel more confident if they share their information with health professionals (n=60; mean=4.15; p=0.000) and privately with other patients (n=62; mean= 3.32; p=0.014), but not publicly (n=59; mean=2.97; p=0.821). They will also feel more confident to receive that information privately from other patients (n=58; mean=3.29; p=0.026) and not publicly (n=56; mean=3.02; p=0.898). All of this leads to the conclusion that there is indeed an impact on patients' well-being and to conclude for the non-rejection of **RP3** ("Patients consider that the existence of a virtual community would bring benefits to their emotional well-being.").

The **RP4** ("A virtual community will enable to improve the doctor-patient relationship.") was tested with physicians and patients. As for physicians, the answers have already been analyzed earlier in this chapter, the conclusion being that this community can effectively improve the doctor-patient relationship. As for patients, the results obtained lead to the conclusion that, for a significance level of 5%, there is an agreement with the possible relationship improvement (n=63; mean=4.14; p=0.000). Thus, considering both parts of the study, we do not reject RP4.

For **RP5** - **"Patients want the 'Profiles' feature."** four nominal scale questions were asked to understand how to build profiles. Most respondents said that their profiles should only have their names (45.5%), although most respondents said they prefer other patients' profiles (46.8%) and health professionals' profiles (75.4%) to have their names and photography. As for the other data to be used in the profile, 84.8% of respondents said they wanted to include their location in the profile, followed by cancer location (69.7%) and age (59.1%). Thus, RP5 is not rejected.

Patients reported willing to exchange private messages with other users (n=3.61; mean=3.61; p=0.000), to comment on information shared by other users (n=64; mean=3.63; p=0.000) and that other users comment on their shared information (n=64; mean=3.51; p=0.000). No statistically significant difference was found between the desire to comment and to have the information commented on by others (p=0.197). Having said this, **RP6** ("Patients want the 'Messages' and 'Comments' features.") is not rejected.

Concerning **RP7** ("Patients want the 'Connections' functionality."), patients answered that they want to choose who can connect with their profiles (n=64; mean=4.15; p=0.000), concluding that RP7 was not rejected.

Questioned patients reported they want to share information (n=61; mean=3.85; p=0.000) and to receive shared information from other users (n=61; mean=3.77; p=0.000). Thus, it is important to understand what kind of information is more likely to be shared by users. As seen in RP3, patients want to share, and other patients share their cancer testimonials, with no significant difference between the importance of giving and receiving these lived experiences (p=0.000). Also, patients want to see other users' publications (or posts) about the treatment or the disease (n=63; mean=3.59; p=0.000), symptoms (n=62; mean=3.73; p=0.000), and experiences with the hospital services (n=61; mean=3.90; p=0.000). Having this in mind, **RP8** ("Patients want the 'Sharing' feature.") should not be rejected.

Regarding the presence functionality, respondents want to know if other users are online (n=63; mean=3.69; p=0.000) and do not deny that their status will be disclosed (n=59; mean=3.50; p=0.000), leading to the not rejection of **RP9** ("Patients want the functionality 'Presence'.").

Patients reported that the presence of health professionals would give the network credibility (n=65; mean=4.45; p=0.000) and believe that the information that health professionals share is credible (n=64; mean=4.45; p=0.000). Participants in this questionnaire do not attribute the same credibility to information shared by patients as compared to information shared by health professionals (n=64; mean= 2.86; p=0.327). That said, patients feel more confident knowing whether their peers consider certain information important (n=61; mean= 3.60; p=0.000), thus leading to the non-rejection of **RP10** ("Patients want the functionality 'Reputation'.").

When asked about their willingness to join groups, patients answered positively to groups dedicated to specific cancers (n=64; mean=3.60; p=0.000) and other more general groups (n=62; mean=3.49; p=0.000), and it was not possible to find a statistically significant difference in the willingness between belonging to general or specific groups (p=0.527). All of this leads to non-rejection of **RP11** ("Patients want the functionality 'Groups'.").

Regarding **RP12**, "Patients want a digital diary.", 77.3% of respondents said they are willing to share, with health professionals, information regarding diet through a digital diary. Also, 72.7% of respondents said they are willing to share their emotional state and daily activity data through this tool, and these three categories are the most consensual among patients. The least consensual information to be shared in this diary is the sexual information (e.g., lack of desire, changes in well-being, etc.), with only 48.5% of patients willing to report this data. Only 4.5% of participants said they refuse to share any kind of information, thus allowing us to conclude the non-rejection of RP12.

To test **RP13,** "Patients want to control the privacy of their information.", it was asked if patients would like to control who could see their information and posts, and the answers were positive (n=59; mean=3.93; p=0.000), not rejecting this research proposition.

Finally, for **RP14,** "Access to the community should be restricted to IPO Porto patients and health professionals.", the majority of respondents included health professionals (70.3%) and patients (64.1%) from other IPOs in the list of potential users of this community, leading to the rejection of RP14.

5. FINAL CONSIDERATIONS

This exploratory study adopted a mixed methodological approach, with the application of questionnaires to patients and semi-structured interviews with health professionals from several areas, all belonging to the IPO Porto, to explore the main tools found in the literature.

By being conducted in partnership with the IPO Porto, this study ensured compliance with high standards of data protection and ethical defense of patients, while guaranteeing a seal of trust from the Institution.

5.1. Contributions

This innovative study aggregated transversal theories of social media and marketing and allowed it to fill a gap in the bibliography. By identifying and understanding the latent needs of health professionals and patients at the IPO Porto, it was possible to identify the tools of an oncologic social environment, and its characteristics, considered most relevant for the integration of parts.

The study also allowed us to understand how to provide health professionals with critical information for patient follow-up, constituting an added value for the hosting institutions. It is, thus, of great importance to highlight the urgency of collecting this data, which may contribute to establishing rigorous causality between the patient's recovery and the different groups of information collected, forming a database with high economic and social value.

This study enables institutions to implement support platforms for their patients that correspond to what they expect and that are useful for their professionals. This is, therefore, a pressing issue that opens doors to new lines of research.

5.2. Conclusion

Health professionals were favorably unanimous regarding the creation of this social environment, with a special focus on the personalized collection of patients' data. Half of these professionals stated that they do not have working hours available to participate, which indicates that health institutions may reflect on it, for the success of these social means.

The impact of data collection occurs on several levels: on the one hand, it positively affects decision-making and allows better patient follow-up, facilitating patient involvement and early detection of adverse events. On the other hand, it allows the creation of science and of reach databases, with scientific, social, economic, and political implications.

Although it was not possible to define the most suitable type of social media, it was possible to conclude that patients want to have a profile and, to connect their profiles, a two-way relationship should be used. Private messaging and commenting functionalities are desired. Healthcare professionals enjoy a reputation that attributes credibility to their shared information. However, knowing whether other patients have found the information useful makes it more credible.

In this social environment should be allowed to participate health professionals and patients from all IPOs in Portugal (Coimbra, Lisbon, and Porto), enhancing the contact between users, and the exchange of knowledge and resulting in a larger database, collected through digital diaries, well accepted by the patients surveyed.

The formation of groups within the community is desired, and it should have a dedicated team to avoid the circulation of inappropriate or malicious content, enabling users to report profiles and information they consider suspicious. Users should be given control over the privacy of their data and shared information.

This type of social environment is, therefore, an added value for health institutions, allowing their patients greater emotional well-being and improving their relationship with the institution and its professionals.

Overall, this oncology social environment shows promise from a Value-Based Healthcare perspective, as it has enormous potential to impact patients, and can enable cost efficiencies of services provided with the personalization and tailoring of treatments to the patient's actual condition.

5.3. Limitations

The exploratory nature of the study proves to be a limitation due to the lack of proven models and the generalized nature of the analysis of the tools, using mainly descriptive statistics. The pandemic of COVID-19 also presented itself as a restrictive factor for the study, due to the complexity of all the processes, and the impact that the virus had on data collection, leading to reduced samples.

5.4. Recommendations for Future Research

Notwithstanding the restrictions encountered, the study proves to be very promising, opening the door to new lines of investigation in this area. As mentioned earlier, it was not possible to determine in this study which type of social environment is most suitable, so it should be studied in depth for its concrete determination.

A latent desire was revealed on the part of health professionals to collect data to allow a more personalized follow-up of patients, although adapted to the type of cancer and professional category in question. It is therefore important to specifically study the data sought by each professional category and specialty, as well as its real impact on treatments and their cost-effectiveness. Also latent was the patients' desire to participate in such a social environment, making it necessary in the future to study which devices would be most effective for this social environment (Web, Smartphone, ...) and whether it should be a new application or be integrated into existing hospital applications for patients and health professionals.

The data to be collected constitutes a real possibility of knowledge creation through the formation of databases that aggregate this information, so there is a need to study the methodology for its creation, safeguarding the security of this delicate information and, at the same time, guaranteeing the ease of analysis. No less important is the study, through clinical trials, to validate the perceived gain in patients' psychological well-being obtained with the use of these platforms and its impact on disease outcomes and costs.

It would also be very interesting to study the impact of the availability of this platform on the evaluation of the quality of services provided, to confirm the added value of this tool.

REFERENCES

Aceto, G., Persico, V., & Pescapé, A. (2020). Industry 4.0 and Health: Internet of Things, Big Data, and Cloud Computing for Healthcare 4.0. *Journal of Industrial Information Integration*, *18*, 100129. doi:10.1016/j.jii.2020.100129

Al-Muhtadi, J., Shahzad, B., Saleem, K., Jameel, W., & Orgun, M. A. (2019). Cybersecurity and privacy issues for socially integrated mobile healthcare applications operating in a multi-cloud environment. *Health Informatics Journal*, *25*(2), 315–329. doi:10.1177/1460458217706184 PMID:28480788

Anand, P., Kunnumakkara, A. B., Sundaram, C., Harikumar, K. B., Tharakan, S. T., Lai, O. S., Sung, B., & Aggarwal, B. B. (2008). Cancer is a preventable disease that requires major lifestyle changes. *Pharmaceutical Research*, *25*(9), 2097–2116. doi:10.100711095-008-9661-9 PMID:18626751

Baccarella, C. V., Wagner, T. F., Kietzmann, J. H., & McCarthy, I. P. (2018). Social media? It's serious! Understanding the dark side of social media. *European Management Journal*, *36*(4), 431–438. doi:10.1016/j.emj.2018.07.002

Benetoli, A., Chen, T. F., & Aslani, P. (2018). How patient's use of social media impacts their interactions with healthcare professionals. *Patient Education and Counseling*, *101*(3), 439–444. doi:10.1016/j.pec.2017.08.015 PMID:28882545

Boyd, D. M., & Ellison, N. B. (2007). Social Network Sites: Definition, History, and Scholarship. *Journal of Computer-Mediated Communication*, *13*(1), 210–230. doi:10.1111/j.1083-6101.2007.00393.x

Britten, N. (1995). Qualitative interviews in medical research. *BMJ (Clinical Research Ed.)*, *311*(6999), 251–253. doi:10.1136/bmj.311.6999.251 PMID:7627048

Chida, Y., Hamer, M., Wardle, J., & Steptoe, A. (2008). Do stress-related psychosocial factors contribute to cancer incidence and survival? *Nature Clinical Practice. Oncology*, *5*(8), 466–475. doi:10.1038/ncponc1134 PMID:18493231

Chida, Y., & Steptoe, A. (2008). Positive psychological well-being and mortality: A quantitative review of prospective observational studies. *Psychosomatic Medicine*, *70*(7), 741–756. doi:10.1097/PSY.0b013e31818105ba PMID:18725425

Dey, N., Borah, S., Babo, R., & Ashour, A. S. (2019). *Social Network Analytics Computational Research Methods and Techniques*. Academic Press.

Dholakia, U. M., Bagozzi, R. P., & Pearo, L. K. (2004). A social influence model of consumer participation in network- and small-group-based virtual communities. *International Journal of Research in Marketing*, *21*(3), 241–263. doi:10.1016/j.ijresmar.2003.12.004

Dicicco-Bloom, B., & Crabtree, B. F. (2006). The qualitative research interview. *Medical Education, 40*(4), 314–321. doi:10.1111/j.1365-2929.2006.02418.x PMID:16573666

Erfani, S. S., Abedin, B., & Blount, Y. (2017). The effect of social network site use on the psychological well-being of cancer patients. *Journal of the Association for Information Science and Technology, 68*(5), 1308–1322. doi:10.1002/asi.23702

Evans, J. R., & Mathur, A. (2005). The value of online surveys. *Internet Research, 15*(2), 195–219. doi:10.1108/10662240510590360

Eysenbach, G. (2003). The Impact of the Internet on Cancer Outcomes. *CA: a Cancer Journal for Clinicians, 53*(6), 356–371. doi:10.3322/canjclin.53.6.356 PMID:15224975

Fu, S., Li, H., Liu, Y., Pirkkalainen, H., & Salo, M. (2020). Social media overload, exhaustion, and use discontinuance: Examining the effects of information overload, system feature overload, and social overload. *Information Processing & Management, 57*(6), 102307. doi:10.1016/j.ipm.2020.102307

Furstrand, D., Pihl, A., Orbe, E. B., Kingod, N., & Sondergaard, J. (2021). "Ask a Doctor About Coronavirus": How Physicians on Social Media Can Provide Valid Health Information During a Pandemic. *Journal of Medical Internet Research, 23*(4), e24586. doi:10.2196/24586 PMID:33835935

Garcia, D. O., & Thomson, C. A. (2014). Physical activity and cancer survivorship. *Nutrition in Clinical Practice, 29*(6), 768–779. doi:10.1177/0884533614551969 PMID:25335787

Gold, H. T., Karia, R. J., Link, A., Lebwohl, R., Zuckerman, J. D., Errico, T. J., Slover, J. D., Buckland, A. J., Mann, D. M., & Cantor, M. N. (2020). Implementation and early adaptation of patient-reported outcome measures into an electronic health record: A technical report. *Health Informatics Journal, 26*(1), 129–140. doi:10.1177/1460458218813710 PMID:30516095

Gupta, P., Khan, A., & Kumar, A. (2020). Social media use by patients in health care: A scoping review. *International Journal of Healthcare Management, 15*(2), 121–131. doi:10.1080/20479700.2020.1860563

Gupta, T., & Schapira, L. (2018). Online Communities as Sources of Peer Support for People Living With Cancer: A Commentary. *Journal of Oncology Practice / American Society of Clinical Oncology, 14*(12), 725–731. doi:10.1200/JOP.18.00261 PMID:30335558

Hlavac, R. (2014). *Social IMC: Social Strategies with Bottom-line ROI*. CreateSpace Independent Publishing Platform.

Johansson, V., Islind, A. S., Lindroth, T., Angenete, E., & Gellerstedt, M. (2021). Online Communities as a Driver for Patient Empowerment: Systematic Review. *Journal of Medical Internet Research, 23*(2), e19910. doi:10.2196/19910 PMID:33560233

Kane, G. C., Alavi, M., Labianca, G., & Borgatti, S. P. (2014). What's Different about Social Media Networks? A Framework and Research Agenda. *Management Information Systems Quarterly, 38*(1), 274–304. doi:10.25300/MISQ/2014/38.1.13

Kaplan, A. M., & Haenlein, M. (2010). Users of the world, unite! The challenges and opportunities of Social Media. *Business Horizons, 53*(1), 59–8. doi:10.1016/j.bushor.2009.09.003

Kietzmann, J. H., Hermkens, K., McCarthy, I. P., & Silvestre, B. S. (2011). Social media? Get serious! Understanding the functional building blocks of social media. *Business Horizons*, *54*(3), 241–251. doi:10.1016/j.bushor.2011.01.005

Laurenza, E., Quintano, M., Schiavone, F., & Vrontis, D. (2018). The effect of digital technologies adoption in healthcare industry: A case based analysis. *Business Process Management Journal*, *24*(5), 1124–1144. doi:10.1108/BPMJ-04-2017-0084

Leimeister, J. M., Ebner, W., & Krcmar, H. (2005). Design, Implementation, and Evaluation of Trust-Supporting Components in Virtual Communities for Patients. *Journal of Management Information Systems*, *21*(4), 101–135. doi:10.1080/07421222.2005.11045825

Li, Y., Wang, X., Lin, X., & Hajli, M. (2018). Seeking and sharing health information on social media: A net valence model and cross-cultural comparison. *Technological Forecasting and Social Change*, *126*, 28–40. doi:10.1016/j.techfore.2016.07.021

Lutgendorf, S. K., & Sood, A. K. (2011). Biobehavioral Factors and Cancer Progression: Physiological Pathways and Mechanisms. *Psychosomatic Medicine*, *73*(9), 724–730. doi:10.1097/PSY.0b013e318235be76 PMID:22021459

Malhotra, N. K., & Birks, D. F. (2003). Marketing Research: An Applied Approach (2end ed.). Pearson Education Limited.

McGlynn, K. A., Petrick, J. L., & El-Serag, H. B. (2021). Epidemiology of Hepatocellular Carcinoma. *Hepatology (Baltimore, Md.)*, *73*(S1), 4–13. doi:10.1002/hep.31288 PMID:32319693

Molina, J. R., Yang, P., Cassivi, S. D., Schild, S. E., & Adjei, A. A. (2008). Non-small cell lung cancer: Epidemiology, risk factors, treatment, and survivorship. *Mayo Clinic Proceedings*, *83*(5), 584–594. doi:10.1016/S0025-6196(11)60735-0 PMID:18452692

Obar, J. A., & Wildman, S. (2015). Social Media Definition and the Governance Challenge: An Introduction to the Special Issue. *Telecommunications Policy*, *39*(9), 745–750. doi:10.1016/j.telpol.2015.07.014

OECD. (2007). *Participative Web and User-Created Content*. OECD. http://browse.oecdbookshop.org/oecd/pdfs/free/9307031e.pdf

Pantuck, A. J., Leppert, J. T., Zomorodian, N., Aronson, W., Hong, J., Barnard, R. J., Seeram, N., Liker, H., Wang, H., Elashoff, R., Heber, D., Aviram, M., Ignarro, L., & Belldegrun, A. (2006). Phase II study of pomegranate juice for men with rising prostate-specific antigen following surgery or radiation for prostate cancer. *Clinical Cancer Research*, *12*(13), 4018–4026. doi:10.1158/1078-0432.CCR-05-2290 PMID:16818701

Papa, A., Mital, M., Pisano, P., & Del Giudice, M. (2020). E-health and wellbeing monitoring using smart healthcare devices: An empirical investigation. *Technological Forecasting and Social Change*, *153*, 119226. doi:10.1016/j.techfore.2018.02.018

Patel, S. A., & Kondratov, R. V. (2021). Clock at the Core of Cancer Development. *Biology (Basel)*, *10*(2), 150. doi:10.3390/biology10020150 PMID:33672910

Rajkomar, A., Dean, J., & Kohane, I. (2019). Machine Learning in Medicine. *The New England Journal of Medicine*, *380*(14), 1347–1358. doi:10.1056/NEJMra1814259 PMID:30943338

Robinson, O. C. (2013). Sampling in Interview-Based Qualitative Research: A Theoretical and Practical Guide. *Qualitative Research in Psychology*, *11*(1), 25–41. doi:10.1080/14780887.2013.801543

Schweizer, K. J., Leimeister, J. M., & Krcmar, H. (2006). The Role of Virtual Communities for the Social Network of Cancer Patients. In *Proceedings of the Twelfth Americas Conference on Information Systems* (pp. 4470–4479), Acapulco, Mexico.

Servan-Schreiber, D. (2009). *Anticancer: A new way of life*. Viking Penguin.

Song, M., Garrett, W. S., & Chan, A. T. (2015). Nutrients, Foods, and Colorectal Cancer Prevention. *Gastroenterology*, *148*(6), 1244–1260.e1216. doi:10.1053/j.gastro.2014.12.035 PMID:25575572

Topol, E. J. (2019). High-performance medicine: The convergence of human and artificial intelligence. *Nature Medicine*, *25*(1), 44–56. doi:10.103841591-018-0300-7 PMID:30617339

Wallace, T. C., Bailey, R. L., Blumberg, J. B., Burton-Freeman, B., Chen, C. O., Crowe-White, K. M., Drewnowski, A., Hooshmand, S., Johnson, E., Lewis, R., Murray, R., Shapses, S. A., & Wang, D. D. (2020). Fruits, vegetables, and health: A comprehensive narrative, umbrella review of the science and recommendations for enhanced public policy to improve intake. *Critical Reviews in Food Science and Nutrition*, *60*(13), 2174–2211. doi:10.1080/10408398.2019.1632258 PMID:31267783

ENDNOTE

1 Available at https://www.dgs.pt/qualidade-e-seguranca/reconhecimento-da-qualidade/acreditacao-em-saude/manuais-de-standards.aspx

Chapter 3
Analyzing Perspectives on Lifestyle M-Health Apps:
User and Non-User Insights

Veronika Keller
https://orcid.org/0000-0002-7759-7613
Széchenyi István University, Hungary

Ida Ercsey
Széchenyi István Egyetem, Hungary

ABSTRACT

The aim of the research is to explore the theoretical background and experiences of using lifestyle (LS) applications from a user perspective. The objective is to identify the reasons for non-usage. To accomplish these research goals, four focus group interviews were conducted with students studying recreation management in the autumn of 2022. The focus group research findings indicated that sports and fitness apps were the participants' most favoured. The evaluation of LS applications identified usefulness, features, accessibility, and accuracy as the most significant factors. More students reported positive effects on their physical and mental health; however, they viewed the applications and smart devices as auxiliary tools. The main reasons for non-use included personal, technical, and usability issues, as discovered by the authors. This chapter provides an in-depth insight into alterations in health practices, incentives and encounters with mobile devices and LS apps, contributing to the field of service literature.

1. INTRODUCTION

Overweight and obesity are an epidemic that appears in the developed countries of the world but also in developing countries. This phenomenon can be explained by inappropriate eating habits and a sedentary lifestyle. Based on statistical data, overweight and obesity is a serious problem among young people, as the proportion of obese young people (below 35) is constantly increasing in the developed regions of the world. Considering the national health survey of KSH (Central Statistical Office) from

DOI: 10.4018/978-1-6684-8984-0.ch003

2019 (European Health Interview Survey, 2019). Generations Z and Y (18-34-year-old Hungarians) have an unhealthy lifestyle than older generations. The proportion of obese and overweight people among young people (aged 18-34) in 2019 was as follows: 46.2% for men and 32.3% for women, although the survey found that women underestimated their weight and overestimated their height, as the calculation of the body mass index was based on self-reporting. Underweight was more common among women (5.5%) than men (1.4%). Looking at trends, there has been a slight decrease among young men and a slight increase among young women over the course of the 21st century (European Health Interview Survey, 2019).

According to Alves et al. (2021), one of the most important social marketing themes is health and well-being and the promotion of healthy food consumption, especially the reduction of fat, sugar and sodium, and the promotion of physical activity and healthy habits. M-health apps can be defined as "*software embedded in smartphones to improve health outcomes, health research and health services*" (Nouri, et al., 2018). The use of different mobile devices for health purposes has become increasingly common (Müller et al., 2018; Nacinovich, 2013). More authors (Nouri, et al., 2018; Villinger et al., 2019) have explored that mobile app-based interventions are effective in improving diet-related health outcomes and reducing the risk of obesity (Tong et al., 2021; Vlahu-Gjorgievska et al., 2018). Furthermore, these interventions are more useful than traditional non-digital interventions (Alnasser et al., 2015, Lieffers et al., 2021). The most common health-related apps are lifestyle (LS) apps, which include fitness, nutrition and meditation apps. The use of fitness apps is the most popular and has increased significantly over the years. The use of fitness apps is highest in the EU Member States (12.49%), followed by Hungary (10.38%) and finally the international penetration rate (7.7%) (Statista, 2022). However, only a small part of the population uses diet apps (Ernsting et al., 2017; König et al., 2018), as people expect them to incorporate self-management techniques into their daily lives. In Hungary, the use of diet apps is less than four per cent. Globally, the use of meditation apps is not significant, only between two and three per cent. However, if we take the average of the countries of the European Union and Hungary, the proportion of people using meditation apps is between 8 and 10 per cent (Statista, 2022). Domestic data on the use of applications clearly show that Hungarians prefer free applications to paid ones, both in terms of fitness, meditation, and nutrition (Statista, 2022). In terms of statistics, the use of LS applications in Hungary (17.1%) is positive compared to the global penetration rate (11.06%), but lags behind the average of EU member states (21.29%).

M-health apps are an effective form of health promotion even by mental healthcare (Sawyer et al., 2023) and this topic has been widely researched by several disciplines (psychology, sociology, medicine, computer science) from theoretical and practical perspectives. Kellen and Saxena (2020) has already explored the motivations for and barriers to adoption and usage of meditation apps during times of crisis. They interviewed 17 college students who had full time jobs and found that job-related factors, changing lifestyles, psychological conditions and worries, perceived outcomes were motivators, and price was a barrier. This paper analyses lifestyle apps from a marketing perspective. There is little research in the international (Sabbir et al., 2021; Sawyer et al., 2023) and national literature on how to disseminate their use (Meskó et al., 2017; Kovács & Várallyai, 2021; Szűcs, 2021). Intention to use, attitude, and motivation to use mobile health apps have already been studied among Hungarian young adults based on the Unified Theory of Acceptance and Use of Technology model (Kovács & Várallyai, 2021). The UTAUT 2 model was developed by Venkatesh et al. (2012) as an extension of the original UTAUT model for the consumer market. This model took into consideration both utilitarian and hedonic aspects of technology use, as well as considering factors like habit and price value. Therefore, the primary objective of this research is to explore the motivations and barriers for using lifestyle (LS) applications from the user's perspective and to develop a potential model for the acceptance of lifestyle applications. On the other hand, this research aims to uncover the reasons for non-use. The present study is considered exploratory, and the respondents were students, who are considered digital natives, and the technology adoption was higher among them. Lieffers et al. (2021) emphasize that university students have poor dietary choices, limited physical activity, and high stress and digital applications can cause behavior change. Therefore, two main research questions were defined:

Q1: Which motivational factors can be distinguished when it comes to using lifestyle applications among the younger generation?

Q2: What are students' main barriers to using lifestyle applications?

After the theoretical background, the authors discuss the methodology and then summarize the results of the focus group interviews. Finally, they conclude with the implications, describe the limitations of this study, and offer directions for future research.

2. THEORETICAL BACKGROUND

2.1. Motivation

"Motivation is an internal state that moves people towards specific goals, and thus they engage in goal-directed behavior" (Hofmeister-Tóth, 2006, p. 199). It is therefore a state, a drive that motivates individuals to act to achieve their goals. Motivation is a three-stage process. The first is the state that motivates behavior, also known as motives. The second is the behavior that is driven by these drives and needs. The final step is the goal itself (Hofmeister-Tóth, 2006, p. 199). Motivation research is linked to the discipline of psychology, as it was Deci and Ryan (2002) who extensively analyzed extrinsic and intrinsic motivations, as well as projected and identification motivation. As more authors (Oc & Plangger, 2022; Smirnova et al., 2021) emphasized that people use lifestyle apps mainly because they want to live a healthier life, use the app regularly, and find features that motivate them and help them to adopt good habits.

Ewais and Alluhaidan (2015) analyzed stress management apps and their gamification features. The authors found that extrinsic motivators such as rewards, points and badges can engage users, but this does not necessarily mean that users will use the apps in the long term. The design of the app should incorporate elements of empowerment, such as a sense of choice and voluntary autonomy. This gamification component is very important to allow users to develop a sense of autonomy and satisfaction. Woldaregay et al. (2018) concluded that privacy and trust are important issues in the case of long-term adoption, and they highlighted the importance of providing value to users. Vlahu-Gjorgievska et al. (2018) highlighted the importance of self-management for better obesity treatment. Amagai et al (2022) conducted a systematic literature review and concluded that factors related to specific elements of the app (e.g. feedback, appropriate reminders and in-app support from peers or coaches) and research strategies (e.g. compensation and niche samples) contributed to retention. In addition, they found that perceived usefulness, validation, and satisfaction had a positive effect on retention intentions. They also highlighted the importance of gamification in the continued use of applications. Byambasuren et al (2020) concluded that effectiveness and physician recommendation of apps were important motivators. Zhou et al. (2020) found that strong but easy-to-use security features could encourage people to use m-health apps in their health management. In their empirical study, Mustafa et al (2022) found that sports and fitness activity tracking were the most popular apps among heavy and light users. They suggested that m-health developers need to consider gamification strategies to maintain user engagement, as well as psychological variables such as intrinsic motivation (Table 1).

2.2. Barriers

Considering barriers, understanding perceived risks perceptions about the potential drawbacks or negative outcomes is important (Cox, 1967). In consumer behavior usually seven different types of risks are usually considered (1) financial, (2) performance, (3) physical, (4) social, (5) psychological (6) time and (7) privacy and security in online context (Norberg, 2007).

More authors have focused on wearable health devices and have presented various reasons for device adoption, sustained use, (un)engagement and abandonment, such as accessibility, convenience, (de)motivation, health status, health-related goals, perceived utility, privacy, and usability (Attig & Franke, 2020; Canhoto & Arp, 2017; Choi et al., 2022; Keeling et al., 2019; Lee & Lee, 2020; Santos-Vijande et. al., 2022; Simblett et al., 2018). Previous studies have shown that nearly half of m-health app users abandon a particular m-health app for a variety of reasons (Krebs & Duncan, 2015). Among these factors, high data entry burden is a usability issue, while loss of interest can be triggered by poor usability of the apps. These facts indicate the importance of good usability of mobile applications.

Alnasser et al. (2015) identified barriers to weight loss applications among Saudi women such as motivation, support (social and professional), boring diets, customs, and lifestyle. Kwon et al. (2017) confirmed the effect of attitude and usefulness, and age and reading news articles about health predicted the use of m-health apps. They found that older age was the main barrier to using m-health apps. Zhou et al. (2019) and Lydinia et al. (2019) identified lack of security features as a barrier to usage, but on the other hand, Byambasuren et al. (2020) found that people were not concerned about privacy and data security issues. Mustafa et al. (2022) identified demotivation, loss of interest and experimenting with different apps as reasons for rejecting an app. They also highlighted the importance of the financial cost of apps, as users prefer free apps. Amagai et al (2022) found that lack of support features, technical difficulties and usefulness of the app hindered retention (Table 2).

Table 1. Some noted studies on motivation of LS apps

Author/s	Main findings / results
Ewais and Alluhaidan (2015)	Extrinsic motivators such as rewards, points and badges can engage users but do not necessarily mean that they will use the apps in the long term.
Vlahu-Gjorgievska et al. (2018)	Self-monitoring, professional feedback, social media support, nutritional menus, goal setting, physical activity and calorie counting are key to the success of diet apps.
Zhou et al. (2020)	Clear privacy policies could encourage users to use m-health apps for health management.
Mustafa et al. (2022)	Developers need to consider gamification strategies to maintain user engagement, as well as psychological variables such as intrinsic motivation.

Source: Own compilation.

Table 2. Some noted studies on abandonment of LS apps

Author/s	Main findings / results
Krebs and Duncan (2015)	High data entry burden, loss of interest, poor usability
Kwon et al. (2017)	Attitude and usefulness, age (older)
Zhou et al. (2019)	Lack of security features
Mustafa et al. (2020)	Demotivation, loss of interest and experimentation with different applications, financial costs
Amagai et al. (2022)	Lack of support features, technical difficulties, and usefulness of the application

Source: Own compilation

3. METHODOLOGY

More studies analyzing LS apps with empirical methods have applied qualitative (Alnasser et al., 2015; Castro et al., 2020; Kellen & Saxena, 2020; Krishnan & Lokachari, 2019; Peng et al., 2016; Simons et al., 2018;) approaches, particularly focus group interviews. In this study, we used the focus group method, and this approach allowed for in-depth insights, rich qualitative data, and group dynamics and synergy.

Forty-nine students participated in focus group interviews during the autumn semester of the 2022/2023 academic year, with one of the four focus groups focusing on the experiences of users and the other three groups exploring the views of non-users and former users. The interview guide was prepared based on previous studies and focused on two general topics, (1) the participants' health behavior and its changes, (2) their health awareness, and two main topics related to LS applications, (3) the use of LS applications, and (4) their experiences and evaluations of LS applications.

Participants were full-time BA students studying '*Recreation and Lifestyle Programme*' courses. Previous studies have highlighted the influential role of age and education. In addition, the researchers assumed that students studying leisure and lifestyle management would have a more positive attitude towards LS applications. Therefore, university students (young and educated people) were selected to participate in the focus groups. The focus group interviews were conducted in quiet places, in the seminar rooms in November 2022, and each interview lasted about 80-90 minutes. The interviews were recorded and then typed. All transcripts were reviewed and checked by the authors. Thematic analysis was used to identify themes in the data. This paper presents the findings of this qualitative research.

4. FINDINGS

In this chapter we first describe the characteristics of the participants in the focus group interviews and then analyze their opinions and experiences with the LS applications. In the focus group research, we discussed four main topics with the participants who used LS applications. Two general themes emerged from the focus group discussion, which focused on the participants' health behavior and its changes, and their health awareness. We then focused on the main topic, the use of LS applications, and the students' experiences and evaluations of LS applications.

Students are enrolled in a 6-semester course at the university with a strong focus on lifestyle, health, and health promotion. Core subjects include the structure and function of the human body, health promotion and lifestyle. The study of physical activity and sport is emphasized in the curriculum, with 12 subjects related to this topic, in which both the theoretical and practical aspects are taught. The course is complemented by summer and winter excursions where students are introduced to sporting activities outside the university walls that they cannot experience inside, such as skiing, hiking, rowing, and cycling.

The second-year students studying recreation and lifestyle were selected because we expected the group to have a high use of LS apps, as the students' future professions will prioritize healthy lifestyles and related physical activity and sports. By the second year, they will already have sufficient knowledge about healthy lifestyles. In selecting the three groups, we also considered the optimal ratio of homogeneity to heterogeneity for the research, which we wanted to increase the transfer of free information on the topic.

4.1. Usage of LS Applications

Twelve students who currently use different LS applications participated in this focus group research. The participants were between 19 and 23 years old and mostly female (8 students). As Hahn et al. (2022) found that women are more likely than men to use physical activity- and dietary-focused apps. Pontin et al. (2021) also reinforced that fitness app usage is higher in females and individuals aged 25-50. Some students live in the university town (4 students), while others live in a student hostel or commute between home and university. The place of residence plays a role in the choice of the location of the participants' sports life.

First, the participants shared their opinions about their health-related behavior and thinking. It can be concluded that they are very informed and have adequate knowledge, which is also reflected in their behavior, they have a healthy lifestyle. We found some differences in the interpretation and manifestation of *health awareness* among the participants based on gender. For women, mental health, and inner harmony play an important role in a healthy lifestyle, along with exercise and optimal nutrition. They live healthily by finding moderation and balance. Mental health is also important for the men, along with exercise and a healthy diet, but they emphasized the importance of rest and avoiding the harmful passions that often arise in university situations. Two of the men believe that physical activity can compensate for dietary 'fluctuations', they do not give up the tasty snacks and do not consider themselves to be health conscious.

Within the focus group, sporting life takes different forms and is present at different levels in terms of frequency and intensity. Three participants lead a very active life, reporting vigorous physical activity 5-6 times a week, including competition. At the next level, 3-4 sessions per week are typical for female participants, and in addition to team sports or group exercises, individual exercises (running, swimming, walking, cycling) also play a role. In the lifestyle of two men, participation in training (football, judo) ensures regular exercise, which is supplemented by individual exercise (walking, cycling, gym). Several people engage in cycling, running, and walking as a hobby or leisure activity in their free time. Table 3 shows the types and frequency of physical activity of students using LS applications.

All participants reported that their sporting lifestyle dates back to their childhood and that during these years the *main motivation* was provided by external factors (family, parents, siblings, school). Adolescence can be seen as a *milestone* in the participants' sporting activities. The talented pupils continued with the sports they had started (horse riding, football, and volleyball), then already at a "higher level", as competitors. In addition to external motivations, the need to improve their body image was an important motivation for them. The next milestone came with university studies, in the field of leisure. As a result of the increase in professional knowledge and the recreational approach, leisure-time physical activities (walking, running, fitness, cycling) came to the fore. Competitive sports and the competitive

Table 3. Physical activity of participants using LS applications

Participants' gender	Forms of exercise	Exercise/week
F3 female	Boxing, rowing, gym training, cycling	5-6 times
M3 male	Bodybuilding, fitness	6 times
F1 female	Swimming, dancing, and jogging	3-4 times and daily
F2 female	Basketball, running, cycling	3-4 times
F7 female	Jogging	3-4 times
M1 male	Judo, Jogging, cycling	2 times
M4 male	Football, gym training	2 times
F4 female	Volleyball trainer	2 times
F5 female	Cycling	2 times
F6 female	Stopped climbing the wall, jogging	2 times
F8 female	Running and gym training	2 times
M2 male	Cycling and jogging	2-3 times and daily

Source: Own compilation.

spirit remained in the lives of a few participants, to whom the inner impulse gave strength and motivation. Some participants were forced to give up their previous sporting activities because they had outgrown the sport, but this was also an example of a continuation of the training work. Family background and positive examples from coaches contributed to the acquisition of knowledge about sporting life and health. In addition, the treatment of childhood illnesses and developmental disorders contributed to the acquisition of knowledge about health promotion. The theoretical and practical training received in the recreational program is particularly useful in health management and disease prevention. We can say that the knowledge and skills related to health literacy can be acquired continuously, at every stage of life.

Several participants use two applications, with women preferring sports and fitness activity measures, as well as apps that contribute to wellbeing (wellbeing, sleep quality). In addition, it is typical for women to use apps that support stress reduction and relaxation, which contributes to good mental health. It is less common for participants to use an app to monitor their eating behavior, or not to use it regularly. The male participants in the focus group prefer apps to measure sports and fitness activities. In terms of mobile devices, all technical solutions are used by the participants, Android device, iPhone and the smartwatch are always at hand when they want to check steps, pulse or blood oxygen. The duration and frequency of use of the applications varied widely, with Strava being used for 2-3 years for fitness and Fiton for one year for training and meditation. Bike monitors were generally used by women for a longer period of time, ranging from 1-3 years to 6 years. We conclude that the participants actively and confidently use the selected LS applications, as they are more health literate. The characteristics of the LS applications used by the focus group participants can be seen in the following Table 4.

Seven participants reported that they had previously used smartphone apps to support physical activity, nutrition, and water management. The reasons for stopping use were varied: moving to an iPhone, feeling the calorie counter was a limitation, distraction from the many notifications, lost its appeal, lack of motivation to exercise, found a better application, chose a different sport.

Table 4. Characteristics of participants' usage of the LS app

Participants' gender	Lifestyle apps usage		
	Number of apps	Type of apps	Period of use (Year)
F1 female	3	Pedometer Female cycle monitor, fitness application	2 years 1-3 years
F2 female	2	For running, cycling (Strava), cycle monitoring (Flow)	1-3 years
F3 female	4	Meditation, yoga, training (Fiton), sleep and heart rate (smart watch)	1 year
F4 female	2	Step, pulse, blood oxygen level (smart watch) Women's cycle monitor	2 years 6 years
F5 female	2	Fitness (Strava), smart watch	2-3 years
F6 female	4	Female cycle monitor (Flow) Nutrition app Health app (iPhone) Pedometer (2 years)	6 years Not regular 4-5 years 2 years
F7 female	2	Sleep and female cycle monitor	2 years
F8 female	2	Pedometer Women's cycle monitor (PT)	6 years 3 years
M1 male	1	Pedometer for running	1 year
M2 male	2	Sleep cycle (smart watch), Running, cycling, step counting	2 years
M3 male	2	Pedometer (smartwatch) and for cardio	5 years
M4 male	3	Calorie Calculator (iPhone Fit), Heart rate and pedometer	2-3 years

Source: own compilation.

It is also important to know what *source of information* the users of the LS app used to get their information and what *criteria* they used to choose the most suitable app for them. There are other aspects to this issue: *social, utilitarian and individual factors*. For females, other people's opinions, ease of use, the possibility of being challenged and personal motivation came up. Male students expressed a technical aspect as an expectation, namely compatibility. In the process of gathering information and selecting applications, the opinions of users of various LS applications in the Google Play Store are a potential source. Several members of the group took this opportunity to say that they usually read the comments. However, they do not share or comment on their experience with the LS application they are using. "*Many people don't comment, there's no need to change what's good, I wasn't dissatisfied.*" (M4)

Participants agreed that there is negative as well as positive aspects to online information sources used for health management. The women felt that there was often conflicting information on the internet about different diets. Comments shared on social media, especially Facebook, are not appropriate from a professional point of view and there are people in the background who are not competent. Both positive and negative effects of influencers were discussed in the group. Some people follow fitness influencers because they expect them to be authentic. However, the perfect appearance and lifestyle of influencers can lead to a lack of self-confidence in followers. On the positive side of online information sources, YouTube videos that help with physical activity and nutrition were mentioned.

We can see that students perceive the importance of other people's opinions in relation to using LS apps. In particular, the opinions of friends, classmates, teachers, and parents have a significant influence on the students' decision to use the applications. In addition, people who comment in the participants' online social network also have an impact, which can be positive or negative (Table 5).

Table 5. Types of perceived benefits mentioned by users

Category of benefits	Motivations
Ease of use	*"I downloaded some apps and checked which ones were easy to use and which were better."* F4
Perceived usefulness	*"I can also monitor my objectives, whether I run the marathon or the half marathon which I have previously accomplished."* F4
	"Ican perceive the velocity, adjust it to go faster or slower, and confirm the alteration." F2
Perceived enjoyment	*"Gamification is good, although it is a fundamental element in other applications."* M4
Perceived value	*"It is a good measuring tool, I look at the data and use it for my training work."* M3
Facilitating conditions	*"I use an iPhone for my applications."* F5, F6, F8, M4 *"I have an android phone and the internet connection works."* F1, F2, F3, F4, F7, M1 *"I use also a smart watch, it's always at hand."* F3, F4, F5, M2, M3

Source: own compilation.

For the fourth topic of the focus group interview, we asked what makes an *application good*, what makes the participant not delete it and accept the app. Women value the following usability features: ease of use, statistics, interesting articles, recipes, ad-free content, important features. "*It doesn't have a lot of features, it shows the steps exactly, it measures my heart rate, it knows how much I've walked. It compares statistics so I can learn from it." "When searching in Google Play, information, articles, training, e.g. how difficult they are and know the extras." "It should meet my needs, be useful."* Men also mentioned several factors. *"Show the number of steps accurately." "It knows the essential things that I don't, and it should be able to give something extra."*

In the next sub-theme, we asked the participants to give their opinion on what would make them satisfied. The participants highlighted some important *expectations* in terms of usability and effort.

"Suit my needs." (M2) "Don't change. I don't like that when I download it and then use it for 3 weeks, and everything is fine. Then it updates itself and the previous version is no longer available. You can only use the updated version, it is more complicated, and you need so much extra information." (F4) "It should be simple and transparent, less is more. The usability should be good, the search is usually not in Hungarian, so easy search is important." (F2)

To ensure continued use of lifestyle applications, they need to be integrated into daily life. Participants identified some perceived risks such as time, performance, financial and psychological ones (Table 6).

In the case of the younger generation, it can be assumed that the fun nature of the apps can be important, but the students denied this and gamification is not important in the evaluation of mobile health apps. "*Gamification is fun, but not important... After a while it doesn't motivate me...*" (M1)

Finally, the researchers wanted to know how the use of the LS application contributed to the positive change in their health. The participants' responses reflect that they lead an active lives and that they believe that the use of the applications has an indirect effect on their health, rather than playing a complementary role.

"I noticed that I was more muscular than I was, but not just because of the app. I do the tracking with the app." (M4) "I tried to lose weight, but it didn't work with the app. ... I saw in the Yazio group that some people I know were able to lose weight with the application." (F1)

Students mentioned various risks associated with the use of LS applications (Table 6). Performance risk was mentioned by the majority of participants. Protection of personal data was not highlighted by the students, nor was it a major concern in the quantitative research, although it was highlighted in the international research (Zhou et al., 2019). However, the authors believe that the risk of personal data being compromised, misused, or stolen is a particularly cautious issue in the case of applications.

Several participants see the application as a measurement tool, for example, to measure running performance, check set goals (step counter, running performance, goal completion, calorie counter, Strava). As noted by Vlahu-Gjorgievska et al. (2018), weight management apps are powerful tools to empower users to make behavioral and lifestyle changes.

Participants' intentions to adopt a new LS app are influenced not only by its usefulness, but also by the risks and individual and social factors of using the app. Focus group research suggests that an LS app that is easy to use in the early stages has a positive impact on consumers' intentions to use it. Participants can benefit from using LS apps if their experience meets their expectations.

We found that among the usability factors, perceived ease of use, perceived usefulness and among the hedonic factors, perceived enjoyment can act as driving influences on the attitude towards adopting a LS application for students. The focus group participants use free LS applications, but the price-performance ratio also plays a role in the selection and use of the application, as highlighted by Mustafa et al. (2022) in their research. The facilitating conditions, the technical and environmental factors, such as the devices needed to use the app, contribute to the regular use of apps. Among the external factors, social interactions were explored as drivers of behavioral intention and continuous use. The perceived risk of personal data, time commitment and limited achievement of performance goals were highlighted as barriers to engagement with LS apps.

The ability to use lifestyle applications influences their effectiveness and health-promoting behaviour. The ability to use a mobile phone, obtain LS information, interpret the information and make decisions is directly or indirectly influenced by individual characteristics, namely socio-demographic variables

Table 6. Types of perceived risks mentioned by users

Category of risks	Sources of potential risks
Time	"*I think half an hour a day to watch and manage the app is enough. No more.*" (M1)
Performance	"*If it sends the notifications, it will help... the notification should be for information, not for cheating*". (F3, F4)
	"*I think it's a matter of choice whether I use it or not. For example, if I decide to pay attention to my meals, I measure how many calories I eat, then I do it properly, enter the data, scan the code, etc*". "*I have found that not all applications are reliable and this has influenced my use and non-use*" (F6)
	"*I'm really bothered by all the advertising. I'll delete it if I'm not happy*". (F5)
	"*It keeps asking for the GPS coordinates. This really bothers me, I don't know why they ask for it.*" (F6)
	"*My running data disappeared after the update.*" (M2)
Financial	"*No, it has to be very unique and extra for me, otherwise it would only be a small amount of money.*" (F3)
Social	"*It would be motivating, where are teammates and friends.*" (F4)
	"*A social function would be nice for a pedometer.*" (F1)
Psychological	"*Fitness influencers on Instagram can make people feel self-conscious. In my opinion, focusing too much on physical appearance in today's world can be harmful. I view the spiritual side as a negative aspect.*" F2 "*FB groups can have commenters who have no idea what is going on and that is wrong, it can be damaging to anyone who reads it.*" F4

Source: Own compilation.

(gender, age), level of health knowledge and previous experience with information technology. Our focus group research has shown that other factors influence participants' intentions to use e-health applications and their actual usage behavior. These factors are related to perceived benefits, risks, social and individual factors. Based on the results of the focus group interviews, we summarized the external and internal factors that influence the actual use of LS apps, which is an updated version of UTAUT 2 model (Figure 1).

The results of the focus group research indicated that usefulness, features, free access, and accuracy were the most important factors in the evaluation of LS applications. Further research is needed to explore different factors, namely perceived benefits, perceived risks and social factors, that influence behavioral intention and actual use of e-health applications. Previous studies have examined the moderating role of personal factors in the use of lifestyle applications by specific groups. It is an interesting question to investigate how, in addition to socio-demographic characteristics, health-related knowledge and previous experience with mobile technologies influence the use of LS applications. The group discussion also revealed that among lifestyle applications, sports and fitness apps are the most popular among students,

Figure 1. The factors influencing the actual use behavior of LS apps
Source: own compilation based on UTAUT 2 model developed by Venkatesh (2012).

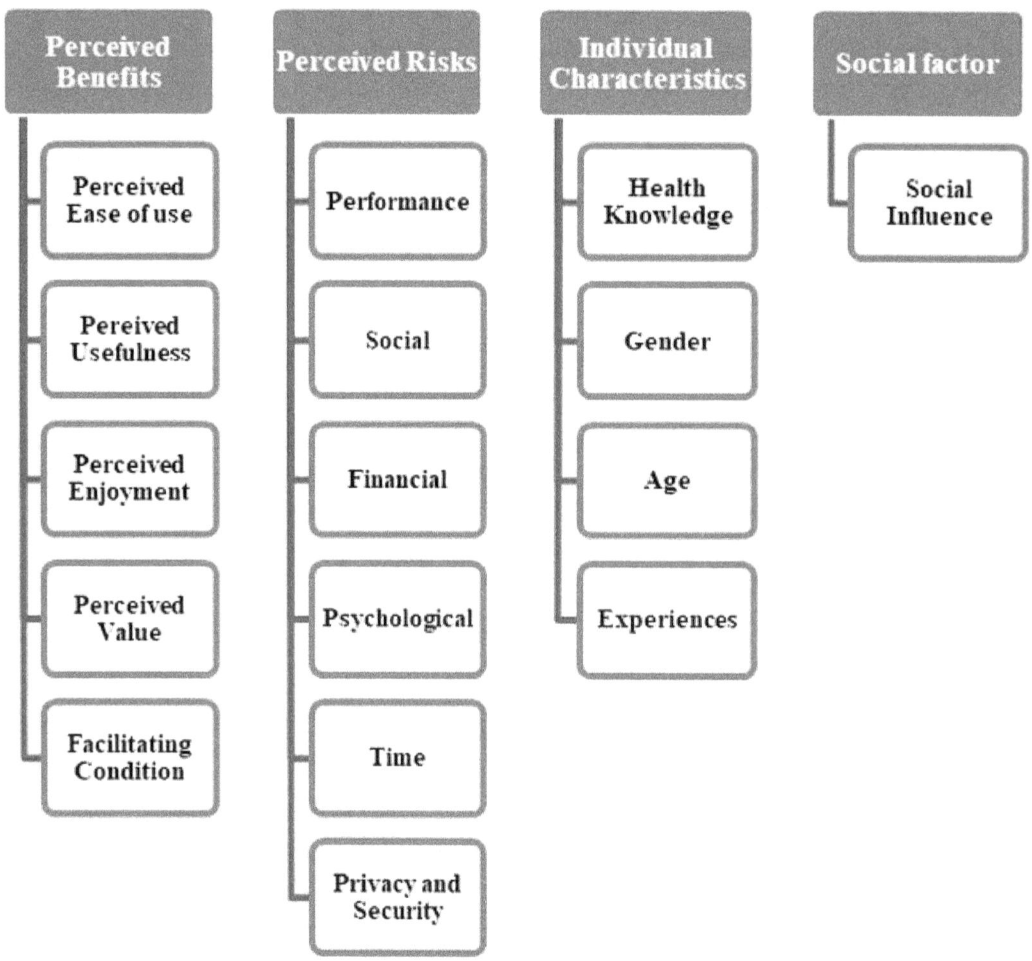

and that online and offline opinions also contribute to the selection of the appropriate application. We are planning further research to know more about the relationship between the offline and online information used and the personal factors of the users. Finally, as a next step, we tend to identify the main drivers of the actual and continuous use of LS applications that have an impact on the users' expectation of health improvement.

4.2. Non-Users

Regular physical activity accompanies us throughout our lives and is a key focus of education from kindergarten to secondary school. Physical activity is not compulsory during university studies, except in some universities. At Széchenyi István University, students must take 4 subjects related to physical activity, except for students of Leisure and Lifestyle, where the subjects are substituted.

31 students participated at least 5 times a week and 6 at least 3 times a week in sports that lasted at least half an hour and caused sweating (WHO guidelines for physical activity were considered). Males were more likely to exercise 5 times a week than females. Women said that they would like to do more exercise, but that they face some kind of obstacle, such as fatigue or health reasons. They mentioned gym activities, weight training, football, running, table tennis, cycling and water sports. Women also reported similar sports activities, such as running, going to the gym, dancing, horse riding, body shaping, health maintenance and boxing. The high rate of sports participation was also due to the high number of students who played sports competitively or chose sports as a profession. Among those who played competitive sports, football, martial arts and water sports were the most popular.

Men who exercised 5 times a week noted the importance of taking a rest day to recover. 17 Of the reasons given for exercising and playing sport, health maintenance and health promotion were the most important, but mental health and relaxation were also mentioned. Men also highlighted broader shoulders and a bolder appearance. Female participants mentioned aesthetic appearance, weight maintenance, better figure and healthy living. Sport as a source of happiness and pleasure was also mentioned, along with '*work capacity, workload*' and in one case the need to be true to oneself. Health awareness and factors related to the development of a holistic approach were mentioned, in line with the training objectives of the course.

A milestone in sports participation has been the age factor of moving from primary to secondary school or from secondary to university education. This has also manifested itself in either a change of sport or a greater involvement in sport or even a greater activity in sport. It was mentioned that changes in social relations have also played a role in the development of sporting behavior. Adolescence has made people more aware of health promotion. In terms of sporting careers, moving from a junior team to an adult championship or even to the Hungarian national team has changed sporting and related lifestyle habits. By then, they had already changed their lifestyle with the help of professionals to optimize their performance, eat consciously and take time to recover. Another milestone was changing teams or clubs within their own sport, or leaving a sports club, which contributed to a more conscious and healthier life (5 students). Choosing a new sport was mentioned by three students. Changing from one sport to another, even taking up boxing as a girl. University studies are the most important stage or even milestone in the lives of the group members, who have to choose between doing sport or going to university/studies. Two women said that it was impossible to combine sport with important studies, and that they had even postponed their studies. However, once they had finished playing elite sport, they felt it was important to balance their lives with work, sport and study, and they completed their lives with a hobby sport of their own choosing. Two of them were recovering from illness or sports injuries, when their attention was on themselves and sport was not compulsory, but they did it for the pleasure of sport itself and continued to participate in hobby sports. One woman in a couple relationship had a partner who played sports and set an example for her to follow. Another woman was motivated to take up sport in order to achieve a higher level of performance (from an advanced level of physical education). As a private student, she managed her own life and was aware of her own development.

Four students had previously used lifestyle apps but had stopped. One male used it briefly while cycling during COVID, but thought he no longer needed it. Another male used it to calculate the energy and nutritional value of food but prefers to look at the table on the packaging. Consciously decides what to buy and what not to buy when shopping. One man used it as a competitive athlete, but no longer competes and sees no need to use it. One person used to use it but found that he was "phoning it in" more and more and was distracted and not doing what I should have been doing.

All non-users had a smartphone and 5 had a smartwatch. 13 did not like the devices, but 7 thought they were necessary. The development of technology affects everyone. The students' use of mobile phones ranged from administration, contact, entertainment, part of their lives and part of their education. There were many positive and negative effects. A balance needs to be found in their use. The students' phones had health-related functions, but they did not use them for anything other than counting steps after a long walk.

Students gave different reasons for not using LS applications. Most of them emphasized the personal contact and the lack of information. Many students felt that there was no need to use such applications. However, technical constraints and time constraints were also cited as reasons for not using them (Table 7).

Table 7. Reasons for non-usage of LS apps

Category of reasons	Number of mentioning	Reasons for non-usage
Personal	9	*'I prefer personal contact. Professionals can better explain and personalize training plans and their application.'*
	4	*'I design my own training plan, which is important because I like to plan my own sporting activities, it gives me pleasure.'*
	1	*'I trust myself more'*
Unnecessary (Performance)	2	*'I don't think an app is necessary for recreational sports.'*
	2	*'I don't need an app to run.'*
	1	*'I am motivated to run without an app.'*
	2	*'I don't feel it adds anything to my knowledge.'*
	1	*'I know the terrain I am running on.'*
	1	*'I can read afterwards, I can go deeper into the planning.'*
	1	*'I can make corrections and improvements if I do it on paper.'*
Not suitable	4	*'Information given is not credible (does not measure what is real).'*
	3	*'I could not find a suitable application that would have been useful.'*
	1	*'I tried a free one but it was not suitable. I will not pay for it until I can try it.'*
Technical	6	*'I probably don't have enough information on how to use it.'*
	1	*'I am not a fan of the digital world.'*
	1	*'I did not have storage space on my phone. If I did, I might reconsider the application.'*
Time	1	*'I am not a fan of the digital world.'*
	1	*'It would have taken me out of my training routine.'*

Source: Own compilation.

5. CONCLUSION

LS apps aim to prevent users from contracting diseases. Global user penetration will be 11.06% in 2022. After using lifestyle apps, patients perceive health benefits such as improved health behaviors and are likely to start using them (Desveaux et al., 2018; Ross et al., 2020). The perceived usefulness is not always related to the condition but can provide various health benefits such as improved physical condition or relaxation, better mental state, and improved sleep quality. Shabir et al (2022) examined lifestyle apps, including apps related to sports and fitness, diet and nutrition, stress management and disease prevention, by reviewing qualitative studies. These preventive apps present both opportunities and challenges for both parts of the health market. Public health can be greatly improved through participation and engagement with these applications.

Q1: Which motivational factors can be distinguished when it comes to using lifestyle applications among the younger generation?

Based on the results of the focus group interview, it can be summarized that participants' intrinsic motivation encourages them to engage in physical activity and that the use of LS app features promotes a physically active lifestyle. The exploratory research highlighted that the adoption and current use of a new LS app is influenced not only by features that support individual interactions, but also by features that support social interactions. Among the features that support individual interactions, goal setting, feedback, performance monitoring, and follow-up are useful to participants. They miss the information content that reflects changes in personal health status. And among the features that support social interactions, competition with friends, teammates, social sharing, and challenges are considered interesting and motivating.

The focus group research conducted shows that the initial ease of use of the LS app positively influences students' intention to use the app and to use it regularly. We found that among the features used by the participants, those that support individual interaction have a stronger influence and contribute to the intrinsic motivation of the athletes than external motivators.

The ability to use LS apps influences their effectiveness and health-promoting behaviors. Mobile phone management skills, acquisition of mHealth information, interpretation of relevant information and decision making are directly or indirectly influenced by individual characteristics such as socio-demographic variables (gender, age), level of health literacy and previous experience with information technology.

Q2: What are students' main barriers to using lifestyle applications?

Mobile health apps, especially lifestyle apps, are becoming increasingly popular worldwide, in Europe especially the free versions. Their impact on health has been proven and they can play a particularly important role in preventing, maintaining, or achieving good health (Ernsting et al., 2017; Müller et al., 2018; Ross et al., 2020; Villinger et al., 2019; Vlahu-Gjorgievska et al., 2018). Motivations have been studied extensively (Kovács & Várallyai, 2021; Kwon et al., 2017; Mustafa et al., 2022), but the study of barriers has been mainly focused on the international literature. The novelty of our research was that we used a qualitative methodology to study university students whose studies have a strong focus on sport and health sciences. Loss of interest and poor usability appeared among the barriers, as previously highlighted by several international studies (Amagai et al., 2022; Krebs & Duncan, 2015; Mustafa et al., 2022). Interestingly, the protection of personal data was not highlighted by the students, nor was it a major concern in the quantitative research, although it was highlighted in the international research (Lydinia et al., 2019; Zhou et al., 2019;). Demotivation, boredom, and loss of interest were prominent among the reasons for not using the tool, as shown by previous findings (Krebs & Duncan, 2015; Mustafa et al., 2022). Kwon et al (2017) emphasized that individual, socio-demographic factors such as age also play a role in the adoption of apps, and these individual aspects are not examined in the present study.

This study makes several notable contributions to the existing literature. First, it used existing users of lifestyle applications to investigate their underlying motivations in a naturalistic manner. Secondly, the research was conducted among university students who consider health and healthy lifestyle important. The motivations for app use identified included perceived benefits, like ease of use, perceived usefulness, enjoyment and value, and facilitating conditions. Usefulness, features, free access, and accuracy were the most important factors in the evaluation of LS applications. More students reported positive effects through improved physical and mental health, but the applications and smart devices were seen as complementary tools. Interestingly, perceived risks - time, performance, financial, social, and psychological - were identified, too. The authors also found that the main reasons for non-use were personal, technical and usability ones.

This study is useful for the health sector (doctors, dieticians, and food experts) and the government, as targeted marketing programs can be planned to change healthy lifestyles. It is also important to raise the health awareness of the Hungarian population. To improve the quality of life and well-being of people, it is necessary to improve their health. Health is not only the state of being free from disease or injury but is a much more complex category. A healthy mind in a healthy body should be emphasized in social marketing campaigns. Reducing overweight and obesity is a goal of all societies (especially in developed countries, where this phenomenon is considered an epidemic), so it is necessary to educate people and use social marketing campaigns. Informing people about the use of lifestyle applications (sports management, nutrition and diet, mindfulness, and other health management) that should be communicated to people. It is in the interest of society to educate people and change their unhealthy habits. The focus should be not only on education, but also on making people aware of the consequences of bad eating habits. The social marketing campaign aims to change people's attitudes and behavior. Behavior is driven by many factors and two factors - benefits and costs - are at the heart of the change process. Non-profit managers try to increase benefits and reduce costs to get target groups to behave in a certain way, for example in terms of health. Often people have social support and belief in the benefits of behaviors such as eating healthily, reducing stress, being more physically active, but are unable to adopt them because they believe they cannot actually succeed.

As a limitation of our research, we would like to point out that in our qualitative research, we only interviewed students of Recreation and Lifestyle. However, our goal was to explore the opinions of individuals interested in the topic of health. On the other hand, the penetration rate of lifestyle applications in Hungary is quite low (17.1%). Previous studies (Pontin et al., 2021) found that women and individuals aged 25-50 were more likely to use fitness apps. In this study, the motivations, and experiences of a younger generation (aged between 19 and 23 years) were analyzed.

As a future extension of the research, we would like to conduct expert interviews with physicians, nutritionists, and dietitians. In the future we plan to recruit a diverse population with a range of ages, occupations, socioeconomic statuses, and levels of education. In addition, we would be interested in conducting an experiment on the physical and mental changes that result from long-term app use over a period of 3-4 months and which dimensions determine the continued use of an app and analyze behavior change and satisfaction with the app. Further research is needed to examine the relationship between factors influencing the use of LS applications and current behavior and continued use in a larger sample using a quantitative research methodology.

REFERENCES

Alnasser, A. A., Alkhalifa, A. S., Sathiaseelan, A., & Marais, D. (2015). What overweight women want from a weight loss app: A qualitative study on Arabic women. *JMIR mHealth and uHealth*, *3*(2), e4409. doi:10.2196/mhealth.4409 PMID:25993907

Alves, H., Galan-Ladero, M. M., & Rivera, R. G. (2021). Theoretical Background: Social Marketing and Quality of Life. *Applied Social Marketing and Quality of Life: Case Studies from an International Perspective*, 3-25. doi:10.1007/978-3-030-83286-5_1

Amagai, S., Pila, S., Kaat, A. J., Nowinski, C. J., & Gershon, R. C. (2022). Challenges in participant engagement and retention using mobile health apps: Literature review. *Journal of Medical Internet Research*, *24*(4), e35120. doi:10.2196/35120 PMID:35471414

Attig, C., & Franke, T. (2020). Abandonment of personal quantification: A review and empirical study investigating reasons for wearable activity tracking attrition. *Computers in Human Behavior*, *102*, 223–237. doi:10.1016/j.chb.2019.08.025

Byambasuren, O., Beller, E., Hoffmann, T., & Glasziou, P. (2020). Barriers to and facilitators of the prescription of mHealth apps in Australian general practice: Qualitative study. *JMIR mHealth and uHealth*, *8*(7), e17447. doi:10.2196/17447 PMID:32729839

Canhoto, A. I., & Arp, S. (2017). Exploring the factors that support adoption and sustained use of health and fitness wearables. *Journal of Marketing Management*, *33*(1-2), 32–60. doi:10.1080/0267257X.2016.1234505

Castro, P. C., Romano, L. B., Frohlich, D., Lorenzi, L. J., Campos, L. B., Paixão, A., Bet, P., Deutekom, M., Krose, B., Dourado, V. Z., & Angélica de Oliveira Gomes, G. (2020). Tailoring digital apps to support active ageing in a low income community. *PLoS One*, *15*(12, e0242192), e0242192. doi:10.1371/journal.pone.0242192 PMID:33301455

Choi, H. Y., Keil, M., & Baird, A. M. (2022). Intention to use smartwatch health applications: A regulatory fit and locus of control perspective. *Information & Management*, *59*(6), 103687. doi:10.1016/j.im.2022.103687

Cox, D. F. (1967). Risk Handling in Consumer Behavior: An Intensive Study of Two Cases. *JMR, Journal of Marketing Research*, *4*(2), 111–116.

Deci, E. L., & Ryan, R. M. (2002). *Handbook of self-determination research*. University of Rochester Press.

Desveaux, L., Shaw, J., Saragosa, M., Soobiah, C., Marani, H., Hensel, J., Agarwal, P., Onabajo, N., Bhatia, R. S., & Jeffs, L. A. (2018). A mobile app to improve self-management of individuals with type 2 diabetes: Qualitative realist evaluation. *Journal of Medical Internet Research*, *20*(3), e81. doi:10.2196/jmir.8712 PMID:29549070

Ernsting, C., Dombrowski, S. U., Oedekoven, M., Kanzler, M., Kuhlmey, A., & Gellert, P. (2017). Using smartphones and health apps to change and manage health behaviors: A population-based survey. *Journal of Medical Internet Research*, *19*(4), e101. doi:10.2196/jmir.6838 PMID:28381394

Ewais, S., & Alluhaidan, A. (2015). Classification of stress management mHealth apps based on Octalysis framework. In *Twenty-first Americas Conference on Information Systems*. AMCIS. https://aisel.aisnet.org/amcis2015/HealthIS/GeneralPresentations/16/

Hahn, S. L., Hazzard, V. M., Larson, N., Klein, L., Loth, K. A., & Neumark-Sztainer, D. (2022). Correlates of weight-related self-monitoring application use during emerging adulthood in a population-based sample. *Eating and Weight Disorders*, *27*(6), 2107–2119. doi:10.100740519-021-01349-4 PMID:35040079

Hofmeister-Tóth Ágnes. (2006). *Fogyasztói magatartás*. Aula Kiadó.

Keeling, D. I., de Ruyter, K., Mousavi, S., & Laing, A. (2019). Technology push without a patient pull: Examining digital unengagement (DU) with online health services. *European Journal of Marketing*, *53*(9), 1701–1732. doi:10.1108/EJM-10-2017-0692

Kellen, M., & Saxena, D. (2020). Calm my headspace: Motivations and barriers for adoption and usage of meditation apps during times of crisis. In *Proceedings of The 20th International Conference on Electronic Business* (pp. 37–46). IEEE.

König, L. M., Sproesser, G., Schupp, H. T., & Renner, B. (2018). Describing the process of adopting nutrition and fitness apps: Behavior stage model approach. *JMIR mHealth and uHealth*, *6*(3), e8261. doi:10.2196/mhealth.8261 PMID:29535078

Kovács, T., & Várallyai, L. (2021). Egészségügyi mobilapplikációkra történő használati szándék mérése UTAUT-modellben: Tanulmány egy online felmérés eredményei alapján. *INFORMÁCIÓS TÁRSADALOM: TÁRSADALOMTUDOMÁNYI FOLYÓIRAT*, *21*(1), 166–187. doi:10.22503/inftars.XXI.2021.1.7

Krebs, P., & Duncan, D. T. (2015). Health app use among US mobile phone owners: A national survey. *JMIR mHealth and uHealth*, *3*(4), e4924. doi:10.2196/mhealth.4924 PMID:26537656

Krishnan, G., & Lokachari, P. S. (2019). Adoption of health and fitness apps by mobile users: Interactive qualitative analysis. In *Proceedings of the 2019 Portland International Conference on Management of Engineering and Technology (PICMET)*, Portland, OR, USA.

KSH. (2019). *European Health Interview Survey, 2019*. KSH. https://www.ksh.hu/docs/hun/xftp/idoszaki/pdf/egeszsegugyi_helyzetkep_2019.pdf

Kwon, M. W., Mun, K., Lee, J. K., McLeod, D. M., & D'Angelo, J. (2017). Is mobile health all peer pressure? The influence of mass media exposure on the motivation to use mobile health apps. *Convergence (London)*, *23*(6), 565–586. doi:10.1177/1354856516641065

Lee, S. M., & Lee, D. (2020). Healthcare wearable devices: An analysis of key factors for continuous use intention. *Service Business*, *14*(4), 503–531. doi:10.100711628-020-00428-3

Lidynia, C., Schomakers, E. M., & Ziefle, M. (2019). What are you waiting for?–perceived barriers to the adoption of fitness-applications and wearables. In *Advances in Human Factors in Wearable Technologies and Game Design: Proceedings of the AHFE 2018 International Conferences on Human Factors and Wearable Technologies, and Human Factors in Game Design and Virtual Environments,* (pp. 41–52). Springer International Publishing.

Lieffers, J. R., Quintanilha, M., Trottier, C. F., Johnson, S. T., Mota, J. F., & Prado, C. M. (2021). Experiences with and perception of a web-based mindfulness, nutrition, and fitness platform reported by first-year university students: A qualitative study. *Journal of the Academy of Nutrition and Dietetics*, *121*(12), 2409–2418. doi:10.1016/j.jand.2021.04.019 PMID:34119458

Luo, Y., Wang, G., Li, Y., & Ye, Q. (2021). Examining protection motivation and network externality perspective regarding the continued intention to use m-health apps. *International Journal of Environmental Research and Public Health*, *18*(11), 5684. doi:10.3390/ijerph18115684 PMID:34073247

Meskó, B., Drobni, Z., Bényei, É., Gergely, B., & Győrffy, Z. (2017). Digital health is a cultural transformation of traditional healthcare. *mHealth*, *3*, 3. doi:10.21037/mhealth.2017.08.07 PMID:29184890

Müller, A. M., Maher, C. A., Vandelanotte, C., Hingle, M., Middelweerd, A., Lopez, M. L., DeSmet, A., Short, C. E., Nathan, N., Hutchesson, M. J., Poppe, L., Woods, C. B., Williams, S. L., & Wark, P. A. (2018). Physical Activity, Sedentary Behavior, and Diet-Related eHealth and mHealth Research: Bibliometric Analysis. *Journal of Medical Internet Research*, *20*(4), e122. doi:10.2196/jmir.8954 PMID:29669703

Mustafa, A. S., Ali, N. A., Dhillon, J. S., Alkawsi, G., & Baashar, Y. (2022). User engagement and abandonment of mHealth: A cross-sectional survey. *Health Care*, *10*(2), 221. doi:10.3390/healthcare10020221 PMID:35206837

Nacinovich, M. (2013). Defining mHealth. *Journal of Communication in Healthcare*, *4*(1), 1–3. doi:10.1179/175380611X12950033990296

Norberg, P. A., Horne, D. R., & Horne, D. A. (2007). The Privacy Paradox: Personal Information Disclosure Intentions versus Behaviors. *The Journal of Consumer Affairs*, *41*(1), 100–126. doi:10.1111/j.1745-6606.2006.00070.x

Nouri, R., Kalhori, S. R. N., Saeedi, M. G., Marchand, G., & Yasini, M. (2018). Criteria for assessing the quality of m-health apps: A systematic review. *Journal of the American Medical Informatics Association : JAMIA*, *25*(8), 1089–1098. doi:10.1093/jamia/ocy050 PMID:29788283

Oc, Y., & Plangger, K. (2022). GIST do it! How motivational mechanisms help wearable users develop healthy habits. *Computers in Human Behavior*, *128*, 107089. doi:10.1016/j.chb.2021.107089

Peng, W., Kanthawala, S., Yuan, S., & Ali Hussain, S. (2016). A qualitative study of user perceptions of mobile health apps. *BMC Public Health*, *16*(1158), 1158. doi:10.118612889-016-3808-0 PMID:27842533

Pontin, F., Lomax, N., Clarke, G., & Morris, M. A. (2021). Socio-demographic determinants of physical activity and app usage from smartphone data. *Social Science & Medicine*, *284*, 114235. doi:10.1016/j.socscimed.2021.114235 PMID:34311392

Ross, E. L., Jamison, R. N., Nicholls, L., Perry, B. M., & Nolen, K. D. (2020). Clinical integration of a smartphone app for patients with chronic pain: Retrospective analysis of predictors of benefits and patient engagement between clinic visits. *Journal of Medical Internet Research*, *22*(4), e16939. doi:10.2196/16939 PMID:32297871

Sabbir, M. M., Taufique, K. M. R., & Nomi, M. (2021). Telemedicine acceptance during the COVID-19 pandemic: User satisfaction and strategic healthcare marketing considerations. *Health Marketing Quarterly*, *38*(2-3), 168–187. doi:10.1080/07359683.2021.1986988 PMID:34645357

Santos-Vijande, M. L., Gómez-Rico, M., Molina-Collado, A., & Davison, R. M. (2022). Building user engagement to mhealth apps from a learning perspective: Relationships among functional, emotional and social drivers of user value. *Journal of Retailing and Consumer Services*, *66*, 102956. doi:10.1016/j.jretconser.2022.102956

Sawyer, C., Hassan, L., Sainsbury, J., Carney, R., Bucci, S., Burgess, H., Lovell, K., Torous, J., & Firth, J. (2023). Using digital technology to promote physical health in mental healthcare: A sequential mixed-methods study of clinicians' views. *Early Intervention in Psychiatry*, 1–13. doi:10.1111/eip.13441 PMID:37318221

Simblett, S., Greer, B., Matcham, F., Curtis, H., Polhemus, A., Ferrão, J., Gamble, P., & Wykes, T. (2018). Barriers to and facilitators of engagement with remote measurement technology for managing health: Systematic review and content analysis of findings. *Journal of Medical Internet Research*, *20*(7), e10480. doi:10.2196/10480 PMID:30001997

Simons, D., De Bourdeaudhuij, I., Clarys, P., De Cocker, K., Vandelanotte, C., & Deforche, B. A. (2018). Smartphone App to Promote an Active Lifestyle in Lower-Educated Working Young Adults: Development, Usability, Acceptability, and Feasibility Study. *JMIR mHealth and uHealth*, *6*(2, e44), e44. doi:10.2196/mhealth.8287 PMID:29463491

Smirnova, E., Eriksson, N., & Fagerstrøm, A. (2021). Adoption and Use of Health-related Mobile Applications: A Qualitative Study with Experienced Users. In *Proceedings of the 14th International Joint Conference on Biomedical Engineering Systems and Technologies*. SCITEPRESS-Science and Technology Publications. 10.5220/0010185902880295

Statista. (2022). *Digital Fitness & Well-Being Apps*. Statista. https://www.statista.com/outlook/dmo/digital-health/digital-fitness-well-being/digital-fitness-well-being-apps/worldwide

Szűcs, R. K. (2021). Mobil egészség–áttekintés. *Biztonságtudományi Szemle*, *3*, 79–91.

Tong, H. L., Quiroz, J. C., Kocaballi, A. B., Fat, S. C. M., Dao, K. P., Gehringer, H., Chow, C. K., & Laranjo, L. (2021). Personalized mobile technologies for lifestyle behavior change: A systematic review, meta-analysis, and meta-regression. *Preventive Medicine*, *148*, 106532. doi:10.1016/j.ypmed.2021.106532 PMID:33774008

Vaghefi, I., & Tulu, B. (2019). The continued use of mobile health apps: Insights from a longitudinal study. *JMIR mHealth and uHealth*, *7*(8), e12983. doi:10.2196/12983 PMID:31469081

Venkatesh, V., Thong, J. Y., & Xu, X. (2012). Consumer acceptance and use of information technology: Extending the unified theory of acceptance and use of technology. *Management Information Systems Quarterly*, *36*(1), 157–178. doi:10.2307/41410412

Villinger, K., Wahl, D. R., Boeing, H., Schupp, H. T., & Renner, B. (2019). The effectiveness of app-based mobile interventions on nutrition behaviours and nutrition-related health outcomes: A systematic review and meta-analysis. *Obesity Reviews*, *20*(10), 1465–1484. doi:10.1111/obr.12903 PMID:31353783

Vlahu-Gjorgievska, E., Mulakaparambil Unnikrishnan, S., & Win, K. T. (2018). mHealth applications: A tool for behaviour change in weight management. *Studies in Health Technology and Informatics*, *252*, 158–163. PMID:30040699

Wang, T., Fan, L., Zheng, X., Wang, W., Liang, J., An, K., Mei, J., & Lei, J. (2021). The impact of gamification-induced Users' feelings on the continued use of mHealth apps: A structural equation model with the self-determination theory approach. *Journal of Medical Internet Research*, *23*(8), e24546. doi:10.2196/24546 PMID:34387550

Woldaregay, A. Z., Issom, D. Z., Henriksen, A., Marttila, H., Mikalsen, M., Pfuhl, G., Sato, K., Lovis, C., & Hartvigsen, G. (2018). Motivational Factors for User Engagement with mHealth Apps. In pHealth, 249, 151–157.

Zhou, L., Bao, J., Watzlaf, V., & Parmanto, B. (2019). Barriers to and Facilitators of the Use of Mobile Health Apps from a Security Perspective: Mixed-Methods Study. *JMIR mHealth and uHealth*, *7*(4), e11223. doi:10.2196/11223 PMID:30990458

Zhou, Y., Su, Y., Chen, T., Huang, Z., Gall, H. C., & Panichella, S. (2020). User review-based change file localization for mobile applications. *IEEE Transactions on Software Engineering*, *47*(12), 2755–2770. doi:10.1109/TSE.2020.2967383

KEY TERMS AND DEFINITIONS

Abandonment: People stop using m-health apps because of different causes.

Facilitating Conditions: Facilitating condition measures whether the user has the necessary resources and assistance available to use m-health apps.

Health Behavior: Health behaviors are practices related to health, such as diet and exercise, that have the potential to either enhance or harm the health of individuals or members of the community.

Lifestyle (LS) Application: Lifestyle apps concentrate on products and services that allow users to monitor and track their fitness behavior. LS apps include fitness, nutrition and meditation apps.

M-health Apps: M-health apps are mobile applications designed to enhance health outcomes, provide healthcare services, or facilitate health research.

Motivation: An internal state that drives individuals towards specific objectives, resulting in purposeful actions.

Usability: Means how easy it is to use a product and complete tasks with it. The ease-of-use impacts how users perceive the quality of the application.

Usefulness: Describes anything that helps users closer to or meet their goals. Usefulness is one of the many dimensions that influences and contributes to a product's usability.

Wearable Health Devices: These are any kind of electronic device designed to be worn on the user's body.

Chapter 4
Social Media and NPOs:
An Integrative Literature Review

Ana Isabel Canavarro
https://orcid.org/0000-0001-9249-6864
Instituto Português de Administração de Marketing, IPAM PORTO, Portugal

Susana Cristina Santos
Instituto Português de Administração de Marketing, IPAM PORTO, Portugal

Joana Vagaroso Tiago
Instituto Português de Administração de Marketing, IPAM PORTO, Portugal

ABSTRACT

The nonprofit sector has been growing around the world. In addition, non-profit organizations (NPOs) are an essential piece of a healthy society. It's undeniable that NPOs (also known as voluntary, independent third sector, or nongovernmental societal sectors) are a relevant part of our society. The activities of fundraising are vital. Following the digital transformation, NPOs have operated in a digital context. These organizations need digital marketing strategies, since the competition is high. This chapter was written with the purpose of elucidating the following research questions: which is the actual state of the art regarding the use of social media marketing in NPOs? In the midst of the various social media tools, which are the ones most successful for NPOs, regarding securing donors and fundraising goals? A qualitative approach was elected, involving an integrative literature review, from 2013 to 2021. Inclusion and exclusion criteria were applied. The authors hope to contribute to a synthesis of knowledge and applicability of results of significant studies into practice.

1. INTRODUCTION

The purpose of this chapter is to analyze, on the one hand, what is the current state of the art regarding the use of social media marketing by NPOs and, on the other hand, to identify, among the various social media tools and strategies, which are the most successful for NPOs in terms of securing donors and achieving fundraising goals.

DOI: 10.4018/978-1-6684-8984-0.ch004

The authors believe that social media and NPOs is an area of knowledge with a rapidly growing body of literature that has not benefited from a comprehensive review and update over an extended period of time.

To fulfil the above intentions, the available literature on the subject (both original studies and theoretical reviews and case reports, from 2013 to 2023) was considered to understand the nuances of various aspects of digital marketing strategies related to NPOs.

It's undeniable that non-profit organisations (also known as voluntary, independent third sector or non-governmental social sectors) are an important part of our society. These organizations operate in the market and don't pursue profit, but the well-being of society, and their founders and shareholders do not receive a share of the profits (Milla et al., 2018).

It's interesting to note that characteristics such as trust, solidarity, reciprocity and cohesion are part of non-profit social networks (Atouba & Shumate, 2020; Bixler & Springer, 2018; McPherson et al., 2001 cit. in. Oliveira et al., 2021).

The truth is that not-for-profit organizations (NPOs) live with the resources they receive from government agencies and private donors. These organizations should then use their resources strategically to achieve their mission-related goals (Richter et al., 2019 cit. in. Gartner et. al., 2021).

With the acceleration of digital transformation, NPOs are increasingly operating in a digital context (Gartner et. al, 2021).

In the early 1990s, communication via the Internet was one-way. Consumers could not express their feedback in real time, nor could they spread their message for a cause (Milla et al., 2017).

In this sense, social media sites have helped in this digitization process by increasing the level of networking and interactivity with friends and donors (Lovejoy & Saxton, 2012).

Moreover, according to Gartner et al. (2021), the existing knowledge, experience and skills from traditional marketing have not lost their value in the context of digital transformation and can still be applied in a digital environment. The principles of service marketing regarding the positive impact of brand trust on service quality are still valid in the era of social media (p. 584).

2. METHODOLOGY

An integrative literature review is proposed in order to gain an overall understanding of the current state of the art in the use of social media marketing by NPOs and, more specifically, which are the most successful social media tools and strategies.

An integrative review is a specific review method that critiques and synthesizes literature in order to gain a comprehensive understanding of a specific topic (Whittemore & Knafl, 2005). In this sense, the use of literature review is chosen to answer specific research questions about a topic (Torraco, 2016). These research questions define the boundaries of the literature to be reviewed and the issues to be investigated. As a bibliographic search was carried out, the following sources of academic and scientific research were used: Academic Search Complete, Web of Science, Business Source Complete (EBSCO), Coimbra University Press, Elsevier, Sage Premier, Springer, Taylor & Francis, Wiley, Teacher Reference Center (EBSCO) and also Google Scholar.

The descriptors and their combinations in English used to search the articles were as follows: "non-profit organizations - NPOs", "digital marketing", "digital marketing and non-profit organizations - NPOs". In general, a comprehensive search for an integrative review identifies the maximum number of eligible primary sources using at least two to three strategies (Whittemore & Knafl, 2005).

The inclusion criteria defined for the selection of articles were:

1. Articles published in English.
2. Full articles on the above topics, original studies and theoretical reviews and case reports.
3. Indexed in the above databases in the last eight years (2013 to 2021).
4. Articles must have been published in journals as Q1, Q2, Q3 or Q4 according to the Journal of Citations Report (JCR).

The initial sample consisted of 43 articles. After applying the above inclusion/exclusion criteria, a total of 17 articles were eligible. Selected articles that did not meet the inclusion criteria described above were excluded from the analysis.

3. LITERATURE REVIEW

3.1. Sectoral Specifics of NPOs

Non-profit organisations provide services to disadvantaged populations, mobilise collective action and advocate for civil rights (Marwell, 2004; McCarthy & Castelli, 2002 cit. in Paxton et al., 2020).

Another feature is that membership of NPOs is not compulsory, and they attract voluntary contributions in terms of time and money (Milla et al., 2017).

Recent decades have seen a significant increase in the number of NPOs involved in the provision of health, welfare and other social services (Agranoff, 2005; Agranoff, 2006; Appleton, 2005; Bryce, 2006; Henriksen et al., 2012; Kendall & Knapp, 2000; Milward & Proven, 2000; Neville et al., 2011; O'Toole, 1997; Robbins & Lapsley, 2008; Salamom, 1995; Selden et al., 2006; Young, 2000 cit. in. Conaty & Robbins, 2021).

From the literature review, there is evidence that the context is favorable for NPOs. Opportunities are emerging for the development of innovative small businesses, social economy start-ups and non-governmental organizations (NGOs) at local, regional, or national level (Paul, 2020 cit. in Vrontis et al., 2021). Indeed, the population of the European Union (EU) is ageing and by 2030 there will be 88 million people over the age of 65. This age group is expected to increase from 17.5% of the population in 2010 to 29.5% in 2060 (European Commission, 2014 cit. in Vrontis et al., 2021).

In the context of NPOs, there are three main external stakeholders: 'donors' (contractual and non-contractual), the 'regulator' and 'beneficiaries' (service users) (Hyndman & McDonnell, 2009 cit. in Conaty & Robbins, 2021).

The effectiveness of NPOs in fulfilling their important functions depends on their organizational capacity in terms of leadership, management, planning, operations, and other factors (Eisinger, 2002 cit in. Sun & Asencio, 2018).

3.2. Marketing for Non-Profit Organizations

Marketing has evolved from a traditional production- and transaction-based concept to a more customer-, stakeholder- and society- (or citizen-) oriented concept (Bagozzi, 1975; Bhattacharya & Korschun, 2008; Feldman, 1971; Lazer, 1969; Webster & Lusch, 2013 cited in. Bandyopadhyay & Ray, 2019).

The application of marketing theory and practice from the commercial sector to the not-for-profit context is increasingly common (Modi & Mishra, 2010 cit in. Mitchell & Clark, 2021) as competition for resources (volunteer time, financial donations, service users and quality staff) increases. However, the sector has unique characteristics, such as volunteer resources and a non-economic mission, which require a different way of thinking (Mitchell & Clark, 2021).

Paxton et al, (2020) argue that nonprofits attract donors and volunteers by appealing to their emotions. Indeed, people weigh factors other than financial and rational motives when deciding whether to donate to a nonprofit. It is a special feature of NPOs.

Research in psychology and neuroscience supports the importance of emotions in guiding decisions, both consciously and unconsciously (Damasio, 1994; Gray 1990; Zajonc, 1980 cit. in Paxton et al., 2020).

In general, emotions, particularly positive emotions, had a stronger effect on volunteering than on giving, as volunteering is a more social, effortful and physically immersive experience than giving (Paxton et al., 2020).

Cause-related marketing (CRM) campaigns have also emerged as a way for companies to differentiate themselves in a highly competitive environment and are increasingly being adopted and implemented by many organizations to gain a competitive advantage (Vrontis et al., 2020).

CRM is "the business partnership of a for-profit company with a not-for-profit organization to promote the former's products and services while raising funds for a charitable cause" (Vrontis et al., 2020). It is clear that today's consumer is looking for product benefits that go beyond quality and functionality (etc.) to include intangible values.

3.3. Secure of Donors and Fundraising of NPOs

Fundraising campaigns are essential for NPOs. In fact, private donations raised by NPOs are influenced by and proportional to the investment NPOs make in fundraising campaigns. The higher the investment in fundraising, the higher the private donations raised (Nageswarakurukkal et al., 2020).

In terms of these fundraising initiatives, mass marketing techniques are expensive and require a large financial investment that small and medium-sized organisations cannot afford (Nageswarakurukkal et al., 2019).

It is also known that there are key variables that influence the level of giving: the age of the organization, the longevity of fundraising, the type of cause, the location, and the commitment of senior management. The economic and political environment can also affect the level of giving (Nageswarakurukkal et al., 2020).

Younger audiences are statistically less likely to give (Generosity for Life, 2019). Despite this, it's important to note that they are rapidly becoming the fundamental donor base for nonprofits around the world.

3.4. Social Media Marketing for NPOs

Online communication is considered a strategic resource for the success of nonprofit organizations (del Mar Galvez-Rodriguez et al., 2016).

Nonetheless, nonprofit organizations have an incentive to reduce barriers that could potentially disrupt the donation process, for example by accepting online donations (Waters, 2007).

A careful review of the literature reveals that few studies have addressed the issues associated with social media from the perspective of NPOs.

Findings suggest that the larger the social network of the NPO, the greater the amount of donations received. A large social network enables the dissemination of the fundraising campaign and reaches more people to donate (Nageswarakurukkala et al., 2019).

Gartner et al. (2021) explain that the specific characteristics of the service provided by the NPO determine the suitability of a particular social media channel, as each social media channel has a specific set of media elements that prioritize different types of communication.

Saxton and Wang (2014) also defend that social media has enabled NPOs to strategically engage new, larger and younger audiences in a cost-effective manner.

Lovejoy and Saxton (2012) attribute the emergence of social networking sites such as Facebook and Twitter as free tools that helped NPOs, large and small, to build a network of friends or followers, maintaining interactivity and real-time contact. This didn't happen with the old sites, which lacked this interactivity.

In the case of Twitter, it can give NPOs the opportunity to be more effective in communicating credibility to their current audience, as well as attracting new audiences. In order to make the best use of this channel, one should implement one-way and two-way communication strategies both in their Twitter profile and in their tweets (Del Mar Galvez-Rodriguez et al., 2016).

In terms of content, it is also important to consider that emotional language shows returns on donations and volunteers across a wide range of nonprofit organizations (Paxton et al., 2020), which we believe is relevant to consider in social media content strategies.

Due to the civil war in Syria and the large number of Syrian immigrants, many NPOs are developing humanitarian work in the Middle East and Jordan. These NPOs are increasingly adopting social media strategies to reach and engage with the communities they serve. Many of these NPOs have developed websites, discussion channels and social networking pages on Facebook, LinkedIn, and Twitter (Albanna et al., 2022).

In the United Kingdom (UK), some small cancer charities use Facebook as a channel to keep in touch with their supporters and to strengthen this relationship in the long term. This is a way they have found to humanize their brands, encourage social interaction, and ultimately raise more donations, although they lack some competencies such as monitoring social media metrics such as return on investment (ROI) (Lucas, 2017).

On the other hand, it's important to note that the smallest NPOs usually have less capacity in terms of income and staff and are therefore the most vulnerable to the demands and pressures of organizations and groups. Therefore, these entities use, for example, Twitter to enrich and strengthen their public relations, disseminate information, and also develop interactive communication with their stakeholders (del Mar Galvez-Rodriguez et al., 2016).

Consumer brand engagement (CBE) is also a construct of great value for social media communication. Telepresence, social presence, and involvement are the main antecedents of CBE. Therefore, Algharabat et al. (2018) advise non-profit organizations to use the social media platform Facebook and correctly design their Facebook pages to reflect sensory information and provide a sense of human warmth (telepresence and social presence).

In the opinion of Sun & Asencio (2018), NPOs that lack resources and social media expertise should learn, namely through online resources on social media training, to learn the best practices. According to these authors, having a presence on social media such as Twitter and making video posts without fully understanding and knowing how to use them can be counterproductive to organizational goals. For example, writing a Twitter post in 140 (now 280) characters requires tactics and practice (Sun & Asencio, 1018).

When preparing content, NPOs should consider stakeholder needs and demographics and recognize staff as internal ambassadors. They should also be considered and can contribute to an integrated social media approach (Swart et al., 2021, p. 8).

Nevertheless, NPOs should adopt an integrated approach to social media communication (SMC) to increase its impact by creating and sharing content on social media platforms. (Swart et al., 2021).

4. CONCLUSION

An integrative literature review is proposed to provide an overall understanding of the current state of the art in the use of social media marketing by NPOs and, more specifically, the most successful social media tools and strategies.

The authors believe this integrative literature review will contribute to the synthesis of knowledge and the applicability of the findings of key studies to practice and to a further understanding of this particular area of study, helping NPOs to develop a strategic vision of their digital communications and practices, particularly with regard to social media marketing.

First of all, the authors conclude that NPOs are growing exponentially around the world and are essential to a healthy society.

A careful review of the literature also reveals that few studies have addressed social media issues from the perspective of NPOs.

On the state of the art in the use of social media marketing by NPOs, the literature analysed confirms that online communication is seen as a strategic resource for the success of non-profit organizations.

The truth is that traditional mass marketing techniques are expensive and require a large financial investment that small and medium sized organizations cannot afford.

On the most successful social media tools and strategies, in terms of securing donors and fundraising goals, it is registered that social networking sites such as Facebook and Twitter, as free tools, have helped NPOs, large and small, to start building a network of friends or followers, while maintaining interactivity and real-time contact.

As also mentioned above, many NPOs have developed websites, discussion channels and social networking pages on Facebook, LinkedIn and Twitter.

These social networks have enabled NPOs to strategically engage new, larger and younger audiences in a cost-effective way.

Indeed, the smallest NPOs, with less capacity in terms of income and staff, use, for example, Twitter to enrich and strengthen their public relations, to disseminate information and also to develop interactive communication with their stakeholders.

Nevertheless, it is important to note that NPOs that lack resources and social media expertise should learn, through online social media training resources, to learn best practices.

A major conclusion of this analysis is that an integrated approach to social media is needed. NPOs should combine traditional and SMC methods to ensure this integrated approach and greater impact.

This study has some limitations:

- The lack of a combined empirical research (which could be of great value to identify the practice of NPOs in the field of digital marketing communications).
- The inclusion/exclusion criteria adopted left out articles of interest.

In terms of future research, as Nageswarakurukkal et al. (2020) maintain, future studies could collect qualitative data (e.g. interviews) to shed light on the reasons for donors' reluctance to donate online. This research, we believe, is important to help NPOs strategically address its donors' and other relevant stakeholders. potential fears regarding the level of trust in digital platforms.

REFERENCES

Albanna, H., Alalwan, A. A., & Al-Emran, M. (2022). An integrated model for using social media applications in non-profit organizations. *International Journal of Information Management*, *63*, 102452.

Bandyopadhyay, C., & Ray, S. (2019). Responsible marketing: Can social enterprises show the way? *Journal of Nonprofit & Public Sector Marketing*, *31*(2), 164–183. doi:10.1080/10495142.2018.1526738

Conaty, F., & Robbins, G. (2021). A stakeholder salience perspective on performance and management control systems in non-profit organizations. *Critical Perspectives on Accounting*, *80*, 102052. doi:10.1016/j.cpa.2018.07.001

del Mar Galvez-Rodriguez, M., Caba-Pérez, C., & López-Godoy, M. (2016). Drivers of Twitter as a strategic communication tool for non-profit organizations. *Internet Research*, *26*(5), 1052–1071. doi:10.1108/IntR-07-2014-0188

Gartner, J., Fink, M., Floh, A., & Eggers, F. (2021). Service quality in social media communication of NPOs: The moderating effect of channel choice. *Journal of Business Research*, *137*, 579–587. doi:10.1016/j.jbusres.2021.08.026

Lovejoy, K., & Saxton, G. D. (2012). Information, community, and action: How nonprofit organizations use social media. *Journal of Computer-Mediated Communication*, *17*(3), 337–353. doi:10.1111/j.1083-6101.2012.01576.x

Milla, A., Mataruna, L., & Ristic, M. R. (2018). Adopting social Media for Nonprofits as a Main marketing tool: Analysis of a youth non-profit organization. *Int J Appl Bus Econ Res*, *22*(2), 741–752.

Nageswarakurukkal, K., Gonçalves, P., & Moshtari, M. (2020). Improving fundraising efficiency in small and medium sized non-profit organizations using online solutions. *Journal of Nonprofit & Public Sector Marketing*, *32*(3), 286–311. doi:10.1080/10495142.2019.1589627

O'Neil, G. (2013). Evaluation of international and non-governmental organizations' communication activities: A 15 year systematic review. *Public Relations Review*, *39*(5), 572–574. doi:10.1016/j.pubrev.2013.07.005

Oliveira, M., Oliveira, J., Borges, A. P., & Lopes, J. M. (2021). Social networks in the non-profit sector: Social support practices. *International Review on Public and Nonprofit Marketing*, *18*(4), 523–552. doi:10.100712208-021-00283-6

Paxton, P., Velasco, K., & Ressler, R. W. (2020). Does use of emotion increase donations and volunteers for nonprofits? *American Sociological Review*, *85*(6), 1051–1083. doi:10.1177/0003122420960104

Sun, R., & Asencio, H. D. (2018). Using social media to increase nonprofit organizational capacity. *International Journal of Public Administration*, *42*, 1–12.

Swart, C., du Plessis, C., & Greeff, E. (2021). An integrated social media communication view on content marketing by South African non-profit sectors. *South African Journal of Information Management*, *23*(1), 1–9. doi:10.4102ajim.v23i1.1366

Thomas, S., & Jadeja, A. (2021). Psychological antecedents of consumer trust in CRM campaigns and donation intentions: The moderating role of creativity. *Journal of Retailing and Consumer Services*, *61*, 102589. doi:10.1016/j.jretconser.2021.102589

Vrontis, D., Morea, D., Basile, G., Bonacci, I., & Mazzitelli, A. (2021). Consequences of technology and social innovation on traditional business model. *Technological Forecasting and Social Change*, *170*, 120877. doi:10.1016/j.techfore.2021.120877

Vrontis, D., Thrassou, A., Christofi, M., Shams, R., & Czinkota, M. R. (2020). Cause-related marketing in international business: What works and what does not? *International Marketing Review*, *37*(4), 593–601. doi:10.1108/IMR-05-2019-0144

Yalçin, Z., & Canoğlu, M. (2021). Social Media Marketing Effectiveness of Non-Profit Organizations: An Analysis on Environmentalist Organizations. *OPUS International Journal of Society Researches*, *18*, 1136-1163.

Chapter 5
Search Engine Optimisation for Social Marketing

Gonzalo Díaz Meneses
University of Las Palmas de Gran Canaria, Spain

Sol Castellanos Pérez Lasala
University of Las Palmas de Gran Canaria, Spain

Maica Amador-Marrero
University of Las Palmas de Gran Canaria, Spain

ABSTRACT

Social marketing is among the scientific disciplines whose professional and scientific institutions have grown significantly in recent years. However, there are still only twelve national and regional institutions worldwide whose online presence must be made more visible insofar as the keyword 'social media marketing' shadows it. Moreover, when labelled correctly as 'social marketing associations,' there is less visibility than other professional associations concerning the same social problems. Therefore, the present chapter sets out the objective of analysing the main SEO metrics of the most important social marketing associations worldwide. With this aim in mind, this book chapter is divided into five sections. Firstly, there is an introduction to set out the research objectives. Secondly, a section on theoretical systematisation. Thirdly, a methodological section. Fourthly, the authors share the empirical evidence obtained and answer the research questions. Fifthly, we indicate the practical implications. Finally, it acknowledges the limitations and suggests future lines of research.

1. INTRODUCTION

Social marketing is among the scientific disciplines whose professional and scientific institutions have seen significant growth in recent years. However, there are fewer than fifteen national and regional institutions worldwide, and their online presence needs more visibility. For this, it is important for social marketing institutions to digitalise and employ a good SEO strategy. This technique is based on a no-cost advertising strategy. Which, according to some authors, is based on keyword optimisation (Tewari, 2023;

DOI: 10.4018/978-1-6684-8984-0.ch005

Yalçın, 2010;). Keywords are the terms that are used to perform a navigational search (Chen, 2023). Therefore, it is important that the website contains certain specific terms to position a website in the first results of search engine result pages (SERPs) (Erdmann et al., 2022; Oliveira & Teixeira, 2023). Hence, certain metrics and technical conditions are based on the website to be ranked highly (Mladenović et al., 2023) so that it increases its visibility.

The present case study aims to analyse the main SEO metrics of the most important social marketing associations worldwide. Moreover, it hopes to give some pointers to improve the social marketing positions on the internet and, in turn, bring the benefit of employing social marketing technologies and approaches to enhance people's quality of life effectively and efficiently.

To structure and drive the steps followed by this paper, eight sets of research questions are raised as follows:

(1) Social marketing? What is social marketing?
(2) What are the structural SEO similarities between the social marketing organisations? This question will be answered by considering structural, performance and output metrics.
(3) What are the performance SEO similarities between the social marketing organisations?
(4) What are the output SEO similarities between the social marketing organisations?
(5) What are the structural SEO differences between the social marketing and psychology organisations?
(6) What are the performance SEO differences between the social marketing and psychology organisations?
(7) What are the output SEO differences between the social marketing and psychology organisations?
(8) Is it possible to aggregate and segment the social marketing and psychology organisations by considering the SEO features?

In addition to the introduction, this case study is divided into four sections. Firstly, the case development section aims to define and systematise key search engine notions. Also, we will define what social marketing is and outline why we have chosen to establish a comparison between the social marketing and psychology associations. Secondly, it deals with methodological content to describe the fieldwork, the measuring instruments, and the research context. Thirdly, we show the statistical analysis and share the obtained empirical evidence. Fourthly, we draw some conclusions by attempting to answer the research questions and so ignite insightful thinking, highlight practical implications, and encourage future courses of action. Finally, we offer a list of bibliographical references whose inspirational sources are therein acknowledged.

2. THE CASE DEVELOPMENT SECTION

Undoubtedly, it is not social marketing's online ranking that matters most, but rather how Search Engine Optimisation for social marketing associations can help solve a wide range of social problems. Insofar as the term 'social marketing' is hugely misused on the internet, we need help putting solutions into orbit. To address the problem, there must be a wide range of measures. However, it all starts with two simple steps. Firstly, we need to raise awareness about what social marketing is so that we get to grips with this scientific discipline. Secondly, we need to build a theoretical framework that might especially be employed by those involved with social marketing's professional associations.

2.1. Social Marketing? What is Social Marketing?

It is worth noting from the start that there is a glaring difference between *social marketing* and *social media marketing*. However, social marketing has much more to do with social media marketing than is typically acknowledged by Internet users worldwide. Unfortunately, social marketing is wrongly labelled by those who often misuse the term owing to blatant confusion with social media.

While social marketing is fundamentally about changing behaviours, social media marketing focuses on search engine optimisation. So as not to go too fast, it is worth the effort to define these terms. We understand *social marketing* as a branch of marketing that "seeks to develop and integrate marketing concepts with other approaches to influence behaviours that benefit individuals and communities for the greater social good" (Lee & Kotler, 2019). Conversely, when talking about social media marketing, the concept refers to a "company's process of creating and promoting online marketing-related activities on social media platforms that offer value to its stakeholders", according to Pham and Gammoh (2015). Furthermore, SEO "is developing a marketing/technical plan to improve visibility within one or more search engines" with quantitative variables, translating into a more closely related metric area (AMA, 2023).

The term 'social marketing' is often confused with 'social media marketing'. Firstly, social marketing studies consumer behaviour in areas such as education, health and environment, among many others. Social media marketing is based on social media strategies to promote a product or to increase a brand's awareness. Consequently, social marketing faces a Search Engine Optimisation stumbling block. Both professionals and trainees are unaware that there is a branch of marketing aimed at solving social issues because there is little "publicity" about it.

Social marketing has been present for centuries (arguably dating back to Ancient Greece), with the campaigns against slavery and the promotion of women's suffrage (Kotler & Roberto, 1992) being two obvious historical examples. However, it is only more recently that campaigns like these have been labelled as such. Social marketing was formally defined in the early 1970s, which is why, although it is a discipline with a long history, it has little trajectory as a marketing branch. Thus, there is still a long way to go. It is worth noting that one of the pioneering social marketing institutions is the International Association of Public and Non-Profit Marketing, created in 2002 in Spain. However, the Spanish association works on more than social marketing. For this reason, it is worth acknowledging that it was only when the National Social Marketing Centre was launched in 2006 that social marketing started its institutionalisation. Still, it implies a considerable step forward since it was born from the merger between the British Health Promotion and consumer governmental units. Another is the Australian Social Marketing Association, founded in 2009. As these and other institutions represent vital social marketing providers in the online marketplace, it is worth pondering how they optimise their search engine activities.

However, the keyword "social marketing" has a disadvantage when it comes to benchmarking once known, it needs to be clarified with other disciplines and activities, such as digital marketing and psychology practices, hindering its ability to assist in resolving social issues. Therefore, it is important to point out the connection between psychology and social marketing. It is a fact that social marketing is based on applying marketing strategies to encourage social causes that are appropriate for society, usually intending to influence and change public behaviour. For example, promoting recycling or reducing alcohol consumption in the adolescents (Beerli-Palacio et al., 2011). On the other hand, psychology studies mental processes in terms of cognitive, behavioural, and affective aspects. Therefore, there is a significant relationship between psychology and social marketing. Also, psychology is essential since it can shed light on the confusion between social marketing and social media marketing.

It should be noted that the term "psychology" plays an important role in society after highly stressful events, such as Covid-19 or the current emerging wars in Ukraine or Israel. Whereas the term "social marketing", which is fundamental for dealing with social stress, has been overlooked regarding visibility or recognition. Hence, the impact of SEO on social marketing associations and psychology institutions should be studied. To find out whether the lack of visibility of social marketing today is due to a positioning technique or a matter of misunderstanding. Therefore, we have chosen the most relevant institutions in social marketing and psychology to analyse their websites (the selected institutions are listed in the methodology section). Thus, we will get to know their SEO, as well as their similarities and differences. To overcome the misunderstanding of the social marketing concept and to find out if it can be recognised through SEO and gain visibility.

2.2. The 'On-Page' and 'Off-Page' Metrics for Social Marketing

We distinguish between 'off-page' and 'on-page' SEO indicators (see Table 1). Firstly, off-page SEO refers to the external optimisation of the website, which is an important SEO element that focuses on backlinks or external links (Alfiana et al., 2023). For example, links from social media to the website. Hence, the off-page indicators are those metrics whose origin is external and refer to link building, penalisations, and social media. Several key concepts play a vital role in optimising websites for search engines. On the other hand, off-page variables, such as link building, are based on the set of actions to generate external or outbound links to promote the authority of the website and social media, such as Facebook and Instagram, this external data can drive traffic to a specific site and improve the positioning (Ahmad et al., 2022). However, Google penalises websites that use aggressive SEO techniques to manipulate its rules in order to show better results in less time. Common errors that call for penalisations include broken links, slow page loading speeds and duplicate content. Such issues can lead to a poor user experience and negatively affect search engine rankings, ranking the website at the bottom of SERPs (Camargo et al., 2022). An example of a penalty involves the use of bots to try to rank the website. Another important concept is *indexability*, which "*refers to adding a webpage's content to Google to be considered for rankings,*" as Davies (2023) explained. It is a process where search engines store the collected data from URLs and group them accordingly to different and changeable variables. The goal is to make the content easily and quickly available to a related search.

On the other hand, on-page SEO concerns the optimisation of certain settings, such as keywords or meta descriptions, within the internal metrics of the website (Alfiana et al., 2023). Those changes directly influence the search engine optimisation of the website. So, the on-page indicators are those metrics that refer to internal, technical aspects and contents ranging from URL and domain, and website hosting, to website design and contents (see Table 1). Firstly, keywords allow to increase organic search traffic through words or short phrases (Garcia et al., 2022) and are fundamental elements that help search engines understand a webpage's relevance to a particular search query (Hermanson, 2021). It allows one to understand what the content of the website is about and to display it to the relevant audience. Also, there is a common confusion between the definitions of 'URL' and 'domain' due to their co-dependency. To contrast them, the *domain* is the website's name (what comes after "www"), and the *URL* is the internet address where the user can find the various pages of the domain. Moreover, good website design, meaning, planning, and content delivering can play a major role when positioning in search results. Also, web design allows determining a wise use of the density keywords (Erdmann et al., 2022). Furthermore, web hosting concerns the servers where the website is stored (Britvin et al., 2022) and available for the users. Though not directly an SEO technique, it plays a crucial role in the performance and visibility on search engines. So, web hosting is an essential component to guarantee the technical functioning of a webpage, i.e., for page speed (Fadli et al., 2023) and security.

Hence, *domain ranking*, *traffic* and *authority* are crucial concepts in search engine optimisation (SEO). Domain ranking refers to the position or prominence of a website on search engine results pages (SERPs) for specific keywords (Erdmann et al., 2022; Rumeliotis et al., 2022). It indicates a domain's overall authority and relevance in relation to other websites. A higher domain ranking is often associated with increased visibility and organic search traffic (Rumeliotis et al., 2022), as it indicates to search engines that the website has valuable and trustworthy information (Moz, 2023). Furthermore, domain authority (DA) (Mladenović et al., 2023) to the perceived expertise, credibility, and trustworthiness of a website in a particular niche or industry. This is established through various factors, such as high-quality content, backlinks from reputable websites, positive user engagement metrics, and a strong online presence. Authority plays a significant role in search engine algorithms in off-page SEO components (Rumeliotis et al., 2022), as search engines aim to provide users with reliable and relevant information. Websites with greater authority are more likely to rank higher in search results and attract organic traffic (Moz, 2023). Finally, in SEO, traffic represents the number of visitors or users accessing a specific website. However, proper SEO can generate several advantages, such as improving the user experience through website structure, segmenting the audience through web performance, or reducing the cost-per-click (CPC) of Search Engine Marketing (SEM) (Erdmann et al., 2022), among others. Therefore, establishing a successful SEO strategy to attract users is essential.

In addition to distinguishing between on-page and off-page links, it is worth noting the existence of causal and consequent metrics. Likewise, SEO metrics are used to measure and analyse a website's performance on the SERPs. Some of the metrics used for SEO strategy are clickthrough rate (CTR) (Yang & Zhai, 2022), organic traffic, bounce rate, backlinks, main keywords, visibility index (CTR + ranking position), domain authority (DA), conversion rate (Miikkulainen et al., 2023), time spent on the website, and search engine position. These metrics are used by SEO experts, and you can see the tools that are used for their websites and these concepts in the practice of digital marketing (see Table 2).

At this point, search engine optimisation is less transparent than a published mathematic formulation, given that search engine brands do not disclose their algorithms. Be that as it may, we can guess a distinction between factors determining a particular position in the search engine result pages, such as *content*, and factors resulting from ranking first, such as *traffic*. However, this is

Table 1. On-page and off-page metrics

On-page	Off-page
☐ URL & domain	☐ Link building
☐ Website hosting	☐ Penalizations
☐ Website design	☐ Social media
☐ Content quality	☐ Indexability
☐ Keyword optimization	
☐ Page Speed	

Table 2. SEO Metrics how to do them

Metric	Measure	Tool
Clickthrough Rate (CTR)	Shows the percentage of users who click on the website link that appears in the SERPs.	Google Search Console
Organic Traffic	Display the number of users who visits the webpage from the search engine results and social media.	Google Analytics or SEMrush
Bounce Rate	Calculates the rate of users who exit a website after viewing a specific page.	Google Analytics
Backlinks	Calculates the quality and quantity of authority.	Moz
Keywords	Track the keywords, to check the amount of driving traffic.	Moz or SEMrush
Page Indexing	Shows if search engines index correctly the webpage.	Google Search Console
Conversion Rate	Calculates the percentage of visitors who perform certain actions on the website.	Google Analytics
Time Spent	Track the user behavior on the website. Calculate the engagement of the content.	Google Analytics
Domain Authority	Predicts the rank on SERPs	Moz

more a systematisation to ease the predominant functioning of search engine optimisation than a classification containing exclusive categories. In other words, causal and consequent factors are variables operating in a recursive model in which, for example, traffic is not only a resultant factor of positioning first in the search engine results, but also a causal factor, since the more visits a website gets, the better it will be positioned in the search engine results. To be precise, this theoretical systematisation is displayed in Figure 1. First, there are structural features regarding how the website is built, such as web hosting and design, and URL & domain, as well as content quality such as keywords, video, audio, and other content formats. Second, performance metrics regarding how the website operates include timings, indexability and accessibility, outbound, social media, outreach, backlinks, errors and penalisations. Third, essential positioning outputs include URL, domain ranking, and traffic and authority.

Figure 1. Theoretical metrics systematisation

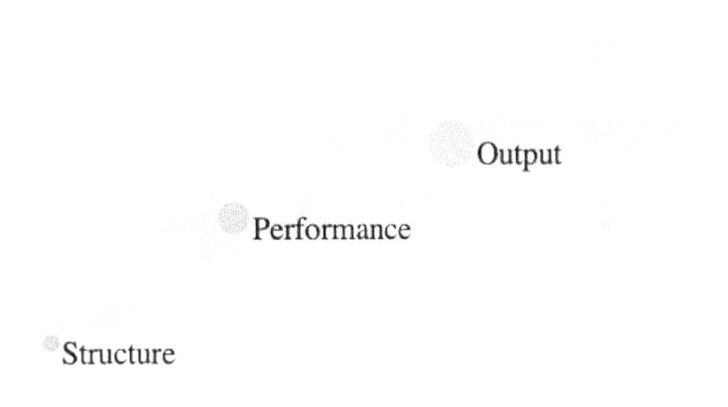

3. METHODOLOGY

Some methodological features need to be planned before social marketing's ranking in search engines can improve. First, we need to pin down the primary social marketing associations indicating their name, geographical scope and URL. Similarly, we must identify other corresponding organisations in the field of Psychology to benchmark. Second, we should select the SEO metrics to monitor distinguishing on-page and off-page variables. Third, we have to choose suitable software to gather this information and describe the survey. Fourth, we must advance the fieldwork planning and pinpoint the research context.

Not only is there a social marketing confusion problem, but the social marketing professional associations should also seek to improve their positions in the natural listings given by the search engine results pages when they are googled. Therefore, there is the question of what these associations are. The answer is displayed in Table 3, in which their URL, names and countries are shown.

In addition to weighing up how serious the confusion is and at what rate the search engine optimisation is, it is worth acknowledging the psychology associations to benchmark against (see table 4).

Another methodological planning task consists of finding a match between the metrics and software to employ. This phase is crucial for carrying out the survey, but it is also vital to address a market intelligence procedure with a continuous and exhaustive monitoring approach. Therefore, in addition to linking software and metrics, it seems essential to describe the database dimensionality so that we pin down the variables to gather and collate during the fieldwork and the consequent monitoring tasks. We display this information in Table 5.

In addition, we should find out how to gauge the social marketing positioning and, thus, clarify that there is a misuse drawback. A social listening tool has been employed to address the shortcoming of the social marketing term misuse. This software is called Webcollector and is made by Provalis Research. The keyword to monitor is "social marketing". On the other hand, the selected monitoring tools allow the analysis of competitor websites or websites one is not part of as their webmaster. Therefore, these programmes were chosen because they allow you to analyse institutions outside of your organisation in a safe and effective way.

Table 3. Social marketing associations

INSTITUTION	ACRONYMS	COUNTRY	URL
International Association on Public and Non Profit Marketing	IAPNM	Spain	https://www.aimpn.org
National Social Marketing Centre	NSMC	UK	https://www.thensmc.com
Portuguese Social Marketing Association	PSMA	Portugal	https://marketingsocialportugal.net/
French Social Marketing Institute	FSMI	France	https://institutdumarketingsocial.org
Italian Social Marketing Association	ItSMA	Italy	https://marketingsociale.net/
The Social Marketing Behaviour Change Institute	SMBCI	Greece	https://www.social-marketing.gr
European Social Marketing Association	ESMA	Europe	https://europeansocialmarketing.org/
Social Marketing Association of North America	SMANA	USA	https://smana.org
Australian Association of Social Marketing	AASM	Australia	https://aasm.org.au
Latin-American Association on Social Marketing	LAASM	Latin America	http://www.mercadeosocial.org
Pacific Northwest Social Marketing Association	PNSMA	Oceania	https://pnsma.org
International Social Marketing Association	ISMA	World	https://isocialmarketing.org

Table 4. Psychology associations

INSTITUTION	ACRONYMS	COUNTRY	URL
The British Psychological Society	BPS	UK	https://www.bps.org.uk/
Ordem dos Psicólogos	OP	Portugal	https://www.ordemdospsicologos.pt/
Fédération Française Psychologues Psychologie	FFPP	France	https://ffpp.net
Associazione Italiana de Psicologi	AIP	Italy	https://www.asp-psicologia.it
National Organisation for Psychotherapy of Greece	NOPG	Greece	https://nopg.gr
European Federation of Psychologists' Associations	EFPA	Europe	https://www.efpa.eu
American Psychological Association	APA	USA	https://www.apa.org
Australian Psychological Society	APS	Australia	https://psychology.org.au/
Sociedad Interamericana de Psicología	SIP	Latin America	https://sipsych.org
Asia Pacific Psychological Alliance	APPA	Asia	https://appa-psy.org
International Union of Psychological Science	IUPS	Worldwide	https://www.iupsys.net

Table 5. Describing the on-page and off-page metrics and software

PHASE	SOFTWARE	METRICS	DESCRIPTION
Structure	IP Neighbour	Website hosting	Qualitative to detect conflictive neighbours
	Screaming Frog	Depth and clicks from start URL	Site structure
	Manual	URL	Uniform resource locator and web address
	Manual	Domain	Identification brand name on the internet
	Website Auditor	Number of resources	Contents
	Website Auditor	Internal resources	Java, HTML, CSS, images, videos, flash, PDF, other internal resources
	Website Auditor	External resources	Java, HTML, CSS, images, videos, flash, PDF, other external resources
	Keyword everywhere	URL word count	Keywords number
	Siteliner	Originality content	Duplicate, common and unique content
Performance	Page speed insight	Speed load	First contentful paint, Largest contentful paint, total blocking time, cumulative layout shift and performance score
	Website Auditor	Indexability	Total number of indexed pages, indexed pages on Google, Yahoo, Bing
	Keyword everywhere	Accessibility	Contents problems
	Page speed insight	Accessibility	Technical problems
	Doctor link check	Link building	Total number of links, outbound links and blocked links
	Website auditor	Penalisations and errors	It stems from indexing, crawlability and faulty redirections
	Phlanx	Social media awareness, interactions and engagement	Reaches, likes, CTR and comments on Facebook, Twitter, Instagram, TikTok, Pinterest, LinkedIn
Output	Keyword Everywhere	URL Searp position	Organic URL ranking
	Keyword Everywhere	Domain Searp position	Organic domain ranking
	Keyword Everywhere	URL traffic	Keyword URL traffic
	SemRush	Domain traffic	Number of visitors
	Moz	Domain authority (DA)	Domain score

Finally, it is worth describing the fieldwork context regarding when and where it occurred and unfolding the target study variables. In this vein, it seems important to explain that the survey took place during two different periods. Firstly, we explored the term "social marketing" on the Google Search Engine and observed the organic results to ponder how serious the confusion was. To do so, we employed the above-mentioned software to gather, collate and interpret the term "social marketing" on Twitter and we built a database with more than 10,000 tweets and three dimensions regarding how correctly the term was used (correct, incorrect, no applicable), the date and 'user identity'. Secondly, we carried out a second survey during the second part of May 2023 from a desktop in the Canary Islands. This survey was carried out by one operator who tabulated the data acknowledging 86 variables whose characteristics are displayed in Table 5. In this case, the aim was to gather information about SEO metrics related to social marketing organisations. As it turns out, we designed a database with multidimensional variables covering a wide range of SEO indicators.

The first four variables identify and classify social marketing and psychology associations by their *database key variable*, *names*, *URL* and *countries*. These variables are qualitative and nominal.

The second twenty-five variables refer to structural characteristics such as *website hosting*, *site structure*, *keywords* and *contents*. Equally, these variables are qualitative.

The third sixteen variables regard performance features such as *accessibility*, *speed load contents*, *indexed pages*, *link building*, *penalisations*, *errors* and *alerts*. These variables are quantitative and continuous.

The fourth thirty variables touch upon information about social media, such as *awareness*, *interaction* and *engagement* on Facebook, Twitter, Instagram, TikTok, Pinterest and Linkedin. Similarly, these variables are qualitative.

Finally, there are five variables to gather information about SEO 'outputs' - *URL* and *domain* (SEARPs positions) - 'outcomes' - *URL* and *domain traffic* - and 'impact' - *domain authority*. Equally, these variables are continuous.

To clarify the grouping of these variables, Table 6 has been designed as an outline for the coding of each variable and its measurement.

In addition, statistical techniques were used to analyse these indicators, such as standardisation, analysis of ANOVA, and student's t-test.

4. ANALYSIS OF THE RESULTS

This section is divided into two subheadings: *preliminary analyses* and *research questions linked to evidence*. While the preliminary section is dedicated to descriptive tests related to the SEO metrics for all the associations, the subsequent part attempts to answer the research questions. First, we gathered and collated data from Twitter to present the data reflecting the social media positioning misuse term problem. Second, we ranked the Social Marketing Organisations in order of Search Engine Optimisation features. Third, the analysis of the results was divided into three consequent subsections.

To answer the first research question, we obtained the count and frequency of the term 'social marketing' used on the internet. To respond to the second set of research questions, we described how similar social marketing associations are. To address the third set of research questions, we compared social marketing organisations' Search Engine Optimisation features and those corresponding associations in

Table 6. Coding scheme

Codes for each variable	Content	Codification (type)	Tool
Identify and classify social marketing and psychology associations	Database key variable, names, URL, and countries.	Qualitative and nominal	Google Search Engine
Structural characteristics	Website hosting, site structure, keywords, and contents.	Qualitative	Ip Neighbours, Screaming Frog, Keyword Everywhere, Website Auditor and Siteliner
Regarding performance features	Accessibility, speed load contents, indexed pages, link building, penalisations, errors, and alerts.	Quantitative and continuous	Keyword Everywhere, PageSpeedInsight, Website Auditor and Doctor link check
Information about social media	Awareness, interaction and engagement on Facebook, Twitter, Instagram, TikTok, Pinterest and Linkedin.	Qualitative	Media Tool Kit, Phlanx,
SEO 'outputs', 'outcomes' and 'impact'	SEARPs positions, URL and domain traffic and domain authority (DA)	Continuous	Keyword Everywhere, Semrush and Moz.

psychology. We then carried out a hierarchical segmentation analysis to aggregate and systematise all of these organisations.

4.1. Preliminary Analyses

Firstly, we developed some pre-processing tasks to transform the variables' original values. These transformations included putting the original 86 variables, which were grouped and analysed in Table 6, into only 17 dimensions, as shown in Table 7. Overall, these transformations came down to mere summing-up and subtraction operations, and, in exceptional cases, it was necessary to standardise the original values to make viable comparisons. With the aim of studying each variable in order to optimise SEO indicators. For this reason, to better understand each variable's content, we employed standardization to compare the variables. We also performed an ANOVA for a causal analysis where the independent variable is discrete and the dependent variable is continuous. In addition, we also employed a students t-test, which is a statistical technique to determine the causality between two variables (independent dichotomous and dependent continuous).

4.2. RQ1: Social Marketing, What Is Social Marketing?

Once we found theoretical ground for delimiting the concept of 'social marketing', it stood to reason that we would try to apply it. However, surprisingly, this notion is misused worldwide. To ponder how serious social marketing misuse is, we gathered and collated more than 10,000 tweets during the last three months of 2020. As seen in Table 8, close to seven out of 10 tweets needed to be corrected. Moreover, 90 per cent of those followers are exposed to this misleading use of the keyword 'social marketing' worldwide. Finally, it was evident that the ill-informed influencers had greater audience numbers. The value on the Y-axis of the graph shows whether the keyword has been used correctly or incorrectly. If this cannot be analysed, it does not apply.

Similarly, we tested the social marketing association's organic results and resulted in first and second positions, as seen in Figure 2, to recognise the abbreviation of the associations see Table 4. In detail,

Table 7. Transformation of old variables into new variables

NEW VARIABLE	FORMULA WITH OLD VARIABLES
V1 Danger	While value 1 indicates that there can be risky neighbours serving the web host, value o indicates free of dangerous neighbours such as drug dealers, pornographic services, weapon dealers, etc
V2 Click depth	(Depth clicks from URL 0)*1+(Depth clicks from URL 1)*2+(Depth clicks from URL 2)*3+(Depth clicks from URL 3)*4+(Depth clicks from URL 4)*5+(Depth clicks from URL 5)*6+(Depth clicks from URL 6)*7+(Depth clicks from URL 7)*8
V3 Number of keywords	URL word count
V4 Number of content formats	Total number of internal format resources + total number of external format resources by considering Java, HTML, CSS, images, videos, flash, PDF and others.
V5 Originality	Percentage of unique content – percentage of duplicate content
V6 Accessibility	Sum up accessibility cell phone and desktop percentages
V7 Cellphone loading time	First Contenful Paint (FCP)+Speed Index (SI)+Largest Contenful Paint (LCP)+Total Blocking Time (TBT)+Cumulative Layout Shift (CLS)
V8 Desktop loading time	First Contenful Paint (FCP)+Speed Index (SI)+Largest Contenful Paint (LCP)+Total Blocking Time (TBT)+Cumulative Layout Shift (CLS)
V9 Cellphone loading time performance	Sum up First Contenful Paint (FCP)*0.1+ Speed Index (SI)*0.1+ Largest Contenful Paint (LCP)*0.25+ Total Blocking Time (TBT)*0.3+ Cumulative Layout Shift (CLS)*0.25
V10 Desktop loading time performance	Sum up First Contenful Paint (FCP)*0.1+ Speed Index (SI)*0.1+ Largest Contenful Paint (LCP)*0.25+ Total Blocking Time (TBT)*0.3+ Cumulative Layout Shift (CLS)*0.25
V11 Engine indexing	Sum up pages indexed on Google, Yahoo and Bing
ZV12 Effort in linkbuilding	Standardised sum up total and outbound links – standardised blocked links
V13 Errors and alerts	Total errors+Total warnings
V14 Number of social networks	If social media profile exists =1; If it does not exist = 0 1/0 (Facebook)+ 1/0 (Twitter)+ 1/0(Instagram)+ 1/0(Tik Tok)+1/0(Pinterest)+1/0(Linkedin)
V15 Number of interactions	Sum up average likes interaction on Facebook, Twitter, Instagram and Linkedin + Sum up average comments interaction on Facebook, Twitter and Instagram + Retweets + sum up average interactions on TikTok, Pinterest and Youtube + average share interactions on Linkedin
V16 Total engagement of social networks	Engagement rate (Facebook)+engagement rate (Twitter)+engagement rate (Instagram)+engagement rate (TikTok)+engagement rate (Pinterest)+engagement rate (Linkedin)+engagement rate (Youtube)
V17 Outcome impact	Standardised summation of URL traffic, domain traffic and authority – Standardised summation of SERPs URL and domain positions,

Greece's Association (SMBCI) always appears in second position. On the other hand, the URL SERPs position of the Social Marketing Association of North America (SMANA) appears in the second position. Therefore, both institutions should improve their SEO strategies.

4.3. RQ2: What Are the Structural SEO Similarities Between the Social Marketing Organisations?

We carried out a correlation test to find out more about how similar social marketing organisations are. First, we performed a correlation test by considering the structural search engine optimisation features. While the correlation test was performed between standardised values (see Table 9), the descriptive results are presented with the original values (see Table 10).

Table 8. Measuring what serious the misuse looks like

Tweets with the Social marketing term	Total	%
Correct	830	7.98614452
Incorrect	7116	68.4691619
Not Applicable	2447	23.5446935
	10393	100

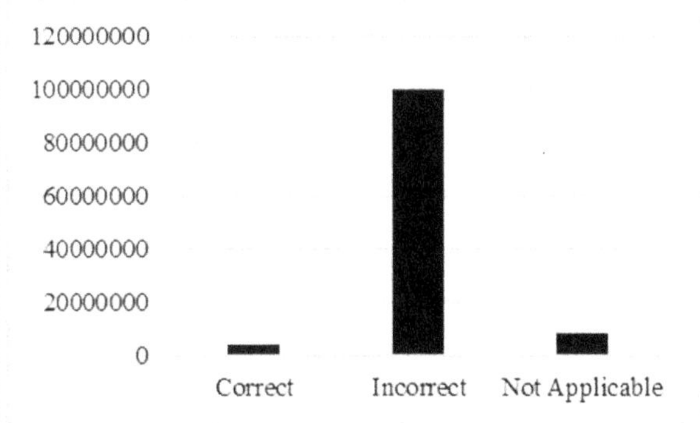

Followers exposed to tweets with the Social Marketing term	Total	%
Correct	22033432	5.29376596
Incorrect	374795702	90.0486465
Not Applicable	19385564	4.65758756
Total general	416214698	100

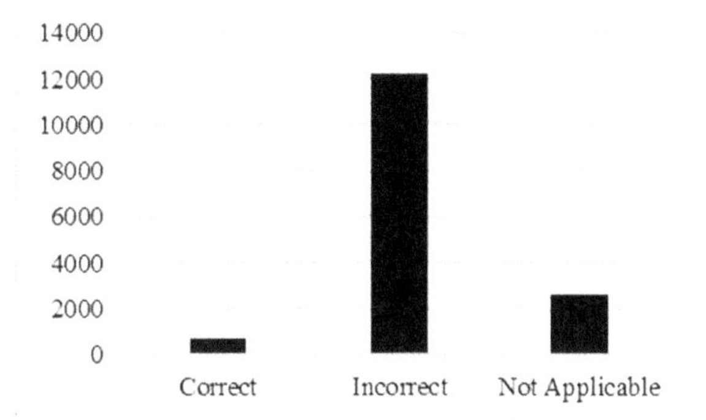

Followings for tweets with the social marketing term	Total	%
Correct	3829685	3.42773323
Incorrect	99784109	89.3110808
Not Applicable	8112666	7.26118594
Total general	111726460	100

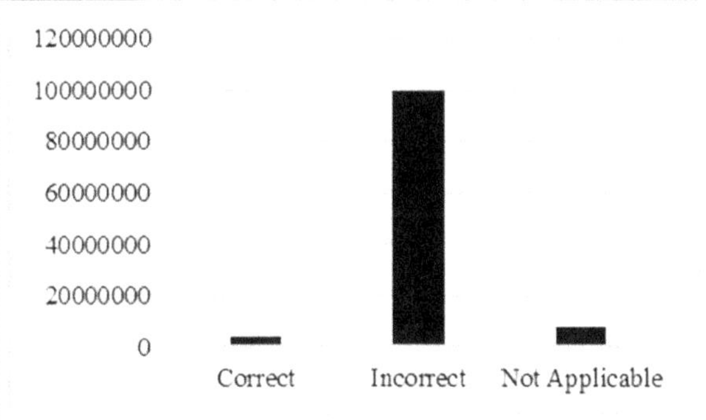

Retweets for tweets with the social marketing term	Total	%
Correct	698	4.48932339
Incorrect	12214	78.5567276
Not Applicable	2636	16.9539491
Total general	15548	100

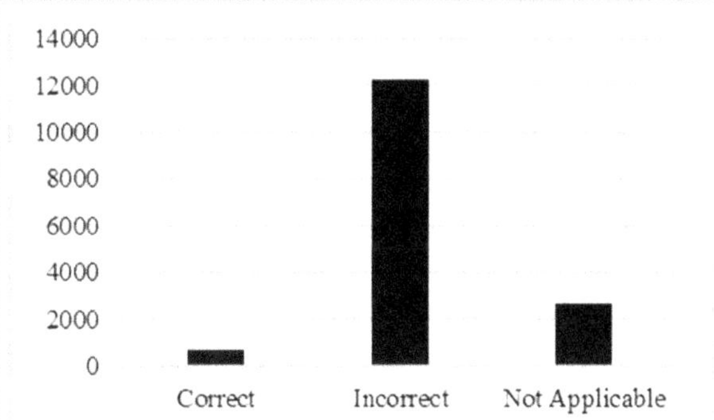

Figure 2. Social marketing association organic results

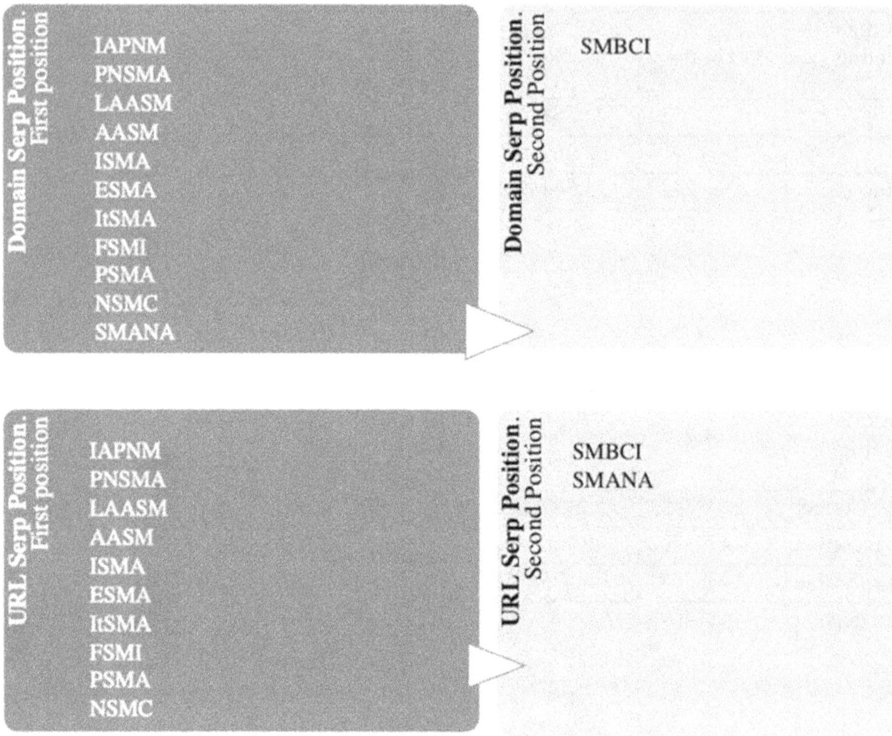

As seen in Table 9, we performed a correlation analysis to determine whether there is any relationship between the dimensions of *structural search engine optimisation* and *social marketing organisations*. As illustrated, there is no statistically significant association; hence, not all the organisations show the same differences regarding the degree of *risky neighbours*, *click depth*, *word number*, *resources* and *originality*.

As far as observing the descriptive data is concerned (see Table 10), there are only a few social marketing associations with 'risky neighbours', such as the AASM and the PNSMA. Similarly, while there are websites with deep paths to click, such as PNSMA and IAPNM, other associations' websites need fewer clicks, such as SMANA. Likewise, the word count is quite different, given that IAPNM and SMANA barely reach 200. The rest go higher, with FSMI on top. Equally, the format content figures are somewhat dissimilar since IASM, ESMA, ISMA, and AASM are leading, and SMANA is the lowest. Finally, it is worth noting that the social marketing association is devoid of similarities in terms of originality. On the one hand, FSMI soars up to a very high originality degree. On the other hand, SMBCI, PNSMA, IAPNM and ESMA plummet very low with negative values since their duplication rate is too high.

4.4. RQ3: What Are the Performance SEO Similarities Between the Social Marketing Organisations?

Furthermore, we tested the similarity rate these social marketing organisations perform for SEO. As seen in Table 11, we carried out a correlation test. Table 10 displays descriptive indicators.

Table 9. Correlation test to find out how similar the search engine optimisation structural metrics are in the social marketing associations

		Zv2	Zv3	Zv4	Zv5
Zv1	P	,503	-,274	-,112	-,193
	Sig.	,095	,388	,728	,549
	N	12	12	12	12
Zv2	P		-,157	,086	-,452
	Sig.		,625	,791	,141
	N		12	12	12
Zv3	P			,156	,471
	Sig.			,629	,122
	N			12	12
Zv4	P				-,063
	Sig.				,845
	N				12
Zv1: Danger, Zv2: Depth, Zv3: No. of words, Zv4: resources, Zv5: Originality					

Table 10. The structural Search engine optimisation metrics description in the social marketing organisations

Associations	V1	V2	V3	V4	V5
International Association on Public and Non-Profit Marketing	0	340.00	195	436	-23.00
National Social Marketing Centre	0	194.12	633	103	51.00
Portuguese Social Marketing Association	0	331.55	634	270	8.00
French Social Marketing Institute	0	239.29	1263	336	73.00
Italian Social Marketing Association	0	245.95	419	1441	36.00
The Social Marketing Behaviour Change Institute	0	235.69	786	366	-55.00
European Social Marketing Association	0	279.69	531	2922	-21.00
Social Marketing Association of North America	0	100.00	193	1	0.00
Australian Association of Social Marketing	1	243.39	499	1382	25.00
Latin American Association on Social Marketing	0	233.34	826	438	19.00
Pacific Northwest Social Marketing Association	1	506.97	322	780	-45.00
International Association of Social Marketing	0	289.97	754	24024	0.24
V1: danger; V2: click depth; V3: number of keywords; V4: number of content formats; V5: originality					

As indicated in Table 11, a correlation analysis determines whether there is any relationship between the dimensions of *search engine optimisation performance* and *social marketing organisations*. As displayed, cell phone and desktop loading times - moreover, the cell phone and desktop *performance* times - show significant similarities. Furthermore, it is noteworthy that errors and alerts are associated with loading times regarding cell phones and desktops. Besides, two metrics are strongly correlated: the

Table 11. Correlation test to find out how similar the search engine optimisation performance metrics are in the social marketing associations

		Zv7	**Zv8**	**Zv9**	**Zv10**	**Zv11**	**Zv12**	**Zv13**	**Zv14**	**Zv15**	**Zv16**
	P	-,075	,034	-,254	-,110	,440	,471	-,023	-,372	-,154	-,232
Zv6	**Sig.**	,816	,917	,426	,734	,153	,123	,945	,234	,633	,469
	N	12	12	12	12	12	12	12	12	12	12
	P		,893**	-,816**	-,787**	-,046	-,076	,520	,238	,034	-,206
Zv7	**Sig.**		**<,001**	**,001**	**,002**	,887	,814	,083	,456	,917	,520
	N		12	12	12	12	12	12	12	12	12
	P			-,823**	-,836**	,205	,094	,712**	,325	,078	-,110
Zv8	**Sig.**			**<,001**	**<,001**	,523	,771	,009	,302	,810	,733
	N			12	12	12	12	12	12	12	12
	P				,816**	-,373	-,233	-,487	-,375	-,138	,397
Zv9	**Sig.**				**,001**	,233	,466	,109	,230	,668	,201
	N				12	12	12	12	12	12	12
	P					-,168	-,157	-,628*	-,469	-,245	,358
Zv10	**Sig.**					,601	,627	,029	,124	,443	,253
	N					12	12	12	12	12	12
	P						,828**	,300	,097	-,028	-,055
Zv11	**Sig.**						**<,001**	,344	,763	,930	,866
	N						12	12	12	12	12
	P							,392	-,105	-,077	-,241
Zv12	**Sig.**							,208	,746	,811	,450
	N							12	12	12	12
	P								,336	,304	-,009
Zv13	**Sig.**								,286	,337	,979
	N								12	12	12
	P									,819**	,174
Zv14	**Sig.**									**,001**	,588
	N									12	12
	P										,396
Zv15	**Sig.**										,203
	N										12

Zv6: accessibility, Zv7: cell phone loading time, V8: desktop loading time, Zv9: cell phone performance time, Zv10: desktop performance time, Zv11: engine indexing, Zv12: link building and effort, Zv13: errors and alerts, Zv14: number of networks, Zv15: interactions in networks, Zv16: engagement

number of networks and interactions in these social media platforms. The more social media profiles the social marketing associations posse, the more active they are on it. Conversely, it is worth noting that there is only one metric without any statistical relation, and that is *accessibility*.

Paradoxically, though accessibility is the most different metric compared to the rest, social marketing associations show relatively similar levels. Conversely, social marketing associations are quite different in degree in terms of loading times as regards cell phones and desktops. While PSMA and ItSMA obtain the best performances, the worst is reached by PNSMA and ISMA. In addition, the most indexed websites are the NSMC, ISMA and ItSMA and the least, SMANA and PSMA. Making an effort in link building is excellent for ItSMA and NSMC, but it seems to need to be noticed by SMANA, PSMA, FSMA, IAPNM, SMBC and LAASM. Concerning errors and alerts, it is worth pointing out that while ISMA faces the most serious threats, SMANA enjoys the least score. For social media, while FSMA, AASM and ISMA show a higher degree of social networks and interactions, IAPNM, PSMA and SMCI are the lowest. Finally, the best engagement is achieved by associations such as the FSMA, IAPN and ISMA; the worst is obtained by PSMA, ItSMA and SMBC (see Table 12).

4.5. RQ4: What Are the Output SEO Similarities Between the Social Marketing Organisations?

Similarly, we assessed the social marketing organisations' search engine optimisation for output metrics (see Table 13). In Table 14, we display the descriptive indicators for all the associations.

As observed in Table 13, we performed a correlation analysis to learn whether there is any relationship between the dimensions of output metrics within social marketing organisations. There is no statistically significant association; hence, all the organisations do not show similar characteristics in terms of *URL traffic*, *domain traffic last month worldwide* and *domain authority*. Conversely, URL SERPs and domain positions show some similarities.

For the SERPs positions, it is worth noting that all the associations obtained the first rank, the SMBCI excepted. Likewise, SMANA is also poorly ranked in the second position. Concerning traffic,

Table 12. The performance of search engine optimisation metrics in the social marketing organisations

V1	V2 entity	V6	V7	V8	V9	V10	V11	ZV12	V13	V14	V15	V16
1	IAPNM	160	7.283	2.101	88	99	142	-1.90	104	1	4.0	72.62
2	NSMC	188	85.653	75.402	30	80	3749	3.23	227	3	7.0	17.84
3	PSMA	177	225.8	13.3	63	96	54	-, 2.01	157	1	0.0	0.0
4	FSMI	162	602.291	53.245	59	97	183	-1.98	46	4	23.0	81.74
5	ItSMA	193	63.6	2.878	62	95	1485	4.14	2847	0	0.0	0.0
6	SMBCI	166	1539.545	135.518	37	85	134	-1.60	53	1	0.0	0.0
7	ESMA	184	280.75	49.399	53	57	616	0.70	2517	3	16.0	0.94
8	SMANA	176	1735.505	212.406	29	52	48	-2.45	2	3	5.0	0.95
9	AASM	129	354.442	5.221	64	83	194	-0.64	2233	4	11.0	0.34
10	LAASM	180	1066.109	17.732	33	72	106	-1.32	67	3	18.0	2.45
11	PNSMA	168	3087.087	224.531	17	49	768	0.09	1952	2	2.0	1.16
12	ISMA	170	2855.075	378.39	7	32	1748	1.76	18976	4	17.0	24.0

V6: accessibility, V7: cell phone loading time, V8: desktop loading time, V9 cell phone loading time performance, V10: desktop loading time performance, V11: engine indexing, ZV12: effort in linkbuilding, V13: errors and alerts, V14: number of social networks, V15: number of interactions, V16: total engagement of social networks.

Table 13. Correlations between output metrics for the social marketing associations

		Zv88	Zv89	Zv90	Zv91
Zv87	P	,674*	-,243	-,150	-,076
	Sig.	,016	,499	,661	,813
	N	12	10	11	12
Zv88	P		-,162	-,101	-,307
	Sig.		,655	,767	,332
	N		10	11	12
Zv89	P			,414	,176
	Sig.			,268	,627
	N			9	10
Zv90	P				,582
	Sig.				,061
	N				11
Zv87: URL SERPs position, Zv88: domain SERPs position, Zv89: URL traffic, Zv90: domain traffic last month worldwide, Zv91: domain authority					

NSMC and ISMA are the most attractive website, while the rest of the associations barely host visits. Regarding authority, NSMC and ItSMA scored highest, followed by SMANA, AASM and IAPNM. The rest of the associations barely reach considerable authority, with PSMA and LAASM in the final position (see Table 14).

Table 14. The output search engine optimisation metrics in the social marketing organisations

V1	V2 organisation	V87	V88	V89	V90	V91
1	International Association on Public and Non Profit Marketing	1	1	0	0	28
2	National Social Marketing Centre	1	1	28	9265	42
3	Portuguese Social Marketing Association	1	1	n/a	5	7
4	French Social Marketing Institute	1	1	n/a	1	12
5	Italian Social Marketing Association	1	1	0	9	33
6	The Social Marketing Behaviour Change Institute	2	2	0	0	10
7	European Social Marketing Association	1	1	0	8	27
8	Social Marketing Association of North America	2	1	0	15	29
9	Australian Association of Social Marketing	1	1	0	23	29
10	Latin American Association on Social Marketing	1	1	1	n/a	4
11	Pacific Northwest Social Marketing Association	1	1	0	5	16
12	International Association of Social Marketing	1	1	49	42	20
V87: URL SERPs position, V88: domain SERPs position, V89: URL traffic, V90: domain traffic last month worldwide, V91: domain authority						

4.6. RQ5: What Are the Structural SEO Differences Between the Social Marketing and Psychology Organisations?

Furthermore, in Table 15, we carried out a student T. test analysis to determine whether there is any relationship between the structural metrics for social marketing and psychology associations. Furthermore, there is only a statistically significant association between the degree of 'risky neighbours'. Besides, there is a small difference in terms of content formats. Finally, in the absence of evidence to the contrary, all the organisations show some equivalent degree concerning *click depth, word number* and *originality.*

In light of the data displayed in Tables 15 and 16, the most significant difference between social marketing and psychology associations is that conflictive neighbours threaten the latter. Similarly, it is worth noting that all the psychology association's websites overcome the social marketing counterpart with content format numbers. OP, EFPA and APA are particularly outstanding, owing to their wide range of resources.

Table 15. Student T. test between social marketing and psychology associations for structural metrics

Descriptive					
		N	**Mean**	**Sd**	**St.Er.Desv.**
Zv1	SM	12	-,8273595	,77291823	,22312228
	P	12	,8273595	,00000000	,00000000
Zv2	SM	12	,0262035	1,20187467	,34695133
	P	12	-,0262035	,80306182	,23182398
Zv3	SM	12	-,2775152	,87568290	,25278788
	P	12	,2775152	1,07520066	,31038370
Zv4	SM	12	-,3242363	,31007075	,08950972
	P	12	,3242363	1,32868073	,38355709
Zv5	SM	12	-,2513060	1,23473392	,35643698
	P	12	,2513060	,65463664	,18897732

		F	**Sig.**	**T**	**Gl**	**Sig.**	
						P of a factor	**Two-factor P**
Zv1	Similar	13,750	**,001**	-7,416	22	<,001	<,001
	Disimilar			-7,416	11,000	<,001	<,001
Zv2	Similar	1,027	,322	,126	22	,451	,901
	Disimilar			,126	19,190	,451	,901
Zv3	Similar	,485	,493	-1,387	22	,090	,179
	Disimilar			-1,387	21,134	,090	,180
Zv4	Similar	8,931	,007	-1,646	22	,057	,114
	Disimilar			-1,646	12,195	,063	,125
Zv5	Similar	3,112	,092	-1,246	22	,113	,226
	Disimilar			-1,246	16,731	,115	,230

Zv1: danger, Zv2: depth, Zv3: no. of words, Zv4: resources, Zv5: originality,

Table 16. The structural search engine optimisation metrics in the psychology organisations

Associations	V1	V2	V3	V4	V5
Consejo General de Psicología de España	1	320.66	1019	4728	8.00
The British Psychological Society	1	277.76	722	26153	7.00
Ordem dos Psicólogos	1	371.43	722	97998	56.00
Fédération Française Psychologues Psychologie	1	265.88	1506	1486	23.00
Associazione Italiana de Psicologi	1	100.00	526	1	6.00
National Organisation for Psychotherapy of Greece (NOPG)	1	278.49	845	1	0.00
European Federation of Psychologists' Associations	1	273.08	579	35119	34.00
American Psychological Association	1	278.61	638	33016	0.00
Australian Psychological Society	1	234.15	1208	1	0.00
Sociedad Interamericana de Psicología	1	310.71	138	840	42.00
Asia Pacific Psychological Alliance	1	230.77	415	294	45.00
International Union of Psychological Science	1	247.36	1035	2566	33.00
V1: danger; V2: click depth; V3: number of keywords; V4: number of content formats; V5: originality					

4.7. RQ6: What Are the Performance SEO Differences Between the Social Marketing and Psychology Organisations?

On the other hand, in Table 17, we executed a student t. analysis to determine whether there is any relationship between the dimensions of performance metrics for social marketing and psychology associations. As shown, there is no statistically significant association; hence, all the organisations show the same differences in accessibility, cell phone loading time, desktop loading time, cell phone performance time, desktop performance time, engine indexing, link building and effort, errors and alerts, number of networks, interactions in networks and engagement.

Concerning performance SEO metrics, both types of organisations show the same differences. It is hard to point out the best organisation. However, APA and APS are particularly outstanding in terms of indexing. If *alerts and errors* are considered, AIP, APS and NOPG operate brilliantly. For social media, the APS engages quite well. None of this is relevant as there are no statistically significant differences (see Table 18).

4.8. RQ7: What Are the Output SEO Differences Between the Social Marketing and Psychology Organisations?

In Table 19, we performed a student T. test analysis to determine whether there is any relationship between the dimensions of output metrics for social marketing organisations and psychology associations. As displayed, there is only one key difference regarding *domain authority*. Nonetheless, there is no statistically significant association regarding other metrics; hence, all the organisations show similar characteristics concerning the *URL SERPs position*, *domain SERPs position*, *URL traffic* and *domain traffic last month worldwide*.

Table 17. Student T. test between social marketing and psychology associations for performance metrics

Group statistics					
	social vs. psico	N	Mean	Standard Deviation	Std error mean
Zv6	SM	12	-,0063191	,84658203	,24438718
	P	12	,0063191	1,17222900	,33839337
Zv7	SM	12	,0761147	1,12995599	,32619020
	P	12	-,0761147	,89524762	,25843573
Zv8	SM	12	-,1042528	,73088912	,21098951
	P	12	,1042528	1,23814248	,35742095
Zv9	SM	12	-,0456369	1,21807885	,35162907
	P	12	,0456369	,77630463	,22409984
Zv10	SM	12	-,0153380	1,17334829	,33871648
	P	12	,0153380	,84477784	,24386636
Zv11	SM	12	-,2091167	,00001828	,00000528
	P	12	,2091167	1,41262120	,40778862
Zv12	SM	12	-.6047	2.50598	.72341
	P	12	.6047	1.48693	.42924
Zv13	SM	12	-,2651374	,09592478	,02769110
	P	12	,2651374	1,38864336	,40086681
Zv14	SM	12	-,1418314	,93877940	,27100227
	P	12	,1418314	1,07968169	,31167726
Zv15	SM	12	-,3108708	,02649259	,00764775
	P	12	,3108708	1,37089566	,39574349
Zv16	SM	12	,2169756	1,25937461	,36355013
	P	12	-,2169756	,63416728	,18306833

		F	Sig.	t	gl	Sig	
						P factor	Two-factor P
Zv6	Similar	1,508	,232	-,030	22	,488	,976
	Dissimilar			-,030	20,021	,488	,976
Zv7	Similar	1,750	,199	,366	22	,359	,718
	Dissimilar			,366	20,906	,359	,718
Zv8	Similar	,891	,356	-,502	22	,310	,620
	Dissimilar			-,502	17,836	,311	,622
Zv9	Similar	3,489	,075	-,219	22	,414	,829
	Dissimilar			-,219	18,670	,415	,829
Zv10	Similar	2,104	,161	-,073	22	,471	,942
	Dissimilar			-,073	19,989	,471	,942
Zv11	Similar	4,836	,039	-1,026	22	,158	,316
	Dissimilar			-1,026	11,000	,164	,327

continued on following page

Table 17. Continued

Group statistics							
		social vs. psico		N	Mean	Standard Deviation	Std error mean
Zv12	Similar	1.112	.303	-1.438	22	.082	.165
	Dissimilar			-1.438	17.891	.084	.168
Zv13	Similar	5,747	,025	-1,320	22	,100	,201
	Dissimilar			-1,320	11,105	,107	,214
Zv14	Similar	,293	,594	-,687	22	,250	,499
	Dissimilar			-,687	21,583	,250	,500
Zv15	Similar	6,038	,022	-1,571	22	,065	,131
	Dissimilar			-1,571	11,008	,072	,145
Zv16	Similar	3,860	,062	1,066	22	,149	,298
	Dissimilar			1,066	16,242	,151	,302

Zv6: accessibility, Zv7: cell phone loading time, Zv8: desktop loading time, Zv9: cell phone performance time, Zv10: desktop performance time, Zv11: engine indexing, Zv12: link building and effort, Zv13: errors and alerts, Zv14: number of networks, Zv15: interactions in networks, Zv16: engagement

Table 18. The performance of search engine optimisation metrics in the psychology organisations

V1	V2 entity	V6	V7	V8	V9	V10	V11	ZV12	V13	V14	V15	V16
13	BPS	124	19.1	9.97	50	68	295010100	0.67	5010	5	101.5	9.49
14	OP	188	658.0	104.2	67	98	104500	0.26	29301	4	327.5	0.25
15	FFPP	182	130.98	4.12	55	76	0	0.39	268913	5	1493	5.65
16	AIP	186	779.39	128.24	22	57	0	0.05	585	2	77.5	0.0
17	NOPG	170	157.7	2.6	56	73	977	-2.76	1	2	5.5	0.006
18	EFPA	157	755.38	66.22	41	78	139	-0.66	3	0	0.0	0.0
19	APA	166	1198.33	83.21	62	97	838	0.21	66018	2	5.0	0.39
20	APS	193	3149.81	646.31	25	54	6810000	1.47	11425	4	246	0.284
21	SIP	131	828.7	17.21	40	72	51700	0.48	1	4	129.5	51.49
22	APPA	192	1477.01	433.41	31	52	21280	2.60	677	3	7.0	12.98
23	IUPS	186	58.3	5.6	59	85	123	-2.23	12	1	0.0	0.0
24	BPS	181	931.4	74.7	55	94	3469	1.51	787	2	3.0	0.26

V6: accessibility, V7: cell phone loading time, V8: desktop loading time, V9 cell phone loading time performance, V10: desktop loading time performance, V11: engine indexing, ZV12: effort in link building, V13: errors and alerts, V14: number of social networks, V15: number of interactions, V16: total engagement of social networks.

Tables 19 and 20 show that all the Psychology associations are better at domain authority than social marketing associations. APA, BPS, CGPE and APS are of particular interest given that their domain authority is over 50. In contrast, APPA, NOPG and AIP show the lowest authority scores.

Table 19. Student t-test between social marketing and psychology associations for output metrics

Group statistics					
		N	Mean	Standard Deviation	Std error mean
Zv87	SM	12	,1233355	1,15219848	,33261105
	P	12	-,1233355	,85449326	,24667096
Zv88	SM	12	,0000000	1,02247472	,29516303
	P	12	,0000000	1,02247472	,29516303
Zv89	SM	10	-,2328434	,00140366	,00044388
	P	9	,2587149	1,45152598	,48384199
Zv90	SM	11	-,2198231	,00212761	,00064150
	P	12	,2015045	1,38107868	,39868307
Zv91	SM	12	-,5487316	,50406441	,14551086
	P	12	,5487316	1,08621772	,31356405

		F	Sig.	T	gl	Sig	
						P factor	Two-factor P
Zv87	Similar	1,497	,234	,596	22	,279	,557
	Dissimilar			,596	20,290	,279	,558
Zv88	Similar	,000	1,000	,000	22	,500	1,000
	Dissimilar			,000	22,000	,500	1,000
Zv89	Similar	5,828	,027	-1,074	17	,149	,298
	Dissimilar			-1,016	8,000	,170	,339
Zv90	Similar	4,401	,048	-1,010	21	,162	,324
	Dissimilar			-1,057	11,000	,157	,313
Zv91	Similar	3,515	,074	-3,175	22	,002	,004
	Dissimilar			-3,175	15,528	,003	,006

Zv87: URL SERPs position, Zv88: domain SERPs position, Zv89: URL traffic, Zv90: domain traffic last month worldwide, Zv91: domain authority

4.9. RQ8: Is it Possible to Aggregate and Segment the Social Marketing and Psychology Organisations by Considering the SEO Features?

Whereas we display the Euclidean distance between the cases in Table 21, the best match between every couple of cases is shown in Table 22. As can be seen, the 'most likeable' segment comprises psychology associations such as BPS, EFPA and IUPS. After these, a group of social marketing associations such as NSMC and ItSMA appears. Conversely, the 'most different' organisations and 'less likeable' to aggregate are the IAPNM and the APA.

Examining Figure 3, there emerges APA as the most different organisations and so the outlier is visualised.

Table 20. The output search engine optimisation metrics in the psychology organisations

V1	V2entidad	V87	V88	V89	V90	V91
13	Consejo General de Psicología de España	1	1	1	57161	65
14	The British Psychological Society	1	1	540	153285	80
15	Ordem dos Psicólogos	1	1	n/a	26982	49
16	Fédération Française Psychologues Psychologie	1	1	0	5214	36
17	Associazione Italiana de Psicologi	2	2	n/a	49	23
18	National Organisation for Psychotherapy of Greece (NOPG)	1	1	n/a	208	17
19	European Federation of Psychologists' Associations	1	1	42	402	46
20	American Psychological Association	1	1	52600	6302796	91
21	Australian Psychological society	1	1	180	91877	63
22	Sociedad Interamericana de Psicología	1	1	0	2644	47
23	Asia Pacific Psychological Alliance	1	1	0	0	5
24	International Union of Psychological science	1	1	46	262	41
V87: URL SERPs position, V88: domain SERPs position, V89: URL traffic, V90: domain traffic last month worldwide, V91: domain authority						

Table 21. Hierarchical segmentation for social marketing and psychology associations: Similarity matrix

Caso	Proximity matrix by Square Euclidean Distance																	
	1:1	**2:1**	**5:1**	**6:1**	**7:1**	**8:1**	**9:1**	**11:1**	**12:1**	**13:2**	**14:2**	**16:2**	**19:2**	**20:2**	**21:2**	**22:2**	**23:2**	**24:2**
1:1	,00	57,0	56,7	48,3	29,4	50,8	28,8	55,8	71,5	68,67	38,1	55,3	32,0	129,8	39,0	64,8	26,4	41,7
2:1	57,0	,00	10,4	65,2	17,0	53,8	33,8	56,1	29,5	55,	27,4	25,5	25,5	85,8	30,2	17,8	41,9	13,2
5:1	56,7	10,4	,00	72,4	24,3	74,9	45,3	64,7	52,5	73,0	35,9	42,3	29,0	105,9	51,3	29,4	47,0	17,5
6:1	48,3	65,2	72,4	,00	36,7	28,4	46,1	49,3	57,4	82,3	54,1	45,1	46,6	117,3	53,4	70,1	42,7	48,1
7:1	29,4	17,0	24,3	36,7	,00	30,1	18,6	27,8	23,8	45,5	18,8	18,2	18,4	82,5	24,9	22,9	22,7	15,0
8:1	50,8	53,8	74,9	28,4	30,1	,00	36,	49,9	42,5	77,7	47,2	40,5	41,6	97,3	49,1	50,3	31,1	47,7
9:1	28,8	33,8	45,3	46,1	18,6	36,3	,00	41,6	45,9	33,7	19,1	26,8	12,1	98,4	15,4	38,0	16,7	17,2
11:1	55,8	56,1	64,7	49,3	27,8	49,9	41,6	,00	23,7	66,3	45,7	33,4	37,4	78,6	44,5	29,3	47,2	39,8
12:1	71,5	29,5	52,5	57,4	23,8	42,5	45,9	23,7	,00	63,3	45,8	26,8	39,1	63,7	34,7	19,0	59,	35,5
13:2	68,6	55,4	73,0	82,3	45,5	77,7	33,7	66,3	63,3	,00	42,4	46,4	44,0	111,0	30,5	60,7	63,4	43,0
14:2	38,1	27,4	35,9	54,1	18,8	47,2	19,1	45,7	45,8	42,4	,00	23,3	8,3	70,8	22,3	29,5	27,6	11,1
16:2	55,3	25,5	42,3	45,1	18,2	40,5	26,8	33,4	26,8	46,4	23,3	,00	21,4	77,3	19,4	28,4	25,2	11,1
19:2	32,0	25,5	29,0	46,6	18,4	41,6	12,1	37,4	39,1	44,0	8,3	21,4	,00	79,0	22,7	26,9	17,2	7,9
20:2	129,8	85,8	105,	117,3	82,5	97,3	98,4	78,6	63,7	111,0	70,8	77,3	79,0	,00	86,3	59,5	111,4	78,8
21:2	39,0	30,2	51,3	53,4	24,9	49,1	15,4	44,5	34,7	30,5	22,3	19,4	22,7	86,3	,00	38,5	40,1	18,7
22:2	64,8	17,8	29,4	70,1	22,9	50,3	38,0	29,3	19,0	60,7	29,5	28,4	26,9	59,5	38,5	,00	44,8	21,4
23:2	26,4	41,9	47,0	42,7	22,7	31,1	16,7	47,2	59,9	63,4	27,6	25,2	17,2	111,4	40,1	44,8	,00	21,6
24:2	41,7	13,2	17,5	48,1	15,0	47,7	17,2	39,8	35,5	43,0	11,1	11,1	7,9	78,8	18,7	21,4	21,6	,00

Table 22. Hierarchical segmentation for social marketing and psychology associations

Conglomeration history						
Phase	Combination		Coefficients	First appearance		Following phase
	Cluster 1	Cluster 2		Cluster 1	Cluster 2	
1	19	24	7,986	0	0	2
2	14	19	9,725	0	1	5
3	2	5	10,436	0	0	12
4	9	21	15,449	0	0	8
5	7	14	17,457	0	2	6
6	7	16	18,556	5	0	8
7	12	22	19,090	0	0	10
8	7	9	20,233	6	4	9
9	7	23	24,490	8	0	12
10	11	12	26,560	0	7	13
11	6	8	28,435	0	0	15
12	2	7	31,745	3	9	13
13	2	11	37,688	12	10	14
14	1	2	45,934	0	13	15
15	1	6	49,374	14	11	16
16	1	13	56,072	15	0	17
17	1	20	90,244	16	0	0

5. CONCLUSION

The most significant of the problems for Social Marketing SEO is how often its name is misused. It is unfortunate that most users confuse *social marketing* with *social media marketing*. As this is clearly wrong, a broad range of measures should be taken. Firstly, we should filter the wrong messages out on social media. To do so, we should clinch an agreement with Facebook, Twitter, YouTube, Instagram, TikTok, and so forth, to become allies against this misunderstanding. Secondly, it is advisable to detect the main websites muddling the social marketing name and persuade the main search engines, such as Google, Yahoo and Bing, to apply penalisations and alerts. AI can be used to automatize operations and optimise results. Otherwise, not only would social marketing need clarification, but social media marketing would also be the culprit.

As far as statistically non-significant correlations are concerned, we need to implement differentiated strategies. First, we should go back over the AASM and PNSMA host neighbours and switch to another server. Second, PNSMA and IAPNM website architecture could be better since they show a deep click path. Conversely, SMANA is better; hence, all social marketing associations should pay careful attention to this paradigm. Third, we recommend that IAPNM and SMANA increase their word count. Fourth, as SMANA lacks content format diversity, we suggest enriching the effort with content. Finally, it is a necessary that some associations overcome duplication shortcomings, such as SMBCI, PNSMA and ESMA.

Figure 3. Dendrogram in hierarchical segmentation for social marketing and psychology associations

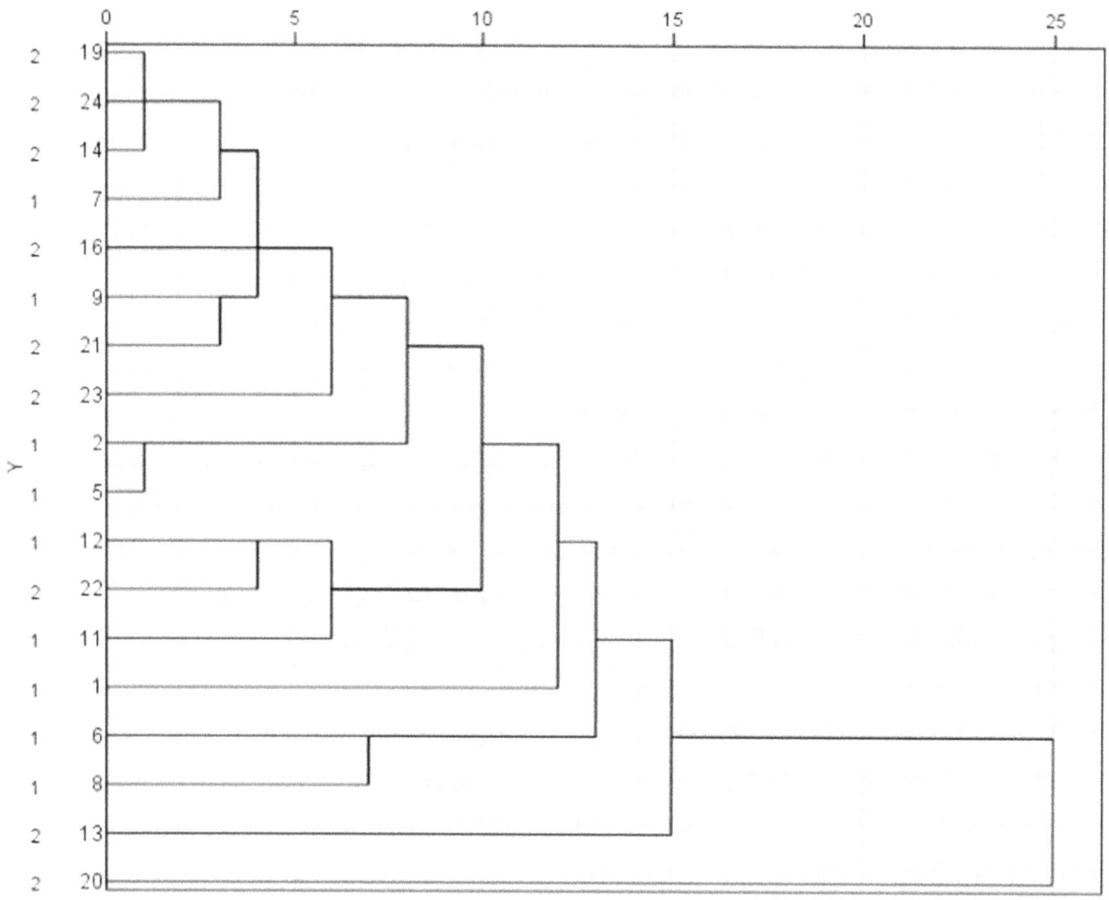

Social marketing associations can be treated with heterogeneity where performance metrics are concerned as they attain varying degrees in terms of *loading times*, *social media profiles* and *interactions*. Nevertheless, the accessibility level is similar. Hence, this feature does not add anything significant. Specifically, we need to revise the *loading times* for PNSMA and ISMA because they are the most sluggish. Likewise, we need to ramp up indexation for SMANA and PSMA. Equally, ISMA must be repaired because it shows the highest level of *alerts and errors*. Concerning social media, it is important to focus on how poorly IAPNM, PSMA and SMCI perform in terms of *social media profile resources* and *interactions*. As far as *engagement* is concerned, PSMA, ItsMA and SMBC come to mind.

In addition, social marketing associations should raise the issues of *traffic* and *authority* in order to become more similar. To be precise, we should make much better use of the huge traffic attracted by NSMC and ISMA so as to share their visitors across all the social marketing associations. Furthermore, PSMA and LAASM ought to engage in more link-building, driven towards NSMC and ItSMA. It goes without saying that the aim is to increase traffic and centralise authority for social marketing's sake.

Comparing social marketing and psychology associations, more insightful implications can be gained. It is important to point out that social marketing associations should avoid the host servers of the psychology associations because they have more risky neighbours than their social marketing counterparts - the former sets an example where the content format is considered, in particular, OP, EFPA and APA. There is less to learn from psychology websites' structure in terms of *click depth*, *word number* and *originality* since the design of their websites is so similar. Concerning *performance*, they are also quite similar. Nonetheless, there are significant differences concerning *authority*, so it would be advisable to start link-building towards APA, BPS, CGPE and APS. It seems more urgent for APPA, NOPG and AIP because these social marketing associations need better levels of authority.

All these things considered, and additionally based on the hierarchical segmentation, it is evident that BPS, EFPA and IUPS – moreover, the social marketing associations such as NSMC and ItSMA - are the most similar websites in terms of SEO. Therefore, they share the same level of advancement, and their practices for participating in courses, seminars and conferences whose main topic is the matter of improving SEO can be easily understood. Nevertheless, IAPNM and APA are the outliers, the former showing problems solving patterns owing to its pioneering coverage countries and the latter representing the most successful model to benchmark against. For example, it is admirable how IAPNM has reached such an enviable degree of engagement on social media platforms, and almost beyond excellent is the high level of authority achieved by APA. Shall we pay careful attention to these achievements in order to gain insight and set forth benchmarking approaches?

In addition to these managerial implications, this research work contributes to the digital marketing literature by putting forward a particular SEO metrics systematisation. It allows us to show new indicators and proposes tools with academic validity to analyse SEO, a relevant aspect for future studies and academic works. Not only does it highlight the terminology problem related to social marketing, but it also distinguishes structural, performance and output indicators. Concerning practical implications, we believe that establishing SEO strategies for social marketing organisations will help address this lack of knowledge about the concept. As a result, SEO experts will be able to learn which indicators, metrics, formulas and tools can be employed to give visibility and optimise SEO. However, this research work assumes several limitations. First, it uses software without webmaster property and, hence, the data validity and reliability might be challenged. Second, the survey took place during a particular week and, consequently, the extracted metrics were averaged to avoid volatility. All the same, this research work can be continued and further developed by considering certain future lines. In this vein, it is worth noting that it is not the social marketing organisations' online position that matters most, but rather the social problems they can potentially help solve if they improve the public's awareness of their existence. With this aim in mind, upcoming works should bring into focus these environmental, health and security-related problems rather than the organisations themselves. Similarly, it should be noted that in today's world, Artificial intelligence (AI) is increasingly used in digital marketing. More and more, SEO specialists are using this technology. In this way, they can use AI to help analyse keywords, generate optimised content, analyse competitors, and even personalise the user experience. Therefore, it might be interesting to gain a deeper understanding of how AI helps and brings benefits to SEO and increases its effectiveness.

REFERENCES

Ahmad, U. F., Mahdee, J., & Abu Bakar, N. (2022). Search engine optimisation (SEO) strategy as determinants to enhance the online brand positioning. *F1000 Research*, *11*, 714. doi:10.12688/f1000research.73382.1

American Marketing Association. (2023). *What Is SEO Marketing?* AMA. https://www.ama.org/marketing-news/what-is-seo-marketing/

Beerli-Palacio, A., Díaz-Meneses, G., Fernández-Monroy, M., Galván-Sánchez, I., & Martín-Santana, J. D. (2011). *The Influence of Gender & Reference Groups on the Irresponsible Alcohol Consumption Behaviour Model Among Young People* (No. 313). Academic Public Administration Studies Archive-APAS.

Britvin, A., Alrawashdeh, J. H., & Tkachuk, R. (2022). Client-Server System for Parsing Data from Web Pages. *Advances in Cyber-Physical Systems, 7*(1), 8–13. doi:10.23939/acps2022.01.008

Camargo, J. L., Miranda, M. E. C., Chávez, R. A. P., Quispe, F. K. V., Muñoz, I. J. T., & Flores, L. J. R. (2022, June). Proposal of the methodology oriented to the automatic generation of content in SEO positioning. In *2022 17th Iberian Conference on Information Systems and Technologies (CISTI)* (pp. 1–7). IEEE. 10.23919/CISTI54924.2022.9820263

Chen, J.-C., & Sénéchal, S. (2023). The reciprocal relationship between search engine optimization (SEO) success and brand equity (BE): An analysis of SMEs. *European Business Review, 35*(5), 860–873. doi:10.1108/EBR-02-2023-0045

Davies, D. (2023). Website Indexing for Search Engines: How Does It Work? *Search Engine Journal.* https://www.searchenginejournal.com/search-engines/website-indexing/

Erdmann, A., Arilla, R., & Ponzoa, J. M. (2022). Search engine optimization: The long-term strategy of keyword choice. *Journal of Business Research, 144*, 650–662. doi:10.1016/j.jbusres.2022.01.065

Fadli, I. S., Lestari, N. P., & Putri, A. A. (2023). Implementation of White Hat SEO-Based Digital Incubator Platform. *International Transactions on Education Technology, 1*(2), 122–130.

Garcia, J. E., Lima, R., & da Fonseca, M. J. S. (2022, April). Search engine optimization (SEO) for a company website: A case study. In *World Conference on Information Systems and Technologies* (pp. 524–531). Cham: Springer International Publishing. 10.1007/978-3-031-04829-6_47

Hermanson, T. (2021). Why Keywords Are Still So Very Important for SEO. *Search Engine Journal.* https://www.searchenginejournal.com/seo/why-keywords-important-seo/

Kotler, P., & Roberto, E. L. (1992). *Marketing social: Estrategias para cambiar la conducta pública.* Ediciones Díaz de Santos, S.A.

Lee, N., & Kotler, P. (2019). *Social Marketing: Behavior Change for Social Good* (6th ed.). SAGE Publications.

Miikkulainen, R., Iscoe, N., Shagrin, A., Cordell, R., Nazari, S., Schoolland, C., & Lamba, G. (2017, July). Conversion rate optimization through evolutionary computation. In *Proceedings of the Genetic and Evolutionary Computation Conference* (pp. 1193–1199). ACM. 10.1145/3071178.3071312

Mladenović, D., Rajapakse, A., Kožuljević, N., & Shukla, Y. (2023). Search engine optimization (SEO) for digital marketers: Exploring determinants of online search visibility for blood bank service. *Online Information Review, 47*(4), 661–679. doi:10.1108/OIR-05-2022-0276

Moz. (2023). *Domain Authority: What is it and how is it calculated.* Moz. https://moz.com/learn/seo/domain-authority

Oliveira, B., & Teixeira Lopes, C. (2023). The Evolution of Web Search User Interfaces-An Archaeological Analysis of Google Search Engine Result Pages. In *Proceedings of the 2023 Conference on Human Information Interaction and Retrieval* (pp. 55–68). ACM. 10.1145/3576840.3578320

Pham, P., & Gammoh, B. (2015). Characteristics of social-media marketing strategy and customer-based brand equity outcomes: A conceptual model. *International Journal of Internet Marketing and Advertising*, *9*(4), 321–337. doi:10.1504/IJIMA.2015.072885

Romano, J. (2023). What is web design? A comprehensive guide. *Wix Blog*. https://www.wix.com/blog/web-design

Roumeliotis, K. I., Tselikas, N. D., & Nasiopoulos, D. K. (2022). Airlines' sustainability study based on search engine optimization techniques and technologies. *Sustainability (Basel)*, *14*(18), 11225. doi:10.3390u141811225

Tewari, S. (2023). Achieve Branding Excellence in the Digital World by Capitalizing on Search Engine Optimization (SEO). *Academy of Marketing Studies Journal*, *27*(S4).

Yalçın, N., & Köse, U. (2010). What is search engine optimization: Seo? *Procedia: Social and Behavioral Sciences*, *9*, 487–493. doi:10.1016/j.sbspro.2010.12.185

Yang, Y., & Zhai, P. (2022). Click-through rate prediction in online advertising: A literature review. *Information Processing & Management*, *59*(2), 102853. doi:10.1016/j.ipm.2021.102853

Chapter 6
Potential Applications of Transmedia Storytelling for Fostering SDG Awareness and Action

Jamie Neil Coles
ESCI-UPF, Spain

ABSTRACT

Transmedia storytelling is a method of reaching fandoms and communities by telling interconnected stories across different platforms and mediums, offering audiences a multitude of touchpoints through which to enter the story for a unique experience of how a narrative unfolds. This method of storytelling has been successfully employed by entertainment franchises such as Marvel, Star Wars, and Game of Thrones, but has also proven beneficial as marketing and even educational approaches. In this chapter, the author will discuss the foundations of transmedia storytelling and how such an approach could be used to better understanding and attitudes towards SDGs.

1. INTRODUCTION

"The medium is the message. This is merely to say that the personal and social consequences of any medium - that is, of any extension of ourselves - result from the new scale that is introduced into our affairs by each extension of ourselves, or by any new technology" (McLuhan, 1964, p. 7).

Within the dynamic landscape of global transition, the United Nations Sustainable Development Goals (SDGs)—a courageous and forward-thinking blueprint for a better tomorrow—hold a prominent position. Conceived in 2015, these seventeen intertwined ambitions bravely confront the planet's most acute trials: poverty, inequality, climate change, and environmental degradation, with a deadline set for 2030. As we collectively steer through the difficulties and challenges of this century, the call to activate these goals intensifies. Yet, imparting information about the SDGs to the connected masses, and fostering engagement with these crucial goals, poses considerable challenges. To cultivate a deeper comprehension and

DOI: 10.4018/978-1-6684-8984-0.ch006

global ownership, we need to employ inventive, creative and engaging communication strategies, such as transmedia storytelling—a technique that spins tales across multiple platforms, stimulates audience involvement in a participatory way, and nurtures a dynamic habitat for mutual learning and exploration.

Transmedia storytelling is not an alien concept in the domains of entertainment and marketing. For years, it has provided a potent approach to captivate audiences, immersing them in riveting narratives that span diverse media channels, in traditional media, new media on and offline. By exploiting the distinctive advantages of each platform, transmedia storytelling has the capacity to craft a unified and mesmerizing experience that resonates with people from all life paths. In the United Nations Sustainable Development Goals' landscape, such storytelling could ignite collective curiosity, inspire action, and ultimately, catalyze profound transformation.

This chapter delves into the intellectual infrastructure of transmedia storytelling and explores and discusses its potential to champion the SDGs. It examines the core principles of this storytelling approach, informed by thought leaders in media and transmedia theory, such as Henry Jenkins and Marsha Kinder. It also scrutinizes unique challenges and opportunities the SDGs introduce, exploring how transmedia storytelling can tackle the intricacy and interconnectedness of these global objectives.

Case studies will demonstrate successful instances where transmedia storytelling has been employed and how lessons from those cases could be used to promote the SDGs, pinpointing areas requiring enhancement and further innovation. The role of transmedia storytelling in fostering empathy and comprehension, stimulating individuals to act within their spheres of influence, is explored. Additionally, the potential of this storytelling form to cultivate a global community rallying around the SDGs, powered by social media platforms and digital technologies, is discussed.

The efficacy of transmedia storytelling in advancing the United Nations Sustainable Development Goals hinges on a strategic and thoughtful application of its principles. The chapter discusses the significance of collaboration and audience-centric design in learning from producers, marketers and franchises to develop transmedia campaigns for the SDGs, exploring how storytelling can be fine-tuned to meet the distinct needs and preferences of diverse audiences, fostering increased engagement and impact. Moreover, it deliberates ethical considerations of transmedia storytelling in the context of the SDGs, addressing pertinent issues like representation, cultural sensitivity, and authenticity.

Ultimately, this chapter seeks to augment the expanding body of research around transmedia storytelling and the United Nations Sustainable Development Goals. By combining insights from theory and practice, it offers a holistic and nuanced launchpad for transmedia storytelling to function as a formidable instrument for communication, engagement, and social transformation.

2. THE CHALLENGES OF LINEAR STORYTELLING?

Navigating the labyrinth of the United Nations Sustainable Development Goals (SDGs)—a tangled network of 17 goals aiming to confront global adversities and cultivate a sustainable future—is no mean feat. The task of effectively conveying the essence of the SDGs becomes an uphill battle, and the traditional storytelling methods reveal their limitations more starkly when grappling with the complexities embedded in these goals. The stumbling blocks traditional storytelling encounters spring from a plethora of sources, including the varied interests and apprehensions of audiences, the wide spectrum of familiarity with the SDGs, and the uphill task of making abstract notions tangible and relatable.

A prominent limitation of traditional storytelling lies in its linear progression. Often, traditional narratives trail a clear-cut trajectory—a beginning, middle, and end. Although this format may adeptly transmit straightforward messages, it risks glossing over the intricate weave and mutual reliance of the SDGs. This linear approach could trivialize the issues or foster a misleading perception that the goals are standalone challenges, thereby inhibiting a holistic understanding of their interconnected nature.

Furthermore, traditional storytelling tends to depend on a single medium—be it print, television, or radio—for message dissemination. However, in our fast-paced, digital, and globalized world, this method may fall short in engaging diverse audiences spanning various cultures and demographics. Traditional media channels, with their limited reach, might fail to provide the necessary interactivity or flexibility to address the specific concerns and interests of different audience segments.

The digital age's relentless pace of information consumption, and availability of evermore convincing and disinformation, further complicates the task for traditional storytelling methods. The transient nature of digital content, coupled with the ceaseless surge of fresh information (or disinformation), can make it challenging for communicators to sustain relevance and engagement over time. Traditional media outlets may find it hard to match the brisk information diffusion on digital platforms, leading to a potential dilution of their narrative impact.

Additionally, traditional storytelling might struggle to effectively communicate the urgency and significance of the SDGs. As Mulholland (2018) observed, "Knowledge alone does not motivate action. Communication needs to consider everyday concerns of people and decision-makers, encourage social norms and identities that promote desired actions, increase perceptions of response-efficacy, and move from communications of sustainability to promoting communication about sustainability." Traditional media channels might lack the agility to tailor their messages and strategies to echo the diverse needs and worries of their audiences, thereby limiting their capacity to galvanize action towards the SDGs.

To surmount these hurdles, communicators should consider venturing into innovative storytelling avenues that can encapsulate the SDGs' complexity, captivate diverse audiences, and incite action. One such strategy is transmedia storytelling, which harnesses multiple media platforms and formats to weave a more immersive and cohesive narrative tapestry. By adopting transmedia storytelling, communicators can address the constraints of traditional methods and nurture a deeper understanding of, and engagement with, the SDGs across a wide range of cultures and demographics.

3. DECODING TRANSMEDIA STORYTELLING

Transmedia storytelling has evolved as a revolutionary narrative mechanism, pushing the confines of traditional storytelling methods beyond recognition. As Lam and Tegelberg (2019) state, "Although a transmedia story may originate in one medium, its creators utilize other media to broaden the narrative scope and draw a larger audience to their tale." This narrative tactic has witnessed an upward trajectory, invigorated by a world increasingly laced with media connections.

Characterized by the deployment of multiple media platforms and formats to weave a single tale, each contributing uniquely to the overarching narrative, transmedia storytelling stands apart from traditional storytelling (Jenkins, 2006). The story isn't merely replicated across diverse platforms but is enriched, dissected, and remixed in novel ways, amplifying the narrative experience (Hills, 2017). Leading theorists like Marsha Kinder and Henry Jenkins have played instrumental roles in framing our comprehension of transmedia storytelling, heralding it as a potent device for both amusement and societal impact.

Transmedia storytelling boasts an ability to engage a more extensive audience. By employing various media channels, transmedia narratives can offer more touch points and cater to different audience predilections and consumption habits (Scolari, 2009). This platform diversification allows the story to resonate with more individuals, thus escalating the potential for audience engagement and involvement in the narrative.

Pont (2013) underlines the potential of transmedia storytelling, stating, "Parallel and non-linear timelines, 'multi-verses', grand narratives with crazy-rich character arcs, 'back-story' has become 'more story', the opportunity to add rich layers of meaning and depth. You don't create a story world by stripping away, but by layering".

One significant advantage of transmedia storytelling, when juxtaposed with traditional digital media storytelling methods, is its capacity to sculpt immersive and captivating experiences for audiences. By spreading the touch points of narrative threads across various media platforms, transmedia storytelling facilitates an in-depth exploration of story worlds, offering audiences the chance to participate actively in the narrative and having unique experiences of the story depending on their entry point and the order in which the content is consumed (Jenkins, 2006; Kinder, 1991). This immersive feeling fosters a deeper emotional connection with the story and its characters, rendering the narrative more memorable and impactful (Klastrup & Tosca, 2004).

Transmedia storytelling also provides increased opportunities for audience interaction and collaboration. By offering multiple entry points and platforms for participation, transmedia narratives can stimulate the creation of fan communities and user-generated content (Jenkins, 2006). This participatory culture not only intensifies engagement with the story but also fosters creativity, collaboration, and critical thinking among audience members (Jenkins, 2009).

Beyond its entertainment value, transmedia storytelling has shown efficacy as a tool for social impact and addressing societal issues (Gürel & Tigli, 2014; Lam & Tegelberg, 2019; Viloria-González, 2022). Transmedia campaigns can create more immersive and impactful experiences by using multiple media platforms, reaching wider audiences, and nurturing communities around shared narratives (Jenkins, 2006, 2009).

4. TRANSMEDIA STORYTELLING CASE STUDIES

4.1. The Dark Knight: "Why So Serious?" Campaign

The marketing campaign for Christopher Nolan's "The Dark Knight" (2008) revolutionized movie marketing through an immersive transmedia narrative. The campaign, known as "Why So Serious?" was a sprawling alternate reality game (ARG) that transformed fans into active participants in the narrative universe of Gotham City. A variety of media platforms, including websites, emails, mobile phones, real-world (offline) events, and even physical artifacts, were used to expand the film's storyline and generate anticipation for the movie's release.

What made it distinctly transmedia was the narrative's expansion across different media channels, providing a unique and immersive experience that each contributed to the overall understanding of the narrative universe.

The success of this campaign can be attributed to the deep level of fan engagement it fostered. It not only generated anticipation for the film but also created a dedicated fan community, actively participating in the narrative. The campaign's transmedia approach resonated with the audiences' media consumption habits, making it a groundbreaking example of effective transmedia storytelling.

4.2. Star Wars Universe

Arguably one of the most successful and most written about transmedia franchises, Star Wars seamlessly integrates films, TV series, books, comics, video games, toys, and more to create an expansive narrative universe, allowing fans to explore as much or as little as they wish. Each medium contributes to the overarching narrative and allows for a more profound understanding of the Star Wars universe, but each piece of content stands alone as a high-quality production with its own engaging narrative.

Star Wars has remained a transmedia phenomenon due to its ability to consistently introduce new narrative elements and expand its boundaries across various media channels, all while maintaining the continuity and richness of the established universe. This has allowed for an immersive and engaging fan experience, with each medium offering a unique entry point into the Star Wars universe.

The success of the Star Wars transmedia franchise can be attributed to its expansive narrative universe, which has cultivated a dedicated fan base across a wide variety of platforms and mediums. The continual expansion of the narrative across various media platforms has kept the franchise relevant and engaging, contributing to its enduring popularity.

4.3. Pottermore: Harry Potter Universe

Pottermore, the digital publishing, e-commerce, entertainment, and news company from J. K. Rowling, is another fantastic example of transmedia storytelling. It extends the Harry Potter narrative beyond the seven books and eight films into an online platform that offers additional content, including new stories, character backstories, and explanations of the wizarding world.

Pottermore stands out as a transmedia storytelling campaign due to its use of engaging and interactive, gamified, digital technology to expand the narrative universe of Harry Potter. This digital platform offers fans an interactive experience, where they can be sorted into Hogwarts houses, learn spells, explore the wizarding world, far beyond the books and films.

The success of Pottermore is primarily due to the global appeal of the Harry Potter franchise and the desire of fans to continue engaging with the narrative universe. The interactive elements of the platform, combined with the additional narrative content, has allowed fans to experience the wizarding world in a new and immersive way.

4.4. The Marvel Cinematic Universe (MCU)

The Marvel Cinematic Universe is an exemplary instance of transmedia storytelling. The MCU, initiated with "Iron Man" in 2008, now spans over two dozen films, multiple television series, comics, video games, and even themed amusement park attractions. Each of these outlets offers a different piece of the overarching narrative puzzle, but standalone, allowing both casual and the most committed fans to engage with the world and enjoy the Marvel experience.

The MCU's strength lies in its intricate narrative webs, where standalone stories interweave to form a larger, cohesive universe. Characters crossover between films and series, and plotlines ripple out across the different media. This approach offers audiences multiple points of entry and keeps them engaged over time, anticipating the next piece of the narrative.

The MCU's success demonstrates the power of narrative continuity and character development across various platforms. By weaving a shared universe that extends beyond individual films or series, Marvel has cultivated a dedicated and active fanbase that eagerly follows the narrative across different media channels (Scolari et al., 2014).

4.5. The Matrix Franchise

The Matrix franchise, created by the Wachowskis, leveraged transmedia storytelling to expand its narrative beyond the initial trilogy of films. The story world of The Matrix was expanded through animated short films ("The Animatrix"), video games ("Enter the Matrix" and "The Matrix Online"), and comic books, each contributing unique elements to the overall coherent narrative.

The video game "Enter the Matrix", for example, was released simultaneously with the second film, "The Matrix Reloaded", and features over an hour of original filmed content that provides additional narrative insights and overlaps with the film's story. Players' experiences in the game align with and enhance the narrative of the film, even impacting its plot, demonstrating the potential for interactivity in transmedia storytelling (Jenkins, 2003).

The Matrix franchise underscores the potential of transmedia storytelling to create an immersive narrative universe that engages audiences across various media platforms. The Wachowskis' innovative approach demonstrates how each medium can contribute uniquely to the overall narrative, offering a richer and more interactive audience experience.

4.6. Similarities

Across these successful media franchises and their engaging transmedia approach, there are similarities which could owe to their success.

Expanding Universe: All five narratives – from Gotham City to the farthest reaches of space – have built intricate, expansive universes that extend well beyond a single medium. Whether through films, games, books, or digital platforms, they have each created unique, multilayered narrative environments that offer a rich tapestry of story elements to explore, but all contribute to the larger, coherent story.

Engaging Audiences: Each narrative has succeeded in transforming its audience from passive consumers to active participants. The Matrix's video games, the Star Wars universe, Pottermore's interactive features, the MCU's narrative interweaving which spawned investigative fan communities, and "Why So Serious?" campaign's alternate reality game, have all offered fans unique ways to engage with and immerse themselves in the narrative world.

Community Creation: Each of these narratives has successfully fostered a dedicated, engaged and participatory fan community. These communities have become significant contributors to the narrative world, actively sharing, discussing, and even creating their own content, thus enriching the overall narrative experience.

4.7. Lessons

Drawing from these case studies and looking at what each of them has in common, we can attempt to draw some lessons that led to their success and what we could apply to transmedia storytelling approach to better communicate about the SDGs.

Medium Matters: Integrating multiple media platforms to craft a cohesive narrative across a variety of entry and touch points is crucial to successful transmedia storytelling. However, merely replicating the same story across platforms is not enough; each platform should contribute uniquely to the overall narrative, as seen in the MCU's careful interplay between films and series, and The Matrix's use of video games to enhance the narrative.

Interactive Narratives: Each case study highlights the importance of fostering interactivity and audience participation. By giving fans the ability to influence or engage with the narrative, storytellers can create more immersive and memorable experiences, as demonstrated by Pottermore's wizarding world or the Star Wars fan-created content.

Sustained Engagement: All of these narratives underscore the importance of long-term engagement. Whether through the continual expansion of the Star Wars universe or the consistent release of new narrative elements in the MCU, these narratives have managed to keep audiences invested and engaged over an extended period.

Community-Driven Approach: Lastly, the power of a community-driven approach shines through in each of these case studies. Building a dedicated fan community not only deepens engagement but also serves as a powerful promotional tool, as fans become advocates for the narrative, as exemplified by the dedicated communities surrounding "The Dark Knight", Star Wars, Pottermore, MCU, and The Matrix.

5. PARTICIPATORY CULTURE: A CORNERSTONE IN TRANSMEDIA STORYTELLING

Coined by Henry Jenkins (2006), Participatory Culture is one where individuals aren't merely passive spectators, quietly consuming media content, but active contributors who produce, remix, and disseminate it. This participatory culture, nourished by the advent of social media platforms, connected digital technologies and ever more accessible (in ease of use and in cost) prosumer technology, allows an environment of creative engagement, where collaborations occur with an ease and reach hitherto unknown (Jenkins, 2006). In the midst of this participatory culture, transmedia storytelling is bolstered as a powerful tool that harnesses audience engagement.

In a circular effect, the participatory and immersive experience, engaging audiences on various levels and pulling them into the narrative's heart, pushes that audience to create their own communities, new narratives, fan theories and content, which they themselves take ownership over.

In the grand tapestry of transmedia narratives, the threads of participatory culture weave in critical engagement, collaboration, and social change. This could prove especially poignant when transmedia storytelling is utilized to promote the United Nations' Sustainable Development Goals (SDGs).

Engagement, that essential spark that kindles interest and commitment, is enriched by participatory culture. It invites audiences into the narrative, nurturing a sense of ownership and investment in the story (Brough & Shresthova, 2012) and could be leveraged in the same way for Social Development Goals.

The "World's Largest Lesson" initiative (Project Everyone, 2015), for example, where interactive quizzes and activities transformed the audience from passive learners to active participants. This deepened their understanding of the SDGs, cultivating a sense of responsibility and a readiness to act.

Participatory culture also fosters collaboration, bridging individuals and communities together. It provides spaces for dialogue, shared learning, and collective action, thus shaping alliances that propel progress towards a common goal (Ito et al., 2009). The "Global Goals Week" (United Nations, 2016), with its worldwide call for collaborative projects, events, and campaigns, is a stellar example. It formed a platform for collective action, creating a global sense of community and solidarity in the quest for sustainable development.

At the heart of participatory culture lies a powerful force for social change. It empowers diverse voices, often unheard, to reverberate across media platforms (Jenkins et al., 2013). This amplification of varied perspectives can give rise to grassroots movements and campaigns centered on a shared goal, catalyzing policy changes and societal transformations (Jenkins, 2016).

The "Humans of New York" project (Stanton, 2010) leveraged participatory culture to narrate personal stories from diverse backgrounds, sparking dialogue on social issues, including those related to the SDGs. Such endeavors allow participatory culture to foster a more inclusive discourse around sustainable development, propelling social change.

Moreover, participatory culture provides fertile ground for learning and skill development. As individuals participate in creating and disseminating media content, they hone essential skills — critical thinking, problem-solving, communication, collaboration, and digital literacy (Ito et al., 2009). This has been noted in fan communities where skill-sharing has emerged, and fans have helped one another to improve their writing of fan fiction or even developing video editing skills to remix their favorite series, or coding skills to develop a new game or app to expand their beloved story universe (Jenkins, 2008).

These skills can equip individuals to contribute effectively to the global effort to realize the SDGs. The "World's Largest Lesson" initiative (Project Everyone, 2015), for example, didn't merely aim to raise SDG awareness, but also sought to empower young people with the necessary knowledge and skills to contribute to their achievement. Thus, participatory culture, by nurturing an informed, skilled, and engaged citizenry, can steer us towards a sustainable future.

The power of participatory culture and transmedia storytelling, however, does not remain confined within the spheres of engagement, collaboration, or skill development. It extends to the realm of collective intelligence, where knowledge is shared and expanded upon by the community. Through such collective problem-solving, participatory culture facilitates the spread of innovative ideas and strategies to tackle the challenges posed by the SDGs (Jenkins, 2006).

The "Mission 1.5" campaign (United Nations Development Programme, 2020), used an interactive mobile game to educate players about climate change and collect data on people's attitudes towards different climate policies. By leveraging the participatory nature of gaming, with global ranking and leadership boards, the initiative not only promoted learning but also harnessed collective intelligence to inform climate action.

Yet, as potent as participatory culture can be in promoting the SDGs through transmedia storytelling, it comes with its challenges. These include issues related to digital divide, media literacy, and the quality of user-generated content (Jenkins et al., 2016). Ensuring inclusive participation becomes crucial, particularly considering the discrepancies in access to digital technologies across different socio-economic groups.

However, these challenges also present opportunities for innovation and growth. By addressing these issues, communities can work towards creating a more inclusive and equitable participatory culture, where diverse voices are heard, and everyone has the opportunity to contribute to the narrative of sustainable development (Jenkins et al., 2016).

6. BEST PRACTICES AND OVERCOMING ASSOCIATED CHALLENGES

This innovative and engaging approach, however, is not without its obstacles and challenges, including issues of budget constraints, resource scarcity, and the sometimes-fickle audience engagement (Beuhring & Vittachi, 2020; Evans, 2014; Hazboun, 2014).

The art of transmedia storytelling is akin to conducting a symphony. Each medium is an instrument that contributes to the overall composition, requiring a conductor to ensure harmony and synchronicity. Herein lies the challenge, how to wield a maestro's baton on a budget.

Jenkins (2006) offers an insight: focus on "world-building" instead of content replication. The idea is to allocate resources strategically, crafting a coherent narrative across platforms, even with limited funds. Evans (2014) further suggests prioritizing platforms that resonate with the core audience and support the narrative's goals. This approach, complemented by the phased rollout of platforms, can help stretch budgets without compromising on the story's integrity (Beuhring & Vittachi, 2020).

In addition, the advent of AI technologies such as ChatGPT introduces a new player to the orchestra, one that can mitigate budget constraints by automating parts of the content creation process (Sharma, 2021). Such generative AI technologies can also be used to repurpose content for different platforms (Long, 2007), adapting texts or videos to appropriate lengths, creating audio from text and even creating unique character dialogues.

The challenge of resource scarcity extends beyond financial limitations to encompass the varying skills required for transmedia production. A broad palette of expertise, from storytelling and marketing to technical abilities is needed. But the workforce is becoming ever-more polyvalent, and overlaps can be created leveraging individuals' strengths and upskilling team members, as well as tapping into crowd wisdom of audiences and external partners (Phillips, 2012) to find solutions to this challenge.

Engaging the audience in any digital storytelling activity can be an intimidating task, as audiences can grow slowly for years then takeoff overnight. The intricacy and abundance of content can both enthrall and overwhelm, potentially diluting the narrative's impact (Evans, 2014). Jenkins (2006) recommends providing distinct entry points for different audience segments and designing "drillable" content that allows audiences to delve into the narrative at their discretion (Jenkins, 2009). The inclusion of interactive elements, in this context, can foster a sense of ownership and deepen the audience's connection with the narrative (Scolari, 2009), whilst fostering communities can turn audiences into ambassadors, who look to involve their wider communities.

The need for narrative consistency in a transmedia story is perhaps the biggest challenge to overcome. Coordinating storylines across platforms, especially when different teams are involved, can be a dizzying endeavor (Evans, 2014). The solution it would seem comes from Kinder's (1991) "master document" or "bible," inspired by soap opera scriptwriting and production (Zaluczkowska, 2018), outlining the narrative structure and key elements. This universal guide can be used in the digital age, when coupled with a centralized project management system (Phillips, 2012), to help maintain the narrative's integrity amidst the chaos of varying platforms and types of content.

It's important to note that intellectual property rights issues can occur with this sometimes-decentralized approach to storytelling, with multiple stakeholders involved in content creation and distribution.

Infringement may not only tarnish relationships but also bring legal repercussions. Clear agreements with stakeholders and early involvement of legal experts are essential to keeping a cohesive and living transmedia experience for the audience (Dena, 2009; Beuhring & Vittachi, 2020).

Finally, the success of a transmedia campaign can be difficult to quantify. Traditional metrics like ratings or page views may fail to capture the essence of the transmedia experience (Evans, 2014). Adopting a holistic approach that melds quantitative and qualitative metrics can offer a more comprehensive view of campaign performance (Beuhring & Vittachi, 2020). This includes platform-specific metrics such as social media engagement, as well as broader indicators of narrative impact, such as audience sentiment and brand affinity. Regular evaluations throughout the campaign can ensure a responsive strategy, agile enough to adapt to evolving audience needs and campaign dynamics (Phillips, 2012).

Transmedia storytelling isn't a one-size-fits-all approach, but a versatile framework that can be tailored to various contexts. It demands a cohesive narrative structure, engaging characters, and careful selection of platforms. Crafting a transmedia production bible can guide the narrative journey, ensuring coherence and consistency (Zaluczkowska, 2018). Strategic content distribution, coupled with active audience participation and constant innovation, can keep the narrative alive and evolving.

A well-planned campaign is instrumental in achieving objectives such as raising awareness, driving engagement, or boosting conversions. It starts with identifying the target audience and developing personas to understand their preferences, habits, and motivations. Resources - budget, personnel, and time - need to be allocated thoughtfully to ensure the campaign's smooth execution.

Content, the core output of the campaign, needs to be high-quality, compelling, and in alignment with campaign objectives. A variety of formats - text, images, audio, and video (of different ratios and lengths) - can cater to diverse audience preferences and platform requirements. Interactive elements, user-generated content, polls, or quizzes can stir audience participation, while regular updates can sustain interest and engagement.

Strategic content distribution is as crucial as its creation. Identifying the most effective channels and platforms to reach the target audience, creating a content distribution schedule, and using platform-specific features can maximize content reach and visibility. This strategy may need constant monitoring and adjustments based on audience engagement and feedback.

In essence, the keys to successful transmedia storytelling lie in the intricate balance of creativity and strategic planning, character development, and audience engagement. And while the challenges may be many, the potential rewards - in terms of audience engagement, brand loyalty, and narrative impact - make the journey worthwhile. As digital marketers continue to explore and experiment with this medium, the art and science of transmedia storytelling will undoubtedly continue to evolve.

7. POSSIBLE APPLICATIONS FOR FOSTERING SDG AWARENESS AND INCITING ACTION

Transmedia storytelling perhaps has the unique ability to amplify the visibility of global campaigns like the Sustainable Development Goals (SDGs), transforming them from abstract concepts into tangible realities.

By leveraging multiple platforms such as videos, podcasts, social media, and interactive websites, the SDGs can be presented in a myriad of perspectives, reaching audiences previously untouched.

7.1. Developing Empathy Through Character-Driven Narratives

Transmedia storytelling could serve as a catalyst for empathy and urgency around the SDGs and inspire action. It has the power to transport audiences into the lives of those affected by these goals, evoking emotions, and fostering a deeper understanding of global challenges (Rose, 2011). By developing character-driven narratives and real-life stories related to the SDGs, and presenting them through varied media formats like documentaries, photo essays, and podcasts, audiences can engage with the content on multiple levels. Fictional characters brought together in a story world affected by one or more of the SDGs could have their own fictional podcast, that audiences could actually listen to, or even follow the characters on their favorite social media platforms.

7.2. Fostering Interactivity: The Power of Participation

Transmedia storytelling is a potent tool for fostering interactivity, giving people a stake in the story and encouraging participation (Gee, 2004). This creates a sense of ownership and personal investment in the SDGs, inciting action. The "Global Goals Week" (United Nations, 2016), with its global call to share ideas and actions related to the SDGs, exemplifies this interactive approach. Social media campaigns like these can significantly amplify the reach and impact of the SDGs, inspiring individuals and communities to take action.

Audiences could engage with fictional characters via social media platforms, or even be solicited or inspired to create their own content, feeding the narrative, and engaging actively with the related SDG, learning more about it and connecting with it on a more meaningful level.

7.3. Sustaining Engagement: The Power of Episodic Storytelling

Transmedia storytelling, with its capacity to create long-term engagement, holds the potential to inspire action and collaboration for a better world (Dena, 2009). By crafting narratives across multiple platforms, it sustains audience interest over time.

An episodic series exploring the interconnected nature of the SDGs, presented through various media channels, and supplemented with interactive content, could maintain audience interest and encourage ongoing engagement.

8. ORCHESTRATING A TRANSMEDIA SYMPHONY: THE ANATOMY OF TRANSMEDIA PRODUCTION

Assembling a transmedia narrative is akin to conducting a symphony orchestra, with each section playing a crucial part in the overall performance. The beauty of a transmedia production lies not only in the captivating stories it tells but also in the intricate choreography of its construction and its telling. It's a dance that requires a deft blend of diverse skillsets, innovative minds, and collaborative spirits.

8.1. The Conductor: The Transmedia Producer

At the helm of any transmedia production is the transmedia producer, an individual (or team) that Long (2007) refers to as "the conductor of the orchestra". They are the visionaries who see the larger narrative arc and understand how it can be dissected and distributed across various platforms to create an engaging, immersive experience. Their role requires a blend of creative acumen, strategic thinking, and leadership skills, as they must coordinate the diverse talents and elements involved in the project while keeping the overarching narrative vision intact.

8.2. The Composers: Writers and Storytellers

The writers and storytellers are the composers of the transmedia world. Jenkins (2006) famously posited that "transmedia storytelling represents a process where integral elements of a fiction get dispersed systematically across multiple delivery channels for the purpose of creating a unified and coordinated entertainment experience." Hence, the writers must craft narratives that are compelling in isolation yet contribute to a more profound, interconnected story when combined, just like the Star Wars or Marvel films, games, and TV series. The writers must understand each platform's unique language and strengths, tailoring the story elements to fit accordingly.

8.3. The Musicians: The Content Creators

Content creators are the musicians of the transmedia symphony. They translate the writers' scripts into engaging content, be it a riveting video series, a gripping podcast, an interactive website, or an intriguing social media campaign. They are the digital artists, filmmakers, graphic designers, sound engineers, web developers —each contributing their expertise to bring the narrative to life across diverse platforms. They must be adaptable and fluent in the language of multiple media, capable of crafting content that resonates with the intended audience.

8.4. The Stagehands: The Technologists

The technologists set the stage where the transmedia performance unfolds. They are the software developers, data analysts, and digital strategists who ensure the seamless integration of various story components across multiple platforms. Scolari (2009) highlighted the importance of the digital environment in transmedia narratives, stating that "the deployment of a storyworld across different media requires a new aesthetic and a specific narratological model." Therefore, the technologists' role is pivotal in ensuring the functionality and navigability of the transmedia narrative, enhancing audience engagement and interaction.

8.5. The Critics: The Analysts

The analysts play the role of the critics, gauging the success of the transmedia narrative by analyzing audience reception and engagement metrics. They assess what works and what doesn't, providing valuable insights to fine-tune the narrative, enhance audience engagement, and ensure the longevity of the transmedia campaign. Green and Jenkins (2011) emphasized the iterative nature of transmedia narratives, where audience feedback and participation play a significant role in shaping the ongoing story. Therefore, the analysts must have a keen understanding of audience analytics and the skill to interpret these data in a meaningful way to inform the evolution of the narrative.

8.6. The Concertmaster: Community Managers

Community managers are the concertmasters of the transmedia narrative orchestra. They are the primary point of contact for the audience, facilitating dialogue and fostering a sense of community among participants. According to Ford, Green, & Jenkins (2013), transmedia narratives are inherently participatory and depend on the active engagement of the audience. The community managers are responsible for cultivating this participation, moderating discussions, and engaging with audience members to enhance their experience and deepen their immersion in the narrative.

Their role extends beyond merely managing interactions; they also play a vital role in gathering audience feedback and insights, which are then shared with the analysts and storytellers to shape the ongoing narrative. They must possess exceptional interpersonal and communication skills, a keen understanding of the narrative and its themes, and a passion for fostering meaningful connections.

In the context of the SDGs, community managers could help facilitate important conversations around these goals, encourage user-generated content, and inspire action among audience members. By nurturing an active and engaged community, they can amplify the impact of the transmedia narrative and foster a sense of collective responsibility towards achieving the SDGs.

Assembling a transmedia production is a complex, collaborative endeavor that necessitates a plethora of skills and a shared vision. Each player's contribution is invaluable in crafting an immersive, participatory narrative that resonates with the audience and amplifies the impact of the story.

8.7. Unleashing the Potential of Transmedia Storytelling for the SDGs

Here are some hypothetical scenarios of how transmedia storytelling approaches could enhance societal attitudes toward the SDGs:

SDG Interactive Web Series: A weekly, informative, interactive web series that explores different aspects of the SDGs, with clickable elements inviting viewers to engage with supplementary information, quizzes, and challenges. This could raise awareness about the SDGs, facilitate a deeper understanding, and inspire viewers to adopt sustainable practices.

Global Goals Social Media Challenge: A global social media challenge where participants organize and share their SDG-related actions, encouraging a sense of collective responsibility. This could amplify individual stories and inspire others to act, fostering a sense of global community.

SDG-themed Alternate Reality Game (ARG): Through a mobile phone app, an ARG immersing players in a fictional world based around the SDGs, where they solve puzzles, collaborate, and complete real-life tasks. This could promote sustainable behaviors and foster a sense of global citizenship.

SDG Storytelling Festival: An on and offline, multi-day, multi-location storytelling festival celebrating the SDGs through artistic performances, workshops, and exhibitions. This could engage audiences with thought-provoking art, inspiring reflection, dialogue, and action on both local and global scales.

SDG Education Toolkit: A free-to-use educational toolkit incorporating video lessons, interactive games, and e-books, designed for various classroom settings. This could empower young people with knowledge and understanding of the SDGs, fostering a generation committed to a more sustainable future.

The reality is that a single transmedia campaign could involve all of these potential scenarios in a cohesive way, creating a sustained and coordinated approach for better SDG comprehension, engagement and action.

9. CRAFTING A TRANSMEDIA PLAN FOR THE SDGS

Putting together a transmedia production is a task involving scriptwriting, storytelling, production, distribution, and community management, all of which have to be well coordinated. Here is what a plan to enhance SDG awareness and engagement could look like, focusing on creating a compelling narrative, innovative distribution techniques, and sustainable funding models.

9.1. Narrative Creation

Storyworld Development: Developing a rich, immersive story world that places the SDGs at its core is a good first step in the process (Zalucskowsa, 2015). This story world should depict the challenges faced and solutions discovered by communities across the globe, providing a framework for audiences to relate to the goals on a personal level. Real-world stories from SDG initiatives could be woven into the narrative to enhance its authenticity and relatability.

Character Creation: Characters are the heart of any story and a transmedia narrative could have many, each offering someone that an audience could empathize and identify with. Create compelling, relatable characters who embody different SDG themes. Their struggles and triumphs can serve as an emotional bridge between the audience and the issues at hand, fostering empathy and engagement.

Story Arcs: Craft episodic story arcs for each SDG, showcasing their importance in addressing global challenges. Connect these arcs through a larger narrative that demonstrates the interconnectedness of the SDGs and their collective impact. This strategy not only maintains audience interest over time but also emphasizes the holistic nature of the SDGs.

9.2. Varied Media Types and Localization

Media Types: The power of transmedia storytelling lies in its ability to span across various media formats, each offering unique storytelling possibilities. Develop content in the form of film and television series, podcasts, interactive web content, mobile apps, games, and print materials. Each medium can target different aspects of the SDGs, providing a comprehensive exploration of the goals and encouraging users to go out looking for more content on other platforms.

Localization: Collaborate with local creators to adapt content for various cultures, languages, and regions. This ensures that the narrative remains relevant and accessible to diverse audiences. Encourage local initiatives and communities to share their SDG stories, fostering a sense of ownership and pride in the goals.

9.3. Multiplatform Distribution and Partnerships

Multiplatform Strategy: Utilize both traditional and digital media platforms to reach a broad audience. Traditional media like TV, radio, and print can ensure extensive reach, while digital platforms like social media, streaming services, and websites can provide interactive and engaging experiences. Collaborating with schools, libraries, and community centers can further extend the reach of educational materials and events.

Partnerships: Form strategic partnerships to amplify the SDGs and the story world. Global and local media networks can ensure the content reaches diverse audiences. Influencers and celebrities can further amplify the message, while NGOs, governments, and businesses can offer resources and reach. Each partnership should be based on shared values and goals, ensuring a synergistic relationship.

9.4. Sustainable Funding

Grants and Donor Funding: Identify and apply for relevant grants from foundations, governments, and international organizations. These can provide substantial funding for development and distribution. Crowdfunding campaigns can also be a great way to raise funds while fostering a sense of community and participation among the public.

Sponsorships and Partnerships: Seek sponsorships from businesses and organizations that align with the SDGs. These sponsorships can provide funding, while also expanding the reach of the content. Developing co-branded content with partners can generate additional funding and audience reach and incentivize the sponsors or partners to participate.

Revenue Generation: Monetize the content through various channels' native platform (YouTube, for example), including licensing, subscription models, and merchandize sales. Additionally, hosting paid events, workshops, and conferences related to the SDGs and the story world could generate revenue while promoting engagement.

9.5. Monitoring and Evaluation

Objectives and KPIs: Set clear, measurable objectives and key performance indicators (KPIs) to track the progress and impact of the transmedia plan. These could be related to audience reach, engagement levels, or actions taken as a result of the campaign.

Evaluation: Regular evaluations provide crucial insights into the effectiveness of the transmedia plan. This involves a comprehensive assessment of whether the objectives and KPIs are being met, along with an analysis of what's working and what's not. Use these insights to refine and adapt the approach and improve on strategies.

Success Stories and Lessons Learned: Share success stories and lessons learned throughout the campaign. This not only provides transparency but also serves as a source of inspiration for further SDG engagement and collaboration, whilst serving as further content in itself. Use case studies, testimonials, and impact reports to highlight the difference your project is making.

9.6. Continuous Engagement

Ongoing Content Release: Maintain audience interest by consistently releasing new content across the varying media platforms. Regular updates keep the narrative fresh and exciting, and also provide opportunities for the audience to engage with both the story and the SDGs on a continuous basis.

Community Engagement: Foster a sense of community among the audience. Encourage interaction through social media discussions, contests, and live events (both on and offline). Highlight community contributions and let the audience see the impact of their actions. This could create a sense of ownership and personal investment in the SDGs, driving long-term commitment.

Staying Relevant: Keep the narrative and content relevant by staying informed about the latest SDG developments and global trends. Incorporate relevant news and updates into the story arcs in an agile way and adapt the content to reflect evolving social contexts.

By implementing a thorough and strategic transmedia plan, it could be possible to effectively raise SDG awareness, build empathy, foster interactivity, and drive long-term engagement, all while inspiring individuals and communities to take action towards a more sustainable future.

10. CONCLUSION: TAPPING INTO THE TRANSMEDIA STORYTELLING MATRIX FOR SUSTAINABLE PROGRESS

As we turn the final page on this exploration of the Sustainable Development Goals (SDGs), we find ourselves standing on the precipice of a remarkable opportunity: harnessing the transmedia storytelling revolution. Since Jenkins (2003) spotlighted its potential to invigorate creativity, ensnare broader audiences, and cultivate unwavering loyalty, this narrative approach has blossomed into a commanding force in our multimedia-infused world.

Transmedia storytelling, with its multidimensional approach, provides a unique platform to decode the intricate and intertwined narratives of the SDGs for the layperson. It invites them into a rich, participatory sphere that nurtures empathy, fosters understanding, and ignites action. The SDGs, by their very nature, resonate with the transmedia approach, allowing their multifaceted narratives to be dissected, reassembled, and presented through various media forms, thereby casting a wider net on the audience sea.

Our expedition through various case studies demonstrates that successful consumer and entertainment campaigns can be repurposed to address global challenges. These transmedia narratives have the potency to leave an indelible impact on societal issues.

The crux of successful transmedia storytelling for the SDGs lies in fostering a participatory culture. By offering multiple avenues for interaction and inspiring user-generated content, audiences transition from passive spectators to active contributors, instilling a sense of agency and ownership. This participatory dynamic is the key that unlocks the door to inspiring individuals and communities to contribute to the actualization of the SDGs.

However, the road to success isn't merely a case of copy-pasting techniques from entertainment campaigns onto the SDG platform. It necessitates a profound comprehension of storytelling's art and science, along with a keen understanding of the unique challenges and opportunities presented by the SDGs. Our voyage has shown us that compelling storytelling is the heart that pumps action-inducing blood into the veins of the audience, motivating them to take up the global challenges gauntlet.

The potential challenges and best practices discussed in this chapter form the foundation for organizations and practitioners seeking to wield the transmedia storytelling sword. By acknowledging and navigating potential pitfalls, such as digital divides, access, and representation, we can foster more inclusive and equitable transmedia narratives that effectively champion the SDGs.

The roadmap outlined in this chapter—ranging from novel campaign ideas to comprehensive plans for SDG engagement—provides the blueprints to harness the transformative power of transmedia storytelling. By weaving compelling narratives, developing engaging content, and strategizing distribution and funding models, we can inspire diverse audiences to contribute to the creation of a more equitable and sustainable world.

As the curtain falls on this chapter, it is imperative that theorists, practitioners, and organizations continue to investigate the potential of transmedia storytelling for the SDGs, learning from both triumphs and setbacks, and adapting to the ever-evolving media landscape. By leveraging the knowledge and experience amassed over the past 20 years and capitalizing on the affordability of cross-platform production, we can engage a larger audience in a participatory dialogue for societal and planetary betterment.

In sum, the power of transmedia storytelling for the SDGs resides in its ability to shatter conventional communication barriers, crafting immersive, participatory experiences that cultivate empathy and incite action. With this powerful tool at our disposal, we can mobilize a global brigade of informed and engaged citizens, rallying together to confront our era's most urgent challenges and breathe life into the vision of the Sustainable Development Goals.

Transmedia storytelling, in essence, is not just a tool; it's a beacon of hope—a compass guiding us towards a more sustainable and equitable future. Let us, then, harness this power, for it is through our collective narratives that we will write the next chapter of human development—one that speaks of unity, resilience, and progress.

REFERENCES

Dena, C. (2009). *Transmedia practice: Theorizing the practice of expressing a fictional world across distinct media and environments*. University of Sydney.

Emerson, S. (2018). Great examples of multiplatform storytelling. [Blog post]. *Echo Stories*. https://www.echostories.com/great-examples-multiplatform-storytelling/

Ford, S., Green, J., & Jenkins, H. (2013). *Spreadable media: Creating value and meaning in a networked culture*. New York University Press.

Gee, J. P. (2004). *Situated language and learning: A critique of traditional schooling*. Routledge.

Green, M. C., & Jenkins, H. (2011). Spreadable media: How audiences create value and meaning in a networked culture. In V. Nightingale (Ed.), *The handbook of media audiences* (pp. 109–127). Wiley-Blackwell. doi:10.1002/9781444340525.ch5

Gürel, M. O., & Tigli, M. (2014). New World Created by Social Media: Transmedia Storytelling. *Journal of Media Critiques*, *1*(1), 35–65. doi:10.17349/jmc114102

Hills, M. (2017). From Transmedia Storytelling to Transmedia Experience. In *Star Wars and the History of Transmedia Storytelling* (pp. 213–225). Amsterdam University Press.

Jenkins, H. (2003). Transmedia Storytelling: Moving Characters from Books to Films to Video Games Can Make Them Stronger and More Compelling. *MIT Technology Review*. https://www.technologyreview.com/news/401760/transmedia-storytelling/

Jenkins, H. (2006). *Convergence culture: Where old and new media collide*. New York University Press.

Jenkins, H. (2009). *If it doesn't spread, it's dead (Part One): Media viruses and memes. Confessions of an Aca-Fan*. Henry Jenkins. http://henryjenkins.org/blog/2009/02/if_it_doesnt_spread_its_dead_p.html

Jenkins, H. (2010). Transmedia storytelling and entertainment: An annotated syllabus. *Continuum (Perth), 24*(6), 943–958. doi:10.1080/10304312.2010.510599

Jenkins, H., & Deuze, M. (2008). Editorial: Convergence Culture. *Convergence (London), 14*(1), 5–12. doi:10.1177/1354856507084415

Jenkins, H., Ford, S., & Green, J. (2013). *Spreadable media: Creating value and meaning in a networked culture*. New York University Press.

Kinder, M. (1991). *Playing with power in movies, television, and video games: From Muppet Babies to Teenage Mutant Ninja Turtles*. University of California Press. doi:10.1525/9780520912434

Klastrup, L., & Tosca, S. (2004). Transmedial worlds – rethinking cyberworld design. In *Proceedings from the 2004 International Conference on Cyberworlds*. 10.1109/CW.2004.67

Lam, A., & Tegelberg, M. (2019). Witnessing glaciers melt: Climate change and transmedia storytelling. *JCOM, Journal of Science Communication, 18*(02), A05. doi:10.22323/2.18020205

Long, G. (2007). *Transmedia storytelling: Business, aesthetics, and production at the Jim Henson Company*. Unpublished doctoral dissertation, Massachusetts Institute of Technology.

Lucas, G. (Creator). (1977-present). *Star Wars* [Film series]. Lucasfilm.

Marvel Studios. (2008-present). *Marvel Cinematic Universe* [Film series]. Marvel Studios.

McLuhan, M. (1964). *Understanding media: The extensions of man*. McGraw Hill.

Mulholland, E., Dimitrova, A., & Hametner, M. (2018). *SDG Indicators and Monitoring: Systems and Processes at the Global, European, and National Level. ESDN Quarterly Report 48*. ESDN Office.

Mulholland, E., Dimitrova, A., & Hametner, M. (2018). *SDG Indicators and Monitoring: Systems and Processes at the Global, European, and National Level*. ESDN Office.

Nolan, C. (Director). (2008). *The Dark Knight* [Film]. Warner Bros. Pictures.

Phillips, A. (2012). *A creator's guide to transmedia storytelling: How to captivate and engage audiences across multiple platforms*. McGraw-Hill Education.

Pont, S. (2013). *Digital state: How the Internet is changing everything*. Kogan Page Project Everyone. https://www.project-everyone.org/

Rose, F. (2011). *The art of immersion: How the digital generation is remaking Hollywood, Madison Avenue, and the way we tell stories*. W. W. Norton & Company.

RowlingJ. K. (n.d.). *Pottermore* [Website]. https://www.pottermore.com

Ruggill, J. E., & McAllister, K. S. (2009). *Inside the video game industry: Game developers talk about the business of play*. Routledge.

Scolari, C. A. (2009). Transmedia storytelling: Implicit consumers, narrative worlds, and branding in contemporary media production. *International Journal of Communication*, *3*, 586–606.

Scolari, C. A., Bertetti, P., & Freeman, M. (2014). *Transmedia archaeology: Storytelling in the borderlines of science fiction, comics and pulp magazines*. Palgrave Pivot. doi:10.1057/9781137434371

Stanton, B. (2010). *Humans of New York*. Humans of New York. https://www.humansofnewyork.com/

United Nations. (2015). *Transforming our world: the 2030 Agenda for Sustainable Development*. UN. https://sdgs.un.org/2030agenda

United Nations. (2016). *Global Goals Week*. UN. https://globalgoalsweek.org/

Viloria-González, J. (2022). Transmedia Storytelling Applied to Science, Technology and Society. *The Turkish Online Journal of Educational Technology*, *2*(1), 1–10.

Wachowski, L., & Wachowski, L. (Creators). (1999-2003). *The Matrix* [Film series]. Warner Bros. Pictures.

Zaluczkowska, A. (2018). *Red Branch Heroes – Writing with my Audiences*. Doctoral thesis, Leeds Beckett University.

Chapter 7
Digital Marketing Through a Diversity, Equity, and Inclusion Lens:
Embracing a New Paradigm for Success

Edna Mngusughun Denga
https://orcid.org/0000-0002-2121-242X
American University of Nigeria, Nigeria

ABSTRACT

Digital marketing has become an integral part of modern business strategies, enabling organizations to reach a wide and diverse audience. However, the lack of diversity, equity, and inclusion (DEI) within digital marketing practices has limited its effectiveness and hindered its potential to connect with diverse consumer groups. This chapter explores the concept of digital marketing through a DEI lens, emphasizing the significance of diversity in campaigns, content creation, and overall marketing strategies. By acknowledging and incorporating DEI principles, organizations can enhance their digital marketing efforts and foster a more inclusive and representative online presence. Embracing diversity, equity, and inclusion in digital marketing is not only a moral imperative but also a strategic advantage. By adopting a DEI lens, organizations can unlock new opportunities, strengthen their brand reputation, and build meaningful connections with diverse audiences in the digital landscape.

1. INTRODUCTION

Digital content plays a pivotal role in both our personal and professional lives. Although traditional marketing methods like print, billboard, and television ads still have their place, most businesses nowadays rely heavily on digital content to build and promote their brands (Burgess et al., 2023). However, a company's success or failure can hinge on the creation and distribution of potentially offensive digital content (Robner et al., 2021a). Consumers today seek out brands that they can connect with, just as they would in the physical world. They want to see their values and identities reflected in the marketing of

DOI: 10.4018/978-1-6684-8984-0.ch007

products and services they wish to purchase (Robner et al., 2021a; Madera, 2013). Promoting diversity, equity, and inclusion (DEI) in digital content is critical not only to increase lead generation, social media engagement, and consumer base but also to protect businesses from experiencing unexpected and potentially irreversible setbacks (Arsel et al., 2022).

Fundamentally, DEI in marketing is about celebrating and supporting people from diverse backgrounds through content. DEI is crucial in marketing because it promotes inclusivity and helps consumers identify brands that align with their values. According to Chaudhry (2023), more and more customers are looking for brands that embrace diversity and support various identities. While many businesses claim to prioritize DEI goals, they need to go beyond mere lip service and integrate diversity and inclusion ideas into their everyday practices and digital marketing content.

The first step in any marketing effort is to identify the target audience and tailor the offer to meet their unique demographics. Over time, the process of identifying the target group has evolved with the help of technology. These days, marketers have access to a vast amount of customer data, thanks to marketing automation systems, tools for tracking and analyzing customer behaviour, and customer data platforms. With big data and innovative techniques for data processing and analysis, marketers can now leverage cutting-edge audience segmentation models with predictive capabilities based on AI algorithms. This technology allows marketers to estimate future consumer purchase trends based on a range of factors such as browser cookies, mobile location data, internet surfing history, social media activity, brand preferences, and online purchasing behaviour (Arsel et al., 2022).

Most brands recognize that their target audiences are made up of consumers from diverse cultural backgrounds, religions, educational levels, socioeconomic statuses, genders, sexual preferences, and physical and mental disabilities (Burgess et al., 2023). This is something to be proud of, as brands that value DEI are better able to facilitate effective interactions between customers of different cultures (Madera, 2013). The ultimate goal of any marketing strategy is to establish a positive brand reputation (Chaudhry, 2023). It's essential to have a brand that consumers can connect with, view positively, and feel good about. Incorporating DEI principles into digital marketing helps ensure that a brand communicates with the broadest possible audience while also helping existing customers forge stronger ties to the brand.

Diversity, Equity, and Inclusion (DEI) have a significant impact on a brand's customer base as well as its employees. According to Madera (2013), having diversity in leadership enables a brand to better reflect the ideals of its target market, create a more diverse workplace, and allow customers to identify with the brand's personalities. As the current generation starts to control the vast majority of consumer spending, DEI in digital marketing is anticipated to become an essential approach for both marketers and companies. Without it, businesses will be powerless to interact with consumers in a way that motivates them to become loyal consumers and potential brand ambassadors, as noted by Robner et al. (2021a). Therefore, it's time to start emphasizing DEI in long-term planning and begin implementing empirically supported techniques. Doing so would be a wise investment that will yield results over the long term for any brand.

2. BACKGROUND

Marketing has historically leveraged diversity and inequality to segment the market, but as society becomes more aware of the negative impacts of racial and income inequality, discrimination becomes less acceptable (Chandy et al. 2021; Johnson & Chichirau 2020; Rust 2020). As a result, discussions about the principles of DEI have gained momentum in the business community and academia (Bennett et al., 2013; Bryan 2020; Bernstein et al., 2020). Inclusive marketing is increasingly gaining traction among consumers, and businesses and brands that showcase diversity in their campaigns are being rewarded by customers who support equality and advocate for diversity (Daya & April 2017). This is particularly true for those who share similar ideals. According to recent studies, 62% of consumers believe that diversity plays a crucial role in brand perception.

As consumers increasingly prioritize inclusivity, marketers need to recognize the value of embracing real-world diversity and supporting those who have historically been underrepresented, excluded, or stereotypically portrayed. Shockingly, only 52% of marketers worldwide recall minority ethnicities being positively represented in their most recent campaigns, and just 15% of positive representation is for people with physical or mental disabilities (Daya & April, 2017). Despite this, numerous brands are undoubtedly benefiting from diverse and inclusive initiatives. As consumers worldwide look at brands in a much broader context, those that fall short of expectations or are associated with counterproductive exclusive acts face the danger of losing consumer appeal in comparison to their more inclusive peers, tarnishing their brand reputation (Burgess et al., 2023).

In today's ever-expanding digital landscape, brands must ensure that their marketing campaigns reach a wide audience (Demangeot et al. 2019). Utilizing digital tools to create diverse and inclusive campaigns is the best way to connect with target consumers. The concept of diversity, equity, and inclusion (DEI) has gained widespread acceptance in all aspects of society in the 21st century (Robner et al., 2021b). In digital marketing, this means developing campaigns that reflect the interests of a broad range of people who engage with a business. According to a 2018 Shutterstock survey, a significant number of Generation X and millennial consumers believe that a brand's reputation is enhanced when its campaigns include diverse representation.

Diversity ensures that a marketer invites everyone to the party. In other words, the message and offer are designed for a diverse target group. Equity can be interpreted as being fair to a brand's target market. Delivering offers through several channels will ensure that everyone has an equal opportunity to receive them. Although marketers generally understand this aspect of the DEI concept, there are still certain holes that need to be addressed (e.g., an elderly person who is not on Instagram or TikTok may never have the opportunity to learn more about the trendy Gen Z-focused offers on healthy food, yoga retreats, or online shopping experiences).

Diversity is crucial to ensure that marketers cater to a wide range of individuals. The message and offer should be designed to appeal to a diverse target group. Equity is about being fair to a brand's target market; by delivering offers through multiple channels, everyone has an equal opportunity to receive them. Although marketers generally understand this aspect of the DEI concept, there are still certain gaps that need to be addressed. For example, an elderly person who is not on popular social media platforms may miss out on trendy Gen Z-focused offers on healthy food, yoga retreats, or online shopping experiences.

The topic of diversity, equity, and inclusion (DEI) has been explored in consumer behaviour literature, with a focus on how factors such as stigma, procedural and distributive fairness, and market structure affect diverse and vulnerable customers (Arsel et al., 2022). Management studies, on the other hand, have looked at how DEI impacts the workforce (Johnson and Chichirau 2020) and customers (McKay et al., 2013), highlighting the importance of this issue for marketing. However, academic marketing literature has paid less attention to DEI, with no studies conducted thus far on the diversity of the digitalization context or the factors that influence it. To address this gap, this chapter aims to explore the role of digital marketing in promoting DEI, which is an increasingly significant societal issue that is closely tied to the marketing function.

3. DIVERSITY, EQUITY, AND INCLUSION IN MARKETING

Diversity, equity, and inclusion are important organizational frameworks that promote fair and equal treatment for all people, especially those who have historically been underrepresented or discriminated against based on their identity or disability (Johnson & Chichirau, 2020). Customer diversity is a fundamental aspect of this, highlighting the need to address the needs of marginalized and underrepresented populations Bernstein et al., 2020; Demangeot et al., 2013). Equity is about ensuring that everyone has an equal opportunity to succeed, without systemic inequalities holding them back. In marketing, DEI means creating campaigns that are inclusive, representative, and accessible to diverse audiences, celebrating the diversity of both the target audience and society as a whole (Daya & April, 2017).

Achieving equity is an imperative aspect of customer inclusion. Diversity, equity, and inclusion (DEI) are essential for ensuring that historically underrepresented, underprivileged, and marginalized market segments are equitably represented in a firm's customer base. The DEI framework is used by companies to institutionalize these three values, which are closely interlinked. While it is essential for change to begin at the highest levels, the field of marketing also has a vital role to play. Marketers are storytelling experts and can create conversations that express the beliefs, thoughts, and feelings of specific individuals, marginalized groups, and cultures (Chaudhry, 2023).

DEI in marketing is all about ensuring that content represents, welcomes, and elevates diverse identities. The ultimate objective is to create an environment where everyone feels accepted and capable of contributing, regardless of differences in gender, age, race, sexual orientation, economic and social status, and ability. It is recognizing the systems that have led to injustice and division and creating new ones that empower everyone to participate equally. According to a report by the American Marketing Association (AMA), DEI in marketing involves acknowledging and addressing the unique experiences and perspectives of different groups of people in the marketing industry. These groups may be based on race, ethnicity, gender, sexual orientation, age, ability, religion, and socioeconomic status. DEI also entails creating a workplace culture that is welcoming and inclusive of people from diverse backgrounds: this culture promotes equality and fairness in hiring, promotion, and compensation practices.

A burgeoning number of consumers rely on the values that a brand espouses to make their purchasing decisions. This is because they believe that the brands they choose to support are consistent with their values. Inclusive marketing efforts aim to integrate people from different backgrounds or narratives that unique audiences can relate to (Demangeot et al. 2019). Some inclusive marketing initiatives seek to dispel stereotypes, while others merely reflect or embrace people in the real world (Daya & April, 2017). By showcasing individuals or groups that may be under or misrepresented in ad campaigns, such as people of color, LGBTQ+ individuals, people who identify as members of particular religions, the disabled, or even people of a particular age or gender, marketers hope to challenge conventional thinking about advertising (Arsel et al., 2022). However, executing inclusive marketing effectively isn't always easy. Inclusive marketing initiatives highlight our many similarities, which necessitates a global perspective.

Consumers believe inclusive marketing is paramount as they reward brands that reflect their values, and the reality of the society they live in to ensure these views not only in marketing but also across the firm itself. Customers are genuinely embarking a step further and examining the organizational structure of businesses that purport to be committed to inclusion making sure that the board of directors, senior management, and other roles are also upholding similar ideals (Arsel et al., 2022). At its foundation, inclusive marketing is nothing revolutionary; it is neither a fad nor a trendy slogan. Marketers have recognized for years that using words and visuals that appeal to a specific group to reach them is indispensable. Give them what they want and know what they appreciate.

It's becoming increasingly clear that modern consumers are changing and evolving, not only in the way they shop and conduct research (Richard et al., 2017). Inclusive marketing is also becoming more prevalent as the global market continues to diversify and become more inclusive of various groups. By moving beyond preconceived notions of gender, age, ethnicity, income, sexual orientation, language, location, and religion, among other things, inclusive marketing aims to emphasize shared pain points and experiences to generate sales and attract a wider group of potential customers. Inclusive marketing challenges traditional ideas about a brand's customer base and how a product is used, allowing it to cast a wider net and include a demographic it may not have previously considered (Zhang, 2020).

3.1. Guidelines for Incorporating DEI Into Marketing

Deliberate efforts must be made to target extremely specific audiences and meet them where they will interact with brands, even though the term "DEI" suggests an umbrella covering a large audience (Bryan, 2020). There are numerous strategies to assist brands in starting to embrace diversity in an effective approach that has previously gone undetected and unappreciated. A company's social consciousness and willingness to integrate minorities and other groups of people who, in the past, were often not represented in advertising is becoming increasingly indispensable (Chaudhry, 2023). This is especially true when social media marketing on the internet is more fixated on targeting specific (and possibly sensitive) demographics like weight and marital status. Increasing visibility and representation is imperative for achieving higher conversion rates since it has an enormous effect on how prospective customers view a brand when deciding where to invest their money (Raggiotto et al., 2020). Here are some tips to help brands embrace DEI in their marketing practices:

- *Build a diverse team:* working with a varied team of marketers who represent the customers who make up the target demographic is essential for understanding the various nuances. Brands will be better able to offer content that connects rather than offends if there are more personnel with extensive target audience knowledge. Employing a team that accurately portrays the audience is the best technique to ensure that consumers see themselves represented in businesses (Richard et al. 2017). Brands require staff that can capitalize on their own life experience to create messages and imagery relevant to extremely niche demographics to connect with and understand what consumers want. Brands following will naturally diversify as consumers gravitate toward others who share their beliefs, perspectives, and appearance (Robner et al., 2021b). A diverse workforce will inevitably attract a diverse fan base, and a diverse fan base can provide brands with even more insights and suggestions to strengthen initiatives (Patel & Feng, 2021). In a global market where events might occasionally change in the blink of an eye, brands must develop resilience and agility. The more viewpoints a brand incorporates into its marketing strategy the more visibility it can achieve. Diversified teams benefit a company in many ways, not just in terms of consumer preference (Bryan, 2020).

- *Make data a* centerpiece: understanding the target segment intimately is one of the most crucial things a marketer can do to create a DEI marketing strategy. The secret to doing that is to gather as much data as possible and apply cutting-edge data analytics tools to derive insightful conclusions. Brands can leverage a variety of strategies to obtain the most accurate image but ought not to disregard what the data reflects. To develop a relatable marketing strategy, brands may utilize market research and data analytics to track positive, negative, and neutral responses to advertising and pinpoint marketing pitfalls. As social awareness evolves, the value of extensive market research only increases (Patel & Feng, 2021). Brands must develop pertinent marketing tactics to connect with consumers with specific beliefs and backgrounds, and the only way to do this is to analyze the data objectively and with an unbiased eye. Brand messages will be ineffective and possibly detrimental if surveys, focus groups, and field trials are not conducted with participants from various target markets (Johnson & Chichiran, 2020). For hyper-specific demographics, brands must go straight to the source to derive any useful information from the data being gathered (Raggiotto et al., 2020). Utilizing the marketing technology available nowadays, which automates processes and offers data insights that can be implemented in DEI marketing campaigns, pays off.

Surveying customers is another technique to clearly understand the variability among customers in addition to the data marketing and sales teams gather from them (Johnson & Chichiran, 2020). Building trust with customers requires direct engagement, whether it is through website surveys or social media conversations with the community (Richard et al. 2017). This information will aid the team in determining the kinds of visuals and marketing messages that will successfully reach target consumers, which is even more crucial for marketing strategy.

- *Prioritize intimacy with customers and let them have a voice: i*nvestment in the neighborhood is also strongly correlated with close customer intimacy. While getting to know customers is significant, brands should also consider the community around them. The only way for brands to change and build an inclusive atmosphere is through developing a deeper awareness of the beliefs, needs, and problems of the target audience and the local community (Johnson & Chichiran, 2020). Whether it be through time, tools, or training, marketers need to have a strong desire and willingness to interact more with their target audience in their natural environment to make sure that everyone on the marketing team has what they require to get acquainted with the audience they are serving intimately. Giving the target audience a say in the campaign is one of the finest methods to assure authenticity in a diversity marketing effort (Bryan, 2020). To ensure the success of a campaign, it is crucial to gather and consider customer feedback throughout the entire process - from planning to execution and even after. Allowing customers, the freedom to create content that accurately represents their relationship with the brand can be an effective strategy when possible. This not only serves as a compelling pitch that resonates with the target audience but also provides valuable real-world data that can be utilized for future campaigns.
- *Build from the ground up:* it's essential to avoid the common mistake of using a cut-and-paste approach when developing a cohesive brand message for different target groups in DEI marketing. Organic messaging that caters to the unique requirements, desires, and connection of each group with the brand is the way to go (Johnson & Chichiran, 2020). DEI marketing involves understanding and addressing various groups with content and advertising that resonates with them (Demangeot et al., 2019). Fortunately, there are several marketing software tools available that

allow businesses to segment their customers and create customized content or digital experiences for them.

- *Welcome contributions from underrepresented groups:* some audiences will feel forgotten by a brand's marketing when DEI is ignored, even if this was never the brand's purpose. When it comes to collaborating with individuals outside of your usual network, it's important to engage with content creators or influencers. This means partnering with freelancers and minority influencers from underrepresented and marginalized communities more frequently (Bryan, 2020). There are countless diverse cultures with endless untold stories that can make people feel valued and understood.
- *Understand the language of inclusivity:* knowing the target demographic is imperative when developing DEI marketing efforts, but it's also fundamental to develop messages that don't exclude others. To do that, brands must have a thorough awareness of how a campaign's language might unintentionally erect barriers or reinforce unconscious biases. Adopt inclusive language throughout each campaign to make it both target-specific and welcoming to others to prevent that. Perhaps more importantly, figure out how to craft a diversity statement to highlight the efforts the business is undertaking (Bryan, 2020). Review the previous emails, social media posts, and website content. What are the presumptions regarding both current and potential customers? Making individuals of marginalized communities feel noticed, included, and appreciated can be done simply by employing inclusive language.

To sum it up, Brands need to be genuinely authentic if they are to be regarded as authentic, and the truth is that marketers must do some soul-searching and reframe what diversity means from a thoroughly fundamental perspective (Raggiotto et al., 2020). The hiring process is where practices to become more genuine and inclusive begin. From there, they spread to the workplace and corporate standards, are squeezed out through branding, and are perceived by audiences through marketing and ad campaigns. The economic and social effects of the pandemic have only exacerbated the issues with race and gender income gap (Patel & Feng, 2021). Potential customers are becoming more and more conscious of the social issues that people from various beliefs, cultures, and nationalities are dealing with.

4. DEI IN DIGITAL MARKETING

The term "digital marketing" is a component of marketing that markets products and services leveraging the Internet and online-based digital technology like desktop computers, mobile phones, and other digital media and platforms (Denga & Rakshit, 2023). The way brands and businesses utilize technology for marketing has altered as a function of its development in the 1990s and 2000s. Digital marketing campaigns have proliferated due to the integration of digital platforms into marketing strategies and daily life, as well as the surge in the adoption of digital devices by consumers in place of physical stores. Digital marketing campaigns often involve a combination of different strategies, including search engine optimization (SEO), search engine marketing (SEM), data-driven marketing, e-commerce marketing, content marketing, influencer marketing, content automation, campaign marketing, social media marketing, and more (Crockett, 2017).

Although businesses frequently profess admirable objectives concerning diversity and inclusion, turning words into deeds, and investigating ways to transform narrative from a marketing exercise into something more cultural is pivotal. This entails incorporating diversity and inclusion principles into day-to-day goals and actions alongside digital marketing content (Bryan, 2020). To address this, some businesses create specialized task forces, while others incorporate diversity and inclusion into their mission statements and strategic goals. Others incorporate it into every aspect of their business operations, such as by forbidding contact with organizations that fail to uphold these values (Chandry, 2021).

More brands are participating in the conversation about DEI utilizing digital marketing by posting in recognition of Pride Month, Hispanic Heritage Month, or Black History Month (Crockett, 2017). Although being aware of these diversity holidays is a good start, firms must move beyond one-time declarations to demonstrate a genuine and sincere commitment to DEI. DEI should be incorporated into the long-term marketing strategy, without it, brands run the risk of being deemed performative or, worse, of alienating the same consumers they are attempting to engage (Burgess et al., 2023). Words matter (Bryan, 2020). Specifically, the tone and sensitivity brands display when it comes to matters of diversity and inclusion can position their organization as a welcome place for audiences of all types. However, when these issues are not addressed sensitively, they can lead to public relations nightmares — especially on social media, where an organization can suddenly find itself amid a crisis following a single errant post (Crockett, 2017).

The promotion of diversity and inclusion requires the critical contribution of digital marketers. This may entail expanding the demographics of the people shown in their advertisements or designing ads that are expressly directed at groups of people who may have previously been left out of mainstream advertising. A notable illustration of this is Microsoft's "We All Win" campaign (Zhang, 2020). It notably draws attention to the requirements of gamers with impairments, challenging preconceived notions about gamers. Small-budget businesses might start a discussion about whether their advertising accurately portrays contemporary culture or reinforces archaic stereotypes (Crockett, 2017). Advertising will undoubtedly appeal to more individuals if it is more diverse. The challenge for digital marketers is to develop communications that resonate with the target audience without offending or dismissing non-target audiences. Marketing must reach out beyond the core audience and embrace new potential customers.

If they are not aware of their own biases, digital marketers may find it challenging to produce diverse content. When striving for more inclusivity in advertising, it's crucial to first develop self-awareness. Moreover, it's essential to have a deeper understanding of brand advertising (Denga & Rakshit, 2023). What are the characteristics that make a brand meaningful to consumers? Identify traits that are universally shared by people, irrespective of their ethnicity, gender, ability, or any other differences. It's also important to think outside the box and explore new ways in which the brand might resonate with consumers of all demographics (Crockett, 2017). In digital marketplaces, it's common to respond to changes and ensure that communications are relevant and up to date (Nishii et al., 2018).

5. DEI IN DIGITAL MARKETING BEST PRACTICES

As marketers, brands can no longer choose to remain silent about the dearth of diversity as consumers, shareholders, employees, and other stakeholders expect brands to show up and exhibit inclusion. Brands can now influence diversity from any position, even though true diversity begins at the top and requires a long-term commitment. There is an enormous opportunity to inspire new audiences that might not have connected with specific brands, products, or services in the past as consumers are increasingly inclined to participate in communities and act as brand ambassadors. A recent survey indicated that 94% of consumers expect firms to take a stance on significant social issues when it comes to DEI and representation in marketing content (Nishii et al., 2018). Authentic and varied storytelling that accurately depicts modern reality can have an advantageous effect on meaningful connections and brand loyalty. The necessity to develop multiple narratives in short form is a responsibility that comes with this new era of digital marketing content creation — which is a task that many seem to find easier said than done.

According to Bernstein et al. (2020), companies that implement representation programs tend to see an increase in their stock value. This suggests that prioritizing the voices of diversity, equity, and inclusion (DEI) can have a positive impact on a brand's bottom line. Additionally, these companies are likely to attract a wider range of intersectional consumers, which can have measurable and beneficial effects. Consumers are continually exploring opportunities to make purchases that are consistent with their underlying values and beliefs, both consciously and unconsciously, based on the human-interest perspective. DEI digital marketing content enables organizations with a clear purpose to create dependable retention strategies and set themselves up for lasting consumer interactions that are consistent with those messages and values Bernstein et al., 2020). DEI initiative implementation is intricate and subtle. Making a difference through diverse content and putting in place the proper steppingstones, however, has an impact on numerous organizational aspects, both internal and external (Zhang, 2020). Here are three excellent techniques. The following are best practices for incorporating DEI into digital marketing initiatives:

- *Empower diverse decision-makers:* when formulating plans to represent and connect with audiences, due diligence is key, but it's essential to go deeper in terms of representation. In today's society, it's all too common for there to be a demand for digital marketing content that reflects a certain demographic that isn't represented on the leadership team. A significant contribution to fulfilling DEI creation goals can be made by elevating leaders who drive the discourse about initiative ideation and creative direction, as well as all aspects of campaigns, including promotions, publicity, and digital media assets (Leslie, 2019). By taking this action, businesses can effectively push engagement by moving beyond the terminology of allies and into that of accomplices. Decision-makers must continue to make suggestions and have influence that allows the right individuals to flourish and make incremental decisions to implement DEI digital marketing and storytelling.
- *Take nuance into account*: making DEI digital marketing content more diverse can be achieved by thinking beyond the binary of lived experience as well as beyond the present. This nuance can take a variety of forms. It shows that members of historically marginalized populations either collaborated during the creation of a piece of digital marketing content or were already a part of it. Consider the LGBTQIA+ community as an example while this population should be represented and taken into consideration all year long, many brands only think about it during Pride Month in June. Implementing pride initiatives year-round, for example, demonstrates that brands walk the talk by upholding their values consistently, as opposed to only paying attention to a trending hashtag or a particular period (Leslie, 2019). If an organization lacks the structural and policy infrastructure to support marginalized communities, it should not be advocating on their behalf (Zhang, 2020).
- *Diverse teams equal diverse marketing content:* to create engaging, diversified narrative or digital marketing content, it is imperative to have a diverse team working on it. Building internal reviews and concept development teams with as many diverse viewpoints and historically excluded voices as possible, in addition to hiring diverse teams when generating marketing content, can

aid brands in creating more inclusive work (Leslie, 2019). Hiring outside experts from nonprofit organizations or public interest groups can also help authentically advance more inclusive digital marketing messaging when it comes to the ideation and validation of creative initiatives (Nishii et al., 2018). Teams who are creating content frequently feel unprepared to address launches that include various communities and lived experiences in which they may not have a solid grounding. Recruiting creators and collaborators who can offer project assistance is indispensable. Brands can avoid the pitfalls of creating work that falls flat by utilizing wider networks to connect with real professionals who can create a stronger marketing campaign or narrative using the various digital tools and platforms (Bernstein et al., 2020).

6. DEI AS A KEY DIFFERENTIATOR IN MARKETING STRATEGY

In today's increasingly diverse and socially conscious marketplace, Diversity, Equity, and Inclusion have emerged as key differentiators in marketing strategy. Businesses that prioritize DEI in their marketing efforts not only foster a more inclusive society but also gain a competitive advantage. By embracing and showcasing diversity, promoting equity, and practicing inclusion, companies can build stronger connections with their target audience, differentiate themselves from competitors, and drive business growth (Leslie, 2019). DEI serves as a key differentiator in marketing strategy, amidst its significance and potential impact on brand reputation, customer loyalty, and market share. Finding the target audience and tailoring the offer to fit the audience's characteristics is the first step in the lifecycle of a marketing campaign. Identification of the target group has evolved (Nishii et al., 2018).

Recently, technology has made it possible for marketers to gather a vast amount of customer data. Marketers nowadays have access to a 360-degree view of the consumer attributable to marketing automation platforms, customer behavior tracking and analytics tools, and customer data platforms. Marketers now leverage innovative audience segmentation models with predictive capabilities based on artificial intelligence (AI) algorithms attributable to big data, new data processing and analysis approaches (Bernstein et al., 2020). AI goes as far as predicting future consumer purchase behaviors, thanks to browser cookies, mobile geo-location positioning, online browsing history, social media sharing, brand likes, and online shopping experiences. In essence, the idea of hyper-personalization allows marketers to offer personalized data and consumer experiences in real-time, wherever and at any time. Today's marketers are far more knowledgeable of the identities, lifestyles, activities, habits, and preferences of their target audience than the consumers are cognizant of themselves.

54% of consumers surveyed said they did not feel their culture was reflected in online advertising, according to research by the Geena Davis Centre on Gender in Media. Furthermore, 71% of customers anticipate that firms will emphasize diversity and inclusion in their online advertising (Nishii et al., 2018). The investigation demonstrates that there are still significant issues with the representation of what is called "minority" groups:

- Women are 6.9 times more likely to be objectified verbally or visually, and they are shown in revealing clothing 14.1 times more frequently.
- Males are 2.4 times more likely to display anger than they are to show happiness, a difference of 1.4 times.
- Only 1.1% of online advertisements studied include images of disabled individuals.

- Just 0.3% of web advertisements specifically targeted the LGBTQ+ community (let us not forget that this particular group has immense purchasing power).

These statistics unequivocally demonstrate the huge potential marketers have to tap into. In an automated world, brands can be human and allow target audiences to identify with their branding efforts. The argument is stronger now than ever! There is little doubt that online marketing with greater representation of various groups has higher recall rates: 90% of the ads with diversity strategies experience higher recall rates (Nishii et al., 2018). Here are some ways in which DEI can be a key differentiator in marketing strategy:

- *Targeting diverse audiences:* by incorporating DEI principles into marketing strategies, businesses can effectively reach and engage diverse consumer segments. This includes considering the specific needs, preferences, and cultural nuances of different groups. Such inclusivity can help companies expand their customer base and build brand loyalty among underrepresented communities.
- *Authenticity and brand reputation:* consumers are increasingly seeking authenticity and transparency from the brands they support. by demonstrating a genuine commitment to DEI, companies can enhance their brand reputation and establish trust with consumers. Authenticity is crucial in DEI efforts, and consumers can quickly recognize when companies engage in performative or superficial practices (Daya, 2014).
- *Differentiating from competitors:* in industries where competition is high, integrating DEI into marketing strategy can help a business stand out from competitors. By actively promoting diversity and inclusion and showcasing how these values are embedded in their brand, products, and services, companies can differentiate themselves in the market and attract customers who prioritize these values.
- *Attracting and retaining talent:* DEI is not only important to consumers but also to employees. Companies that prioritize diversity and inclusion tend to be more attractive to top talent. By incorporating DEI into marketing efforts, businesses can showcase their commitment to creating an inclusive work environment, which can help attract diverse talent and retain employees who value such principles (Bernstein et al., 2020).
- *Social impact and advocacy:* incorporating DEI into marketing strategy allows companies to position themselves as advocates for social change. By aligning their brand with important social issues and initiatives, businesses can show that they are invested in making a positive impact on society. This can generate positive PR, enhance brand reputation, and attract socially conscious consumers. It is important to note that incorporating DEI into marketing strategy requires a genuine commitment to change and not simply tokenistic gestures. Authenticity, inclusivity, and a long-term commitment to ongoing improvement are essential for successfully leveraging DEI as a key differentiator in marketing strategy (Daya, 2014).

7. BENEFITS OF DEI IN DIGITAL MARKETING

Diversity, equity, and inclusion (DEI) are fundamental principles that promote fairness, representation, and equal opportunities for all individuals, regardless of their backgrounds or characteristics. Digital marketing, which encompasses various online strategies and platforms, can play a significant role in advancing DEI initiatives. In today's diverse and interconnected world, businesses and organizations are increasingly recognizing the importance of DEI in various aspects of their operations. One area where DEI has significant benefits is marketing. DEI in marketing refers to strategies and practices that embrace diversity, ensure equity, and promote inclusivity in all marketing efforts. This approach has proven to be not only ethically sound but also highly advantageous for businesses (Leslie, 2019). Below are the key benefits of incorporating DEI principles into digital marketing strategies:

- *Reach a broader audience:* digital marketing enables organizations to reach a diverse range of audiences across different demographics, locations, and backgrounds. By leveraging digital channels such as social media, search engine optimization, and online advertising, companies can engage with individuals who might otherwise be inaccessible through traditional marketing methods (Daya, 2014). This broad reach helps in promoting inclusivity and ensuring that diverse voices are heard.
- *Targeted messaging:* digital marketing allows for precise targeting of specific audience segments. By leveraging data analytics and user insights, organizations can tailor their messages to resonate with diverse groups. This approach enables companies to create personalized and culturally relevant content that speaks directly to different communities, fostering a sense of inclusivity and representation.
- *Amplify underrepresented voices:* digital platforms provide an opportunity for underrepresented individuals and communities to amplify their voices and share their experiences. Social media, blogs, and online forums empower individuals to express their perspectives and engage in discussions around diversity, equity, and inclusion. Companies can actively support and collaborate with influencers, content creators, and thought leaders from diverse backgrounds to ensure their voices are heard and valued (Choi & Yang, 2021).
- *Showcase diversity in marketing campaigns:* digital marketing campaigns can showcase diversity by featuring people from different backgrounds, ethnicities, genders, and abilities. By consciously representing diverse individuals in advertisements, websites, and other promotional materials, organizations demonstrate their commitment to inclusivity and send a powerful message to their audience. This approach helps in challenging stereotypes, promotes acceptance, and inspires positive change (Zhang, 2020).
- *Gather and analyze data:* digital marketing provides robust data collection and analysis capabilities. By tracking user interactions, engagement metrics, and feedback, organizations can gain insights into the preferences and behaviors of diverse audience segments. This data-driven approach helps in identifying gaps, understanding challenges, and making informed decisions to improve DEI efforts (Leslie, 2019).
- *Collaborate with diverse influencers and partners:* digital marketing offers opportunities for collaborations with diverse influencers, content creators, and partner organizations. By partnering with individuals and organizations that champion diversity and equity, companies can tap into their networks and leverage their expertise to amplify their DEI messages and initiatives.
- *Continuous learning and improvement:* digital marketing allows organizations to engage in ongoing conversations and receive feedback from their audience. By actively listening to diverse perspectives and engaging in dialogue, companies can continuously learn, adapt, and improve their DEI strategies. Online surveys, social media listening tools, and community engagement

platforms facilitate this iterative process and foster an environment of continuous growth (Golom & Cruz, 2021).

- *Increased brand reputation and loyalty:* consumers today are increasingly conscious of brands' commitment to diversity and inclusivity. By showcasing their DEI efforts through digital marketing, organizations can enhance their brand reputation and attract loyal customers (Zhang, 2020). Consumers are more likely to support brands that align with their values and demonstrate a genuine commitment to diversity, equity, and inclusion.
- *Talent acquisition and retention:* digital marketing can support organizations in attracting and retaining diverse talent. By highlighting their inclusive workplace culture, diversity initiatives, and employee resource groups through online platforms, companies can attract a wider range of candidates and create a more diverse workforce (Golom & Cruz, 2021). This, in turn, fosters innovation, creativity, and different perspectives within the organization.
- *Education and awareness:* digital marketing can be used as a powerful tool to educate and raise awareness about diversity, equity, and inclusion. Organizations can leverage their digital platforms to share educational content, resources, and stories that promote understanding and empathy. By providing accessible information and fostering dialogue, digital marketing contributes to creating more inclusive and informed communities (Chandry, 2021).
- *Online accessibility:* digital marketing can enhance accessibility for individuals with disabilities. Organizations can optimize their websites, content, and online platforms to ensure they are compliant with accessibility standards, making it easier for people with disabilities to access information and engage with digital content. This commitment to accessibility aligns with the principles of inclusion and equal access for all individuals (Rust, 2020).
- *Social media activism and support:* social media platforms have become powerful tools for promoting social justice and advancing DEI causes. Through digital marketing on social media, organizations can support and amplify social justice movements, raise funds for charitable causes, and encourage community engagement (Chandry, 2021). This active participation in online activism demonstrates a commitment to diversity, equity, and inclusion beyond organizational boundaries.
- *Measurable impact and accountability:* digital marketing provides organizations with the ability to track and measure the impact of their DEI efforts. Through analytics and reporting tools, companies can monitor the effectiveness of their diversity-focused campaigns, initiatives, and strategies. This data-driven approach allows for ongoing evaluation, improvement, and accountability in promoting diversity and inclusion (Zhang, 2020).
- *Global reach and cultural exchange:* digital marketing transcends geographical boundaries, enabling organizations to engage with diverse audiences on a global scale. This presents an opportunity for cultural exchange and learning, fostering mutual understanding and appreciation for different perspectives and experiences. Digital marketing can facilitate cross-cultural dialogue, breaking down barriers and promoting a more inclusive global community (Chandry, 2021).

It is important to note that while digital marketing can be a powerful tool for promoting diversity, equity, and inclusion, it must be accompanied by genuine commitment, cultural competence, and inclusive practices within organizations. Combining digital marketing efforts with comprehensive DEI strategies can lead to more inclusive workplaces, diverse customer bases, and a positive societal impact (Bernstein et al., 2020). The year 2020 highlighted that tokenism, whitewashing, and one-size-fits-all marketing were no longer acceptable. Even while the necessity for underrepresented minorities to be exposed isn't about returns on investment, research from McKinsey demonstrates that brands with a more diverse workforce fare better financially than those that don't (Choi & Yang, 2021). When compared to their respective national industry medians, brands that rank in the top quartile for gender, racial, and ethnic diversity are approximately 35% more likely to experience profitability (Daya, 2014).

Businesses with diverse and inclusive personnel generate superior ideas, more genuine customer engagements, and greater financial gains. In turn, this enables a business to forge deeper connections with its customers and create a robust sense of brand identity. Inclusion is quickly evolving into a standard within advertising, and the value placed on varied and ethical messaging is beyond measure, with 62% of consumers rewarding brands that accurately portray real-world diversity (Rust, 2020). Ignoring the influence that marketers and advertisers have in promoting diversity and inclusivity would be shortsighted. For real-world change to occur, there must be continuous incremental representation in advertising. When comparing Google search data from January 2021 and January 2020, the industry observed an 18% surge in consumers searching for "diverse brands" in the previous year alone as people all around the world began actively searching for inclusive brands (Rust, 2020).

By leveraging the power of digital marketing, organizations can make significant strides in advancing diversity, equity, and inclusion. However, it is important to remember that digital marketing should be used as a complement to comprehensive DEI strategies and a commitment to creating inclusive environments both online and offline.

8. STRATEGIES TO INCORPORATE DEI IN DIGITAL MARKETING CAMPAIGNS

Sales and valuation, two critical business metrics, have been shown to benefit from DEI. In a 2019 survey, it was shown that 64% of participants acted after viewing a DEI advertisement culminating in an effect on the call to action (CTA). Additionally, including DEI in digital marketing initiatives improves consumer engagement; it is more than just a hyped-up jargon; it's a business approach (Choi &Yang, 2021).

DEI in digital marketing campaigns is not always easy to achieve, it requires a dedication to comprehending and embracing diverse points of view, as well as ongoing initiatives to make sure that marketing campaigns are inclusive and reflective of a variety of experiences. Incorporating diversity, equity, and inclusion (DEI) in digital marketing campaigns requires thoughtful planning and execution (Rust, 2020). Here are some strategies to consider when aiming to infuse DEI principles into your digital marketing efforts:

- *Create diverse and inclusive marketing content*: ensure that your digital marketing campaigns feature diverse representation in terms of race, ethnicity, gender, age, ability, and other relevant characteristics. Use images, videos, and testimonials that reflect the diversity of your target audience and society as a whole. Avoid tokenism and strive for authentic and meaningful representation. In the past years, marketers have made substantial attempts to support or change social issues such as encouraging racial, gender, and LGBTQ+ equality. Spending on DEI marketing activities that enhance brands and marketing communications is soaring by 8.8% One method to make a difference is to demand that the photography and imagery employed in digital marketing campaigns as well as internal communications be reflective of diverse types of employees and customers (Rust, 2020). According to Golom and Cruz (2021), marketing teams are increasingly relying on digital asset management (DAM) systems to locate photos and track their usage. This helps ensure that a more equitable representation is achieved in marketing contents.

- *Representation in imagery*: to truly integrate inclusion into brands, it's important to avoid relying on unreliable and exclusive messaging. Even if a brand uses all the right influencers and visuals, it can still lose credibility with its audience. Instead, brands must actively work to provide minority groups with a platform and challenge conventional messages. This is the key to mastering the art of inclusivity in branding. Marketing professionals can create a welcoming and targeted message and imagery that is more effective than using the same old brand messaging. Simply claiming to be transparent or diverse is no longer enough to win over customers. In industries such as technology, healthcare, and finance, creating an inclusive work environment is still a challenge, and this is often reflected in their marketing. However, using imagery solely for aesthetic purposes, such as using stock photos, is unlikely to be beneficial for a business. Customers will eventually see through this kind of façade. To connect with consumers, representational imagery must accurately reflect the target market.
- *Language usage*: when creating digital marketing campaigns, it's essential to be mindful of the language and terminology used. To ensure that brands' messaging is inclusive, they should avoid using exclusionary language, stereotypes, and assumptions. Instead, the usage of gender-neutral language and respect for diverse identities and experiences should be maintained. It's important to be considerate of different cultures and backgrounds to catch as many segments of a potential market as possible. A company that wants to build a solid marketing campaign should avoid sending signals that its products are not meant for a certain category. While such exclusionary signaling may work for a niche brand, the majority of products across the world cater to the masses (Kipnis et al., 2021). Hence, it becomes imperative to use the right words to create a loyal customer base. Adopting inclusive language that is "politically correct" and does not insult any members of the potential market is necessary for achieving DEI. Some strategies for utilizing inclusive language consist of employing words with no specific gender connotation (such as "Y'all," "friends," or "folks"), avoiding phrases having negative connotations, and keeping up with the vocabulary that young people are employing. One excellent illustration of inclusive marketing is the 1971 Coca-Cola advertisement, in which 65 people from all backgrounds sat on a hilltop and drank a refreshing beverage (Daya, 2014). Coca-Cola positioned itself as a company that championed DEI in the world through this advertisement.
- *Website accessibility:* ensure that digital marketing campaigns are accessible to people with disabilities. Optimize website and digital content to meet accessibility standards, including alt text for images, closed captions for videos, and proper heading structure. This enables individuals with disabilities to engage with content and participate in campaigns. The DEI pitch might be explored on a website that allows access to a diverse audience. The most effective way for businesses to demonstrate their concern for all of their potential consumers, including people with disabilities, is through their websites. In actuality, a website accessible is also a fantastic public relations exercise for any business seeking to increase the value of its brand (Choi & Yang, 2021). For businesses intending to expand their customer base, implementing the POUR (Perceivable, Operable, Understandable, Robust) approach for website accessibility is strongly advised. Besides being user-friendly, having an accessible website helps with search engine optimization (SEO). Maintaining a disabled-friendly interface assists businesses in avoiding legal snags as 15% of the world's population has some sort of disability, and numerous nations have strict internet acces-

sibility laws. People value seeing representations of various racial, ethnic, and socioeconomic groups in advertising in addition to seeing themselves reflected in it (Choi & Yang, 2021). From now on, marketing will be impacted by embracing consumer diversity, therefore firms must stay on the bleeding edge of advertising to show viewers how they are paving the way for awareness and inclusivity (Golom & Cruz, 2021).

- *Collaborate with diverse influencers*: partner with influencers and content creators from diverse backgrounds who have a genuine interest in an industry or product. Collaborating with influencers can help brands reach new audiences, tap into different communities, and amplify the DEI message. Prioritize long-term partnerships based on shared values rather than one-off collaborations (Rust, 2020).
- *Measure and analyze impact*: it's important to establish key performance indicators (KPIs) to measure the impact of DEI-focused digital marketing campaigns. Tracking metrics such as engagement, conversions, and sentiment analysis can help gauge the effectiveness of marketing initiatives. This data can then be used to refine strategies, make informed decisions, and continuously improve DEI efforts. (Kipnis et al., 2021).
- *Foster inclusive storytelling and engage in social listening*: tell compelling stories that reflect the diversity and lived experiences of your target audience. Incorporate narratives that highlight the challenges, triumphs, and aspirations of underrepresented communities. Use storytelling to foster empathy, break down stereotypes, and inspire positive change (Leslie, 2019). Consider sharing user-generated content that celebrates diversity and inclusion. Actively monitor social media and online platforms to listen to conversations around diversity, equity, and inclusion. Engage in meaningful dialogue with your audience, respond to their concerns, and address any feedback or questions. This demonstrates your commitment to inclusivity and creates opportunities for learning and improvement (Kipnis et al., 2021).
- *Internal alignment and collaboration with diverse organizations*: ensure that the organization's internal practices align with DEI-focused digital marketing campaigns. Foster an inclusive and diverse work environment, establish diverse hiring practices, and provide training and education on unconscious bias and cultural competence. When an organization embraces diversity and inclusion internally, it naturally reflects the brand's external marketing efforts. Remember that DEI in digital marketing is an ongoing process (Golom & Cruz, 2021). Regularly assess and update strategies to stay responsive to evolving societal needs and to ensure that digital marketing campaigns continue to foster diversity, equity, and inclusion. Forge partnerships with organizations and nonprofits that champion diversity, equity, and inclusion. Collaborate on joint initiatives, events, or social campaigns that align with the brands' values. This collaborative approach not only expands brands' reach but also showcases commitment to DEI and fosters positive change beyond marketing efforts (Robner et al., 2021a).

9. CONCLUSION

To successfully develop an ecosystem of diverse digital marketing campaigns and storytelling, it is important to examine both internal procedures and external failures. An intersectional marketing strategy accurately reflects the realities and truths of the modern world, creates a positive emotional connection with target audiences, and drives a financial advantage in differentiation strategies as opposed to approaching diversity from a clout-chasing perspective. It shouldn't be a hasty process to implement more varied digital marketing initiatives (Kipnis et al., 2021). The journey in front of and behind the content continually evolves, and brands are required to take the time to create a successful and relevant intersectional strategy. This journey keeps evolving and involves learning, doing, making mistakes, and recovering. In addition, it is fundamental to take proactive measures to address social inequities if brands want to attract consumers. Leveraging politically correct terminology and steering clear of any words with a pejorative connotation is imperative to appeal to a wider audience. Furthermore, it is integral to make use of the technologies already available to create digital marketing campaigns that cater to individuals of diverse genders, races, ethnicities, sexual orientations, and abilities and keep an eye on discussions on social media as well as handle any instances of prejudice or discrimination.

In the end, the expanding populations of various groups and future generations are demanding more. The fastest-growing companies are also closing the gap in culture and demographics between their team members and the target markets. Marketers may support their companies' transformation towards a more egalitarian, diverse, and inclusive organization in addition to helping them refine their messaging, which will give their brand messaging more credibility. To reach target markets, a varied and inclusive marketing campaign must make use of digital tools. DEI digital marketing campaigns may experience an increase in client preference, revenues, and stock gains. Representational images, online accessibility, and inclusive language are important strategies for achieving this goal. Brands must make sure to include a variety of ethnicities, genders, and cultures in their marketing approach, among other things. Businesses can aid in fostering greater understanding and respect between diverse groups by purposefully integrating DEI into marketing strategies.

REFERENCES

American Marketing Association. (2021). *Diversity, equity and inclusion in marketing*. AMA. https://www.ama.org/diversity-equity-and-inclusion-in-marketing/

Arsel, Z., Crockett, D., & Scott, M. L. (2022). Diversity, equity, and inclusion (DEI) in the Journal of Consumer Research: A curation and research agenda. *The Journal of Consumer Research*, *48*(5), 920–933. doi:10.1093/jcr/ucab057

Bennett, A. M., Hill, R. P., & Oleksiuk, D. (2013). The impact of disparate levels of marketplace inclusion on consumer–brand relationships. *Journal of Public Policy & Marketing*, *32*(Special Issue), 16–31. doi:10.1509/jppm.12.023

Bernstein, R. S., Bulger, M., Salipante, P., & Weisinger, J. Y. (2020). From diversity to inclusion to equity: A theory of generative interactions. *Journal of Business Ethics*, *167*(3), 395–410. doi:10.100710551-019-04180-1

Boyd, C. S., Ritch, E. L., Dodd, C. A., & McColl, J. (2020). Inclusive identities: Re-imaging the future of the retail brand? *International Journal of Retail & Distribution Management*, *48*(12), 1315–1335. doi:10.1108/IJRDM-12-2019-0392

Burgess, A., Wilkie, D. C. H., & Dolan, R. (2023). Brand approaches to diversity: A typology and research agenda. *European Journal of Marketing*, *57*(1), 60–88. doi:10.1108/EJM-09-2021-0696

Chaudhry, S. (2023). Measuring diversity, equity and inclusion: A holistic approach. *Development and Learning in Organizations*, *37*(2), 4–6. doi:10.1108/DLO-04-2022-0068

Choi, H., & Yang, J. (2021). Embracing diversity and inclusion in marketing: How firms can avoid backlash and gain support. *Journal of Business Research*, *129*, 151–161. doi:10.1016/j.jbusres.2021.02.005

Crockett, D. (2017). Paths to respectability: Consumption and stigma management in the contemporary Black middle class. *The Journal of Consumer Research*, *44*(3), 554–581. doi:10.1093/jcr/ucx049

Crockett, D. (2021). Racial oppression and racial projects in consumer markets: A racial formation theory approach. *The Journal of Consumer Research*, ucab050. doi:10.1093/jcr/ucab050

Daya, P. (2014). Diversity and inclusion in an emerging market context. *Equality, Diversity and Inclusion*, *33*(3), 293–308. doi:10.1108/EDI-10-2012-0087

Daya, P., & April, K. (2017). Practical Considerations for the Management of Diversity and Inclusion in an Emerging Market Context: A South African Case Study. In *Management and Diversity* (Vol. 3, pp. 191–225). Emerald Publishing Limited. doi:10.1108/S2051-233320160000003008

Demangeot, C., Kipnis, E., Pullig, C., Cross, S. N., Emontspool, J., Galalae, C., Grier, S. A., Rosenbaum, M. S., & Best, S. F. (2019). Constructing a bridge to multicultural marketplace well-being: A consumer-centred framework for marketer action. *Journal of Business Research*, *100*, 339–353. doi:10.1016/j.jbusres.2018.12.026

Denga, E. M., & Rakshit, S. (2023). Digital Marketing and the Sustainable Performance of Small and Medium Enterprises. In R. Potluri & N. Vajjhala (Eds.), *Advancing SMEs Toward E-Commerce Policies for Sustainability* (pp. 213–234). IGI Global. doi:10.4018/978-1-6684-5727-6.ch011

Golom, F. D., & Cruz, M. (2021). Context-levels-culture: A diagnostic framework for consulting to diversity, equity, and inclusion change in organizations. In Research in Organizational Change and Development (Vol. 29, pp. 201-234). Emerald Publishing Limited. doi:10.1108/S0897-301620210000029009

Johnson, M. P., & Chichirau, G. R. (2020). Diversity, equity, and inclusion in operations research and analytics: A research agenda for scholarship, practice, and service. *Pushing the boundaries: Frontiers in impactful OR/OM research*, 1-38.

Kipnis, E., Demangeot, C., Pullig, C., Cross, S. N., Cui, C. C., Galalae, C., Kearney, S., Licsandru, T. C., Mari, C., Ruiz, V. M., Swanepoel, S., Vorster, L., & Williams, J. D. (2021). Institutionalizing diversity-and-inclusion-engaged marketing for multicultural marketplace well-being. *Journal of Public Policy & Marketing*, *40*(2), 143–164. doi:10.1177/0743915620975415

Leslie, L. M. (2019). Diversity initiative effectiveness: A typological theory of unintended consequences. *Academy of Management Review*, *44*(3), 538–563. doi:10.5465/amr.2017.0087

Madera, J. M. (2013). Best practices in diversity management in customer service organizations: An investigation of top companies cited by Diversity Inc. *Cornell Hospitality Quarterly*, *54*(2), 124–135. doi:10.1177/1938965513475526

Nishii, L. H., Khattab, J., Shemla, M., & Paluch, R. M. (2018). A multi-level process model for understanding diversity practice effectiveness. *The Academy of Management Annals*, *12*(1), 37–82. doi:10.5465/annals.2016.0044

Patel, P. C., & Feng, C. (2021). LGBT workplace equality policy and customer satisfaction: The roles of marketing capability and demand instability. *Journal of Public Policy & Marketing*, *40*(1), 7–26. doi:10.1177/0743915620945259

Raggiotto, F., Scarpi, D., & Moretti, A. (2020). Advertising on the edge: Appeal effectiveness when advertising in extreme sports. *International Journal of Advertising*, *39*(5), 655–678. doi:10.1080/02650487.2019.1653009

Richard, O. C., Stewart, M. M., McKay, P. F., & Sackett, T. W. (2017). The impact of store-unit-community racial diversity congruence on store-unit sales performance. *Journal of Management*, *43*(7), 2386–2403. doi:10.1177/0149206315579511

Rößner, A., Gvili, Y., & Eisend, M. (2021). Explaining consumer responses to ethnic and religious minorities in advertising: The case of Israel and Germany. *Journal of Advertising*, *50*(4), 391–407. doi:10.1080/00913367.2021.1939201

Rößner, A., Kämmerer, M., & Eisend, M. (2017). Effects of ethnic advertising on consumers of minority and majority groups: The moderating effect of humour. *International Journal of Advertising*, *36*(1), 190–205. doi:10.1080/02650487.2016.1168907

Zhang, L. (2020). An institutional approach to gender diversity and firm performance. *Organization Science*, *31*(2), 245–534. doi:10.1287/orsc.2019.1297

ADDITIONAL READING

Cateriano-Arévalo, E., Alrakhayes, S., Foote, L., Hussain, T., Lai, K., & Nyundo, L. (2022). Social marketing at 50: Towards an epistemological expansion of the discipline to embrace diversity. A Viewpoint. *Journal of Social Marketing*, *12*(3), 315–336. doi:10.1108/JSOCM-09-2021-0223

Murray, J. A., O'Driscoll, A., & Torres, A. (2002). Discovering diversity in marketing practice. *European Journal of Marketing*, *36*(3), 373–390. doi:10.1108/03090560210417183

KEY TERMS AND DEFINITIONS

Digital Marketing: Digital marketing refers to the promotion of brands using various online and digital communication channels to reach out to potential customers.

Diversity: The act of including or involving individuals from a variety of different social and ethnic origins, as well as those with various genders and sexual orientations.

Equity: The attribute of being unbiased and fair.

Inclusion: The practice of giving those who might otherwise be excluded or marginalized equitable access to opportunities and resources.

Marketing: An activity, a group of organizations, and a system of procedures for developing, disseminating, delivering, and exchanging products and services that are valuable to clients, partners, and society as a whole.

Chapter 8
Activist Brands:
Exploring the Boundaries of Controversy

Fabio Shimabukuro Sandes
https://orcid.org/0000-0002-2349-7123
Universidade Lusófona, Portugal

ABSTRACT

Recent events triggered consumer outrage towards brands taking a stand on controversial matters. However, the response to low controversial topics marketing's definition of controversy requires an understanding of consumers' subjective perceptions shaped by cognitive processes, emotions, experiences, and cultural backgrounds. Subjectivity influences consumer behavior, while cognitive processing facilitates information comprehension. An experimental study using controversy level and brand presence as independent variables and consumer perceptions as dependent variables revealed that consumers associate branded content with irritation. A statistically significant interaction indicated that controversial topics are perceived as more disturbing with brand presence, while noncontroversial topics are more disturbing without a brand.

1. INTRODUCTION

The most recent definition of Marketing states that it's important for companies to consider "society at large" as a key stakeholder in their marketing efforts (AMA, 2022). Marketing should play a role in helping societies improve over time (Sarkar & Kotler, 2020; Sidibe, 2020). However, recent cases, such as Nike's Kaepernick campaign and Gillette's anti-toxic masculinity campaign, suggest that consumers may react negatively when a brand's values clash with their own (Kim et al., 2020; Vredenburg et al., 2020).

We might expect that discussing less controversial issues, like environmental concerns, would generate less disagreement and impact compared to more controversial topics, such as gender identity or LGBTQIA+ (Mukherjee & Althuizen, 2020). However, this difference isn't clearly addressed in the existing literature, which is what this study focuses on. The term "controversy" isn't well-defined in the literature, especially regarding its use in brand management (Mukherjee & Althuizen, 2020).

DOI: 10.4018/978-1-6684-8984-0.ch008

In this study, we start by briefly summarizing the main ideas behind brand activism and the varying levels of controversy. Then, we share the results of an experiment we conducted to see how different levels of controversy might affect how consumers perceive brands engaging in activism in the market. Our findings indicate that consumers often expect brands to take a stance on controversial issues. They view brands more positively when they actively participate in such topics. Additionally, a brand discussing non-controversial issues might influence consumers to ponder if the topic is indeed non-controversial. This study represents a partial exploration of the subject, acknowledging that there are numerous unexplored facets and diverse perspectives that merit further investigation and inclusion in this discourse.

2. LITERATURE REVIEW

Vredenburg et al. (2020) proposed a definition for brand activism that differentiates it from Cause Marketing, Corporate Social Marketing, and Advocacy Advertising - similar and earlier versions of classification for brands addressing societal issues – specifically because in Brand Activism, brands choose to take a stand and speak up their brand voices on controversial topics (such as racism, gender equality, LGBTQIA+, among others), generating a mix of different reactions amongst consumers (Mukherjee & Althuizen, 2020). In the framework proposed by Vredenburg et al. (2020), consumers' responses may vary from delight to outrage, depending on how these values are intertwined.

Looking deeper into this definition, we see two points that need further exploration to be better understood in marketing literature. One is the definition of controversial and how scholars can address this concept when analyzing and discussing brand activism (Aaker et al. (2004). The second point to address is if there is a way to measure – or at least consider – different levels of controversy (Mukherjee & Althuizen, 2020). Topics may be too much or too little controversial, and these differences may lead to different outcomes for brands that take a stand related to these matters (Vredenburg et al, 2020).

2.1. The Definition of Controversy

Defining what is controversy is a complex task, as it entails different perspectives. One common perception of controversy is that it is defined by the hegemonic ideology (Camicia, 2008) as they would help define the norms in which consumers – and people – live. As we are discussing from a marketing perspective, it is important to include consumers' perception of controversy, as they are the ones we are interested in understanding if and how much one topic may be controversial. We are adopting, thus, a subjective understanding, interpretation, and evaluation perspective that individuals have regarding issues that elicit diverse and often conflicting perspectives, opinions, and emotions. It refers to how consumers perceive, process, and make sense of controversial subjects based on their beliefs, values, attitudes, experiences, and sociocultural context (Gupta & Gould, 1997; Jennings et al., 2015; Treise et al., 1994).

We first need to consider the **subjectivity** of consumers' perceptions, influenced by their unique cognitive processes, emotions, and personal experiences. It varies from person to person and may be shaped by their perspectives and biases (Hornik, 1984). One controversial topic is, thus, related to consumers' subjective beliefs and norms. One study that addressed how subjectivity influences consumer behavior was conducted by Alsaad (2021). The author found evidence to support the hypothesis that consumers act according to their subjective norms when there is a strong ethical identification. One example from the market that we can use to illustrate this hypothesis is the "Share a Coke" campaign, where Coca-

Cola printed different popular names in their cans of Coke and Diet Coke, prompting consumers to buy the product when they found their names on a can of Coke (for more information, please read Vincent & Kolade, 2019).

How consumers process the messages is also relevant when discussing the subjective perception of controversy, as consumers need to process the information to understand and interpret the message (Megehee, 2009). Their **cognitive process of a message** is thus important to include in the discussion of consumers' perception of a controversy. On that matter, Kitchen et al. (2014) proposed an intricate model to understand consumers' elaboration of messages. Creating catchy phrases, songs, and sounds is used by marketers as a resource to ease consumers' cognition and elaboration processes. One global example is McDonald's "I am loving it" campaign (for more information, please read Graakjær, 2019).

Consumers' emotional response is also one relevant topic to include in the discussion, as controversial topics often evoke strong emotions in consumers (e.g. Krishna, 2012). These emotions, such as anger, fear, empathy, or excitement, can influence how individuals perceive and evaluate the topic, shaping their attitudes and behavioral responses. This is a broad topic that has been extensively discussed in the literature. Schindler et al. (2017) extensively reviewed aesthetic consumption, including emotions, and proposed a tool to measure aesthetic emotion. Nike's "Dream Crazier" campaign uses emotion to connect with consumers and improve their relationship with the brand (for more information, please read Hoffmann et al., 2020).

Consumers' underlying **values, beliefs, and cultural backgrounds** significantly shape their perception of controversial topics. These factors can act as filters through which information is processed, and judgments are made. Hassan et al. (2022) conducted an extensive literature review on how ethics influence consumer behavior, showing that cultural values play a decisive role in consumers' perception of any marketing tactics and actions and, therefore, maybe a part of the discussion of consumers' perception of a controversy. The Body Shop is an established beauty brand that, since its entrance to the market, has focused on its position against animal testing in the Cosmetics and Beauty Industry, appealing to consumers' ethical and moral values.

Social interactions and group dynamics can influence **consumers' perceptions of controversial topics**. Social norms, peer pressure, and conformity can impact how individuals perceive and align themselves with certain viewpoints or positions. Several studies have addressed how peer pressure influences consumer behavior (e.g., Johnstone & Hopper, 2016; Huang et al., 2012), and it is also expected to influence consumers' perception of a controversial topic.

When considering the definition of consumers' perspective of controversy, it is essential to include consumers' subjectivity, cultural norms, cognitive processing, peer influence, and their values, beliefs, and cultural backgrounds (Mukherjee & Althuizen, 2020; Aaker et al., 2004), as they likely impact the way consumers perceive, process, and signify the messages they receive.

2.2. Range of Topics That May be Controversial in the Marketing Arena

When discussing contentious subjects within the marketing field, a wide range of potential topics emerges that can be deemed controversial. We have meticulously chosen eight distinct topics to explore, accompanied by real-world marketing examples that exemplify how brands adeptly navigate through these intricate waters.

1. Ethical Considerations: A crucial aspect involves delving into the ethical implications associated with marketing practices, encompassing deceptive advertising, data privacy concerns, targeting vulnerable populations, and promoting potentially harmful products or services. Brands must carefully address advertising to children and substance-dependent consumers, as well as privacy matters and marketing products or services that could potentially harm consumers. An example that sparked substantial debate is Spotify's "Embrace People's Weirdness" campaign, which humorously exposed peculiar user behaviors on their platform. This campaign incited discussions regarding how companies may exploit user data as valuable assets.
2. Social Responsibility: Another pivotal area to explore is how companies tackle social and environmental issues. This encompasses their commitment to sustainability, diversity and inclusion, labor practices, and corporate social responsibility initiatives. An exemplary illustration of a brand demonstrating social impact is TOMS Shoes' "One for One" campaign, wherein they pledged to donate shoes to a child in need for every pair purchased, exemplifying their dedication to effecting positive change in society.
3. Cultural Sensitivity: Respecting diverse cultures and avoiding cultural appropriation, stereotyping, or offensive representations in marketing campaigns is paramount. Nike's "Juntas Imparables" campaign serves as an enlightening example, successfully portraying Mexican and Latin American cultures while expressing support for women's rights. This video resonated with the target audience by capturing the essence of their cultural identity.
4. Gender and Sexuality: Examining how marketing perpetuates or challenges gender norms, stereotypes, and heteronormativity is crucial to the controversy. Brands must address issues of inclusivity, representation, and LGBTQ+ rights in their advertising campaigns. Diesel's "Francesca" campaign provides an intriguing case study, showcasing the gender transition journey of a trans woman, including her religious transformation as she ultimately becomes a nun.
5. Body Image and Beauty Standards: Exploring the impact of marketing on body image and self-esteem, including the portrayal of unrealistic beauty standards and the promotion of unhealthy practices, requires careful examination. Dove's "Real Beauty" campaign offers a fresh perspective on how the advertising industry often fosters women's insecurities about their bodies. By promoting a more authentic perception of beauty, Dove aims to empower and inspire consumers.
6. Political and Social Activism: Analyzing the role of brands in supporting or engaging with political and social movements necessitates a comprehensive evaluation. The potential risks, benefits, and authenticity of brands taking a stance on controversial issues must be considered. Airbnb's "We Accept" campaign exemplifies how a brand responds to immigration policies while promoting inclusivity by featuring diverse individuals. This campaign raised awareness and emphasized the importance of acceptance in society.
7. Greenwashing and Sustainability Claims: Thoroughly discussing the potential for misleading or exaggerated environmental claims by companies and the significance of authentic sustainability efforts is essential. H&M's "Conscious Collection" campaign, highlighting its endeavors to promote sustainable fashion through organic cotton and recycled materials, faced criticism for potentially stimulating an increase in clothing consumption. In response, H&M launched the "Bring It On" campaign, reaffirming its commitment to collecting all used products in its stores and responsibly recycling them.
8. Targeting Children and Vulnerable Populations: Scrutinizing the ethical concerns associated with marketing to children encompasses examining manipulative techniques, unhealthy food market-

ing, and the potential impact on their well-being. McDonald's "Happy Meal" campaigns, featuring healthier menu options and educational initiatives that promote exercise and nutrition for children, exemplify how brands can proactively address these concerns and contribute to positive change.

The marketing arena presents a myriad of controversial topics that warrant careful consideration. The selected examples offer valuable insights into how brands effectively navigate these complex issues. By thoroughly exploring these areas, marketers can understand the intricate dynamics involved, enabling them to make informed decisions that align with ethical values and societal expectations.

Does it mean brands must always address controversial items to be considered activists? Brands must be cautious when affirming their values in all the topics society is interested in, or is it specific to controversial matters? This question is especially important in a context where Generation Z has become the largest one in society. One of their main characteristics is expecting brands to act positively toward constructing a better world (Spitznagel, 2020). This research aims to answer questions like "How does a brand know if they can enter into the discussion of a specific matter?" and "What makes consumers perceive a brand as authentic when taking a stand in specific matters?".

In this work, we discuss if brand authenticity and image are affected by the presence of activism in a brand campaign on highly controversial and low-controversial topics. We selected these constructs as they are most connected to brand activism discussion in the literature.

2.3. Brand Authenticity

Brand authenticity is a vastly discussed topic in the literature (Key et al., 2021; Sibai et al., 2021; Södergren, 2021) and may offer a valid lens for this discussion. Brand authenticity refers to the genuineness, transparency, and credibility a brand exhibits in its interactions with consumers and stakeholders (Key et al., 2021). It refers to the alignment between a brand's identity, values, and actions, creating a sense of trust and reliability among its consumers. Authenticity is especially relevant in a competitive marketplace (Södergren, 2021), where consumers increasingly seek meaningful connections and experiences with the brands they support. It goes beyond surface-level marketing tactics and extends to the core of a brand's purpose, culture, and relationships. An authentic brand stays true to its essence, consistently delivering on its promises and remaining loyal to its values, even in the face of challenges or changing market trends.

Some elements contribute to brand authenticity: Purpose and Values (Södergren, 2021, Vredenburg et al, 2020). An authentic brand has a clear sense of purpose and operates according to a set of core values that guide its decisions and actions. This purpose goes beyond profit-making and reflects a genuine commitment to positively impacting society or the lives of its customers. In other words, a brand must invest in showcasing its values in the topics they choose to support, and they need to be consistent with how they position itself in the market. One of the greatest examples we can find in the market is Patagonia (Michael et al., 2019). Their values are in the core communication strategy they offer to the market. To be sustainable is a key value at the center of all marketing and communication strategies Patagonia offers to its customer base and the market at large.

Another element that is essential to be seen as authentic is consistency (Södergren, 2021). Consistency builds trust and reinforces the brand's identity in the minds of consumers, and it also helps shapes consumers' expectations (Hernandez-Fernandez & Lewis, 2019). To be consistent means delivering a consistent brand experience across all touchpoints, including messaging, visuals, customer service, and product quality. Apple is one of the most consistent brands in the marketplace, as its product lines, communication, and marketing strategy are aligned and behave in an expected matter. The experience of owning an Apple product is the same, regardless of the product you use. They are all integrated into one system, consistent with their services, in-store experience, and communication strategy.

To be an authentic brand, it is mandatory to be transparent in its communications and operations. Brands must be open and honest about their processes, ingredients, sourcing, and any other relevant information consumers may value. Transparency builds trust and fosters a sense of credibility and reliability (Hernandez-Fernandez & Lewis, 2019), especially if consumers are experts in finding information about the brands in the online environment. Any noise they find in the communication process reverberates quickly in social media. ISTO, a Portuguese brand, is the first 100% transparent brand. They expose all their costs to produce and distribute their products, including sensitive information such as the name and contacts of their supplier and the profit margin they operate in the distribution channels.

Authentic brands prioritize their customers' needs and strive to create meaningful connections. They actively listen to customer feedback, engage in open dialogue, and continuously improve their products or services based on customer insights. Authentic brands aim to build strong and lasting relationships by putting the customer at the center. Amazon is known in the market (H Oh et al., 2019). They operate as a customer-centered brand, offering excellent levels of consumer service and constantly innovating in providing different formats of service and customer experience.

Storytelling is one of the key elements that brands use to build and foster authenticity. Creating stories where their values are intertwined with their personality is a valuable tool to be perceived as authentic by their customers. They ought to find ways to create and communicate a compelling story that resonates with their audience (Hong et al., 2022). They effectively communicate their brand narrative, origins, and values, allowing consumers to connect emotionally. Storytelling helps create an authentic brand identity and fosters a sense of shared values and experiences. Nike uses their tagline – Just Do It – as a connector of different stories they tell in their Marketing and Communication strategies. It began in 1984 when they first released the tagline to the market in an advertisement where a 75 years-old man talks about their running routine, showing a just-do-it attitude.

While consistency is crucial, authentic brands also understand the importance of evolving and adapting to changing market dynamics and consumer preferences. They stay true to their core values but are willing to embrace innovation, respond to feedback, and improve their offerings to remain relevant. Levi's is one example of such adaptability. Their Marketing and Communication strategies adapt to the demand of the youth generation of more than 100 years old. Their main product, 501®, has been in the market since 1890, with hundreds of different commercials and campaigns adapted to the youth market's needs.

To be authentic, brands need to establish a unique and genuine relationship with their customers. Consumers are more likely to trust, support, and advocate for authentic brands because they perceive them as reliable, credible, and aligned with their values. Authenticity is essential to resonate with an activist campaign.

3. METHODOLOGY

We conducted a study employing a 2 (brand x no brand) x 2 (controversial high x low controversial) design, where participants were randomly assigned to different scenarios. Our objective was to manipulate high controversy by using gender equality and gender issues as the topic of manipulation in the study.

This commercial explicitly expresses Gillette's stance against toxic masculinity, which generated significant consumer backlash. In the brand-high controversy condition, we utilized Gillette's "The Best a man can be" commercial (https://bit.ly/exp1Brand) as the brand-related stimulus. On the other hand, in the high controversy, no brand condition, we employed the commercial for the #PowerlessQueen movement (https://bit.ly/expNoBrand). This commercial juxtaposes the game of Chess, where the Queen holds significant power, with the unfortunate reality that women in India lack power, facing discrimination and limited access to education and independent careers. The message conveyed is that society suffers when women lack power.

We focused on sustainable and socially responsible production issues for the low controversial scenarios. In the brand condition, we presented H&M's "Bring It On" commercial (https://bit.ly/explowcontrov), encouraging consumers to return their used items for reutilization, reducing their environmental impact. As for the no-brand condition, we showcased the "2 Euro T-shirt" commercial (https://bit.ly/expnoncontrov2), emphasizing that consumers, aware of the unethical production practices behind cheap clothing, opt not to purchase them. The duration of each commercial ranged from 93 to 118 seconds, and participants were randomly assigned to one of the conditions, watching one of the commercials at the beginning of the experiment. Participants were asked to provide their perceptions of brands before and after watching the video, including the brands featured in the experiment. Additionally, to account for potential covariates, participants responded to scales assessing ecological behavior, gender issues, and regulatory focus.

4. RESULTS AND DISCUSSION

We collected 192 responses. Seven needed to be completed, four did not pass the attention check, and we had 181 valid responses. Respondents were mainly women (67.4%), the mean age was 22, and 91.7% were from the Gen Z generation (166 respondents from 18-26). This is since we recruited respondents from undergraduate courses, resulting in a sample predominantly composed of Gen Z consumers with an average age of around 21 years. It is important to highlight that these consumers are recognized for their critical perspective on the role of brands in society (Rue, 2018), often expecting brands to take a stance on relevant social issues.

A two-way ANOVA was conducted to analyze the main effects of brand presence and topic nature, as well as the interaction effect between these variables on participants' ratings of "it bothers people." The results demonstrated a statistically significant interaction effect ($p < 0.001$) between consumers' perceptions of controversy and brand involvement. In the No Brand condition, participants rated the noncontroversial topic moderately bothersome ($M = 4.7$). However, in the Brand condition, participants rated the same noncontroversial topic as significantly more bothersome, indicating a higher perceived level of controversy.

The observed statistically significant interaction effect between consumers' perception of controversy and brand involvement suggests that a brand's presence significantly influences the degree to which a noncontroversial topic is perceived as controversial. The finding that participants in the Brand condition rated the noncontroversial topic as significantly more bothersome highlights the power of brand presence in altering consumers' perception of the topic's controversial nature.

This outcome could be attributed to several factors. First, the association of a brand with a particular topic might trigger pre-existing beliefs or attitudes held by consumers, leading to a heightened perception of controversy. Second, the presence of a well-established brand may increase the salience and credibility of the message, making consumers more receptive to perceiving the topic as controversial. Additionally, including brand elements in the commercial might elicit emotional responses that further contribute to perceiving the topic as more bothersome. These nuanced responses shed light on the intricate dynamics between brand presence, consumer perceptions, and the perceived controversy of the presented topic, suggesting a rich area for future research and exploration.

These findings hold significant practical implications for marketers and advertisers, emphasizing the critical importance of thoughtfully considering the potential outcomes of associating a brand with sensitive or noncontroversial topics. Marketers should recognize that brand presence can profoundly influence consumers' perceptions of controversy, subsequently impacting their attitudes, behaviors, and evaluations of the brand. Responsible and ethical branding practices should prioritize alignment with consumers' expectations and values.

The results from our study suggest that brands should actively engage in controversial matters, and the degree of alignment with the discussed topic significantly affects consumers' perception of brand authenticity. Utilizing ANOVA to analyze the data, we identified a statistically significant interaction between brand presence and controversial subjects ($F=8.18$, $p=0.005$) when participants were queried about their opinions regarding brands taking a stance on controversial matters and their perception of the discomfort experienced by consumers ($F=18.75$, $p<0.001$).

However, this interaction did not reach statistical significance when participants were informed that their perception of brands improved after taking a stand ($F=0.21$, $p=0.65$). Intriguingly, respondents displayed an overall improved perception of brands across all scenarios when the brands took a stand on the respective issues. This finding suggests a preference among consumers for brands that actively participate in controversial topics.

The interaction between brand presence and controversial topics significantly influenced the dependent variable associated with the level of disturbance experienced by consumers ($F(1,181)= 18.75$, $p<0.001$). This indicates that when a brand is present, controversial topics tend to be perceived as more disturbing, while noncontroversial topics are considered more disturbing in the absence of a brand. Thus, a brand's presence may lead consumers to view controversial subjects as more unsettling. Furthermore, the results indicate that participants perceived that brands should involve themselves in controversial scenarios ($F=5.56$, $p=0.019$), rating brands higher in the noncontroversial scenarios.

These findings offer valuable insights and suggest pathways for further research. Future studies should delve into the specific conditions under which brands should take a stand, further exploring the factors influencing consumer perceptions of brand authenticity in controversial contexts. By gaining a deeper understanding of these dynamics, marketers can make well-informed decisions regarding their brand's involvement in societal debates, ensuring alignment with consumer expectations and enhancing brand-consumer relationships.

5. CONCLUSION

The main focus was understanding how brand presence and topic nature influence consumer perceptions of controversy. A significant interaction effect ($p < 0.001$) was found, indicating that a brand's presence alters how consumers perceive a topic's controversy. This is possibly attributed to triggering pre-existing beliefs, enhancing credibility, and evoking emotions through brand association, revealing a rich area for further research. Practically, this underscores the need for responsible branding practices aligning with consumer values.

This study suggests that brands should engage with controversial matters, impacting brand authenticity perception. The analysis revealed a preference for brands actively involved in controversial topics. Moreover, the interaction between brand presence and controversial topics significantly influenced perceived disturbance by consumers. Controversial topics were seen as more disturbing in the presence of a brand. Participants favored brands engaging in controversial scenarios, reflecting evolving consumer expectations.

5.1. Limitations and Discussions for Future Research

This study was conducted exclusively with Generation Z consumers, which may be a limitation that generalizes other generations of consumers as a complex and risky task. If this study were replicated with consumers from different generations, the results would be more interesting and compelling.

For future research, we suggest further investigating a more in-depth perspective on consumer attitudes and perceptions towards brands that stance their positions in the market, trying to understand the underlying mechanisms that explain different outcomes brands may expect from consumers. Future studies must investigate the effectiveness of different approaches brands can employ when addressing controversial matters, considering factors such as messaging styles, tonalities, and creative executions. Another potential topic to explore is the role of brand authenticity in navigating controversial topics, as consumers seek genuine and credible brand involvement. However, the way these concepts interact needs to be clarified in the literature. By examining these interconnected areas, brand managers and marketing scholars can gain insights into authentically connecting with consumers while effectively navigating the complexities of controversial issues.

REFERENCES

Aaker, J., Fournier, S., & Brasel, S. A. (2004). When good brands do bad. *The Journal of Consumer Research*, *31*(1), 1–16. doi:10.1086/383419

Alsaad, A. K. (2021). Ethical judgment, subjective norms, and ethical consumption: The moderating role of moral certainty. *Journal of Retailing and Consumer Services*, *59*, 102380. doi:10.1016/j.jretconser.2020.102380

Camicia, S. P. (2008). Deciding what is a controversial issue: A case study of social studies curriculum controversy. *Theory and Research in Social Education*, *36*(4), 298–316. doi:10.1080/00933104.2008.10473378

Faircloth, J. B., Capella, L. M., & Alford, B. L. (2001). The Effect of Brand Attitude and Brand Image on Brand Equity. *Journal of Marketing Theory and Practice*, *9*(3), 61–75. doi:10.1080/10696679.2001.11501897

Graakjær, N. J. (2019). Sounding out i'm lovin'it–a multimodal discourse analysis of the sonic logo in commercials for McDonald's 2003–2018. *Critical Discourse Studies*, *16*(5), 569–582. doi:10.1080/17405904.2019.1624184

Gupta, P. B., & Gould, S. J. (1997). Consumers' perceptions of the ethics and acceptability of product placements in movies: Product category and individual differences. *Journal of Current Issues and Research in Advertising*, *19*(1), 37–50. doi:10.1080/10641734.1997.10505056

Hassan, S. M., Rahman, Z., & Paul, J. (2022). Consumer ethics: A review and research agenda. *Psychology and Marketing*, *39*(1), 111–130.

Hernandez-Fernandez, A., & Lewis, M. C. (2019). Brand authenticity leads to perceived value and brand trust. *European Journal of Management and Business Economics*, *28*(3), 222–238. doi:10.1108/EJMBE-10-2017-0027

Hoffmann, J., Nyborg, K., Averhoff, C., & Olesen, S. (2020). The contingency of corporate political advocacy: Nike's 'dream crazy' campaign with Colin Kaepernick. *Public Relations Inquiry*, *9*(2), 155–175. doi:10.1177/2046147X20920802

Hong, J., Yang, J., Wooldridge, B. R., & Bhappu, A. D. (2022). Sharing consumers' brand storytelling: Influence of consumers' storytelling on brand attitude via emotions and cognitions. *Journal of Product and Brand Management*, *31*(2), 265–278. doi:10.1108/JPBM-07-2019-2485

Hornik, J. (1984). Subjective vs. objective time measures: A note on the perception of time in consumer behavior. *The Journal of Consumer Research*, *11*(1), 615–618. doi:10.1086/208998

Huang, Y., Wang, L., & Shi, J. (2012). How attachment affects the strength of peer influence on adolescent consumer behavior. *Psychology and Marketing*, *29*(8), 558–567. doi:10.1002/mar.20543

Jennings, P. L., Mitchell, M. S., & Hannah, S. T. (2015). The moral self: A review and integration of the literature. *Journal of Organizational Behavior*, *36*(S1), S104–S168. doi:10.1002/job.1919

Johnstone, M. L., & Hooper, S. (2016). Social influence and green consumption behavior: A need for greater government involvement. *Journal of Marketing Management*, *32*(9–10), 827–855. doi:10.1080/0267257X.2016.1189955

Key, T. M., Keel, A. L., Czaplewski, A. J., & Olson, E. M. (2021). Brand activism change agents: Strategic storytelling for impact and authenticity. *Journal of Strategic Marketing*, 1–17. doi:10.1080/0965254X.2021.1904435

Kim, J. K., Overton, H., Bhalla, N., & Li, J. Y. (2020). Nike, Colin Kaepernick, and the politicization of sports: Examining perceived organizational motives and public responses. *Public Relations Review*, *46*(2), 101856. doi:10.1016/j.pubrev.2019.101856

Kitchen, J. P., Kerr, G. E., Schultz, D., McColl, R., & Pals, H. (2014). The elaboration likelihood model: Review, critique, and research agenda. *European Journal of Marketing*, *48*(11/12), 2033–2050. doi:10.1108/EJM-12-2011-0776

Krishna, A. (2012). An integrative review of sensory marketing: Engaging the senses to affect perception, judgment and behavior. *Journal of Consumer Psychology*, *22*(3), 332–351. doi:10.1016/j.jcps.2011.08.003

Megehee, C. M. (2009). Advertising time expansion, compression, and cognitive processing influences on consumer acceptance of message and brand. *Journal of Business Research*, *62*(4), 420–431. doi:10.1016/j.jbusres.2008.01.019

Michel, G. M., Feori, M., Damhorst, M. L., Lee, Y. A., & Niehm, L. S. (2019). Stories we wear: Promoting sustainability practices with the case of Patagonia. *Family and Consumer Sciences Research Journal*, *48*(2), 165–180. doi:10.1111/fcsr.12340

Mukherjee, S., & Althuizen, N. (2020). Brand activism: Does courting controversy help or hurt a brand? *International Journal of Research in Marketing*, *37*(4), 772–788. doi:10.1016/j.ijresmar.2020.02.008

Oh, H., Prado, P. H. M., Korelo, J. C., & Frizzo, F. (2019). The effect of brand authenticity on consumer–brand relationships. *Journal of Product and Brand Management*, *28*(2), 231–241. doi:10.1108/JPBM-09-2017-1567

Ramesh, K., Saha, R., Goswami, S., Sekar, & Dahiya, R. (2019). Consumer's response to CSR activities: Mediating role of brand image and attitude. *Corporate Social Responsibility and Environmental Management*, *26*(2), 377–387. doi:10.1002/csr.1689

Rue, P. (2018). Make way, millennials; here comes Gen Z. *About Campus: Enriching the Student Learning Experience*, *23*(3), 5–12. doi:10.1177/1086482218804251

Sarkar, C., & Kotler, P. (2020). *Brand activism: From purpose to action*. Idea Bite Press.

Schindler, I., Hosoya, G., Menninghaus, W., Beermann, U., Wagner, V., Eid, M., & Scherer, K. R. (2017). Measuring aesthetic emotions: A review of the literature and a new assessment tool. *PLoS One*, *12*(6), e0178899. doi:10.1371/journal.pone.0178899 PMID:28582467

Sibai, O., Mimoun, L., & Boukis, A. (2021). Authenticating brand activism: Negotiating the boundaries of free speech to make a change. *Psychology and Marketing*, *38*(10), 1651–1669. doi:10.1002/mar.21477

Sidibe, M. (2020). Marketing Meets Mission. *Harvard Business Review*. https://hbr.org/2020/05/marketing-meets-mission

Södergren, J. (2021). Brand authenticity: 25 Years of research. *International Journal of Consumer Studies*, *45*(4), 645–663. doi:10.1111/ijcs.12651

Spitznagel, E. (2020, January 25). Generation Z is bigger than millennials, and they are out to change the world. *NYpost.com*. https://nypost.com/2020/01/25/generation-z-is-bigger-than-millennials-and-theyre-out-to-change-the-world/

Treise, D., Weigold, M. F., Conna, J., & Garrison, H. (1994). Ethics in advertising: Ideological correlates of consumer perceptions. *Journal of Advertising*, *23*(3), 59–69. doi:10.1080/00913367.1994.10673450

Vincent, E., & Kolade, A. (2019). Persuasive communication: Semiotic analysis of "Share-a-Coke" advertising campaign. *World Journal of Innovative Research*, *7*(2), 1–6.

Vredenburg, J., Kapitan, S., Spry, A., & Kemper, J. A. (2020). Brands Taking a Stand: Authentic Brand Activism or Woke Washing? *Journal of Public Policy & Marketing*, *39*(4), 444–460. doi:10.1177/0743915620947359

Chapter 9

Perceived Organizational Support – Effectuating Digital Marketing Communication and Facilitating Sustainable Development Goals 3, 8 and 16:

An Integrative Literature Review

Deeba Hasan
https://orcid.org/0000-0001-9583-2536
Indian Institute of Technology, Madras, India

T. J. Kamalanabhan
Indian Institute of Technology, Madras, India

ABSTRACT

Rapidly proliferating organizational digital marketing communications (DMC) can adversely affect employees and, in turn, organizational success. Past research indicates that perceived organizational support (POS) engenders employee attitudinal and behavioral outcomes that warrant organizational success. However, studies evaluating the effects of POS on DMC employees are lacking. This study conducted an integrative literature review on POS to increase understanding related to it, determine how POS leads to DMC success, and facilitate organizational contribution towards SDGs 3, 8, and 16. Sixty-three papers were reviewed to conduct a qualitative thematic template analysis that identified significant themes of POS. The psychology of reciprocity was determined to engender DMC success. The mechanisms through which POS facilitates SDGs 3, 8, and 16 were illustrated. A conceptual framework is proposed delineating the pathway from POS to outcomes, including enablers, barriers, mediators, moderators, and boundary conditions. Future studies could identify more factors operating in this pathway.

DOI: 10.4018/978-1-6684-8984-0.ch009

1. INTRODUCTION

Digital marketing communication (DMC) is a fast-growing practice in marketing. It has received the attention of practitioners and scholars alike by dint of exhibiting important outcomes positively associated with organizational marketing goals. The benefits comprise rapid information gains, enhanced organizational productivity, knowledge expansion, quicker outcome measurements and feedback (Tiago & Veríssimo, 2014). DMC is formally defined as any communication between businesses and consumers that is accomplished via digital or electronic media (Shankar et al., 2022). Recent years have witnessed a remarkable increase in organizations' DMC activities. The Statista Research Department (SRD, 2023) has estimated global digital advertising expenses in 2021 to have clocked 522.5 billion U.S. dollars. This is forecasted to escalate to 836 billion dollars by 2026. Global spending on social media advertising in 2021 cost an estimated 116 billion U.S. dollars (SRD, 2023). It is estimated that this figure would reach record levels of 262 billion by 2028. These figures bear testimony to the rapid expansion of DMC endeavors of organizations.

Nonetheless, when extolling the virtues of digital marketing activities, one should not overlook the fact that these activities are touched by a *"dark side"* (Tarafdar et al., 2014). Prior research informs us that whenever there has been an unrestrained and invasive exposure to digital technologies, employees have suffered from adverse physical and mental consequences like technostress, burnout, job dissatisfaction, turnover intentions (Fuglseth & Sørebø, 2014), role ambiguities and role conflicts (Tarafdar et al., 2014). Sadly, this dark side of DMC, wherein it takes its toll on the employees that perpetuate it, is often brushed away in scholarly discourse. When delineating the determinants of success of an organization's DMC, the dimension that most often tends to be overlooked is the humane one. This is ironical because strategies, resources, and innovations notwithstanding, it is the human resource that forms the mainstay of an organization's functioning. A marketing strategy no matter how good, can only be as good as the employees responsible for operationalizing it. Furthermore, employees form salient points of contacts between organizations and customers via engagement in customer services and complaints resolutions. Hence, their contribution in eliciting organizational DMC success cannot be ignored. It is incumbent on organizations to recognize employees' contribution and support them in the face of unique job challenges. Marketing employees are especially vulnerable to experiencing job-stress (Tarafdar et al., 2014). This is on account of the diverse professional roles they are expected to play in servicing multiple groups, and the unnatural expectations held of them to grapple IS as well as interpersonal relationships with equal ease. Increasingly permeable work-family boundaries and changing market dynamics compound the problem and mark a predisposition for them to suffer from role-conflicts and role-ambiguities. This impacts sales adversely (Tarafdar et al., 2014). Besides, employees engaged in DMC (henceforth referred to as DMC employees) face the added burden of being constantly exposed to technology, and consequent technostress with subdimensions of techno-overload, techno-insecurity, techno-invasion, techno-uncertainty, and techno-complexity (Ragunathan et al., 2008). Against these complex contexts, it is imperative that organizations cultivate HR and offer them support. Importantly, this support should be 'perceived' by employees in a positive light.

Perceived organizational support (POS) is a popular concept in organizational and psychology literature. It refers to the generalized beliefs that employees develop about the extent of their organization's concern for them and how it values their contribution (Eisenberger et al., 1986). In forming such beliefs, employees anthropomorphize the organization and attempt to reciprocate its level of concern. High POS leads to a felt obligation amongst employees to requite with equal effort on their parts, thus facilitating organizational goal achievement. There has been a significant rise in interest in POS in industrial organizational and psychology research as witnessed by a one thousand percent growth in published literature on POS in Scopus and Web of Science from its first conceptualization in 1986 to January 2023 (Hasan & Kamalanabhan, 2023). The reason behind the rise in popularity of POS is its evidence-based linkages with important attitudinal and behavioral employee outcomes like organizational citizenship behavior (Wayne et al., 2002), commitment (McBey et al., 2017), knowledge sharing (Imamoglu et al., 2022), enhanced job-performance (Eisenberger et al., 2001) and reduced turnover intentions (Edwards & Peccei, 2010). Interestingly, POS can help employees gain significant psychological benefits even when organizations cannot compensate for exhaustive workloads and elevated levels of stress (Prysmakova & Lallatin, 2021). Based on these findings, we expect that DMC employees would be apt to particularly benefit from POS.

Surprisingly, a review of literature reveals that despite POS's popularity in other streams like industrial and organizational psychology, marketing literature has paid little attention to it. Specifically, research evaluating the effects of POS on DMC employees is sadly lacking. This is a cause for concern since DMC employees' predilection for adverse job consequences has been established by past studies. Organizations need to understand that what influences the success of digital communication the most is the attitude and behavior of its own employees. This study argues that, for successful DMC, organizations first and foremost need to ensure the growth and wellbeing of their employees by offering them POS; effectively, organizations should first look 'within' before looking 'without'. Doing so will not only ensure DMC success but will also contribute towards UN Sustainable development goal (SDG) 3, which is ensuring healthy life and wellbeing, SDG 8, which is promoting decent work and economic growth, and SDG 16 which is building effective institutions.

The research objectives of the study are:

- *Research Objective 1 - Provide a comprehensive understanding of the POS construct through analysis and synthesis of the findings of the integrative review.*
- *Research Objective 2 - Demonstrate how POS helps in determining the success of organizational DMC.*
- *Research Objective 3 - Provide a conceptual framework illustrating the pathway from POS-to-POS outcomes delineating the operant internal and external forces in the pathway.*
- *Research Objective 4 - Demonstrate how POS facilitates organizational contribution towards United Nations SDG 3, SDG 8 and SDG 16.*

The article is structured in the following manner: the next section provides a review of relevant literature. This is followed by the methodology used to conduct the integrative review. Analysis, results, and discussion follow. The article concludes with theoretical and practical implications, limitations, and future research directions.

2. LITERATURE REVIEW

POS as an organizational construct was formally defined as "employee beliefs concerning the extent to which the organization values their contribution and cares about their well-being" (Eisenberger at al., 1986, p. 501). Their work drew heavily from the social exchange theory and described how POS extended to employees is construed by them in a manner that confers human-like characteristics to the organization. Employees develop perceptions about how much their organization 'cares' about them and their contributions. These perceptions go on to influence employee attitudes and determination to 'repay' their organization, again anthropomorphizing it. These interesting revelations and the significant organizational benefits accruing from the exchange ideology created a stir in academic circles and the construct has since been tested under varying contexts and outcomes. POS has consistently demonstrated a spectrum of organizationally beneficial employee-outcomes such as improved in-role (Eisenberger et al., 2001) and extra-role performance (Shanock & Eisenberger, 2006), reduced turnover (Wang & Wang, 2020), affective commitment (Kim et al., 2016) organizational citizenship behavior (Bhatti et al., 2022), creativity (Tang et al., 2017) and innovation (Eisenberger et al., 1990). Rhoades and Eisenberger's meta-analysis (2002) demonstrated the antecedents of POS to be organizational rewards, favorable conditions, and supervisor fairness. These, through POS, lead to job satisfaction, commitment, performance, and continuance intentions. These findings were supported by Wayne et al. (2002) and Kurtessis et al. (2017) who found organizational support theory to successfully predict the antecedents and consequences of POS. Tang et al. (2017) found a positive relationship between high performance work systems and POS that increases employee creativity.

Most research have utilized the organizational support (OS) theory as their overarching framework, which itself is based on the social exchange theory. This idea of exchange plays an instrumental role in employee reciprocation efforts to help the organization attain its objectives. Some concerns, however, have been raised about this *"idée fixe"* of POS being a single-directional, or individual level construct. Zagenczyk et al. (2010) criticized the OS theory for focusing on 'individual level' psychological explanations of outcomes. They claimed that this bounded perspective restricted the theory's predictive power. Matusik et al. (2022) argued that organizational support can take various forms. They offered the Teleological, Personalized, Collectivistic, and Monistic Organizational Support (PCMT) model where organizational support could take four different approaches: teleological, personalized, collectivistic, and monistic. Each approach was defined by whether it was targeted at the individual or the group, and whether motivated by organizational self-interest or not. Employee interpretation of POS was found to be strongest when the support was personalized. The PCMT model thus, gave a nuanced depth to POS that was lacking earlier. Organizations thus, need to understand that different interpretations can be given to support and should take care to fashion it in a manner that invokes positive interpretations. Some inconsistencies have also been observed in literature regarding POS's association with gender, job-tenure, and job-satisfaction. Riggle et al. (2009) found only a moderate association between POS and job-performance. Suthatorn and Charoensukmongkol (2022) demonstrated that experienced and passionate employees needed lesser POS to achieve organizational identification. Gender has also exhibited contrasting associations with POS. Thompson et al. (2020) claimed that men needed more POS than women to elicit the same amounts of felt obligation. This was believed to be on account of women feeling obligated to their organizations even at lesser POS levels. These findings, however, were not replicated by Foley et al. (2005) who found no association between gender and POS. Also, POS effects logically will be more pronounced in employees with a strong exchange ideology (Eisenberger et al., 1986). What is the effect on those with weaker ideologies remains unanswered. The present review aims to uncover such open questions and inconsistencies and attempts to unearth the reasons therein. The findings suggest that there are operant boundary conditions that determine the differential POS effects. Specific boundary conditions are offered that would potentially explain the differences in support perceptions at the individual and larger levels of analysis. These are explained in upcoming sections.

3. METHODOLOGY

3.1. Study Design

The integrative literature review design was used as it was determined to be most suitable for the purposes of this study. This study aimed to synthesize the state of extant research on POS and determine the ways in which it contributes to the success of organizational DMC. A conceptual framework was also intended that would illustrate the pathway from POS to POS-outcomes delineating the operant internal and external forces. For these purposes, it was required to integrate concepts from information science, industrial organizational psychology, and marketing literatures. An integrative review design offers the advantage of spanning multiple disciplines and consolidating the strength of scientific evidence. It also establishes core issues in a field and identifies conceptual frameworks (Russell, 2005).

3.2. Review Methods

Russell's (2005) five stage process for conducting integrative reviews was followed. It comprised (1) Problem formulation, (2) Search for relevant literature (3) Data evaluation (4) Data analysis, and (5) Presentation of main findings.

1. **Problem Formulation and Justification**

These have been covered in the Introduction section.

2. **Search for Relevant Literature**

The search was conducted in the following databases: EBSCO Business, Springer, Scopus, Web of Science, Taylor & Francis online, Emerald Insight, APA, Science Direct and Google Scholar. These databases were selected because they index high-quality and peer-reviewed contemporary research articles.

The keywords were *"perceived organizational support" and "perceived organizational support AND marketing"*. The Boolean operator 'AND' was incorporated to make the results precise and relevant to context.

3. **Study Selection Process**

An initial search of the identified databases generated 408571 results. Later, sequential steps were followed to select the final sample of primary studies (PS). This incorporated first reading the titles, then abstracts, followed by introductions and conclusions, and finally, full texts of articles. The articles were then subjected to quality evaluation that resulted in 63 PS being selected for review. The search was conducted between1986 when POS was first conceptualized to March 2023. Table 1 depicts the databases, search term(s) number of initial search results, and sequential steps followed to select final PS.

4. **Data Evaluation**

Data was evaluated on the following inclusion criteria:

Table 1. Databases, search term(s) number of initial search results, and sequential steps followed to select final PS

	Database	Search term(s)	n = number of results in initial search
I.	APA	Perceived organizational support	90
		Perceived organizational support AND marketing	3
	Web of Science	Perceived organizational support	7177
		Perceived organizational support AND marketing	560
	SCOPUS	Perceived organizational support	9026
		Perceived organizational support AND marketing	177
	Taylor & Francis	Perceived organizational support	75567
		Perceived organizational support AND marketing	58836
	Springer	Perceived organizational support	13300
		Perceived organizational support AND marketing	11532
	Science Direct	Perceived organizational support	54770
		Perceived organizational support AND marketing	28832
	Emerald Insight	Perceived organizational support	81000
		Perceived organizational support AND marketing	66000
	EBSCO Business Source	Perceived organizational support	1570
		Perceived organizational support AND marketing	126
	Articles identified from Google Scholar		5
	Total = 408571		
I.	Articles retained after reading titles		903
II.	Articles retained after reading Abstracts		273
III.	Articles retained after reading Introductions and Conclusions		104
IV.	Articles retained after reading full texts		90
V.	Articles retained after application of quality criteria		63
Total sample of Primary Studies = 63			

a. Peer-reviewed: All articles should be peer-reviewed.
b. English: All articles should be accessible in English.
c. Temporal criteria: Articles from 1986 to March 2023 were included making this review both comprehensive and contemporary.
d. Discipline: The search was limited to business, management, accounting, and industry disciplines.
e. Quality: The selected databases ensure article quality. Articles were further subjected to authors' quality criteria for relevance, methodology, answers to research questions, discussion, and interpretation.
f. Complete text should be available.

Any article that did not meet these criteria was excluded from analysis.

5. Data Analysis

Data analysis is the step that carries the highest risk of bias, yet it is, perhaps the least developed facet of the integrative review process. To increase the rigor of the study and reduce the risk of bias, guidelines provided by Whittemore and Knafl (2005) were followed. These consist of data reduction, display, comparison, conclusion drawing, and verification.

a. Data reduction

Data was extracted from PS and categorized in bibliographic information, author(s), journals, databases, publication year, type of study (qualitative/quantitative), sample size, context, country of research, findings, theoretical framework, scope, future directions, and number of citations. This was fitted in a study-characteristics table. At the end of this stage, each study was reduced to a single page, as recommended by Whittemore and Knafl (2005).

b. Data display

The extracted data was further categorized in sub-groups and a visual display was created. Visualizing the categories made it easier to contrast and identify patterns between categories.

c. Data comparison

This step comprised of comparing data across categories. The visual display helped identify patterns, relationships, departures from routine, and outliers. This was the starting point of theme building. At this stage theme-building was an iterative process subject to changes. Relationships among themes were analyzed.

d. Conclusion drawing

This phase marked the end of the iterative theme-building process. Themes were isolated based on clear relationships with sub-themes and a lack of overlapping dimensions. It was ensured that as much of data was extracted as possible in the creation of themes. Departures from normal patterns represented literature gaps.

e. Verification

Final themes and interpretive conclusions were brought back and checked against PS that provided the initial data for thematic analysis to corroborate the accuracy of data.

6. Presentation of Main Findings

The final step of data analysis consisted of integrating all information and presenting a novel conceptualization.

4. FINDINGS AND DISCUSSION

This section presents the main findings and implications of the review process. It provides answers to the four research objectives of the study.

4.1. Research Objective One: Understanding POS

Detailed findings on the contemporary state of research on POS makes it possible to gain a comprehensive understanding of the construct.

4.1.1. Growth in Publications

POS has garnered marked scholarly interest as evinced by more than a 1000 percent growth rate in the number of publications in Scopus and Web of Science databases from 1986, when the construct was first conceptualized to January 2023 (Hasan & Kamalanabhan, 2023). This interest accrues from evidence-based organizational benefits of POS outcomes. POS leads to positive employee outcomes that help organizations attain their objectives. The mechanism through which this happens is explained later.

4.1.2. Theoretical Frameworks

Theories used to explain POS can be segregated into four major categories. The first category is the social-exchange category. This includes the majority of studies and comprises of employer-employees social reciprocations, support, roles and cognitions that take place following POS. The second category is the matching of job with rewards/ resources/ conditions. This includes conditions where employees compare services offered with recompense received. This is also a kind of exchange, but it does not lead to an obligation amongst employees to repay organizations. It is, in a sense, more a 'balancing of scales' where a judgement is made whether efforts and recompense are equally balanced. The third category is based on individual traits and characteristics. These differ from person to person and include traits like self-concept, self-determination, and self-leadership. The individual self is an important construct to be kept in mind when analyzing POS effects. Employees' self-beliefs and exchange ideologies determine, to a large extent, the interpretation and consequences of POS. Table 2 depicts the categorization of theoretical frameworks used to study POS.

4.1.3. Professions Studied for POS Effects

Diverse population samples have been used to study POS ranging from hotel employees to healthcare and police personnel. However, it is noteworthy that marketing employees have seldom been used as study samples. Only DeConinck et al. (2018), Piercy et al. (2006) and Maan et al. (2020) have studied sales personnel in the context of POS. This denotes a significant gap in marketing research that needs to be bridged by more studies on marketing personnel to help identify their unique concerns. Table 3 represents the different professions in the PS sample that have been studied for POS effects.

Table 2. Categorization of theoretical frameworks used to study POS

Social Exchanges	Job vs Rewards/ Conditions Matching	Individual Characteristics	Role of the Leader
OS theory	Optimal matching theory	PsyCap theory	Leadership theory
Social exchange theory	Herzberg's Motivation-hygiene theory	Learning development goal orientation	Servant leadership
Reciprocation norms	Effort-reward imbalance	Self-construal	Gender role socialization
Social support theory	Job-demands-resources	Self-leadership	Disparity research
Social role theory	Job-demands-control-support	Self-determination	
Contagion effect	Leader-member exchange	Collectivism/ Individualism	
Trust repair	Conservation of resources	Creativity	
	Work-family theory	Workplace deviance	
	Boundary theory	Ethical ideology	
	Stakeholder theory	Moral development	

Source: *Authors.*

Table 3. Professions studied for POS effects

Professions	Reference
Healthcare personnel	Edwards and Peccei (2010), Zou et al. (2021), Ilyas et al. (2022)
Postal services personnel	Eisenberger et al. (2001)
Metal fabrication workers	Wayne et al. (2002)
Flight attendants	Suthatorn and Charoensukmongkol (2022)
Hotel employees	Akgunduz et al. (2018), Karatepe (2015), Lee (2021)
Bank officers and managers	Poon et al. (2007), Bhatti et al. (2022)
Police officers	Adebayo (2005)
Teachers	Imamoglu et al. (2022)
Manufacturing plant employees	Hofmann and Morgeson (1999)
Pesticide chemical farmers	Tang et al. (2017)
Salaried workers in private and government sectors	Lee (2021)
Managers	Webber et al. (2012)
Military personnel	Russell et al. (2022)
Fast food firm employees	Vandenberghe et al. (2007)
Community mental health centre	Pullen et al. (2023)
Salespersons	Piercy et al. (2006)
Manufacturing & Service sector employees	Maan et al. (2020)
Car dealers	Wang et al. (2011)
Gas-station employees	Wang and Wang (2020)
Protestant clergy	Foley et al. (2005)
Business-to-business-salespeople	DeConinck et al. (2018)
Transgenders and non-binaries	Cancela et al. (2022)

Source: *Authors.*

4.1.4. Differences in POS Perspective in East and West

Though there is a generalized scarcity of muti-cultural and cross-cultural studies to compare the effects of POS across nations and cultures, a few studies have attempted this. Malaeb et al. (2022) studied the effects of POS across two nations: UAE and Lebanon. They found that POS enhanced self-leadership in UAE but not in Lebanon, indicating that differences in nationality and culture may play a role in determining POS impacts. Rockstuhl et al. (2020) found differences between Eastern and Western nations in the way employees associate with POS. They found that in Western nations, POS was associated with social exchange processes whereas in Eastern nations POS was associated with organizational identification. These differences were attributed to the East having a vertical-collectivistic culture as opposed to the West which has a horizontal-individualistic culture.

A template analysis depicting the themes and sub-themes generated from the review is presented.

Template Analysis

1). Theoretical frameworks
- 1.1 Social exchanges
- 1.2 Job vs conditions matching
- 1.3 Individual characteristics
- 1.4 Role of leader

2). Contexts
- 2.1 Social context
- 2.1.1 Shaping employee POS
- 2.2.2 Social comparisons
- 2.2.3 Socio-emotional resources
- 2.2 Administrative context
- 2.2.1 Admin
- 2.2.2 Voluntary/ non-profit
- 2.3 Self
- 2.3.1 Self-efficacy
- 2.3.2 Self-leadership
- 2.3.3 Propensity to trust
- 2.3.4 Personal resources
- 2.3.5 Prosocial behavior
- 2.3.6 Self-enhancement
- 2.3.7 Depressive symptoms
- 2.4 Customer context
- 2.4.1 Service quality
- 2.4.2 Needs' knowledge
- 2.5 Employee perceptions
- 2.5.1 POS inference
- 2.5.2 Perceived org. competence
- 2.5.3 Perceived philanthropy
- 2.5.4 Trust in top management

2.6 Work relationships
2.6.1 Supervisor support
2.6.2 Co-workers' support
2.6.3 Ethical leadership
2.6.4 Servant leadership
2.7 Ethics
2.7.1 Unethical attitude
2.7.2 Deviant behavior
2.7.3 Ethical climate
2.7.4 Ethical leadership
2.7.5 Questionable actions
2.7.6 Unethical behavior
2.7.7 Organizational CSR
2.8 Safety
2.8.1 Psychological safety
2.8.2 Safety communications
2.9 Theoretical arguments
2.10 Boundary conditions
2.11 Racial disparity
2.12 Mental health

3). POS Enablers
3.1 Devolved management
3.2 CSR towards employees
3.3 High performance work systems
3.4 Developmental experiences
3.5 Task flexibility
3.6 Communication
3.7 CSR towards employees
3.8 Leadership
3. 9 Rewards
3.10 Employee voice
3.11 Org. philanthropy
3.12 Health and safety
3.13 HR practices
3.14 Social support

4). POS barriers
4.1 Role-conflict
4.2 Role-ambiguity
4.3 Perceived inequity in POS
4.4 Perceived upwards social comparison

5). Mediators
5.1 Affective commitment
5.2 PsyCap
5.3 Perceived ethical CSR

5.4 Customer needs knowledge
5.5 Personal resources
5.6 Overcommitment
5.7 Org. competence
5.8 Occupational stress
5.9 Work calling
5.10 Effort-reward ratio
5.11 Positive mood
5.12 Subjective wellbeing

6). Moderators
6.1 Devolved management
6.2 POS from unit
6.3 Job type
6.4 Psychological entitlement
6.5 Self-construal
6.6 Burnout
6.7 Nationality
6.8 Collectivism
6.9 Experience and passion for work
6.10 Embeddedness
6.11 Perceived org. competence
6.12 Self-identity

7). Differences in POS perspective between the East and the West
7.1 East-Vertical - collectivistic culture
7.2 West-Horizontal - individualistic culture

4.2. Research Objective Two: How Does POS Lead to DMC Success?

Based on an exhaustive analysis of published research, it is submitted that the underlying mechanism through which POS leads to organizational DMC success is through the psychological norm of reciprocity, where employees exchange hard work, commitment and other organizationally beneficial attributes and behaviors in exchange for support, recognition, and rewards.

Like any other organizational endeavor, DMC success depends on positive employee behaviors and attitudes. This section explains the specific ways in which POS engenders attitudinal and behavioral employee outcomes that ensure DMC success.

4.2.1. Employee Outcomes That Lead to DMC Success

4.2.1.1. Affective Organizational Commitment

Several studies demonstrate significant positive associations between POS and affective organizational commitment (AOC) (Eisenberger et al., 1986, 2001; Sumardjo & Supriadi, 2023). Prysmakova and Lallatin (2021) found that POS is particularly helpful in inducing employee commitment when organizations cannot compensate for high workloads and high stress levels by other means. Wang (2022) showed that

POS is positively associated with AOC, which enhances employee performance and creativity. These positive associations suggest a serial benefit for organizations. McBey et al. (2017) claimed that self-expression mediates between POS and AOC. Zagenczyk et al. (2021) found that perceived ethical climate of the organization moderates between POS and AOC. Bhatti et al. (2022) claimed that POS and AOC are sequential mediators between employee-directed CSR and organizational citizenship.

4.2.1.2. Organizational Citizenship Behavior

Van Knippenberg et al. (2015) demonstrated a positive relationship between POS and organizational citizenship behavior (OCB). This relationship was found to be moderated by collectivism. Stinglhamber et al. (2020) found that focal-employee's POS is positively related to co-workers' POS. This relationship is stronger when the focal employee had a low voice. Piercy et al. (2006) demonstrated that POS is strongly related to salespersons' OCB. Moreover, sales manager control on OCB was greater when channeled through POS, rather than directly.

4.2.1.3. Creativity

Multiple studies have found a positive relationship between POS and employee creativity. Choi et al. (2018) found that POS is positively related to creativity. They indicated that the effects are greater in employees with higher learning development goal orientation. Duan et al. (2020) showed that 'calling' for a profession and POS led to heightened creativity. Tang et al. (2017) found high-performance work systems to enhance POS which increases creativity.

4.2.1.4. Job-Satisfaction

Poon et al. (2007) and Riggle et al. (2009) found a strong positive relationship between POS and job-satisfaction. Maan et al. (2020) concurred that POS increases job-satisfaction. Cheng et al. (2021) found that work-connectivity after hours decreased job-satisfaction, but the presence of POS mitigated this effect. Stinglhamber et al. (2020) found associations between co-worker and employee POS resulting in job-satisfaction. Prysmakova and Lallatin (2021) and Cancela et al. (2022)'s findings are consistent with past research and show that POS increases job-satisfaction.

4.2.1.5. Job-Performance

Eisenberger et al. (2001) found that POS improves employee in-role performance. Wang et al. (2011) examining the effect of salespersons' POS on job-satisfaction, found that salespersons' customer's needs knowledge mediates the relationship between POS and job-performance. Maan et al. (2020) claimed that the increase in job-satisfaction resulting from POS is less pronounced in employees with proactive personalities. This suggests that job-satisfaction due to POS should be greater in less proactive employees. A meta-analysis conducted by Riggle et al. (2009) found only a moderate association between POS and performance. However, Wang (2022) and Kurtessis et al. (2017) revealed a strong positive association between the two.

4.2.1.6. Decreased Turnover Intention

POS exhibits a positive and consistent relationship with continuance intention, especially amongst those in public services (Prysmakova & Lallatin, 2021). Edwards and Peccei (2010) found that extending POS boosts employees' organizational identification, which decreases turnover intention. Riggle et al. (2009), in their meta-analysis, identified a strong negative relationship between POS and intent to leave. DeConinck et al. (2018) demonstrated that servant leadership indirectly reduces turnover through POS. Cancela et al. (2022) found that POS mediates between co-worker support and intent to stay. In effect, both organizations and co-employees need to be seen as supportive for employee's continuance intention. There are two subdimensions of continuance commitment- lack of alternatives, and perceived high sacrifice. Perceived high sacrifice increases continuance commitment (Vandenberghe et al., 2007). Corroborating this, Wang and Wang (2020) depicted a strong negative association of POS with turnover. Moreover, they found that other job-resources cannot substituted for POS. This establishes the unique position of POS in decreasing turnover intention.

4.2.1.7. Decreased Work-Family Conflict

POS decreases both work-to-family conflict as well as family-to-work conflict (Foley et al., 2005). Perceived organizational-supervisory support and family support enhances organizational identity which decreases work-family conflict. This effect is stronger in employees with higher cognitive emotion regulation (Demirtaş, 2019). Chan et al. (2022) studied the underlying mechanism behind this finding and identified that self-efficacy in the presence of POS acts as a mediator and motivates workers to balance their work and family lives.

4.2.1.8. Employee Individual Growth and Wellbeing

POS is linked with employees' individual growth, motivation (Prysmakova & Lallatin, 2021) and subjective wellbeing (Ilyas et al., 2022; Kurtessis et al., 2017). It also enhances other facets of wellbeing such as psychological empowerment (Demirtaş et al., 2019), psychological safety (Lee, 2021),finding meaning in work (Akgunduz et al., 2018), decreasing job insecurity during external threats (Zhou, 2023), and job anxiety (Cancela et al., 2022). POS is interestingly found to be directly or indirectly associated with employee ethics. Eisenberger et al. (1990) found that POS positively predicts conscientiousness. Singh (2019) and Cancela et al. (2022) found that POS negatively predicts deviance and counter-productive work behavior. Demirtaş et al. (2019) found that POS decreases psychological contract breaches. Employees who perceive greater organizational support also exhibit greater trust in top management (Webber et al., 2012).

4.2.1.9. Other Organizational Benefits

Besides the above-mentioned benefits, there are other advantages that incur from POS. Some notable ones are knowledge sharing (Yang et al., 2020), employee engagement (Malaeb et al., 2022), improved service quality, helpful behavior of employees towards customers (Vandenberghe et al., 2007), and an enhanced knowledge of customer-needs (Wang et al., 2011). Now, that it is clear that POS is a significant predictor of DMC success, it becomes important to identify its enablers and barriers. This is important for managers so that they may take steps to enhance POS in organizations and prevent factors that impede it.

4.2.2. Understanding POS Enablers and Barriers

4.2.2.1. POS Enablers

POS enablers are those policies, practices or job characteristics that facilitate POS in organizations. This review has identified the following POS enablers as listed in table 4.

4.2.2.2. POS Barriers

POS barriers are those policies, practices or job characteristics that hinder POS in organizations. This review has identified the following POS enablers as listed in Table 5.

4.2.3 Boundary Conditions That Operate in the POS-Employee Outcome Pathway

Based on a comprehensive review of literature, the authors suggest the existence of certain boundary conditions operating in the POS-outcome pathway as listed below. These would explain the inconsistencies observed amongst employees subjected to similar levels of POS. Some of these have been identified by past studies, whereas some warrant further research to be established firmly as boundary conditions.

Table 4. POS enablers

POS Enablers
1. Type of leadership- Proactive, Transformational, Ethical, Servant
2. Fairness, Organizational justice
3. Employee inclusiveness and recognition
4. Organizational rewards and promotions
5. Favorable job conditions and task flexibility
6. HR practices
7. Developmental experiences
8. Communication; managerial online communication
9. Health, safety, social support
10. Perceived downwards social comparisons
11. High performance work-systems
12. Perceived ethical philanthropic CSR
13. CSR towards employees
14. Devolved management
15. Co-workers' POS
16. Employee voice

Source: *Authors.*

Table 5. POS barriers

POS Barriers
1. Perceived downwards social comparisons
2. Perceived inequity in POS
3. Role-conflict
4. Role-ambiguity

Source: *Authors.*

4.2.3.1. Type of Job: Frontline vs. Non-Frontline

Zou et al. (2021) identified that frontline healthcare workers suffered from greater fatigue and insomnia than non-frontline workers, even though POS mitigated it. Ilyas et al. (2022) found a positive impact of POS on professional commitment of frontline doctors and nurses. Wang and Wang (2020) identified a significant negative relationship between POS and frontline employees' turnover intention and burnout. These findings indicate that frontline employees benefit from POS. However, the meta-analysis by Riggle et al. (2009) claimed that POS' positive effects on performance, commitment and turnover intentions are stronger in cases of non-frontline workers. Clearly, there is a differential impact of POS on frontline and non-frontline workers. Hence, job type as a boundary condition determining the intensity of POS is posited. Further studies should make the relationship clearer.

4.2.3.2. Demographics

National and cultural differences play a part in determining the effects of POS. Malaeb et al. (2022) found that for the same degree of POS, employee engagement and self-leadership increased in UAE but not in Lebanon. Thompson et al. (2020) demonstrated that women developed a felt-obligation towards organizations at lower levels of POS compared to men. Prysmakova and Lallatin (2021) and Foley et al. (2005) could not find a congruous pattern of POS with demographics. These inconsistencies suggest a need for further exploration of demographics positioned as a boundary condition operating at the POS-outcomes pathway.

4.2.3.3. Employee Self-System

Employee self-system is suggested to play a role in determining the impacts of POS. For instance, Yang et al. (2020) identified that individuals with a low independent or high interdependent self are inclined to knowledge-share in the presence of POS. Van Knippenberg et al. (2015) found that POS positively predicts OCB in workers with individualistic self-construal. Gu et al. (2020) identified that self-efficacy moderates between POS and depressive symptoms. Malaeb et al. (2022) depicted that POS enhances self-leadership in individualistic workers. Karatepe (2015) claimed self-efficacy to be a personal resource moderating the effects of POS on extra-role customer service, intent to leave and emotional exhaustion. McBey et al. (2017) found that POS enhances self-expression which, in turn, mediates organizational commitment arising from POS. Clearly, the individual self-concept is a significant determiner of POS' effects and needs to be studied as a boundary condition in conjunction with POS.

4.2.3.4. Role of Emotions: An Open Question

Emotions have been studied in association with POS by multiple authors but to conflicting findings. Demirtaş et al. (2019) revealed that cognitive emotion regulation in employees leads to organizational identification in the presence of POS. Karatepe (2015) found that POS indirectly influences emotional exhaustion of employees through personal resources. Lee (2021) identified POS to engender emotional reactions in employees during crisis. Task flexibility, communication, safety, and social support were found to be socio-emotional resources that act as a kind of organizational support. These findings beg the question- does POS lead to emotional reactions that result in positive outcomes, or is POS itself a form of emotional resource? The lack of clear answers leads to the suggestion that emotions and emotion regulation should be analysed as boundary conditions which would make their role in the POS-outcomes pathway clearer.

4.3. Research Objective Three: Provide a Conceptual Framework Illustrating the Path From POS-TO-POS Outcomes Delineating the Operant Internal and External Forces in the Pathway

Figure 1 illustrates the conceptual framework that is drawn following a comprehensive analysis and synthesis of the review findings. The framework depicts the complete pathway from POS-to-POS-outcomes. This pathway comprises of the psychological mechanism of felt obligation that leads to positive outcomes. POS enablers, barriers, mediators, moderators, and boundary conditions that operate in this route are depicted. Suggestions to increase POS by making efforts to enhance enablers are also shown.

4.4. Research Objective Four: Demonstrate How POS Facilitates Organizational Contribution Towards SDG 3, SDG 8, and SDG 16

The SDGs are global goals adopted by the United Nations in 2015 as a universal call to end poverty, protect the Earth, and secure peace, health and happiness for everyone by 2030. This section showcases how POS facilitates organizational contribution towards SDGs 3, 8, and 16.

4.4.1. SDG 3: Good Health and Well-Being

By extending POS to their employees, organizations effectively ensure that employee wellbeing and good health is taken care of. Multiple studies have established POS as a positive predictor of subjective wellbeing. The meta-analysis of OS theory by Kurtessis et al. (2017) showed employee wellbeing was a POS consequence. This was consistent with the findings of Ilyas et al. (2022) where POS was identified as a sequential mediator between ethical leadership and subjective wellbeing of healthcare workers. Zou et al. (2021) and Wang et al. (2022) found that POS leads to decrease in insomnia symptoms in workers. Wang and Wang (2020) corroborated this by revealing a significant negative effect of POS on burnout and fatigue. POS has been related to safety behaviors and a decrease in accidents (Hofmann & Morgeson, 1999), psychological safety (Lee, 2021) and psychological empowerment (Maan et al., 2020). It has shown positive associations with motivation (Prysmakova & Lallatin, 2021) meaning of work (Akgunduz et al., 2018), employee engagement (Malaeb et al., 2022), trust in management (Webber et al., 2012), and work-family balance (Chan et al., 2022). The multifarious benefits extended by POS show beyond a reasonable doubt that when an organization offers POS, it promotes good health and wellbeing among its workers and contributes categorically to SDG 3.

4.4.2. SDG 8: Promote Decent Work and Economic Growth

SDG 8 focusses on promoting decent work and economic growth. Economic growth can only take place in a workplace where employees feel psychologically empowered, their families and safety taken care of, and creativity encouraged. POS is an ideal facilitator of SDG 8, since it provides employees with an atmosphere of psychological as well as physical safety (Lee, 2021; Hofmann & Morgeson, 1999), it enhances passion for and engagement in jobs (Malaeb et al., 2022), encourages creativity (Wang, 2022)

Figure 1. Conceptual framework of POS-to-POS outcomes pathway depicting underlying psychological mechanism, enablers, barriers, mediators, moderators, boundary conditions and suggestion to enhance outcomes
Source: Authors.

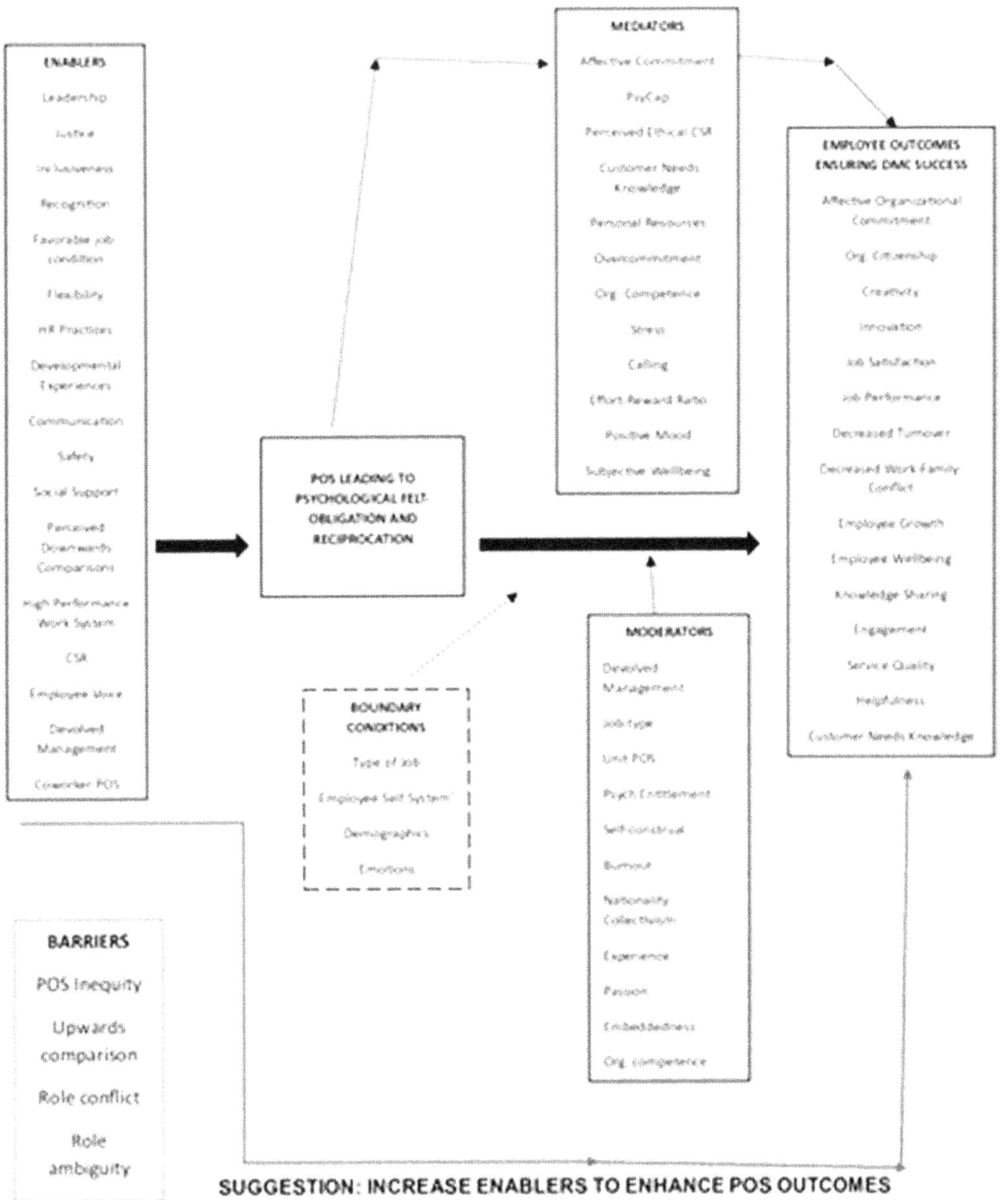

innovation (Eisenberger et al., 1990), and flexibility (Lee, 2021). It also ensures gender and racial parity (Pullen et al., 2023), and equitable distribution of resources, rewards, and promotions. Under these conducive conditions, employees become ethical and refrain from deviant behaviors. They engage in knowledge sharing (Yang et al., 2020) and demonstrate organizational commitment (Zagenczyk et al.,

2021). They dutifully assist customers, raise service quality, and work hard to help organizations reach their goals. All this ensures economic growth at multiple levels: individual, organizational, and national. Hence, by extending POS, an organization promotes decent workplaces, and enables economic growth, thus, facilitating SDG 8.

4.4.3. SDG 16: Build Effective Institutions

SDG 16 aims at building effective institutions. An essential characteristic of an effective institution is employee perception of being supported and cared for. Previous body of work has established that employees develop global beliefs about their organizations. These beliefs are built progressively. From an organizational point of view, it is crucial that these beliefs are built-up to be favorable towards the organization as this would warrant employee loyalty, hard work, commitment, leading to an 'effective' functioning organization. This leads to the question- how can organizations ensure positive employee perceptions? The answer lies in offering support to employees when they need it. Further, the support should not only be received by employees, but perceived positively as well. For this to occur, support should be employee-directed and personalized (Matusik et al., 2022). Positive perceptions of support induce individual and organizational-level outcomes that build "effective" institutions where employees work committedly and feel safe, and organizations prosper. Some of the noteworthy outcomes are offering developmental experiences to employees leading to personal growth (Wayne et al., 1997), better work-family balance, (Chan et al., 2022) job-satisfaction (Cancela et al., 2022) and psychological empowerment (Maan et al., 2020). Moreover, the benefits are not just focal-employee specific. The ramifications are felt in reciprocal organizational growth depicted in profitability, enhanced job-performances, lessened employee complaints and psychological contract breaches.

Thus, POS provides a dual-pronged approach towards SDG 16, firstly, by producing outcomes benefitting employees, and secondly, by engendering organizationally beneficial outcomes. The win-win situation leads to a high-functioning, effective organization.

5. CONCLUSION

This study conducted an integrative literature review on POS by analyzing sixty-three papers from select, high-quality databases. Russel (2005) and Whittemore and Knafl's (2005) recommendations were followed for the review process and data analysis. The first research objective was to provide an up-to-date and thorough understanding of POS. This was accomplished through a qualitative thematic template analysis which identified pertinent themes around the construct. The second research objective was to determine how POS leads to organizational DMC success. This was confirmed to be through the psychological mechanism of reciprocity where POS engenders organizationally beneficial outcomes such as employee commitment, citizenship, improved job-performance, continuance commitment, creativity and innovation which lead to DMC success. Review findings evince that simply extending support will not induce positive results. It is critical that the offered support is perceived positively as well. Employee traits, supervisor leadership and co-worker perceptions all play a part in determining outcomes. It is hence suggested that POS is a complex construct that operates at multiple levels. Although recent studies have started discussing the role of mediators and moderators, there is a long way to go before we zero-in on all the forces that operate in the dynamic organizational support landscape. Specific boundary conditions are offered that could potentially impact POS outcomes. The third research objective was fulfilled by denoting POS facilitation of organizational contribution towards SDGs 3,8 and 16. The fourth objective of the study was attained by offering a conceptual framework illustrating the pathway from POS to POS-outcomes. The framework delineates the psychology underlying POS, barriers, enablers, mediators, moderators and suggested boundary conditions. An even richer and more layered understanding of the construct can be achieved by including boundary conditions and increasing qualitative and longitudinal studies in the field. It is hoped that this review provides a relevant reference for academicians and spurs holistic studies on POS traversing multi-disciplinary perspectives.

5.1. Implications for Research and Practice

The theoretical contributions of this article are that firstly, it examines POS in the context of DMC activities and illustrates how POS steers organizational digital communication successfully. To the best of our knowledge, this has not been attempted before. Secondly, it integrates concepts from multi-disciplinary fields and summarizes current knowledge on POS through a template analysis that identifies relevant themes around the construct. A major contribution of this study is the proposal of a conceptual framework illustrating the pathway from POS to outcomes delineating the operant internal and external forces in the pathway. It includes the psychological mechanism underlying POS, enablers, mediators, moderators, and boundary conditions. It identifies POS barriers and provides suggestions to escalate POS by increasing enablers. This framework can serve as a ready reference for scholars in the field. Thirdly, the study highlights how POS facilitates organizational contribution towards SDGs 3, 8 and 16. The practical contribution of this article lies in providing managers with an understanding of the psychology underlying employee reciprocation of organizational support. Organizations are advised to make POS an integral part of HR and marketing policies to ensure DMC success. Recommendations to improve POS are provided.

5.2. Limitations

The first limitation of this study is that the review findings are limited to the sixty-three papers analyzed in the review. Though steps were taken to make the search strategy as comprehensive as possible by including latest and foundational articles from reliable databases, as well as conducting manual searches on Google Scholar to not miss out on suitable studies, it cannot be ascertained that all relevant studies have been included. A second limitation is inherent to the nature of integrative reviews which combine different study designs and methodologies. This may lead to inaccuracies in interpretations. This threat was limited by following guidelines recommended by Russel (2005) and Whittemore and Knafl (2005). Adhering to recommended guidelines reduces threats of biases and inaccuracies. Keywords used for the search and final extracted themes were reported to ensure reliability. The third limitation is the threat of researcher bias. Preventative measures to limit this were taken, firstly, by limiting the search to reputable databases that include peer-reviewed and quality-controlled articles, and secondly, by subjecting articles to quality evaluation before final selection. Data was extracted independently by two authors to limit bias. These measures increase the rigor of a study. It still cannot be claimed, however, that the study is free of limitations. Future scholars are urged to use this study as a reference and replicate the results to extend the field.

5.3. Future Research Directions

The review findings reveal conflicting reports of POS outcomes depending on variations in demographics, employee self-construal, job, and emotions. These departures from the previously one-dimensional understanding of POS indicate that it is a multi-faceted construct and should be understood as such to avoid its underrepresentation. Based on these inconsistencies, four boundary conditions likely to influence the impact of POS are suggested as future research avenues. These are: frontline versus non-frontline work, demographic differences, emotion regulation, and employee self-system of self-construal, self-leadership, and self-expression. Future studies incorporating these factors as boundary conditions should contribute towards a richer understanding of POS.

An overwhelming 87.3% studies in this review were quantitative in nature revealing a lack of qualitative studies. In a field like POS dealing with subjective social phenomenon, more qualitative studies need to be included to ask layered questions that get to the core of the human experience. Longitudinal studies that mark changes in outcomes over time also promise a fulfilling future research avenue.

REFERENCES

Adebayo, D. O. (2005). Ethical attitudes and prosocial behaviour in the Nigeria police: Moderator effects of perceived organizational support and public recognition. *Policing*, *28*(4), 684–705. doi:10.1108/13639510510628767

Akgunduz, Y., Alkan, C., & Gök, Ö. A. (2018). Perceived organizational support, employee creativity and proactive personality: The mediating effect of meaning of work. *Journal of Hospitality and Tourism Management*, *34*, 105–114. doi:10.1016/j.jhtm.2018.01.004

Bhatti, S. H., Iqbal, K., Santoro, G., & Rizzato, F. (2022). The impact of corporate social responsibility directed toward employees on contextual performance in the banking sector: A serial model of perceived organizational support and affective organizational commitment. *Corporate Social Responsibility and Environmental Management*, *29*(6), 1980–1994. doi:10.1002/csr.2295

Cancela, D., Hulsheger, U. R., & Stutterheim, S. E. (2022). The role of support for transgender and nonbinary employees: Perceived co-worker and organizational support's associations with job attitudes and work behavior. *Psychology of Sexual Orientation and Gender Diversity*, *9*(1), 49–57. doi:10.1037gd0000453

Chan, X. W., Kalliath, T., Brough, P., Siu, O., & Timms, C. (2022). Examining the mediating role of self-efficacy in the relationship between perceived organizational support and work–family enrichment. *International Journal of Stress Management*, *29*(3), 281–291. doi:10.1037tr0000263

Cheng, K., Cao, X., Guo, L., & Xia, Q. (2021). Work connectivity behaviour after-hours and job satisfaction: Examining the moderating effects of psychological entitlement and perceived organizational support. *Personnel Review*, *59*(9), 2277–2293. doi:10.1108/PR-06-2020-0413

Choi, W., Madjar, N., & Yun, S. (2018). Suggesting creative solutions or just complaining: Perceived organizational support, exchange ideology, and learning goal orientation as determining factors. *Psychology of Aesthetics, Creativity, and the Arts*, *12*(1), 68–78. doi:10.1037/aca0000143

DeConinck, J. B., Moss, H. K., & Deconinck, M. B. (2018). The relationship between servant leadership, perceived organizational support, performance, and turnover among business to business salespeople. *Global J management and marketing, 2*(1), 38–52. doi:10.14738/abr.510.3730

Demirtaş, Ö., Arslan, A., & Karaca, M. (2019). Why perceived organizational and supervisory family support is important for organizations? Evidence from the field. *Review of Managerial Science, 13*(4), 841–869. doi:10.100711846-017-0264-x

Duan, W., Tang, X., Li, Y., Cheng, X., & Zhang, H. (2020). Perceived organizational support and employee creativity: The mediation role of calling. *Creativity Research Journal, 32*(4), 403–411. doi:10.1080/10400419.2020.1821563

Edwards, M. R., & Peccei, R. (2010). Perceived organizational support, organizational identification, and employee outcomes: Testing a simultaneous multifoci model. *Journal of Personnel Psychology, 9*(1), 17–26. doi:10.1027/1866-5888/a000007

Eisenberger, R., Armeli, S., Rexwinkel, B., Lynch, P. D., & Rhoades, L. (2001). Reciprocation of perceived organizational support. *The Journal of Applied Psychology, 86*(1), 42–51. Advance online publication. doi:10.1037/0021-9010.86.1.42 PMID:11302232

Eisenberger, R., Fasolo, P., & Davis-LaMastro, V. (1990). Perceived organizational support and employee diligence, commitment, and innovation. *The Journal of Applied Psychology, 75*(1), 51–59. doi:10.1037/0021-9010.75.1.51

Eisenberger, R., Huntington, R., Hutchison, S., & Sowa, D. (1986). Perceived organizational support. *The Journal of Applied Psychology, 71*(3), 500–507. doi:10.1037/0021-9010.71.3.500

Foley, S., Hang-Yue, N., & Lui, S. (2005). The effects of work stressors, perceived organizational support, and gender on work-family conflict in Hong Kong. *Asia Pacific Journal of Management, 22*(3), 237–256. doi:10.100710490-005-3568-3

Fuglseth, A. M., & Sørebø, Ø. (2014). The effects of technostress within the context of employee use of ICT. *Computers in Human Behavior, 40*, 161–170. doi:10.1016/j.chb.2014.07.040

Gu, Z. H., Qiu, T., Tian, F. Q., Yang, S. H., & Wu, H. (2020). Perceived organizational support associated with depressive symptoms among petroleum workers in China: A cross-sectional study. *Psychology Research and Behavior Management, 13*, 97–104. doi:10.2147/PRBM.S232635 PMID:32095086

Hasan, D., & Kamalanabhan, T. J. (2023). Perceived Organizational Support- A Systematic Literature Review and Future Research Agenda. *Manager-The British Journal of Administrative Management, 59*(1), 71–95.

Hofmann, D. A., & Morgeson, F. P. (1999). Safety-related behavior as a social exchange: The role of perceived organizational support and leader–member exchange. *The Journal of Applied Psychology, 84*(2), 286–296. doi:10.1037/0021-9010.84.2.286

Ilyas, S., Abid, G., & Ashfaq, F. (2022). The impact of perceived organizational support on professional commitment: A moderation of burnout and mediation of well-being. *The International Journal of Sociology and Social Policy, 43*(7/8), 710–726. doi:10.1108/IJSSP-06-2022-0170

Imamoglu, S. Z., Erat, S., & Turkcan, H. (2022). *How organizational identity relates to knowledge sharing and creativity: moderating effect of perceived organizational support.* Kybernetes. doi:0.1108/K-02-2022-0169

Karatepe, O. M. (2015). Do personal resources mediate the effect of perceived organizational support on emotional exhaustion and job outcomes? *International Journal of Contemporary Hospitality Management*, *27*(1), 4–26. doi:10.1108/IJCHM-09-2013-0417

Kim, K. Y., Eisenberger, R., & Baik, K. (2016). Perceived organizational support and affective organizational commitment: Moderating influence of perceived organizational competence. *Journal of Organizational Behavior*, *37*(4), 558–583. doi:10.1002/job.2081

Kurtessis, J. N., Eisenberger, R., Ford, M. T., Buffardi, L. C., Stewart, K. A., & Adis, C. S. (2017). Perceived organizational support: A meta-analytic evaluation of organizational support theory. *Journal of Management*, *43*(6), 1854–1884. doi:10.1177/0149206315575554

Lee, H. (2021). Changes in workplace practices during the COVID-19 pandemic: The roles of emotion, psychological safety and organisation support. *Journal of Organizational Effectiveness: People and Performance*, *8*(1), 97–128. doi:10.1108/JOEPP-06-2020-0104

Maan, A. T., Abid, G., Butt, T. H., Ashfaq, F., & Ahmed, S. (2020). Perceived organizational support and job satisfaction: A moderated mediation model of proactive personality and psychological empowerment. *Future Business Journal*, *6*(1), 1–12. doi:10.118643093-020-00027-8

Malaeb, M., Dagher, G. K., & Messarra, L. C. (2022). The relationship between self-leadership and employee engagement in Lebanon and the UAE: the moderating role of perceived organizational support. Personnel Review. doi:10.1108/PR-12-2021-0862

Matusik, J. G., Ferris, D. L., & Johnson, R. E. (2022). The PCMT model of organizational support: An integrative review and reconciliation of the organizational support literature. *The Journal of Applied Psychology*, *107*(3), 329–345. doi:10.1037/apl0000922 PMID:34060884

McBey, K., Karakowsky, L., & Ng, P. (2017). Can I make a difference here? The impact of perceived organizational support on volunteer commitment. *Journal of Management Development*, *36*(8), 991–1007. doi:10.1108/JMD-05-2015-0078

Piercy, N. F., Cravens, D. W., Lane, N., & Vorhies, D. W. (2006). Driving organizational citizenship behaviors and salesperson in-role behavior performance: The role of management control and perceived organizational support. *Journal of the Academy of Marketing Science*, *34*(2), 244–262. doi:10.1177/0092070305280532

Poon, J. M., Salleh, A. H. M., & Senik, Z. C. (2007). Propensity to trust as a moderator of the relationship between perceived organizational support and job satisfaction. *International Journal of Organization Theory and Behavior*, *10*(3), 350–366. doi:10.1108/IJOTB-10-03-2007-B004

Prysmakova, P., & Lallatin, N. (2021). Perceived organizational support in public and nonprofit organizations: Systematic review and directions for future research. *International Review of Administrative Sciences*, *89*(2), 467–483. doi:10.1177/00208523211033822

Pullen, E., Fischer, M. W., Morse, G., Garabrant, J., Salyers, M. P., & Rollins, A. L. (2023). Racial disparities in the workplace: The impact of isolation on perceived organizational support and job satisfaction. *Psychiatric Rehabilitation Journal*, *46*(1), 45–52. doi:10.1037/prj0000543 PMID:36809015

Ragu-Nathan, T. S., Tarafdar, M., Ragu-Nathan, B. S., & Tu, Q. (2008). The consequences of technostress for end users in organizations: Conceptual development and empirical validation. *Information Systems Research*, *19*(4), 417–433. doi:10.1287/isre.1070.0165

Rhoades, L., & Eisenberger, R. (2002). Perceived organizational support: A review of the literature. *The Journal of Applied Psychology*, *87*(4), 698–714. doi:10.1037/0021-9010.87.4.698 PMID:12184574

Riggle, R. J., Edmondson, D. R., & Hansen, J. D. (2009). A meta-analysis of the relationship between perceived organizational support and job outcomes: 20 years of research. *Journal of Business Research*, *62*(10), 1027–1030. doi:10.1016/j.jbusres.2008.05.003

Rockstuhl, T., Eisenberger, R., Shore, L. M., Kurtessis, J. N., Ford, M. T., Buffardi, L. C., & Mesdaghinia, S. (2020). Perceived organizational support (POS) across 54 nations: A cross-cultural meta-analysis of POS effects. *Journal of International Business Studies*, *51*(6), 933–962. doi:10.105741267-020-00311-3

Russell, C. L. (2005). An overview of the integrative research review. *Progress in Transplantation (Aliso Viejo, Calif.)*, *15*(1), 8–13. doi:10.1177/152692480501500102 PMID:15839365

Russell, D. W., Russell, C. A., & Hill, R. P. (2022). Mental health service utilization after military missions: The double-edged consequences of unit-level organizational support. *Psychological Services*, *19*(2, Suppl 2), 113–125. doi:10.1037er0000542

Shankar, V., Grewal, D., Sunder, S., Fossen, B., Peters, K., & Agarwal, A. (2022). Digital marketing communication in global marketplaces: A review of extant research, future directions, and potential approaches. *International Journal of Research in Marketing*, *39*(2), 541–565. doi:10.1016/j.ijresmar.2021.09.005

Shanock, L. R., & Eisenberger, R. (2006). When supervisors feel supported: Relationships with subordinates' perceived supervisor support, perceived organizational support, and performance. *The Journal of Applied Psychology*, *91*(3), 689–695. doi:10.1037/0021-9010.91.3.689 PMID:16737364

Singh, R. (2020, February). Organisational embeddedness as a moderator on the organisational support, trust and workplace deviance relationships. *Evidence-based HRM: a Global Forum for Empirical Scholarship, 8*(1), 1–17. 10.1108/EBHRM-03-2019-0025

Statista-The Statistics Portal. (2023). *Digital advertising spending worldwide from 2021 to 2026(in billion U.S. dollars)*. Statista Research Department. https://www.statista.com/statistics/237974/online-advertising-spending-worldwide/

Statista-The Statistics Portal. (2023). *Social media advertising spending worldwide from 2021 to 2028 (in billion U.S. dollars)*. Statista Research Department. https://www.statista.com/statistics/271406/advertising-revenue-of-social-networks-worldwide/#statisticContainer

Stinglhamber, F., Ohana, M., Caesens, G., & Meyer, M. (2020). Perceived organizational support: The interactive role of coworkers' perceptions and employees' voice. *Employee Relations*, *42*(1), 107–124. doi:10.1108/ER-05-2018-0137

Sumardjo, M., & Supriadi, Y. N. (2023). Perceived Organizational Commitment Mediates the Effect of Perceived Organizational Support and Organizational Culture on Organizational Citizenship Behavior. *Calitatea*, *24*(192), 376–384. doi:10.47750/QAS/24.192.45

Suthatorn, P., & Charoensukmongkol, P. (2022). How work passion and job tenure mitigate the effect of perceived organizational support on organizational identification of flight attendants during the COVID-19 pandemic. *Asia Pacific Management Review*, *28*(3), 347–357. doi:10.1016/j.apmrv.2022.12.003

Tang, G., Yu, B., Cooke, F. L., & Chen, Y. (2017). High-performance work system and employee creativity: The roles of perceived organisational support and devolved management. *Personnel Review*, *46*(7), 1318–1334. doi:10.1108/PR-09-2016-0235

Tarafdar, M., D'arcy, J., Turel, O., & Gupta, A. (2014). The dark side of information technology. *MIT Sloan Management Review*.

Thompson, P. S., Bergeron, D. M., & Bolino, M. C. (2020). No obligation? How gender influences the relationship between perceived organizational support and organizational citizenship behavior. *The Journal of Applied Psychology*, *105*(11), 1338–1350. doi:10.1037/apl0000481 PMID:32118460

Tiago, M. T. P. M. B., & Veríssimo, J. M. C. (2014). Digital marketing and social media: Why bother? *Business Horizons*, *57*(6), 703–708. doi:10.1016/j.bushor.2014.07.002

Van Knippenberg, D., Van Prooijen, J. W., & Sleebos, E. (2015). Beyond social exchange: Collectivism's moderating role in the relationship between perceived organizational support and organizational citizenship behaviour. *European Journal of Work and Organizational Psychology*, *24*(1), 152–160. doi:10.1080/1359432X.2013.858699

Vandenberghe, C., Bentein, K., Michon, R., Chebat, J. C., Tremblay, M., & Fils, J. F. (2007). An examination of the role of perceived support and employee commitment in employee-customer encounters. *The Journal of Applied Psychology*, *92*(4), 1177–1187. doi:10.1037/0021-9010.92.4.1177 PMID:17638475

Wang, C. J. (2022). Exploring the Mechanisms Linking Transformational Leadership, Perceived Organizational Support, Creativity, and Performance in Hospitality: The Mediating Role of Affective Organizational Commitment. *Behavioral Sciences (Basel, Switzerland)*, *12*(10), 406. doi:10.3390/bs12100406 PMID:36285975

Wang, G., Liu, D., & Wang, X. (2011). Effects of perceived organizational support and guanxi on salesperson performance: The mediation of customer need knowledge. *Frontiers of Business Research in China*, *5*(3), 422–435. doi:10.100711782-011-0138-z

Wang, M. F., He, Q., Liu, Z., Du, Y. L., Wu, C., Lang, H. J., & Du, J. (2022). The relationship between perceived organizational support and insomnia in Chinese nurses: The Serial multiple mediation analysis. *Frontiers in Psychology*, *13*, 1026317. doi:10.3389/fpsyg.2022.1026317 PMID:36591078

Wang, Q., & Wang, C. (2020). Reducing turnover intention: Perceived organizational support for frontline employees. *Frontiers of Business Research in China*, *14*(1), 1–16. doi:10.118611782-020-00074-6

Wayne, S. J., Shore, L. M., Bommer, W. H., & Tetrick, L. E. (2002). The role of fair treatment and rewards in perceptions of organizational support and leader-member exchange. *The Journal of Applied Psychology*, *87*(3), 590–598. doi:10.1037/0021-9010.87.3.590 PMID:12090617

Wayne, S. J., Shore, L. M., & Liden, R. C. (1997). Perceived organizational support and leader-member exchange: A social exchange perspective. *Academy of Management Journal*, *40*(1), 82–111. doi:10.2307/257021

Webber, S. S., Bishop, K., & O'Neill, R. (2012). Trust repair: The impact of perceived organisational support and issue-selling. *Journal of Management Development*, *31*(7), 724–737. doi:10.1108/02621711211243917

Whittemore, R., & Knafl, K. (2005). The integrative review: Updated methodology. *Journal of Advanced Nursing*, *52*(5), 546–553. doi:10.1111/j.1365-2648.2005.03621.x PMID:16268861

Yang, H., van Rijn, M. B., & Sanders, K. (2020). Perceived organizational support and knowledge sharing: Employees' self-construal matters. *International Journal of Human Resource Management*, *31*(17), 2217–2237. doi:10.1080/09585192.2018.1443956

Zagenczyk, T. J., Purvis, R. L., Cruz, K. S., Thoroughgood, C. N., & Sawyer, K. B. (2021). Context and social exchange: Perceived ethical climate strengthens the relationships between perceived organizational support and organizational identification and commitment. *International Journal of Human Resource Management*, *32*(22), 4752–4771. doi:10.1080/09585192.2019.1706618

Zagenczyk, T. J., Scott, K. D., Gibney, R., Murrell, A. J., & Thatcher, J. B. (2010). Social influence and perceived organizational support: A social networks analysis. *Organizational Behavior and Human Decision Processes*, *111*(2), 127–138. doi:10.1016/j.obhdp.2009.11.004

Zou, X., Liu, S., Li, J., Chen, W., Ye, J., Yang, Y., Zhou, F., & Ling, L. (2021). Factors associated with healthcare workers' insomnia symptoms and fatigue in the fight against COVID-19, and the role of organizational support. *Frontiers in Psychiatry*, *12*, 652717. doi:10.3389/fpsyt.2021.652717 PMID:33841214

KEY TERMS AND DEFINITIONS

Boundary Conditions: The conditions describing the limits of generalizability of a theory or causal model. They denote the boundaries in time or space or research contexts and depict when an effect becomes pronounced.

Competing Interests and Funding Statements: The authors of this publication declare there are no competing interests. This research received no specific grant from any funding agency in the public, commercial, or not-for-profit sectors.

Digital Marketing Communication: Communications by organizations to potential customers using digital means. These may include social media advertising, web-based advertising, text messaging, e-mailing, and multi-media messaging.

Perceived Organizational Support: Employee perception of being supported by the organization and assignation of the degree of being cared for and valued by the organization.

Chapter 10
The Global Implications of Diversity and Inclusion:
Exploring Economic, Image, and Meaning Dimensions

Marcia Siqueira Costa Marques
https://orcid.org/0000-0002-3824-2975
Grupo Design e Convergencia, Brazil

ABSTRACT

This chapter provides a comprehensive examination of the multifaceted implications of diversity and inclusion within business and societal contexts. This elucidates the economic, image, and meaning dimensions of diversity and inclusion, highlighting their potential to foster social progress, enhance reputation, and improve financial performance. The chapter further delves into the challenges faced by organizations in implementing these initiatives, such as resistance to change, lack of diversity in leadership, and the need for greater accountability. Future directions for enhancing the effectiveness of diversity and inclusion efforts were also explored. This chapter aims to provide a deeper understanding of these concepts, emphasizing their critical role in the current globalized and interconnected world.

1. INTRODUCTION

In the contemporary landscape of global business, the imperatives of diversity and inclusion have transcended buzzwords to become fundamental pillars for organizational success. The evolution of economies, technological advancements, and shifting societal norms has underscored the critical need for organizations to cultivate inclusive environments. Beyond merely addressing social justice concerns, diversity and inclusion fuel innovation, nurture creativity, and facilitate adaptation to diverse customer bases. So, there is necessary a more comprehensive exploration of the chapter's foundational concepts. To address this, the following section delves into the nuanced meanings of diversity and inclusion, prevalent trends in their implementation, and their interconnectedness with organizational growth.

DOI: 10.4018/978-1-6684-8984-0.ch010

This chapter, titled "The Global Implications of Diversity and Inclusion: Exploring Economic, Image, and Meaning Dimensions," aims to provide a multidimensional exploration of these crucial concepts. We begin by examining the economic implications of diversity and inclusion and demonstrating how they foster access to a wider talent pool, improve financial performance, decrease turnover, and enhance an organization's reputation. We then delve into the role that these principles play in shaping an organization's image and discuss how they affect corporate identity, customer perception, and brand value. To further deepen our understanding, we navigate the complex terrain of meaning-making by exploring how diversity and inclusion contribute to cultural competency, social justice, and equity.

Significant attention has also been paid to the challenges encountered in the implementation of diversity and inclusion initiatives. These challenges, including resistance to change, lack of diversity in leadership, and the call for greater transparency and accountability, are analyzed in depth. By exploring these issues, we aim to stimulate critical thought and inspire innovative solutions that can help organizations overcome these hurdles and move towards a more inclusive and equitable future.

1.1. Understanding Diversity and Inclusion

According to the program Global Diversity Practice, diversity encapsulates the acknowledgment and celebration of the multifaceted differences among individuals within a workforce. These distinctions encompass but are not limited to race, gender, age, ethnicity, sexual orientation, physical ability, religion, and socioeconomic background. The core of diversity lies in recognizing that each individual's unique background contributes to a rich tapestry of experiences, perspectives, and talents. The practical manifestation of diversity involves creating an environment where these differences are not only accepted but actively leveraged to drive organizational success.

Inclusion complements diversity by focusing on fostering an environment in which every individual feels respected, valued, and empowered to contribute their unique insights. Inclusive workplaces prioritize equity, ensuring that everyone has equitable access to opportunities and resources regardless of their background. Inclusion is not just about being present in the room; it is about creating a space where every voice is heard, perspectives are sought, and contributions are recognized.

1.2. Main Trends in Diversity and Inclusion

Over the years, according to reports and publications from organizations such as the International Labor Organization (IOT), Society for Human Resource Management (SHRM), the World Economic Forum (WEF) and the Center for Creative Leadership (CCL), several trends were used to discuss Diversity and Inclusion. We believe that some prevailing trends are reshaping the landscape of diversity and inclusion, prompting organizations to adapt and evolve:

1. **Holistic Diversity:** Beyond demographic characteristics, organizations are embracing broader forms of diversity, including cognitive diversity, which encompasses different thinking styles, problem-solving approaches, and cognitive processes. This expanded perspective recognizes that diverse thought patterns enhance creativity and innovation. Diversity and inclusion can also lead to better decision-making in global organizations. When a diverse group of people come together to make decisions, they can consider a wider range of perspectives and ideas. This can lead to better decisions that consider the needs and perspectives of a diverse range of stakeholders.

2. **Intersectionality:** Acknowledging that individuals often hold multiple dimensions of diversity, the concept of intersectionality has gained prominence. Organizations now consider how various aspects of an individual's identity interact and influence their experiences within the workplace.
3. **Inclusive Leadership:** Effective leadership involves actively championing diversity and inclusion. Organizations are emphasizing the need for leaders who demonstrate inclusive behaviors, set an example, and promote a culture where diversity is celebrated at all levels.
4. **Data-Driven Approaches:** The application of data analytics has enabled organizations to identify diversity gaps, measure inclusion levels, and assess the impact of diversity initiatives. Data-driven strategies facilitate evidence-based decision-making in shaping inclusive environments. Diversity and inclusion in global organizations can lead to increased creativity and innovation. When people from different backgrounds come together, they bring unique perspectives and ideas that can lead to new and innovative solutions to problems. This can result in a competitive advantage for the organization, as they are able to offer products and services that are more innovative and better meet the needs of a diverse customer base.
5. **Global and Cultural Competence:** In an increasingly interconnected world, organizations are recognizing the importance of understanding diverse cultures and global nuances. Cultivating cultural competence equips organizations to navigate international markets and diverse customer bases more effectively. Diversity and inclusion can help global organizations to build a positive reputation and brand image. In today's global marketplace, consumers are increasingly looking for organizations that are committed to diversity and inclusion. By promoting diversity and inclusion, global organizations can build a positive reputation and attract customers who value these principles.
6. **Flexible Work Arrangements:** Embracing diversity extends to accommodating various work styles and needs. Flexible work arrangements, such as remote work and flexible hours, cater to different preferences, enabling individuals to contribute effectively.
7. **Inclusive Product Development:** Organizations are realizing that diverse teams are better equipped to develop products and services that resonate with diverse customer bases. This trend emphasizes the importance of diversity in all aspects of business, including innovation. Another economic benefit of diversity and inclusion is increased employee engagement and retention. When employees feel valued and included, they are more likely to be engaged in their work and committed to the organization. This can lead to increased productivity and decreased turnover, which can save the organization money in recruitment and training costs.

1.3. Global Implications of Diversity and Inclusion

Nowadays, diversity and inclusion have transcended buzzwords to become integral tenets of successful and socially responsible organizations. Their impact resonates across different aspects of business and society, influencing economic performance, shaping the organizational image, and playing a pivotal role in the creation of meaning. Having a diverse and inclusive workforce can also help organizations better understand and connect with their customers. In today's globalized world, companies need to appeal to a wide range of consumers with different cultural backgrounds and values. By having employees who reflect this diversity, organizations can better understand the needs and preferences of their customers and tailor their products and services accordingly.

In the era of social media and digitalization, the ways in which we communicate and interact have been revolutionized. This chapter explored the transformative impact of these platforms on business communication, product creation, and promotional strategies. It unravels emerging communication paradigms steered by changes in user ethos, which are significantly shaped by social media landscapes.

1.4. Embracing the Digital Revolution: A New Landscape of Business Communication and Cultural Integration

In this buzzing era of social media and digitalization, the rulebook for communication and interaction has been rewritten. These platforms have had a transformative impact on business communication, product creation, and promotional strategies, giving rise to new paradigms in communication steered by changes in user ethos.

The landscape of social media has significantly shaped these changes. A critical focal point is the incorporation of cultural elements into advertising. Historically, cultures of marginalized groups have often been used as marketing tools, but without the due respect or genuine representation. However, the contemporary market recognizes the need to respect and authentically represent producers of meaning rather than merely appropriating their cultural symbols. For instance, using symbols from refugees or LGBTQ+ cultures should involve those who live with these experiences, ensuring that narratives are authentically represented.

By comprehending and acknowledging the expectations and perceptions of different communities, we can strategize more effective, inclusive, and respectful communication that champions diversity and equality. By exploring these dimensions, we aim to deepen our understanding of the significance of diversity and inclusion with insights and strategies to foster a culture that celebrates diversity, promotes inclusion, and drives success in today's dynamic business environment. This chapter aims to provide readers with a comprehensive understanding of the global significance of diversity and inclusion. It underscores the importance of strategic and proactive approaches that effectively address stakeholder interests and community values, stimulate critical thought, and inspire innovative solutions for a more inclusive and equitable future.

2. THE ECONOMIC IMPLICATIONS OF DIVERSITY AND INCLUSION

In today's rapidly evolving global landscape, diversity and inclusion have emerged as crucial pillars of success for organizations. The increasing interconnectedness of economies, technological advancements, and changing societal expectations has spotlighted the need for organizations to foster diverse and inclusive environments. Beyond being mere buzzwords, diversity and inclusion are essential components for thriving businesses and progressive societies.

Historically, organizations have often faced criticism for their lack of representation and inclusivity. Marginalized groups, including women, racial and ethnic minorities, individuals with disabilities, and the LGBTQ+ community, are underrepresented and face barriers to advancement and equal opportunities. This lack of diversity not only perpetuates inequality, but also hampers innovation, stifles creativity, and limits organizations' ability to adapt to diverse customer bases.

In recent years, there has been a paradigm shift in our understanding of diversity and inclusion. Organizations have come to recognize the significant benefits of embracing diversity and fostering an inclusive culture. A diverse workforce brings together individuals with a range of backgrounds, experiences, and perspectives, leading to increased creativity, broader problem-solving capabilities, and improved decision-making processes. Moreover, an inclusive culture that values and respects individual differences fosters a sense of belonging, engagement, and loyalty among employees, resulting in higher productivity and reduced turnover.

The social landscape also plays a vital role in shaping the importance of diversity and inclusion. Activism, social movements, and increased public awareness have raised expectations for organizations to go beyond tokenistic gestures and commit to creating diverse and inclusive spaces. Customers, employees, and investors are increasingly demanding transparency, accountability, and authentic representation in organizational practices and policies.

Understanding the multifaceted implications of diversity and inclusion is essential for organizations to navigate challenges and leverage the opportunities they present. This chapter delves into the economic, image, and meaning implications of diversity and inclusion, providing a comprehensive analysis of their impact on organizations and society.

The economic benefits of diversity and inclusion are no longer seen as merely ancillary; they are now understood to be central to the health and vitality of organizations across industries. In this section, we delve into the multifaceted economic implications of diversity and inclusion, exploring how these practices contribute to the overall success and sustainability of organizations. This exploration focuses on four key areas: access to a wider talent pool, improved financial performance, reduced turnover, and enhanced reputation. By understanding these economic implications, we can further appreciate the tangible benefits diversity and inclusion bring to the corporate world, beyond their intrinsic value in promoting fairness and equity.

2.1. Access to a Wider Talent Pool

Embracing diversity and inclusion in the workplace expands an organization's access to a broader talent pool, yielding numerous advantages in a globalized world. Talents are no longer confined to specific demographic segments or geographical areas. By valuing diversity and inclusion, organizations can attract a wider variety of candidates with unique perspectives, experiences, and skills, which can fuel innovation and creativity within the company (Hunt et al., 2018).

When organizations prioritize diversity and inclusion, they signal to potential candidates that they value different backgrounds, perspectives, and ideas. This attracts individuals from diverse backgrounds, who might bring fresh insights and approaches to problem-solving. In 2020, 47% of millennials considered a company's diversity and inclusion policies when job searching, and 76% of job seekers said that a diverse workforce was important when evaluating companies and job offers. Kochhar, 2020)

By assembling teams with diverse perspectives and skill sets, organizations can tap into a wealth of collective knowledge and foster a culture of collaboration and creativity. Moreover, having diverse teams allows organizations to better understand and cater to their increasingly diverse customer bases, providing them with a competitive advantage in the market (Gotsis & Kortezi, 2015). With globalization and increased connectivity, companies now operate in multicultural environments. By embracing diversity and inclusion, organizations can draw on the insights and cultural competencies of their diverse workforce to tailor products, services, and marketing strategies that resonate with a wide range of customers. Understanding and responsiveness to diverse customer needs and preferences can lead to improved customer satisfaction, loyalty, and market share.

In essence, embracing diversity and inclusion broadens an organization's talent pool, enabling it to attract individuals with diverse backgrounds, perspectives, and skills. This diversity drives innovation, creativity, and problem-solving, positioning the organization for long-term success. By understanding and meeting the needs of a diverse customer base, organizations can gain a competitive edge in the marketplace. Access to a wider talent pool through diversity and inclusion has become an essential asset for organizations seeking to thrive in a globalized and interconnected world.

2.2. Improved Financial Performance

A growing body of research has highlighted the positive correlation between diversity and improved financial performance. Organizations that prioritize diversity and inclusion have demonstrated potential for enhanced profitability and sustainable growth. These findings underline the crucial link among diversity, innovation, and financial success.

Research conducted by McKinsey & Company reveals compelling evidence of the financial benefits associated with diversity. Companies in the top quartile of racial and ethnic diversity are 35% more likely to outperform their industry peers in terms of financial returns (Hunt et al., 2018). This indicates that embracing diversity and creating an inclusive environment can translate into tangible economic gain. And inclusive companies are 57% more likely to improve their reputation and brand image. (Delloite, 2021)

Diverse perspectives, experiences, and backgrounds within an organization foster a dynamic and innovative culture, enabling companies to adapt and thrive in an increasingly complex and competitive marketplace.

Furthermore, a study by the Peterson Institute for International Economics provides additional support for the positive relationship between diversity and financial performance. This study found a significant correlation between the presence of women in leadership roles and profitability. Companies with a higher representation of women in executive positions experienced, on average, a 15% increase in profitability (Noland et al., 2016). This finding suggests that gender diversity in leadership brings about unique perspectives and decision-making approaches that contribute to improved financial outcomes.

The positive impact of diversity on financial performance can be attributed to several factors. First, diversity fosters a broader range of ideas and viewpoints, leading to more comprehensive problem solving and innovative strategies. Diverse teams challenge conventional thinking, stimulate creativity, and promote out-of-the-box solutions for complex business challenges.

Second, diversity and inclusion contribute to a better understanding of and connections with diverse customer segments. As organizations become more representative of their customer base, they gain insight into different preferences, needs, and cultural nuances. This understanding enables them to develop products and services that resonate with a diverse range of consumers, expanding their market reach and potential revenue stream.

Moreover, diverse teams promote effective decision-making through constructive debate and the consideration of multiple perspectives. This inclusive approach reduces the risk of groupthink and fosters critical analysis, leading to informed and balanced business decisions.

In conclusion, an increasing body of evidence supports a positive correlation between diversity and improved financial performance. Organizations that prioritize diversity and inclusion create an environment that fosters innovation, enhances problem-solving capabilities, and better connects with diverse customer bases. By leveraging the unique perspectives and talents of a diverse workforce, organizations can unlock new opportunities, drive growth, and achieve sustainable financial success. Embracing diversity is not only a social imperative, but also a strategic advantage that contributes to improved financial outcomes and long-term competitiveness in the dynamic business landscape.

2.3. Reduced Turnover

Creating an inclusive and diverse workplace environment contributes to reducing employee turnover. Employees who feel included, valued, and respected are more likely to develop a strong sense of loyalty and commitment to the organization. This, in turn, leads to reduced turnover costs, including expenses associated with hiring and training new employees as well as productivity losses resulting from vacant positions.

A study conducted by Delloite University Press (2017) emphasized the impact of diversity and inclusion on employee retention. This study shows that 78 percent of respondents now believe diversity and inclusion is a competitive advantage (39 percent say it is a "significant" competitive advantage). In 2017 survey, the proportion of executives who cited inclusion as a top priority has risen by 32 percent compared with the 2014 survey. And over two-thirds (69 percent) of the executives rate diversity and inclusion an important issue (up from 59 percent in 2014). "As awareness around diversity and inclusion grows, diversity and inclusion have become more important for talent acquisition and a company's employment brand. Many organizations operate in an environment of high transparency, which employees demand." About the Millennials, the study shows that "inclusion is not just about assembling diverse teams but also about connecting team members so that everyone is heard and respected. And companies should align their approach with the expectations of Millennials and others, or they will likely lose talent". (Delloite UP, 2017). This indicates that when employees feel a sense of belonging and see themselves represented within the workplace, they are more inclined to remain committed and engaged, thereby reducing their turnover rates.

Several factors contribute to the relationship between diversity, inclusion, and turnover. First, when employees feel included and valued, they experience a strong sense of job satisfaction. This satisfaction stems from the recognition and appreciation of their unique contributions and perspectives within the organization. These positive experiences enhance employee engagement, motivation, and overall job commitment.

Moreover, an inclusive workplace fosters an environment in which individuals from diverse backgrounds can fully contribute their skills and talent. This sense of empowerment and opportunities for growth and advancement can significantly affect employee retention. When employees perceive that their contributions are valued and that they have equal access to opportunities for career development, they are more likely to stay with the organization and invest in their long-term professional growth.

Additionally, inclusive culture promotes positive relationships and effective communication among employees. When individuals from diverse backgrounds collaborate, share ideas, and learn from one another, they develop a sense of belonging and camaraderie. This positive social environment enhances job satisfaction and strengthens the bonds between employees and the organization, making them less inclined to seek opportunities elsewhere.

Reducing employee turnover offers numerous benefits to organizations. This helps minimize the costs associated with recruiting, hiring, and training new employees. It also contributes to the preservation of institutional knowledge and continuity of productivity and efficiency within the organization. Furthermore, a stable workforce improves team dynamics, fosters stronger relationships, and facilitates collaboration.

In conclusion, fostering an inclusive and diverse workplace has a direct impact on reducing employee turnover. When employees feel included, valued, and respected, they are more likely to remain committed and engage within the organization. This, in turn, decreases turnover costs and helps to create a more stable and productive workforce. By prioritizing diversity and inclusion, organizations can foster a workplace culture that supports employee retention and strengthens their overall human capital.

2.4. Enhanced Reputation

Organizations that prioritize diversity and inclusion often enjoy an enhanced reputation among stakeholders, including employees, customers, and investors. These organizations are socially responsible and progressive, which can significantly enhance their brand image, customer loyalty, and overall market position.

In today's socially conscious world, consumers are becoming increasingly aware of the values and practices of the companies they support. Organizations that demonstrate genuine commitment to diversity and inclusion are perceived as socially responsible entities that value fairness, equality, and inclusivity. This positive reputation can contribute to increased customer loyalty, as consumers are more likely to align themselves with organizations that share their values and ideals.

Furthermore, employees are attracted to organizations that prioritize diversity and inclusion. A strong reputation for embracing diversity and creating an inclusive work environment can serve as a magnet for top talents. Prospective employees seek organizations aligned with their personal values and aspirations. They are more likely to be attracted to companies that are known for their inclusive practices and reputation, resulting in a larger pool of high-quality candidates.

Investors also consider an organization's reputation when making their investment decisions. Companies that prioritize diversity and inclusion are often viewed as forward-thinking, adaptable, and better-positioned to navigate the complexities of a rapidly changing business landscape. Investors recognize the long-term value of organizations that promote diversity and inclusion, as these factors contribute to innovation, resilience, and sustainability.

A study conducted by Corporate Responsibility Magazine underscores the significance of reputation in attracting talent. The research found that 76% of the surveyed individuals refused to work for a company with a poor reputation (Fombrun et al., 2019). This highlights the importance of reputation in attracting and retaining top talent, as employees seek organizations that align with their values and ethical standards.

In conclusion, the economic implications of diversity and inclusion are substantial, and extend beyond financial performance and reduced turnover. Organizations that embrace diversity and inclusion can also enjoy an enhanced reputation among stakeholders. By prioritizing diversity and inclusion, organizations are seen as socially responsible and progressive, leading to improved brand image, customer loyalty, and attractiveness to investors. This positive reputation provides a competitive edge and strengthens the overall market position of organizations committed to diversity and inclusion.

2.5. Enhanced Problem-Solving and Innovation

One of the significant benefits of diversity and inclusion in the workplace is the enhancement of problem-solving capabilities and fostering of innovation. Research indicates that diverse teams are more effective in solving problems and generating innovative solutions than teams composed of individuals with similar cognitive backgrounds.

A study conducted by Harvard Business Review found that diverse teams can solve problems faster than groups comprising cognitively similar individuals (Phillips, 2014). When people from diverse backgrounds and experiences come together, they bring along a wide range of perspectives, insights, and approaches to problem-solving. This diversity of viewpoints allows for a more comprehensive analysis of complex challenges and opens new avenues for innovative thinking. Companies with more diverse management teams have 19% higher revenue due to innovation. (GrowthForce. Human Capital, n.d.)

Diverse teams are better equipped to identify and examine problems from multiple perspectives, which can lead to more robust and creative solutions. Each team member contributes a unique expertise and experience, resulting in a more comprehensive understanding of the problem at hand. This diversity of perspectives fosters a culture of critical thinking and constructive debate, stimulates creativity, and enables teams to explore innovative approaches.

Diverse teams benefit from a phenomenon known as cognitive diversity. This refers to a range of individual thinking styles, problem-solving techniques, and cognitive processes within a group. Cognitive diversity broadens the range of potential solutions and increases the likelihood of finding unconventional or breakthrough ideas. By leveraging the collective intelligence of diverse team members, organizations can tap into a vast pool of knowledge and generate innovative solutions that might not be achievable within homogenous teams.

Inclusive work environments, in which value diversity creates a sense of psychological safety, where individuals feel comfortable expressing their ideas, challenging conventional thinking, and taking calculated risks. Psychological safety nurtures a culture of experimentation and continuous learning, fostering an environment that encourages innovation and creativity.

In conclusion, diversity and inclusion in the workplace enhances problem-solving capabilities and fuel innovation. Diverse teams bring together a variety of perspectives and experiences, enabling a comprehensive analysis of problems and development of innovative solutions. By embracing diversity and fostering inclusive environments, organizations can tap into the collective intelligence of their diverse workforce, generating fresh ideas and breakthrough innovations that contribute to their competitive advantage and long-term success.

2.6. Broadened Market Understanding

Diversity and inclusion play vital roles in broadening an organization's understanding of the global market. By embracing diversity and creating an inclusive work environment, organizations can gain valuable insights into diverse customer segments, allowing them to cater to a wide range of needs, preferences, and cultural nuances. This deepened understanding of the market contributes to product innovation, customization, and ultimately, customer satisfaction and loyalty.

A diverse workforce brings together individuals from varied backgrounds, experiences, and perspectives. This diversity of viewpoints helps organizations to better comprehend the complexities and nuances of different customer segments. By having employees who reflect on the diversity of their customer base, organizations can develop a deeper understanding of customers' cultural, social, and behavioral dynamics (Herring, 2009). This insight is crucial in creating products and services that resonate with diverse markets.

Understanding the unique needs and preferences of diverse customer segments enables organizations to tailor their offerings more effectively. This allows them to develop products and services that align with customers' cultural values, language preferences, and specific requirements. This customization not only increases the relevance and appeal of the organization's offerings but also strengthens the bond between the organization and its customers. Organizations can enhance customer satisfaction, loyalty, and retention by addressing the unique needs of diverse market segments.

Furthermore, an organization that values diversity and inclusion is more likely to foster a culture of empathy and customer-centricity. Employees from diverse backgrounds can bring a heightened sense of empathy and understanding when interacting with customers who may come from different cultural or socioeconomic contexts. This empathetic approach enables organizations to build stronger connections with their customers, leading to increased trust and brand loyalty.

Moreover, diverse teams can serve as valuable resources for market research and consumer insights. Diverse perspectives and experiences within the team enable a more comprehensive analysis of market trends, consumer behavior, and emerging opportunities. These insights can guide organizations in identifying untapped market segments, uncovering emerging needs, and developing innovative solutions to meet evolving customer demands.

In conclusion, diversity and inclusion broaden an organization's market understanding by fostering insights into diverse customer segments. By leveraging the diverse perspectives and experiences of their employees, organizations can gain a deeper understanding of customer needs, preferences, and cultural nuances. This understanding facilitates product innovation, customization, and the development of customer-centric strategies. Ultimately, organizations that prioritize diversity and inclusion are better equipped to navigate and succeed in a diverse and rapidly evolving global market.

2.7. Risk Management

Diversity and inclusion play critical roles in risk management within organizations. By fostering a diverse and inclusive workforce, organizations can enhance their ability to anticipate, identify, and effectively respond to a wide range of challenges and risks. Diverse teams bring different perspectives, experiences, and knowledge to the table, enabling them to recognize potential threats from various angles and devise comprehensive strategies to mitigate them.

Diverse teams offer a wider array of insights and viewpoints when assessing risks and making decisions. Individuals from different backgrounds and experiences possess unique expertise and knowledge that can help identify blind spots, consider alternative scenarios, and uncover potential risks that might otherwise go unnoticed. This diverse perspective allows organizations to adopt a more holistic and comprehensive approach to risk management.

Research conducted by McKinsey & Company highlights the benefits of diversity in risk management. Hunt et al. (2015) found that diverse companies are better equipped to attract top talent, improve customer orientation, enhance employee satisfaction, and enhance decision-making processes. This virtuous cycle of increasing returns contributes to a stronger risk management framework within organizations.

In addition, a diverse and inclusive workforce promotes a culture of open communication and constructive debates. Employees who feel valued, respected, and included are more likely to express their concerns and opinions regarding potential risks or issues. This open dialogue allows organizations to identify and address risks proactively, reducing the likelihood of potential problems escalating into significant crises.

Moreover, diverse teams can draw upon their collective knowledge and experience to develop innovative and effective risk-mitigation strategies. Different perspectives can shed light on alternative approaches and potential solutions, enabling organizations to consider a broader range of options. This diversity of thought enhances an organization's ability to adapt to changing circumstances, navigate uncertainties, and effectively manage risks.

Furthermore, a diverse and inclusive work environment can help organizations anticipate and respond to risks related to changing demographics, cultural shifts, and evolving market dynamics. By reflecting on the diversity of the communities they serve, organizations can stay attuned to emerging trends, anticipate potential challenges, and adjust their strategies accordingly. This proactive approach to risk management enables organizations to be more agile, resilient, and better prepared to navigate the complexities of an ever-changing business landscape.

In conclusion, diversity and inclusion contribute to effective risk management by leveraging the collective insights, perspectives, and experiences of diverse workforces. By embracing diversity, organizations can better anticipate, identify, and respond to a wide range of challenges and risks. Diverse teams enhance decision-making processes, foster open communication, and promote innovative risk mitigation strategies. Consequently, organizations can establish a robust risk management framework that enables them to navigate uncertainties and safeguard their long-term success.

2.8. Promoting Corporate Social Responsibility (CSR)

Embracing diversity and inclusion within an organization goes hand in hand with promoting corporate social responsibility (CSR). A diverse and inclusive workplace is often regarded as a reflection of an organization's commitment to equality, fairness, and respect for all individuals, aligned with the principles of CSR. By prioritizing diversity and inclusion, organizations not only enhance their reputation, but also become more attractive to socially conscious investors, customers, and potential employees.

Corporate social responsibility entails conducting business in an ethical and responsible manner, considering the impact of organizational actions on various stakeholders, including employees, customers, communities, and the environment. By fostering diversity and inclusion, organizations demonstrate their dedication to creating an inclusive and equitable work environment that respects and values the unique contributions of every individual.

A diverse and inclusive workplace promotes a culture of fairness, equality and respect. This ensures that all individuals, regardless of their background, identity, or characteristics, are provided with equal opportunities, recognition, and support. By valuing diversity and inclusion, organizations send powerful messages to their stakeholders about their commitment to social responsibility.

Moreover, organizations that prioritize diversity and inclusion are more likely to adopt policies and practices that promote social and environmental sustainability. They are inclined to develop inclusive hiring practices, provide equal opportunities for professional growth and development, and foster workplace cultures that celebrate diversity. These initiatives contribute to a more inclusive and equitable society, while addressing the social and economic disparities that exist within communities.

The promotion of diversity and inclusion also has a positive impact on an organization's reputation, which is a crucial aspect of corporate social responsibility. Organizations recognized for their commitment to diversity and inclusion are viewed as socially responsible entities that value fairness, equality, and respect. This positive reputation enhances stakeholders' perceptions of the organization's values and practices, ultimately strengthening its position in the market.

Additionally, embracing diversity and inclusion can attract socially conscious investors, customers, and employees. In today's socially aware and value-driven society, individuals are increasingly seeking organizations that align with their own principles and beliefs. Organizations that prioritize diversity and inclusion are attractive choices for socially conscious investors interested in supporting companies that uphold ethical standards and promote social justice.

Customers are also drawn to organizations that demonstrate commitment to diversity and inclusion. Studies have shown that consumers prefer to engage with businesses that have diverse and inclusive practices and are more likely to support brands that align with their values (Sood & Nasu, 2018). By fostering diversity and inclusion, organizations can build a loyal customer base and strengthen their market position.

Furthermore, organizations that promote diversity and inclusion are more likely to attract talent. Talented individuals increasingly prioritize workplaces that foster an inclusive environment in which they can bring their authentic selves, feel valued, and have equal opportunities for growth and advancement. By embracing diversity and inclusion, organizations can attract a diverse pool of talented individuals who are passionate about contributing to socially responsible and inclusive organizations.

In conclusion, embracing diversity and inclusion promotes corporate social responsibility by demonstrating an organization's commitment to equality, fairness, and respect. It enhances an organization's reputation and makes it more attractive to socially conscious investors, customers, and potential employees. By prioritizing diversity and inclusion, organizations not only contribute to a more inclusive and equitable society, but also align themselves with the principles of corporate social responsibility, fostering a positive impact on both the organization and its stakeholders.

To summarize, the economic implications of diversity and inclusion extend beyond financial performance. They play a significant role in enhancing problem-solving capabilities, promoting innovation, broadening market understanding, managing risk, and promoting corporate social responsibility. Embracing diversity and inclusion can therefore provide organizations with a competitive advantage in the global market, fostering long-term sustainability and growth. By valuing and leveraging the diverse perspectives, talents, and experiences of individuals, organizations can foster a culture of inclusivity, drive positive change, and create a prosperous and equitable future for all.

3. IMAGE IMPLICATIONS OF DIVERSITY AND INCLUSION

As organizations strive to become more inclusive and diverse, their impact on their image becomes increasingly pronounced. In a world where social consciousness is on the rise, the image of a company project can greatly influence its relationships with its stakeholders, including its employees, customers, investors, and the wider community.

3.1. Internal Image

A positive internal image is crucial for the healthy functioning of an organization. A diverse and inclusive workplace can create a strong sense of belonging among employees, increasing their engagement with and commitment to the company. In such an environment, every individual feels valued and respected, which can lead to improved morale, enhanced productivity, and overall job satisfaction (Dobbin & Kalev, 2016). The perception of the organization as a place that truly values diversity and inclusion can be a powerful factor in attracting and retaining a talented workforce. Research suggests that employees are more attracted to employers who demonstrate commitment to diversity and inclusion (Pichler et al., 2017). When employees feel valued and included, they are more likely to be advocates for the organization, leading to positive word-of-mouth and a favorable internal image.

3.2. External Image

Externally, a strong commitment to diversity and inclusion can considerably enhance a company's reputation among consumers and the public. Companies perceived as inclusive, and representative of diverse communities tend to enjoy more favorable public sentiment. This positive image can lead to increased customer loyalty and a larger market share (Brands & Fernandez-Mateo, 2017). Today, consumers are increasingly conscious of a company's stance on social issues and are more likely to support organizations that align with their values. In 2020, 81% of consumers said they would stop buying from a company if they learned it was engaging in discriminatory practices (Alemany, 2022).

Moreover, companies that prioritize diversity and inclusion can receive more positive media coverage and recognition from external ranking entities, further elevating their public image. A positive external image enhances trust, credibility, and brand value, ultimately contributing to long-term success. In 2020, 62% of consumers said they would buy from a brand that took a stand on social issues they cared about (Ipsos, 2021).

3.3. Investor Relations

The image of a company project also significantly influences investor relationships. In recent years, investors have begun to factor in diversity and include decision-making processes. Companies demonstrating a commitment to these principles are often seen as more innovative, adaptable, and ready to meet changing market conditions (Eccles, Ioannou, & Serafeim, 2014). Investors recognize the value of diversity in driving creativity, fostering different perspectives, and enhancing problem-solving capabilities within organizations. Thus, strong commitment to diversity and inclusion can enhance a company's attractiveness to investors, potentially leading to increased investment and financial stability.

The image implications of diversity and inclusion have far-reaching consequences. Companies that embrace these principles can cultivate positive internal and external images, attract and retain high-quality talent, foster customer loyalty, and appeal to a wider pool of investors. Through these benefits, diversity and inclusion can strengthen a company's market position and contribute to long-term sustainability. By projecting an image of inclusivity, fairness, and respect, organizations can position themselves as socially responsible entities that value diversity and contribute positively to society. This alignment with stakeholder expectations and societal values fosters a positive image, which can lead to a competitive advantage in the global market. In 2020, the global market for diversity and inclusion consulting was valued at $31.9 billion. (Research and Markets, 2022).

4. MEANING IMPLICATIONS OF DIVERSITY AND INCLUSION

Understanding the implications of diversity and inclusion extends beyond economic and image perspectives. It also encompasses the deeper and more profound layers of meaning that these concepts bring to an organization and society as a whole.

4.1. Cultural Competency

Diversity and inclusion initiatives foster cultural competencies within organizations. This means acknowledging, appreciating, and leveraging the wide array of cultural backgrounds, languages, experiences, and worldviews employees bring to the workplace. By doing so, organizations create a richer, more dynamic environment that is more capable of innovation and problem-solving. Culturally competent organizations tend to be more effective in serving diverse customer bases and operating in global markets.

4.2. Social Justice

Promoting diversity and inclusion is a concrete step towards addressing systemic social injustices. It challenges biases, stereotypes, and discriminatory practices that have historically marginalized certain groups (Pless & Maak, 2011). By creating an inclusive environment, organizations send powerful messages about their commitment to fairness, equity, and social justice.

4.3. Equity

Diversity and inclusion are central to promoting equity in organizations. Equity is about ensuring fair treatment, equality of opportunity, and fairness in access to information and resources for all (Choi & Rainey, 2010). By prioritizing diversity and inclusion, organizations can create a workplace in which all individuals have the opportunity to contribute, advance, and succeed.

In summary, the implications of diversity and inclusion are both profound. They touch on the vital aspects of cultural competency, social justice, and equity. Therefore, embracing diversity and inclusion is not just a business strategy, it is also a commitment to creating a more equitable and just society.

4.4. Inclusion as a Catalyst for Change

Diversity and inclusion can act as catalysts for organizational and societal changes. By valuing diversity, organizations can disrupt homogenous thinking and create a space for multiple perspectives to thrive. This can lead to more innovative problem solving and decision-making processes (Phillips, 2014). Similarly, inclusion can challenge power structures within organizations, giving voice to individuals who have traditionally been marginalized or excluded. Inclusive companies are 1.7 times more likely to be innovation leaders in their market. (Together equal, n.d.)

4.5. Sense of Belonging

A diverse and inclusive workplace fosters a sense of belonging among all employees regardless of their backgrounds or identities. Employees who feel like they belong are more likely to feel engaged and committed to their work, which can lead to increased productivity and job satisfaction (Walton & Brady, 2017). Moreover, a sense of belonging can contribute to employees' overall well-being as they feel valued, respected, and supported in their work environment.

In conclusion, the implications of diversity and inclusion are far-reaching, touching on the vital aspects of our societal fabric. By embracing diversity and inclusion, organizations not only enrich their cultural competence and promote equity, but also become agents of social justice, fostering a sense of belonging and acting as catalysts for change.

4.6. Social and Cultural Awareness

Organizations inherently cultivate social and cultural awareness by investing in diversity and inclusion. This enhanced awareness can lead to greater understanding, respect, and value for different cultures, social groups, and perspectives within the organization. It broadens the collective mindset and fosters an environment that appreciates the richness of diverse experiences (Özbilgin, Tatli, Ipek, & Sameer, 2014).

4.7 Corporate Social Responsibility

Diversity and inclusion are increasingly being seen as key components of corporate social responsibility (CSR). Organizations that are committed to diversity and inclusion fulfill their ethical and societal obligations by recognizing and valuing the diversity of the communities they serve. Diversity and inclusion can have a significant impact on a company's brand image. By promoting diversity and inclusion, a company can position itself as a socially responsible organization that values and respects differences. This can help attract customers who prioritize diversity and inclusion in their purchasing decisions. Emphasizing diversity and inclusion in CSR strategies signals to stakeholders that the organization is committed to equitable practices and is actively working to reduce social and economic disparities (Dahlsrud 2008).

4.8. Positive Impact on Society

Finally, diversity and inclusion initiatives can have broad and positive impacts on society. By promoting and valuing diversity, organizations can help challenge stereotypes, combat discrimination, and foster greater social cohesion. Moreover, by ensuring that a wide array of voices and experiences are included and valued, organizations can contribute to a more equitable and inclusive society (Page, 2017).

In conclusion, the meaning of diversity and inclusion extends beyond the boundaries of an organization, playing a crucial role in promoting social and cultural awareness, embodying corporate social responsibility, and positively impacting society as a whole.

5. THE MEANING DIMENSION OF DIVERSITY AND INCLUSION:

Diversity and inclusion hold profound significance beyond their evident benefits to organizational performance and reputation. They signify a broader social context and an understanding of human relationships and interactions within organizations and society.

5.1. Creating a Shared Understanding

Diversity and inclusion initiatives aim to create a shared understanding of the value of unique experiences, identities, and perspectives. They promote the idea that individual differences are a source of strength and creativity, rather than division (Shore et al., 2018). By fostering such understanding, organizations can break down barriers, promote empathy, and facilitate collaboration across diverse teams. By valuing diverse perspectives and incorporating them into decision-making processes, organizations can tap into a wider range of ideas, insights, and solutions.

5.2. Enhancing Human Dignity

At their core, diversity and inclusion initiatives emphasize respect for human dignity. They echo the fundamental belief that everyone, regardless of their background or identity, deserves to be treated with respect and fairness and that their contributions should be valued. By promoting diversity and inclusion, organizations reinforce the significance of human dignity in the workplace and beyond. They create an environment in which individuals feel safe, accepted, and empowered to express their authentic selves, fostering a sense of belonging and psychological well-being.

5.3. Shaping Organizational Identity

Diversity and inclusion significantly shape an organization's identity. They define how an organization sees itself and how it wants to be perceived by others. An organization that values diversity and inclusion sends a strong message about its values, culture, and vision for the future (Hatch and Schultz 2002). By embracing diversity and inclusion, organizations not only reflect on the diverse societies in which they operate, but also demonstrate their commitment to social progress, equality, and inclusivity. This can attract like-minded individuals, customers, and stakeholders, who align with their values and contribute to their overall success.

5.4. Promoting Social Progress

Diversity and inclusion initiatives play crucial roles in advancing social progress. They challenge societal norms, combat discrimination, and promote social cohesion. Organizations become agents of change by fostering inclusive environments and promoting fairness, equality, and justice. They help forge a more inclusive, equitable, and just society in which everyone has the opportunity to thrive (Page, 2017). Through their actions, organizations can influence social norms, break down barriers, and create a ripple effect that extends beyond their boundaries.

In summary, the meaning of the dimensions of diversity and inclusion are broad and profound. It touches upon creating a shared understanding, enhancing human dignity, shaping organizational identity, and promoting social progress. By embracing diversity and inclusion, organizations are not just improving their performance or reputation; they also contribute to a more inclusive and equitable world. Through their commitment to diversity and inclusion, organizations can foster positive social change, empower individuals, and create environments where diversity is celebrated, respected, and harnessed for the benefit of all.

6. CHALLENGES AND FUTURE DIRECTIONS OF DIVERSITY AND INCLUSION INITIATIVES

While the benefits of diversity and inclusion are well documented, organizations may face several challenges when implementing these initiatives. This chapter also explores potential future directions for enhancing the effectiveness of diversity and inclusion efforts.

6.1. Resistance to Change

One of the significant challenges in implementing diversity and inclusion initiatives is the resistance to change. Employees may resist new policies or practices because of fear of the unknown, perceived threats to their status, or deeply held biases and stereotypes (Ford et al., 2008). Overcoming this resistance requires organizations to address these challenges. It is crucial to communicate the benefits of diversity and inclusion, provide training and education to foster awareness and understanding, and create an environment that supports and embraces changes. By addressing resistance to change, organizations can create a culture that embraces diversity and inclusion as catalysts for growth and innovation.

6.2. Lack of Diversity in Leadership Positions

Despite progress in many areas, there is still a lack of diversity in leadership positions in many organizations. This underrepresentation can hinder the effectiveness of diversity and inclusion initiatives as it sends a message that only certain groups are suited for leadership roles (Cook & Glass, 2014). To address this challenge, organizations need to prioritize the development and advancement of diverse talents. This includes implementing strategies to reduce bias in promotional decisions, fostering inclusive leadership behaviors, and providing mentorship and sponsorship opportunities to individuals from underrepresented groups. By creating a diverse leadership pipeline, organizations can ensure that diverse perspectives are represented at the decision-making level.

6.3. Need for Greater Accountability and Transparency

Another challenge for diversity and inclusion initiatives is the need for greater accountability and transparency. Without clear metrics and regular reporting, it can be difficult to track progress and hold individuals and teams accountable. Organizations should establish clear diversity and inclusion goals, measure progress, and communicate their results to all stakeholders. Transparency and accountability help to create a culture of trust and ensure that diversity and inclusion efforts are consistently prioritized and evaluated. By fostering a culture of accountability, organizations can demonstrate their commitment to diversity and inclusion and drive continuous improvement.

In terms of future directions, organizations should continue to innovate and adapt their diversity and inclusion practices to changing societal norms and expectations. This could include expanding the understanding of diversity beyond traditional categories to encompass dimensions, such as neurodiversity and intersectionality. Leveraging technology can also play a crucial role in promoting inclusion such as remote work options, virtual collaboration platforms, and inclusive AI tools. Additionally, organizations should integrate diversity and inclusion considerations into all aspects of the organization, including talent acquisition, performance management, and leadership development. By embedding diversity and inclusion as core values and practices, organizations can create an inclusive and equitable culture that drives sustainable success.

In summary, while there are challenges in implementing diversity and inclusion initiatives, these can be overcome through strategic planning, effective communication, and unwavering commitment. By continually evolving and adapting, organizations can ensure that their diversity and inclusion efforts remain effective and relevant in the future. By addressing resistance to change, promoting diversity in leadership, fostering accountability and transparency, and embracing future directions, organizations can create a workplace that celebrates diversity, fosters inclusion, and drives innovation and success.

7. DIVERSITY AND INCLUSION MAKE THE WORKPLACE MORE COMPETITIVE

IBM has been a leader in diversity and inclusion initiatives for decades. In 2018, they launched their Reinvention Program which aimed to retrain and reskill their employees who were at risk of losing their jobs due to technological changes. This program was specifically targeted towards older employees and those without a college degree, groups that are often underrepresented in the tech industry. (IBM Careers, n.d.)

Unilever has also been recognized for their diversity and inclusion efforts. They have implemented a Diversity and Inclusion Strategy which includes initiatives such as unconscious bias training, flexible work arrangements, and employee resource groups. In 2019, they were named the top global employer by the Top Employers Institute. (Unilever, n.d.)

Salesforce is another company that has made significant strides in diversity and inclusion. They have implemented a Women's Surge program which aims to increase the number of women in leadership positions within the company. They have also established employee resource groups for underrepresented groups and have committed to achieving equal pay for all employees. (Salesforce, n.d.)

Accenture has been recognized for their diversity and inclusion initiatives, particularly in regard to gender equality. They have set a goal to achieve a gender-balanced workforce by 2025 and have implemented programs such as unconscious bias training and mentorship programs for women. In 2019, they were named the top company for gender equality by the Equileap Gender Equality Global Report and Ranking. (Accenture, n.d.)

Coca-Cola is a global company that has also implemented successful diversity and inclusion initiatives. The company has a Chief Diversity and Inclusion Officer and has set a goal to create a more diverse and inclusive workforce. Coca-Cola has implemented various programs to support this goal, including unconscious bias training, diversity recruiting initiatives, and employee resource groups. As a result, the company has seen an increase in the percentage of women and minorities in leadership positions and has been recognized as a top employer for diversity and inclusion. (The Coca-Cola Company, n.d.)

8. CONCLUSION: EMBRACING THE MULTIFACETED IMPLICATIONS OF DIVERSITY AND INCLUSION

Exploration of diversity and inclusion in this academic discourse reveals the multifaceted and far-reaching implications of these concepts. It is evident that diversity and inclusion are not mere buzzwords or superficial initiatives but hold deep significance for businesses and society. From the economic benefits of increased performance and enhanced reputation to the social progress they foster, diversity and inclusion are indispensable in our current globalized and interconnected world.

However, it is important to recognize that the journey towards true diversity and inclusion is complex and challenging. The challenges of resistance to change, lack of diversity in leadership roles, and need for greater transparency and accountability pose significant obstacles. These hurdles require deliberate effort and an unwavering commitment to overcome. Organizations must engage in strategic planning, clear communication, and proactive measures to foster an inclusive culture that embraces diversity.

Moreover, the power of diversity and inclusion extends beyond the confines of the business metrics. They have the potential to challenge societal norms and to promote social and cultural awareness. By fostering a sense of belonging and respect for individual differences, organizations can contribute to a more inclusive, equitable, and just society. Diversity and inclusion act as catalysts for social progress, dismantling barriers, and opening doors for marginalized individuals and communities.

In the future, it is crucial for organizations to continually innovate and adapt their diversity and inclusion practices to align with changing societal norms and expectations. This requires expanding our understanding of diversity beyond traditional categories, embracing intersectionality, and fostering an environment of genuine inclusion in which everyone is unique perspectives and experiences are valued.

In conclusion, the journey towards diversity and inclusion is ongoing and dynamic. It requires collective effort from organizations, leaders, employees, and society as a whole. The benefits of embracing diversity and inclusion to businesses, individuals, and society make the journey well worth undertaking. By understanding and embracing the multifaceted implications of diversity and inclusion, we can work towards a world that values and celebrates differences, where diversity is not just tolerated but embraced, and where everyone has the opportunity to thrive. It is a challenging journey, but one that holds the promise of a more inclusive, equitable, and vibrant future.

REFERENCES

Accenture. (n.d.). Advancing gender equality program. *Accenture.* https://www.accenture.com/us-en/about/inclusion-diversity/gender-equality

Alemany, C. (2022). 3 Ways Marketers Can Earn — and Keep — Customer Trust. *Harvard Business Review.* https://hbr.org/2022/06/3-ways-marketers-can-earn-and-keep-customer-trust

Choi, S., & Rainey, H. G. (2010). Managing diversity in US federal agencies: Effects of diversity and diversity management on employee perceptions of organizational performance. *Public Administration Review, 70*(1), 109–121. doi:10.1111/j.1540-6210.2009.02115.x

Cook, A., & Glass, C. (2014). Women and top leadership positions: Towards an institutional analysis. *Gender, Work and Organization, 21*(1), 91–103. doi:10.1111/gwao.12018

Dahlsrud, A. (2008). How corporate social responsibility is defined: An analysis of 37 definitions. *Corporate Social Responsibility and Environmental Management, 15*(1), 1–13. doi:10.1002/csr.132

Delloite insights. (2021). *Authentically inclusive marketing. Winning future customers with diversity, equity, and inclusion.* Deloitte. https://www2.deloitte.com/uk/en/insights/topics/marketing-and-sales-operations/global-marketing-trends/2022/diversity-and-inclusion-in-marketing.html

Delloite University Press. (2013). *Diversity's new frontier. Diversity of thought and the future of the workforce.* Deloitte. https://www2.deloitte.com/content/dam/insights/us/articles/diversitys-new-frontier/DUP426_Cognitive-diversity_vFINAL1.pdf

Delloite University Press. (2017). Diversity and inclusion: The reality gap -2017 Global Human Capital Trends. https://www2.deloitte.com/xe/en/insights/focus/human-capital-trends/2017/diversity-and-inclusion-at-the-workplace.html

Dobbin, F., & Kalev, A. (2016). Why Diversity Programs Fail. *Harvard Business Review*, *94*(7), 2–10.

Eccles, R. G., Ioannou, I., & Serafeim, G. (2014). The impact of corporate sustainability on organizational processes and performance. *Management Science*, *60*(11), 2835–2857. doi:10.1287/mnsc.2014.1984

Fombrun, C., Gardberg, N. A., & Barnett, M. L. (2019). Reputation and corporate social responsibility aberrations, trends, and hypocrisy: Reactions to firm choices in the stock option backdating scandal. *Journal of Management Studies*, *46*(7), 1319–1337.

Ford, J. D., Ford, L. W., & D'Amelio, A. (2008). Resistance to change: The rest of the story. *Academy of Management Review*, *33*(2), 362–377. doi:10.5465/amr.2008.31193235

Gotsis, G., & Kortezi, Z. (2015). The business case for diversity in the workplace: An empirical review. *Business Ethics (Oxford, England)*, *24*(2), 157–175.

GrowthForce. (n.d.) Busin*esses with Workplace Diversity Have 19% Higher Revenue. Here's Why*. GrowthForce. https://www.growthforce.com/blog/business-workplace-diversity-revenue

Hatch, M. J., & Schultz, M. (2002). The dynamics of organizational identity. *Human Relations*, *55*(8), 989–1018. doi:10.1177/0018726702055008181

Herring, C. (2009). Does Diversity Pay? Race, Gender, and the Business Case for Diversity. *American Sociological Review*, *74*(2), 208–224. doi:10.1177/000312240907400203

Hunt, V., Layton, D., & Prince, S. (2015). *Why Diversity Matters*. McKinsey & Company. https://www.mckinsey.com/business-functions/organization/our-insights/why-diversity-matters

Hunt, V., Yee, L., Prince, S., & Dixon-Fyle, S. (2018). *Delivering through diversity*. McKinsey & Company. https://www.mckinsey.com/capabilities/people-and-organizational-performance/our-insights/delivering-through-diversity

Ipsos. (2021). *Consumers want deeper social-justice commitments from brands*. Ipsos. https://www.ipsos.com/en-us/knowledge/society/Consumers-want-deeper-social-justice-commitments-from-brands

Kochhar, S. (2020). *Millenials@work: perspectives on diversity & inclusion*. Institute for Public Relations. https://instituteforpr.org/millennialswork-perspectives-diversity-inclusion/

McKinsey & Company. (2020) *Diversity wins. How inclusion matters. May 2020 report*. McKinsey. https://www.mckinsey.com/~/media/mckinsey/featured%20insights/diversity%20and%20inclusion/diversity%20wins%20how%20inclusion%20matters/diversity-wins-how-inclusion-matters-vf.pdf

Noland, M., Moran, T., & Kotschwar, B. (2016*). Is Gender Diversity Profitable?* Evidence from a Global Survey. *Peterson Institute for International Economics Working Paper, 16(*3).

Özbilgin, M., Tatli, A., Ipek, G., & Sameer, M. (2014). *Four approaches to accounting for diversity in global organizations*. Deloitte Case Studies. https://www2.deloitte.com/au/en/pages/human-capital/articles/four-approaches-accounting-diversity-global-organisations.html

Page, S. E. (2017). *The diversity bonus: How great teams pay off in the knowledge economy*. Princeton University Press. doi:10.2307/j.ctvc77c0h

Phillips, K. W. (2014). How Diversity Makes Us Smarter. *Harvard Business Review*. https://hbr.org/2014/10/how-diversity-makes-us-smarter

Pichler, S., Ruggs, E., & Trau, R. (2017). Worker outcomes of LGBT-supportive policies: A cross-level model. *Equality, Diversity and Inclusion*, *36*(1), 17–32. doi:10.1108/EDI-07-2016-0058

Pless, N. M., & Maak, T. (2011). *Responsible leadership: Pathways to the future*. Research Gate. https://www.researchgate.net/publication/227451528_Responsible_Leadership_Pathways_to_the_Future

Research and Markets. (2022). *Global Diversity and Inclusion (D&I) Market Report 2021*. Research and Markets. https://www.globenewswire.com/news-release/2022/01/27/2374060/28124/en/Global-Diversity-and-Inclusion-D-I-Market-Report-2021-Market-is-Estimated-at-7-5-Billion-in-2020-and-is-Projected-to-Reach-15-4-Billion-by-2026-Growing-at-a-CAGR-of-12-6.html

Rogers, R. A. (2006). *From cultural exchange to transculturation: A review and reconceptualization of cultural appropriation*. Research Gate. https://www.researchgate.net/publication/227630287_From_Cultural_Exchange_to_Transculturation_A_Review_and_Reconceptualization_of_Cultural_Appropriation

Salesforce. (n.d.). *Bring Women back to work. (BWBW)*. Salesforce. https://www.salesforce.com/eu/campaign/bwbw/

Shore, L. M., Randel, A. E., Chung, B. G., Dean, M. A., Ehrhart, K. H., & Singh, G. (2018). Inclusion and diversity in workgroups: A review and model for future research. *Journal of Management*, *37*(4), 1262–1289. doi:10.1177/0149206310385943

The Coca-Cola Compay. (n.d.). *Diversity, Equity & Inclusion. Creating a culture of diversity, equity and inclusion*. Coca-Cola. https://www.coca-colacompany.com/social/diversity-and-inclusion

Together Equal. (n.d.) *Diversity at Work. The 10 benefits of diversity*. Together Equal. https://www.togetherequal.com/diversity-at-work

Unilever. (n.d.). *Equity, diversity and inclusion*. Unilever. https://www.unilever.com/planet-and-society/equity-diversity-and-inclusion/

Walton, G. M., & Brady, S. T. (2017). The Many Questions of Belonging. In Andrew J. Elliot, Carol S. Dweck, and David S. Yeager (Eds.), Handbook of Competence and Motivation: Theory and Application (2end ed.) (pp. 272–293). Guilford Publications.

World Economic Forum (WEF). (2020). *Systemic Racism - 5 ways intersectionality affects diversity and inclusion at work*. WEF. https://www.weforum.org/agenda/2020/07/diversity-inclusion-equality-intersectionality/

KEY TERMS AND DEFINITIONS

Accountability and Transparency: The principle that organizations should be responsible for their actions and open in their communications. In the context of diversity and inclusion, this can involve clear reporting of diversity and inclusion metrics and progress.

Corporate Social Responsibility (CSR): The principle that businesses should act in ways that have a positive impact on society, beyond their basic economic functions. This can include efforts to promote diversity and inclusion.

Cultural Appropriation: The adoption or borrowing of elements of one culture by members of another culture, particularly when the culture being borrowed from is a marginalized or less dominant group.

Diversity: The presence of differences within a given setting. In the context of the workplace, diversity can refer to differences in race, ethnicity, gender, age, religion, ability, sexual orientation, and other attributes.

Inclusion: The practice of ensuring that people feel valued, respected, and supported. It involves creating an environment where everyone has an equal opportunity to contribute and succeed.

Marginalized Groups: Social groups that are systematically disadvantaged or excluded, often due to factors such as race, gender, sexual orientation, or socio-economic status. The inclusion of marginalized groups is a key focus of diversity and inclusion efforts.

Organizational Identity: How an organization sees itself and how it wants to be perceived by others. Diversity and inclusion can significantly shape an organization's identity.

Resistance to Change: The opposition or reluctance to alter existing norms, processes, or behaviors. In the context of diversity and inclusion, this can refer to resistance to new policies or practices aimed at promoting diversity and inclusion.

Social and Cultural Awareness: The understanding and respect for different cultures, social groups, and perspectives. This awareness can be cultivated through diversity and inclusion initiatives.

Social Progress: The process of societal improvement towards more equitable, inclusive, and just conditions. Diversity and inclusion initiatives can contribute to social progress.

Chapter 11
A Survey About the Gamification of the Relations Among Companies and Stakeholders

Ascensão Maria Martins Braga
University Polytechnic of Guarda, Portugal

Paulo Alexandre Vieira
https://orcid.org/0000-0003-4692-5546
University Polytechnic of Guarda, Portugal

ABSTRACT

One of the most important concerns of companies is engagement with stakeholders. One of the main ways of engaging is using gamification. To create engagement is the principal aim of a gamification system. In this work, and from literature, the authors survey how it has gamified the relationship between companies and stakeholders. The aim is to gather data to create a dataset for training an artificial neural network model. Among the artificial intelligence (AI) models, this kind of model has been the one that has been shown to increase human analytical capacity and is responsible for the emergence of generative AI. The final aim of this work is to create a generative AI that enables the design gamification system to create engagement between stakeholders and companies in the more diverse areas. This AI will be used as a service in a platform as a service (PaaS), where companies can get the best way to engage the stakeholders.

1. INTRODUCTION

Faced with a globalized world, a complex business environment, in which markets are constantly changing, more demanding and competitive, managing stakeholders is essential to the company's success. Placing successful products on the market depends greatly on the level of stakeholders engaged,

DOI: 10.4018/978-1-6684-8984-0.ch011

managing the different interests and influences of stakeholder's groups. In this sense, stakeholder engagement is a key to the company's success, and all stakeholders will get better results as a result of this engagement.

One of the techniques recently used to increase employee engagement is the application of game elements in companies - gamification - in other words, providing playful and fun moments for employees that enable them to achieve company objectives and better results.

In this introduction we start by talking about stakeholders and the importance for companies to engage with stakeholders. After referring shortly, what is the methodology that we follow to get scientific literature about the problem and, for last, we describe how the paper is organized.

1.1. The Stakeholders Concepts

Companies, in developing their activities, are surrounded by an environment (internal and external) that, in part, influences the way they act and to achieve their goals, they increasingly have to identify their stakeholders, that is, the interested parties that have a relationship with them.

There are several definitions about Stakeholders, some broader than others. According to Freeman (2010) the concept was originally defined as "those groups without whose support the organization would cease to exist". Include employees, environmentalists near the company's plants, vendors, governmental agencies, and more. And this definition is fundamental to the theory of stakeholder's management. This is a perspective opposite to Friedman (1962) for whom the only stakeholders a company should care about are its shareholders (inspired in shareholder theory of capitalism: that a company's sole responsibility is to make money for its shareholders). But to Freeman, the shareholders are merely one of many stakeholders in a company. The several definitions of stakeholders include just about anyone affected by the company and its workings, and are, therefore, essential pieces in strategic business planning, to the extent that they affect or are affected by the companies' decisions. However, if stakeholders feel the direct or indirect impacts of a company's decisions, the reverse may also be true.

Also, we can find various typologies of stakeholders, depending on the criteria used: primary stakeholders (those directly affected by a business and its activities or decisions) and secondary stakeholders (those who are indirectly affected by the business and may be connected with the main stakeholders). But Post, Preston and Sachs (2002) developed the idea that stakeholders can be classified into three categories: primary stakeholders, secondary stakeholders, and marginal stakeholders, those with minimal or casual interest.

More important than identifying stakeholders is to integrate them in a strategic management company. To Freeman (2010) the stakeholder's approach to strategic management suggests that the companies must formulate and implement processes which satisfy the interested groups and manage and integrate the relationships and interest of shareholders, employees, customers, suppliers, communities and other groups in a way that ensures the long-term success of the firm. And to achieve success in any business it needs to add value for all its stakeholders, so it is necessary to find out what the common ground is between all the interested parties, so that decisions can be made to meet/exceed the satisfaction of their expectations. The stakeholder's management develops trusting relationships based on "principles of distributional, procedural, and interactional justice" (Harrison et al., 2010).

1.2. The Importance of the Stakeholder's Engagement

The stakeholders play a crucial role in a company and have significant importance in several dimensions and the strategy of gaining competitive advantage by developing intrinsic relationships among stakeholders is called stakeholder engagement. The importance of these engagement was evident in crucial organizational activities such as: strategic planning and decision-making: having a clear understanding of their expectations and interests allows the company to make strategic decisions that consider these stakeholders (Noland & Phillips, 2010); value creation: "the best deal for all is if managers try to create as much value for stakeholders as possible" (Freeman et al., 2004; Freudenreich et al., 2020); access to resources: maintaining positive relationships with stakeholders is vital to ensuring continued access to capital (investors), revenue (customers), inputs (suppliers), and labor and knowledge (employees) (Harrison et. Al., 2010); innovation and competitiveness: the feedback of ideas from stakeholders can be good sources of innovation (Alvarez & Sachs, 2021); minimizing risk: a good understanding of stakeholders interests is helpful to companies anticipate potential problems and develop strategies to reduce risks (Mitchell et al., 2022); corporate social responsibility and sustainability: the adoption of corporate social responsibility involves the concerns of stakeholders and the contribution to the well-being of society (Arenas et al., 2009; Castelló et al., 2016; Westberg et al., 2014). In addition, there is research that explains the politics and democratic principles of stakeholder engagement and examines how stakeholder activism influences organizational activities" (Kujala et al., 2022).

According to ChatGPT (ChatGPT, personal communication, june 29, 2023), the stakeholder engagement is critical to the success of companies in that it can translate into:

- customer loyalty (greater brand loyalty and they themselves can help increase company visibility and attract new customers);
- increased employee productivity (engaged employees are more motivated and work more efficiently, hence perform better);
- increased support from the local community (can gain more support and loyalty from the community which will contribute to success);
- improved corporate governance (engaged shareholders improve corporate governance and in turn their efficient and responsible management).

1.3. The Methodology Followed

Our final aim is to build a generative AI. This generative Ai must generate designs of gamification systems to engage stakeholders with companies in different areas. To build generative AI we need a dataset. The datasets of this kind of generation will be a prompt-dataset. Thus, we oriented the methodology to this aim. Then we search in Scopus for publications where the words: 'companies', 'stakeholders', 'engagement', appear in abstract, keywords or in the title. This search is sorted by relevance, and we get the first 20 publications for our analysis, human analysis. The 20 papers selected from this methodology are described in Table 1, Section 3.

1.4 The Paper Organization

This paper is organized in 6 sections. After the first section, called Introduction, we have section two that is titled as "What is gamification?". In it we explain the concept of gamification. In the following section we talked about the methodology used for searching scientific literature about the theme companies, stakeholders and gamification and we published a descriptive table about them. The literature selected is analyzed in section four. The analysis is focused on the design of gamified systems already existing in their components, dynamics, and mechanics. Using this analysis, we present a first design of an automatic system that enables us to present a proposal of how to gamify the relation between stakeholders and a certain company. For last we present a conclusion and the future work.

2. WHAT IS GAMIFICATION?

Gamification is a concept that is being used in a wide range of entrepreneurial contexts. The term gamification is used to refer to the application of game elements on non-game environments (Deterding et al, 2011). Game elements are elements used in game design. The aim of the gamification intervenes in a system or area through the design of motivational systems that allow amplifying values of intrinsic engagement factors of that system or area (Figure 1).

Games can be powerful experiences, leveraging both motivation and engagement. The recent trend toward "gamifying" applications, however, often reduces the complexity of a well-designed and balanced game to its simplest components, such as badges, levels, points, and leaderboards. The resulting implementations don't just fail to engage players; they can actually damage existing interest or engagement with the service or product (Rigby & Ryan, 2011).

3. SEARCH BY RELEVANCE IN SCOPUS

The research question of this work is:

How to gamify the relation between companies and stakeholders?

To answer the question, we search in scopus for publications where the words companies, stakeholders, engagement appear in abstract, keywords or in the title. The document finds were sorted by relevance, and we get the first 20 publications for our analysis. The papers selected are described in Table 1.

What are stakeholders in a company context? Stakeholders are all the agents that have some kind of involvement with a company. They can be divided into internal stakeholders and external stakeholders (Figure 2):

i) internal stakeholders are: employees, manager, owners, and so on.
ii) external stakeholders are: customers, employers, governments, communities, society, suppliers, creditors, investors, and so on.

The literature found in Scopus, January 2023, presents the following distribution (Figure 3) by the different study areas. The area of computer science, decision science, engineering and social sciences is where it produced more studies respectively with 28.2%,12.8%,12.8% and 12.8%.

Figure 1. "Gamification" between game and play, whole and parts
Source: Drawn from Deterding et al., 2011.

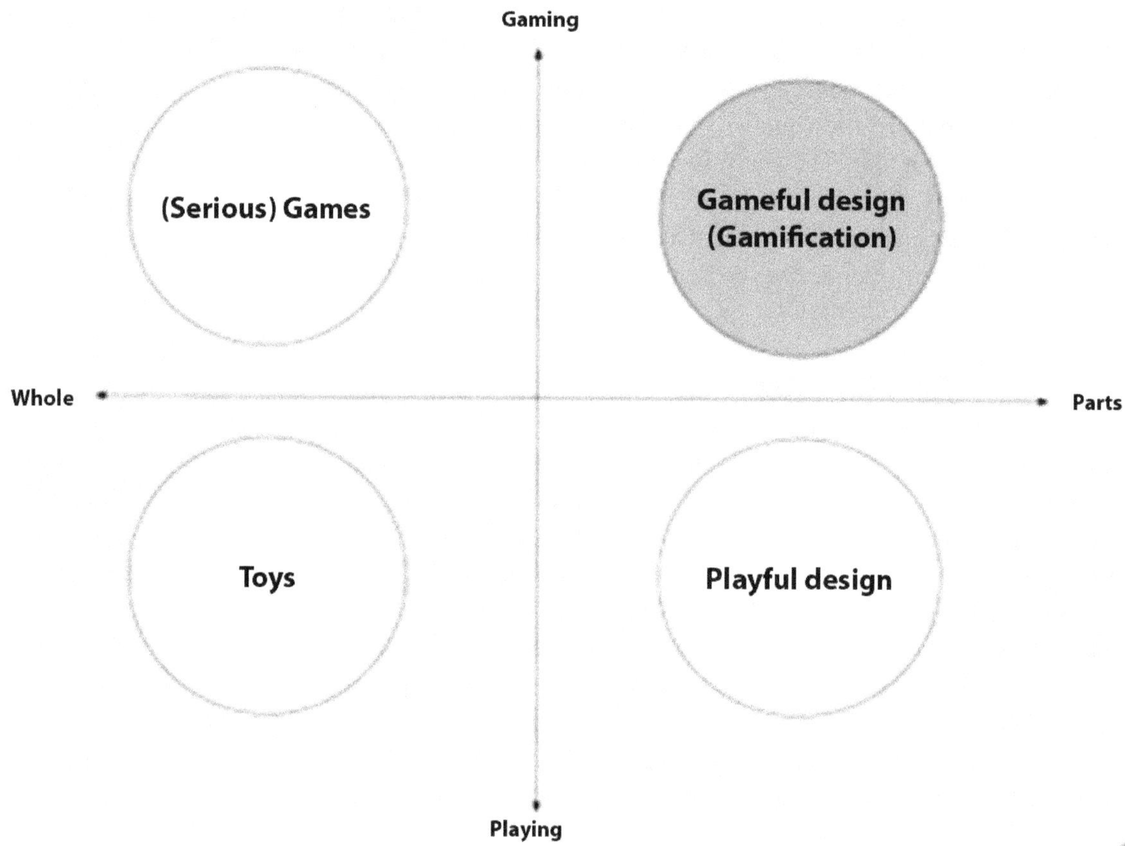

The analysis of each article is done in two items. The aim, what is the aim of the stakeholder engagement intervention? and the engagement produced or pretended.

Article 1:

Aim: growing emphasis in many countries on matters such as participation in e-government, e-democracy, the provision of forums for online debate, and so on.

Engagement: engagement across a broad spectrum of potentially interested parties and stakeholders. It is an ethnographic study of an online event, designed to encourage debate, to explore some critical issues in how the mechanisms productive of debate have shifted in company with the Web 2.0 phenomenon.

Article 2:

Aim: looking to engage employees and customers because it is one of the key factors in running a successful business.

Figure 2. Graphic about companies, stakeholders
Source: Drawn from https://www.google.com/imgres?imgurl=https%3A%2F%2Fcanny.io%2Fblog%2Fwp-content%2Fuploads-%2F2019%2F10%2Fstakeholders.png&tbnid=xHZyC2MPqfx9jM&vet=10CKkBEDMosgFqFwoTCKiN4YCshYIDFQAAAAA-dAAAAABAD..i&imgrefurl=https%3A%2F%2Fcanny.io%2Fblog%2Fcommunicate-product-roadmap%2F&docid=BNmhEY-dSoWaC_M&w=678&h=629&q=stakeholders&ved=0CKkBEDMosgFqFwoTCKiN4YCshYIDFQAAAAAdAAAAABAD and https://www.google.com/imgres?imgurl=https%3A%2F%2Fupload.wikimedia.org%2Fwikipedia%2Fcommons%2F5%2F56-%2FStakeholder_%2528en%2529.svg&tbnid=eQlcwcH20nM3TM&vet=12ahUKEwjeuJSArIWCAxVSUqQEHeflBH8QMy-gJegQIARBk..i&imgrefurl=https%3A%2F%2Fen.wikipedia.org%2Fwiki%2FStakeholder_theory&docid=Veqc6GTJayjH-4M&w=720&h=443&q=stakeholders&ved=2ahUKEwjeuJSArIWCAxVSUqQEHeflBH8QMygJegQIARBk

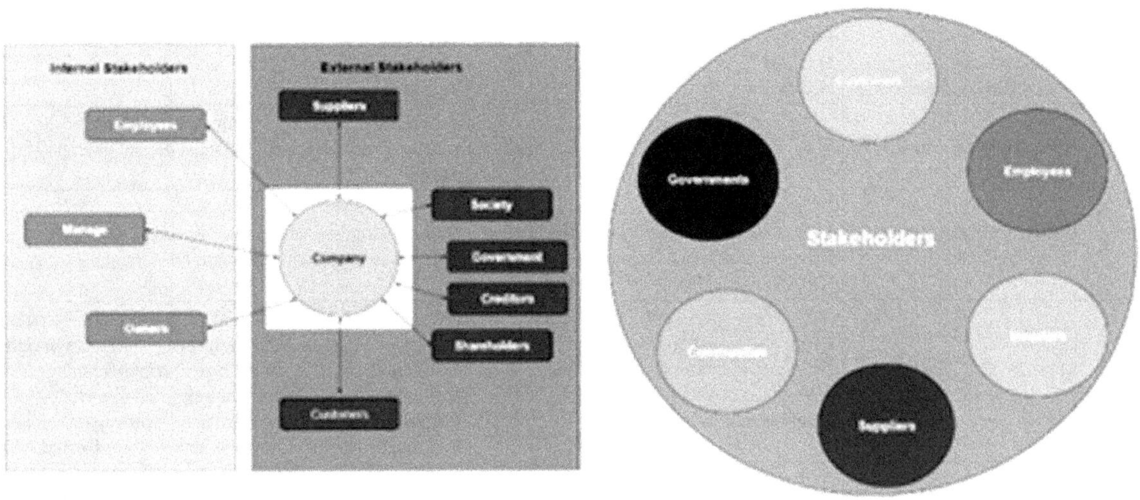

Figure 3. Documents by subject area
Source: Scopus's documents data analysis graphic.

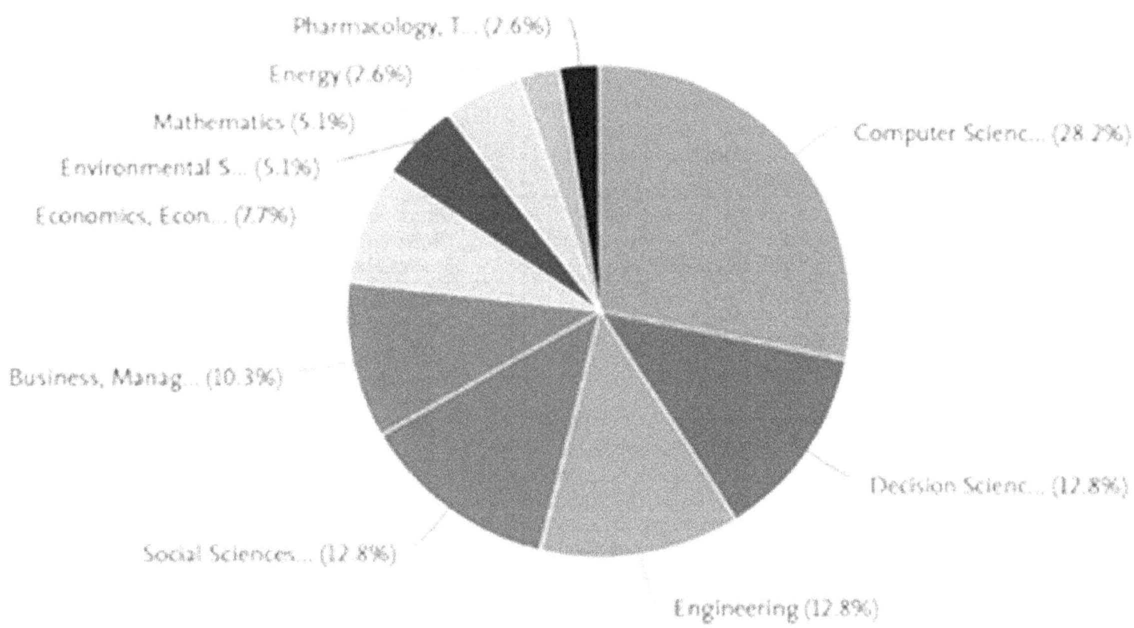

Table 1. Scopus articles papers

Article	Authors	Title	Year	Index Keywords
1	Tolmie P.; Chamberlain A.; Benford S.	Designing for reportability: sustainable gamification, public engagement, and promoting environmental debate.	2014	E-government; Public policy; E-democracy; Ethnographic study; Ethnomethodology; Online debate; Pervasive game; Reportability; Web 2.0; Human computer interaction.
2	Dolatabadi S.H.; Budinskai I.	A New Method Based on Gamification Algorithm to Engage Stakeholders in Competitive Markets	2020	Computer games; Customer satisfaction; Gamification; Human resource management; Sales; Competitive markets; Data mining algorithm; Statistical computing; Data mining.
3	Gasca-Hurtado G.P.; Gómez-Álvarez M.C.; Muñoz M.; Betancur S.H.	Gamified Strategy Oriented to Decrease SPI Change Resistance: A Case Study.	2020	Gamification; Process engineering; Best practices; Change management; Employee behavior; Resistance increase; Study case; Software design.
4	Brandes N.; Evans C.	Connected health: The future of effective drug delivery.	2016	Article; drug delivery system; drug industry; health program; medication compliance; patient care; patient compliance; smartphone.
5	Khan S.; Charissis V.; Harrison D.K.	Utilising Gamification and Virtual Environments to Present Digitally Enhanced Advanced Services (DEAS) for the Financial Sector.	2023	Gamification; serious games; servitization; user experience virtual environment; DEAS.
6	Picanço C.T.; dos Santos, S.	Promoting Collaboration and Creativity in Process Improvement: A Proposal based on Design Thinking and Gamification.	2022	Enterprise resource management; Information systems; Information use; Process engineering; Software design; Business Process; Business process improvement; Customer values; Design thinking; End to end; Gamification; In-process; Process Improvement; Process management; Process stakeholder; Design.
7	Ünal A.E.; İnce G.; Ay K.; Öztürk S.; Gezer C.	An Easily Configurable Customer Loyalty Framework Using Distributed Ledger Technologies.	2022	Loyalty program; Distributed ledger technologies; graphical programming interface; mobile application.
8	Weerasekara M.; Smedberg Å.	Felix the digibud: unveiling the design of an ict-supported intervention for occupational stress management.	2022	Design; Human resource management; Occupational risks; Social networking (online); User interfaces; Digital micro intervention; Ehealth; Empirical studies; Gamification; Health interventions; Management IS; Occupational stress; Occupational stress management; Stakeholder groups; Stress management; eHealth.
9	Prasad K.D.V.; Mruthyanjaya Rao M.; Vaidya R.	Gamification and resource pooling for improving operational efficiency and effective management of human resources: A case study with an ecommerce company.	2019	Gamification, resource pooling, motivation, behavioural change, employees.
10	Richter T.; Albers A.; Birk C.; Rapp M.; Bursac N.	A Training Framework for the Synthesis of a Consistent System of Objectives in Modular Design	2018	Change management; Conflicting Systems of Objectives; Design method; Knowledge transfer; Modular designs; Knowledge management
11	Marcao R.P.; Pestana, G.; Sousa M.J.	Gamification framework for management practice.	2021	Benchmarking; Human resource management; % reductions; Business architecture; Business models; Engagement; Enterprise Architecture; Gamification; Management practises; Performance; Professional services; Service sectors; Profitability.
12	Negrușa, A.L.: Toader, V.; Sofică, A.; Tutunea M.F. ; Rus, R.V.	Exploring Gamification Techniques and Applications for Sustainable Tourism.	2015	economic growth; ecotourism; ethics; nongovernmental organization; recreational activity; stakeholder; sustainability; tourism development; tourism marketing.
13	Silva J.; Raposo D.; Neves J.; Silva F.; Ribeiro R.; Fernandes M.E.	Gamification in Communicating the Concept of Circular Economy - A Design Approach.	2021	Gamification; Circular Economy; Communication design.

continued on following page

Table 1. Continued

Article	Authors	Title	Year	Index Keywords
14	Marcão R.P.; Pestana G.; Sousa M.J.	Gamifying the product quality reviews in the pharmaceutical industry	2019	Accident prevention; Commerce; Controlled drug delivery; Digital storage; Health care; Knowledge management; Quality management; Regulatory compliance; Risk assessment; Supply chains; Effectiveness and efficiencies; European medicines agencies; Food and Drug Administration; Gamification; Pharmaceutical industry; Quality management systems; Quality reviews; Situational awareness; Quality control.
15	Breuer H.; Bessant J.; Gudiksen S.	Gamification for innovators and entrepreneurs: using games to drive innovation and facilitate learning.	2022	Business management; business and economics; entrepreneurship.
16	Donath L.; Mircea G.; Rozman T.	E-learning platforms as leverage for education for sustainable development	2020	E-learning, education, sustainable development, gamification, LMS.
17	Haziri F.; Chovancová M.; Fetahu F.	Game mechanics and aesthetics differences for tangible and intangible goods provided via social media.	2019	Aesthetics, game mechanics, online buying behavior, products, services, social media, user behavior.
18	Seiffert-Brockmann J.; Weitzl W.; Henriks M.	Stakeholder engagement through gamification: Effects of user motivation on psychological and behavioral stakeholder reactions.	2018	Communication Technologies; Electronic media; Marketing communications; Stakeholders management.
19	Busetta P.; Kifetew F.M.; Munante D.; Perini A.; Siena A.; Susi A.	Tool-Supported Collaborative Requirements Prioritization	2017	Application programs; Decision making; Iterative methods; Automated decision making; Collaborative decision making; Decision making process; Exploratory case studies; Gamification; Requirements prioritization; Small software companies; Stakeholder engagement; Computer software.
20	Robson, K.; Plangger, K.; Kietzmann, J.H.; Ian McCarthy; Leyland Pit	Game on: Engaging customers and employees through gamification.	2016	Gamification; Employee engagement; Customer engagement; Mechanics; Dynamics; Emotions; Behavior change.

Engagement: in this study, we will introduce a new technique for designing gamification in servicing companies in which customers and employees interact with each other and also examine the principles of setting up a game site based on statistical computing and data mining algorithm (Figure 4).

Article 3

Aim: influencing employee behavior, allowing them to improve the SPI (Software Process Improvement) initiatives.

Engagement: gamification is an alternative for influencing employee behavior, allowing them to improve the SPI initiatives. This paper shows a case study of the application of a gamified strategy oriented to decrease change resistance.

The methodology for the strategy definition:

i) includes a sequence of steps for selecting and associating change resistance causes,
ii) change management models, and
iii) gamification principles.

Figure 4. Gamification system
Source: Dolatabadi et al., 2020.

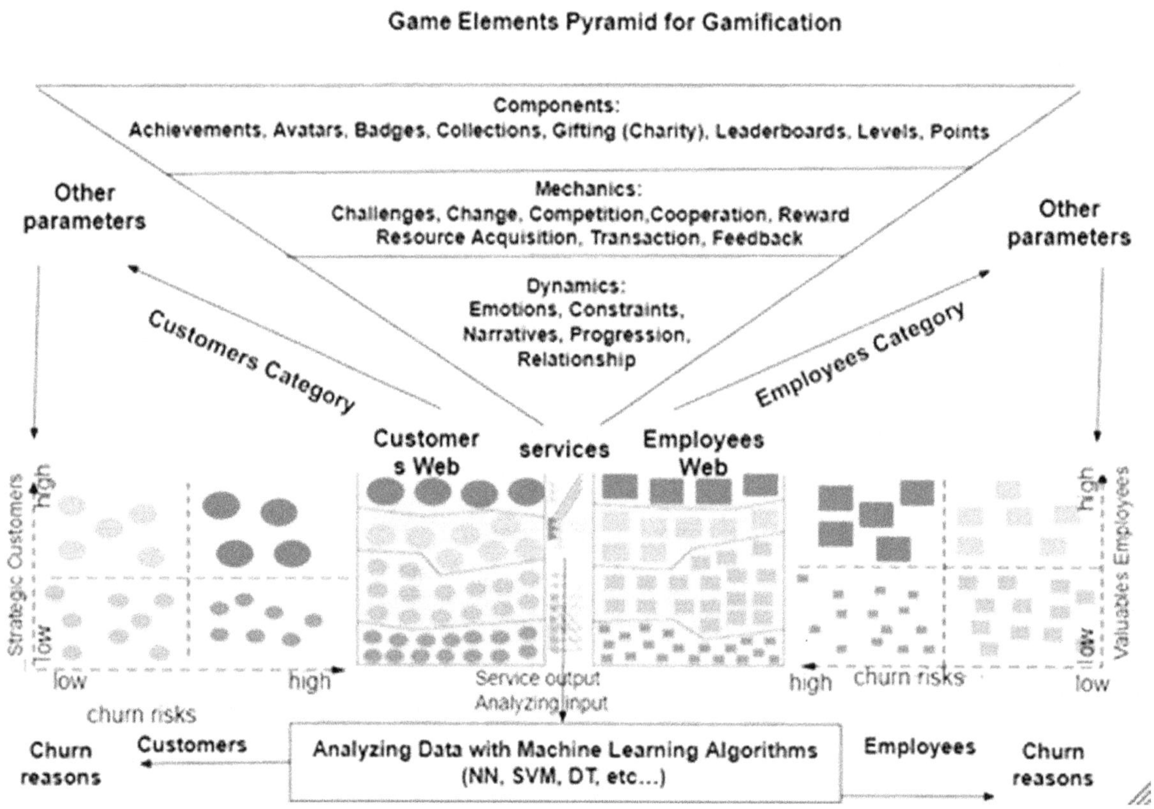

The study case evidences a positive impact on causes like:

i) lack of commitment management, and
ii) a general improvement in the change resistance in SPI initiatives

when the gamification is the central element of the strategy.

Article 4

Aim: leveraging gamification, the HealthPrize platform rewards patients for medication adherence. helping patients find a new way to meet the daily challenges of chronic disease management.

Engagement: as a concept, gamification has made inroads in online marketing by applying elements of game playing, such as scoring points, competing with others, setting a hierarchy of rules and, of course, reaping rewards for success. But it is showing promise in other sectors as well, including fitness and healthcare, and for helping patients find a new way to meet the daily challenges of chronic disease management.

Connected health programs such as HealthPrize and other systems that "gamify" treatment regimens – and allow doctors and nurses to monitor patient data and medication adherence – show promise in giving patients better reasons for caring for themselves, in both incentive and accountability.

Article 5

Aim. utilizing Gamification and Virtual Environments to Present Digitally Enhanced Advanced Services (DEAS) for the Financial Sector.

Engagement: this paper presents a prototype Serious game application designed for the financial sector which enables the customers to experience a variety of construction scenarios and weather conditions that affect the progress and cost of the in-game building.

Article 6

Aim: "How to promote collaboration and creativity among stakeholders in improving business processes?"

Engagement: to answer this question, it is to propose a method based on the Design Thinking (DT) process, called Boomerang, including a creative game to involve people while generating insights and ideas. It is carried out as a case study, collecting the perceptions of professionals engaged in improving a business process in a public education institution.

So, the Boomerang method combined gamification with the DT approach to stimulate member engagement by promoting more ideas for solving companies' problems with focus on process improvements.

Article 7

Aim: an Easily Configurable Customer Loyalty Framework Using Distributed Ledger Technologies. In this paper, it is proposed a system for the user-friendly generation and deployment of loyalty programs by using a graphical programming interface.

Engagement: the loyalty programs are one of the effective marketing and business development strategies. Solutions offered for loyalty programs are generally tailor-made and created by sector-specific software.

Existing loyalty program solutions cannot offer campaign creation tools which can be used by teams, such as sales and marketing often lacking software knowledge.

Personalization of campaigns for end-users, on the other hand, can be done in a limited way within the scope of existing tools.

In loyalty programs where transactions and data are kept distributed among different stakeholders, establishing a trust relationship involves several difficulties.

The system consists of distributed ledger technologies such as Hyperledger Fabric and Ethereum, an API gateway backend structure with micro-service architecture, campaign definition interface with drag-and-drop and gamification capabilities, and a mobile application with interaction methods such as OCR, Bluetooth communication, NFC, QR code scanning, interactive map-based services, and augmented reality.

The proposed system is evaluated under different loyalty use cases such as point, barter, checklist, and tier campaigns. In open, query and transfer transactions, required time to finalize transactions and transaction per second are measured and compared in different DLTs.

Article 8

Aim: the Design of an ICT-Supported Intervention for Occupational Stress Management.

Engagement: digital stress management is an evolving yet promising approach to the continuum of stress management programs. There are shreds of evidence on the benefits that could be achieved. However, numerous studies discuss the challenges that hinder the potential benefits of digital stress management interventions. Such challenges mainly include less engagement, insufficient theoretical underpinning, high attrition, and lack of personalization.

Felix, the DigiBud platform, was co-designed and developed using a multidisciplinary team based on empirical and literature evidence. All the empirical studies were carried out in Sri Lanka, applying quantitative and qualitative approaches. The designers made a comprehensive effort to embed gamification and digital micro intervention concepts in the intervention design to increase user engagement.

Article 9

Aim: improve operational efficiency and effective management of human resources: a case study with an ecommerce company.

Engagement: the authors of this article attempted combining two methodologies the gamification and the resource pooling with a view to derive the maximum productivity from the organization drawing certain significant commonalities.

Article 10

Aim: a Training Framework for the Synthesis of a Consistent System of Objectives in Modular Design.

Engagements: the training is based on a multi-media approach with participative learning and gamification elements.

Article 11

Aim: to understand how the commitment of stakeholders evolves and if the application of gamification techniques and/ or frameworks enhances the performance profitability (Table 2).

Table 2. Game elements and their motivation

Motivation	Game Mechanics	Game Dynamics
Intellectual curiosity	Documentation about behavior	Exploration
Achievement	Scoring systems and awards	Collection
Social recognition	Rankings	Competition
Final goal	Levels and reputation	Status acquisition
Social exchange	Group tasks	Collaboration
Cognitive stimulation	Pressure and challenges	Challenge
Self-determination	Characters and world/virtual trading	Development/Organization

Source: Blohm et al., 2013.

Article 12

Aim: the main objective of this study is to identify gamification techniques and applications used by organizations in the hospitality and tourism industry to improve their sustainable activities (Table 3).

Article 13

Aim: to present a paradigm regarding the circular economy (CE) concept's communication, referring to the difficulty presented by the type of reflexivity involved in the circular economy process.

Engagements: draw the hypothesis, in DesignThinking (DT) context, that gamification can induce a reflexivity thinking on CE, specifically on Agrofood entrepreneurs in the Portuguese context. Reflexivity could empower the connection between the company and its local context and stakeholders dissuading the drivers for abroad markets positioning.

Article 14

Aim: projection of a Gamification model related to managing activities of a PQR (Product Quality Reviews) development project at the level of the active substance.

Table 3. Gamification Platforms used in hospitality and travel

Product	Vendor/Producer	User	Game Mechanics Features	Social Features
Badgeville	Badgeville Inc. (Redwood City, CA, USA) (badgeville.com)	Customer engagement Marketing campaign	Competition Feedback Levels & missions Profiles Ranks & badges	Activity feed Ratings & reviews Social media login
Bigdoor	Bigdoor Media Inc. (Seatle, WA, USA) (bigdoor.com)	Customer engagement	Economy/Marketplace Feedback Profiles Progress Bar Ranks & badges	Activity feed Community forums Likes & comments Ratings & reviews Share plugin
Gigya	Gigya Inc. (Mountain View, CA. USA) (gigya.com)	Customer engagement Marketing campaign	Economy/Marketplace Levels & missions Profiles Ranks & badges	Activity feed Likes & comments Live chat Ratings & reviews Share plugin Social login
Keas	Keas Inc. (San Francisco, CA, USA) (Keas.com)	Customer engagement	Competition	Likes & comments Ratings & reviews Social login
Bamboo	Manumatix Inc. (Redwood City, CA, USA) (manumatix.com)	Customer engagement Marketing campaign	Competition	Activity feed Social login
Pluck	Demand Media Inc. (Santa Mónica, CA, USA) (demandmedia.com)	Customer engagement Marketing campaign	Competition Economy/Marketplace Feedback Ranks & badges	Community forums Likes & comments Ratings & reviews

Source: Negruşa,. et al., 2015.

Engagements: gamification can be used to monitor and improve the performance of different business activities related to the stages of the development of PQRs. Regarding the activities of the project, it is necessary to understand how the commitment of stakeholders evolves and if the application of Gamification techniques allows enhancing this variable, taking the evolution of the performance as another variable that could be evaluated.

Article 15

Aim: to introduce the potential of gamification and games to solve the great societal and organizational challenges that corporations and public institutions are dealing with today.

Engagements: The key attributes games have to support the learning cycle: create a temporary alternative world with boundaries in time and space; involve rules and other play structures and elements; allow interactivity between players and game objects; allow multiple simulations in which players can experiment with different strategies; provide motivation, the fun element of a game which draws people in; permit experimentation within the game context; involves participants in teams competing; the players have limited resources so they need to be creative, and have time restrictions; they are judged on a number of performance criteria; teams have to do activities to achieve other step; they are interactions and competition; we can see the role the gameplays in allowing experimentation and exploration; the risks they take in design are calculated; the reflection phase after the game is completed allows participants to straddle both the game world and the real world.

Article 16

Aim: to develop a conceptual approach to education for sustainable development using an e-learning platform.

Engagements: a conceptual design of the learner's journey and a mapping from gamification concepts to Moodle LMS elements. To engage online learners, various gamification techniques were used in the course design phase, such as recording and presenting the learner's progress, role-playing and similar (Figure 5, Table 4).

Article 17

Aims: to identify the differences within consumers who purchase via social media when game mechanics and aesthetics are applied, the chi-square test for independence has been employed.

Engagements: the results estimate that the association between purchasing products or services via social media and game mechanics (such as fun, joy, rewards points, badges, leaderboards) and aesthetics (such as positive feelings, emotions, satisfaction and delight) is not statistically significant and the relationship is weak or moderate.

Article 18

Aim: to research the role of stakeholder motivation in the context of gamification.

Engagements: to examine stakeholder engagement through gamification, the authors propose a research model that links gamer types, i.e. a gamer's motivation, with engagement and potential effects

Figure 5. Gamification levels of abstraction
Source: Donath et al, 2020.

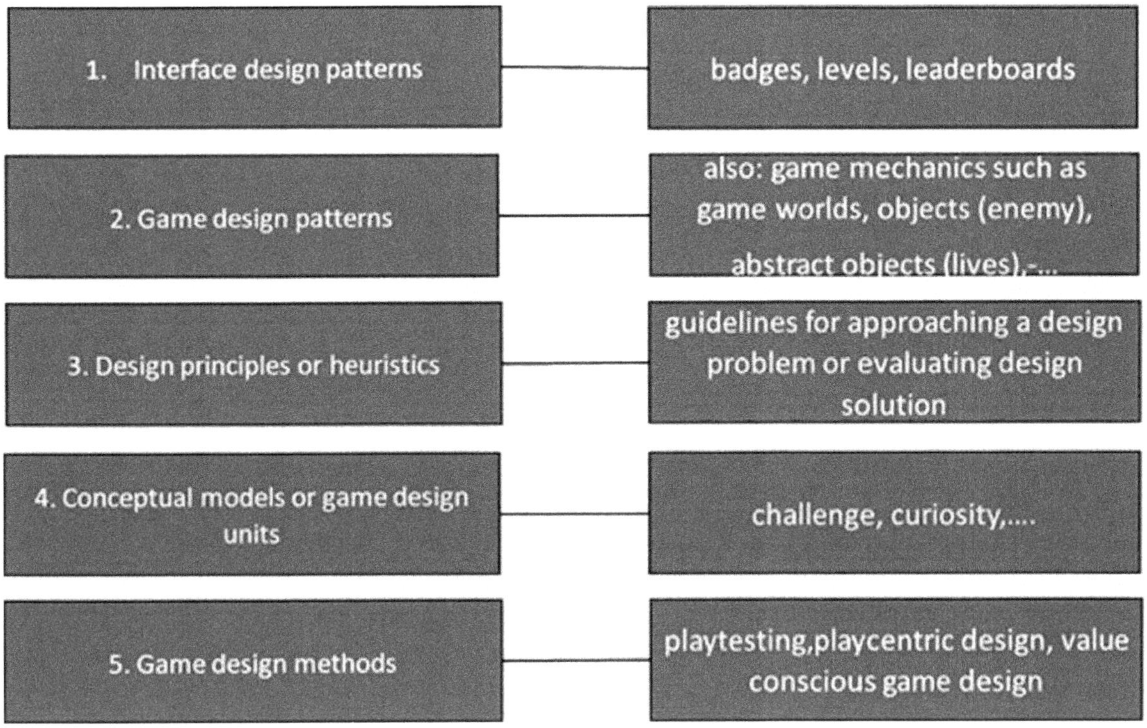

Table 4. Game and moodle activity

GAME ACTIVITY	MOODLE ACTIVITY
Accomplishement of personal adventure	Studying learning resources. Accomplishment of personal Assignment. Solving tests (quizzes)
Accomplishement of team adventure	Accomplishment of group assignments
Repetition of adventure	Repetition of learning resource/activity (with permission for repetition) in order to achieve better results (points)
Passage of level	Passage to the next learning section when a given criteria is met
Level repetition	Repetition of learning resources/activities (with permission) in order to achieve missed badges
Obtaining of badge	Obtaining of badges, certifying successfully completion of learning activities and achieving some learning objectives
Obtaining of reward	Obtaining acess to additional optional learning material
Obtaining of points	Obtaining points from assessed learning activities
Discover hidden treasures	Opening of hidden or grayed-out learning resources/activities when some other learning resources/activities are successfully completed
Feedback when progression is noticed	Obtaining a badge or points. Teacher feedback
Time restriction for accomplishment of adventure	Setting up a time restriction of a learning resource or activity
Personal communication	Chat/forum/shared files with another student or teacher
Common communication	Chat/forum/shared files with other students and teachers

Source: Donath et al, 2020.

beyond the gamified content. The findings of the study suggest that a gamer's typology, i.e. her underlying motivation, positively influences psychological stakeholder engagement toward gamified content and indirectly behavioral stakeholder engagement toward the communication instrument (i.e. the app) itself.

Article 19

Aim: to propose a tool-supported Collaborative Requirements Prioritization process, called CRP, which exploits gamification elements to engage distributed stakeholders to contribute to the overall decision-making process.

Engagements: engagement to integrated on organizational context automated decision-making techniques.

Article 20

Aim: to discuss how gamification can aid customer and employee engagement, and delineate between four different types of customers and employees who act as 'players' in gamified experiences. Included illustrative examples of gamification (1- how gamification can create engaging customer experiences to improve the way customers interact with a brand or firm-Jay-Z's Decoded; 2- a helpdesk software program for customer support centers that aims to improve not only employee productivity but also customer satisfaction, thus creating value for the client firm and customers by reducing costs and boosting service quality).

Engagements: help guide designers and managers in using appropriate gamification mechanics to engage different types of employees and customers: slayers, strivers, socialites, and scholars (Table 5).

4. ANALYZING SOME GAMIFIED SYSTEMS

To answer the research question, we conducted a survey in which we investigated how relations between companies and their stakeholders can be gamified. The survey was based on a set of 20 articles, the

Table 5. Key gamification mechanics for player types

	Slayers	Strivers	Socialities	Scholars
Leaderboards, Badges, and Points	✓	✓		
Increasing Task Difficulty	✓	✓		
Finite End	✓	✓		
Multiplayer Orientation	✓		✓	
Infinite Play			✓	✓
New Levels		✓		✓
Team Playing	✓	✓	✓	✓
Online Playing	✓	✓	✓	✓
Real World Playing	✓	✓	✓	✓

Source: Robson et al., 2016.

most relevant ones, found in scopus through a search using the words companies, stakeholders, and engagement. The analysis of these 20 articles was carried out looking for the existence of gamification. In almost all of them it was possible to establish the existence of gamification, even if it is sometimes incipient. This shows that there is a strong correlation between engagement and gamification. In several articles there are even gamification systems designed for engagement. The correlation is so strong that we were able to construct the following table (Table 6).

Table 6. Analyze of the game elements presented in each article

Context of the Gamification Elementos	Gamification Elements	Article																				
		1	2	3	4	5	6	7	8	9	10	11	12	13	14	15	16	17	18	19	20	
																					20a	20b
Game Dynamics	Emotions		x										x				x				x	x
	Narrative	x	x					x									x				x	x
	Progression		x						x			x	x			x	x			x	x	x
	Relationship	x	x									x	x			x	x				x	x
	Restrictions		x																			
Game Mechanisms	Resources acquisition		x					x					x			x					x	x
	Evaluation (feedback)	x	x						x		x	x		x		x	x			x		x
	Chance			x																	x	x
	Cooperation and Competition	x	x		x				x		x		x			x					x	x
	Challenges	x	x	x	x		x	x		x	x		x			x	x				x	x
	Rewards		x		x				x				x			x	x				x	x
	Transactions		x					x														
	Shits															x						
	Victory																				x	
	Time restriction	x					x	x								x				x		
	Loss aversion						x	x														
Game Components	Avatar	x	x			x				x												
	Virtual goods		x										x								x	x
	Boss		x						x	x							x					
	Collections		x																		x	x
	Combat	x																				x
	Dispute												x			x	x				x	x
	Unlockable contents																				x	
	Badges/medals		x						x				x			x					‘	x
	Social graphs	x										x	x				x					x
	Mission	x															x				x	x
	Levels		x					x	x	x							x					x
	Points		x		x			x	x	x			x				x			x		x
	Gifts																					
	Ranking																x					x
	Times												x			x					x	x

Having established the existence of correlation between gamification and engagement, we begin to think that the design of a gamification system to engage a stakeholder should at least be automatically sketched. Thus, we think about the "design" of an Artificial Intelligence (AI) system for the prediction of a draft of how to gamify the interaction between a company and a stakeholder. This system is a draft for later human analysis.

Once thought of the development of an AI for prediction, the idea immediately arises of the need to create a dataset and the identification of its component variables. This is what was done in the following section.

The analysis done here shows that for build a dataset it is necessary human annotation because:

- there are elements of game that appear through synonymous;
- there are elements of game that appear through excerpt of text;
- to find the aim of the pretended stakeholder engagement;
- to find the description of the engagement;
- to allow understanding and design of the gamification system implemented;

To help this work we are designing software to do the future analysis.

5. HOW TO ADD GAMIFICATION TO COMPANIES' STRATEGY: OUR PROPOSAL

We are starting to design an Artificial Intelligence system that will be working as a service for companies. This service will consist of a draft of designing gamification strategies to engage with the company stakeholders. The requisites of this system come to us from the analysis done in this survey and from our knowledge of what Artificial Intelligences Models are and working. But to have a predictor model we need a dataset.

The datasets are tables whose columns are variables and each row is an entry or instance of each one of the variables. The sensibility of the dataset variables arose from the literature analysis that we have done to write this survey. We define the following variables for the dataset from our analysis.

Variable: company intervention area, aim, stakeholder, game element context, game element, synonymous, engagement (Table 7).

This dataset must be a dataset with human annotation. This conviction comes to us from this survey, section 3 and 4 (Table 8).

The artificial intelligence model that will be used is an Artificial Neural Network (ANN). The kind of ANN used is still in study, but we are walking fast (Figure 6).

Table 7. Dataset of the AI gamification system predictor

index	area	aim	stakeholder	game element context	game element	synonymous	engagement
1	...	...	...	...	...	...	...
2	...	...	...	...	...	...	...
...	...	...	...	...	...	...	...

Table 8. Interpretability of the dataset

Dataset variables	Description
index	the number of the entry in the dataset
area	which is the intervention area of the company must be considered?
aim	what is the aim of the intervention?
stakeholder	the stakeholder target
game element context	what is the area (component, dynamic, mechanism) of the gamification element used (see column 1 of the table 1)
game element	which of the element of gamification used (see the column 2 of the table 1)
synonymous	if it is used, the synonymous of the game element that allow to categorize the document
engagements	the engagement produced or pretended

Figure 6. Example of a simple ANN
Source: https://scikit-learn.org/stable/about.html#citing-scikit-learn.

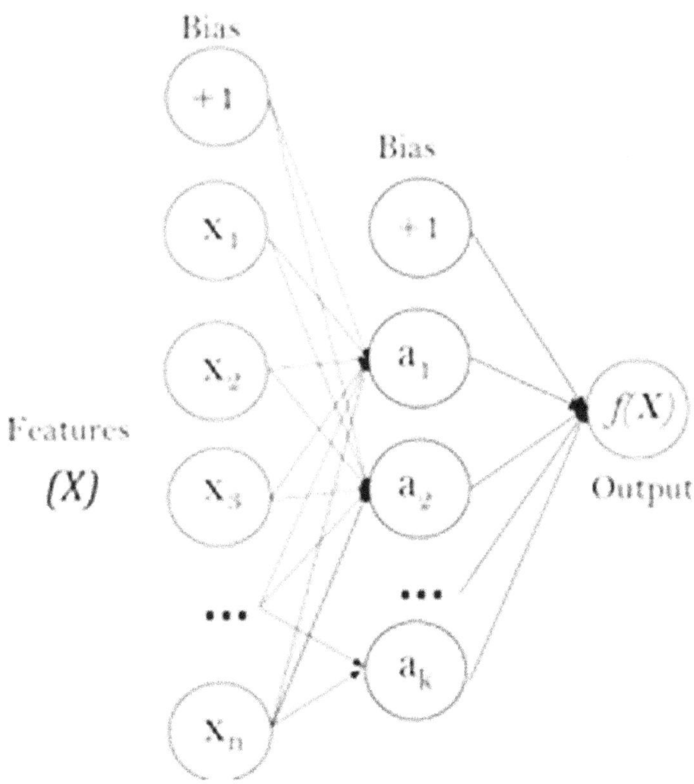

The AI model will contain an encoder. The encoder is doing a translation of implemented numbers and from numbers to different realities in our case text reality. To know the architecture of the AI can be taken (Figure 7).

Using this architecture, it will be possible to know the impact of an implementation of a gamification system calculating the correlation between the variables the aim and the engagement, this can be done using its translation by the encoder to numbers.

Figure 7. Draft of the Architecture of the Artificial Intelligence for predict how to gamify
Source: https://www.compthree.com/blog/autoencoder/.

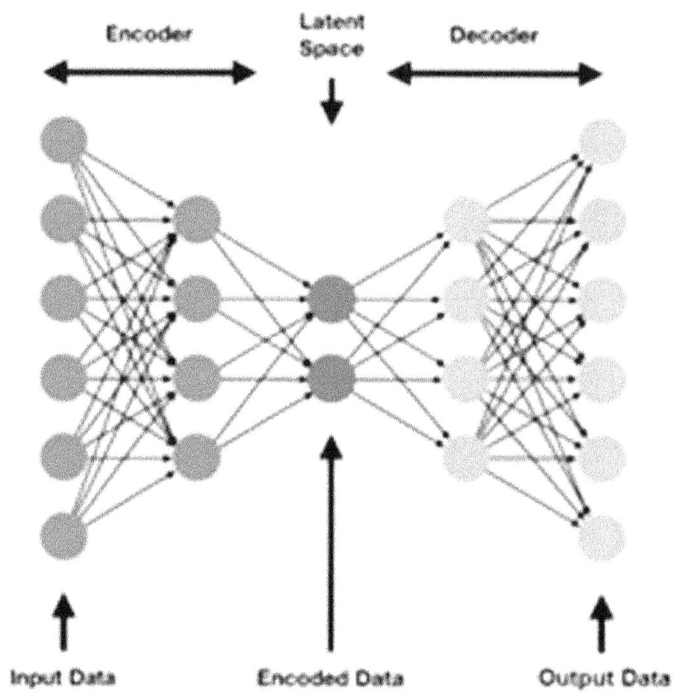

6. CONCLUSION AND FUTURE WORK

At the end of this paper, it will be possible to have a comprehensive understanding of stakeholder management importance and the engagement strategies.

In conclusion, this work allows gathering information about the design of gamification systems already carried on relative to the engagement of stakeholders with companies. From these systems already designed we will build a dataset prompt oriented with the aim of designing an architecture to a machine learning and training that for prediction.

The following steps of this project will be create the dataset prompt-oriented, design the architecture of the Artificial Neural Network (the AI), implement the AI design, train it and create a predictor. Then, to get a more accurate predictor, the dataset will be expanded from other databases. After all this it will develop a platform to be used as a service PaaS - Platform as a Service to produce gamification systems drafts between a company and the stakeholders. The AI developed will be deployed for this platform to be used as a generative AI for the gamification systems produced.

REFERENCES

Alvarezand, S., & Sachs, S. (2021). Where do stakeholders come from? *Academy of Management Review*. doi:10.5465/amr.2019.0077

Arenas, D., Lozano, J. M., & Albareda, L. (2009). The role of NGOs in CSR: Mutual perceptions among stakeholders. *Journal of Business Ethics*, *88*(1), 175–197. doi:10.100710551-009-0109-x

Blohm, I., & Leimeister, J. M. (2013). Gamification: Design of IT-based enhancing services for motivational support and behavioral change. *Business & Information Systems Engineering*, *5*(4), 275–278. doi:10.100712599-013-0273-5

Castelló, I., Etter, M., & Årup, F. (2016). Strategies of legitimacy through social media: The networked strategy. *Journal of Management Studies*, *53*(3), 402–432. doi:10.1111/joms.12145

Deterding, S., Dixon, D., Khaled, R., & Nacke, L. (2011). From game design elements to gamefulness: defining" gamification". In *Proceedings of the 15th international academic MindTrek conference: Envisioning future media environments* (pp. 9-15). ACM. 10.1145/2181037.2181040

Dobele, R., Westberg, K., Steel, M., & Flowers, K. (2014). An examination of corporate social responsibility implementation and stakeholder engagement: A case study in the Australian mining industry. *Business Strategy and the Environment*, *23*(3), 145–159. doi:10.1002/bse.1775

Dolatabadi, S. H., & Budinskai, I. (2020). A New Method Based on Gamification Algorithm to Engage Stakeholders in Competitive Markets. In *2020 IEEE 24th International Conference on Intelligent Engineering Systems (INES)* (pp. 11-18). IEEE. 10.1109/INES49302.2020.9147196

Donath, L., Mircea, G., & Rozman, T. (2020). E-learning platforms as leverage for education for sustainable development. *European Journal of Sustainable Development*, *9*(2), 1–1. doi:10.14207/ejsd.2020.v9n2p1

Freeman, E., Wicks, A., & Parmar, B. (2004). Stakeholder Theory and "The Corporate Objective Revisited". *Organization Science*, *15*(3), 364–369. doi:10.1287/orsc.1040.0066

Freeman, R. (2010). *Strategic Management Approach*. Cambridge University Press. doi:10.1017/CBO9781139192675

Freudenreich, B., Lüdeke-Freund, F., & Schaltegger, S. (2020). A stakeholder theory perspective on business models: Value creation for sustainability. *Journal of Business Ethics*, *166*(1), 3–18. doi:10.100710551-019-04112-z

Friedman, M. (1962). *Capitalism and Freedom* (40th ed.). University of Chicago Press.

Harrison, J., Bosse, D., & Phillips, R. (2010). Managing for stakeholders, stakeholder utility functions, and competitive advantage. *Strategic Management Journal*, *31*(1), 58–74. doi:10.1002mj.801

Kujala, J., Sachs, S., Leinonen, H., Heikkinen, A., & Laude, D. (2022). Stakeholder Engagement: Past, Present, and Future. *Business & Society*, *61*(5), 1136–1196. doi:10.1177/00076503211066595

Mitchell, R., Hunt, R., Townsend, D., & Lee, J. (2022). Stakeholder engagement, knowledge problems and ethical challenges. *Journal of Business Ethics*, *175*(1), 75–94. doi:10.100710551-020-04550-0

Noland, J., & Phillips, R. (2010). Stakeholder engagement, discourse ethics and strategic management. *International Journal of Management Reviews*, *12*(1), 39–49. doi:10.1111/j.1468-2370.2009.00279.x

Piras, L., Dellagiacoma, D., Perini, A., Susi, A., Giorgini, P., & Mylopoulos, J. (2019). Design thinking and acceptance requirements for designing gamified software. In *2019 13th International Conference on Research Challenges in Information Science (RCIS)* (pp. 1-12). IEEE. 10.1109/RCIS.2019.8876973

Post, J., Preston, L., & Sachs, S. (2002). *Redefining the Corporation Stakeholder Management and Organizational Wealth*. Stanford University Press. doi:10.1515/9781503619692

Rigby, S., & Ryan, R. M. (2011). *Glued to games: How video games draw us in and hold us spellbound*. AbC-CLIo.

Robson, K., Plangger, K., Kietzmann, J. H., McCarthy, I., & Pitt, L. (2016). Game on: Engaging customers and employees through gamification. *Business Horizons*, *59*(1), 29–36. doi:10.1016/j.bushor.2015.08.002

Chapter 12
Influence Drivers of Food Waste Platforms Within Their Circular Economy Contribution: A Portuguese Analysis

Cristina Castro
Higher School of Technology and Management, Polytechnic Institute of Guarda, Portugal

Gil Manuel Costa Inácio
Higher School of Technology and Management, Polytechnic Institute of Guarda, Portugal

Hugo Mendes
Higher School of Technology and Management, Polytechnic Institute of Guarda, Portugal

Teresa Paiva
https://orcid.org/0000-0002-1721-9813
Higher School of Technology and Management, CI&DEI, Polytechnic Institute of Guarda, Portugal

ABSTRACT

Every year, 1.3 billion pieces of food are wasted, which impacts the circular economy's (CE) effective transition, and greater knowledge of the consumer's opinion and valorisation of food waste has positive consequences on food safety, the environment and sustainable consumption. There are different platforms and apps for improving food waste behaviour, some linked to social concerns and others trying to achieve circular economy goals. This study aims to analyse the influence drivers of users' motivation to use these food waste technologies in Portugal. It follows a qualitative approach to fully understand the user's motivation and link to their social and environmental concerns. Results revealed that most of the interviewees who used these platforms/apps were driven by economic influences and had environmental concerns. Identifying the users' drivers of influence on food waste and reflecting on the consequences for businesses and their marketing strategies on positioning and communication was possible, so promoting behaviour to facilitate the social dimension of the CE transition.

DOI: 10.4018/978-1-6684-8984-0.ch012

1. INTRODUCTION

The transition towards a circular economy requires more than a focus on engineering or production, manufacturing, business and industry processes (Lehtokunnas et al., 2022). As Circular Economy (CE) is defined (Santagata et al., 2021), it is a paradigm to overcome the linear model to reinforce a responsible approach to resource exploitation and utilisation, aiming at the environmental charge and improving human well-being. Specifically, CE aims to create a better waste management system, reduce the use of fossil resources and reduce production. But this perspective also implies a societal change and a change in everyday practices, which consists of understanding the transition in the socio-material foundations of everyday life (Lehtokunnas et al., 2022). What are the responsibilities and possibilities of acting that society has to contribute to a circular economy, like the practices of food consumption (e.g., reusing leftovers; less food waste), as a moral and ethical behaviour that overall contributes a stronger transition to a circular economy since it addresses the living of abundance and overconsumption of food to deal with this excess production at an individual level in society that should motivate people to find environmentally sustainable ways to address food waste (Lehtokunnas et al., 2022).

As stated by several authors (Al-Obadi et al., 2022; Shankar et al., 2022; Talwar et al., 2023), food waste is a social, environmental, and economic problem that affects sustainability challenges that have risen to 32% of the global food production (Octavia et al., 2022; Santagata et al., 2021; Tamasiga et al., 2022;). It affects the environment through gas emissions and global warming, the economy with the loss of resources (e.g., water and energy) and socially through the increasing food poverty (Octavia, 2022). Around 1.3 billion tons of food per year is wasted worldwide (FAO, 2019; Tamasiga et al., 2022), which could be enough to feed up to 815 million people. Consumers are pointed out to be a major source of food waste (40%) since they tend to purchase excessive food, which often remains unconsumed, followed by household (25%) and agriculture (35%) (Al-Dhabi, 2020; Gustavsson et al., 2011; Octavia et al., 2022; Shankar et al., 2022).

Several studies highlight the consumers' role in reducing food waste (Al-Obadi et al., 2022; van Geffen et al., 2020; Vittuari et al., 2021), and it is said that consumers' perceptions of their behaviours, beliefs, and values on food waste are the main drivers of food waste and loss (Al-Obadi et al., 2022). Therefore, there is an emphasis on the education of consumers and strong communication campaigns to alert them to the food waste problem (Al-Obadi et al., 2022). This social innovation approach is not the only one used. Economic innovation, through different business models associated with technology, can also help to increase food sustainability and support a circular economy.

The balance between the economic and environmental development focused on CE context and perspective helps to design or redesign the possibilities better to create an economy less harmful to the environment, protecting resources and promoting the economy loop (preserving natural capital, optimising resource yields and fostering system effectiveness) (Frey et al., 2017; UNEP, 2022). Several pathways for food waste improvements are linked to CE (Teigiserova et al., 2020). For example, in the case of edible food waste is suggested the intervention of food banks (to reuse), retail stage (when food is sent to secondary retailers) and consumption and services (restaurants and other redistribution systems of leftovers) (Teigiserova et al., 2020). This CE concept advocates waste as a resource and reinforces the need to optimise systems (Frey et al., 2017). This focus on preventing and reducing food waste, included as one of the UN Sustainable Development Goals (SGD 21), led to initiatives for sharing economy and the creation of different platforms and apps that try to answer the food waste problem in diverse approaches.

Due to the exposure, it is important to analyse how the consumers in Portugal address food waste and also, specifically, if the existing facilitating technologies (platforms and apps) help consumers to engage in a more ethical behaviour work as influence drivers to use them. With this chapter proposal, it is possible to understand how consumers can be motivated to take an ethical role in the social process towards a CE context, contributing to the implementation of a food waste strategy within CE.

2. THEORETICAL BACKGROUND

2.1. Food Waste and Circular Economy

Circular Economy (CE) is connected to food waste since 2014 by Papargyropoulou et al. (Viscardi et al., 2023), that argue that facing the food waste problem has a clear impact on sustainability. At the environmental level, the food produced and not consumed represents resource waste and is commonly associated with greenhouse gases (around 8% of the global greenhouse gas emissions) (Viscardi et al., 2023). On a social level, food waste reduces food security and availability which means that decreasing food waste could mitigate world hunger. And finally, on the economic level, food waste not only can limit businesses' profitability (higher operational costs) and it is linked to higher prices (Viscardi et al., 2023).

From a consumer perspective, CE relies on consumers' acceptance and attitudes towards food goods (Viscerdi et al., 2023). Several strategies emerged in the literature about the best way to deal with and impact food waste behaviour within CE problematic. Prevention and reuse (human and animal consumption) are two of the most popular ones, along with nutrient recycling, energy recovery and disposal (Teigiserova et al., 2020). Several authors (e.g., Stelick et al., 2021; Wang et al., 2020) have demonstrated the positive effects of information and education about purchase behaviour and consumption. Understanding the consumer's opinion and valorisation of food waste seems important, particularly for the food safety implications, a better knowledge of the environmental consequences and how and why a reused food product can be achieved (Aschemann-Witzel & Stangherlin 2021; Coderoni & Perito 2020; Goodman-Smith et al., 2021). Consumers are willing to accept programmes that reward their behaviour and do not see positive any type of behaviour penalisations or actions that aren't convenient (Borrello et al., 2017). The social and technological transformation seems to be appealing and engaging in the consumer's behaviour to contribute to reducing food waste and therefore contribute to CE (Souza et al., 2021). Also, a well-known brand can help the purchase behaviour and increase the consumption of circular food products (Aschemann-Witzel and Peschel 2019). This may happen in terms of the platforms and apps consumers may use or the food chain supplier.

2.2. Consumer Influence Drivers

The field of consumer behaviour is the study of individuals, groups or organisations and the processes they use to select, protect, use and discard products, services, experiences or ideas to satisfy needs and the impacts that these processes have on the consumer and society (Mothersbaugh & Hawkins, 2016). Their model is divided into four interrelated parts: external and internal influences affect the consumer's idea of themselves and their lifestyle, which in turn affects the decision-making process; external influences include culture, reference groups, demographics and marketing activities; internal influences include perception, emotions, attitudes, and personality; self-concept is the totality of an individual's thoughts and feelings about himself. External and internal factors act to influence self-concept and lifestyle, which in turn influences the decision process. The study and understanding of consumer behaviour allow to raise awareness and change attitudes throughout the chain, causing an impact on all stakeholders.

Several studies have analysed the drivers and barriers of food waste behaviour on consumers. Stangherlin and De Barcellos (2018) supported the main findings of Stancu et al. (2016) and defended that the main drivers of food waste reduction can be categorised as societal factors (historical; regulatory; and supply chain factors), behavioural factors (linked to food purchase and consumption in its various phases - planning, purchasing, storage, preparing, consumption, leftover storage and disposal.) and personality factors (demographic and psychological). Canali et al. (2016) already systematised the food waste drivers in Europe, emphasising that there are three main types of motivations in the literature for consumers' behaviour and reduction of food waste. The economic motivation (saving money by reducing food waste), the personal gratification (making good food management and reducing the waste and therefore not feeling guilty and being in control), and the environmental and humanitarian motivations (contributing to food waste reduction and consequently having a better environmental impact and helping reducing hunger and economic constraints) (Graham-Rowe et al., 2014; Jagau & Vyrastekova, 2017; Quested et al., 2011).

More recently, and according to Moltene & Orsato (2021), the factors influencing the use of food waste reduction platforms can be divided into extrinsic and intrinsic factors. The extrinsic factors can be: i) Economic: the final consumer can benefit from a reduction in the price of products, while companies can benefit through the revenue generated by products that, if not sold on these platforms, would be considered waste and a loss. It also makes it possible to balance the seasonal demand for certain products, particularly in the primary sector; ii) Environmental: reduction of pollution through waste reduction, saving of natural resources, human resources and logistics. Also, the environmental regulation/legislation implemented by countries can influence the adoption of this type of platform; iii) Social: increased access and availability of food while allowing for greater cultural and social interaction, as it allows consumers to have access to offers that would not normally be options. The ease of use also allows greater social inclusion by making food reach those who need it most, which would otherwise be very difficult. And the intrinsic factors might be: i) Personal beliefs: the pleasure of being part of a new platform and the spirit of empathy, solidarity and cooperation. Social and environmental concerns are also one of the main drivers in using these platforms; ii) Personal desires: the convenience in using these services, autonomy and independence that these platforms provide.

With this model in mind and regarding the research focus, we aim to identify and understand which of the influence drivers (extrinsic or intrinsic) are influencing the users of the food waste platforms.

2.3. Food Waste Platforms and Apps

As stated, consumption is one of the main causes and, therefore, the most critical in preventing waste, especially in purchasing food products (Al-Dhabi, 2020; Gustavsson et al., 2011; Octavia et al., 2022; Shankar et al., 2022).

Technologies are essential for sharing economy-focused business models and handling food waste (Frey et al., 2017; Mazzucchelli et al., 2021). The Food Waste Platforms and Apps (FWPA) have the advantages of any Food Delivery Digital Application (FDA). They are convenient, have a list of partners, menus, and rapid delivery (Shankar et al., 2022). These FDA are growing businesses, not only because of social context evolution (increased number of working parents and single-person households) but also because of the technological access people have (increase in internet access and smartphone) (Shankar et al., 2022). Despite these mutual advantages and motivation to use the normal FDA, it can potentially increase the food waste numbers due to its non-consumer purchase control and non-sharing principle.

Food-sharing platforms allow individuals and businesses (e.g. retailers, producers, and local shops) to reduce food waste by redistributing surpluses (Frey et al., 2017; Mazzucchelli et al., 2021; Octavia et al., 2022). The FWDA can help reduce food waste by connecting food donors and receivers and expanding the food stakeholder network. It also controls the stocks, improves management and layout and contributes to monitoring food quality (Mazzucchelli et al., 2021; Octavia et al., 2022).

Michelini et al. (2018) proposed a classification of the sharing models, analysed by Octavia et al. (2022). It consists of four types of models accordingly to the type of provider (peer-to-peer or business-to-peer) and the platform orientation (non-profit or for-profit), namely:

- Social sharing platforms – individuals that share food they are not going to use before it becomes damaged and donate it through a platform user. This type of service is free and aims to fight everyday food waste and raise awareness.
- Corporate social sharing platforms - allow retailers, local shops, and producers to offer, collect and donate food that would otherwise be thrown away. These platforms align with the circular economy principles as they give a solution for food waste disposal, encouraging actions to avoid throwing food away.
- Social eating platforms (SE business model) - social eating platforms allow users (i.e. hosts) to organise meals and events at home to be attended by other users (i.e. guests). The revenue model is such that platforms take a fee every time a match between a host and a guest is booked, but no food waste is pursued.
- Food alerting platform (FAP business model) - platforms allowing shops and supermarkets to advertise products that are close to the expiration date or with cosmetic defects, likely to be wasted, to be sold at a discounted price. It can help food waste reduction, but it is not its main goal.

Another classification developed by Cane and Parra (2020) simplified the findings into two groups:

1. Digital platforms of a social nature – online platforms to store different types of personal and commercial information to become social networks to facilitate relations between friends, family and other social agents, acting as a group in social commitment.
2. Apps for responsible consumption – digital applications to be used on mobile devices, allowing people to manage information and access to services. They can be subdivided into:
   a) Apps that educate in food management
   b) Apps that avoid waste and help manage surplus products
   c) Apps to promote savings in food consumption

Applying the classification above, it is possible to find both social and corporate social sharing platforms in Portugal, as shown in Table 1.

The effectiveness of some of these platforms depends on the users and if they feel comfortable sharing or meeting other people, not worrying about being judged for their food-related behaviours or other potential barriers (Octavia et al., 2022). The literature does not yet answer all the questions about the consumer's use of FWDA. There is research on consumers' intentions in using the platforms, their

Table 1. Social and corporate-social sharing platforms focused on food waste prevention and reduction

United Movement Against Waste (MUCD – Movimento Unido Contra o Desperdício)	**A digital platform, originally from 10 founding entities from various sectors, that aggregates important information and aims to be the reference site in Portugal in the fight against food waste**	**The main goal is to create awareness for an indispensable change in attitudes and behaviours.**
LISBOA ZERO	It is a collaborative digital application whose mission is to combat food waste.	The goal will be to allow companies to donate the surpluses to charities.
OLIO	is a food-sharing platform where you can give or receive food at no cost. The information is placed online, and the receivers can contact the givers directly to collect the food.	The initial goal was to create a sharing network between neighbours, but it was used by shops, grocery stores, bakeries or others so that the surplus food was not wasted.
REFOOD	The Refood Movement is a daily activity and has immediate effects: food is not wasted, and people do not go hungry, anyone can donate a part of their time to change the world, and local businesses can activate their duty of social and environmental responsibility, and everyone can actively participate in a circular economy that produces a social good in their own local community.	The goal is to reduce food waste and feed people.
PHENIX	It is an online platform where you can buy baskets from the most varied restaurants, pastry shops and grocery stores at a symbolic price.	The goal is to save food from waste and save money with it.
GoodAfter	It is a Portuguese platform to prevent food waste prevention, residing of an online supermarket focused on products near their recommended consumption date or, in certain cases, even after the "best before" date, that they sell at lower prices.	The goal is to prevent food waste and sell products at a lower price.
Too Good to Go	It is a platform to avoid food waste by being able to order, at lower prices, food that would otherwise be wasted by not being sold in hotel establishments (restaurants, bakeries) or supermarkets, fruit shops or even producers. These orders consist of "surprise boxes" (Magic Boxes). Here the customer does not know what the contents of the boxes are.	The goal is to reduce food waste and feed people at lower prices.

quality services, barriers to usage, perceived risks, and even food waste reduction intentions, but studies on the use of digital platforms to mitigate the food waste problem are still largely lacking (Shankar et al., 2022). Our goal is to address one of the perspectives on FWDA use and understand what motivates consumers to use them.

3. METHODOLOGY

Besides a deep theoretical review and an empirical identification and characterisation of the digital platforms and applications available to the target of the study, the Portuguese, a qualitative approach to better understand the influence drivers of the Portuguese consumers and their food waste behaviour and environmental concern.

Semi-structured interviews allowed the interviewees to give their opinion and reflection on the subject in question with the advantage of not losing focus (Knot et al., 2022). Thirty people were interviewed, covering different demographic features to allow the identification of any possible different influences and an interview guide was defined (see Appendix). The pre-structured questions were defined within two subdivided categories, as seen in Table 2.

Table 2. Categories and subcategories of the questions of the semi-structured interviews

Categories	Subcategories
FWDA knowledge and use	Aware of FWDA Use of FDWA
FWDA Extrinsic motivation/influence	Economic Environmental Social
FWDA Intrinsic motivation/influence	Personal beliefs Personal desires

The sample chosen for the interviews was based on the profile characteristics identified in the literature as the most probable to have consumer behaviour on food waste reduction (e.g., Stangherlin & De Barcellos, 2018). When analysing food waste reduction practices by gender, the literature indicates that women are responsible for grocery shopping, so the amount of waste generated by this gender is higher (Stangherlin& De Barcellos, 2018). That is, although women are more alert to the issue of food waste, previous studies point out that they are the ones who produce more of it, given that they are usually the ones in charge of grocery shopping. Men are more open when talking about the price being their primary driver.

Several authors state that age has been shown to affect food waste production, with young people wasting more than older people (Grainger et al., 2018; Thyberg and Tonjes, 2016). Other studies indicate that younger generations are more aware of these environmental problems (Comber & Thieme, 2013; Zepeda & Balaine, 2017), which explore the awareness of the younger generations of problems such as food waste, and report that younger generations are concerned about the environmental and financial costs of food waste and are hence less likely to waste themselves. Given that, age is an important factor that affects the amount of food waste.

Other important demographic characteristics are income and education. Regarding income levels, high levels of income inequality may generate a larger polarisation in declared food waste behaviour (Grainger et al., 2018), and richer citizens tend to waste more (Secondi et al., 2015). In regards to the relationship between academic qualifications and environmental concerns, according to Stangherlin and De Barcellos (2018), households with individuals with high education tend to produce more waste. People with lower education levels may be less aware of the environmental and economic impacts of food waste, which can lead to higher levels of food waste.

Therefore the thirty interviewees were chosen to represent several characteristics or demographic profiles (men and women, different age groups, levels of income and education) that could be compared to the groups typically described in the literature as more compelling to practice food waste reduction. So, the sample of individuals was selected for research convenience.

The data collected individually was transcripted, inserted, and analysed through NVivo software. The main structures of an NVivo project are the Nodes or nodes, which can be of type Free Node (an isolated node) or Tree Node (a tree of nodes). A node is a structure for storing coded information and can take on different meanings depending on the methodological approach used in the research. In this research, the content analysis implied that the nodes received the codes (fragments of text) forming categories of information. If these categories have subcategories, then a node tree structure is used (Lage, 2011).

As the Appendix of this article shows, the foreseen structure of the interview was already organised in terms to be examined in this software.

4. RESULTS

4.1. Knowledge and Use of Food Waste Reduction Platforms (FWPs)

The empirical data collection focused on the Portuguese platforms already identified, and it was possible t observe that from the 30 interviews made, 19 of the respondents know and use these platforms. Eight interviewees did know them but did not use them, and three people interviewed did not have prior knowledge of them. Therefore, the study ended with 27 interviews with usable results.

It was possible to understand that of the 27 interviewees, most said they learned about the food waste platforms through friends and advertising (see Figure 1). The most mentioned platforms were "Too Good To Go", followed by "ReFood" and "GoodAfter".

The main reasons for the respondent's awareness are the concerns about reducing food waste, followed by trying to save money and getting product quality simultaneously (see Table 3). The most frequent keywords used are "waste, food, price, and cheap".

The respondents believe that most FWPs are simple, intuitive, and easy to use, providing a review system that allows them to evaluate which businesses provide the best customer experience. Regarding platform features, the most mentioned factors were "digital, easy, and price" (Figure 2). Although the environmental issue is the most valued in the interviews, when the keywords are analysed, price is the common factor in analysing the usability and consumption factors.

Several limitations were pointed out, such as a complaint system that is too bureaucratic and sometimes the focus is more on the business side of things than on reducing food waste, with some interviewees mentioning that partnered businesses don't look at these platforms as an instrument that's going to help them in their food waste reduction, they look at it as a way to make a profit on things they weren't able

Figure 1. Source of information about de FWPs

Table 3. Awareness and usability factors of FWPs

Categories	Results - Statements or words used
Awareness factors	Reduced food waste by using food that would otherwise be discarded. Reduced price compared to other options. Proximity - "There are several stores near where I live, which ends up being more comfortable than going to the supermarket, which is further away". Several pick-up locations are available. The message that the platforms transmit is about being environmentally friendly.
Platform features	Quickness/Agility/Speed. Price. Let me reach smaller businesses. Provides user interaction. Sends useful notifications. Has relevant information. Variety. There are partnered businesses in my area of residence. They let me discover new businesses. Has a "favourite" feature. The schedules are explicit and well-advertised. Easy-to-use payment methods. The review system.
Platform limitations	At times the payment is not as fluid as it seems. Fixed schedules and awkward hours. The fact there's no delivery. Bureaucratic complaint system. "It doesn't have a great variety, but I think it depends on the partnered businesses". "I think that it ends up paying off in big cities". "There is the issue of buying products that aren't exactly reliable". "...it would be better if baskets said what products they offer, people may be intolerant to something". "The only thing they don't say is what products come in the basket. I think that might be a limitation". It should be more publicised. "...lack of encouragement to evaluate establishments makes people weary of buying". Too many notifications, and very repetitive. "They should warn people that the packaging is not included in the price". No delivery option.

Figure 2. Platform features keywords

to sell conventionally. Some respondents pointed out as a limitation the fact that the platforms do not reveal the products that come inside the food boxes in the platforms that have them. Also, some of the interviewees mentioned that the hours available for collection are not the most convenient.

Finally, even though advertising is one of the most common ways customers learn about FWPs, most interviewees believe that the platforms should be more publicised, especially on different channels other than digital ones. It was suggested to create a scoring system in which users could obtain benefits through continued use, that is, gamification of the platform.

4.2. Influential Drivers for Experimentation and Use

Regarding the influential drivers behind using FWPs, it was conducted a comprehensive consumer behaviour analysis to meet the research questions defined.

A summary of the respondents' answers concerning extrinsic factors can be found in Table 4. The extrinsic factor most frequently mentioned is the economic one, having been declared by a considerable portion of the respondents. Many interviewees alluded to the fact that they solely use the platforms because they can enjoy considerable savings when pursuing a certain product. Some of the interviewees use these platforms as alternatives to the "usuals" supermarkets and restaurants, being able to purchase products and/or meals at a reduced cost, satisfying the need to go shopping and eat out.

Social motivations are the least mentioned by the interviewees. However, those who addressed the social topic talked about the message, the attitude, and the contribution to the awareness of this problem in society. Some of the respondents understand that these types of platforms are a way for those who have less economic conditions to acquire meals, and, therefore, feel important the platform information as a social education contribution in order to create informed communities that add value to society.

The environmental driver directly relates to the base concept of these types of platforms. Although it is the second most mentioned influence, respondents showed concern about food waste reduction and resource-saving. Most respondents indicate that they use these platforms with the purpose of reducing food waste, considering that their use is a way to reduce their ecological footprint and a way to maintain previously acquired sustainable practices. The information these platforms provide is again important for these users, considering that their use helps to promote sustainable practices.

When questioned about the intrinsic factors, personal beliefs and desires, respondents showed a clear desire to use the platform out of curiosity's sake, which led them to discover new establishments and new products they had never tried before and probably, never would if it weren't for this business model. The joy of using the platform found and the not guilty feeling of reducing food waste were two important factors that influenced the platform's use. Generally, using FWPs makes them feel good about themselves, knowing that they are consuming products that would otherwise be discarded.

A summary of the respondent's answers concerning intrinsic factors can be found in Table 5. It is possible to observe the personal beliefs mentioned before and the personal desire for convenience, mentioned again here, of the savings that this kind of solution provides. This convenience is possible to be observed, also in the usability and simplicity of these platforms use, as stated before.

Table 4. Summary of responses about extrinsic factors regarding the use of FWPs

	Categories	Results
Extrinsic Factors	Economic Drivers	· "...especially the savings"; · "The amount of food that I can get for very little money"; · "The real incentive is really the monetary part of it, and the cheaper it is, the more people will want to join. Most people don't care much about the waste reduction part"; · "I use it almost every week, and I can get a 12 to 4 € reduction in price, which is a lot; · "I have done dinners with friends solely with boxes, while if we went to restaurants, we would have spent three times as much"; · "You can save, on average, 30 € a month"; · "The business will feel the benefit, even if they sell things cheaper. Whoever buys is benefiting because they buy cheap things. There are only benefits, no downsides"; · "For us students that don't have a car, to go to the supermarket can be more expensive and more bothersome. Plus, I'm saving money."
	Social Drivers	· "The message and the attitude we convey"; · "Maybe we're contributing to at least creating awareness about this problem that is food waste"; · "These platforms can help those that have little"; · "Honestly, I think it's more of a need since the cost of things is lower"; · "I agree with the fact that these businesses are avoiding food waste, but it shouldn't be just these businesses; we should do that at home too"; · "I think that people are concerned about these problems, but it isn't enough"; · "It gives people who have less than us the possibility of buying a meal"; · "It lets us contribute towards sustainability, towards the environment, and towards social education"; · "Through these initiatives and the existing partnerships, they create incentives for other businesses to join in and collaborate." Refood, for example, goes to restaurants and supermarkets at the end of the day, so they can then distribute the goods to people that are in need"; · "I think the communities built around these platforms have a lot of value for our society".
	Environmental drivers	· "We have to think about the future—about the future of our children and grandchildren"; · "Decrease my ecological footprint"; · "I think there is something missing. I think they try to make the process convenient for the people that go pick up the products, but they end up generating a lot of packaging waste. I think that a "bring your own container" policy should be implemented; · "The purpose of the platform is not to sell things at a reduced price, but to reduce food waste"; · "I buy fewer products because I use these types of platforms"; · "I think the platform is very much geared towards people who have a different kind of awareness. I think the issue of knowing that if I don't buy it, it will go to waste is stronger than the economic issue; · "I think my motivation to use these platforms comes from behaviours I had beforehand. I was already concerned about food waste, so in a way, this is an extension of my own sustainable practices"; · "I think that, aside from saving money, I become more aware of what I'm doing, that I'm not wasting food".

5. DISCUSSION

Despite the growing concern for environmental factors, economic drivers are predominant in the decision-making process and in the use of FWPs. By themselves, economic drivers were the most mentioned, while environmental ones were most mentioned in tandem but not as a priority. Social drivers are the least relevant in using FWPs (see Table 6). The findings also suggest that the interviewees are in accordance with Borrello et al. (2017) results when stating that their main driver is economical and, therefore, seeking to be awarded, somehow, for their behaviour.

This study found that convenience is an important intrinsic factor in the decision-making process, motivating users to join the platform. The users whose values are aligned with those of FWPs have had their wishes met by using these platforms. If not, however, they will only use the platform if they are motivated by the economic driver. It was possible to understand that those concerned about sustainable practices continued with their behaviour. In contrast, subjects who had no prior awareness about this

Table 5. Summary of responses about intrinsic factors regarding the use of FWPs

	Categories	Results
Intrinsic factors	Personal Desires	· "I think people try it out for curiosity's sake and end up discovering products they don't usually buy"; · "It's new, something I had never seen or tried before. I wanted to know if it worked as advertised if they did what they said they did"; · "Mainly the quality of the products, and it pays off. The first time I tried it, I had a good experience. My box had a lot of products"; · "The lack of consistency of some of the partnered businesses makes me a bit irritated"; · "The locations of one of the businesses were incorrect, and the products that I bought were not in the best condition"; · "I get to find new businesses in my city"; · "I value the information we get exposed to regarding food waste. I was aware, but I had no idea of the whole economic system around food waste"; · "I save money, and I feel good about myself, that's very important"; · "I think the biggest benefit is being exposed to new businesses".
	Personal Beliefs	· "The information that is made available to me has led me to become more aware of the nuances of this topic"; · "Even if it's just one person, it makes a difference"; · "I had a situation where I had booked a box at a cafe, and when I went to pick it up, the people at the cafe had nothing available and didn't know that there was a box available in the application. They had signed up but didn't know how to use the application"; · "The price I paid for the box matched the value of its contents when I was supposed to pay less"; · "I saved money and worked towards my self-fulfilment"; · "I am more careful when I do my monthly shopping. I look at the products that are going bad and make sure to use them instead of throwing them in the trash. I am more mindful of my waste"; · "I had access to food that was perishable and was still in good condition; that was the main benefit"; · "My lifestyle influences the use of these platforms, seeking a healthy lifestyle and fighting waste"; · "Using this platform ends up being an extension of how I live"; · "I've always been very concerned about not wasting food. Doing as much as possible with our resources, optimising the use of all the resources".

Table 6. Main findings of the qualitative research

Subcategories	Main Results
Aware of FWDA **Use of FDWA**	The 27 interviewees revel awareness mainly of three platforms. The main motives for their awareness are food prices and waste concerns. The platforms are easy to use but have some limitations.
Economic **Environmental** **Social**	A strong influence on the platform's usability. It is important, but it is not a priority influence on using the FWPs. The least mentioned influence, but because of the importance of social equity
Personal beliefs **Personal desires**	Good and satisfying feelings about having social and sustainable behaviour when seeking to save money and get the products they need and want. The convenience (savings and usability) of using the platforms is high.

matter have not had their behaviour changed. Most respondents believe their food waste reduction behaviours did not change due to the use of these platforms. However, some respondents mentioned that their behaviour was impacted, being more aware of their actions while cooking and grocery shopping. This finding contradicts some authors (de Souza et al., 2021), as stated in the literature review that technology can be a driver to reduce food waste and therefore contribute to CE. In this case, it seems that technology can help, but it is not a driver of food waste reduction behaviour.

The results of the interviews confirm that, in fact, economic motivation and personal gratification are two of the key factors to influence consumer behaviour on food waste reduction (Graham-Rowe et al., 2014; Jagau &Vyrastekova, 2017; Quested et al., 2011).

To better understand the interviewees and to try to understand the pertinence and impact on the results of the sample chosen for this study, a further analysis was made regarding the consumer profile, even if it is clear that a qualitative study will not give us a strong profile analysis. It was possible to observe that the male respondents tend to value economic factors more and talk about them without limitations or if their thought process is "politically correct", even though they also refer to the environmental factor. Social factors are not taken into account by male respondents. In addition, they report that their beliefs have not been changed but strengthened, which influences their use of FWPs. As for their personal desires, some deceptions were cited. Female respondents tend to value environmental factors, discussing and exploring the subject in great detail. However, they also refer to the economic factor, although they seem to be bothered when referring to it as a driver. Social factors were mentioned as being very important. They also report that their beliefs have not been changed but have been reinforced and that they also influence their use of FWPs. As for their personal desires, some disappointments were mentioned.

In the presented study, the younger respondents refer to price as the biggest driver. They also mention the social factor as being very important, but in correlation with price, referring to the fact that in times of crisis, these platforms have a very important role. The environmental factor is seldom mentioned. Their beliefs have not changed due to their use of these platforms. They also mention that their desires have not been satisfied as a result of some limitations of the platform. The interviewees between 30 and 40 years old state as the first driver environment, followed by social and economic influence is the last one to be mentioned. As for their beliefs, some mention that they have felt a change regarding meal planning and have been more alert in their day-to-day lives regarding food waste. As age increases, the price factor tends to be devalued.

Regarding income, it was observed that the lower the income, the bigger the concern with savings, therefore, the greater the necessity for using this type of platform. People with a monthly income lower than 750€ value the price to the detriment of environmental and social factors, which are only mentioned in passing and in addition to the price. They believe that these platforms help them save money and raise awareness of the issue of food waste. In addition, they say that these platforms are intuitive and satisfy their desire for convenience. The respondents who earn between 750€ and 1200€/month are the ones who use the platform the least and who have savings as their main driver, followed by environmental factors, with the social factor being the least referred to as the main reason for using FWPs. Respondents who earn above 1200€/month state that they have more of an environmental concern when using these platforms but do not underestimate the savings factor. The social factor is the least important.

The interviewees with high school education have the economic factor as their main driver, even if they refer to the environmental factor. The social factor was never mentioned. They believe that if the platforms were more publicised, they could reach a larger percentage of the population. The need and desire to save money are fulfilled through the use of the platforms. Bachelors point to price as their main driver, valuing savings above environmental concerns or social utility. Their beliefs are reflected in the values by which the platforms are governed, although they mention that other features could be introduced, mentioning some limitations. People with a Master's degree or PhD use this type of platform to reduce the environmental impact caused by food waste, garnering savings as an extra benefit. Again, social concerns are not considered. They believe that they can contribute to a more sustainable form of living, helping the planet while still saving some money. They point out some improvements that could make these platforms more friendly, but they don't point out any limitations.

The results achieved seem to say that Portuguese consumers are not yet fully aware of the food waste problem and its effect on CE. Strategies of information and education should be put into practice (Aschemann-Witzel & Stangherlin, 2021; Coderoni & Perito, 2020; Goodman-Smith et al., 2021; Stelick et al., 2021; Wang et al., 2020) to increase consumer knowledge, overcome the paradox between environmental and social concern and effective proactive behaviour about food waste, enhancing the impact that it has in CE. The promotion of these types of platforms and apps can induce convenience of use, an important factor in driving consumer behaviour (Borrello et al., 2017) that even might create a brand awareness marketing strategy (Aschemann-Witzel & Peschel, 2019).

6. CONCLUSION

Our findings contribute to the understanding of the motivations beyond the use of FWPs. They could be valuable in improving the customer experience of these platforms, as well as helping food waste reduction efforts and raising awareness about the topic. It is clear that Portuguese consumers think that these platforms are useful to save money while satisfying their product's desires and making them feel good since there are helping to reduce the impact of food waste. They believe that FWPs are convenient to use and satisfying.

This study did not find a direct relationship between age and FWPs use. The female gender appears to value environmental issues more, while the male gender values economic factors. Higher-income respondents tend to place more importance on environmental and social drivers, while lower-income respondents place more value on economic factors. Finally, respondents with higher educational qualifications tend to value environmental drivers more, while those with lower educational qualifications value economic factors.

Despite the usual limitations of a qualitative study, it was possible to deeply understand the Portuguese consumers and their influence drivers regarding using FWPs. In doing so, it was possible to observe that the contribution to the circular economy of these platforms in the Portuguese case might be poor since it is not the influence driver that leads to consumer usage. It seems to be a natural consequence that makes the consumers feel gratified and fulfilled, but it does not engage massive behaviour since it is not a major concern.

The contribution of food waste in Portugal to CE seems to be inefficient since so few consumers really engage in these types of behaviours through the platforms and apps provided. These technologies are not drivers of behaviour (food waste reduction) by themselves, even if there is recognition of their convenience for the consumers, which is important to the effectiveness of the behaviour. Therefore, not only should businesses improve the information given to consumers about their practices of food waste reduction, but also government can make policies to promote this type of behaviour, enhancing the tangible and intangible award to be achieved if consumer behaviour is accordingly.

FWPs could probably explore more of the consumer's pain of losing and the transmitted feeling of self-fulfilment to increase the use of platforms and solutions that decrease food waste. Although FWPs expose users to relevant information about food waste reduction, there is a need to revamp how it is presented, to whom it is presented, and when it is presented. In conclusion, these types of platforms have a key role in helping to reduce food waste, saving resources while saving money for consumers, and holding great value for stakeholders and society in general.

It seems to be crucial to address the social dimension of CE that argues that the engagement of consumers in reducing food waste will contribute to its improvement (Lehtokunnas et al., 2022). In doing so, definitively, there is a need for information and education campaigns to induce consumers behaviour and effectivey contribute to CE.

REFERENCES

Al-Dhabi, N. A., Esmail, G. A., Ghilan, A. K. M., Arasu, M. V., Duraipandiyan, V., & Ponmurugan, K. (2020). Characterization and fermentation optimization of novel thermo stable alkaline protease from Streptomyces sp. Al-Dhabi-82 from the Saudi Arabian environment for eco-friendly and industrial applications. *Journal of King Saud University. Science*, *32*(1), 1258–1264. doi:10.1016/j.jksus.2019.11.011

Al-Obadi, M., Ayad, H., Pokharel, S., & Ayari, M. A. (2022). Perspectives on food waste management: Prevention and social innovations. *Sustainable Production and Consumption*, *31*, 190–208. doi:10.1016/j.spc.2022.02.012

Aschemann-Witzel, J., & Peschel, A. O. (2019). How Circular Will you eat? The Sustainability Challenge in Food and Consumer Reaction to Either Waste-to-Value or yet Underused Novel Ingredients in Food. *Food Quality and Preference*, *77*, 15–20. doi:10.1016/j.foodqual.2019.04.012

Aschemann-Witzel, J., & Stangherlin, I. D. C. (2021). Upcycled by-Product use in Agri-Food Systems from a Consumer Perspective: A review of what we know, and what is missing. *Technological Forecasting and Social Change*, *168*, 120749. doi:10.1016/j.techfore.2021.120749

Borrello, M., Caracciolo, F., Lombardi, A., Pascucci, S., & Cembalo, L. (2017). Consumers' perspective on circular economy strategy for reducing food waste. *Sustainability (Basel)*, *9*(1), 141. doi:10.3390u9010141

Canali, M., Amani, P., Aramyan, L., Gheoldus, M., Moates, G., Östergren, K., Silvennoinen, K., Waldron, K., & Vittuari, M. (2016). Food Waste Drivers in Europe, from Identification to Possible Interventions. *Sustainability (Basel)*, *9*(1), 37. doi:10.3390u9010037

Cane, M., & Parra, C. (2020). Digital platforms: Mapping the territory of new technologies to fight food waste. *British Food Journal*, *122*(5), 1647–1669. doi:10.1108/BFJ-06-2019-0391

Coderoni, S., & Perito, M. A. (2020). Sustainable Consumption in the Circular Economy. An Analysis of Consumers' Purchase Intentions for Waste-to-Value Food'. *Journal of Cleaner Production*, *252*, 119870. doi:10.1016/j.jclepro.2019.119870

Comber, R., & Thieme, A. (2013). Designing beyond habit: Opening space for improved recycling and food waste behaviors through processes of persuasion, social influence and aversive affect. *Personal and Ubiquitous Computing*, *17*(6), 1197–1210. doi:10.100700779-012-0587-1 de Souza, M., Pereira, G. M., de Sousa Jabbour, A. B. L., Jabbour, C. J. C., Trento, L. R., Borchardt, M., & Zvirtes, L. (2021). A digitally enabled circular economy for mitigating food waste: Understanding innovative marketing strategies in the context of an emerging economy. *Technological Forecasting and Social Change*, *173*, 121062. doi:10.1016/j.techfore.2021.121062

FAO. (2019). *The State of Food and Agriculture 2019*. Moving Forward on Food Loss and Waste Reduction. Food and Agriculture Organization—United Nations, Rome. https://www.fao.org/3/ca6030en/ca6030en.pdf

Frey, M., Gusmerotti, N. M., Corsini, F., & Sarti, S. (2017). Food sharing: Making sense between new business models and responsible social initiatives for food waste prevention, 123–134.

Goodman-Smith, F., Bhatt, S., Moore, R., Mirosa, M., Ye, H., Deutsch, J., & Suri, R. (2021). Retail potential for upcycled foods: Evidence from New Zealand. *Sustainability (Basel)*, *13*(5), 2624. doi:10.3390u13052624

Graham-Rowe, E., Jessop, D. C., & Sparks, P. (2014). Identifying motivations and barriers to minimising household food waste. *Resources, Conservation and Recycling*, *84*, 15–23. doi:10.1016/j.resconrec.2013.12.005

Grainger, M. J., Aramyan, L., Logatcheva, K., Piras, S., Righi, S., Setti, M., Vittuari, M., & Stewart, G. B. (2018). The use of systems models to identify food waste drivers. *Global Food Security*, *16*, 1–8. doi:10.1016/j.gfs.2017.12.005

Gustavsson, J., Cederberg, C., Sonesson, U., Van Otterdijk, R., & Meybeck, A. (2011). *Global food losses and food waste*.

Jagau, H. L., & Vyrastekova, J. (2017). Behavioral Approach to Food Waste: An experiment. *British Food Journal*, *119*(4), 882–894. doi:10.1108/BFJ-05-2016-0213

Lage, M. C. (2011). Utilização do software NVivo em pesquisa qualitativa: Uma experiência em EaD. *ETD Educação Temática Digital*, *12*(03), 198–226.

Lehtokunnas, T., Mattila, M., Närvänen, E., & Mesiranta, N. (2022). Towards a circular economy in food consumption: Food waste reduction practices as ethical work. *Journal of Consumer Culture*, *22*(1), 227–245. doi:10.1177/1469540520926252

Mazzucchelli, A., Gurioli, M., Graziano, D., Quacquarelli, B., & Aouina-Mejri, C. (2021). How to fight against food waste in the digital era: Key factors for a successful food sharing platform. *Journal of Business Research*, *124*, 47–58. doi:10.1016/j.jbusres.2020.11.055

Michelini, L., Principato, L., & Iasevoli, G. (2018). Understanding Food Sharing Models to Tackle Sustainability Challenges. *Ecological Economics*, *145*, 205–217. doi:10.1016/j.ecolecon.2017.09.009

Moltene, L., & Orsato, R. J. (2021). Economia compartilhada na prática: um estudo exploratório sobre aceitação e uso de plataformas digitais para a redução do desperdício de alimentos. *Revista de Administração de Empresas*, 61.

Mothersbaugh, D. L., & Hawkins, D. I. (2016). *Consumer behavior: Building marketing strategy*. McGraw-Hill.

Octavia, D., Nasution, R. A., & Yudoko, G. (2022). A Conceptual Framework for Food Sharing as Collaborative Consumption. *Foods*, *11*(10), 1422. doi:10.3390/foods11101422 PMID:35626993

Principato, L., Secondi, L., & Pratesi, C. A. (2015). Reducing Food Waste: An investigation on the behaviour of Italian youths. *British Food Journal*, *117*(2), 731–748. doi:10.1108/BFJ-10-2013-0314

Quested, T. E., Parry, A. D., Easteal, S., & Swannell, R. (2011). Food and drink waste from households in the UK. *Nutrition Bulletin*, *36*(4), 460–467. doi:10.1111/j.1467-3010.2011.01924.x

Santagata, R., Ripa, M., Genovese, A., & Ulgiati, S. (2021). Food waste recovery pathways: Challenges and opportunities for an emerging bio-based circular economy. A systematic review and an assessment. *Journal of Cleaner Production*, *286*, 125490. doi:10.1016/j.jclepro.2020.125490

Shankar, A., Dhir, A., Talwar, S., Islam, N., & Sharma, P. (2022). Balancing food waste and sustainability goals in online food delivery: Towards a comprehensive conceptual framework. *Technovation*, *117*, 102606. doi:10.1016/j.technovation.2022.102606

Silvennoinen, K., Katajajuuri, J.-M., Hartikainen, H., Heikkilä, L., & Reinikainen, A. (2014). Food Waste Volume and composition in Finnish households. *British Food Journal*, *116*(6), 1058–1068. doi:10.1108/BFJ-12-2012-0311

Stancu, V., Haugaard, P., & Lähteenmäki, L. (2016). Determinants of consumer food waste behaviour: Two routes to food waste. *Appetite*, *96*, 7–17. doi:10.1016/j.appet.2015.08.025 PMID:26299713

Stangherlin, I. D. C., & De Barcellos, M. D. (2018). Drivers and barriers to food waste reduction. *British Food Journal*, *120*(10), 2364–2387. doi:10.1108/BFJ-12-2017-0726

Stelick, A., Sogari, G., Rodolfi, M., Dando, R., & Paciulli, M. (2021). 9 Impact of Sustainability and Nutritional Messaging on Italian Consumers' Purchase Intent of Cereal Bars Made with Brewery Spent Grains'. *Journal of Food Science*, *86*(2), 531–539. doi:10.1111/1750-3841.15601 PMID:33462803

Talwar, S., Kaur, P., Ahmed, U., Bilgihan, A., & Dhir, A. (2023). The dark side of convenience: How to reduce food waste induced by food delivery apps. *British Food Journal*, *125*(1), 205–225. doi:10.1108/BFJ-02-2021-0204

Tamasiga, P., Miri, T., Onyeaka, H., & Hart, A. (2022). Food waste and circular economy: Challenges and opportunities. *Sustainability (Basel)*, *14*(16), 9896. doi:10.3390u14169896

Teigiserova, D. A., Hamelin, L., & Thomsen, M. (2020). Towards transparent valorization of food surplus, waste and loss: Clarifying definitions, food waste hierarchy, and role in the circular economy. *The Science of the Total Environment*, *706*, 136033. doi:10.1016/j.scitotenv.2019.136033 PMID:31855638

UNEP. (2022). *Food Waste Index Report 2021*. United Nations Environment Programme Nairobi. https://wedocs.unep.org/bitstream/handle/20.500.11822/41679/Annual_Report_2022.pdf?sequence=3

van Geffen, L., van Herpen, E., Sijtsema, S., & van Trijp, H. (2020). Food waste as the consequence of competing motivations, lack of opportunities, and insufficient abilities. *Resources, Conservation & Recycling: X*, *5*, 100026.

Viscardi, S., Colicchia, C., & Creazza, A. (2023). Circular economy and food waste in supply chains: A literature review. *International Journal of Logistics*, *26*(5), 589–614. doi:10.1080/13675567.2022.2128095

Vittuari, M., Masotti, M., Iori, E., Falasconi, L., Toschi, T. G., & Segrè, A. (2021). Does the COVID-19 external shock matter on household food waste? The impact of social distancing measures during the lockdown. *Resources, Conservation and Recycling*, *174*, 105815. doi:10.1016/j.resconrec.2021.105815 PMID:36569117

Wang, Y., Zhu, Q., Krikke, H., & Hazen, B. (2020). How product and process knowledge enable consumer switching to remanufactured laptop computers in circular economy. *Technological Forecasting and Social Change*, *161*, 120275. doi:10.1016/j.techfore.2020.120275

Zepeda, L., & Balaine, L. (2017). Consumers' perceptions of food waste: A pilot study of US students. *International Journal of Consumer Studies*, *41*(6), 627–637. doi:10.1111/ijcs.12376

APPENDIX

Figure 3. Semi-structure interview guidelines

Categories	Subcategory	Indicators	Questões
Knowledge and use of waste reduction platforms	Knowledge of the platform	No	Would you use a platform that allows you to access products that would be discarded if they were not sold through these alternatives? What are the reasons that would lead you to disregard this type of service? What are the reasons why you would use this type of service? (extrinsic motivations - economic, social and environmental; intrinsic motivations - personal beliefs and desires
		Yes, but don't use	How did you first become aware of digital platforms for reducing food waste? Why don't you use it? What are the reasons why you would use this type of service? (extrinsic motivations - economic, social and environmental; intrinsic motivations - personal beliefs and desires)
	Usability and consumption factors		What factors do you consider most important when you buy a product on the platforms? What features do you appreciate most about this type of platform? Is there a specific digital platform that you have found particularly effective in reducing food waste? Are there any limitations to the use of digital platforms for the reduction of food waste that you have encountered or are aware of?
(for those who know and use the platforms) Drivers of influence of the use of the food waste reduction platform What motivated you to try this type of service?	Extrinsic Factors	Economic (if they indicate economic reasons)	How much money do you think you've saved by using digital food waste reduction platforms? How is the philosophy of this type of platform aligned with your financial management? Do you think consumers are more likely to use these platforms if they see that they save money? What are the economic benefits of this type of service? Do you think that using these platforms has changed your shopping behaviour and meal planning?
		Social (if they indicate social reasons)	To what extent can reducing food waste benefit society? What is the importance of the social interaction provided by these services in reducing food waste? To what extent is the use of these platforms aligned with your values in relation to social responsibility and sustainability? Have you noticed any social impact caused by the use of food waste reduction platforms? What incentives would motivate more people to use these platforms? What role does "social awareness" play in reducing food waste?
		Environmental (if they indicate environmental reasons)	Can food waste reduction platforms contribute to the sustainable development of the sector? Have you noticed any changes in your environmental behaviour as a result of using these platforms?
	Intrinsic Factors	Personal desires (the convenience in the use of these services, autonomy and independence that these platforms provide)	What benefits have you obtained from using this type of service? To what extent have they affected your personal habits? Have you noticed any changes in your behavior? Does your lifestyle influence the use of these platforms?
		Personal beliefs (the pleasure of being part of a new platform and the spirit of empathy, solidarity and cooperation)	Have you ever come across a situation where a digital platform doesn't meet your expectations? If so, can you describe what happened? Do you believe that digital platforms for reducing food waste have had any impact on reducing it? If so, how?

Chapter 13
When Sustainability Goes Wrong:
A Critical Perspective About Consumer Behaviour, Greenwashing, and its Impact on Sustainability

Anna Carolina Boechat
https://orcid.org/0000-0002-9252-6602
UNIDCOM/IADE, Portugal

Nuno Baptista
Universidade Lusíada, Comegi, Portugal

Mariana dos Reis Torgal
Universidade Católica Portuguesa, CECC - Research Centre for Communication and Culture, Portugal

ABSTRACT

Based on a conceptual discussion, this chapter focused on current consumer behavior, with a special emphasis on its relationship with sustainability, and on the recent sustainable practices of companies. Through the analysis of these two pillars, this narrative review aimed to frame sustainability and emphasize the greenwashing processes that take place in this context. To this end, some reasons why sustainability has been a major subject of debate in recent decades and also evidence on consumer behavior about this discussion were pointed out. The role of companies was also outlined – through corporate social responsibility practices – bridging the issue of greenwashing. As a negative aspect associated with sustainability, greenwashing was observed in depth, with a special focus on the digital environment, and in the context of marketing and influence.

1. INTRODUCTION

The global society has faced several challenges in the last decades, and forecasts point out critical damages related to social, economic, and environmental issues – such as civil conflicts, global warming,

DOI: 10.4018/978-1-6684-8984-0.ch013

and poverty, for example, just to name a few. As a natural consequence, consumer behavior has been changing drastically, and sustainability has been elevated as an important drive to lead change (Boechat et al., 2022).

This urge to provide a more sustainable context for current and future generations is applying pressure among organizations to enhance their sustainable behavior to fulfill stakeholders' expectations (Li et al., 2023), creating a better environmental reputation (Mazur-wierzbicka, 2022). Consequently, there has been an explosion of green initiatives (Shanor & Light, 2022) usually represented by "eco-friendly", "sustainable" or "organic" labels (Schmuck et al., 2018).

Greenwashing emerges when an organization has limited transparency (Dong et al., 2023) i.e., when it discloses positive environmental actions but "hides" those negative ones, giving an overall positive positioning regarding this matter (Arouri et al., 2021). This attempt to spend money promoting green actions instead of actually implementing them (Anand, 2022) creates a divergency between communication and practice (Li et al., 2023).

Based on these assumptions, this chapter develops a critical perspective on consumer behavior, greenwashing, and its impact on sustainability, considering that greenwashing is a practice that denotes the dark side of sustainable practices.

To fundament this point of view, the chapter starts explaining why sustainability is a global and common speech nowadays, highlighting the debate regarding a sustainable crisis. In sequence, it highlights the current consumerism process and the reasons why sustainability is a challenge to regular global consumption habits. In other words, this chapter presents the misalignment of consumers' sustainability intentions and actual behavior.

Following this rationale, Corporate Social Responsibility (CSR) is discussed as an important asset to any organization, due to its positive impact on several aspects of the brand and the organization itself. A current state of art of this concept is provided to enhance its importance and, also, greenwashing's emergence. Thus, greenwashing is the topic that follows this discussion, being deeply analyzed through literature, current examples, its performance in the digital fields, and the close relationship established between greenwashing and marketing techniques.

2. SUSTAINABILITY AS GLOBAL SPEECH: WHY SOCIETY CAN'T STOP TALKING ABOUT IT

Technology has benefited everyday life in many ways, but it has also brought disadvantages and serious problems. At the beginning of the 20th century, humanity became aware that in the moral domain there was a dark side in scientific and technological advances (Coutinho, 2009). The evolution of technology brought advantages but has encouraged the unrestrained exploitation of the planet's natural resources and caused high levels of pollution (Coutinho, 2009). As society and economy developed, the environment began to suffer from certain actions by human beings (ElHaffara et al., 2020).

According to Brahami et al. (2022), industrialization, urbanization, population explosion, wild capitalism programmed to obtain ever-increasing levels of productivity, consumption and profits are depleting the planet's resources, sending excessive amounts of carbon monoxide into the atmosphere, which is responsible for the destruction of the ozone layer and the consequent greenhouse effect. Moreover, these factors are depleting the oceans, annihilating the equatorial forests, as well as inflating non-biodegradable waste on land and in the seas: cement, polystyrene, plastics, tires, glass.

The alliance between science and practice has allowed man to understand more precisely the planet where he lives, to make the most of its natural resources, to create more improved machines, and to maximize levels of productivity and comfort – registered above all in populations from the most developed countries, located in the longitudes of the northern hemisphere. The truth is that this allegedly brave new world has gradually made the planet more degraded, more contaminated, more polluted, and, in short, more uninhabitable (Brahami et al., 2022; Figuers & Rivett-Carnac, 2020). Proof of this is the number of animal and plant species that have become extinct at supersonic speed (United Nations, 2022), and also the environmental disasters (heat waves, droughts, fires forests, floods, hurricanes, etc.) increasingly frequent, largely resulting from the accelerated climate change we have been witnessing, and which are exacerbating social problems in many latitudes of the world (Borrell, 2021; Elkington, 1998).

All these worrying signs, which are multiplying at a galloping pace, prove that planet Earth is experiencing a dramatic threat, which seems to be irreversible. Inevitably, this path will lead to an even more unregulated and unpredictable world, marked by catastrophes, even more acute inequalities, revolts, and social revolutions. According to Figuers and Rivett-Carnac (2020), the solution to reverse this self-destructive trend is to opt for sustainable policies, build a more sustainable world economy, and instill more sustainable behaviors in citizens.

The behavior that human societies decide to adopt in the 2020s/2030s will be decisive in combating and mitigating the problems and managing to decrease the average global temperature below 2º C, as suggested by *The 2015 Paris Agreement* (Borrell, 2021). The transition to sustainable capitalism could be the answer, according to Elkington (1998), but it will be one of the most complex challenges that the human species will have to overcome. With all this, the design and development of ecological products grew up with the aim of answering these questions but at the same time brought new challenges both in the management of the resource chain and in the development of products (Katsikeas et al., 2016). It is a complex theme that has been investigated by several psychologists and marketing professionals, more specifically in the area of consumer behavior (Prothero et al., 2011). So, green consumption may be the key to mitigating the threat of destruction of planet Earth (Prothero et al., 2011), however, finding ways to make people change their behavior and their routines and start to act more consciously may seem like an easy solution, but it is not as easy as it seems (Prothero et al., 2011). Will global society be prepared and available to fight the battle and overcome this challenge?

3. TO BE (SUSTAINABLE) OR NOT TO BE: A CONSUMERISM CHALLENGE

Because of the presented scenario, environmental awareness has evolved to be a dominant topic. One of the main consequences of this development is the clear effort by companies to become increasingly "green", as a way of responding to the growing consumer demand for more sustainable and ecological products and services (Gleim & Lawson, 2014). In other words, many consumers who are more enlightened and concerned about environmental issues opt for a more ecologically responsible lifestyle, seek to purchase products and services from companies that have been focusing on production processes that are less harmful to the environment, more sustainable, more recyclable, and soon, respectful of the planet (Borger & Costa, 2022).

However, and although sustainable behaviors seem to be the right path to be followed, some consumers seem reluctant to change their consumption habits. Consumption patterns continue to be a significant driver of growing socio-economic disparities and environmental harm, and without substantive changes in consumer behavior, the United Nations (UN) objectives of achieving broader sustainable development will not be attainable (Majer et al., 2022; Toussaint et al., 2021). Policymakers, activists and researchers have called for a better understanding of the factors that explain consumers' apparent lack of interest and research on how to elicit sustainable consumer behavior (Han, 2021). In reality, understanding consumer behavior in the context of sustainability is fraught with difficulties and complications (Papasolomou et al., 2022).

First and foremost, there is no consensus on what sustainable consumption is and the state of knowledge continues to be fragmented without unifying paradigms (Dos-Santos et al., 2021). The term 'sustainable consumption' is often confused with similar concepts, such as 'ethical consumption', 'green consumption', 'socially conscious consumption', and 'ethical consumerism' (Dos-Santos et al., 2021). Second, besides marketing efforts, there are multiple factors that affect consumers' purchasing choices and the consequent consumption of sustainable products, including socio-demographic characteristics, psychological factors, social drivers, and contextual and situational forces (Chirilli et al., 2022; Nguyen & Johnson, 2020).

Studies have examined socio-demographic characteristics, such as gender, age, and education level to characterize sustainability-sensitive consumers, yielding very divergent results (Chirilli et al., 2022; Palacios-González & Chamorro-Mera, 2020). It became clear that there is not one unique type of socially responsible consumer; moreover, a consumer may exhibit differentiated levels of commitment to social, economic, and environmental problems (Palacios-González & Chamorro-Mera, 2020) and there may be a trade-off between sustainability decisions in some situations (Baptista et al., 2022). There is also the well-established phenomenon designated alternately as the 'attitude–behavior', 'intention–behavior' or 'words–deeds gap', a concept that refers to the frequent misalignment of consumers' sustainability intentions and actual behavior (Carrington et al., 2014; Yeow et al., 2014).

Most consumers realize that there is a problem, and that urgent action is needed (Stoknes, 2015). Why do they not join the sustainable movement? One of the reasons given for this not happening is the fact that environmentalists in their marketing communication end up attributing the blame for the accelerated destruction of the planet to all human beings – well, it seems, that making people feel guilty is not a good strategy (Stoknes, 2015). Gleim and Lawson (2014) give a very interesting practical example: the use of seat belts in road vehicles. According to the authors, most people admit to feeling safer with the seat belt fastened correctly. However, they don't always put it on. The 'green gap' reflects a similar idea – consumers care about the planet but are rarely willing to make significant changes in their behavior and consumption habits. They are not willing to deal with the hassle of recycling, to pay more for a green product, nor to risk buying and using ecological products (Gleim & Lawson, 2014).

From a social perspective, social pressure can lead consumers to adopt sustainability values, but can also imply detrimental effects. For example, consumers who buy sustainable products can be negatively judged by peers, who can frame them as hippie or feminine (Acuti et al., 2022). On the other side, consumers that reveal an apparent concern for societal goods such as sustainability, may be mostly motivated by self-interests. Studying anti-consumption practices, motivations, and values within the attempts to live a more sustainable lifestyle, Black and Cherrier (2010) found that anti-consumption for sustainability is affected by the subjectivity of the consumer, due to consumers' multiple identities and conflicting values, and a focus on personal needs, including the need to secure a better world for their descendants, to save money and improve health conditions. Hence, these authors concluded that, contrary to the general notion that sustainability will be associated with socially aware consumers, that are prepared to sacrifice personal pleasure for communal well-being, sustainability does not require sacrificing personal pleasure. In addition, and as highlighted by Soper (2007), we should not overlook the extent to which consumption for sustainability is motivated by a social interest in acquiring status and distinction rather than altruistic concerns for collective well-being.

When looking at sustainability though a consumption point of view, it can be stated that sustainable consumption barriers are complex, diverse, and interrelated. Common barriers cited in the literature include the lack of information, information overload or information asymmetry between consumers and producers, and supply-chain complexity – making it difficult to monitor and track products' origins –, price barriers, lack of trust and consumers' association of sustainability with a compromise in terms of product functionality, aesthetics or healthiness (Acuti et al., 2022; Majer et al., 2022; Toussaint et al., 2021).

Some specialists believe that it would be preferable to start by changing simpler everyday habits. Consequently, the sum of all these actions could be translated into considerably more sustainable behavior. Starting with more conscious consumption is a key step, since the current relationship that most people in the middle and upper-middle classes have with consumption is reduced to the expression "buy, use and throw away" (Figuers & Rivett-Carnac, 2020). On the other side, communication to achieve short-term changes in consumer behavior has been criticized in the literature. Recycling and the use of your own bag on a shopping trip are examples of actions that are quite popular among more developed societies. Stoknes (2015) admits that these actions will have some benefits, but also states that these are the most insignificant way to really reduce polluting emissions – since they are only small individual actions. This author believes that individual recycling actions have, above all, the purpose of alleviating the burden on the conscience of those who practice them, since they only have an impact if they are catalysts for other larger actions.

4. CORPORATE SOCIAL (AND SUSTAINABLE!) RESPONSIBILITY

The already discussed context of severe socio-environmental challenges at a global level call for urgent intervention by organizations and, in this context, Corporate Social Responsibility (CSR) emerges (Oliveira et al., 2020). To better understand this concept, it is important to go back in time. Historically, CSR emerged during reflections on whether top managers in organizations should have concerns other than profit (Mohr et al., 2001). According to Mohr et al. (2001), as early as 1863, Adam Smith argued that the owners of big businesses would realize for themselves that it would be advantageous to adhere to social initiatives, ultimately because of the "invisible hand" of the market – which, allegedly, regulates supply and the demand. However, other authors argue that the theoretical concept of CSR was born in the 1950s, when the literature on this topic grew, both in the United States of America and in Europe (Borger & Costa, 2022). This concept developed because some academics concluded that certain companies were too independent of society and, consequently, were not really concerned with helping to solve problems in fields such as: sustainability, ethics, social solidarity, gender equality, and workers' rights, among others (Borger & Costa, 2022; Mohr et al. 2001).

Later, around 1980, there was an evident growth of the Third Sector (private, non-governmental, non-profit organizations) (Bordin & Pasqualotto, 2013). In this way, the number of partnerships that this sector began to develop with the Second Sector (private organizations sector) also grew and, naturally, this gave rise to CSR policies within large companies (Bordin & Pasqualotto, 2013).

That said, it is important to precisely define the concept of CSR, a task that appears to be intricate. CSR is a very broad concept, so there are several ways to define it (Mohr et al., 2001). Moreira (2002 in Levek et al., 2002) designates CSR as the "ethics based on actions with the public with which the organization can interact, that is, its stakeholders (customers, employees, suppliers, shareholders, government, society, environment)" (p. 16). A neoclassical definition in the field of economics, given by Friedman (1962), highlights that CSR is a way to increase the profits of an organization acting within the game rules, that is, in open and free competition, without deceit or fraud. However, this perspective has been criticized and considered reductive by several authors (Ebner & Baumgartner, 2006), since CSR cannot be viewed from a purely economic perspective. To corroborate this last statement, Wood (1991) believes that CSR is the major way of interconnecting society and business and proving that these are not distinct and completely independent entities. The author also adds that, for this reason, society has the right to create expectations regarding the way organizations act.

In short, and in a simple way, it can be said that CSR is essentially dedicated to the relationship between organizations and society, thus being strongly related to the management of *stakeholders* (Borger & Costa, 2022).

CSR is already regulated by law and there is a legal minimum of what companies need to comply within this area. For example, in many countries, investments in CSR must be mandatorily disclosed in companies' annual reports (Nalband & Kelabi, 2014). However, to gain the trust of *stakeholders*, and for reasons of social sanction, several companies are implementing CSR actions beyond of what is required by law (Hlioui & Yousfi, 2022). CSR is undoubtedly a very important area and one that must be considered when building the organizational culture (Schick et al., 2002). According to Hlioui and Yousfi (2022), there was an effort on the part of interested sectors to gradually make CSR more strategic. The dynamic market, where companies face increasing competition, has also pressured organizations to redefine their philanthropy and adhere to CSR as a way of guaranteeing competitive advantages (Burke & Logsdon, 1996).

Nevertheless, it is important to mention that, with the evolution of time, several researchers revisited these themes, updating and adapting them to the contemporary world. There are many scientific publications about CSR aimed at identifying possible future scenarios. According to Sharp et al. (2019), in 2015 Carroll predicted that in the future we would see an increase in *stakeholder engagement*, the prevalence of ethically sensitive consumers, the rise in the level of sophistication of non-governmental organizations (NGOs) and, finally, the increase in employees who value CSR more. However, the future of this concept needs to take technological advances into account and clearly define its role in building new structures and in the business strategy itself (Latapí Agudelo et al., 2019). In this sense, companies will have to adapt and evolve in order to embrace the most recent tools marketing tools, and they will have to do so through a comprehensive and holistic framework based on the principles of social responsibility, in order to defend sustainability, generation of shared value, and the belief that companies can redefine their purpose based on what is best for the world (Latapí Agudelo et al., 2019).

After understanding the concept of CSR, it is important to understand how it relates to sustainability. Firstly, sustainability has been a concept that has been increasingly highlighted in corporate communication and, consequently, in CSR (Gatti & Seele, 2014).

About CSR and its implementation much has been done in recent years. Top managers and CEOs themselves have begun to show more sensitivity to the risks and opportunities associated with CSR and, of course, to the impact of their organizations on society (Rake & Grayson, 2009). It can be said that one of the main tools for implementing CSR is the "Annual CSR Report" or "Annual Sustainability

Report" (Gatti & Seele, 2014). This document has gained special relevance in the last 10 years and is very important for several audiences - namely for the scientific community (since it offers "material" for studies and investigations), for the government, for shareholders, for *consumers,* and even for other companies in the market (Gatti & Seele, 2014). This is a valuable document, which is normally published both internally and externally, whose main objective is to communicate the CSR actions that the company carried out during the year of publication, whether in the environmental, ethical, philanthropic, and economic spheres (Cote, 2021). These reports are an excellent communication tool, allowing the company to inform the public about the mission, efforts, and results of the organization (Cote, 2021). Cote (2021) states that 90% of companies listed in the *Standard & Poor's 500 (S&P 500) Index* published a CSR report in 2019 – surpassing the percentage of 86% of companies in 2018 and 20% in 2011. Thus, it is possible to consider this communication tool as a trend that has been gaining prominence and importance over the last 12 years.

This information is relevant because as previously mentioned, sustainability has taken root in the corporate environment through CSR practices (Boechat et al., 2022). The literature carried out within the scope of this project points to the preponderance of transparency in the sustainable context as a very current theme. In other words, this explosion of green initiatives (Shanor & Light, 2022) means that organizations want to comply with sustainability policies – as they can face various criticisms if their actions are interpreted as not sustainable – and, for this, they make transparency a fundamental and necessary element (Svendsen, 2010) for their stakeholders so that they will have the perception that they are making considered and conscious consumption choices (Elkington & Zeitz, 2014; Rodrigues et al., 2021).

Even though sustainable consumption cannot be considered a transversal and uniform pattern in different societies, as debated before, it is undeniable that market choices have been changing over the years, which can be observed through the increased demand for ecological products (Mazur-wierzbicka, 2022): there has been a remarkable growth of these new purchase habits aligned with environmental causes, a preference for products identified as "eco-friendly", "sustainable" or "organic" emerged (Schmuck et al., 2018). This scenario applied considerable pressure among organizations, elevating sustainability as a corporate signal of responsibility (Arouri et al., 2021) and ethical behavior (Chen et al., 2022; Robertson et al., 2023).

By enhancing their sustainable performance, companies can improve their image (Dong et al., 2023), competitive advantage, and financial aspects (Sun & Zhang, 2019). A positive green reputation can also simplify decision-making processes and purchase decisions (Adamkiewicz et al., 2022), while attracting value chain partners (Li et al., 2023). By promoting a "green talk", companies are trying to promote better identification with investors and customers (Shanor & Light, 2022). These are just a few assumptions found in the broad literature regarding sustainability because the contribution of several authors throughout many years leaves no room for doubt: by implementing sustainability, organizations harvest several benefits (Boechat et al., 2022).

Following this reasoning line, it is important to address the fact that these changing consumption patterns to achieve a more sustainable world have become part of the political agenda. National and local governments have implemented a large range of sustainability-related policy measures (Acuti et al., 2022; Nguyen & Johnson, 2020). Supra national organizations and activist movements contributed by exercising pressure on governments and the corporate world, and by developing information campaigns to raise consumers' awareness (Nguyen & Johnson, 2020). Many governments are taking measures, articulated at a global level, and producing laws that aim to stop, reverse or, at least, soften the worst projections (Domingues & Remoaldo, 2012). The Sustainable Development Goals (SDGs) are a great example: created by the United Nations (UN) in 2015, they represent a global purpose based on social, economic, and environmental measures to ensure that by 2030 all countries can benefit from a better life quality (UNDP, 2023). The 17 SDGs are connected and destined to fulfill several gaps in the global society, and this task is assigned to governments, companies, families, citizens, etc., representing thus a collective compromise (UNDP, 2023). By eliminating poverty, hunger, and inequalities; creating good health, well-being, quality education, gender equality, clean water and sanitation, affordable and clean energy, decent work and economic growth; promoting sustainable cities and communities, responsible consumption and production, climate action, life below water and on land, peace, justice and strong institutions, and partnerships (UNPD, 2023); society – and especially companies can benefit from the SDGs, once they are able to associate their images with global responsible actions, elevating themselves as main actors in the global sustainable arena.

In sum, when considering all aspects mentioned before – an alarming environmental scenario, a slow but steady consumption behavior change towards a sustainable path, and a bigger compromise from governments, society, and firms –, all conditions are created to a phenomenon that will be explored in the next section of this chapter: greenwashing.

5. GREENWASHING: WHEN SUSTAINABILITY GOES WRONG

Several authors (Lee & Raschke, 2023; Pizzetti et al., 2021; Seele & Schultz, 2022) identify the environmental activist Jay Westerveld as the creator of the 'greenwashing' term, in 1986, when he brought attention to false environmental claims made by companies (Sun & Zhang, 2019). Since then, the literature about greenwashing has been growing considerably (Seele & Gatti, 2017).

Greenwashing represents an advertisement or a label for companies that are not honest about their environmental behavior (Sun & Zhang, 2019); it is a speculative strategic behavior that misleads consumers (Zhang, 2022), deceiving them to believe that their products or services are aligned with environmental practices (Dong et al., 2023). Thus, greenwashing is a practice based on limited transparency (Dong et al., 2023) i.e., when companies disclose positive environmental actions but "hide" those negative ones, giving an overall positive positioning regarding this matter (Arouri et al., 2021).

If organizations present themselves as sustainable and they are not so, there is the possibility of being seen as a 'pseudo-green' company, based on the infraction of lack of transparency (Parguel et al., 2011; Rodrigues et al., 2021). Pseudo-green companies are those that manage to create a "green" image and reputation in the minds of consumers to compete with true green brands (Jog & Singhal, 2019). It is important to highlight, at this point, that green companies are those that act according to concerns about well-being, quality of life, development, and progress (Pérez et al., 2016). For truly sustainable companies to differentiate themselves from pseudo-green ones, they must make consumers aware of greenwashing practices, highlight environmental aspects, expose pseudo-green companies and their deceptive practices, demonstrate and prove their ecological behavior, by adopting socially and ecologically responsible practices on resources and throughout the chain, in addition to adopting the 3R's of sustainability, that is, reducing, reusing, and recycling all possible waste (Jog & Singhal, 2019).

When managing brands through a green path, there is an attempt of companies to spend money promoting green actions instead of actually implementing them (Nidhi & Anand, 2022), which creates a divergency between communication and practice (Li et al., 2023) or, as posited by Walker and Wan (2012), a practice of "not walking the talk" (Pizzetti et al., 2021).

By obscuring negative activities (Adamkiewicz et al., 2022) or exaggerating an environmental performance (Shanor & Light, 2022), firms try to enhance their public image (Sun & Zhang, 2019), and to align their practices with society's expectations regarding ESGs conduct (Lee & Raschke, 2023). As explained by Chen et al. (2022), concepts such as cheating, misleading, selective disclosure, or false manipulation represent greenwashing actions, once the organization's goal is to be seen as more environmentally friendly than it actually is (Seele & Schultz, 2022).

This 'eco-washing', 'green makeup', 'green sheen' (Mazur-wierzbicka, 2022), or even 'exaggerated CSR strategy' (Li et al., 2023) can be identified in several ways. Literature in this regard highlight some important cases, as in China for example, where the government implemented specific regulation to prevent greenwashing due to a high number of fraudulent cases (Li et al., 2023), or in Japan, when Oji Paper – a paper company – claimed to have products with 50% of recycled paper when it actually was only less than 10% (Dong et al., 2023). At this point, it is important to highlight that, besides this Chinese example, the US government created a Guide for the Use of Environmental Marketing Claims in 2012 (Lee & Raschke, 2023). Overall, the main goal of these initiatives is to use public power in order to avoid misleading (Zhang, 2022) and several negative consequences to businesses, consumers, and markets.

Adamkiewicz et al. (2022) emphasize that in the fashion industry, for example, there are several certifications, labels, and initiatives (such as EU Ecolabel, Textile Exchange, The Microfibre Consortium, OEKO-TEX) that enable greenwashing in a massive scale. It is interesting to note that, by using these certifications and alternative materials, the greenwashing narrative helps to incentivize guilt-free fashion consumption (Adamkiewicz et al., 2022). It is not just in these sectors that flagrant cases of greenwashing are found. In the food sector, media websites highlight that Coca-Cola and Unilever were accused of misleading greenwashing due to their "recyclable" packaging claims (Laville, 2022).

In literature it is common to find examples of sustainable initiatives that may not be considered greenwashing but certainly do not promote sustainability through a correct perspective. In other words, it can be stated that different research evidence cases that initially seem to promote sustainability, unintentionally end up bringing a non-sustainable sign. Moskal (2022) took a deeper look at Uber's business model, aiming to verify if the company really enhances a greener economy or if this is another greenwashing example. The author claims that "Uber does not facilitate gratuitous sharing of goods and services with a view to use an excess capacity. It places profit maximization above the core values of the sharing economy such as collaboration, openness, and sources reusage. Due to these reasons, Uber hardly qualifies as a representative example of sharing economy business model. This also explains why Uber is referred to by some as a 'pseudo-sharing economy' and is accused of using greenwashing empty slogans to distort its real image and impact on the environment" (p. 273). To this extent, its 'Green Recovery Plan' might be the chance to clarify if Uber's actions are really sustainable or a simple greenwashing effect (Moskal, 2022).

On the other hand, Beste (2021) highlights the scope of regenerative agriculture, which emerged as a concept highly used in greenwashing processes. Although this type of agriculture does represent positive and well-known practices to benefit the environment, it was found that a coalition with members such as L'Oréal, Mars, Nestlé, Unilever, and other multinational companies – called "One Planet Business for Biodiversity" – was using the 'regenerative agriculture' concept as a common practice, but without any concrete evidence of its implementation (Beste, 2021). The author mentions PepsiCo and Crop Life as other similar examples regarding the same practice.

Obviously, companies that practice greenwashing are the most affected by its consequences, and literature regarding this issue presents several perspectives. Greenwashing can harm companies' market share and financial performance (Lee & Raschke, 2023; Sun & Zhang, 2019); prejudice credibility, market value, and competitive advantage (Sun & Zhang, 2019); cause negative reactions from different stakeholders (Arouri et al., 2021); create sustainability conflicts (Adamkiewicz et al., 2022), negative reputation, share price (Robertson et al., 2023), and word-of-mouth (Chen et al., 2022); it affects negatively consumers' trust, evaluation, attitudes, product quality perceptions, and performance towards the brand, manifesting thus corporate hypocrisy (Robertson et al., 2023).

Greenwashing can also affect consumers' green satisfaction and perceived value, which can lead to an idea that most stakeholders will not support it anymore, due to its fake foundation (Chen et al., 2022). Pizzetti et al. (2021) also bring information to this debate, by adding that greenwashing can generate online discussion against a company due to stakeholders' skepticism, leading to brand avoidance. The authors highlight also that it affects employees' performance and jobseekers' opinions. In sum, although greenwashing can encompass several damaging consequences as negative media promotion, customer litigation (Jhamb & Fiegl, 2022), customer distrust, and dissatisfaction (Chen et al., 2022), it is noted that this practice is far from being extinguished (Robertson et al., 2023).

Academics are giving an important contribution to the greenwashing debate, clarifying some new applications of greenwashing, like bluewashing – that do not evolve only environmental aspects but also social (Adamkiewicz et al., 2022) as poverty, disaster relief, and human rights (Ruiz et al., 2022); the vocal green organizations – that keep a good level of both communications and practices in the green field; the silent green organizations – that maintain a good environmental practice with low communication; and the silent brown – a company that does not a have a positive green performance but don't try to communicate it in a positive way (Shanor & Light, 2022).

6. GREENWASHING IN THE DIGITAL CONTEXT

Based on the discussion achieved so far, it seems important to bring a digital aspect to this conceptual narrative, by showing some examples of greenwashing through a digital point of view. First, it is relevant to address that companies with an undeniable presence in the digital field, such as Apple, Microsoft, and Google – commonly known as part of the Big Five – are already communicating their carbon neutrality when, in fact, their allegations represent only 3% of their carbon emissions (Baruah, 2023) – which can be interpreted as a greenwashing sign.

In line with Baruah (2023) information, Hazel and Brittany (2020) did interesting research by evaluating the information industry and taking a deeper look at Amazon and Google, for example. The first, although regularly communicate its efforts – on renewable energy, for example –, fails to provide report status or updated information. By doing so, it weakens the legitimacy of their compromise. Concerns with plastic waste are also addressed by Amazon, another digital giant, which communicated a huge effort in order to minimize packaging excess; but, as commented by the Hazer and Brittany (2020), it was found out through the media that the packing for small products was not recyclable (Hazel & Brittany, 2020). In sum, "Despite Amazon's reported efforts to environmental change, there are gaps between their policies and their operations, signaling that in order for the company to make substantial change, much still needs to be addressed" (p. 4).

Google, in its turn, faced the same type of accusations regarding its sustainable performance. Even though their effort is clearly communicated, as Amazon's, also there were identified media accusations regarding lobby activities to cover their alleged 'less ethical' actions (Hazel & Brittany, 2020). Additionally, an incongruence between internal and external policies was pointed out concerning sustainable efforts, not to mention other pieces of evidence described in the mentioned research, giving an idea that although there is a sustainable path being constructed, some incongruences need to be addressed so a higher level of transparency and accountability can be achieved by Google.

Meyers and Bittner (2012) approached the ecological intelligence concept implemented in virtual worlds and immersive games developed for children, to understand how these digital tools were able to enhance kids' ecological knowledge. They found out that the tools analyzed certainly provided ecological thinking but were deeply based on consumption activities. By promoting consumerism, these digital games did not fulfill an important aspect of sustainability (Meyers & Bittner, 2012).

Following the same reasoning line, Bohnsack et al. (2022) examined digital technologies and their relation with sustainable development. Even though it is common sense that digital transformations are a driving force towards sustainability, a "dark side" of it should not be ignored: by investing in digital economies there is an increase in energy use, as well as a manufacturing footprint (mainly produced by the Big Five companies), not to mention ethical issues – as fake news and AI excessive usage (Bohnsack et al., 2022).

7. GREENWASHING THROUGH A MARKETING POINT OF VIEW

Because greenwashing evolves a certain distance from truthfulness and is based on misleading communications, marketing has an important role in using communication techniques to mislead its targets (Lee & Raschke, 2023). Also, to reach a profile aligned with customers' sustainable expectations, organizations adopt some actions such as updating their communication and consequent marketing and advertising campaigns, updating production processes, renewing formulas, and the *packaging* of their products (Pérez et al., 2016), enhancing the marketing role as a green tool.

Lee and Raschke's (2023) research indicate that the majority of S&P 500 companies develop ESG reports regularly, communicating their sustainable efforts on websites and social media as a marketing digital strategy. Through verbal appeals (Lee & Raschke, 2023), as mentioned previously, these messages are built with ambiguous words and/or "*keywords (e.g., eco, organic, no chemicals, and sustainable)*" (Adamkiewicz et al., 2022, p. 3), and can include slight exaggeration or even full fabrication (Shanor & Light, 2022).

Once marketing communication is a central point in the greenwashing process (Chen et al., 2022), since the 2000s green advertising has been increasing (Jhamb & Fiegl, 2022; Schmuck et al., 2018). This context is very close to the "marketing myopia" concept mentioned by Nidhi and Anand (2022) in their research: they point out various cases of "*fluffy and exaggerated marketing*" (p. 17), with messages expressing facts that obviously cannot be validated by customers. In other words, this might happen because when signaling their commitment to the green cause, firms are promoting an asymmetric marketing communication, in the sense that consumers might not fully understand the environmental claims (Seele & Gatti, 2017). Thus, signaling theory can help to explain greenwashing, to the extent that there might be differences between the signal sent from the organization and the information processed by the consumer.

Stoica (2021) did a very interesting analysis regarding these sustainable marketing strategies: it became clear that, overall, green marketing has an educational purpose with a strong informative character, and communication to this extent must reinforce credibility through different tools – including, obviously, the digital ones. Once green communications are mostly developed to highlight positive initiatives from companies, this positive continuum can lead to what Shanor and White (2022) call the 'halo effect': *"... the idea is that when individuals learn about certain positive attributes of a product or firm, they come to believe that other attributes of the firm are similarly positive, even in the absence of evidence to that effect. For example, consumers and investors might perceive that a firm that derives all of its energy from solar power is likewise an environmental leader on water use or forestry management, even in the absence of evidence on its water use or forestry practices*" (Shanor & Light, 2022, p. 2046). It is understood, though, that this 'halo effect' can be considered as a marketing force that might feed greenwashing's propagation.

D'Hotman and Schnall (2021) add another layer to this perspective by mentioning 'digital greenwashing', which represents when "*a social media company develops a tool that creates the impression of acting in the interests of users, the public and policy makers are likely to have greater tolerance for actual harms caused by their platforms*" (p. 36). They use Facebook as an expressive example through its AI suicide prevention tool, highly marketed on its platform: although the usage of algorithms seemed to be an interesting way to enhance prevention in these situations, no data related to this initiative was provided, leading to a doubtful and non-transparent scenario (D'Hotman & Schnall, 2021).

Following the same path as the previous authors, Schultz and Seele (2022) adopt the 'digital ethics washing' to introduce misleading (marketing) communications about the use of AI tools and customer data management. As happens with greenwashing, corporate communication in these cases might enhance companies' digital performance by presenting thus a fake scenario (Schultz & Seele, 2022).

Once the internet offers a suitable environment for companies to inform, converse, and engage with the consumer about sustainability CSR issues (Aracil-Jordá et al., 2023), firms can link themselves with sustainable behavior in brand content marketing to obtain more consumer recognition (Zhang et al., 2023). However, these corporate efforts make little sense in cases where the consumer is not willing to pay for companies' sustainable practices.

Additionally, digital marketing tools such as Big data, digital twin, and IoT technology are used to forecast the demands of customers by analyzing their purchase patterns through the data collected by the organization and AI in marketing strategy enables the creation of artificial agents that suggest marketing actions on the basis of customer behavior (Kaur et al., 2022). These tools detect the apparent misalignment between consumers' sustainability intentions and actual purchasing behavior and can lead companies to disinvest in sustainability.

To avoid greenwashing marketing practices, there is a growing debate about how marketers can communicate firms' efforts without compromising transparency. On the American Marketing Association website, Hintermeister (2022) presents some ideas to promote brands' sustainable attributes without associating its image with greenwashing. The author refers education, accuracy, honesty, data usage, and certifications as a positive path to follow. Edwards (2023) go further, presenting a list of marketing practices that should be avoided. Apart from some practices already mentioned in our conceptual narrative, the following can be added: the use of evocative pictures or endorsements that do not exist, not credible designations (such as "eco-friendly cigarettes"), and outright lies.

The European Commission released recently new marketing standards for agri-food products, to provide more transparency to the consumer and, on the other hand, to better guide marketing professionals, in avoiding greenwashing (European Union, 2023). Overall, the guidelines are oriented to origin labelling, food waste, packaging, fruit juices, jams and marmalades, and eggs. The idea is to provide the consumer with more information, avoiding misleading messages. Following the same path, it is known that the US government updated its Green Guides for the use of environmental marketing claims (Boudreau, 2023). The idea is to align current marketing practices with ethical standards.

Mace (2023) took a deeper look at a global survey of the marketing industry developed by The World Federation of Advertisers in partnership with Kantar's Sustainable Transformation Practice. The results indicate that 39% of marketing professionals that answered the survey affirmed that their sustainability journey is still embryonic, once corporate sustainability strategies are still not ambitious enough. By decoupling the report, the author claims that there is a widening capability gap between marketers, related to a lack of knowledge regarding sustainable topics such as carbon emissions, for example (Mace, 2023).

By considering 'what is next' on sustainable marketing, Essen (2023) clarified that sustainability should be addressed with actions, and no longer storytelling. to that extent, the author sees a better marketing performance through a holistic approach, where circular economy is enhanced with CRM (Customer Relationship Management) techniques – moving thus from a traditional CRM process to a circular one. In other words, by managing the relationship with the customer, companies can encourage and reward reusing processes, enhancing products lifecycle (Essen, 2023). Another interesting idea is that companies can invest more in B2B marketing to accelerate sustainable growth through partnerships; in this case, a win-win situation would be beneficial, by improving both companies and the environment.

8. GREENWASHING AND MARKETING INFLUENCE

One noteworthy way to analyse greenwashing through a marketing perspective is by looking at the marketing influence phenomenon, which emerged in the digital context, more specifically via social media (Tafesse & Wood, 2021). It is widely known that marketing influence is a 'hot topic' in the marketing field over the last years due to an organic approach and a need for proximity between brands and consumers (Yesiloglu, 2021). By mediating both, influencers can improve marketing performance and deepen consumers' brand experience (Kim & Kim, 2021). In the wide range of influencers categories, the sustainable influencer can be distinguished as someone whose activity is to promote sustainable brands, products, and services (Taylor, 2021). Quick research can bring a lot of information online about this trend: the website 'The Good Trade' (2022), for example, presents 11 sustainable influencers that help to promote an eco-friendly mindset. As a result, the list highlights ONGs founders, bloggers, environmental educators, intersectional environmentalists, photographers, and digital creators that overall shares information about sustainability and travel, food, companies, job creation, lifestyle, fashion, social impact, nature, products, books, wellness, etc., which gives an idea about the relevance of these individuals in the marketing context.

A dangerous situation might happen if influencers fall into the same process mentioned before – such as the use of exaggerated messages, the lack of knowledge of the audience (and eventually of the influencer itself), or misleading communication – which could be seen as a greenwashing activity propagated by influencers (Taylor, 2021). Breves and Liebers (2022) designate 'greenfluencing' as a process based on the para-social theory aimed to persuade followers to buy green products.

The fashion industry, as earlier identified through Adamkiewicz et al. (2022) outputs, faces challenges in order to promote a better sustainable image, which enhances greenwashing processes. Thus, it is noted that fashion brands are using influencers to vary their marketing strategies and reach a positive reputation among younger generations. As pointed out by Cernansky (2022), by using influencers to promote their images, companies might face the risk to amplify greenwashing messages, corroborating thus to enhancing misleading regarding the fashion industry production, known by its overall not-sustainable production processes (Adamkiewicz et al., 2022).

Jalali and Khalid (2021) indicate that green influencers can have an impact on followers by promoting green WOM, green attitude, and green consumption intention. It is important to highlight, though, that once perceived credibility plays a huge role in the influencing process, green influencers must have reliable and trustworthy messages and behaviors (Jalali & Khalid, 2021), otherwise, they might fall into the greenwashing trap.

9. CONCLUSION

By developing this narrative review, it became clear that sustainability has emerged as a trending topic in the last decades due to several factors related to economic, social, and environmental aspects. The urge for consistent initiatives to mitigate environmental damage led to a scenario that evidently changed consumption behavior and firms' performance. By observing consumers, it was noted that although sustainable products and services are aligned with individuals' beliefs, economic factors and lack of knowledge might be barriers to an overall consistent sustainable behavior. On the other hand, companies are facing a challenge to fulfill society's expectations, which can be one of the reasons why greenwashing has emerged in the last years as a phenomenon based on misleading information communicated through marketing techniques.

By not being transparent, companies are risking customers' and governments' backlash, as well as a negative reputation and other damaging consequences. Unfortunately, greenwashing has grown so much that it can be seen through different categories – e.g. bluewashing or digital washing. To avoid this situation, it is believed that metrics and measurement tools based on emerging technologies should be implemented, thus assessing the authenticity and impact of these sustainable claims. Another sign of growth it's when greenwashing companies use marketing techniques to hide their negative environmental actions and promote a greener image. As a result, companies that really want to be perceived as sustainable face a considerable challenge, mostly because of a lack of trust from different stakeholders.

However, it is important to highlight that there are relevant examples of positive sustainable communications, as indicated by Broom (2019), which designate BP, IKEA, Coca-Cola, Centrica, Lush, Lacoste, and Shell as providers of personal, warm, informative, immersive, and creative communication. Mulholland (2019) adds another layer to this perspective, shedding light on the Finland government and its use of social media to promote awareness about sustainable initiatives, the French Energy Observer Project – which created several documentaries about sustainable topics –, the German Forums and dialogue actions, and the Iceland TV campaign also regarding SDG issues. The same author (2019) presents also Pulse of Europe, Netzwerk Weitblick, and Project 17 as good examples of EU projects that maximize information through compelling storytelling techniques to reach their target audience. Mulholland (2019) concluded that knowing the target audience, developing positive communication and storytelling, connecting, and mainstreaming the SGDs in everyday life, and having adequate resources to communicate are key elements to creating a successful SGDs communication.

In sum, it becomes evident that clear message, consistent commitment, regular communication, education, innovation, and investment in social, environmental, and economic initiatives are some of the strategies to avoid sustainability going wrong.

REFERENCES

Acuti, D., Pizzetti, M., & Dolnicar, S. (2022). When sustainability backfires: A review on the unintended negative side-effects of product and service sustainability on consumer behavior. *Psychology and Marketing*, *39*(10), 1933–1945. doi:10.1002/mar.21709

Adamkiewicz, J., Kochańska, E., Adamkiewicz, I., & Łukasik, R. M. (2022). Greenwashing and sustainable fashion industry. *Current Opinion in Green and Sustainable Chemistry*, *38*, 1–8. doi:10.1016/j.cogsc.2022.100710

Anand, A. (2022). *Greenwashing and the Use of Environmental Appeals in Modern Advertising.*, *11*, 15–26.

Aracil-Jordá, J., Clemente-Almendros, J. A., Jiménez-Zarco, A. I., & González-González, I. (2023). Improving the social performance of women-led microenterprises: The role of social media marketing actions. *Technological Forecasting and Social Change*, *191*(March), 122484. doi:10.1016/j.techfore.2023.122484

Arouri, M., El Ghoul, S., & Gomes, M. (2021). Greenwashing and product market competition. *Finance Research Letters*, *42*, 101927. doi:10.1016/j.frl.2021.101927

Baptista, N., Alves, H., & Matos, N. (2022). Scoping Challenges and Opportunities Presented by COVID-19 for the Development of Sustainable Short Food Supply Chains. *Sustainability (Basel)*, *14*(21), 14475. doi:10.3390u142114475

Baruah, A. (2023). 'Greenwashing' - Think tank criticise climate plans of 24 top firms, including Apple, Amazon. *The Print*. https://theprint.in/environment/greenwashing-think-tanks-criticise-climate-plans-of-24-top-firms-including-apple-amazon/1376920/

Beste, A. (2021). Greenwashing & hight tech! *Gesunderde*. https://www.gesunde-erde.net/media/fake-sustainability_end_english_1.pdf

Black, I. R., & Cherrier, H. (2010). Anti-consumption as part of living a sustainable lifestyle: Daily practices, contextual motivations and subjective values. *Journal of Consumer Behaviour*, *9*(6), 437–453. doi:10.1002/cb.337

Boechat, A. C., Morais, J., Moura, A., & Barreto, A. M. (2022). The impact of corporate social responsibility on brand loyalty and brand attachment: an analysis of the Portuguese brand Delta cafés. In *International Workshop in Marketing*. Sustainability and resilience. Porto: Universidade Lusíada.

Bohnsack, R., Bidmon, C. M., & Pinkse, J. (2022). Sustainability in the digital age: Intended and unintended consequences of digital technologies for sustainable development. *Business Strategy and the Environment*, *31*(2), 599–602. doi:10.1002/bse.2938

Bordin, D., & Pasqualotto, N. (2013). A Importância da Responsabilidade Social Empresarial para a Sustentabilidade e o Papel do Marketing Social. *Revista Capital Científico, 11*(2).

Borger, F., & Costa, A. (2022). Corporate Social Responsibility and Sustainability in Corporate Strategy: Brazilian Cases Studies. In Corporate Social Responsibility (pp. 69–92). IntechOpen. doi:10.5772/intechopen.94414

Borrell, J. (2021). Alterações climáticas: a UE está pronta a assumir as suas responsabilidades a nível mundial. In *European Union - External Action*. https://www.eeas.europa.eu/eeas/alterações-climáticas-ue-está-pronta-assumir-suas-responsabilidades-n%C3%ADvel-mundial_pti

Boudreau, C. (2023). Companies are selling us more stuff by telling us it's 'sustainable'. *Business Insider*. https://www.businessinsider.com/green-shopping-products-government-green-guides-marketing-sustainable-2023-4

Brahami, Y., Saeidi, A., Fiset, M., & Ba, K. (2022). The Effects of the Type and Quantity of Recycled Materials on Physical and Mechanical Properties of Concrete and Mortar. *Sustainability (Basel)*, *14*(22), 14752. doi:10.3390u142214752

Breves, P., & Liebers, N. (2022). #Greenfluencing. The Impact of Parasocial Relationships with Social Media Influencers on Advertising Effectiveness and Followers' Pro-environmental Intentions. *Environmental Communication*, *16*(6), 773–787. doi:10.1080/17524032.2022.2109708

Broom, D. (2019). Communicating sustainability: 7 companies doing it well. *Formative Content*. https://formativecontent.com/communicating-sustainability-7-companies-doing-it-well/

Burke, L., & Logsdon, J. M. (1996). How Corporate Social Responsibility Pays Off. *Long Range Planning*, *29*(4), 495–502. doi:10.1016/0024-6301(96)00041-6

Cernansky, R. (2022). Brands are tapping influencers to make sustainability fashionable. *Vogue Business*. https://www.voguebusiness.com/sustainability/brands-are-tapping-influencers-to-make-sustainability-fashionable

Chen, Y. S., Lin, Y. H., Lo, W. Y., & Lai, P. Y. (2022). Sustainable trick or tactic? The influence of greenwashing on green reputation, green satisfaction and green perceived value. *Coporate Management Review*, *42*(1), 107–139. doi:10.53106/102873102022064201004

Chirilli, C., Molino, M., & Torri, L. (2022). Consumers' awareness, behavior and expectations for food packaging environmental sustainability: Influence of socio-demographic characteristics. *Foods*, *11*(16), 2388. doi:10.3390/foods11162388 PMID:36010389

Cote, C. (2021). *What is a CRS Report & why is it important?* Harvard Business School Online. https://online.hbs.edu/blog/post/what-is-a-csr-report

Coutinho, R. (2009). "Crise Ambiental" e Desenvolvimento Insustentável: A Mitologia da Sustentabilidade e a Utopia da Humanização do Capitalismo "Selvagem". *Revista Praia Vermelha*, *19*(2), 21–36.

D'Hotman, D., & Schnall, J. (2021). A New Type of "Greenwashing"? Social Media Companies Predicting Depression and Other Mental Illnesses. *The American Journal of Bioethics*, *21*(7), 36–38. doi:10.1080/15265161.2021.1926583 PMID:34152910

Domingues, I., & Remoaldo, P. (2012). Responsabilidade Social Organizacional e Sustentabilidade. In I. Domingos & P. Remoaldo (Eds.), *Responsabilidade Social Organizacional: Desenvolvimento e Sustentabilidade* (pp. 93–114). Edições Húmus.

Dong, C., Huang, Q., Pan, Y., Ng, C. T., & Liu, R. (2023). Logistics outsourcing: Effects of greenwashing and blockchain technology. *Transportation Research Part E: Logistics and Transportation Review, 170*(October 2022), 103015. doi:10.1016/j.tre.2023.103015

Dos-Santos, M. J. P. L., Baptista, N., & Nobre, H. (2021). Exploring the relationship between ethical and sustainable consumption in short supply chains: A literature review. In J. I. Kantola, S. Nazir, & V. Salminen (Eds.), *Advances in Human Factors, Business Management and Leadership - Proceedings of the AHFE 2021 Virtual Conferences on Human Factors, Business Management and Society, and Human Factors in Management and Leadership* (pp. 197–203). Springer. 10.1007/978-3-030-80876-1_26

Ebner, D., & Baumgartner, R. J. (2006). The relationship between Sustainable Development and Corporate Social Responsibility. *Corporate Responsibility Research Conference, 4*(5.9). http://wbw.unileoben.ac.at

Edwards, C. (2023). What is Greenwashing? *Business News Daily*. https://www.businessnewsdaily.com/10946-greenwashing.html

ElHaffara, G., Durifa, F., & Dubéb, L. (2020). Towards closing the attitude-intention-behavior gap in green consumption: A narrative review of the literature and an overview of future research directions. *Journal of Cleaner Production*, *275*, 275. doi:10.1016/j.jclepro.2020.122556

Elkington, J. (1998). *Cannibals With Forks: The Triple Bottom Line of 21st Century Business*. Capstone.

Elkington, J., & Zeitz, J. (2014). *The Breakthrough Challenge: 10 Ways to Connect Todays Profits With Tomorrows Bottom Line*. Jossey-Bass: A Wiley Brand.

Essen, B. (2023). Shifting from stories to substance: Here's what is next for sustainable marketing. *Think with Google*. https://www.thinkwithgoogle.com/intl/en-gb/future-of-marketing/digital-transformation/sustainable-marketing-solutions/

European Union (2023). Commission update marketing standards of agri-food products to better address consumer needs and sustainability. *The European Sting*. https://europeansting.com/2023/04/24/commission-updates-marketing-standards-of-agri-food-products-to-better-address-consumer-needs-and-sustainability/

Figuers, C., & Rivett-Carnac, T. (2020). *The Future We Choose: Surviving the Climate Crisis*. Alfred A. Knopf.

Friedman, M. (1962). *Capitalism and Freedom*. University of Chicago Press.

Gatti, L., & Seele, P. (2014). Evidence for the prevalence of the sustainability concept in European corporate responsibility reporting. *Sustainability Science*, *9*(1), 89–102. doi:10.100711625-013-0233-5

Gleim, M., & Lawson, S. J. (2014). Spanning the gap: An examination of the factors leading to the green gap. *Journal of Consumer Marketing*, *31*(6–7), 503–514. doi:10.1108/JCM-05-2014-0988

Han, H. (2021). Consumer behavior and environmental sustainability in tourism and hospitality: A review of theories, concepts, and latest research. *Journal of Sustainable Tourism*, *29*(7), 1021–1042. doi:10.1080/09669582.2021.1903019

Hazel, S., & Brittany, M. (2020). Greenwashing in the Information Industry. *The I Journal. Graduate Student Journal of the Faculty of Information*, *5*(2). Advance online publication. doi:10.33137/ijournal.v5i2.34413

Hintermeister, S. (2022). How Marketers Can Avoid Greenwashing. *American Marketing Association (AMA)*. https://www.ama.org/marketing-news/how-marketers-can-avoid-greenwashing/

Hlioui, Z., & Yousfi, O. (2022). CSR and Innovation: Two Sides of the Same Coin. In Corporate Social Responsibility (pp. 1–29). IntechOpen. doi:10.5772/intechopen.94344

Jalali, S., & Khalid, H. (2021). The Influence of Instagram Influencers' Activity on Green Consumption Behavior. *Business Management and Strategy*, *12*(1), 78–90. doi:10.5296/bms.v12i1.18265

Jhamb, S., & Fiegl, R. (2022). Perceived Greenwashing and Sustainable Business Strategies: Understanding Organizational Roles in Addressing Environmental Issues. *IUP Journal of Business Strategy*, *19*(2), 23–32.

Jog, D., & Singhal, D. (2019). Pseudo green players and their greenwashing practices: A differentiating strategy for real green firms of personal care category. *Strategic Direction*, *35*(12), 4–7. doi:10.1108/SD-07-2019-0143

Katsikeas, C. S., Leonidou, C. N., & Zeriti, A. (2016). Eco-friendly product development strategy: Antecedents, outcomes, and contingent effects. *Journal of the Academy of Marketing Science*, *44*(6), 660–684. doi:10.100711747-015-0470-5

Kaur, R., Singh, R., Gehlot, A., Priyadarshi, N., & Twala, B. (2022). Marketing Strategies 4.0: Recent Trends and Technologies in Marketing. *Sustainability (Basel)*, *14*(24), 1–17. doi:10.3390u142416356

Kim, D. Y., & Kim, H. S. (2021). Influencer advertising on social media: The multiple inference model on influencer-product congruence and sponsorship disclosure. *Journal of Business Research*, *130*, 405–415. doi:10.1016/j.jbusres.2020.02.020

Latapí Agudelo, M. A., Jóhannsdóttir, L., & Davídsdóttir, B. (2019). A literature review of the history and evolution of corporate social responsibility. *International Journal of Corporate Social Responsibility*, *4*(1), 1–23. doi:10.118640991-018-0039-y

Laville, S. (2022, June 30th). Coca-Cola among brands greenwashing over packaging, report says. *The Guardian*. https://www.theguardian.com/environment/2022/jun/30/coca-cola-among-brands-greenwashing-over-packaging-report-says

Lee, M. T., & Raschke, R. L. (2023). Stakeholder legitimacy in firm greening and financial performance: What about greenwashing temptations?☆. *Journal of Business Research*, *155*, 113393. doi:10.1016/j.jbusres.2022.113393

Levek, A., Benazzi, A., Arnone, J., Seguin, J., & Gerhardt, T. (2002). A responsabilidade social e sua interface com o marketing social. *Revista Da FAE*, *5*(2), 15–25.

Li, W., Li, W., Seppänen, V., & Koivumäki, T. (2023). Effects of greenwashing on financial performance: Moderation through local environmental regulation and media coverage. *Business Strategy and the Environment*, *32*(1), 820–841. doi:10.1002/bse.3177

Mace, M. (April 23rd, 2023). Greenwashing concerns: Marketing professionals warn of sustainability knowledge gap. *Edie*. https://www.edie.net/greenwashing-concerns-marketing-professionals-warn-of-sustainability-knowledge-gap/

Majer, J. M., Henscher, H. A., Reuber, P., Fischer-Kreer, D., & Fischer, D. (2022). The effects of visual sustainability labels on consumer perception and behavior: A systematic review of the empirical literature. *Sustainable Production and Consumption*, *33*, 1–14. doi:10.1016/j.spc.2022.06.012

Mohr, L. A., Webb, D. J., & Harris, K. E. (2001). Do consumers expect companies to be socially responsible? The impact of corporate social responsibility on buying behavior. *The Journal of Consumer Affairs*, *35*(1), 45–72. doi:10.1111/j.1745-6606.2001.tb00102.x

Moskal, A. (2022). Moving Towards a Sustainable Digital Future with Uber – a Legitimate Step Towards a Greener Economy or Merely Greenwashing Policy? *Politeja*, *19*(3(78)), 267–282. doi:10.12797/Politeja.19.2022.78.14

Mulholland, E (2019). Communicating Sustainable Development and the SDGs in Europe: Good practice examples from policy, academia, NGOs, and media. *ESDN Quarterly Report 51*.

Nalband, N. A., & al Kelabi, S. (2014). Redesigning Carroll's CSR Pyramid Model. *Journal of Advanced Management Science*, *236–239*, 236–239. doi:10.12720/joams.2.3.236-239

Nguyen, N., & Johnson, L. W. (2020). Consumer behaviour and environmental sustainability. *Journal of Consumer Behaviour*, *19*(6), 539–541. doi:10.1002/cb.1892

Oliveira, I., Figueiredo, J., Cardoso, A., & de Oliveira, E. R. (2021). Gap between sophisticated consumers and sophisticated behaviors: Analysis of The portuguese in social sustainability. *Academy of Strategic Management Journal*, *20*(5), 1–11.

Oliveira, J., Júnior, L., Fernandes De Mesquita, R., Alves, N., Santos, D., Gomes, W., Felipe, F., Fátima, S., & Matos, R. N. (2020). O Futuro Que Nós Criamos: A Perspetiva da Sustentabilidade Para Futuros Gestores. *Revista Gestão e Organizações*, *5*(4), 80–101.

Palacios-González, M. M., & Chamorro-Mera, A. (2020). Analysis of socially responsible consumption: A segmentation of Spanish consumers. *Sustainability (Basel)*, *12*(20), 1–15. doi:10.3390u12208418

Papasolomou, I., Melanthiou, Y., & Tsamouridis, A. (2022). The fast fashion vs environment debate: Consumers' level of awareness, feelings, and behaviour towards sustainability within the fast-fashion sector. *Journal of Marketing Communications*, *29*(2), 191–209. doi:10.1080/13527266.2022.2154059

Parguel, B., Benoît-Moreau, F., & Larceneux, F. (2011). How Sustainability Ratings Might Deter "Greenwashing": A Closer Look at Ethical Corporate Communication. *Journal of Business Ethics*, *102*(1), 15–28. doi:10.100710551-011-0901-2

Pei, J. (2022). Approaches Toward Building the Digital Enterprise and Sustainable Economic Development: The Moderating Role of Sustainability. *Frontiers in Psychology*, *13*(March), 1–11. doi:10.3389/fpsyg.2022.835602 PMID:35360590

Pérez, L. A., Garzón, M. A., & Ibarra, M. A. (2016). Empresa Verde: Diagnostico de la necesidad de un modelo. *Dimensión Empresarial*, *14*(1), 67–78. doi:10.15665/rde.v14i1.425

Pizzetti, M., Gatti, L., & Seele, P. (2021). Firms Talk, Suppliers Walk: Analyzing the Locus of Greenwashing in the Blame Game and Introducing 'Vicarious Greenwashing.'. *Journal of Business Ethics*, *170*(1), 21–38. doi:10.100710551-019-04406-2

Prothero, A., Dobsha, S., Freund, J., Kilbourne, W., Luchs, M., Ozanne, L., & Thøgersen, J. (2011). Sustainable Consumption: Opportunities for Consumer Research and Public Policy Related papers. *Journal of Public Policy & Marketing*, *30*(1), 31–38. doi:10.1509/jppm.30.1.31

Rake, S. M., & Grayson, D. (2009). Overall change dynamics: Embedding corporate responsibility and sustainability - everybody's business. *Corporate Governance (Bradford)*, *9*(4), 395–399. doi:10.1108/14720700910984945

Robertson, J. L., Montgomery, A. W., & Ozbilir, T. (2023). Employees' response to corporate greenwashing. *Business Strategy and the Environment, 2022*(May 2022), 1–13. doi:10.1002/bse.3351

Rodrigues, L., Silva, F., & Romero, C. (2021). "Sou Verde de Verdade": Estratégias Mercadológicas da Economia Criativa para Superar a Desconfiança do Consumidor. *Revista de Gestão Social e Ambiental*, *15*, e02780. doi:10.24857/rgsa.v15.2780

Ruiz, S., Silvia, B., Belen, R., & Feijoo, F. (2022). Characteristics Determine Greenwashing? *Environment, Development and Sustainability*, *24*(3), 4024–4045.

Schick, H., Marxen, S., & Freimann, J. (2002). Sustainability Issues for Start-up Entrepreneurs. *Greener Management International*, *38*, 59–70. doi:10.2307/greemanainte.38.59

Schmuck, D., Matthes, J., & Naderer, B. (2018). Misleading Consumers with Green Advertising? An Affect–Reason–Involvement Account of Greenwashing Effects in Environmental Advertising. *Journal of Advertising*, *47*(2), 127–145. doi:10.1080/00913367.2018.1452652

Seele, P., & Gatti, L. (2017). Greenwashing Revisited: In Search of a Typology and Accusation-Based Definition Incorporating Legitimacy Strategies. *Business Strategy and the Environment*, *26*(2), 239–252. doi:10.1002/bse.1912

Seele, P., & Schultz, M. D. (2022). From Greenwashing to Machinewashing: A Model and Future Directions Derived from Reasoning by Analogy. *Journal of Business Ethics*, *178*(4), 1063–1089. doi:10.100710551-022-05054-9

Shanor, A., & Light, S. E. (2022). Greenwashing and the First Amendment. *Columbia Law Review*, *122*(7), 2033–2118.

Soper, K. (2007). Re-thinking the "Good Life": The citizenship dimension of consumer disaffection with consumerism. *Journal of Consumer Culture*, *7*(2), 205–229. doi:10.1177/1469540507077681

Sun, Z., & Zhang, W. (2019). Do government regulations prevent greenwashing? An evolutionary game analysis of heterogeneous enterprises. *Journal of Cleaner Production*, *231*, 1489–1502. doi:10.1016/j.jclepro.2019.05.335

Svendsen, A. (2010). *The Stakeholder Strategy: Profiting From Collaborative Business Relationships*. Berrett-Koehler.

Tafesse, W., & Wood, B. P. (2021). Followers' engagement with instagram influencers: The role of influencers' content and engagement strategy. *Journal of Retailing and Consumer Services*, *58*, 102303. doi:10.1016/j.jretconser.2020.102303

Taylor, E. (July 19th, 2021). The paradox of the "sustainable influencer". *Remake*. https://remake.world/stories/news/the-paradox-of-the-sustainable-influencer

The Good Trade. (2022). 11 Sustainability Influencers Inspiring Us To Do A Little Bit Better Everyday. *The Good Trade*. https://www.thegoodtrade.com/features/sustainability-influencers/

Toussaint, M., Cabanelas, P., & González-Alvarado, T. E. (2021). What about the consumer choice? The influence of social sustainability on consumer's purchasing behavior in the Food Value Chain. *European Research on Management and Business Economics*, *27*(1), 100134. doi:10.1016/j.iedeen.2020.100134

UNDP. (2023). *United Nations Development Programme*. UNDP. https://www.undp.org/sustainable-development-goals

United Nations. (2022). *The Sustainable Development Goals Report*. UNDP. https://unstats.un.org/sdgs/report/2022/

Wood, D. (1991). Corporate Social Performance Revisited. *Academy of Management Review*, *16*(4), 691–718. doi:10.2307/258977

Yesiloglu, S. (2021). The rise of influencers and influencer marketing. In *Influencer Marketing: Building Brand Communities and Engagement*. Routledge.

Zhang, D. (2022). *Environmental regulation, green innovation, and export product quality*. Elsevier. doi:10.1016/j.irfa.2022.102311

Zhang, Y., Zhou, Y., Liu, Y., & Xiao, Z. (2023). Research on the Influencing Mechanism of the Effect of Brands' Sustainable Behaviors on Consumer Attitudes: An Empirical Study on Clothing Brands. *Sustainability (Basel)*, *15*(3), 2351. doi:10.3390u15032351

Chapter 14
The Usage of Digital Marketing Tools in City Branding

Anna Vaňová
https://orcid.org/0000-0002-0035-9326
Matej Bel University, Slovakia

Darina Rojíková
Matej Bel University, Slovakia

Katarína Vitálišová
https://orcid.org/0000-0002-5830-4862
Matej Bel University, Slovakia

ABSTRACT

The aim of the chapter is to assess and compare the differences in the approach of European and Slovak cities to city branding with focus on utilisation of digital tools of marketing communication tools. The concept of city branding has developed through several stages and nowadays, it is strongly affected by utilization of digital tools. The empirical research verifies the current approaches to urban branding in 13 European and eight Slovak cities which are the administrative and cultural centres of the regions and have the best potential for applying the concept of city branding in Slovakia. By questionnaire survey, the authors have verified in depth the defined approaches to city branding in eight Slovak cities. For inspiration, the process of city branding in one of the best ranked European cities—Amsterdam—is presented. In the conclusion, the chapter defines the measures that should be taken to implement city branding as a comprehensive, systematic and targeted process aimed at shaping the positive image of the city in order to promote it on the market and to ensure comprehensive city development.

1. INTRODUCTION

Since 1975, when the concept of city branding began to develop, society has also been shaped and developed in a significant way. Progressive changes in society and the functioning of cities have occurred mainly as a result of globalisation, in which local traditions and differences have gradually disappeared

DOI: 10.4018/978-1-6684-8984-0.ch014

and a homogenised society has been created, which has also brought uniformity to the territorial market. During this period, the importance of city branding as a tool of achieving sustainable development by building a competitive advantage through a differentiation strategy grew. Although it is a qualitative, intangible, and more or less subjective attribute of the territory, it offers some potential to differentiate cities against the increasing degree of similarity of many traditional localisation factors. In recent decades, the development of digital communication has had significant impact on the tools used to brand cities. In this chapter, we focus on the role and use of digital communication in the concept of city branding in the context of achieving sustainable city development. The work is divided into three chapters. The theoretical section defines the approaches in the development of the concept of city branding and digital tools of marketing communication. In the Material and methodology section, we explain how the research was conducted and what material was used. In the fourth chapter, we present the results of the empirical research conducted to map the approaches of European and Slovak cities to city branding with using digital forms of marketing communication and we characterise in a form of best practice the branding process in one of these cities – Amsterdam. In the conclusion of the paper, we formulate recommendations for the application of the concept of branding in the conditions of Slovak cities.

2. THEORETICAL APPROACHES TO CITY BRANDING

In the context of increasing competition between cities that are subject to comparison and competition, the city brand has become one of the most important elements of their differentiation and recognition (Nogué, 1999; Anholt, 2007; Zenker et al., 2017; Lucarelli, 2018; Ma, 2019; Rinaldi et al., 2021; Oliva et al., 2022).

Cities should focus on branding for three main reasons. The first reason is the importance of connecting the city with the external environment and communicating the city with this environment in a clear, unambiguous, coordinated way so that the general perception of the city among the target groups coincides with the perception of the city itself. The second reason is the fact that the city brand is a relatively significant factor influencing the sustainable development and competitiveness of the city. The third reason is related to the value of the city brand, which has recently become crucial. The city brand is an asset to be managed, valued, and protected in a focused and coordinated way (Anholt, 2007; McCabe, 2017; Frig, Sorsa, 2018; Alexander et al, 2020).

In today's rapidly changing and uncertain times, city branding has become essential for the sustainable development and success of a city in a competitive environment and provides several advantages. The advantages include connecting and developing economic, business, sport and cultural activities, promoting the city's economic and political interests in the internal and external environment, stimulating stronger partnership relations, attracting talent, students and skilled labour, strengthening investor confidence, attracting inward investment, decreasing unemployment and increasing the standard of living of the population and, last but not least, the overall competitiveness of the city (Jaffe & Nebenzahl, 2001; Anholt, 2007, 2014; Hakala & Lemmetyinen, 2011; Vaňová et al., 2017; Giobanardi et al, 2018; Alexander, 2020).

Moreover, the current broad international debate on city branding is not about seeking these advantages, but about answering the question of how to make branding deliver the aforementioned advantages.

Cities have been building their brands for several decades, but this area has long been associated mainly with marketing communication (Olins, 2002; Anholt, 2007; Dzureková, 2009). Anholt (2008) argues that the connection between brands and cities dates to the time of Alexander the Great (356 BC to 323 BC). He was one of the first people to believe that the success or failure of a territory largely depends on how people perceive that territory and what value it has for them.

The origins of modern place brand theory date back to 1969 (Kotler & Levy, 1969), when territory began to be thought of as a product and the object of marketing efforts. The concept of place brand first appeared in Hunt 's work (1975) in the context of tourist destinations, which considered the image of a tourist destination as a place brand. The place brand was identified with place image in other works (e.g., Ashworth & Voogd, 1990), when place brand theory was extended from the field of tourist destinations to territories in general. Vaňová (1996) considers the name of a city as its brand.

Until the late 1980s and early 1990s, the concept of city brand was mainly associated with marketing communication, as it mainly focused on activities promoting the city to create a city image without a long-term strategy (Bartels & Timmer, 1987; Ashworth & Voogd, 1990; Kotler et al., 1993). This approach to the city brand has led to further misinterpretations of the role that the city brand performs (Oliva et al., 2022). Govers and Go (2009) argue the old city brand model needs to be deconstructed because it is closely related to the traditional city image theory, which is inappropriate because it does not link the city's image to aspects of the city's identity. Unlike city promotion, city branding is a highly integrated and strategic activity that is directly related to public policy (Štefčeková & Vaňová, 2013; Lucarelli, 2018).

According to Kavaratzis and Ashworth (2010), city branding is not only about communicating a desired city image but is a strategic response to environmental challenges. Therefore, city branding is considered a new form of territorial governance, which is aimed at satisfying the needs and desires of the city's potential consumers. The concept of city branding thus moved from city communication through city marketing to its current state. The current situation is defined by the city's brand, which can differentiate the city from other cities serving the same purpose, with the main goal of presenting the city's image to external audiences (Vela, 2013) as well as internal audiences, thus ensuring a competitive advantage for its sustainable development (Borseková et al., 2017).

In the analysis of city marketing theory and practice, Kavaratzis, (2004), Kavaratzis and Ashworth (2005), Braun (2008), Chartron, (2013), Giovanardi et al. (2018), Oliva et al. (2022), and Hosper (2020) observe the shift from city marketing to city branding. According to the authors, city branding is a new episode in the application of city marketing. City branding seeks to create a connection with the city through associations that are an emotional, mental, psychological departure from the functional - rational nature of marketing interventions. It implies a change of direction in which desired brand guides marketing measures related to the physical environment and functionality of the city (Kavaratzis, 2004). According to Braun (2008), city branding is the next step or the ultimate goal of the marketing process. According to Eshuis et al. (2014), Vuignier (2016) city branding is a marketing tool for managing cities associated with perception, image, reputation and mental associations in the minds of target audiences.

Ashworth (2011), Eshuis and Klijn (2012), Eshuis et al. (2014) argue that city branding is a very broad strategy that goes beyond the current management of the city. According to the authors, city branding is public governance as it affects all sectors of public life. Anders-Morawska and Rudolf (2015) add that city branding is a management strategy in which public administration builds relationships with the population, fosters civic pride, community participation and social capital. Furthermore, Vaňová (2020) adds that city branding is a type of competitive strategy.

Braun (2008), Janiszewska and Insch (2012), Eshuis and Edwards (2013), Anholt (2014), Hereźniak and Anders-Morawska (2015), McCabe (2017), Lucarelli (2018), and Baker (2019) present city branding as a form of city policy based on strategic management and place sustainable development planning where the use of modern technologies also plays an important role.

Similarly, Sarah Essbai (in Baker, 2019), an urban planner in Amsterdam, drawing on the broader emerging relationship between urban planning and city brands, said that "city brands are a tool for strategic planning. The integrated, strong brand of the city serves as a "guide" for the growth of the city, identifies its priorities in the field of capital investment, services and urban development and is a vehicle for the long-term success of the territory. "

We have summarised the authors' various approaches to city branding in Table 1.

Despite the fact that in the development of the concept of city branding, the authors moved from the perception of the city brand as a form of marketing communication to its perception as a form of management of cities, communication is still considered one of the basic steps and, at the same time, prerequisites in the process city branding.

In this regard, Kavaratzis (2008) developed a city brand communication model that includes three types of city brand communication: primary communication, secondary communication, and tertiary communication. Primary communication includes architecture, city design, infrastructure, but also city management, e.g., city institutions and residents. Secondary communication includes formal communication through various traditional and modern forms (tools and channels) of marketing communication. Tertiary communication refers to the oral presentation of information about the city by residents and visitors to the city. Tertiary communication is largely outside the control of territory management (Kavaratzis, 2008).

Kavaratzis was followed by Baker (2019), who claims that a city brand usually develops and communicates in three successive stages. The first stage is an organic image that develops from the general awareness of the city through influences such as media coverage, books, movies, family and friends, sports, and entertainment. This organic image is even stronger if city has a long and exciting history, a unique cultural fabric, outstanding natural attractions, or an important business or political background. The second phase is the marketing-induced image, which, as the name suggests, is mainly shaped by marketing communication tools. This means that it is developed through controlled marketing-communication processes. The third phase is the experiential phase based on the experiences of the city's consumers. Every city that attracts visitors, new residents, and investors will encounter this phase. However, according to Baker (2019), the third phase is critical since for the city to fulfil its "promises" embedded

Table 1. Approaches to city branding from the perspective of selected authors

Approach	Authors
City brand as a city image	Hunt (1975); Ashworth and Voogd (1990); Vaňová (1996)
City brand as a form of city marketing communication	Bartels and Timmer (1987); Ashworth, Voogd (1990); Kotler et. al. (1993), Kavaratzis (2004, 2008)
City brand as a city marketing tool	Eshuis et al. (2014); Vuignier (2016)
City brand as a superstructure, the goal of city marketing	Kavaratzis (2004); Kavaratzis and Ashworth (2005); Anholt (2007); Brown (2008); Chartron (2013)
City brand as a new form of territorial administration, public administration, and a new form of public policy	Kavaratzis (2005, 2011); Brown (2008); Govers and Go (2009); Ashworth (2011); Eshuis and Klijn (2012); Janiszewska and Insch (2012); Eshuis and Edwards, (2013); Eshuis et al. (2014); Anholt (2014); Hereźniak and Anders-Morawska (2015); McCabe (2017); Lucarelli (2018); Frig, Sorsa (2018); Baker (2019); Hosper (2020); Vaňová (2020)

in the communication in the first and second phases and to strengthen its brand, it must have a strong reality, i.e., strong assets. This means that the reality that the consumers of the city will encounter when visiting it must correspond to the ideas that the consumers of the city had before visiting it. Otherwise, the city's brand may be undermined.

In this regard, the authors Anholt (2007), Govers and Go (2009), Ashworth (2011), Eshuis and Klijn (2012) oppose the claim that it is not possible to build a successful city brand through marketing-communication activities, as they do not bring the desired result when city branding. This claim is substantiated by Anholt (2007) with his research from 2005 to 2007 (when the Brand Index was launched), in which no correlations were found between changes in the brand and spending on so-called marketing-communication campaigns for branding.

However, Anholt (2007, 2014) adds that in this area it is necessary to carry out detailed research that would clarify the position of marketing communication in the concept of city branding.

2.1. The Role of Marketing Communication and Its Digital Forms in the Concept of City Branding

Vaňová et al. (2017) claim that one of the primary tasks of marketing communication in place marketing is to city branding through its tools. The role of marketing communication in the process city branding is to inform about the intended strategy of city branding, to implement the city brand in the internal and external environment, and to gain public support. On the other hand, the two-sidedness of marketing communication makes it possible to get feedback (Vaňová et al., 2017) and involve the public in the creation of a city branding strategy through various surveys and evaluations (Herezniak, 2017).

All these activities should be supported by effective and efficient marketing communication. We live in a time when the communication is strongly depended on the modern technical devices and technologies. They became important source of information, sharing ideas as well as self-promoting. These changes in the communication reflects the new tools of city branding, especially in the field of communication and online media. The success of city branding depends essentially on how the city management turns digitization into a competitive advantage. The focus is on regular and multi-channel communication with all relevant stakeholders, strongly supported by online tools. To the most progressive and more frequently used tools belong websites, discussion forums, blogs, social media, mobile applications, influencers activities, various kinds of events (real or virtual) etc.

According to Scott (2013), Karlíček (2016) and Přikrylová et al. (2019), websites serve primarily to provide various types of information to current and potential consumers of the city, allow building relationships with target groups and create an environment for two-way communication. Social media is a relatively new form of marketing communication used over the Internet. Social networks are the world's most visited websites with significant growth potential, which is why they also find their place in city´s branding. The term social media usually includes the Internet, communication channels of mobile devices, and tools through which users can share opinions and textual, audiovisual, and image content with each other. As the name implies, social networks involve building community and networks and encourage its users to participate and engage (CIPR, 2011), thus greatly expanding the reach of target audiences. Blogs are according to Přikrylová, Jahodová (2010), Janoucha (2014) uncomplicated text websites without or with simple graphics, presenting the author's personal opinions and creating space for further communication. The author often targets a certain group of users with his topics and opinions and deliberately provokes a discussion. The popularity of this form of marketing communication results mainly from people's need to communicate, draw information, present, and confront their opinions with other people. More and more often, blogs are also used by large companies or cities, while not only communication department workers, but also top management representatives and employees contribute their articles to them (Foret, 2011; Přikrylová, Jahodová, 2010; Kim et al., 2019). According to Foret (2011), a discussion forum is a communication tool through which Internet users can discuss various topics with each other in the form of short text messages. Individual contributions (reactions) of users are organised hierarchically, while the rules for adding reactions are clearly defined by the administrator of the discussion forum (Foret, 2011). Authors, inter alia Přikrylová, Jahodová (2010), Frey (2011), Rajčák and Rajčáková (2012), Scott (2013), Kim et al. (2019) and others also include graphic (banner) Internet advertisements, which are the oldest and at the same time the most frequently used form of Internet advertising, among modern forms of marketing communication. Banners are according to Přikrylova and Jahodová (2010), Scott (2013) flashing, moving, or static graphic advertising bars that carry an advertising message and when clicked, the user is redirected to the advertiser's website. According to Přikrylová and Jahodová (2010, p. 227), banners can have "various forms, types, sizes and locations, from a static combination of text and images, through cartoon animations using photos, sound, to videos, which currently have the greatest potential, as far as they are able to best engage users". Frey (2011), Přikrylová and Jahodová (2010), Jurášková et al. (2012), Karlíček (2016) define location placement as the placement of a territory in an audiovisual work (film, television series, computer games), in a live broadcast, theatre performance, radio play, or books, for the purpose of promotion, under clear, precontractual agreed conditions, for a monetary fee compensation or other barter consideration. Pavlik (2008) adds that location placement is a promotional technique, where, unlike classic advertising, it is a nonviolent method that the viewer perceives, but does not consider it intrusive and, in the ideal case, makes him want to visit the advertised territory. In order for location placement to work effectively, the territory should be displayed or mentioned in positive form. The user is often not even aware of the location of the territory in the work, it works subconsciously and influences the consumer's behavior, which the consumer is unable to reasonably justify. With location placement, the problem is the high cost of its implementation, as well as the measurement of its effectiveness. With mobile operators' expansion of the networks and with the increase in the functionality and possibilities of using mobile phones, there was also room for the expansion of mobile communication. In addition to classic mobile communication (SMS, MMS, calling), mobile applications are currently quite often used as one of the modern forms of marketing communication. According to Janssen (2010), mobile applications are a type of small application software, specially designed with regard to the requirements of the operating system used by the mobile device. Some mobile applications, after being downloaded to a mobile device, work via the Internet as separate programs in an offline environment; for other applications, online space is a necessary prerequisite for full functionality. The current market offers many different-orientated mobile applications (from simple games intended for entertainment to applications intended for interaction between users to various applications items intended for work or shopping).

The process of marketing communication starts with a needs and wishes survey and ends with the pre-sale and after-sale marketing communication. This covers plenty of activities in order to attract customers to visit a city, as well as to inform the public about the city and thus to engage stakeholders in developmental activities (Lee, 2022). Vaňová et al. (2017) state that the function of marketing communication in city marketing is to provide information about the city as a whole and about its sub-products, in order to convince society of advantage of the place. Furthermore, it should provide motivation for the target markets to „purchase" the products of the city; or to visit the city; to arouse the interest of the public in solving the problems of the place; to gain public support; to reach a mutual agreement between the actors that influence the sustainable development of the place (Vaňová, 2006; Herezniak et all, 2015; McCabe, 2017; Lee, 2022) and with all this activities help to create city brand (Moilanen & Rainisto, 2009; Vuignier, 2016; Rojíková, 2022). For this purpose, it is inevitable to prepare a comprehensive strategy based on combination of traditional and innovative promotion tools. According to Kotler et al. (2021), Moilanen and Rainisto (2009), Govers and Go (2009), Vaňová et. al. (2017), and others, the tools of the promotion mix include advertising, personal selling, sales promotion, public relations, on-line communication, location placement, guerilla and viral communication, word of mouth, mobile applications, and experiential marketing. Unlike traditional forms of promotion mix, an innovative approach makes it possible to reach target segments both in mass and individually, maintain the interest of target segments, convey individually tailored information, and obtain feedback.

Anholt (2007) and Lucarelli (2018) further adds that systematic, thoughtful, purposeful, and coordinated city branding should become one of the primary areas of city policy in the 21st century. Cities that are unwilling or unable to branding will find it increasingly difficult to gain their share of world markets, capital, investment, talent, cultural exchange, respect, and attention.

3. MATERIAL AND METHODOLOGY

The paper deals with the current topic of city branding, in which there is a significant polarisation of the professional opinions of the authors, inter alia Anholt (2007), Govers and Go (2009), Ashworth (2011), Eshuis and Klijn (2012) on the need, meaning, and importance of the role of marketing communication in city branding.

The aim of the paper is to define the approach to city branding and to identify the role and use of modern digital forms of marketing communication in city branding.

To define the theoretical approaches to city branding we use the method of literature review of foreign and domestic scientific papers and books. This helps us to identify individual development stages and intersections in the approaches to city branding. We have verified the defined approaches to city branding and utilisation of digital tools in this process through empirical research in 13 European cities (London, Paris, Rome, Amsterdam, Vienna, Berlin, Barcelona, Copenhagen, Munich, Madrid, Stockholm, Dublin, Prague), which they place in the top places in the rankings evaluating city brands, i.e. European cities that were ranked in at least one of the city brand rankings in 2020 - The Anholt - Ipsos City Brands Index, Saffron's City Brand Barometer and Bloom Consulting Digital City Index - on one of the first ten ranks and were also part of the research The Anholt – Ipsos City Brands Index (2020) and The Resonance World's Best Cities (2019) and the 8 largest Slovak cities (Bratislava, Nitra, Trnava, Trenčín, Žilina, Banská Bystrica, Prešov and Košice), which are also the capitals and administrative, cultural centres of the regions and have the best potential for the application of the city branding concept in the conditions of Slovakia. The primary research was conducted in the period from 7 September 2020 to 21 September 2020. The research was conducted in a form of a questionnaire survey. The questions were formulated in terms of the established hypothesis H0: Marketing communication and its modern forms play an important role in the city branding, which was established on the basis of the theoretical starting points of the investigated issue. We tested the hypothesis by answering 2 research questions. Q1: Which modern forms of marketing communication and how do European and Slovak cities use them in the process of city branding? Q2: What is the perception and application of the city branding in European and Slovak cities?

The questionnaires were distributed to the cities electronically - with a predefined form to fill in and the possibility to fill it in online via Google Forms. The questionnaire contained 10 questions, 7 of which were closed and combined, 1 open and 2 identification questions of the respondents representing the cities. The respondents were employees of individual cities. In the European cities, 6 respondents (46.15%) were employees in the field of development / development activities of the city, 5 respondents (38.46%) - employees in the field of marketing, city communication, 1 respondent (7.69%) - employee of the section for Smart City and 1 respondent (7.69%) a customer service employee. In the Slovak cities, 100% of the respondents were employees of the communication and promotion / public relations departments. We use the method of analysis, comparison, synthesis and deduction for data processing and presentation. We compared the results of the research from the European cities with the results from the Slovak cities and based on the synthesis and deduction we formulate the measures that should be taken to implement city branding as a comprehensive, systematic and targeted process aimed at forming a positive image of the city in order to promote the city on the market and ensure the comprehensive development of the city. As inspiration for the cities from Central and Eastern Europe (including Slovakia) we present also the best practice example of city branding in Amsterdam.

4. COMPARISON OF THE APPROACHES TO BRANDING OF SELECTED EUROPEAN AND SLOVAK CITIES

European cities have been applying the concept of city branding in their development for several decades, as confirmed by the responses of the European cities to the individual questions of the primary research. All the European cities stated that city branding is important for their development, that city branding should be built in a targeted and systematic way with the concept of city branding as part of several strategic documents. 12 (92.31%) representatives of the European cities said that city branding is part of the city's development strategy and communication strategy. 5 of the surveyed European cities (38.46%) have prepared a separate document for city branding. 5 representatives of the European cities (38.46%) stated that city branding is also part of the city's marketing strategy. None of the European cities indicated that city branding was not part of any document.

Despite the fact that all the Slovak cities agreed that city branding is important for their development and is built in a targeted and systematic way, the answers of the Slovak city representatives in other primary research questions did not confirm these statements. None of the Slovak cities has a separate document for city branding and city branding is not anchored in the main development document of the city – the Economic Development and Social Development Programme of the researched cities. 5 Slovak cities (62.5%) stated that city branding is not part of any document. According to the answers of the representatives of the Slovak cities, city branding is part of the design manual in 1 city and part of the city's communication strategy in 1 city. After reviewing these documents, we found that the documents do not address city branding. The only Slovak city that has city branding captured in a document is the capital city Bratislava (the capital of the Slovak Republic) with a Marketing and Communication Strategy of Destination Bratislava with a focus on source markets, with a time horizon of 2018 - 2022. The strategy focuses on branding and development in the field of tourism. The results of the research aimed at examining the current approaches of European and Slovak cities to city branding are presented in Figure 1.

The strategic approach of the European cities to city branding also confirms their perception and application of the city brand concept itself. European cities currently apply the concept of city branding mainly as a city marketing tool (84.62% of EU cities) and a superstructure, a city marketing goal (69.23% of EU cities). 61.54% of the European cities also perceive city branding as a form of marketing communication and 38.46% of the European cities as a new form of territorial administration, public administration, and a new form of public policy. Representatives of the European cities surveyed excluded the identification of the city brand with the city's image.

Unlike the European cities, the Slovak cities perceive the city brand mainly as a form of marketing communication (75% of Slovak cities). Only 37.5% of the Slovak cities also marked city branding as a city marketing tool. The city of Bratislava is the only one that perceives city branding as a superstructure, a goal of the city's marketing. Representatives of the Slovak cities do not perceive city branding as an image of the city, but as a new form of territorial administration, public administration, and a new form of public policy.

We pay special attention to the analysis of digital forms of marketing communication in the process of city branding of European and Slovak cities.

Based on the answers of representatives of European and Slovak cities, we can conclude that European and Slovak cities use all 10 modern forms of marketing communication to city branding. Despite

Figure 1. The approaches of European and Slovak cities to the implementation of the city branding concept

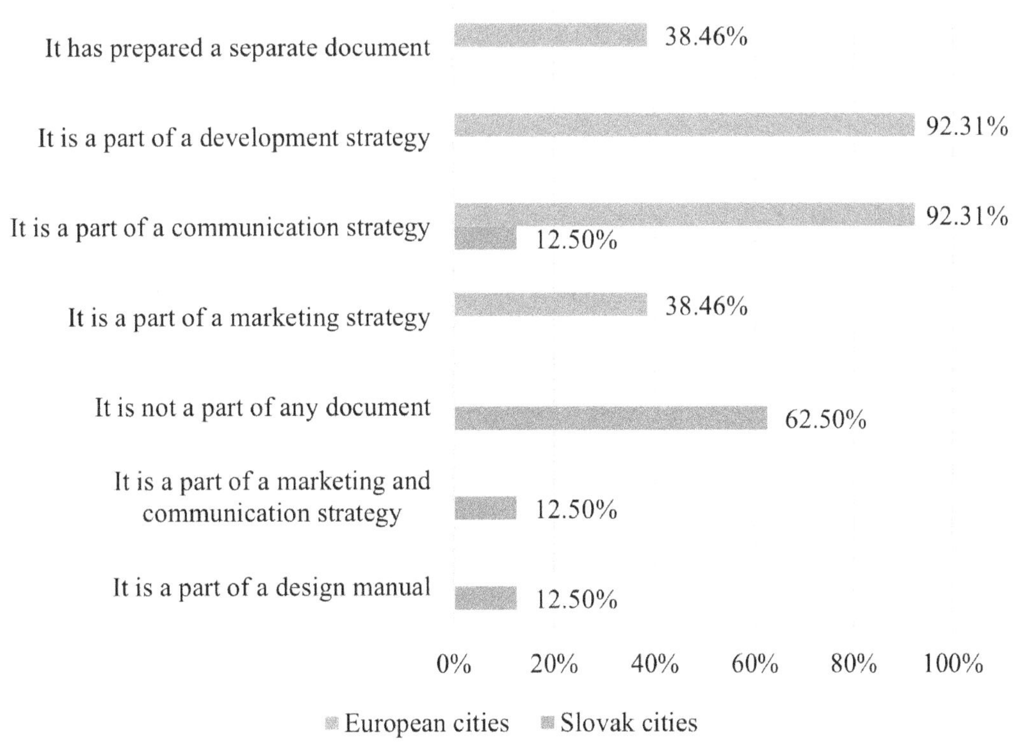

Figure 2. Perception of the city brand concept of European and Slovak cities

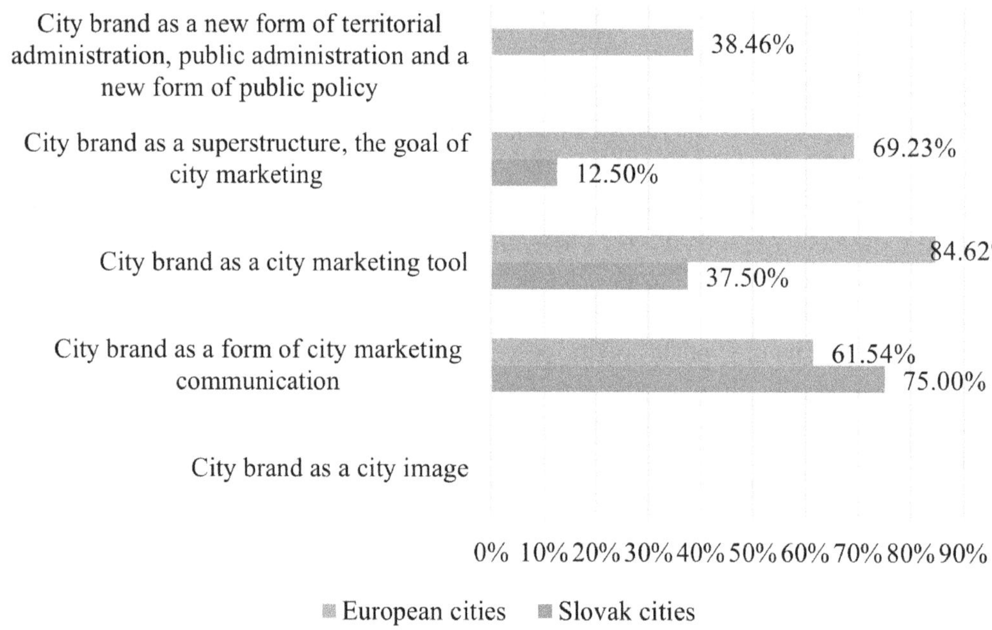

the fact that all European and Slovak cities have a website, only 69.23% of European cities use it for branding. European cities that stated that they use an Internet site for city branding have a separate site for branding, or the focus on city branding is a subpage of the city's official website. Within the website, a subsite focused on city branding, residents and companies operating in the city have the opportunity to participate in the creation and communication of the city brand through questionnaires, surveys, designing and evaluating the visual identity of the city brand (logo, slogan), submitting suggestions, reminders of the city brand, or its strategies. Instructions and guidelines for using the visual identity of the city brand (logo, slogan) in the form of a design manual are also part of such types of websites and subsites. In addition to websites and subsites aimed directly at city branding, all the investigated European cities also have websites focused on city visitors and the city's offer, especially in the field of tourism (history, attractions, events, gastronomy, etc.), while it is in most cases a page marked with the logo and slogan of the city brand. In contrast to European cities, all representatives of Slovak regional cities stated that they use the website to city branding. After a detailed examination of the official websites of Slovak regional cities, we found that the pages and their subpages do not focus on building the city's brand. In addition to official websites, the cities of Bratislava, Košice, Banská Bystrica, Nitra and Trenčín have created websites aimed at visitors and the offer of tourism products in the area (visitnázovmesta.sk/com/eu). Operators of portals focused on the offer of the cities of Košice, Trenčín and Nitra in the field of tourism are not individual cities, but regional tourism organizations. The city of Bratislava, as the only Slovak city, uses the official logo and slogan of the city brand on the portal, as well as the elements of the city brand defined by the Marketing and Communication Strategy of Destination Bratislava 2018 – 2022. Location placement is used in city branding by only 53.84% of European cities and 25% of Slovak cities. The relatively low rate of use of this modern form of marketing communication in city branding is mainly related to its price (Frey, 2011; Přikrylová, Jahodová, 2010; Jurašková et al., 2012; Karlíček, 2016).

All Slovak cities and 69.23% of European cities stated in the primary research that they use online events to city branding. The expansion of the offer of online events by cities (especially in the conditions of the Slovak Republic) is mainly related to the transition of culture to a virtual environment during the Covid-19 pandemic. The online events organized by Slovak cities are mainly based on chamber music concerts, theatre performances, and exhibitions. The city of Bratislava also offers virtual city tours. Compared to Slovak cities, online events in European cities are mainly focused on virtual exhibitions, openings, and city tours, respectively. important cultural and historical monuments.

The use of digital billboards on the Internet is more widespread in European cities to city branding, which, as with location placement, is mainly related to its price. Digital billboards are used by 76.92% of European cities and only 25% of Slovak cities. Discussion forums, chats, and web applications are the least used modern forms of marketing communication in city branding, both in European and Slovak cities. Only 38.46% of European cities and one Slovak city (12.50%) use discussion forums and chats to city branding. Web applications are used by only one Slovak city (12.5%) and 46.15% of European cities to city branding. European cities use web applications in city branding, especially in participatory processes focused on voting, evaluation, commenting, and submission of suggestions related to the city brand.

In contrast to web applications, up to 84.61% of European cities and one Slovak city - the city of Bratislava - use mobile applications to city branding. The European cities investigated, in addition to mobile applications adapted to the needs of city residents, use applications aimed mainly at city visitors and making their stay in the city more pleasant and easier. Applications alert city visitors to monuments, attractions, events, shopping, and accommodation options, etc. Most mobile applications of European cities work in online and offline with the possibility of using the map to facilitate movement around the city. The official mobile application of the city of Bratislava, which is linked to the city's website aimed at visitors to the city, also works on the same principle. Despite the fact that the city of Košice stated that it uses the mobile application to city branding, it is not its operator. The operator of the Košice Region mobile application is the regional organization of the tourism industry, as with the website focused on the field of tourism.

A relatively used modern form of marketing communication in city branding of European cities are blogs, which are used by up to 84.61% of European cities. Blogs of European cities are mainly aimed at potential visitors to the city, while in various language mutations, they convey information about the city and its offer in an engaging way. Unlike European cities, only 2 Slovak cities (25%) use blogs for branding. The cities of Bratislava and Košice have established blogs that are part of the city's websites focused on tourism. The city of Bratislava presents the elements of the city brand defined in the Marketing and Communication Strategy of the destination Bratislava 2018 – 2022 within the blog, as well as with the website.

The phenomenon of current stage of development in city branding are social media. It is confirmed by our and the international researches. E.g., by survey of App Annie in 2022, the people spend 4,8 hours in average by using smart phone, what is 1/3 of daytime. In comparison to 2019, the increase is more than 30%. They use mostly applications for communication and social networks, secondly, applications focused on photos and videos. Approximately the same time period people use TikTok as well as Facebook, cca 19,6 hours per month. To the most used application belongs TikTok, Facebook, WhatsApp Messenger, and Instagram.

Figure 3 shows the use of individual digital forms of marketing communication in city branding of European and Slovak cities.

European cities rate the overall importance of marketing communication in city branding with an average score of 1.23 and Slovak cities with 1.75.

From the point of view of evaluating the importance of individual modern forms of marketing communication1 in city branding, it is social media that are considered the most important, which were rated by representatives of European cities with an average grade of 1.23 and representatives of Slovak cities with an average grade of 1.33. The second best-rated modern form of marketing communication in city branding is the website, which represents European cities with an average grade of 1.85 and representatives of Slovak cities with a grade of 1.38. The three most important modern forms of marketing communication in city branding are completed by mobile applications, which are rated 1.92 for European cities and 2.00 for Slovak cities. The worst-rated modern forms of marketing communication in city branding are digital billboards, chats, discussion forums and location placement.

In the primary research, representatives of European and Slovak cities also commented on the issue of the role of marketing communication in city branding. Representatives of Slovak cities stated that the role of marketing communication in city branding is mainly to inform city visitors about the city's offer, bring information about the city to current and potential customers of the city, communicate and interpret the city's activities, promote the city, provide information about the city, create an interactive space with the public. On the other hand, representatives of European cities stated that the role of marketing communication in city branding consists of informing the public about the process of city branding, obtaining information from city residents, engaging in the process of city branding, communicating significant elements of the city brand, informing potential and current the city's customers

Figure 3. Tools of digital marketing communication used in city branding

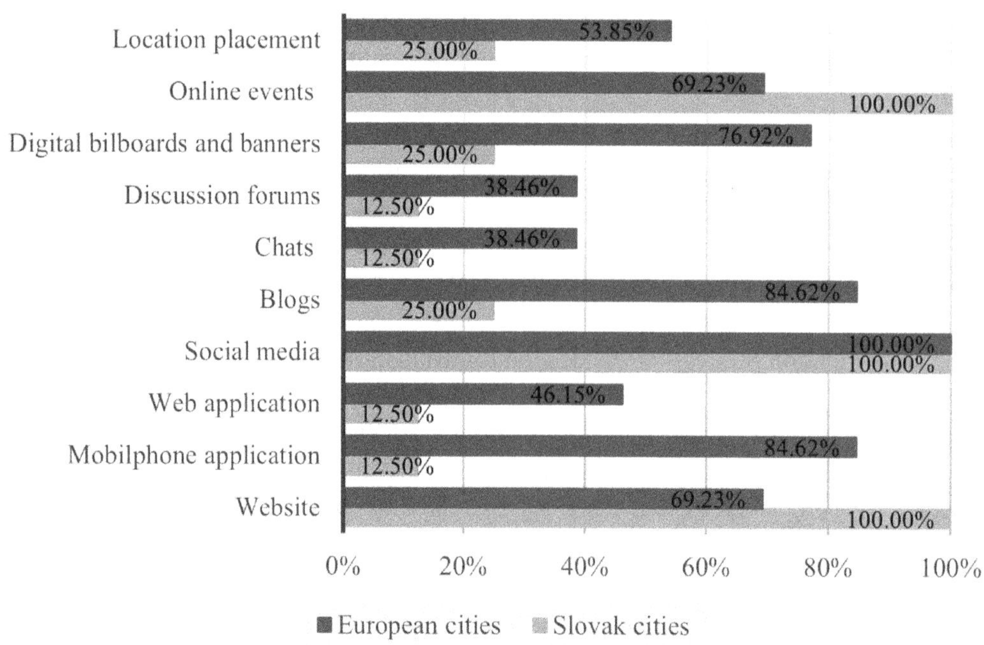

about the city's offer, and evaluation of the city's brand. The significant difference in the responses of representatives of European and Slovak cities to the question of the role of marketing communication in city branding is mainly related to different perceptions and ignorance of the concept of city branding. We therefore summarized the answers to the open question into three tasks resulting from the answers, which we divided into three phases of the city branding process, namely: the city branding phase (informing the public about the city branding process, involvement in the city branding process), city brand communication phase (communication of significant elements of the city brand, informing potential and current customers of the city about the offer), city brand evaluation phase (city brand evaluation).

Based on the results of the primary research aimed at examining the current approaches of European and Slovak cities to city branding, we found that, with the exception of the city of Bratislava, there is no systematic application of the city branding concept in the conditions of Slovak cities. The main reason for this is the lack of knowledge of the city management about the essence of city branding as a concept ensuring the sustainable development of the city. Another reason is to narrow the perception of city branding only to the city's marketing communication. The third reason is the insufficient personnel and professional capacities at the level of strategic urban development departments, as well as the difficulty of overcoming experienced stereotypes within the structures and processes of municipal authorities, which generally hinder the introduction of innovations in strategic urban development planning.

The research results showed that the big European cities, as London, Paris, Amsterdam, Vienna, Barcelona, realised city branding based on the strategical approach gradually, with the exactly defined target groups and continuously passes all stages of city branding development. The lack of knowledge and practice in city branding the cities of Central and Eastern Europe was confirmed, that is why in the last part of the chapter, we present the process of city branding of Amsterdam as a best practice example that can be a source of inspiration for these cities.

5. INSPIRATION HOW TO BRAND CITY: THE CASE OF AMSTERDAM

Amsterdam, the capital of the Netherlands, is situated in the western part of the country within the province of North Holland. Nestled along the banks of the beautiful Amstel River, the city is connected to the North Sea via the renowned North Sea Canal. With its extensive network of picturesque canals spanning over a hundred kilometers, Amsterdam has earned the well-deserved moniker of the "Venice of the North."

The origins of Amsterdam date back to the 12th century when it emerged as a humble fishing village. The city derives its name from two components: "Amstel," representing the river on which it is situated, and "dam," referring to the dam constructed at the mouth of the Amstel. In the early 14th century, Amsterdam was granted city rights, and despite the challenging task of building on marshy terrain, it continued to flourish.

During the 16th century, Amsterdam gained a reputation for religious tolerance, attracting traders and scholars from across Europe. This period, known as the city's Golden Age, marked its ascendancy as a significant commercial hub and the wealthiest city in Europe, rivaling the likes of London and Paris. It was from Amsterdam that ships embarked on expeditions to North America, Indonesia, Brazil, and Africa. The city served as the preeminent port in Europe and a global financial center.

However, the prosperity of Amsterdam waned during the 18th and early 19th centuries due to conflicts between Holland, England, and France. Nonetheless, in the late 19th century, the city experienced a revival with the construction of new museums and a train station, along with the advent of the industrial revolution. Prior to World War I, Amsterdam underwent expansion, resulting in the development of new suburbs. While the city-maintained neutrality during the First World War, it was occupied by German forces during the Second World War (Amsterdam.info, 2012).

Today, Amsterdam is the capital of the Netherlands and with area of 219.32 km2 and population 883 thousand inhabitants it is also the largest Dutch city (Statista, 2023). It is considered the most multicultural city in the world as it is home to people of many nationalities. The official language in the city is Dutch. Amsterdam has a long business tradition and good reputation in respect to culture and innovation. It is one of the most picturesque and liberal cities in Europe.

For a considerable period, Amsterdam was a must-visit destination for travelers traversing Europe. However, in the early 21st century, it experienced a decline in popularity among international tourists, primarily due to the rising allure of Eastern European and Spanish destinations (Mravčák, 2014). This necessitated the creation of a new brand and marketing strategy. The first step involved conducting a comparative study by a communication agency, analyzing the city marketing practices of Barcelona, Berlin, Dublin, and Rotterdam—the perceived strongest competitors of Amsterdam. The analysis showed the position of Amsterdam in the city charts (e.g., conference cities) had been getting worse and its competitors were doing better. Even at the national level Amsterdam was perceived as a city of problems rather than opportunities. General conclusion of the study was the need to intensify marketing in the city of Amsterdam as the lack of responsibility for building and managing the city of Amsterdam brand was proven (Kavaratzis, 2008).

The representatives of the city of Amsterdam assumed the task to suggest specific methods and goals for marketing efforts and to propose a suitable and effective organization structure. On the grounds of the analysis the city representatives defined a vision which included creation of a new brand and establishment of a public-private platform that was supposed to manage and develop it. Extensive research, including interviews with key city representatives, was conducted to identify the unique characteristics of Amsterdam and determine the core values that would underpin the marketing and branding efforts. Sixteen dimensions were derived from the research, effectively representing the city's versatility. Additionally, a questionnaire survey was conducted among city residents to gauge their perception of current and desired associations with Amsterdam. The highest scores were given to the following Amsterdam associations: the city of canals, a meeting place, sex, drugs and rock and roll, the city of events, the city of arts. The goal of the campaign is to strengthen perception of Amsterdam associations as the city of culture, the city of canals, the meeting place, the city of knowledge, the city of business and the residential city.

To ensure effective organization and coordination of marketing activities and city branding, the public-private partnership Amsterdam Partners was established in 2004. This entity served as the primary coordinator, bringing together companies, municipal offices, regional self-governments, and organizations with marketing and promotional objectives (Lombarts, 2011). Other partners were eight neighbouring villages and the province of North Holland plus their self-governing authorities, business communities and contractual partners (eight organizations which had previously been involved in the city marketing and play an active role in support and advice related to strategy and practical issues). The main tasks of Amsterdam Partners were branding, positioning and sales promotion, support and advice regarding marketing festivals and events, enhancement of favourable business environment, relations to the national and international media, hospitality, research, and monitoring (City of Amsterdam, 2004).

The primary objective of branding in Amsterdam has been to attract the attention of target groups from abroad and maintain or enhance the city's position in international rankings. This entails retaining a strong standing in the top three priority dimensions while reinforcing its position in less prominent areas. The process commenced with an assessment of Amsterdam's position in the world, leading to the development of a city profile based on sixteen dimensions. Subsequently, three key values - creativity, innovation, and the "spirit of business"- were identified to form the foundation of the future city brand (Kavaratzis, 2008).

Branding strategy focuses on three primary groups: businesses, residents, and tourists. The first target group comprises the businesses with decision-makers, especially the international business based in the Amsterdam Area, working mainly in creative (media, fashion) and knowledge (talented young people and scientists) sectors. The second groups encompasses active city residents, i.e. the residents attracted by the atmosphere in Amsterdam (students, young professionals or couples). The third group are the international visitors or congress participants (Kavaratzis, 2008).

The need for a new brand stemmed from the mismanagement of Amsterdam's previous branding efforts. The city required a brand that effectively communicated its advantages and values. Previous slogans such as "Amsterdam has it," "Small City, Big Business," or "Cool City" fell short in encapsulating the city's key attributes and benefits. These slogans were often focused on a single dimension or target group. To address this, Amsterdam Partners sought to create a new, universal slogan that encompassed the city's advantages and values. The result was the iconic slogan "I amsterdam," accompanied by a comprehensive manual outlining its proper usage (City of Amsterdam, 2004).

Generally, a logo serves multiple target groups, including entrepreneurs, tourists, and residents. The new slogan, "I amsterdam," is a concise, impactful, and memorable phrase. It represents both the people and the place, allowing individuals to express their pride, self-confidence, support, and love for the city. The slogan should always originate from the people - those who live, work, and visit the city. "I amsterdam" tells the human story of Amsterdam. The logo's colors (red, black, white) and slogan are inspired by the city's flag and coat of arms. The flag features three white crosses on a black strip against a red field. According to the manual, the primary font for the brand is Avenir, a bright and open typeface that reflects the city's character. Avenir offers a range of styles and weights, including Avenir Light, Avenir Book, Avenir Roman, Avenir Medium, Avenir Heavy, and Avenir Black. The standard application involves a black-and-white slogan on a red background. In full-color applications, the slogan should always appear on a red strip. If a red background is used, the slogan can be modified to appear on a white strip. Additionally, there are two gray variants available for black and white applications. The "I amsterdam" brand manual also provides recommendations and suggestions on how to apply specific components of its visual identity.

A variety of marketing activities was a part of the strategy for the city of Amsterdam branding, e.g., a unique international PICNIC festival for creative conversation and cooperation aiming to improve creative and innovative image of the city. In the recent years, Amsterdam International Fashion Week has been very successful. It started in 2004 and its aim was to show Amsterdam as an international fash-

Figure 4. I amsterdam

ion destination. Amsterdam also puts emphasis on its reputation as the international city of commerce. The municipality established The Duisenberg School of Finance, which is the common initiative of the Dutch financial sector and the Dutch University. Its objective is top level studies of finance. Another initiative is a Science Park Amsterdam which has a leading position in research, technology, and science (Lombarts, 2011).

„I amsterdam"campaign was promoted through billboards, posters and on big screens in the city and its surroundings. Physical versions of the brand included red and white 2-metre-long letters. According to Amsterdam Partners, these versions have been a great success and on the day of their installation in 2005 they appeared in about 8000 photos (Stamp, 2012).

"I amsterdam" exhibition titled as The Portray of the City and its People was also open at FOAM, the Amsterdam museum of photography. Along with that a book called "I amsterdam" was published. Since 2005, the exhibition has traveled worldwide, and the book has been distributed internationally. Twenty renowned photographers were commissioned to capture the city from various perspectives, resulting in a personal, diverse, and modern portrayal of Amsterdam. The exhibition and the impressive 308-page book aim to promote Amsterdam to an international audience (This is not advertising, 2012).

There were also some online marketing activities at www.iamsterdam.com providing all important information about the city in English: where to spend your time if you are a visitor, a resident or a businessperson. This website contains information on museums and sights from A to Z, shopping, nightlife, accommodation, study, housing, investment, bars and restaurants, public transport, etc. Extra promotion of the city of Amsterdam is done at social networks - Facebook, Twitter, Instagram, Flickr, and YouTube.

Naturally, printed promotional materials and souvenirs featuring the "I amsterdam" logo, such as T-shirts, bags, and cups, were part of the campaign. The next step involved the creation of the "I amsterdam City Card," which serves as a key to the city and provides an excellent way to explore everything Amsterdam has to offer. The card offers discounts or free admission to top museums and attractions, canal cruises, and local specialties. It also allows unlimited use of public transport for 24, 48, or 72 hours.

Figure 5. I amsterdam city card

Checking and interim evaluation of the I amsterdam brand perception is provided by the Amsterdam Marketing company. It was established in 2013 as a continuator of Amsterdam Partners, Amsterdam Tourism & Convention Board and Amsterdam Uitburo (Iamamsterdam, 2013).

Amsterdam Marketing, established in 2013 as a continuation of Amsterdam Partners, Amsterdam Tourism & Convention Board, and Amsterdam Uitburo (Iamsterdam, 2013), conducts checks and interim evaluations of the perception of the "I amsterdam" brand. The evaluation process enables the measurement of the city's marketing activities and their impact on target groups. By repeatedly assessing associations with Amsterdam every four years, changes in recognition and preferences can be monitored. The success of the "I amsterdam" brand and campaign is evident from the growth in tourist numbers and overnight stays. Since 2004, when the city welcomed around 4 million tourists with almost 8 million overnight stays (City of Amsterdam, 2011), the figures have significantly improved. In 2014, over 7 million tourists visited Amsterdam, resulting in more than 11 million registered overnight stays (European cities marketing, 2015).

Thanks to the great social media revolution, also the Amsterdam branding strategy turned from the traditional one-way flow to more interactive and empowering consumers to co-create the brand. Visitors become "brand ambassadors" that promote the city by various forms of visuals, e. g. visual stories in a form of selves to share with the peers, one-place indicative photo with I Amsterdam sculpture as a possibility to touch and feel the brand. The I Amsterdam letter seems to be the most important marketing tool especially because of its multiple ways of utilization in virtual world. However, after considerable criticism for focusing on tourists, the city council removed the letters from the city center and placed them at the local airport (Asser Institute, 2019).

Amsterdam is one of the most successful destination brands on social media (Hornstein, 2014). Currently, the Instagram profile of @iamsterdam has 297 thousand followers (it was established in January 2016) and shows photos with people in it, with architecture and unknown places around the center and region. The Facebook profile has 914 thousand followers, Twitter profile 392 thousand followers and YouTube channel has 5,8 thousand subscribers.

Amsterdam has consolidated its position in top five European cities based on the brand strength and brand assets. The city has also improved its rating in the Anholt-GfK Roper City Brands Index: in 2013 it took 11th place compared to 2011 when it was 17th. By Anholt-Ipsos City Brands Index 2020 Amsterdam achieved the highest-ever ranking - the 6th position. The great progress is declared also by the Global Power City Index, in 2016, Amsterdam took 8th place and in 2022 the 6th place (Institute for Urban Strategies, 2022).

Amsterdam become an innovative, creative, and commercial city and it is evident that the branding of the city appeals not only to tourists, but also entrepreneurs and citizens. It also opens a new question, what level of tourism is critical and not threat for the city (Albareda, 2018).

6. CONCLUSION

The issue of city branding has been developing for 25 years. During this period, a relatively large number of foreign experts have dealt with the study of its aspects. Nevertheless, experts still agree that there is no uniformly accepted definition and approach to city branding and its construction. The reason for the relatively large number of different definitions and approaches to city branding is a diversity of functions and tasks that city branding performs. In the theories of the concept of city branding, there are also relatively large contradictions in the perception of the role and importance of marketing communication. Considering the ambiguous position of marketing communication in the city branding, we established a hypothesis H0: Marketing communication and its modern forms play an important role in city branding, which we verified by answering 2 research questions. Q1: Which modern forms of marketing communication and how do European and Slovak cities use them in the process of city branding? Q2: What is the perception and application of the city branding in European and Slovak cities?

The research results show that the perception and application of the concept of branding is very different in European and Slovak cities. While the representatives of the European cities perceive the concept of city branding as a tool, a superstructure, a goal of city marketing, a new form of territorial administration and a form of marketing communication of the city, in Slovak conditions the concept of city branding is identified exclusively with marketing communication and especially with promotion, one of a number of tools of the marketing communication mix applied in the communication processes of cities. City branding is implemented in European cities as a comprehensive, systematic and targeted process aimed at forming a positive image of the city in order to promote the city on the market and ensure comprehensive sustainable city development, which is confirmed by the implementation of the city branding concept in several strategic documents of European cities. The distorted perception of the city branding concept by Slovak cities may be mainly due to the undersized personnel capacities in the professional departments of municipal offices focused on urban development planning, marketing and communication. An obstacle to the application of the concept of city branding in the conditions of Slovak cities is the ignorance of the issue of city branding on the part of elected representatives and executive managers, as well as the difficulty of overcoming stereotypes within the structures and processes of municipal authorities, which generally hinder the implementation of innovations in strategic urban development planning.

Despite the different perception and application of the concept of branding in European and Slovak cities, the research results and the case study of the city of Amsterdam confirm the importance of the role of marketing communication and its digital forms in the process of city branding, and not only in the context of communicating significant elements of the city brand and thus influencing the perception of the city brand to the target segments, but also in the process of city branding itself, since its role, in addition to the communication of the city brand itself, also consists in the communication of significant elements of the city brand and thus influencing the perception of the city brand in the target segments. In our opinion, this role is even more important in the process of city branding, as it enables the city's residents to actively participate in the process of city branding, who subsequently identify with the city brand, which is a basic prerequisite for the success of the city brand and the territory itself on the territory market. At the same time, digital forms of marketing communication make it possible to involve a massively large number of residents without distinction in the process of building and communicating the city's brand, which promotes inclusion and prevents exclusion. Digital forms of marketing communication, due to their global character, also attract the attention of a large number of potential consumers of the territory from the external environment. From this point of view, digital forms of marketing communication are not only effective but also sustainable and inclusive.

The success of the city brand declared by the sustainable development of the territory can be ensured only by purposeful, coordinated and systematic activities. We consider the application of a strategic approach in city branding to be a prerequisite for the promotion of the city brand on the territory market, as well as for the development of the city itself. Therefore, the basic starting point for the systematic branding of the city and the sustainable development of the city itself should be a strategic document, which will at the same time fulfill the function of a city development strategy based on the principles of sustainability and competitiveness. The important thing is to perceive the city branding as an approach to the management of the territory not only as a communication tool or some "logo". If it becomes the core of the city strategy, it fosters the value of the territory, creation of the competitive advantage(s) and initiates the further urban development based on the exceptional features of the city.

Marketing communication and its digital forms play an important role in the city branding and represent one of the tools used in the entire process of city branding to achieve the desired goal, which is the sustainable development of the territory.

The results of the research are the starting points for further research that we plan to implement in the conditions of Slovak cities and probably in other Central and Eastern European countries. Also, for the cities from these countries our research results can be a valuable source of information because of partially common history, and similar social and economic background. But it can also be seen as a possibility to inspire changing the management of the city in the right direction.

ACKNOWLEDGMENT

This study has been supported by project Vega 1/0343/23 Modern approaches to the development of cities and regions and Vega 1/0311/23 Open Local Municipality.

REFERENCES

Albareda, J. T. (2018). *Is it the end of the rebranding Amsterdam campaign?* https://www.linkedin.com/pulse/end-rebranding-amsterdam-campaign-judit-turon

Alexander, A., Teller, C., & Wood, S. (2020). Augmenting the urban place brand - On the relationship between markets and town and city centres. *Journal of Business Research*, *116*, 642–654. doi:10.1016/j.jbusres.2019.02.013

Amsterdam.info. (2015). *História mesta Amsterdam*. https://www.amsterdam.info/sk/historia/

Anders-Morawska, J., & Rudolf, W. (2015). *Orientacja rynkowa we współrządzeniu miastem*. Wydawnictwo Uniwersytetu Łódzkiego.

Anholt, S. (2007). What is competitive identity? In *Competitive identity* (pp. 1–23). Palgrave Macmillan.

Anholt, S. (2008). Place branding: Is it marketing, or isn't it? *Place Branding and Public Diplomacy*, *4*(1), 1–6. doi:10.1057/palgrave.pb.6000088

Anholt, S. (2014). *Place Branding Research*. Taking Zour Reputation Places. Public Affairs and Corporate Communicationsan, GfK.

App Annie. (2022). *The State of Mobile in 2022: How to Succeed in a Mobile-First World As Consumers Spend 3.8 Trillion Hours on Mobile Devices*. https://www.data.ai/en/insights/market-data/state-of-mobile-2022/

Ashworth, G., & Kavaratzis, M. (Eds.). (2010). *Towards effective place brand management: Branding European cities and regions.* Edward Elgar Publishing. doi:10.4337/9781849806398

Ashworth, G. J. (2011). Should we brand places? *Journal of Town and City Management, 1*(3), 248-252.

Ashworth, G. J., & Voogd, H. (1990). *Selling the City: Marketing Approaches in Public Sector Urban Planning*. Belhaven Press.

Asser institute. (2017). *Blog post: City-branding and human rights: A win-win combination?* https://www.asser.nl/about-the-asser-institute/news/blog-post-city-branding-and-human-rights-a-win-win-combination/

Baker, B. (2007). *Destination Branding for small cities: The Essentials for Successful Place Branding*. Creative Leap Book.

Baker, B. (2019). *Place Branding for Small Cities, Regions and Downtowns: The Essentials for Successful Destinations.* Independently published.

Bartels, C. P. A., & Timmer, M. (1987). City marketing: Instruments and effects. *European Congress of the Regional Science Association.*

Borseková, K., Vaňová, A., & Vitálišová, K. (2017). Smart specialization for smart spatial development: Innovative strategies for building competitive advantages in tourism in Slovakia. *Socio-Economic Planning Sciences, 58*, 39–50. doi:10.1016/j.seps.2016.10.004

Braun, E. (2008). *City Marketing: Towards an Integrated Approach.* Haveka.

Chartron, G. (2013). *Bienvenue dans l'ère du Place Branding!* https://www.leweboskop.fr/bienvenue-dans-lere-du-place-branding/

City of Amsterdam. (2003). *Choosing Amsterdam. Brand, concept and organisation of the city marketing.* http://www.iamsterdam.com/ en/amsterdam-marketing/marketing/iamsterdam/downloads

Dzureková, M. (2009). *Seriál Marketing krajiny: Kde sa "berie" značka krajiny.* https://www.veldan.sk/serial-marketing-krajiny-kde-sa-berie-znacka-krajiny/

Eshuis, J., & Edwards, A. (2013). Branding the city: The democratic legitimacy of a new mode of governance. *Urban Studies (Edinburgh, Scotland), 50*(5), 1066–1082. doi:10.1177/0042098012459581

Eshuis, J., & Klijn, E. H. (2012). *Branding in Governance and Public Management.* Routledge. doi:10.4324/9780203145159

Eshuis, J., Klijn, E. H., & Braun, E. (2014). Place marketing and citizen participation: Branding as strategy to address the emotional dimension of policy making? *International Review of Administrative Sciences, 80*(1), 151–171. doi:10.1177/0020852313513872

European cities marketing. (2015). *Bolstered international bed nights recovery traditional markets.* http://www.europeancitiesmarketing.com/european- city-tourism-resume-positive-growth-2014-bolstered-international-bednights- recovery-traditional-markets/

Fan, Y. (2010). Branding the nation: Towards a better understanding. *Place Branding and Public Diplomacy*, *6*(2), 97–103. doi:10.1057/pb.2010.16

Frig, M., & Sorsa, V. P. (2018). Nation branding as sustainability governance: A comparative case analysis. *Business & Society*, 1–30.

Giovanardi, M., Lichrou, M., & Kavaratzis, M. (2018). Inclusive place branding: Towards an integrative research agenda. In M. Karavatzis, M. Giovanardi, & M. Lichrou (Eds.), Inclusive place branding: Critical perspectives on theory and practice (pp. 172–181). Academic Press.

Govers, R., & Go, F. M. (2009). *Place Branding: Glocal, Virtual and Physical Identities, Constructed, Imagiden and Experiences*. Palgrave Macmillan. doi:10.1007/978-0-230-24702-4

Hakala, U., & Lemmetyinen, A. (2011). Co-creating a nation brand "bottom -up". *Tourism Review*, *66*(3), 14–24. doi:10.1108/16605371111175294

Hereźniak, M., & Anders-Morawska, J. (2015). City brand strategy evaluation: In search of effectiveness indicators. *Journal of Place Management and Development*, *8*(3), 187–205. doi:10.1108/JPMD-06-2015-0023

Hornstein, D. (2014). *What the 'I amsterdam' letters teach us about destination branding in the social media age*. Reuters Events. https://www.reutersevents.com/travel/social-media-and-marketing/what-i-amsterdam-letters-teach-us-about-destination-branding-social-media

Horváth, M. (2006). *Nation Branding – komplexný prístup k prezentácii Slovenska (Diskusia)*. https://www.trend.sk/spravy/nation-branding-komplexny-pristup-prezentacii-slovenska-diskusia

Hospers, G. J. (2020). A short reflection on city branding and its controversies. *Tijdschrift voor Economische en Sociale Geografie*, *111*(1), 18–23. doi:10.1111/tesg.12386

Hunt, J. D. (1975). Image as a factor in tourism development. *Journal of Travel Research*, *13*(3), 1–7. doi:10.1177/004728757501300301

Iamsterdam. (2013). *Amsterdam marketing*. https://www.iamsterdam.com/en/amsterdam- marketing

Institute for Urban Strategies. (2022). *Global Power City Index*. Author.

Jaffe, E. D., & Nebenzahl, I. D. (2001). *National Image and Competitive Advantage: The Theory and Practice of Country-of-Origin Effect*. Copenhagen Business School Press.

Janiszewska, K., & Insch, A. (2012). The strategic importance of brand positioning in the place brand concept: Elements, structure and application capabilities. *Journal of International Studies*, *5*(1), 2071–8330. doi:10.14254/2071-8330.2012/5-1/2

Kavaratzis, M. (2004). From city marketing to city branding: Towards a theoretical framework for developing city brands. *Place Branding*, *1*(1), 58-73.

Kavaratzis, M. (2008). *From city marketing to city branding: an interdisciplinary analysis with reference to Amsterdam, Budapest and Athens* [Doctoral Thesis]. University of Groningen.

Kavaratzis, M. (2011). The dishonest relationship between city marketing and culture: Reflections on the theory and the case of Budapest. *Journal of Town & City Management, 1*(4).

Kavaratzis, M., & Ashworth, G. J. (2005). City branding: An effective assertion of identity or a transitory marketing trick? *Tijdschrift voor Economische en Sociale Geografie*, *96*(5), 506–514. doi:10.1111/j.1467-9663.2005.00482.x

Kotler, P., Haider, D., & Rein, I. (1993). *Marketing Places: Attracting Investment, Industry and Tourism to Cities, States and Nations*. Free Press.

Kotler, P., Kartajaya, H., & Setiawan, I. (2021). *Marketing 5.0: Technology for Humanity*. John Wiley & Sons.

Kotler, P., & Levy, S. J. (1969). Broadening the concept of marketing. *Journal of Marketing*, *33*(1), 10–15. doi:10.1177/002224296903300103 PMID:12309673

Lee, Y. J. (2022). Social media capital and civic engagement: Does type of connection matter? *International Review on Public and Nonprofit Marketing*, *19*(1), 167–189. doi:10.100712208-021-00300-8

Lombarts, A. (2011). *Amsterdam, a brand that appeals to tourists and business alike*. http://www. citymayors.com/marketing/amsterdam-brand.html

Lucarelli, A. (2018). Place branding as urban policy: The (im)political place branding. *Cities (London, England)*, *80*, 12–21. doi:10.1016/j.cities.2017.08.004

Ma, W., Schraven, D., de Bruijne, M., de Jong, M., & Lu, H. (2019, May 28). Tracing the Origins of Place Branding Research: A Bibliometric Study of Concepts in Use (1980–2018). *Sustainability*, *11*(11), 2999. doi:10.3390u11112999

McCabe, S. (2017). Sustainability and marketing in tourism: Its contexts, paradoxes, approaches, challenges and potential. *Journal of Sustainable Tourism*, *25*(7), 869–883. doi:10.1080/09669582.2017.1301721

Moilanen, T., & Rainisto, S. (2009). *How to Brand Nations, Cities and Destination. A Planning Book for Place Branding*. Palgrave Macmillan. doi:10.1057/9780230584594

Mravčák, A. (2014). *Značkové mestá*. http://profit.etrend.sk/dennik/znackove-mesta.html

Nogué, J. (1999). El retorno al lugar. La creación de identidades territoriales. *Claves de razón práctica, 92*, 9-11.

Olins, W. (2002). Branding the nation – The historical context. *Journal of Brand Management*, *9*(4-5), 241–248. doi:10.1057/palgrave.bm.2540075

Oliva, E. J. D., Sánchez-Torres, J. A., & Niño, J. S. S. (2022). City brand evolution research and future agenda: Bibliometric and science mapping analysis. *Heliyon*, *8*(8). PMID:35991998

Rinaldi, Ch., Giovanardi, M., & Lucarelli, A. (2021). Keeping a foot in both camps: Sustainability, city branding and boundary spanners. *Cities (London, England)*, *115*, 103236. doi:10.1016/j.cities.2021.103236

Rojíková, D. (2022). *Budovanie značky mesta a moderné formy marketingovej komunikácie* [Doctoral dissertations]. Banská Bystrica: Ekonomická fakulta UMB.

Rojíková, D., Vaňová, A. & Borseková, K. (2020). The Role and Position of the Nation Brand in Cultural and Foreign Policy. *Ekonomika a spoločnosť, 21*(1), 68-77.

Stamp, J. (2012) *Rebranding Amsterdam and What it Means to Rebrand a city*. https://ww. smithsonianmag.com/ist/?next=/arts-culture/rebranding-amsterdam-and-what- it-means-to-rebrand-a-city-19539392/

Statista. (2023). *Amsterdam - Statistics & Facts*. https://www.statista.com/topics/9014/amsterdam/#topicOverview

Štefčeková, L., & Vaňová, A. (2013). Comparison of perceived and projected image of Slovakia as a starting point for a country image building strategy. *Responsibility and Sustainability: Socioeconomic, Political, and Legal Issues, 1*(3), 41-50.

This is not advertising. (2012). *I Amsterdam the campaign to rebrand Amsterdam*. https://thisisnotadvertising.wordpress.com/2012/11/05/i- amsterdam-the-campaign-to-re-brand-amsterdam/

Vaňová, A. (1996). Territorial marketing as a component of municipal and regional policy. *Ekonomický časopis: časopis pre ekonomickú teóriu, hospodársku politiku, spoločensko-ekonomické prognózovanie, 44*(7-8).

Vaňová, A. (2020). *Marketingové stratégie rozvoja územia*. Belianum.

Vaňová, A., Vitálišová, K., & Borseková, K. (2017). *Place marketing*. Belianum.

Vela, S.E.J. (2013). Place branding: A conceptual and theoretical framework. *Boletin de la Asociacion de Geografos Espanoles, 62*, 189-211+467-471.

Vuignier, R. (2016). *Place marketing and place branding: A systematic (and tentatively exhaustive) literature review.* Working Paper de l'IDHEAP, 5/2016.

Zenker, S., Braun, E., & Petersen, S. (2017). Branding the destination versus the place: The effects of brand complexity and identification for residents and visitors. *Tourism Management*, *58*, 15–27. doi:10.1016/j.tourman.2016.10.008

Compilation of References

Aaker, J., Fournier, S., & Brasel, S. A. (2004). When good brands do bad. *The Journal of Consumer Research*, *31*(1), 1–16. doi:10.1086/383419

Accenture. (n.d.). Advancing gender equality program. *Accenture.* https://www.accenture.com/us-en/about/inclusion-diversity/gender-equality

Aceto, G., Persico, V., & Pescapé, A. (2020). Industry 4.0 and Health: Internet of Things, Big Data, and Cloud Computing for Healthcare 4.0. *Journal of Industrial Information Integration*, *18*, 100129. doi:10.1016/j.jii.2020.100129

Acuti, D., Pizzetti, M., & Dolnicar, S. (2022). When sustainability backfires: A review on the unintended negative side-effects of product and service sustainability on consumer behavior. *Psychology and Marketing*, *39*(10), 1933–1945. doi:10.1002/mar.21709

Adamkiewicz, J., Kochańska, E., Adamkiewicz, I., & Łukasik, R. M. (2022). Greenwashing and sustainable fashion industry. *Current Opinion in Green and Sustainable Chemistry*, *38*, 1–8. doi:10.1016/j.cogsc.2022.100710

Adebayo, D. O. (2005). Ethical attitudes and prosocial behaviour in the Nigeria police: Moderator effects of perceived organizational support and public recognition. *Policing*, *28*(4), 684–705. doi:10.1108/13639510510628767

Ahmad, U. F., Mahdee, J., & Abu Bakar, N. (2022). Search engine optimisation (SEO) strategy as determinants to enhance the online brand positioning. *F1000 Research*, *11*, 714. doi:10.12688/f1000research.73382.1

Akgunduz, Y., Alkan, C., & Gök, Ö. A. (2018). Perceived organizational support, employee creativity and proactive personality: The mediating effect of meaning of work. *Journal of Hospitality and Tourism Management*, *34*, 105–114. doi:10.1016/j.jhtm.2018.01.004

Albanna, H., Alalwan, A. A., & Al-Emran, M. (2022). An integrated model for using social media applications in non-profit organizations. *International Journal of Information Management*, *63*, 102452.

Albareda, J. T. (2018). *Is it the end of the rebranding Amsterdam campaign?* https://www.linkedin.com/pulse/end-rebranding-amsterdam-campaign-judit-turon

Al-Dhabi, N. A., Esmail, G. A., Ghilan, A. K. M., Arasu, M. V., Duraipandiyan, V., & Ponmurugan, K. (2020). Characterization and fermentation optimization of novel thermo stable alkaline protease from Streptomyces sp. Al-Dhabi-82 from the Saudi Arabian environment for eco-friendly and industrial applications. *Journal of King Saud University. Science*, *32*(1), 1258–1264. doi:10.1016/j.jksus.2019.11.011

Alemany, C. (2022). 3 Ways Marketers Can Earn — and Keep — Customer Trust. *Harvard Business Review.* https://hbr.org/2022/06/3-ways-marketers-can-earn-and-keep-customer-trust

Alexander, A., Teller, C., & Wood, S. (2020). Augmenting the urban place brand - On the relationship between markets and town and city centres. *Journal of Business Research*, *116*, 642–654. doi:10.1016/j.jbusres.2019.02.013

Al-Muhtadi, J., Shahzad, B., Saleem, K., Jameel, W., & Orgun, M. A. (2019). Cybersecurity and privacy issues for socially integrated mobile healthcare applications operating in a multi-cloud environment. *Health Informatics Journal*, *25*(2), 315–329. doi:10.1177/1460458217706184 PMID:28480788

Alnasser, A. A., Alkhalifa, A. S., Sathiaseelan, A., & Marais, D. (2015). What overweight women want from a weight loss app: A qualitative study on Arabic women. *JMIR mHealth and uHealth*, *3*(2), e4409. doi:10.2196/mhealth.4409 PMID:25993907

Al-Obadi, M., Ayad, H., Pokharel, S., & Ayari, M. A. (2022). Perspectives on food waste management: Prevention and social innovations. *Sustainable Production and Consumption*, *31*, 190–208. doi:10.1016/j.spc.2022.02.012

Alsaad, A. K. (2021). Ethical judgment, subjective norms, and ethical consumption: The moderating role of moral certainty. *Journal of Retailing and Consumer Services*, *59*, 102380. doi:10.1016/j.jretconser.2020.102380

Alvarezand, S., & Sachs, S. (2021). Where do stakeholders come from? *Academy of Management Review*. doi:10.5465/amr.2019.0077

Alves, H., Galan-Ladero, M. M., & Rivera, R. G. (2021). Theoretical Background: Social Marketing and Quality of Life. *Applied Social Marketing and Quality of Life: Case Studies from an International Perspective*, 3-25. doi:10.1007/978-3-030-83286-5_1

Amagai, S., Pila, S., Kaat, A. J., Nowinski, C. J., & Gershon, R. C. (2022). Challenges in participant engagement and retention using mobile health apps: Literature review. *Journal of Medical Internet Research*, *24*(4), e35120. doi:10.2196/35120 PMID:35471414

American Marketing Association. (2021). *Diversity, equity and inclusion in marketing*. AMA. https://www.ama.org/diversity-equity-and-inclusion-in-marketing/

American Marketing Association. (2023). *What Is SEO Marketing?* AMA. https://www.ama.org/marketing-news/what-is-seo-marketing/

Amsterdam.info. (2015). *História mesta Amsterdam*. https://www.amsterdam.info/sk/historia/

Anand, A. (2022). *Greenwashing and the Use of Environmental Appeals in Modern Advertising.*, *11*, 15–26.

Anand, P., Kunnumakkara, A. B., Sundaram, C., Harikumar, K. B., Tharakan, S. T., Lai, O. S., Sung, B., & Aggarwal, B. B. (2008). Cancer is a preventable disease that requires major lifestyle changes. *Pharmaceutical Research*, *25*(9), 2097–2116. doi:10.100711095-008-9661-9 PMID:18626751

Anders-Morawska, J., & Rudolf, W. (2015). *Orientacja rynkowa we współrządzeniu miastem*. Wydawnictwo Uniwersytetu Łódzkiego.

Anholt, S. (2007). What is competitive identity? In *Competitive identity* (pp. 1–23). Palgrave Macmillan.

Anholt, S. (2008). Place branding: Is it marketing, or isn't it? *Place Branding and Public Diplomacy*, *4*(1), 1–6. doi:10.1057/palgrave.pb.6000088

Anholt, S. (2014). *Place Branding Research*. Taking Zour Reputation Places. Public Affairs and Corporate Communicationsan, GfK.

App Annie. (2022). *The State of Mobile in 2022: How to Succeed in a Mobile-First World As Consumers Spend 3.8 Trillion Hours on Mobile Devices*. https://www.data.ai/en/insights/market-data/state-of-mobile-2022/

Appel, G., Grewal, L., Hadi, R., & Stephen, A. T. (2020). The future of social media inmarketing. *Journal of the Academy of Marketing Science*, *48*(1), 79–95. doi:10.100711747-019-00695-1 PMID:32431463

Aracil-Jordá, J., Clemente-Almendros, J. A., Jiménez-Zarco, A. I., & González-González, I. (2023). Improving the social performance of women-led microenterprises: The role of social media marketing actions. *Technological Forecasting and Social Change*, *191*(March), 122484. doi:10.1016/j.techfore.2023.122484

Arenas, D., Lozano, J. M., & Albareda, L. (2009). The role of NGOs in CSR: Mutual perceptions among stakeholders. *Journal of Business Ethics*, *88*(1), 175–197. doi:10.100710551-009-0109-x

Arouri, M., El Ghoul, S., & Gomes, M. (2021). Greenwashing and product market competition. *Finance Research Letters*, *42*, 101927. doi:10.1016/j.frl.2021.101927

Arsel, Z., Crockett, D., & Scott, M. L. (2022). Diversity, equity, and inclusion (DEI) in the Journal of Consumer Research: A curation and research agenda. *The Journal of Consumer Research*, *48*(5), 920–933. doi:10.1093/jcr/ucab057

Aschemann-Witzel, J., & Peschel, A. O. (2019). How Circular Will you eat? The Sustainability Challenge in Food and Consumer Reaction to Either Waste-to-Value or yet Underused Novel Ingredients in Food. *Food Quality and Preference*, *77*, 15–20. doi:10.1016/j.foodqual.2019.04.012

Aschemann-Witzel, J., & Stangherlin, I. D. C. (2021). Upcycled by-Product use in Agri-Food Systems from a Consumer Perspective: A review of what we know, and what is missing. *Technological Forecasting and Social Change*, *168*, 120749. doi:10.1016/j.techfore.2021.120749

Ashworth, G. J. (2011). Should we brand places? *Journal of Town and City Management, 1*(3), 248-252.

Ashworth, G. J., & Voogd, H. (1990). *Selling the City: Marketing Approaches in Public Sector Urban Planning*. Belhaven Press.

Ashworth, G., & Kavaratzis, M. (Eds.). (2010). *Towards effective place brand management: Branding European cities and regions*. Edward Elgar Publishing. doi:10.4337/9781849806398

Asser institute. (2017). *Blog post: City-branding and human rights: A win-win combination?* https://www.asser.nl/about-the-asser-institute/news/blog-post-city-branding-and-human-rights-a-win-win-combination/

Attig, C., & Franke, T. (2020). Abandonment of personal quantification: A review and empirical study investigating reasons for wearable activity tracking attrition. *Computers in Human Behavior*, *102*, 223–237. doi:10.1016/j.chb.2019.08.025

Baccarella, C. V., Wagner, T. F., Kietzmann, J. H., & McCarthy, I. P. (2018). Social media? It's serious! Understanding the dark side of social media. *European Management Journal*, *36*(4), 431–438. doi:10.1016/j.emj.2018.07.002

Baglioni, S., de Pieri, B., & Tallarico, T. (2017). Surplus Food Recovery and Food Aid: The Pivotal Role of Non-profit Organisations. *Insights From Italy and Germany. Voluntas*, *28*(5), 2032–2052. doi:10.100711266-016-9746-8

Baker, B. (2019). *Place Branding for Small Cities, Regions and Downtowns: The Essentials for Successful Destinations*. Independently published.

Baker, K. (2022) *The Ultimate Guide to Content Marketing*. HubSpot. https://blog.hubspot.com/marketing/content-marketing

Baker, B. (2007). *Destination Branding for small cities: The Essentials for Successful Place Branding*. Creative Leap Book.

Bala, M., & Verma, D. (2018). A Critical review of Digital Marketing. *International Journal of Mnanagement. IT& Engineering*, *8*(10), 321–329.

Bandyopadhyay, C., & Ray, S. (2019). Responsible marketing: Can social enterprises show the way? *Journal of Nonprofit & Public Sector Marketing*, *31*(2), 164–183. doi:10.1080/10495142.2018.1526738

Baptista, N., Alves, H., & Matos, N. (2022). Scoping Challenges and Opportunities Presented by COVID-19 for the Development of Sustainable Short Food Supply Chains. *Sustainability (Basel)*, *14*(21), 14475. doi:10.3390u142114475

Bartels, C. P. A., & Timmer, M. (1987). City marketing: Instruments and effects. *European Congress of the Regional Science Association*.

Baruah, A. (2023). 'Greenwashing' - Think tank criticise climate plans of 24 top firms, including Apple, Amazon. *The Print*. https://theprint.in/environment/greenwashing-think-tanks-criticise-climate-plans-of-24-top-firms-including-apple-amazon/1376920/

Beerli-Palacio, A., Díaz-Meneses, G., Fernández-Monroy, M., Galván-Sánchez, I., & Martín-Santana, J. D. (2011). *The Influence of Gender & Reference Groups on the Irresponsible Alcohol Consumption Behaviour Model Among Young People* (No. 313). Academic Public Administration Studies Archive-APAS.

Benetoli, A., Chen, T. F., & Aslani, P. (2018). How patient's use of social media impacts their interactions with healthcare professionals. *Patient Education and Counseling*, *101*(3), 439–444. doi:10.1016/j.pec.2017.08.015 PMID:28882545

Bennett, A. M., Hill, R. P., & Oleksiuk, D. (2013). The impact of disparate levels of marketplace inclusion on consumer–brand relationships. *Journal of Public Policy & Marketing*, *32*(Special Issue), 16–31. doi:10.1509/jppm.12.023

Bernstein, R. S., Bulger, M., Salipante, P., & Weisinger, J. Y. (2020). From diversity to inclusion to equity: A theory of generative interactions. *Journal of Business Ethics*, *167*(3), 395–410. doi:10.100710551-019-04180-1

Beste, A. (2021). Greenwashing & hight tech! *Gesunderde*. https://www.gesunde-erde.net/media/fakesustainability_end_english_1.pdf

Bhatti, S. H., Iqbal, K., Santoro, G., & Rizzato, F. (2022). The impact of corporate social responsibility directed toward employees on contextual performance in the banking sector: A serial model of perceived organizational support and affective organizational commitment. *Corporate Social Responsibility and Environmental Management*, *29*(6), 1980–1994. doi:10.1002/csr.2295

Black, I. R., & Cherrier, H. (2010). Anti-consumption as part of living a sustainable lifestyle: Daily practices, contextual motivations and subjective values. *Journal of Consumer Behaviour*, *9*(6), 437–453. doi:10.1002/cb.337

Blohm, I., & Leimeister, J. M. (2013). Gamification: Design of IT-based enhancing services for motivational support and behavioral change. *Business & Information Systems Engineering*, *5*(4), 275–278. doi:10.100712599-013-0273-5

Boechat, A. C., Morais, J., Moura, A., & Barreto, A. M. (2022). The impact of corporate social responsibility on brand loyalty and brand attachment: an analysis of the Portuguese brand Delta cafés. In *International Workshop in Marketing*. Sustainability and resilience. Porto: Universidade Lusíada.

Bohnsack, R., Bidmon, C. M., & Pinkse, J. (2022). Sustainability in the digital age: Intended and unintended consequences of digital technologies for sustainable development. *Business Strategy and the Environment*, *31*(2), 599–602. doi:10.1002/bse.2938

Bordin, D., & Pasqualotto, N. (2013). A Importância da Responsabilidade Social Empresarial para a Sustentabilidade e o Papel do Marketing Social. *Revista Capital Científico, 11*(2).

Borger, F., & Costa, A. (2022). Corporate Social Responsibility and Sustainability in Corporate Strategy: Brazilian Cases Studies. In Corporate Social Responsibility (pp. 69–92). IntechOpen. doi:10.5772/intechopen.94414

Boris, E. T., & Steuerle, C. E. (1999). *Nonprofits and government: Collaboration and conflict*. Urban Institute Press.

Borrell, J. (2021). Alterações climáticas: a UE está pronta a assumir as suas responsabilidades a nível mundial. In *European Union - External Action*. https://www.eeas.europa.eu/eeas/alterações-climáticas-ue-está-pronta-assumir-suas-responsabilidades-n%C3%ADvel-mundial_pti

Borrello, M., Caracciolo, F., Lombardi, A., Pascucci, S., & Cembalo, L. (2017). Consumers' perspective on circular economy strategy for reducing food waste. *Sustainability (Basel)*, *9*(1), 141. doi:10.3390u9010141

Borseková, K., Vaňová, A., & Vitálišová, K. (2017). Smart specialization for smart spatial development: Innovative strategies for building competitive advantages in tourism in Slovakia. *Socio-Economic Planning Sciences*, *58*, 39–50. doi:10.1016/j.seps.2016.10.004

Boudreau, C. (2023). Companies are selling us more stuff by telling us it's 'sustainable'. *Business Insider*. https://www.businessinsider.com/green-shopping-products-government-green-guides-marketing-sustainable-2023-4

Boyd, C. S., Ritch, E. L., Dodd, C. A., & McColl, J. (2020). Inclusive identities: Re-imaging the future of the retail brand? *International Journal of Retail & Distribution Management*, *48*(12), 1315–1335. doi:10.1108/IJRDM-12-2019-0392

Boyd, D. M., & Ellison, N. B. (2007). Social Network Sites: Definition, History, and Scholarship. *Journal of Computer-Mediated Communication*, *13*(1), 210–230. doi:10.1111/j.1083-6101.2007.00393.x

Brahami, Y., Saeidi, A., Fiset, M., & Ba, K. (2022). The Effects of the Type and Quantity of Recycled Materials on Physical and Mechanical Properties of Concrete and Mortar. *Sustainability (Basel)*, *14*(22), 14752. doi:10.3390u142214752

Braun, E. (2008). *City Marketing: Towards an Integrated Approach*. Haveka.

Breves, P., & Liebers, N. (2022). #Greenfluencing. The Impact of Parasocial Relationships with Social Media Influencers on Advertising Effectiveness and Followers' Pro-environmental Intentions. *Environmental Communication*, *16*(6), 773–787. doi:10.1080/17524032.2022.2109708

Britten, N. (1995). Qualitative interviews in medical research. *BMJ (Clinical Research Ed.)*, *311*(6999), 251–253. doi:10.1136/bmj.311.6999.251 PMID:7627048

Britvin, A., Alrawashdeh, J. H., & Tkachuk, R. (2022). Client-Server System for Parsing Data from Web Pages. *Advances in Cyber-Physical Systems*, *7*(1), 8–13. doi:10.23939/acps2022.01.008

Brooks, M. (2022). *Why your Non-Profit should invest in Search Engine Optimisation*. HubSpot. https://blog.hubspot.com/marketing/nonprofit-seo

Broom, D. (2019). Communicating sustainability: 7 companies doing it well. *Formative Content*. https://formativecontent.com/communicating-sustainability-7-companies-doing-it-well/

Burgess, A., Wilkie, D. C. H., & Dolan, R. (2023). Brand approaches to diversity: A typology and research agenda. *European Journal of Marketing*, *57*(1), 60–88. doi:10.1108/EJM-09-2021-0696

Burke, L., & Logsdon, J. M. (1996). How Corporate Social Responsibility Pays Off. *Long Range Planning*, *29*(4), 495–502. doi:10.1016/0024-6301(96)00041-6

Byambasuren, O., Beller, E., Hoffmann, T., & Glasziou, P. (2020). Barriers to and facilitators of the prescription of mHealth apps in Australian general practice: Qualitative study. *JMIR mHealth and uHealth*, *8*(7), e17447. doi:10.2196/17447 PMID:32729839

Camargo, J. L., Miranda, M. E. C., Chávez, R. A. P., Quispe, F. K. V., Muñoz, I. J. T., & Flores, L. J. R. (2022, June). Proposal of the methodology oriented to the automatic generation of content in SEO positioning. In *2022 17th Iberian Conference on Information Systems and Technologies (CISTI)* (pp. 1–7). IEEE. 10.23919/CISTI54924.2022.9820263

Camicia, S. P. (2008). Deciding what is a controversial issue: A case study of social studies curriculum controversy. *Theory and Research in Social Education*, *36*(4), 298–316. doi:10.1080/00933104.2008.10473378

Canali, M., Amani, P., Aramyan, L., Gheoldus, M., Moates, G., Östergren, K., Silvennoinen, K., Waldron, K., & Vittuari, M. (2016). Food Waste Drivers in Europe, from Identification to Possible Interventions. *Sustainability (Basel)*, *9*(1), 37. doi:10.3390u9010037

Cancela, D., Hulsheger, U. R., & Stutterheim, S. E. (2022). The role of support for transgender and nonbinary employees: Perceived co-worker and organizational support's associations with job attitudes and work behavior. *Psychology of Sexual Orientation and Gender Diversity*, *9*(1), 49–57. doi:10.1037gd0000453

Cane, M., & Parra, C. (2020). Digital platforms: Mapping the territory of new technologies to fight food waste. *British Food Journal*, *122*(5), 1647–1669. doi:10.1108/BFJ-06-2019-0391

Canhoto, A. I., & Arp, S. (2017). Exploring the factors that support adoption and sustained use of health and fitness wearables. *Journal of Marketing Management*, *33*(1-2), 32–60. doi:10.1080/0267257X.2016.1234505

Carboni, J. L., & Maxwell, S. P. (2015). Effective social media engagement for nonprofits: What matters? *Journal of Public and Nonprofit Affairs*, *1*(1), 18–28. doi:10.20899/jpna.1.1.18-28

Castelló, I., Etter, M., & Årup, F. (2016). Strategies of legitimacy through social media: The networked strategy. *Journal of Management Studies*, *53*(3), 402–432. doi:10.1111/joms.12145

Castro, P. C., Romano, L. B., Frohlich, D., Lorenzi, L. J., Campos, L. B., Paixão, A., Bet, P., Deutekom, M., Krose, B., Dourado, V. Z., & Angélica de Oliveira Gomes, G. (2020). Tailoring digital apps to support active ageing in a low income community. *PLoS One*, *15*(12, e0242192), e0242192. doi:10.1371/journal.pone.0242192 PMID:33301455

Cernansky, R. (2022). Brands are tapping influencers to make sustainability fashionable. *Vogue Business*. https://www.voguebusiness.com/sustainability/brands-are-tapping-influencers-to-make-sustainability-fashionable

Chan, X. W., Kalliath, T., Brough, P., Siu, O., & Timms, C. (2022). Examining the mediating role of self-efficacy in the relationship between perceived organizational support and work–family enrichment. *International Journal of Stress Management*, *29*(3), 281–291. doi:10.1037tr0000263

Chartron, G. (2013). *Bienvenue dans l'ère du Place Branding!* https://www.leweboskop.fr/bienvenue-dans-lere-du-place-branding/

Chary, S. R. K. (2014). Social media marketing: The paradigm shift in internationalmarketing. *IOSR Journal of Business and Management*, *16*(9), 11–13. doi:10.9790/487X-16921113

Chaudhry, S. (2023). Measuring diversity, equity and inclusion: A holistic approach. *Development and Learning in Organizations*, *37*(2), 4–6. doi:10.1108/DLO-04-2022-0068

Cheng, K., Cao, X., Guo, L., & Xia, Q. (2021). Work connectivity behaviour after-hours and job satisfaction: Examining the moderating effects of psychological entitlement and perceived organizational support. *Personnel Review*, *59*(9), 2277–2293. doi:10.1108/PR-06-2020-0413

Chen, J.-C., & Sénéchal, S. (2023). The reciprocal relationship between search engine optimization (SEO) success and brand equity (BE): An analysis of SMEs. *European Business Review*, *35*(5), 860–873. doi:10.1108/EBR-02-2023-0045

Chen, Y. S., Lin, Y. H., Lo, W. Y., & Lai, P. Y. (2022). Sustainable trick or tactic? The influence of greenwashing on green reputation, green satisfaction and green perceived value. *Coporate Management Review*, *42*(1), 107–139. doi:10.53106/102873102022064201004

Chida, Y., Hamer, M., Wardle, J., & Steptoe, A. (2008). Do stress-related psychosocial factors contribute to cancer incidence and survival? *Nature Clinical Practice. Oncology*, *5*(8), 466–475. doi:10.1038/ncponc1134 PMID:18493231

Chida, Y., & Steptoe, A. (2008). Positive psychological well-being and mortality: A quantitative review of prospective observational studies. *Psychosomatic Medicine*, *70*(7), 741–756. doi:10.1097/PSY.0b013e31818105ba PMID:18725425

Chikwanda, H. K. (2020). Challenges and Strategies in NPOs' Operations during Covid-19 Pandemic. In *Proceedings of the 2nd African International Conference on Industrial Engineering and Operations Management*, Harare, Zimbabwe.

Chirilli, C., Molino, M., & Torri, L. (2022). Consumers' awareness, behavior and expectations for food packaging environmental sustainability: Influence of socio-demographic characteristics. *Foods*, *11*(16), 2388. doi:10.3390/foods11162388 PMID:36010389

Choi, H. Y., Keil, M., & Baird, A. M. (2022). Intention to use smartwatch health applications: A regulatory fit and locus of control perspective. *Information & Management*, *59*(6), 103687. doi:10.1016/j.im.2022.103687

Choi, H., & Yang, J. (2021). Embracing diversity and inclusion in marketing: How firms can avoid backlash and gain support. *Journal of Business Research*, *129*, 151–161. doi:10.1016/j.jbusres.2021.02.005

Choi, S., & Rainey, H. G. (2010). Managing diversity in US federal agencies: Effects of diversity and diversity management on employee perceptions of organizational performance. *Public Administration Review*, *70*(1), 109–121. doi:10.1111/j.1540-6210.2009.02115.x

Choi, W., Madjar, N., & Yun, S. (2018). Suggesting creative solutions or just complaining: Perceived organizational support, exchange ideology, and learning goal orientation as determining factors. *Psychology of Aesthetics, Creativity, and the Arts*, *12*(1), 68–78. doi:10.1037/aca0000143

Choto, P., Iwu, C. G., & Tengeh, R. K. (2020). Non-Profit Organisations and Socio-Economic Development in South Africa: A literature analysis. *Humanities & Social Sciences Reviews*, *8*(2), 689–600. doi:10.18510/hssr.2020.8267

City of Amsterdam. (2003). *Choosing Amsterdam. Brand, concept and organisation of the city marketing.* http://www.iamsterdam.com/ en/amsterdam-marketing/marketing/iamsterdam/downloads

Coderoni, S., & Perito, M. A. (2020). Sustainable Consumption in the Circular Economy. An Analysis of Consumers' Purchase Intentions for Waste-to-Value Food'. *Journal of Cleaner Production*, *252*, 119870. doi:10.1016/j.jclepro.2019.119870

Comber, R., & Thieme, A. (2013). Designing beyond habit: Opening space for improved recycling and food waste behaviors through processes of persuasion, social influence and aversive affect. *Personal and Ubiquitous Computing*, *17*(6), 1197–1210. doi:10.100700779-012-0587-1

Conaty, F., & Robbins, G. (2021). A stakeholder salience perspective on performance and management control systems in non-profit organizations. *Critical Perspectives on Accounting*, *80*, 102052. doi:10.1016/j.cpa.2018.07.001

Cook, A., & Glass, C. (2014). Women and top leadership positions: Towards an institutional analysis. *Gender, Work and Organization*, *21*(1), 91–103. doi:10.1111/gwao.12018

Cote, C. (2021). *What is a CRS Report & why is it important?* Harvard Business School Online. https://online.hbs.edu/blog/post/what-is-a-csr-report

Coutinho, R. (2009). “Crise Ambiental” e Desenvolvimento Insustentável: A Mitologia da Sustentabilidade e a Utopia da Humanização do Capitalismo “Selvagem”. *Revista Praia Vermelha*, *19*(2), 21–36.

Cox, D. F. (1967). Risk Handling in Consumer Behavior: An Intensive Study of Two Cases. *JMR, Journal of Marketing Research*, *4*(2), 111–116.

Crockett, D. (2017). Paths to respectability: Consumption and stigma management in the contemporary Black middle class. *The Journal of Consumer Research*, *44*(3), 554–581. doi:10.1093/jcr/ucx049

Crockett, D. (2021). Racial oppression and racial projects in consumer markets: A racial formation theory approach. *The Journal of Consumer Research*, ucab050. doi:10.1093/jcr/ucab050

Crotty, J. L., & Jubownikow, S. (2019). Restrictive Institutions and Critical Resources:Non-Profit Organisations and Volunteer Resources in the Russian Federation. *Europe-Asia Studies*, *72*(1), 99–116. doi:10.1080/09668136.2019.1686462

D'Hotman, D., & Schnall, J. (2021). A New Type of “Greenwashing”? Social Media Companies Predicting Depression and Other Mental Illnesses. *The American Journal of Bioethics*, *21*(7), 36–38. doi:10.1080/15265161.2021.1926583 PMID:34152910

Dahlsrud, A. (2008). How corporate social responsibility is defined: An analysis of 37 definitions. *Corporate Social Responsibility and Environmental Management*, *15*(1), 1–13. doi:10.1002/csr.132

Davies, D. (2023). Website Indexing for Search Engines: How Does It Work? *Search Engine Journal*. https://www.searchenginejournal.com/search-engines/website-indexing/

Daya, P. (2014). Diversity and inclusion in an emerging market context. *Equality, Diversity and Inclusion*, *33*(3), 293–308. doi:10.1108/EDI-10-2012-0087

Daya, P., & April, K. (2017). Practical Considerations for the Management of Diversity and Inclusion in an Emerging Market Context: A South African Case Study. In *Management and Diversity* (Vol. 3, pp. 191–225). Emerald Publishing Limited. doi:10.1108/S2051-233320160000003008

de Souza, M., Pereira, G. M., de Sousa Jabbour, A. B. L., Jabbour, C. J. C., Trento, L. R., Borchardt, M., & Zvirtes, L. (2021). A digitally enabled circular economy for mitigating food waste: Understanding innovative marketing strategies in the context of an emerging economy. *Technological Forecasting and Social Change*, *173*, 121062. doi:10.1016/j.techfore.2021.121062

Deci, E. L., & Ryan, R. M. (2002). *Handbook of self-determination research*. University of Rochester Press.

DeConinck, J. B., Moss, H. K., & Deconinck, M. B. (2018). The relationship between servant leadership, perceived organizational support, performance, and turnover among business to business salespeople. *Global J management and marketing, 2*(1), 38–52. doi:10.14738/abr.510.3730

Deepa, N., & Deshmukh, S. (2013). Social media marketing: The next generation of business engagement. *International Journal of Management Research and Reviews*, *3*, 2461–2468.

del Mar Galvez-Rodriguez, M., Caba-Pérez, C., & López-Godoy, M. (2016). Drivers of Twitter as a strategic communication tool for non-profit organizations. *Internet Research*, *26*(5), 1052–1071. doi:10.1108/IntR-07-2014-0188

Delloite insights. (2021). *Authentically inclusive marketing. Winning future customers with diversity, equity, and inclusion*. Deloitte. https://www2.deloitte.com/uk/en/insights/topics/marketing-and-sales-operations/global-marketing-trends/2022/diversity-and-inclusion-in-marketing.html

Delloite University Press. (2013). *Diversity's new frontier. Diversity of thought and the future of the workforce.* Deloitte. https://www2.deloitte.com/content/dam/insights/us/articles/diversitys-new-frontier/DUP426_Cognitive-diversity_vFINAL1.pdf

Delloite University Press. (2017). Diversity and inclusion: The reality gap -2017 Global Human Capital Trends. https://www2.deloitte.com/xe/en/insights/focus/human-capital-trends/2017/diversity-and-inclusion-at-the-workplace.html

Demangeot, C., Kipnis, E., Pullig, C., Cross, S. N., Emontspool, J., Galalae, C., Grier, S. A., Rosenbaum, M. S., & Best, S. F. (2019). Constructing a bridge to multicultural marketplace well-being: A consumer-centred framework for marketer action. *Journal of Business Research*, *100*, 339–353. doi:10.1016/j.jbusres.2018.12.026

Demirtaş, Ö., Arslan, A., & Karaca, M. (2019). Why perceived organizational and supervisory family support is important for organizations? Evidence from the field. *Review of Managerial Science*, *13*(4), 841–869. doi:10.100711846-017-0264-x

Dena, C. (2009). *Transmedia practice: Theorizing the practice of expressing a fictional world across distinct media and environments*. University of Sydney.

Denga, E. M., & Rakshit, S. (2023). Digital Marketing and the Sustainable Performance of Small and Medium Enterprises. In R. Potluri & N. Vajjhala (Eds.), *Advancing SMEs Toward E-Commerce Policies for Sustainability* (pp. 213–234). IGI Global. doi:10.4018/978-1-6684-5727-6.ch011

Desai, V. (2019). Digital Marketing: *A Review.* [ijtsrd]. *International Journal of Trend in Scientific Research and Development*, (Special Issue), 196–200. doi:10.31142/ijtsrd23100

Desveaux, L., Shaw, J., Saragosa, M., Soobiah, C., Marani, H., Hensel, J., Agarwal, P., Onabajo, N., Bhatia, R. S., & Jeffs, L. A. (2018). A mobile app to improve self-management of individuals with type 2 diabetes: Qualitative realist evaluation. *Journal of Medical Internet Research*, *20*(3), e81. doi:10.2196/jmir.8712 PMID:29549070

Deterding, S., Dixon, D., Khaled, R., & Nacke, L. (2011). From game design elements to gamefulness: defining" gamification". In *Proceedings of the 15th international academic MindTrek conference: Envisioning future media environments* (pp. 9-15). ACM. 10.1145/2181037.2181040

Dey, N., Borah, S., Babo, R., & Ashour, A. S. (2019). *Social Network Analytics Computational Research Methods and Techniques*. Academic Press.

Dholakia, U. M., Bagozzi, R. P., & Pearo, L. K. (2004). A social influence model of consumer participation in network- and small-group-based virtual communities. *International Journal of Research in Marketing*, *21*(3), 241–263. doi:10.1016/j.ijresmar.2003.12.004

Dicicco-Bloom, B., & Crabtree, B. F. (2006). The qualitative research interview. *Medical Education*, *40*(4), 314–321. doi:10.1111/j.1365-2929.2006.02418.x PMID:16573666

Dobbin, F., & Kalev, A. (2016). Why Diversity Programs Fail. *Harvard Business Review*, *94*(7), 2–10.

Dobele, R., Westberg, K., Steel, M., & Flowers, K. (2014). An examination of corporate social responsibility implementation and stakeholder engagement: A case study in the Australian mining industry. *Business Strategy and the Environment*, *23*(3), 145–159. doi:10.1002/bse.1775

Dolatabadi, S. H., & Budinskai, I. (2020). A New Method Based on Gamification Algorithm to Engage Stakeholders in Competitive Markets. In *2020 IEEE 24th International Conference on Intelligent Engineering Systems (INES)* (pp. 11-18). IEEE. 10.1109/INES49302.2020.9147196

Domingues, I., & Remoaldo, P. (2012). Responsabilidade Social Organizacional e Sustentabilidade. In I. Domingos & P. Remoaldo (Eds.), *Responsabilidade Social Organizacional: Desenvolvimento e Sustentabilidade* (pp. 93–114). Edições Húmus.

Donath, L., Mircea, G., & Rozman, T. (2020). E-learning platforms as leverage for education for sustainable development. *European Journal of Sustainable Development*, *9*(2), 1–1. doi:10.14207/ejsd.2020.v9n2p1

Dong, C., Huang, Q., Pan, Y., Ng, C. T., & Liu, R. (2023). Logistics outsourcing: Effects of greenwashing and blockchain technology. *Transportation Research Part E: Logistics and Transportation Review*, *170*(October 2022), 103015. doi:10.1016/j.tre.2023.103015

Dos-Santos, M. J. P. L., Baptista, N., & Nobre, H. (2021). Exploring the relationship between ethical and sustainable consumption in short supply chains: A literature review. In J. I. Kantola, S. Nazir, & V. Salminen (Eds.), *Advances in Human Factors, Business Management and Leadership - Proceedings of the AHFE 2021 Virtual Conferences on Human Factors, Business Management and Society, and Human Factors in Management and Leadership* (pp. 197–203). Springer. 10.1007/978-3-030-80876-1_26

du Plessis, C. (2017). The role of content marketing in social media content communities. *South African Journal of Information Management*, *19*(1), 1–7. doi:10.4102ajim.v19i1.866

Duan, W., Tang, X., Li, Y., Cheng, X., & Zhang, H. (2020). Perceived organizational support and employee creativity: The mediation role of calling. *Creativity Research Journal*, *32*(4), 403–411. doi:10.1080/10400419.2020.1821563

Dzureková, M. (2009). *Seriál Marketing krajiny: Kde sa "berie" značka krajiny.* https://www.veldan.sk/serial-marketing-krajiny-kde-sa-berie-znacka-krajiny/

Ebner, D., & Baumgartner, R. J. (2006). The relationship between Sustainable Development and Corporate Social Responsibility. *Corporate Responsibility Research Conference*, *4*(5.9). http://wbw.unileoben.ac.at

Eccles, R. G., Ioannou, I., & Serafeim, G. (2014). The impact of corporate sustainability on organizational processes and performance. *Management Science*, *60*(11), 2835–2857. doi:10.1287/mnsc.2014.1984

Edwards, C. (2023). What is Greenwashing? *Business News Daily*. https://www.businessnewsdaily.com/10946-greenwashing.html

Edwards, M. R., & Peccei, R. (2010). Perceived organizational support, organizational identification, and employee outcomes: Testing a simultaneous multifoci model. *Journal of Personnel Psychology*, *9*(1), 17–26. doi:10.1027/1866-5888/a000007

Eisenberger, R., Armeli, S., Rexwinkel, B., Lynch, P. D., & Rhoades, L. (2001). Reciprocation of perceived organizational support. *The Journal of Applied Psychology*, *86*(1), 42–51. Advance online publication. doi:10.1037/0021-9010.86.1.42 PMID:11302232

Eisenberger, R., Fasolo, P., & Davis-LaMastro, V. (1990). Perceived organizational support and employee diligence, commitment, and innovation. *The Journal of Applied Psychology*, *75*(1), 51–59. doi:10.1037/0021-9010.75.1.51

Eisenberger, R., Huntington, R., Hutchison, S., & Sowa, D. (1986). Perceived organizational support. *The Journal of Applied Psychology*, *71*(3), 500–507. doi:10.1037/0021-9010.71.3.500

ElHaffara, G., Durifa, F., & Dubéb, L. (2020). Towards closing the attitude-intention-behavior gap in green consumption: A narrative review of the literature and an overview of future research directions. *Journal of Cleaner Production*, *275*, 275. doi:10.1016/j.jclepro.2020.122556

Elkington, J., & Zeitz, J. (2014). *The Breakthrough Challenge: 10 Ways to Connect Todays Profits With Tomorrows Bottom Line*. Jossey-Bass: A Wiley Brand.

Elkington, J. (1998). *Cannibals With Forks: The Triple Bottom Line of 21st Century Business*. Capstone.

Emerson, S. (2018). Great examples of multiplatform storytelling. [Blog post]. *Echo Stories*. https://www.echostories.com/great-examples-multiplatform-storytelling/

Erdmann, A., Arilla, R., & Ponzoa, J. M. (2022). Search engine optimization: The long-term strategy of keyword choice. *Journal of Business Research*, *144*, 650–662. doi:10.1016/j.jbusres.2022.01.065

Erfani, S. S., Abedin, B., & Blount, Y. (2017). The effect of social network site use on the psychological well-being of cancer patients. *Journal of the Association for Information Science and Technology*, *68*(5), 1308–1322. doi:10.1002/asi.23702

Ernsting, C., Dombrowski, S. U., Oedekoven, M., Kanzler, M., Kuhlmey, A., & Gellert, P. (2017). Using smartphones and health apps to change and manage health behaviors: A population-based survey. *Journal of Medical Internet Research*, *19*(4), e101. doi:10.2196/jmir.6838 PMID:28381394

Eshuis, J., & Edwards, A. (2013). Branding the city: The democratic legitimacy of a new mode of governance. *Urban Studies (Edinburgh, Scotland)*, *50*(5), 1066–1082. doi:10.1177/0042098012459581

Eshuis, J., & Klijn, E. H. (2012). *Branding in Governance and Public Management*. Routledge. doi:10.4324/9780203145159

Eshuis, J., Klijn, E. H., & Braun, E. (2014). Place marketing and citizen participation: Branding as strategy to address the emotional dimension of policy making? *International Review of Administrative Sciences*, *80*(1), 151–171. doi:10.1177/0020852313513872

Essen, B. (2023). Shifting from stories to substance: Here's what is next for sustainable marketing. *Think with Google*. https://www.thinkwithgoogle.com/intl/en-gb/future-of-marketing/digital-transformation/sustainable-marketing-solutions/

European cities marketing. (2015). *Bolstered international bed nights recovery traditional markets*. http://www.europeancitiesmarketing.com/european- city-tourism-resume-positive-growth-2014-bolstered-international-bednights-recovery-traditional-markets/

European Union (2023). Commission update marketing standards of agri-food products to better address consumer needs and sustainability. *The European Sting*. https://europeansting.com/2023/04/24/commission-updates-marketing-standards-of-agri-food-products-to-better-address-consumer-needs-and-sustainability/

Evans, J. R., & Mathur, A. (2005). The value of online surveys. *Internet Research*, *15*(2), 195–219. doi:10.1108/10662240510590360

Ewais, S., & Alluhaidan, A. (2015). Classification of stress management mHealth apps based on Octalysis framework. In *Twenty-first Americas Conference on Information Systems*. AMCIS. https://aisel.aisnet.org/amcis2015/HealthIS/GeneralPresentations/16/

Eysenbach, G. (2003). The Impact of the Internet on Cancer Outcomes. *CA: a Cancer Journal for Clinicians*, *53*(6), 356–371. doi:10.3322/canjclin.53.6.356 PMID:15224975

Fadli, I. S., Lestari, N. P., & Putri, A. A. (2023). Implementation of White Hat SEO-Based Digital Incubator Platform. *International Transactions on Education Technology*, *1*(2), 122–130.

Faircloth, J. B., Capella, L. M., & Alford, B. L. (2001). The Effect of Brand Attitude and Brand Image on Brand Equity. *Journal of Marketing Theory and Practice*, *9*(3), 61–75. doi:10.1080/10696679.2001.11501897

Fan, Y. (2010). Branding the nation: Towards a better understanding. *Place Branding and Public Diplomacy*, *6*(2), 97–103. doi:10.1057/pb.2010.16

FAO. (2019). *The State of Food and Agriculture 2019*. Moving Forward on Food Loss and Waste Reduction. Food and Agriculture Organization—United Nations, Rome. https://www.fao.org/3/ca6030en/ca6030en.pdf

Felix, R., Rauschnabel, P. A., & Hinsch, C. (2017). Elements of strategic social media marketing: A holistic framework. *Journal of Business Research*, *70*, 118–126. doi:10.1016/j.jbusres.2016.05.001

Figuers, C., & Rivett-Carnac, T. (2020). *The Future We Choose: Surviving the Climate Crisis*. Alfred A. Knopf.

Fink, M., Koller, M., Gartner, J., Floh, A., & Harms, R. (2020). Effective entrepreneurial marketing on Facebook–A longitudinal study. *Journal of Business Research*, *113*, 149–157. doi:10.1016/j.jbusres.2018.10.005

Foley, S., Hang-Yue, N., & Lui, S. (2005). The effects of work stressors, perceived organizational support, and gender on work-family conflict in Hong Kong. *Asia Pacific Journal of Management*, *22*(3), 237–256. doi:10.100710490-005-3568-3

Fombrun, C., Gardberg, N. A., & Barnett, M. L. (2019). Reputation and corporate social responsibility aberrations, trends, and hypocrisy: Reactions to firm choices in the stock option backdating scandal. *Journal of Management Studies*, *46*(7), 1319–1337.

Ford, J. D., Ford, L. W., & D'Amelio, A. (2008). Resistance to change: The rest of the story. *Academy of Management Review*, *33*(2), 362–377. doi:10.5465/amr.2008.31193235

Ford, S., Green, J., & Jenkins, H. (2013). *Spreadable media: Creating value and meaning in a networked culture*. New York University Press.

Freeman, E., Wicks, A., & Parmar, B. (2004). Stakeholder Theory and "The Corporate Objective Revisited". *Organization Science*, *15*(3), 364–369. doi:10.1287/orsc.1040.0066

Freeman, R. (2010). *Strategic Management Approach*. Cambridge University Press. doi:10.1017/CBO9781139192675

Freudenreich, B., Lüdeke-Freund, F., & Schaltegger, S. (2020). A stakeholder theory perspective on business models: Value creation for sustainability. *Journal of Business Ethics*, *166*(1), 3–18. doi:10.100710551-019-04112-z

Frey, M., Gusmerotti, N. M., Corsini, F., & Sarti, S. (2017). Food sharing: Making sense between new business models and responsible social initiatives for food waste prevention, 123–134.

Friedman, M. (1962). *Capitalism and Freedom* (40th ed.). University of Chicago Press.

Frig, M., & Sorsa, V. P. (2018). Nation branding as sustainability governance: A comparative case analysis. *Business & Society*, 1–30.

Fuentes, C., & Jimenez, M. (2017). Challenges and Opportunities for non-profit organisations in the digital era. *Social Responsibility Journal*, *13*(4), 833–849.

Fuglseth, A. M., & Sørebø, Ø. (2014). The effects of technostress within the context of employee use of ICT. *Computers in Human Behavior*, *40*, 161–170. doi:10.1016/j.chb.2014.07.040

Furstrand, D., Pihl, A., Orbe, E. B., Kingod, N., & Sondergaard, J. (2021). "Ask a Doctor About Coronavirus": How Physicians on Social Media Can Provide Valid Health Information During a Pandemic. *Journal of Medical Internet Research*, *23*(4), e24586. doi:10.2196/24586 PMID:33835935

Fu, S., Li, H., Liu, Y., Pirkkalainen, H., & Salo, M. (2020). Social media overload, exhaustion, and use discontinuance: Examining the effects of information overload, system feature overload, and social overload. *Information Processing & Management*, *57*(6), 102307. doi:10.1016/j.ipm.2020.102307

Garcia, D. O., & Thomson, C. A. (2014). Physical activity and cancer survivorship. *Nutrition in Clinical Practice*, *29*(6), 768–779. doi:10.1177/0884533614551969 PMID:25335787

Garcia, J. E., Lima, R., & da Fonseca, M. J. S. (2022, April). Search engine optimization (SEO) for a company website: A case study. In *World Conference on Information Systems and Technologies* (pp. 524–531). Cham: Springer International Publishing. 10.1007/978-3-031-04829-6_47

Gartner, J., Fink, M., Floh, A., & Eggers, F. (2021). Service quality in social media communication of NPOs: The moderating effect of channel choice. *Journal of Business Research*, *137*, 579–587. doi:10.1016/j.jbusres.2021.08.026

Gatti, L., & Seele, P. (2014). Evidence for the prevalence of the sustainability concept in European corporate responsibility reporting. *Sustainability Science*, *9*(1), 89–102. doi:10.100711625-013-0233-5

Gee, J. P. (2004). *Situated language and learning: A critique of traditional schooling*. Routledge.

Giovanardi, M., Lichrou, M., & Kavaratzis, M. (2018). Inclusive place branding: Towards an integrative research agenda. In M. Karavatzis, M. Giovanardi, & M. Lichrou (Eds.), Inclusive place branding: Critical perspectives on theory and practice (pp. 172–181). Academic Press.

Gleim, M., & Lawson, S. J. (2014). Spanning the gap: An examination of the factors leading to the green gap. *Journal of Consumer Marketing*, *31*(6–7), 503–514. doi:10.1108/JCM-05-2014-0988

Gold, H. T., Karia, R. J., Link, A., Lebwohl, R., Zuckerman, J. D., Errico, T. J., Slover, J. D., Buckland, A. J., Mann, D. M., & Cantor, M. N. (2020). Implementation and early adaptation of patient-reported outcome measures into an electronic health record: A technical report. *Health Informatics Journal*, *26*(1), 129–140. doi:10.1177/1460458218813710 PMID:30516095

Golom, F. D., & Cruz, M. (2021). Context-levels-culture: A diagnostic framework for consulting to diversity, equity, and inclusion change in organizations. In Research in Organizational Change and Development (Vol. 29, pp. 201-234). Emerald Publishing Limited. doi:10.1108/S0897-301620210000029009

Goodman-Smith, F., Bhatt, S., Moore, R., Mirosa, M., Ye, H., Deutsch, J., & Suri, R. (2021). Retail potential for upcycled foods: Evidence from New Zealand. *Sustainability (Basel)*, *13*(5), 2624. doi:10.3390u13052624

Gotsis, G., & Kortezi, Z. (2015). The business case for diversity in the workplace: An empirical review. *Business Ethics (Oxford, England)*, *24*(2), 157–175.

Govers, R., & Go, F. M. (2009). *Place Branding: Glocal, Virtual and Physical Identities, Constructed, Imagiden and Experiences*. Palgrave Macmillan. doi:10.1007/978-0-230-24702-4

Graakjær, N. J. (2019). Sounding out i'm lovin'it–a multimodal discourse analysis of the sonic logo in commercials for McDonald's 2003–2018. *Critical Discourse Studies*, *16*(5), 569–582. doi:10.1080/17405904.2019.1624184

Graham-Rowe, E., Jessop, D. C., & Sparks, P. (2014). Identifying motivations and barriers to minimising household food waste. *Resources, Conservation and Recycling*, *84*, 15–23. doi:10.1016/j.resconrec.2013.12.005

Grainger, M. J., Aramyan, L., Logatcheva, K., Piras, S., Righi, S., Setti, M., Vittuari, M., & Stewart, G. B. (2018). The use of systems models to identify food waste drivers. *Global Food Security*, *16*, 1–8. doi:10.1016/j.gfs.2017.12.005

Green, M. C., & Jenkins, H. (2011). Spreadable media: How audiences create value and meaning in a networked culture. In V. Nightingale (Ed.), *The handbook of media audiences* (pp. 109–127). Wiley-Blackwell. doi:10.1002/9781444340525.ch5

GrowthForce. (n.d.) Busin*esses with Workplace Diversity Have 19% Higher Revenue. Here's Why*. GrowthForce. https://www.growthforce.com/blog/business-workplace-diversity-revenue

Gruber, T., & Schlegelmilch, B. B. (2017). Digital transformation of nonprofit organisations: A research agenda. *Journal of Business Research*, *70*, 322–326.

Gupta, P. B., & Gould, S. J. (1997). Consumers' perceptions of the ethics and acceptability of product placements in movies: Product category and individual differences. *Journal of Current Issues and Research in Advertising*, *19*(1), 37–50. doi:10.1080/10641734.1997.10505056

Gupta, P., Khan, A., & Kumar, A. (2020). Social media use by patients in health care: A scoping review. *International Journal of Healthcare Management*, *15*(2), 121–131. doi:10.1080/20479700.2020.1860563

Gupta, T., & Schapira, L. (2018). Online Communities as Sources of Peer Support for People Living With Cancer: A Commentary. *Journal of Oncology Practice / American Society of Clinical Oncology*, *14*(12), 725–731. doi:10.1200/JOP.18.00261 PMID:30335558

Gürel, M. O., & Tigli, M. (2014). New World Created by Social Media: Transmedia Storytelling. *Journal of Media Critiques*, *1*(1), 35–65. doi:10.17349/jmc114102

Gustavsson, J., Cederberg, C., Sonesson, U., Van Otterdijk, R., & Meybeck, A. (2011). *Global food losses and food waste*.

Gu, Z. H., Qiu, T., Tian, F. Q., Yang, S. H., & Wu, H. (2020). Perceived organizational support associated with depressive symptoms among petroleum workers in China: A cross-sectional study. *Psychology Research and Behavior Management*, *13*, 97–104. doi:10.2147/PRBM.S232635 PMID:32095086

Hahn, S. L., Hazzard, V. M., Larson, N., Klein, L., Loth, K. A., & Neumark-Sztainer, D. (2022). Correlates of weight-related self-monitoring application use during emerging adulthood in a population-based sample. *Eating and Weight Disorders*, *27*(6), 2107–2119. doi:10.100740519-021-01349-4 PMID:35040079

Hakala, U., & Lemmetyinen, A. (2011). Co-creating a nation brand "bottom -up". *Tourism Review*, *66*(3), 14–24. doi:10.1108/16605371111175294

Han, H. (2021). Consumer behavior and environmental sustainability in tourism and hospitality: A review of theories, concepts, and latest research. *Journal of Sustainable Tourism*, *29*(7), 1021–1042. doi:10.1080/09669582.2021.1903019

Hanna, T. K. 2022. What is a non-profit organisation. *Tech Target.* https://www.techtarget.com/

Harrison, J., Bosse, D., & Phillips, R. (2010). Managing for stakeholders, stakeholder utility functions, and competitive advantage. *Strategic Management Journal*, *31*(1), 58–74. doi:10.1002mj.801

Hasan, D., & Kamalanabhan, T. J. (2023). Perceived Organizational Support- A Systematic Literature Review and Future Research Agenda. *Manager-The British Journal of Administrative Management*, *59*(1), 71–95.

Hassan, S. M., Rahman, Z., & Paul, J. (2022). Consumer ethics: A review and research agenda. *Psychology and Marketing*, *39*(1), 111–130.

Hatch, M. J., & Schultz, M. (2002). The dynamics of organizational identity. *Human Relations*, *55*(8), 989–1018. doi:10.1177/0018726702055008181

Hazel, S., & Brittany, M. (2020). Greenwashing in the Information Industry. *The I Journal. Graduate Student Journal of the Faculty of Information*, *5*(2). Advance online publication. doi:10.33137/ijournal.v5i2.34413

Heaslip, E. (2023) Non-profit vs. Not for profit vs For-profit: What is the difference? *US Chamber.* https://www.uschamber.com/co/start/startegy/

Hereźniak, M., & Anders-Morawska, J. (2015). City brand strategy evaluation: In search of effectiveness indicators. *Journal of Place Management and Development*, *8*(3), 187–205. doi:10.1108/JPMD-06-2015-0023

Hermanson, T. (2021). Why Keywords Are Still So Very Important for SEO. *Search Engine Journal.* https://www.searchenginejournal.com/seo/why-keywords-important-seo/

Hernandez-Fernandez, A., & Lewis, M. C. (2019). Brand authenticity leads to perceived value and brand trust. *European Journal of Management and Business Economics*, *28*(3), 222–238. doi:10.1108/EJMBE-10-2017-0027

Herring, C. (2009). Does Diversity Pay? Race, Gender, and the Business Case for Diversity. *American Sociological Review*, *74*(2), 208–224. doi:10.1177/000312240907400203

Hills, M. (2017). From Transmedia Storytelling to Transmedia Experience. In *Star Wars and the History of Transmedia Storytelling* (pp. 213–225). Amsterdam University Press.

Hintermeister, S. (2022). How Marketers Can Avoid Greenwashing. *American Marketing Association (AMA).* https://www.ama.org/marketing-news/how-marketers-can-avoid-greenwashing/

Hlavac, R. (2014). *Social IMC: Social Strategies with Bottom-line ROI.* CreateSpace Independent Publishing Platform.

Hlioui, Z., & Yousfi, O. (2022). CSR and Innovation: Two Sides of the Same Coin. In Corporate Social Responsibility (pp. 1–29). IntechOpen. doi:10.5772/intechopen.94344

Hoffmann, J., Nyborg, K., Averhoff, C., & Olesen, S. (2020). The contingency of corporate political advocacy: Nike's 'dream crazy' campaign with Colin Kaepernick. *Public Relations Inquiry*, *9*(2), 155–175. doi:10.1177/2046147X20920802

Hofmann, D. A., & Morgeson, F. P. (1999). Safety-related behavior as a social exchange: The role of perceived organizational support and leader–member exchange. *The Journal of Applied Psychology*, *84*(2), 286–296. doi:10.1037/0021-9010.84.2.286

Hofmeister-Tóth Ágnes. (2006). *Fogyasztói magatartás.* Aula Kiadó.

Holliman, G., & Rowley, J. (2014). Business to business digital content marketing: Marketers' perceptions of best practice. *Journal of Research in Interactive Marketing*, *8*(4), 269–293. doi:10.1108/JRIM-02-2014-0013

Hong, J., Yang, J., Wooldridge, B. R., & Bhappu, A. D. (2022). Sharing consumers' brand storytelling: Influence of consumers' storytelling on brand attitude via emotions and cognitions. *Journal of Product and Brand Management*, *31*(2), 265–278. doi:10.1108/JPBM-07-2019-2485

Hornik, J. (1984). Subjective vs. objective time measures: A note on the perception of time in consumer behavior. *The Journal of Consumer Research*, *11*(1), 615–618. doi:10.1086/208998

Hornstein, D. (2014). *What the 'I amsterdam' letters teach us about destination branding in the social media age.* Reuters Events. https://www.reutersevents.com/travel/social-media-and-marketing/what-i-amsterdam-letters-teach-us-about-destination-branding-social-media

Horváth, M. (2006). *Nation Branding – komplexný prístup k prezentácii Slovenska (Diskusia).* https://www.trend.sk/spravy/nation-branding-komplexny-pristup-prezentacii-slovenska-diskusia

Hospers, G. J. (2020). A short reflection on city branding and its controversies. *Tijdschrift voor Economische en Sociale Geografie*, *111*(1), 18–23. doi:10.1111/tesg.12386

Huang, S. L., & Ku, H. H. (2016). Brand image management for nonprofit organizations: Exploring the relationship between websites, brand images and donations. *Journal of Electronic Commerce Research*, *17*(1), 80–97.

Huang, Y., Wang, L., & Shi, J. (2012). How attachment affects the strength of peer influence on adolescent consumer behavior. *Psychology and Marketing*, *29*(8), 558–567. doi:10.1002/mar.20543

Hunt, V., Layton, D., & Prince, S. (2015). *Why Diversity Matters*. McKinsey & Company. https://www.mckinsey.com/business-functions/organization/our-insights/why-diversity-matters

Hunt, V., Yee, L., Prince, S., & Dixon-Fyle, S. (2018). *Delivering through diversity*. McKinsey & Company. https://www.mckinsey.com/capabilities/people-and-organizational-performance/our-insights/delivering-through-diversity

Hunt, J. D. (1975). Image as a factor in tourism development. *Journal of Travel Research*, *13*(3), 1–7. doi:10.1177/004728757501300301

Iamsterdam. (2013). *Amsterdam marketing*. https://www.iamsterdam.com/en/amsterdam- marketing

Idealware. (2012). *Notprofit social media policybook*. Wordpress. https://www.sustainingplaces.fileswordpress.com/2012/10/

Ihm, J. (2015). Network measures to evaluate stakeholder engagement with nonprofit organizations on social networking sites. *Public Relations Review*, *41*(4), 501–503. doi:10.1016/j.pubrev.2015.06.018

Ilyas, S., Abid, G., & Ashfaq, F. (2022). The impact of perceived organizational support on professional commitment: A moderation of burnout and mediation of well-being. *The International Journal of Sociology and Social Policy*, *43*(7/8), 710–726. doi:10.1108/IJSSP-06-2022-0170

Imamoglu, S. Z., Erat, S., & Turkcan, H. (2022). *How organizational identity relates to knowledge sharing and creativity: moderating effect of perceived organizational support*. Kybernetes. doi:0.1108/K-02-2022-0169

Institute for Urban Strategies. (2022). *Global Power City Index*. Author.

Ipsos. (2021). *Consumers want deeper social-justice commitments from brands*. Ipsos. https://www.ipsos.com/en-us/knowledge/society/Consumers-want-deeper-social-justice-commitments-from-brands

Iqbal, M., Khalid, M. N., Manzoor, A., Abid, M. M., & Shakh, N. A. (2022). Search Engine optimisation: A study of key factors in achieving in achieving a better search result page (SERP) position. *Sukkur IBA Journal of Computing and Mathematical Science*, *6*(1), 1–15. doi:10.30537jcms.v6i1.924

Ištvanić, M., Crnjac Milić, D., & Krpić, Z. (2017). Digital marketing in the business environment. *International Journal of Electrical and Computer Engineering Systems*, *8*(2), 67–75. doi:10.32985/ijeces.8.2.4

Jadhav, V. S., & Yallatti, R. M. (2018). A critical study on digital marketing with reference to different components of digital marketing. *International Journal of Trend in Scientific Research and Development*, (Special Issue), 231–233. doi:10.31142/ijtsrd18711

Jaffe, E. D., & Nebenzahl, I. D. (2001). *National Image and Competitive Advantage: The Theory and Practice of Country-of-Origin Effect*. Copenhagen Business School Press.

Jagau, H. L., & Vyrastekova, J. (2017). Behavioral Approach to Food Waste: An experiment. *British Food Journal*, *119*(4), 882–894. doi:10.1108/BFJ-05-2016-0213

Jalali, S., & Khalid, H. (2021). The Influence of Instagram Influencers' Activity on Green Consumption Behavior. *Business Management and Strategy*, *12*(1), 78–90. doi:10.5296/bms.v12i1.18265

Janiszewska, K., & Insch, A. (2012). The strategic importance of brand positioning in the place brand concept: Elements, structure and application capabilities. *Journal of International Studies*, *5*(1), 2071–8330. doi:10.14254/2071-8330.2012/5-1/2

Jenkins, H. (2003). Transmedia Storytelling: Moving Characters from Books to Films to Video Games Can Make Them Stronger and More Compelling. *MIT Technology Review*. https://www.technologyreview.com/news/401760/transmedia-storytelling/

Jenkins, H. (2009). *If it doesn't spread, it's dead (Part One): Media viruses and memes. Confessions of an Aca-Fan.* Henry Jenkins. http://henryjenkins.org/blog/2009/02/if_it_doesnt_spread_its_dead_p.html

Jenkins, H. (2006). *Convergence culture: Where old and new media collide*. New York University Press.

Jenkins, H. (2010). Transmedia storytelling and entertainment: An annotated syllabus. *Continuum (Perth)*, *24*(6), 943–958. doi:10.1080/10304312.2010.510599

Jenkins, H., & Deuze, M. (2008). Editorial: Convergence Culture. *Convergence (London)*, *14*(1), 5–12. doi:10.1177/1354856507084415

Jennings, P. L., Mitchell, M. S., & Hannah, S. T. (2015). The moral self: A review and integration of the literature. *Journal of Organizational Behavior*, *36*(S1), S104–S168. doi:10.1002/job.1919

Jhamb, S., & Fiegl, R. (2022). Perceived Greenwashing and Sustainable Business Strategies: Understanding Organizational Roles in Addressing Environmental Issues. *IUP Journal of Business Strategy*, *19*(2), 23–32.

Jog, D., & Singhal, D. (2019). Pseudo green players and their greenwashing practices: A differentiating strategy for real green firms of personal care category. *Strategic Direction*, *35*(12), 4–7. doi:10.1108/SD-07-2019-0143

Johansson, V., Islind, A. S., Lindroth, T., Angenete, E., & Gellerstedt, M. (2021). Online Communities as a Driver for Patient Empowerment: Systematic Review. *Journal of Medical Internet Research*, *23*(2), e19910. doi:10.2196/19910 PMID:33560233

Johnson, M. P., & Chichirau, G. R. (2020). Diversity, equity, and inclusion in operations research and analytics: A research agenda for scholarship, practice, and service. *Pushing the boundaries: Frontiers in impactful OR/OM research*, 1-38.

Johnstone, M. L., & Hooper, S. (2016). Social influence and green consumption behavior: A need for greater government involvement. *Journal of Marketing Management*, *32*(9–10), 827–855. doi:10.1080/0267257X.2016.1189955

Jones-Smith, V. (2021). *Nonprofifit Leaders' Digital Marketing Strategies to Secure and Sustain Donors* [Doctoral dissertation, Walden university].

Kane, G. C., Alavi, M., Labianca, G., & Borgatti, S. P. (2014). What's Different about Social Media Networks? A Framework and Research Agenda. *Management Information Systems Quarterly*, *38*(1), 274–304. doi:10.25300/MISQ/2014/38.1.13

Kaplan, A. M., & Haenlein, M. (2010). Users of the world, unite! The challenges and opportunities of Social Media. *Business Horizons*, *53*(1), 59–8. doi:10.1016/j.bushor.2009.09.003

Karatepe, O. M. (2015). Do personal resources mediate the effect of perceived organizational support on emotional exhaustion and job outcomes? *International Journal of Contemporary Hospitality Management*, *27*(1), 4–26. doi:10.1108/IJCHM-09-2013-0417

Katsikeas, C. S., Leonidou, C. N., & Zeriti, A. (2016). Eco-friendly product development strategy: Antecedents, outcomes, and contingent effects. *Journal of the Academy of Marketing Science*, *44*(6), 660–684. doi:10.100711747-015-0470-5

Kaur, R., Singh, R., Gehlot, A., Priyadarshi, N., & Twala, B. (2022). Marketing Strategies 4.0: Recent Trends and Technologies in Marketing. *Sustainability (Basel)*, *14*(24), 1–17. doi:10.3390u142416356

Kavaratzis, M. (2004). From city marketing to city branding: Towards a theoretical framework for developing city brands. *Place Branding, 1*(1), 58-73.

Kavaratzis, M. (2008). *From city marketing to city branding: an interdisciplinary analysis with reference to Amsterdam, Budapest and Athens* [Doctoral Thesis]. University of Groningen.

Kavaratzis, M. (2011). The dishonest relationship between city marketing and culture: Reflections on the theory and the case of Budapest. *Journal of Town & City Management, 1*(4).

Kavaratzis, M., & Ashworth, G. J. (2005). City branding: An effective assertion of identity or a transitory marketing trick? *Tijdschrift voor Economische en Sociale Geografie*, *96*(5), 506–514. doi:10.1111/j.1467-9663.2005.00482.x

Keeling, D. I., de Ruyter, K., Mousavi, S., & Laing, A. (2019). Technology push without a patient pull: Examining digital unengagement (DU) with online health services. *European Journal of Marketing*, *53*(9), 1701–1732. doi:10.1108/EJM-10-2017-0692

Kellen, M., & Saxena, D. (2020). Calm my headspace: Motivations and barriers for adoption and usage of meditation apps during times of crisis. In *Proceedings of The 20th International Conference on Electronic Business* (pp. 37–46). IEEE.

Key, T. M., Keel, A. L., Czaplewski, A. J., & Olson, E. M. (2021). Brand activism change agents: Strategic storytelling for impact and authenticity. *Journal of Strategic Marketing*, 1–17. doi:10.1080/0965254X.2021.1904435

Khan, M. N. A., & Mahmood, A. (2018). A distinctive approach to obtain higher page rank through search engine optimization. *sādhanā, 43*(3), 43.

Kietzmann, J. H., Hermkens, K., McCarthy, I. P., & Silvestre, B. S. (2011). Social media? Get serious! Understanding the functional building blocks of social media. *Business Horizons*, *54*(3), 241–251. doi:10.1016/j.bushor.2011.01.005

Kim, D. Y., & Kim, H. S. (2021). Influencer advertising on social media: The multiple inference model on influencer-product congruence and sponsorship disclosure. *Journal of Business Research*, *130*, 405–415. doi:10.1016/j.jbusres.2020.02.020

Kim, J. K., Overton, H., Bhalla, N., & Li, J. Y. (2020). Nike, Colin Kaepernick, and the politicization of sports: Examining perceived organizational motives and public responses. *Public Relations Review*, *46*(2), 101856. doi:10.1016/j.pubrev.2019.101856

Kim, K. Y., Eisenberger, R., & Baik, K. (2016). Perceived organizational support and affective organizational commitment: Moderating influence of perceived organizational competence. *Journal of Organizational Behavior*, *37*(4), 558–583. doi:10.1002/job.2081

Kinder, M. (1991). *Playing with power in movies, television, and video games: From Muppet Babies to Teenage Mutant Ninja Turtles*. University of California Press. doi:10.1525/9780520912434

Kipnis, E., Demangeot, C., Pullig, C., Cross, S. N., Cui, C. C., Galalae, C., Kearney, S., Licsandru, T. C., Mari, C., Ruiz, V. M., Swanepoel, S., Vorster, L., & Williams, J. D. (2021). Institutionalizing diversity-and-inclusion-engaged marketing for multicultural marketplace well-being. *Journal of Public Policy & Marketing*, *40*(2), 143–164. doi:10.1177/0743915620975415

Kirby, J., & Marsden, P. (2006). *Connected Marketing: The Viral, Buzz and Word of Mouth Revolution*. Elsevier.

Kitchen, J. P., Kerr, G. E., Schultz, D., McColl, R., & Pals, H. (2014). The elaboration likelihood model: Review, critique, and research agenda. *European Journal of Marketing*, *48*(11/12), 2033–2050. doi:10.1108/EJM-12-2011-0776

Klastrup, L., & Tosca, S. (2004). Transmedial worlds – rethinking cyberworld design. In *Proceedings from the 2004 International Conference on Cyberworlds*. 10.1109/CW.2004.67

Knater, B., & Paine, K. D. (2012). *Measuring the networked NPO. Using data to change the world*. John Wiley and Sons.

Kochhar, S. (2020). *Millenials@work: perspectives on diversity & inclusion*. Institute for Public Relations. https://instituteforpr.org/millennialswork-perspectives-diversity-inclusion/

König, L. M., Sproesser, G., Schupp, H. T., & Renner, B. (2018). Describing the process of adopting nutrition and fitness apps: Behavior stage model approach. *JMIR mHealth and uHealth*, *6*(3), e8261. doi:10.2196/mhealth.8261 PMID:29535078

Kotler, P., & Roberto, E. L. (1992). *Marketing social: Estrategias para cambiar la conducta pública*. Ediciones Díaz de Santos, S.A.

Kotler, P., Haider, D., & Rein, I. (1993). *Marketing Places: Attracting Investment, Industry and Tourism to Cities, States and Nations*. Free Press.

Kotler, P., Kartajaya, H., & Setiawan, I. (2021). *Marketing 5.0: Technology for Humanity*. John Wiley & Sons.

Kotler, P., & Levy, S. J. (1969). Broadening the concept of marketing. *Journal of Marketing*, *33*(1), 10–15. doi:10.1177/002224296903300103 PMID:12309673

Kovács, T., & Várallyai, L. (2021). Egészségügyi mobilapplikációkra történő használati szándék mérése UTAUT-modellben: Tanulmány egy online felmérés eredményei alapján. *INFORMÁCIÓS TÁRSADALOM: TÁRSADALOMTUDOMÁNYI FOLYÓIRAT*, *21*(1), 166–187. doi:10.22503/inftars.XXI.2021.1.7

Krebs, P., & Duncan, D. T. (2015). Health app use among US mobile phone owners: A national survey. *JMIR mHealth and uHealth*, *3*(4), e4924. doi:10.2196/mhealth.4924 PMID:26537656

Krishna, A. (2012). An integrative review of sensory marketing: Engaging the senses to affect perception, judgment and behavior. *Journal of Consumer Psychology*, *22*(3), 332–351. doi:10.1016/j.jcps.2011.08.003

Krishnan, G., & Lokachari, P. S. (2019). Adoption of health and fitness apps by mobile users: Interactive qualitative analysis. In *Proceedings of the 2019 Portland International Conference on Management of Engineering and Technology (PICMET)*, Portland, OR, USA.

KSH. (2019). *European Health Interview Survey, 2019*. KSH. https://www.ksh.hu/docs/hun/xftp/idoszaki/pdf/egeszsegugyi_helyzetkep_2019.pdf

Kujala, J., Sachs, S., Leinonen, H., Heikkinen, A., & Laude, D. (2022). Stakeholder Engagement: Past, Present, and Future. *Business & Society*, *61*(5), 1136–1196. doi:10.1177/00076503211066595

Kurtessis, J. N., Eisenberger, R., Ford, M. T., Buffardi, L. C., Stewart, K. A., & Adis, C. S. (2017). Perceived organizational support: A meta-analytic evaluation of organizational support theory. *Journal of Management*, *43*(6), 1854–1884. doi:10.1177/0149206315575554

Kwon, M. W., Mun, K., Lee, J. K., McLeod, D. M., & D'Angelo, J. (2017). Is mobile health all peer pressure? The influence of mass media exposure on the motivation to use mobile health apps. *Convergence (London)*, *23*(6), 565–586. doi:10.1177/1354856516641065

Lage, M. C. (2011). Utilização do software NVivo em pesquisa qualitativa: Uma experiência em EaD. *ETD Educação Temática Digital*, *12*(03), 198–226.

Lam, A., & Tegelberg, M. (2019). Witnessing glaciers melt: Climate change and transmedia storytelling. *JCOM, Journal of Science Communication*, *18*(02), A05. doi:10.22323/2.18020205

Latapí Agudelo, M. A., Jóhannsdóttir, L., & Davídsdóttir, B. (2019). A literature review of the history and evolution of corporate social responsibility. *International Journal of Corporate Social Responsibility*, *4*(1), 1–23. doi:10.118640991-018-0039-y

Laurenza, E., Quintano, M., Schiavone, F., & Vrontis, D. (2018). The effect of digital technologies adoption in healthcare industry: A case based analysis. *Business Process Management Journal*, *24*(5), 1124–1144. doi:10.1108/BPMJ-04-2017-0084

Laville, S. (2022, June 30th). Coca-Cola among brands greenwashing over packaging, report says. *The Guardian*. https://www.theguardian.com/environment/2022/jun/30/coca-cola-among-brands-greenwashing-over-packaging-report-says

Lee, H. (2021). Changes in workplace practices during the COVID-19 pandemic: The roles of emotion, psychological safety and organisation support. *Journal of Organizational Effectiveness: People and Performance*, *8*(1), 97–128. doi:10.1108/JOEPP-06-2020-0104

Lee, M. T., & Raschke, R. L. (2023). Stakeholder legitimacy in firm greening and financial performance: What about greenwashing temptations?☆. *Journal of Business Research*, *155*, 113393. doi:10.1016/j.jbusres.2022.113393

Lee, N., & Kotler, P. (2019). *Social Marketing: Behavior Change for Social Good* (6th ed.). SAGE Publications.

Lee, S. M., & Lee, D. (2020). Healthcare wearable devices: An analysis of key factors for continuous use intention. *Service Business*, *14*(4), 503–531. doi:10.100711628-020-00428-3

Lee, Y. J. (2022). Social media capital and civic engagement: Does type of connection matter? *International Review on Public and Nonprofit Marketing*, *19*(1), 167–189. doi:10.100712208-021-00300-8

Lehtokunnas, T., Mattila, M., Närvänen, E., & Mesiranta, N. (2022). Towards a circular economy in food consumption: Food waste reduction practices as ethical work. *Journal of Consumer Culture*, *22*(1), 227–245. doi:10.1177/1469540520926252

Leimeister, J. M., Ebner, W., & Krcmar, H. (2005). Design, Implementation, and Evaluation of Trust-Supporting Components in Virtual Communities for Patients. *Journal of Management Information Systems*, *21*(4), 101–135. doi:10.1080/07421222.2005.11045825

Leslie, L. M. (2019). Diversity initiative effectiveness: A typological theory of unintended consequences. *Academy of Management Review*, *44*(3), 538–563. doi:10.5465/amr.2017.0087

Levek, A., Benazzi, A., Arnone, J., Seguin, J., & Gerhardt, T. (2002). A responsabilidade social e sua interface com o marketing social. *Revista Da FAE*, *5*(2), 15–25.

Levenshus, A. (2010). Online relationship management in a presidential campaign: A case study of the Obama campaign's management of its internet-integrated 177 grassroots effort. *Journal of Public Relations Research*, *22*(3), 313–335. doi:10.1080/10627261003614419

Lidynia, C., Schomakers, E. M., & Ziefle, M. (2019). What are you waiting for?–perceived barriers to the adoption of fitness-applications and wearables. In *Advances in Human Factors in Wearable Technologies and Game Design: Proceedings of the AHFE 2018 International Conferences on Human Factors and Wearable Technologies, and Human Factors in Game Design and Virtual Environments,* (pp. 41–52). Springer International Publishing.

Lieffers, J. R., Quintanilha, M., Trottier, C. F., Johnson, S. T., Mota, J. F., & Prado, C. M. (2021). Experiences with and perception of a web-based mindfulness, nutrition, and fitness platform reported by first-year university students: A qualitative study. *Journal of the Academy of Nutrition and Dietetics*, *121*(12), 2409–2418. doi:10.1016/j.jand.2021.04.019 PMID:34119458

Li, W., Li, W., Seppänen, V., & Koivumäki, T. (2023). Effects of greenwashing on financial performance: Moderation through local environmental regulation and media coverage. *Business Strategy and the Environment*, *32*(1), 820–841. doi:10.1002/bse.3177

Li, Y., Wang, X., Lin, X., & Hajli, M. (2018). Seeking and sharing health information on social media: A net valence model and cross-cultural comparison. *Technological Forecasting and Social Change*, *126*, 28–40. doi:10.1016/j.techfore.2016.07.021

Lombarts, A. (2011). *Amsterdam, a brand that appeals to tourists and business alike.* http://www. citymayors.com/marketing/amsterdam-brand.html

Long, G. (2007). *Transmedia storytelling: Business, aesthetics, and production at the Jim Henson Company.* Unpublished doctoral dissertation, Massachusetts Institute of Technology.

Lovejoy, K., & Saxton, G. D. (2012). Information, community, and action: How non-profit organizations use social media. *Journal of Computer-Mediated Communication*, *17*(3), 337–353. doi:10.1111/j.1083-6101.2012.01576.x

Lucarelli, A. (2018). Place branding as urban policy: The (im)political place branding. *Cities (London, England)*, *80*, 12–21. doi:10.1016/j.cities.2017.08.004

Lucas, G. (Creator). (1977-present). *Star Wars* [Film series]. Lucasfilm.

Luo, Y., Wang, G., Li, Y., & Ye, Q. (2021). Examining protection motivation and network externality perspective regarding the continued intention to use m-health apps. *International Journal of Environmental Research and Public Health*, *18*(11), 5684. doi:10.3390/ijerph18115684 PMID:34073247

Lutgendorf, S. K., & Sood, A. K. (2011). Biobehavioral Factors and Cancer Progression: Physiological Pathways and Mechanisms. *Psychosomatic Medicine*, *73*(9), 724–730. doi:10.1097/PSY.0b013e318235be76 PMID:22021459

Maan, A. T., Abid, G., Butt, T. H., Ashfaq, F., & Ahmed, S. (2020). Perceived organizational support and job satisfaction: A moderated mediation model of proactive personality and psychological empowerment. *Future Business Journal*, *6*(1), 1–12. doi:10.118643093-020-00027-8

Mace, M. (April 23rd, 2023). Greenwashing concerns: Marketing professionals warn of sustainability knowledge gap. *Edie*. https://www.edie.net/greenwashing-concerns-marketing-professionals-warn-of-sustainability-knowledge-gap/

Macedo, I. M., & Pinho, J. C. (2006). The relationship between resource dependence and market orientation. *European Journal of Marketing*, *40*(5/6), 533–553. doi:10.1108/03090560610657822

Madera, J. M. (2013). Best practices in diversity management in customer service organizations: An investigation of top companies cited by Diversity Inc. *Cornell Hospitality Quarterly*, *54*(2), 124–135. doi:10.1177/1938965513475526

Majer, J. M., Henscher, H. A., Reuber, P., Fischer-Kreer, D., & Fischer, D. (2022). The effects of visual sustainability labels on consumer perception and behavior: A systematic review of the empirical literature. *Sustainable Production and Consumption*, *33*, 1–14. doi:10.1016/j.spc.2022.06.012

Malaeb, M., Dagher, G. K., & Messarra, L. C. (2022). The relationship between self-leadership and employee engagement in Lebanon and the UAE: the moderating role of perceived organizational support. Personnel Review. doi:10.1108/PR-12-2021-0862

Malhotra, N. K., & Birks, D. F. (2003). Marketing Research: An Applied Approach (2end ed.). Pearson Education Limited.

Marvel Studios. (2008-present). *Marvel Cinematic Universe* [Film series]. Marvel Studios.

Matusik, J. G., Ferris, D. L., & Johnson, R. E. (2022). The PCMT model of organizational support: An integrative review and reconciliation of the organizational support literature. *The Journal of Applied Psychology*, *107*(3), 329–345. doi:10.1037/apl0000922 PMID:34060884

Ma, W., Schraven, D., de Bruijne, M., de Jong, M., & Lu, H. (2019, May 28). Tracing the Origins of Place Branding Research: A Bibliometric Study of Concepts in Use (1980–2018). *Sustainability*, *11*(11), 2999. doi:10.3390u11112999

Maxim, E. (2016). *Planning strategic marketing for non-profit organizations case study* [Bachelor's Thesis, Laurea university of applied sciences].

Mazzucchelli, A., Gurioli, M., Graziano, D., Quacquarelli, B., & Aouina-Mejri, C. (2021). How to fight against food waste in the digital era: Key factors for a successful food sharing platform. *Journal of Business Research*, *124*, 47–58. doi:10.1016/j.jbusres.2020.11.055

McBey, K., Karakowsky, L., & Ng, P. (2017). Can I make a difference here? The impact of perceived organizational support on volunteer commitment. *Journal of Management Development*, *36*(8), 991–1007. doi:10.1108/JMD-05-2015-0078

McCabe, S. (2017). Sustainability and marketing in tourism: Its contexts, paradoxes, approaches, challenges and potential. *Journal of Sustainable Tourism*, *25*(7), 869–883. doi:10.1080/09669582.2017.1301721

McGlynn, K. A., Petrick, J. L., & El-Serag, H. B. (2021). Epidemiology of Hepatocellular Carcinoma. *Hepatology (Baltimore, Md.)*, *73*(S1), 4–13. doi:10.1002/hep.31288 PMID:32319693

McKinsey & Company. (2020) *Diversity wins. How inclusion matters. May 2020 report*. McKinsey. https://www.mckinsey.com/~/media/mckinsey/featured%20insights/diversity%20and%20inclusion/diversity%20wins%20how%20inclusion%20matters/diversity-wins-how-inclusion-matters-vf.pdf

McLuhan, M. (1964). *Understanding media: The extensions of man*. McGraw Hill.

Megehee, C. M. (2009). Advertising time expansion, compression, and cognitive processing influences on consumer acceptance of message and brand. *Journal of Business Research*, *62*(4), 420–431. doi:10.1016/j.jbusres.2008.01.019

Meskó, B., Drobni, Z., Bényei, É., Gergely, B., & Győrffy, Z. (2017). Digital health is a cultural transformation of traditional healthcare. *mHealth*, *3*, 3. doi:10.21037/mhealth.2017.08.07 PMID:29184890

Michel, G. M., Feori, M., Damhorst, M. L., Lee, Y. A., & Niehm, L. S. (2019). Stories we wear: Promoting sustainability practices with the case of Patagonia. *Family and Consumer Sciences Research Journal*, *48*(2), 165–180. doi:10.1111/fcsr.12340

Michelini, L., Principato, L., & Iasevoli, G. (2018). Understanding Food Sharing Models to Tackle Sustainability Challenges. *Ecological Economics*, *145*, 205–217. doi:10.1016/j.ecolecon.2017.09.009

Miikkulainen, R., Iscoe, N., Shagrin, A., Cordell, R., Nazari, S., Schoolland, C., & Lamba, G. (2017, July). Conversion rate optimization through evolutionary computation. In *Proceedings of the Genetic and Evolutionary Computation Conference* (pp. 1193–1199). ACM. 10.1145/3071178.3071312

Milde, K., & Yawson, R. M. (2017). Strategies for social media use in nonprofits. *Journal of Management Policy and Practice*, *18*(1), 19–27.

Milla, A. C., Mataruna-Dos-Santos, L. J., & Ristic, M. R. (2018). Adopting social media for nonprofits as a main marketing tool: Analysis of a youth non-profit organization. *International Journal of Applied Business and Economic Research*, *22*(2), 741–752.

Milla, A., Mataruna, L., & Ristic, M. R. (2018). Adopting social Media for Nonprofits as a Main marketing tool: Analysis of a youth non-profit organization. *Int J Appl Bus Econ Res*, *22*(2), 741–752.

Mitchell, G. E., & Calabrese, T. D. (2019). Proverbs of nonprofit financial management. *American Review of Public Administration*, *49*(6), 649–661. doi:10.1177/0275074018770458

Mitchell, R., Hunt, R., Townsend, D., & Lee, J. (2022). Stakeholder engagement, knowledge problems and ethical challenges. *Journal of Business Ethics*, *175*(1), 75–94. doi:10.100710551-020-04550-0

Mladenović, D., Rajapakse, A., Kožuljević, N., & Shukla, Y. (2023). Search engine optimization (SEO) for digital marketers: Exploring determinants of online search visibility for blood bank service. *Online Information Review*, *47*(4), 661–679. doi:10.1108/OIR-05-2022-0276

Mohr, L. A., Webb, D. J., & Harris, K. E. (2001). Do consumers expect companies to be socially responsible? The impact of corporate social responsibility on buying behavior. *The Journal of Consumer Affairs*, *35*(1), 45–72. doi:10.1111/j.1745-6606.2001.tb00102.x

Moilanen, T., & Rainisto, S. (2009). *How to Brand Nations, Cities and Destination. A Planning Book for Place Branding*. Palgrave Macmillan. doi:10.1057/9780230584594

Molina, J. R., Yang, P., Cassivi, S. D., Schild, S. E., & Adjei, A. A. (2008). Non-small cell lung cancer: Epidemiology, risk factors, treatment, and survivorship. *Mayo Clinic Proceedings*, *83*(5), 584–594. doi:10.1016/S0025-6196(11)60735-0 PMID:18452692

Moltene, L., & Orsato, R. J. (2021). Economia compartilhada na prática: um estudo exploratório sobre aceitação e uso de plataformas digitais para a redução do desperdício de alimentos. *Revista de Administração de Empresas*, 61.

Moskal, A. (2022). Moving Towards a Sustainable Digital Future with Uber – a Legitimate Step Towards a Greener Economy or Merely Greenwashing Policy? *Politeja*, *19*(3(78)), 267–282. doi:10.12797/Politeja.19.2022.78.14

Mothersbaugh, D. L., & Hawkins, D. I. (2016). *Consumer behavior: Building marketing strategy*. McGraw-Hill.

Moz. (2023). *Domain Authority: What is it and how is it calculated*. Moz. https://moz.com/learn/seo/domain-authority

Mravčák, A. (2014). *Značkové mestá*. http://profit.etrend.sk/dennik/znackove-mesta.html

Mukherjee, S., & Althuizen, N. (2020). Brand activism: Does courting controversy help or hurt a brand? *International Journal of Research in Marketing*, *37*(4), 772–788. doi:10.1016/j.ijresmar.2020.02.008

Mulholland, E (2019). Communicating Sustainable Development and the SDGs in Europe: Good practice examples from policy, academia, NGOs, and media. *ESDN Quarterly Report 51*.

Mulholland, E., Dimitrova, A., & Hametner, M. (2018). *SDG Indicators and Monitoring: Systems and Processes at the Global, European, and National Level*. ESDN Office.

Mulholland, E., Dimitrova, A., & Hametner, M. (2018). *SDG Indicators and Monitoring: Systems and Processes at the Global, European, and National Level. ESDN Quarterly Report 48*. ESDN Office.

Müller, A. M., Maher, C. A., Vandelanotte, C., Hingle, M., Middelweerd, A., Lopez, M. L., DeSmet, A., Short, C. E., Nathan, N., Hutchesson, M. J., Poppe, L., Woods, C. B., Williams, S. L., & Wark, P. A. (2018). Physical Activity, Sedentary Behavior, and Diet-Related eHealth and mHealth Research: Bibliometric Analysis. *Journal of Medical Internet Research*, *20*(4), e122. doi:10.2196/jmir.8954 PMID:29669703

Müller, J., & Christandl, F. (2019). Content is king – But who is the king of kings? The effect of content marketing, sponsored content & user-generated content on brand responses. *Computers in Human Behavior*, *96*, 46–55. doi:10.1016/j.chb.2019.02.006

Musikavanhu, T. B., Asoba, S. N., & Mefi, N. P. (2022). Content Marketing strategies for Non-governmental organisations in a developing nation. *International Journal of Scientific Research*, *78*(4), 17–24. doi:10.5281/zenodo.7269280

Mustafa, A. S., Ali, N. A., Dhillon, J. S., Alkawsi, G., & Baashar, Y. (2022). User engagement and abandonment of mHealth: A cross-sectional survey. *Health Care*, *10*(2), 221. doi:10.3390/healthcare10020221 PMID:35206837

Musungwini, S., Gavai, P. V., Munyoro, B., & Chare, A. (2023). Emerging ICT Technologies for Agriculture, Training, and Capacity Building for Farmers in Developing Countries. *Advances in Environmental Engineering and Green Technologies*, (January), 12–30. doi:10.4018/978-1-6684-6413-7.ch002

Nacinovich, M. (2013). Defining mHealth. *Journal of Communication in Healthcare*, *4*(1), 1–3. doi:10.1179/175380611X12950033990296

Nageswarakurukkal, K., Gonçalves, P., & Moshtari, M. (2020). Improving fundraising efficiency in small and medium sized non-profit organizations using online solutions. *Journal of Nonprofit & Public Sector Marketing*, *32*(3), 286–311. doi:10.1080/10495142.2019.1589627

Nalband, N. A., & al Kelabi, S. (2014). Redesigning Carroll's CSR Pyramid Model. *Journal of Advanced Management Science*, *236–239*, 236–239. doi:10.12720/joams.2.3.236-239

Namisango, F., Kang, K., & Rehman, J. (2019). What do we know about social media in nonprofits? A review. In *Pacific Asia conference on information systems*. AIS e-library.

Nguyen, N., & Johnson, L. W. (2020). Consumer behaviour and environmental sustainability. *Journal of Consumer Behaviour*, *19*(6), 539–541. doi:10.1002/cb.1892

Nishii, L. H., Khattab, J., Shemla, M., & Paluch, R. M. (2018). A multi-level process model for understanding diversity practice effectiveness. *The Academy of Management Annals*, *12*(1), 37–82. doi:10.5465/annals.2016.0044

Nogué, J. (1999). El retorno al lugar. La creación de identidades territoriales. *Claves de razón práctica, 92*, 9-11.

Nolan, C. (Director). (2008). *The Dark Knight* [Film]. Warner Bros. Pictures.

Noland, M., Moran, T., & Kotschwar, B. (2016*). Is Gender Diversity Profitable?* Evidence from a Global Survey. *Peterson Institute for International Economics Working Paper, 16(*3).

Noland, J., & Phillips, R. (2010). Stakeholder engagement, discourse ethics and strategic management. *International Journal of Management Reviews*, *12*(1), 39–49. doi:10.1111/j.1468-2370.2009.00279.x

Norberg, P. A., Horne, D. R., & Horne, D. A. (2007). The Privacy Paradox: Personal Information Disclosure Intentions versus Behaviors. *The Journal of Consumer Affairs*, *41*(1), 100–126. doi:10.1111/j.1745-6606.2006.00070.x

Nouri, R., Kalhori, S. R. N., Saeedi, M. G., Marchand, G., & Yasini, M. (2018). Criteria for assessing the quality of m-health apps: A systematic review. *Journal of the American Medical Informatics Association : JAMIA*, *25*(8), 1089–1098. doi:10.1093/jamia/ocy050 PMID:29788283

O'Neil, G. (2013). Evaluation of international and non-governmental organizations' communication activities: A 15 year systematic review. *Public Relations Review*, *39*(5), 572–574. doi:10.1016/j.pubrev.2013.07.005

Obar, J. A., & Wildman, S. (2015). Social Media Definition and the Governance Challenge: An Introduction to the Special Issue. *Telecommunications Policy*, *39*(9), 745–750. doi:10.1016/j.telpol.2015.07.014

Octavia, D., Nasution, R. A., & Yudoko, G. (2022). A Conceptual Framework for Food Sharing as Collaborative Consumption. *Foods*, *11*(10), 1422. doi:10.3390/foods11101422 PMID:35626993

Oc, Y., & Plangger, K. (2022). GIST do it! How motivational mechanisms help wearable users develop healthy habits. *Computers in Human Behavior*, *128*, 107089. doi:10.1016/j.chb.2021.107089

OECD. (2007). *Participative Web and User-Created Content*. OECD. http://browse.oecdbookshop.org/oecd/pdfs/free/9307031e.pdf

Oh, H., Prado, P. H. M., Korelo, J. C., & Frizzo, F. (2019). The effect of brand authenticity on consumer–brand relationships. *Journal of Product and Brand Management*, *28*(2), 231–241. doi:10.1108/JPBM-09-2017-1567

Olins, W. (2002). Branding the nation – The historical context. *Journal of Brand Management*, *9*(4-5), 241–248. doi:10.1057/palgrave.bm.2540075

Oliva, E. J. D., Sánchez-Torres, J. A., & Niño, J. S. S. (2022). City brand evolution research and future agenda: Bibliometric and science mapping analysis. *Heliyon*, *8*(8). PMID:35991998

Oliveira, B., & Teixeira Lopes, C. (2023). The Evolution of Web Search User Interfaces-An Archaeological Analysis of Google Search Engine Result Pages. In *Proceedings of the 2023 Conference on Human Information Interaction and Retrieval* (pp. 55–68). ACM. 10.1145/3576840.3578320

Oliveira, I., Figueiredo, J., Cardoso, A., & de Oliveira, E. R. (2021). Gap between sophisticated consumers and sophisticated behaviors: Analysis of The portuguese in social sustainability. *Academy of Strategic Management Journal*, *20*(5), 1–11.

Oliveira, J., Júnior, L., Fernandes De Mesquita, R., Alves, N., Santos, D., Gomes, W., Felipe, F., Fátima, S., & Matos, R. N. (2020). O Futuro Que Nós Criamos: A Perspetiva da Sustentabilidade Para Futuros Gestores. *Revista Gestão e Organizações*, *5*(4), 80–101.

Oliveira, M., Oliveira, J., Borges, A. P., & Lopes, J. M. (2021). Social networks in the non-profit sector: Social support practices. *International Review on Public and Nonprofit Marketing*, *18*(4), 523–552. doi:10.100712208-021-00283-6

Özbilgin, M., Tatli, A., Ipek, G., & Sameer, M. (2014). *Four approaches to accounting for diversity in global organizations*. Deloitte Case Studies. https://www2.deloitte.com/au/en/pages/human-capital/articles/four-approaches-accounting-diversity-global-organisations.html

Page, S. E. (2017). *The diversity bonus: How great teams pay off in the knowledge economy*. Princeton University Press. doi:10.2307/j.ctvc77c0h

Palacios-González, M. M., & Chamorro-Mera, A. (2020). Analysis of socially responsible consumption: A segmentation of Spanish consumers. *Sustainability (Basel)*, *12*(20), 1–15. doi:10.3390u12208418

Pantuck, A. J., Leppert, J. T., Zomorodian, N., Aronson, W., Hong, J., Barnard, R. J., Seeram, N., Liker, H., Wang, H., Elashoff, R., Heber, D., Aviram, M., Ignarro, L., & Belldegrun, A. (2006). Phase II study of pomegranate juice for men with rising prostate-specific antigen following surgery or radiation for prostate cancer. *Clinical Cancer Research*, *12*(13), 4018–4026. doi:10.1158/1078-0432.CCR-05-2290 PMID:16818701

Papa, A., Mital, M., Pisano, P., & Del Giudice, M. (2020). E-health and wellbeing monitoring using smart healthcare devices: An empirical investigation. *Technological Forecasting and Social Change*, *153*, 119226. doi:10.1016/j.techfore.2018.02.018

Papasolomou, I., Melanthiou, Y., & Tsamouridis, A. (2022). The fast fashion vs environment debate: Consumers' level of awareness, feelings, and behaviour towards sustainability within the fast-fashion sector. *Journal of Marketing Communications*, *29*(2), 191–209. doi:10.1080/13527266.2022.2154059

Parguel, B., Benoît-Moreau, F., & Larceneux, F. (2011). How Sustainability Ratings Might Deter "Greenwashing": A Closer Look at Ethical Corporate Communication. *Journal of Business Ethics*, *102*(1), 15–28. doi:10.100710551-011-0901-2

Patel, P. C., & Feng, C. (2021). LGBT workplace equality policy and customer satisfaction: The roles of marketing capability and demand instability. *Journal of Public Policy & Marketing*, *40*(1), 7–26. doi:10.1177/0743915620945259

Patel, S. A., & Kondratov, R. V. (2021). Clock at the Core of Cancer Development. *Biology (Basel)*, *10*(2), 150. doi:10.3390/biology10020150 PMID:33672910

Paxton, P., Velasco, K., & Ressler, R. W. (2020). Does use of emotion increase donations and volunteers for nonprofits? *American Sociological Review*, *85*(6), 1051–1083. doi:10.1177/0003122420960104

Pei, J. (2022). Approaches Toward Building the Digital Enterprise and Sustainable Economic Development: The Moderating Role of Sustainability. *Frontiers in Psychology*, *13*(March), 1–11. doi:10.3389/fpsyg.2022.835602 PMID:35360590

Peng, W., Kanthawala, S., Yuan, S., & Ali Hussain, S. (2016). A qualitative study of user perceptions of mobile health apps. *BMC Public Health*, *16*(1158), 1158. doi:10.118612889-016-3808-0 PMID:27842533

Pérez, L. A., Garzón, M. A., & Ibarra, M. A. (2016). Empresa Verde: Diagnostico de la necesidad de un modelo. *Dimensión Empresarial*, *14*(1), 67–78. doi:10.15665/rde.v14i1.425

Pham, P., & Gammoh, B. (2015). Characteristics of social-media marketing strategy and customer-based brand equity outcomes: A conceptual model. *International Journal of Internet Marketing and Advertising*, *9*(4), 321–337. doi:10.1504/IJIMA.2015.072885

Phillips, K. W. (2014). How Diversity Makes Us Smarter. *Harvard Business Review*. https://hbr.org/2014/10/how-diversity-makes-us-smarter

Phillips, A. (2012). *A creator's guide to transmedia storytelling: How to captivate and engage audiences across multiple platforms*. McGraw-Hill Education.

Pichler, S., Ruggs, E., & Trau, R. (2017). Worker outcomes of LGBT-supportive policies: A cross-level model. *Equality, Diversity and Inclusion*, *36*(1), 17–32. doi:10.1108/EDI-07-2016-0058

Piercy, N. F., Cravens, D. W., Lane, N., & Vorhies, D. W. (2006). Driving organizational citizenship behaviors and salesperson in-role behavior performance: The role of management control and perceived organizational support. *Journal of the Academy of Marketing Science*, *34*(2), 244–262. doi:10.1177/0092070305280532

Pinto, L., Loureiro, S. M. C., Rita, P., & Sarmento, E. M. (2019). Fostering online relationships with brands through websites and social media brand pages. *Journal of Promotion Management*, *25*(3), 379–393. doi:10.1080/10496491.2019.1557817

Piras, L., Dellagiacoma, D., Perini, A., Susi, A., Giorgini, P., & Mylopoulos, J. (2019). Design thinking and acceptance requirements for designing gamified software. In *2019 13th International Conference on Research Challenges in Information Science (RCIS)* (pp. 1-12). IEEE. 10.1109/RCIS.2019.8876973

Pizzetti, M., Gatti, L., & Seele, P. (2021). Firms Talk, Suppliers Walk: Analyzing the Locus of Greenwashing in the Blame Game and Introducing 'Vicarious Greenwashing.'. *Journal of Business Ethics*, *170*(1), 21–38. doi:10.100710551-019-04406-2

Pless, N. M., & Maak, T. (2011). *Responsible leadership*: *Pathways to the future*. Research Gate. https://www.researchgate.net/publication/227451528_Responsible_Leadership_Pathways_to_the_Future

Pont, S. (2013). *Digital state: How the Internet is changing everything*. Kogan Page Project Everyone. https://www.project-everyone.org/

Pontin, F., Lomax, N., Clarke, G., & Morris, M. A. (2021). Socio-demographic determinants of physical activity and app usage from smartphone data. *Social Science & Medicine*, *284*, 114235. doi:10.1016/j.socscimed.2021.114235 PMID:34311392

Poon, J. M., Salleh, A. H. M., & Senik, Z. C. (2007). Propensity to trust as a moderator of the relationship between perceived organizational support and job satisfaction. *International Journal of Organization Theory and Behavior*, *10*(3), 350–366. doi:10.1108/IJOTB-10-03-2007-B004

Post, J., Preston, L., & Sachs, S. (2002). *Redefining the Corporation Stakeholder Management and Organizational Wealth*. Stanford University Press. doi:10.1515/9781503619692

Principato, L., Secondi, L., & Pratesi, C. A. (2015). Reducing Food Waste: An investigation on the behaviour of Italian youths. *British Food Journal*, *117*(2), 731–748. doi:10.1108/BFJ-10-2013-0314

Prothero, A., Dobsha, S., Freund, J., Kilbourne, W., Luchs, M., Ozanne, L., & Thøgersen, J. (2011). Sustainable Consumption: Opportunities for Consumer Research and Public Policy Related papers. *Journal of Public Policy & Marketing*, *30*(1), 31–38. doi:10.1509/jppm.30.1.31

Prysmakova, P., & Lallatin, N. (2021). Perceived organizational support in public and nonprofit organizations: Systematic review and directions for future research. *International Review of Administrative Sciences*, *89*(2), 467–483. doi:10.1177/00208523211033822

Pullen, E., Fischer, M. W., Morse, G., Garabrant, J., Salyers, M. P., & Rollins, A. L. (2023). Racial disparities in the workplace: The impact of isolation on perceived organizational support and job satisfaction. *Psychiatric Rehabilitation Journal*, *46*(1), 45–52. doi:10.1037/prj0000543 PMID:36809015

Quested, T. E., Parry, A. D., Easteal, S., & Swannell, R. (2011). Food and drink waste from households in the UK. *Nutrition Bulletin*, *36*(4), 460–467. doi:10.1111/j.1467-3010.2011.01924.x

Quevedo, F. J., & Quevedo-Prince, A. K. (2019). A predictive model for the US non-profit market; a macro to a micro perspective. *Advanced Journal of Social Science*, *5*(1), 1–9. doi:10.21467/ajss.5.1.1-9

Raggiotto, F., Scarpi, D., & Moretti, A. (2020). Advertising on the edge: Appeal effectiveness when advertising in extreme sports. *International Journal of Advertising*, *39*(5), 655–678. doi:10.1080/02650487.2019.1653009

Ragu-Nathan, T. S., Tarafdar, M., Ragu-Nathan, B. S., & Tu, Q. (2008). The consequences of technostress for end users in organizations: Conceptual development and empirical validation. *Information Systems Research*, *19*(4), 417–433. doi:10.1287/isre.1070.0165

Rajkomar, A., Dean, J., & Kohane, I. (2019). Machine Learning in Medicine. *The New England Journal of Medicine*, *380*(14), 1347–1358. doi:10.1056/NEJMra1814259 PMID:30943338

Rake, S. M., & Grayson, D. (2009). Overall change dynamics: Embedding corporate responsibility and sustainability - everybody's business. *Corporate Governance (Bradford)*, *9*(4), 395–399. doi:10.1108/14720700910984945

Ramesh, K., Saha, R., Goswami, S., Sekar, & Dahiya, R. (2019). Consumer's response to CSR activities: Mediating role of brand image and attitude. *Corporate Social Responsibility and Environmental Management*, *26*(2), 377–387. doi:10.1002/csr.1689

Research and Markets. (2022). *Global Diversity and Inclusion (D&I) Market Report 2021*. Research and Markets. https://www.globenewswire.com/news-release/2022/01/27/2374060/28124/en/Global-Diversity-and-Inclusion-D-I-Market-Report-2021-Market-is-Estimated-at-7-5-Billion-in-2020-and-is-Projected-to-Reach-15-4-Billion-by-2026-Growing-at-a-CAGR-of-12-6.html

Rhoades, L., & Eisenberger, R. (2002). Perceived organizational support: A review of the literature. *The Journal of Applied Psychology*, *87*(4), 698–714. doi:10.1037/0021-9010.87.4.698 PMID:12184574

Richard, O. C., Stewart, M. M., McKay, P. F., & Sackett, T. W. (2017). The impact of store-unit-community racial diversity congruence on store-unit sales performance. *Journal of Management*, *43*(7), 2386–2403. doi:10.1177/0149206315579511

Rigby, S., & Ryan, R. M. (2011). *Glued to games: How video games draw us in and hold us spellbound*. AbC-CLIo.

Riggle, R. J., Edmondson, D. R., & Hansen, J. D. (2009). A meta-analysis of the relationship between perceived organizational support and job outcomes: 20 years of research. *Journal of Business Research*, *62*(10), 1027–1030. doi:10.1016/j.jbusres.2008.05.003

Rinaldi, Ch., Giovanardi, M., & Lucarelli, A. (2021). Keeping a foot in both camps: Sustainability, city branding and boundary spanners. *Cities (London, England)*, *115*, 103236. doi:10.1016/j.cities.2021.103236

Robertson, J. L., Montgomery, A. W., & Ozbilir, T. (2023). Employees' response to corporate greenwashing. *Business Strategy and the Environment, 2022*(May 2022), 1–13. doi:10.1002/bse.3351

Robinson, O. C. (2013). Sampling in Interview-Based Qualitative Research: A Theoretical and Practical Guide. *Qualitative Research in Psychology*, *11*(1), 25–41. doi:10.1080/14780887.2013.801543

Robson, K., Plangger, K., Kietzmann, J. H., McCarthy, I., & Pitt, L. (2016). Game on: Engaging customers and employees through gamification. *Business Horizons*, *59*(1), 29–36. doi:10.1016/j.bushor.2015.08.002

Rockstuhl, T., Eisenberger, R., Shore, L. M., Kurtessis, J. N., Ford, M. T., Buffardi, L. C., & Mesdaghinia, S. (2020). Perceived organizational support (POS) across 54 nations: A cross-cultural meta-analysis of POS effects. *Journal of International Business Studies*, *51*(6), 933–962. doi:10.105741267-020-00311-3

Rodrigues, L., Silva, F., & Romero, C. (2021). "Sou Verde de Verdade": Estratégias Mercadológicas da Economia Criativa para Superar a Desconfiança do Consumidor. *Revista de Gestão Social e Ambiental*, *15*, e02780. doi:10.24857/rgsa.v15.2780

Rogers, R. A. (2006). *From cultural exchange to transculturation: A review and reconceptualization of cultural appropriation*. Research Gate. https://www.researchgate.net/publication/227630287_From_Cultural_Exchange_to_Transculturation_A_Review_and_Reconceptualization_of_Cultural_Appropriation

Rojíková, D. (2022). *Budovanie značky mesta a moderné formy marketingovej komunikácie* [Doctoral dissertations]. Banská Bystrica: Ekonomická fakulta UMB.

Rojíková, D., Vaňová, A. & Borseková, K. (2020). The Role and Position of the Nation Brand in Cultural and Foreign Policy. *Ekonomika a spoločnosť, 21*(1), 68-77.

Romano, J. (2023). What is web design? A comprehensive guide. *Wix Blog*. https://www.wix.com/blog/web-design

Rose, R. (2016). *The 2017 Content Marketing Framework: 5 Building Blocks for Profitable, Scalable Operations*. Content Marketing Institute. https://contentmarketinginstitute.com/2016/10/contentmarketing-framework-profitable/

Rose, F. (2011). *The art of immersion: How the digital generation is remaking Hollywood, Madison Avenue, and the way we tell stories*. W. W. Norton & Company.

Rosnerova, Z., & Hraskova, D. (2021). The Application and Importance of Marketing and its Tools in the Conditions of Non-profit Organizations on a Global Scale. In *SHS Web of Conferences* (Vol. 92, p. 02055). EDP Sciences. 10.1051hsconf/20219202055

Ross, E. L., Jamison, R. N., Nicholls, L., Perry, B. M., & Nolen, K. D. (2020). Clinical integration of a smartphone app for patients with chronic pain: Retrospective analysis of predictors of benefits and patient engagement between clinic visits. *Journal of Medical Internet Research, 22*(4), e16939. doi:10.2196/16939 PMID:32297871

Rößner, A., Gvili, Y., & Eisend, M. (2021). Explaining consumer responses to ethnic and religious minorities in advertising: The case of Israel and Germany. *Journal of Advertising*, *50*(4), 391–407. doi:10.1080/00913367.2021.1939201

Rößner, A., Kämmerer, M., & Eisend, M. (2017). Effects of ethnic advertising on consumers of minority and majority groups: The moderating effect of humour. *International Journal of Advertising*, *36*(1), 190–205. doi:10.1080/02650487.2016.1168907

Roumeliotis, K. I., Tselikas, N. D., & Nasiopoulos, D. K. (2022). Airlines' sustainability study based on search engine optimization techniques and technologies. *Sustainability (Basel)*, *14*(18), 11225. doi:10.3390u141811225

RowlingJ. K. (n.d.). *Pottermore* [Website]. https://www.pottermore.com

Rue, P. (2018). Make way, millennials; here comes Gen Z. *About Campus: Enriching the Student Learning Experience*, *23*(3), 5–12. doi:10.1177/1086482218804251

Ruggill, J. E., & McAllister, K. S. (2009). *Inside the video game industry: Game developers talk about the business of play*. Routledge.

Ruiz, S., Silvia, B., Belen, R., & Feijoo, F. (2022). Characteristics Determine Greenwashing? *Environment, Development and Sustainability*, *24*(3), 4024–4045.

Russell, C. L. (2005). An overview of the integrative research review. *Progress in Transplantation (Aliso Viejo, Calif.)*, *15*(1), 8–13. doi:10.1177/152692480501500102 PMID:15839365

Russell, D. W., Russell, C. A., & Hill, R. P. (2022). Mental health service utilization after military missions: The double-edged consequences of unit-level organizational support. *Psychological Services*, *19*(2, Suppl 2), 113–125. doi:10.1037er0000542

Sabbir, M. M., Taufique, K. M. R., & Nomi, M. (2021). Telemedicine acceptance during the COVID-19 pandemic: User satisfaction and strategic healthcare marketing considerations. *Health Marketing Quarterly*, *38*(2-3), 168–187. doi:10.1080/07359683.2021.1986988 PMID:34645357

Salesforce. (n.d.). *Bring Women back to work. (BWBW).* Salesforce. https://www.salesforce.com/eu/campaign/bwbw/

Santagata, R., Ripa, M., Genovese, A., & Ulgiati, S. (2021). Food waste recovery pathways: Challenges and opportunities for an emerging bio-based circular economy. A systematic review and an assessment. *Journal of Cleaner Production*, *286*, 125490. doi:10.1016/j.jclepro.2020.125490

Santos-Vijande, M. L., Gómez-Rico, M., Molina-Collado, A., & Davison, R. M. (2022). Building user engagement to mhealth apps from a learning perspective: Relationships among functional, emotional and social drivers of user value. *Journal of Retailing and Consumer Services*, *66*, 102956. doi:10.1016/j.jretconser.2022.102956

Sarkar, C., & Kotler, P. (2020). *Brand activism: From purpose to action*. Idea Bite Press.

Sawyer, C., Hassan, L., Sainsbury, J., Carney, R., Bucci, S., Burgess, H., Lovell, K., Torous, J., & Firth, J. (2023). Using digital technology to promote physical health in mental healthcare: A sequential mixed-methods study of clinicians' views. *Early Intervention in Psychiatry*, 1–13. doi:10.1111/eip.13441 PMID:37318221

Schick, H., Marxen, S., & Freimann, J. (2002). Sustainability Issues for Start-up Entrepreneurs. *Greener Management International*, *38*, 59–70. doi:10.2307/greemanainte.38.59

Schindler, I., Hosoya, G., Menninghaus, W., Beermann, U., Wagner, V., Eid, M., & Scherer, K. R. (2017). Measuring aesthetic emotions: A review of the literature and a new assessment tool. *PLoS One*, *12*(6), e0178899. doi:10.1371/journal.pone.0178899 PMID:28582467

Schmuck, D., Matthes, J., & Naderer, B. (2018). Misleading Consumers with Green Advertising? An Affect–Reason–Involvement Account of Greenwashing Effects in Environmental Advertising. *Journal of Advertising*, *47*(2), 127–145. doi:10.1080/00913367.2018.1452652

Schrage, R., Hubert, M., & Linzmajer, M. (2019) Content is king? The effectiveness of message content, personalization, and location in mobile in-store advertising. In *Proceedings of the Annual Hawaii International Conference on System Sciences* (pp. 1373–1382). Scholar Space. 10.24251/HICSS.2019.167

Schweizer, K. J., Leimeister, J. M., & Krcmar, H. (2006). The Role of Virtual Communities for the Social Network of Cancer Patients. In *Proceedings of the Twelfth Americas Conference on Information Systems* (pp. 4470–4479), Acapulco, Mexico.

Scolari, C. A. (2009). Transmedia storytelling: Implicit consumers, narrative worlds, and branding in contemporary media production. *International Journal of Communication*, *3*, 586–606.

Scolari, C. A., Bertetti, P., & Freeman, M. (2014). *Transmedia archaeology: Storytelling in the borderlines of science fiction, comics and pulp magazines*. Palgrave Pivot. doi:10.1057/9781137434371

Seele, P., & Gatti, L. (2017). Greenwashing Revisited: In Search of a Typology and Accusation-Based Definition Incorporating Legitimacy Strategies. *Business Strategy and the Environment*, *26*(2), 239–252. doi:10.1002/bse.1912

Seele, P., & Schultz, M. D. (2022). From Greenwashing to Machinewashing: A Model and Future Directions Derived from Reasoning by Analogy. *Journal of Business Ethics*, *178*(4), 1063–1089. doi:10.100710551-022-05054-9

Seelig, M. I., Millette, D., Zhou, C., & Huang, J. (2019). A new culture of advocacy: An exploratory analysis of social activism on the web and social media. *Atlantic Journal of Communication*, *27*(1), 15–29. doi:10.1080/15456870.2019.1540418

Seo, H., & Vu, H. T. (2020). Transnational nonprofits' social media use: A survey ofcommunications professionals and an analysis of organizational characteristics. *Nonprofit and Voluntary Sector Quarterly*, *49*(4), 849–870. doi:10.1177/0899764020908340

Servan-Schreiber, D. (2009). *Anticancer: A new way of life*. Viking Penguin.

Shankar, A., Dhir, A., Talwar, S., Islam, N., & Sharma, P. (2022). Balancing food waste and sustainability goals in online food delivery: Towards a comprehensive conceptual framework. *Technovation*, *117*, 102606. doi:10.1016/j.technovation.2022.102606

Shankar, V., Grewal, D., Sunder, S., Fossen, B., Peters, K., & Agarwal, A. (2022). Digital marketing communication in global marketplaces: A review of extant research, future directions, and potential approaches. *International Journal of Research in Marketing*, *39*(2), 541–565. doi:10.1016/j.ijresmar.2021.09.005

Shanock, L. R., & Eisenberger, R. (2006). When supervisors feel supported: Relationships with subordinates' perceived supervisor support, perceived organizational support, and performance. *The Journal of Applied Psychology, 91*(3), 689–695. doi:10.1037/0021-9010.91.3.689 PMID:16737364

Shanor, A., & Light, S. E. (2022). Greenwashing and the First Amendment. *Columbia Law Review, 122*(7), 2033–2118.

Shin, N. (2019). The impact of the web and social media on the performance of non-profit organizations. *Journal of International Technology and Information Management, 27*(4), 17–35. doi:10.58729/1941-6679.1386

Shore, L. M., Randel, A. E., Chung, B. G., Dean, M. A., Ehrhart, K. H., & Singh, G. (2018). Inclusion and diversity in work-groups: A review and model for future research. *Journal of Management, 37*(4), 1262–1289. doi:10.1177/0149206310385943

Sibai, O., Mimoun, L., & Boukis, A. (2021). Authenticating brand activism: Negotiating the boundaries of free speech to make a change. *Psychology and Marketing, 38*(10), 1651–1669. doi:10.1002/mar.21477

Sidibe, M. (2020). Marketing Meets Mission. *Harvard Business Review*. https://hbr.org/2020/05/marketing-meets-mission

Silvennoinen, K., Katajajuuri, J.-M., Hartikainen, H., Heikkilä, L., & Reinikainen, A. (2014). Food Waste Volume and composition in Finnish households. *British Food Journal, 116*(6), 1058–1068. doi:10.1108/BFJ-12-2012-0311

Simblett, S., Greer, B., Matcham, F., Curtis, H., Polhemus, A., Ferrão, J., Gamble, P., & Wykes, T. (2018). Barriers to and facilitators of engagement with remote measurement technology for managing health: Systematic review and content analysis of findings. *Journal of Medical Internet Research, 20*(7), e10480. doi:10.2196/10480 PMID:30001997

Simons, D., De Bourdeaudhuij, I., Clarys, P., De Cocker, K., Vandelanotte, C., & Deforche, B. A. (2018). Smartphone App to Promote an Active Lifestyle in Lower-Educated Working Young Adults: Development, Usability, Acceptability, and Feasibility Study. *JMIR mHealth and uHealth, 6*(2, e44), e44. doi:10.2196/mhealth.8287 PMID:29463491

Singh, R. (2020, February). Organisational embeddedness as a moderator on the organisational support, trust and workplace deviance relationships. *Evidence-based HRM: a Global Forum for Empirical Scholarship, 8*(1), 1–17. 10.1108/EBHRM-03-2019-0025

Singh, S. (2017). Challenges of digital marketing for non-profit organisations. *International Journal of Social Sciences and Economic Research, 2*(11), 5303–5311.

Smirnova, E., Eriksson, N., & Fagerstrøm, A. (2021). Adoption and Use of Health-related Mobile Applications: A Qualitative Study with Experienced Users. In *Proceedings of the 14th International Joint Conference on Biomedical Engineering Systems and Technologies*. SCITEPRESS-Science and Technology Publications. 10.5220/0010185902880295

Soboleva, A., Burton, S., Daellenbach, K., & Basil, D. Z. (2017). Tweets for tots: Using Twitter to promote a charity and its supporters. *Journal of Consumer Marketing, 34*(6), 515–523. doi:10.1108/JCM-03-2017-2123

Södergren, J. (2021). Brand authenticity: 25 Years of research. *International Journal of Consumer Studies, 45*(4), 645–663. doi:10.1111/ijcs.12651

Song, M., Garrett, W. S., & Chan, A. T. (2015). Nutrients, Foods, and Colorectal Cancer Prevention. *Gastroenterology, 148*(6), 1244–1260.e1216. doi:10.1053/j.gastro.2014.12.035 PMID:25575572

Soper, K. (2007). Re-thinking the "Good Life": The citizenship dimension of consumer disaffection with consumerism. *Journal of Consumer Culture, 7*(2), 205–229. doi:10.1177/1469540507077681

Spitznagel, E. (2020, January 25). Generation Z is bigger than millennials, and they are out to change the world. *NYpost.com*. https://nypost.com/2020/01/25/generation-z-is-bigger-than-millennials-and-theyre-out-to-change-the-world/

Srivastava, J., Saks, J., Weed, A. J., & Atkins, A. (2018). Engaging audiences on social media: Identifying relationships between message factors and user engagement on the American Cancer Society's Facebook page. *Telematics and Informatics*, *35*(7), 1832–1844. doi:10.1016/j.tele.2018.05.011

Stamp, J. (2012) *Rebranding Amsterdam and What it Means to Rebrand a city*. https://ww. smithsonianmag.com/ist/?next=/arts-culture/rebranding-amsterdam-and-what- it-means-to-rebrand-a-city-19539392/

Stancu, V., Haugaard, P., & Lähteenmäki, L. (2016). Determinants of consumer food waste behaviour: Two routes to food waste. *Appetite*, *96*, 7–17. doi:10.1016/j.appet.2015.08.025 PMID:26299713

Stangherlin, I. D. C., & De Barcellos, M. D. (2018). Drivers and barriers to food waste reduction. *British Food Journal*, *120*(10), 2364–2387. doi:10.1108/BFJ-12-2017-0726

Stanton, B. (2010). *Humans of New York*. Humans of New York. https://www.humansofnewyork.com/

Statista. (2022). *Digital Fitness & Well-Being Apps*. Statista. https://www.statista.com/outlook/dmo/digital-health/digital-fitness-well-being/digital-fitness-well-being-apps/worldwide

Statista. (2023). *Amsterdam - Statistics & Facts*. https://www.statista.com/topics/9014/amsterdam/#topicOverview

Statista-The Statistics Portal. (2023). *Digital advertising spending worldwide from 2021 to 2026(in billion U.S. dollars)*. Statista Research Department. https://www.statista.com/statistics/237974/online-advertising-spending-worldwide/

Statista-The Statistics Portal. (2023). *Social media advertising spending worldwide from 2021 to 2028 (in billion U.S. dollars)*. Statista Research Department. https://www.statista.com/statistics/271406/advertising-revenue-of-social-networks-worldwide/#statisticContainer

Štefčeková, L., & Vaňová, A. (2013). Comparison of perceived and projected image of Slovakia as a starting point for a country image building strategy. *Responsibility and Sustainability: Socioeconomic, Political, and Legal Issues, 1*(3), 41-50.

Stelick, A., Sogari, G., Rodolfi, M., Dando, R., & Paciulli, M. (2021). 9 Impact of Sustainability and Nutritional Messaging on Italian Consumers' Purchase Intent of Cereal Bars Made with Brewery Spent Grains'. *Journal of Food Science*, *86*(2), 531–539. doi:10.1111/1750-3841.15601 PMID:33462803

Stinglhamber, F., Ohana, M., Caesens, G., & Meyer, M. (2020). Perceived organizational support: The interactive role of coworkers' perceptions and employees' voice. *Employee Relations*, *42*(1), 107–124. doi:10.1108/ER-05-2018-0137

Sumardjo, M., & Supriadi, Y. N. (2023). Perceived Organizational Commitment Mediates the Effect of Perceived Organizational Support and Organizational Culture on Organizational Citizenship Behavior. *Calitatea*, *24*(192), 376–384. doi:10.47750/QAS/24.192.45

Sun, R., & Asencio, H. D. (2018). Using social media to increase nonprofit organizational capacity. *International Journal of Public Administration*, *42*, 1–12.

Sun, Z., & Zhang, W. (2019). Do government regulations prevent greenwashing? An evolutionary game analysis of heterogeneous enterprises. *Journal of Cleaner Production*, *231*, 1489–1502. doi:10.1016/j.jclepro.2019.05.335

Suthatorn, P., & Charoensukmongkol, P. (2022). How work passion and job tenure mitigate the effect of perceived organizational support on organizational identification of flight attendants during the COVID-19 pandemic. *Asia Pacific Management Review*, *28*(3), 347–357. doi:10.1016/j.apmrv.2022.12.003

Svendsen, A. (2010). *The Stakeholder Strategy: Profiting From Collaborative Business Relationships*. Berrett-Koehler.

Swart, C., du Plessis, C., & Greeff, E. (2021). An integrated social media communication view on content marketing by South African non-profit sectors. *South African Journal of Information Management*, *23*(1), 1–9. doi:10.4102ajim.v23i1.1366

Szűcs, R. K. (2021). Mobil egészség–áttekintés. *Biztonságtudományi Szemle*, *3*, 79–91.

Tafesse, W., & Wood, B. P. (2021). Followers' engagement with instagram influencers: The role of influencers' content and engagement strategy. *Journal of Retailing and Consumer Services*, *58*, 102303. doi:10.1016/j.jretconser.2020.102303

Talwar, S., Kaur, P., Ahmed, U., Bilgihan, A., & Dhir, A. (2023). The dark side of convenience: How to reduce food waste induced by food delivery apps. *British Food Journal*, *125*(1), 205–225. doi:10.1108/BFJ-02-2021-0204

Tamasiga, P., Miri, T., Onyeaka, H., & Hart, A. (2022). Food waste and circular economy: Challenges and opportunities. *Sustainability (Basel)*, *14*(16), 9896. doi:10.3390u14169896

Tang, G., Yu, B., Cooke, F. L., & Chen, Y. (2017). High-performance work system and employee creativity: The roles of perceived organisational support and devolved management. *Personnel Review*, *46*(7), 1318–1334. doi:10.1108/PR-09-2016-0235

Tarafdar, M., D'arcy, J., Turel, O., & Gupta, A. (2014). The dark side of information technology. *MIT Sloan Management Review*.

Taylor, E. (July 19th, 2021). The paradox of the "sustainable influencer". *Remake*. https://remake.world/stories/news/the-paradox-of-the-sustainable-influencer

Teigiserova, D. A., Hamelin, L., & Thomsen, M. (2020). Towards transparent valorization of food surplus, waste and loss: Clarifying definitions, food waste hierarchy, and role in the circular economy. *The Science of the Total Environment*, *706*, 136033. doi:10.1016/j.scitotenv.2019.136033 PMID:31855638

Tewari, S. (2023). Achieve Branding Excellence in the Digital World by Capitalizing on Search Engine Optimization (SEO). *Academy of Marketing Studies Journal*, *27*(S4).

The Coca-Cola Compay. (n.d.). *Diversity, Equity & Inclusion. Creating a culture of diversity, equity and inclusion.* Coca-Cola. https://www.coca-colacompany.com/social/diversity-and-inclusion

The Good Trade. (2022). 11 Sustainability Influencers Inspiring Us To Do A Little Bit Better Everyday. *The Good Trade*. https://www.thegoodtrade.com/features/sustainability-influencers/

This is not advertising. (2012). *I Amsterdam the campaign to rebrand Amsterdam*. https://thisisnotadvertising.wordpress.com/2012/11/05/i- amsterdam-the-campaign-to-re-brand-amsterdam/

Thomas, S., & Jadeja, A. (2021). Psychological antecedents of consumer trust in CRM campaigns and donation intentions: The moderating role of creativity. *Journal of Retailing and Consumer Services*, *61*, 102589. doi:10.1016/j.jretconser.2021.102589

Thompson, P. S., Bergeron, D. M., & Bolino, M. C. (2020). No obligation? How gender influences the relationship between perceived organizational support and organizational citizenship behavior. *The Journal of Applied Psychology*, *105*(11), 1338–1350. doi:10.1037/apl0000481 PMID:32118460

Tiago, M. T. P. M. B., & Veríssimo, J. M. C. (2014). Digital marketing and social media: Why bother? *Business Horizons*, *57*(6), 703–708. doi:10.1016/j.bushor.2014.07.002

Together Equal. (n.d.) *Diversity at Work. The 10 benefits of diversity*. Together Equal. https://www.togetherequal.com/diversity-at-work

Tong, H. L., Quiroz, J. C., Kocaballi, A. B., Fat, S. C. M., Dao, K. P., Gehringer, H., Chow, C. K., & Laranjo, L. (2021). Personalized mobile technologies for lifestyle behavior change: A systematic review, meta-analysis, and meta-regression. *Preventive Medicine*, *148*, 106532. doi:10.1016/j.ypmed.2021.106532 PMID:33774008

Topol, E. J. (2019). High-performance medicine: The convergence of human and artificial intelligence. *Nature Medicine*, *25*(1), 44–56. doi:10.103841591-018-0300-7 PMID:30617339

Toussaint, M., Cabanelas, P., & González-Alvarado, T. E. (2021). What about the consumer choice? The influence of social sustainability on consumer's purchasing behavior in the Food Value Chain. *European Research on Management and Business Economics*, *27*(1), 100134. doi:10.1016/j.iedeen.2020.100134

Treise, D., Weigold, M. F., Conna, J., & Garrison, H. (1994). Ethics in advertising: Ideological correlates of consumer perceptions. *Journal of Advertising*, *23*(3), 59–69. doi:10.1080/00913367.1994.10673450

UNDP. (2023). *United Nations Development Programme*. UNDP. https://www.undp.org/sustainable-development-goals

UNEP. (2022). *Food Waste Index Report 2021*. United Nations Environment Programme Nairobi. https://wedocs.unep.org/bitstream/handle/20.500.11822/41679/Annual_Report_2022.pdf?sequence=3

Unilever. (n.d.). *Equity, diversity and inclusion*. Unilever. https://www.unilever.com/planet-and-society/equity-diversity-and-inclusion/

United Nations. (2015). *Transforming our world: the 2030 Agenda for Sustainable Development*. UN. https://sdgs.un.org/2030agenda

United Nations. (2016). *Global Goals Week*. UN. https://globalgoalsweek.org/

United Nations. (2022). *The Sustainable Development Goals Report*. UNDP. https://unstats.un.org/sdgs/report/2022/

Vaghefi, I., & Tulu, B. (2019). The continued use of mobile health apps: Insights from a longitudinal study. *JMIR mHealth and uHealth*, *7*(8), e12983. doi:10.2196/12983 PMID:31469081

van Geffen, L., van Herpen, E., Sijtsema, S., & van Trijp, H. (2020). Food waste as the consequence of competing motivations, lack of opportunities, and insufficient abilities. *Resources, Conservation & Recycling: X*, *5*, 100026.

Van Knippenberg, D., Van Prooijen, J. W., & Sleebos, E. (2015). Beyond social exchange: Collectivism's moderating role in the relationship between perceived organizational support and organizational citizenship behaviour. *European Journal of Work and Organizational Psychology*, *24*(1), 152–160. doi:10.1080/1359432X.2013.858699

Vandenberghe, C., Bentein, K., Michon, R., Chebat, J. C., Tremblay, M., & Fils, J. F. (2007). An examination of the role of perceived support and employee commitment in employee-customer encounters. *The Journal of Applied Psychology*, *92*(4), 1177–1187. doi:10.1037/0021-9010.92.4.1177 PMID:17638475

Vaňová, A. (1996). Territorial marketing as a component of municipal and regional policy. *Ekonomický časopis: časopis pre ekonomickú teóriu, hospodársku politiku, spoločensko-ekonomické prognózovanie, 44*(7-8).

Vaňová, A. (2020). *Marketingové stratégie rozvoja územia*. Belianum.

Vaňová, A., Vitálišová, K., & Borseková, K. (2017). *Place marketing*. Belianum.

Vela, S.E.J. (2013). Place branding: A conceptual and theoretical framework. *Boletin de la Asociacion de Geografos Espanoles, 62*, 189-211+467-471.

Venkatesh, V., Thong, J. Y., & Xu, X. (2012). Consumer acceptance and use of information technology: Extending the unified theory of acceptance and use of technology. *Management Information Systems Quarterly*, *36*(1), 157–178. doi:10.2307/41410412

Villinger, K., Wahl, D. R., Boeing, H., Schupp, H. T., & Renner, B. (2019). The effectiveness of app-based mobile interventions on nutrition behaviours and nutrition-related health outcomes: A systematic review and meta-analysis. *Obesity Reviews*, *20*(10), 1465–1484. doi:10.1111/obr.12903 PMID:31353783

Viloria-González, J. (2022). Transmedia Storytelling Applied to Science, Technology and Society. *The Turkish Online Journal of Educational Technology*, *2*(1), 1–10.

Vincent, E., & Kolade, A. (2019). Persuasive communication: Semiotic analysis of "Share-a-Coke" advertising campaign. *World Journal of Innovative Research*, *7*(2), 1–6.

Viscardi, S., Colicchia, C., & Creazza, A. (2023). Circular economy and food waste in supply chains: A literature review. *International Journal of Logistics*, *26*(5), 589–614. doi:10.1080/13675567.2022.2128095

Vittuari, M., Masotti, M., Iori, E., Falasconi, L., Toschi, T. G., & Segrè, A. (2021). Does the COVID-19 external shock matter on household food waste? The impact of social distancing measures during the lockdown. *Resources, Conservation and Recycling*, *174*, 105815. doi:10.1016/j.resconrec.2021.105815 PMID:36569117

Vlahu-Gjorgievska, E., Mulakaparambil Unnikrishnan, S., & Win, K. T. (2018). mHealth applications: A tool for behaviour change in weight management. *Studies in Health Technology and Informatics*, *252*, 158–163. PMID:30040699

Vredenburg, J., Kapitan, S., Spry, A., & Kemper, J. A. (2020). Brands Taking a Stand: Authentic Brand Activism or Woke Washing? *Journal of Public Policy & Marketing*, *39*(4), 444–460. doi:10.1177/0743915620947359

Vrontis, D., Morea, D., Basile, G., Bonacci, I., & Mazzitelli, A. (2021). Consequences of technology and social innovation on traditional business model. *Technological Forecasting and Social Change*, *170*, 120877. doi:10.1016/j.techfore.2021.120877

Vrontis, D., Thrassou, A., Christofi, M., Shams, R., & Czinkota, M. R. (2020). Cause-related marketing in international business: What works and what does not? *International Marketing Review*, *37*(4), 593–601. doi:10.1108/IMR-05-2019-0144

Vuignier, R. (2016). *Place marketing and place branding: A systematic (and tentatively exhaustive) literature review.* Working Paper de l'IDHEAP, 5/2016.

Wachowski, L., & Wachowski, L. (Creators). (1999-2003). *The Matrix* [Film series]. Warner Bros. Pictures.

Wallace, T. C., Bailey, R. L., Blumberg, J. B., Burton-Freeman, B., Chen, C. O., Crowe-White, K. M., Drewnowski, A., Hooshmand, S., Johnson, E., Lewis, R., Murray, R., Shapses, S. A., & Wang, D. D. (2020). Fruits, vegetables, and health: A comprehensive narrative, umbrella review of the science and recommendations for enhanced public policy to improve intake. *Critical Reviews in Food Science and Nutrition*, *60*(13), 2174–2211. doi:10.1080/10408398.2019.1632258 PMID:31267783

Walton, G. M., & Brady, S. T. (2017). The Many Questions of Belonging. In Andrew J. Elliot, Carol S. Dweck, and David S. Yeager (Eds.), Handbook of Competence and Motivation: Theory and Application (2end ed.) (pp. 272–293). Guilford Publications.

Wang, C. J. (2022). Exploring the Mechanisms Linking Transformational Leadership, Perceived Organizational Support, Creativity, and Performance in Hospitality: The Mediating Role of Affective Organizational Commitment. *Behavioral Sciences (Basel, Switzerland)*, *12*(10), 406. doi:10.3390/bs12100406 PMID:36285975

Wang, G., Liu, D., & Wang, X. (2011). Effects of perceived organizational support and guanxi on salesperson performance: The mediation of customer need knowledge. *Frontiers of Business Research in China*, *5*(3), 422–435. doi:10.100711782-011-0138-z

Wang, M. F., He, Q., Liu, Z., Du, Y. L., Wu, C., Lang, H. J., & Du, J. (2022). The relationship between perceived organizational support and insomnia in Chinese nurses: The Serial multiple mediation analysis. *Frontiers in Psychology*, *13*, 1026317. doi:10.3389/fpsyg.2022.1026317 PMID:36591078

Wang, Q., & Wang, C. (2020). Reducing turnover intention: Perceived organizational support for frontline employees. *Frontiers of Business Research in China*, *14*(1), 1–16. doi:10.118611782-020-00074-6

Wang, T., Fan, L., Zheng, X., Wang, W., Liang, J., An, K., Mei, J., & Lei, J. (2021). The impact of gamification-induced Users' feelings on the continued use of mHealth apps: A structural equation model with the self-determination theory approach. *Journal of Medical Internet Research*, *23*(8), e24546. doi:10.2196/24546 PMID:34387550

Wang, Y., Ki, E.-J., & Kim, Y. (2017). Exploring the perceptual and behavioral outcomes of public engagement on mobile phones and social media. *International Journal of Strategic Communication*, *11*(2), 133–147. doi:10.1080/1553118X.2017.1280497

Wang, Y., Zhu, Q., Krikke, H., & Hazen, B. (2020). How product and process knowledge enable consumer switching to remanufactured laptop computers in circular economy. *Technological Forecasting and Social Change*, *161*, 120275. doi:10.1016/j.techfore.2020.120275

Waters, R. D. (2008). Applying relationship management theory to the fundraising process for individual donors. *Journal of Communication Management (London)*, *12*(1), 73–87. doi:10.1108/13632540810854244

Waters, R. D., Burnett, E., Lamm, A., & Lucas, J. (2009). Engaging stakeholders through social media: How nonprofit organizations are using Facebook. *Public Relations Review*, *35*(2), 102–106. doi:10.1016/j.pubrev.2009.01.006

Wayne, S. J., Shore, L. M., Bommer, W. H., & Tetrick, L. E. (2002). The role of fair treatment and rewards in perceptions of organizational support and leader-member exchange. *The Journal of Applied Psychology*, *87*(3), 590–598. doi:10.1037/0021-9010.87.3.590 PMID:12090617

Wayne, S. J., Shore, L. M., & Liden, R. C. (1997). Perceived organizational support and leader-member exchange: A social exchange perspective. *Academy of Management Journal*, *40*(1), 82–111. doi:10.2307/257021

Webber, S. S., Bishop, K., & O'Neill, R. (2012). Trust repair: The impact of perceived organisational support and issue-selling. *Journal of Management Development*, *31*(7), 724–737. doi:10.1108/02621711211243917

Werthner, H., & Ricci, F. (2018). Digitalisation challenges and opportunities for nonprofit organisations. *Nonprofit Management & Leadership*, *28*(1), 5–18.

Whittemore, R., & Knafl, K. (2005). The integrative review: Updated methodology. *Journal of Advanced Nursing*, *52*(5), 546–553. doi:10.1111/j.1365-2648.2005.03621.x PMID:16268861

Woldaregay, A. Z., Issom, D. Z., Henriksen, A., Marttila, H., Mikalsen, M., Pfuhl, G., Sato, K., Lovis, C., & Hartvigsen, G. (2018). Motivational Factors for User Engagement with mHealth Apps. In pHealth, 249, 151–157.

Wood, D. (1991). Corporate Social Performance Revisited. *Academy of Management Review*, *16*(4), 691–718. doi:10.2307/258977

World Economic Forum (WEF). (2020). *Systemic Racism - 5 ways intersectionality affects diversity and inclusion at work*. WEF. https://www.weforum.org/agenda/2020/07/diversity-inclusion-equality-intersectionality/

Wymer, W., Knowles, P., & Gomes, R. (2006). *Non-profit Marketing – Marketing Management for Charitable and Nongovernmental Organizations*. Sage Publications.

Xu, W., & Saxton, G. D. (2019). Does stakeholder engagement pay off on social media? A social capital perspective. *Nonprofit and Voluntary Sector Quarterly*, *48*(1), 28–49. doi:10.1177/0899764018791267

Yalçin, Z., & Canoğlu, M. (2021). Social Media Marketing Effectiveness of Non-Profit Organizations: An Analysis on Environmentalist Organizations. *OPUS International Journal of Society Researches, 18*, 1136-1163.

Yalcin, N., & Kose, U. (2011). What is search engine Optimisation: SEO. *Procedia: Social and Behavioral Sciences*, *9*, 487–493. doi:10.1016/j.sbspro.2010.12.185

Yang, H., van Rijn, M. B., & Sanders, K. (2020). Perceived organizational support and knowledge sharing: Employees' self-construal matters. *International Journal of Human Resource Management*, *31*(17), 2217–2237. doi:10.1080/09585192.2018.1443956

Yang, Y., & Zhai, P. (2022). Click-through rate prediction in online advertising: A literature review. *Information Processing & Management*, *59*(2), 102853. doi:10.1016/j.ipm.2021.102853

Yesiloglu, S. (2021). The rise of influencers and influencer marketing. In *Influencer Marketing: Building Brand Communities and Engagement*. Routledge.

Younan, M., Houssein, E. H., Elhoseny, M., & Ali, A. A. (2020). Challenges and recommended technologies for the industrial internet of things: A comprehensive review. *Measurement*, *151*, 107198. doi:10.1016/j.measurement.2019.107198

Zagenczyk, T. J., Purvis, R. L., Cruz, K. S., Thoroughgood, C. N., & Sawyer, K. B. (2021). Context and social exchange: Perceived ethical climate strengthens the relationships between perceived organizational support and organizational identification and commitment. *International Journal of Human Resource Management*, *32*(22), 4752–4771. doi:10.1080/09585192.2019.1706618

Zagenczyk, T. J., Scott, K. D., Gibney, R., Murrell, A. J., & Thatcher, J. B. (2010). Social influence and perceived organizational support: A social networks analysis. *Organizational Behavior and Human Decision Processes*, *111*(2), 127–138. doi:10.1016/j.obhdp.2009.11.004

Zahay, D., & Griffin, A. (2019). Digital Marketing for nonprofits: Challenges and opportunities. *Journal of Nonprofit & Public Sector Marketing*, *31*(1), 1–14.

Zaluczkowska, A. (2018). *Red Branch Heroes – Writing with my Audiences*. Doctoral thesis, Leeds Beckett University.

Zenker, S., Braun, E., & Petersen, S. (2017). Branding the destination versus the place: The effects of brand complexity and identification for residents and visitors. *Tourism Management*, *58*, 15–27. doi:10.1016/j.tourman.2016.10.008

Zepeda, L., & Balaine, L. (2017). Consumers' perceptions of food waste: A pilot study of US students. *International Journal of Consumer Studies*, *41*(6), 627–637. doi:10.1111/ijcs.12376

Zhang, D. (2022). *Environmental regulation, green innovation, and export product quality*. Elsevier. doi:10.1016/j.irfa.2022.102311

Zhang, L. (2020). An institutional approach to gender diversity and firm performance. *Organization Science*, *31*(2), 245–534. doi:10.1287/orsc.2019.1297

Zhang, Y., Zhou, Y., Liu, Y., & Xiao, Z. (2023). Research on the Influencing Mechanism of the Effect of Brands' Sustainable Behaviors on Consumer Attitudes: An Empirical Study on Clothing Brands. *Sustainability (Basel)*, *15*(3), 2351. doi:10.3390u15032351

Zhou, L., Bao, J., Watzlaf, V., & Parmanto, B. (2019). Barriers to and Facilitators of the Use of Mobile Health Apps from a Security Perspective: Mixed-Methods Study. *JMIR mHealth and uHealth*, *7*(4), e11223. doi:10.2196/11223 PMID:30990458

Zhou, Y., Su, Y., Chen, T., Huang, Z., Gall, H. C., & Panichella, S. (2020). User review-based change file localization for mobile applications. *IEEE Transactions on Software Engineering*, *47*(12), 2755–2770. doi:10.1109/TSE.2020.2967383

Zorn, T. E., Flanagin, A. J., & Shoham, M. D. (2011). Institutional and non-institutional influences on information and communication technology adoption and use among non-profit organizations. *Human Communication Research*, *37*(2), 1–33. doi:10.1111/j.1468-2958.2010.01387.x

Zou, X., Liu, S., Li, J., Chen, W., Ye, J., Yang, Y., Zhou, F., & Ling, L. (2021). Factors associated with healthcare workers' insomnia symptoms and fatigue in the fight against COVID-19, and the role of organizational support. *Frontiers in Psychiatry*, *12*, 652717. doi:10.3389/fpsyt.2021.652717 PMID:33841214

About the Contributors

Inês Pereira is a Marketing and Brand manager professor at ISCAP, from Polytechnic of Porto, with expertise in branding, social marketing and corporate social responsibility. Inês has edited books, published chapters and papers in journals and international congresses with referee. She has also organized 2 international congresses on social and non profit marketing. She is the director of Business Communication Degree and Post-graduation on Management and direction of Health care institutions.

Paulo Botelho Pires received his PhD in Management and has a master's degree in marketing.

José Duarte da Rocha Santos received his PhD in Management from Vigo University. He also holds MSc in Marketing and a bachelor's degree in Business Sciences. Between 1987 and 2002, he played various roles in sales, marketing, and management of companies in the information technology sector. From 2003 to 2018, he performed the functions of a management and marketing consultant. Since 1999, he has been a professor in higher education in Portugal in the fields of management and marketing. He is currently a marketing professor at the Accounting and Business School of the Polytechnic of Porto (ISCAP/P.PORTO). He is also a senior researcher at the CEOS.PP - Centre for Organizational and Social Studies of the Polytechnic of Porto, Portugal. His principal research area is customer relationship management through digital marketing.

***

Maica Amador Marrero (1998) is a dedicated doctoral student in Management at the University of Las Palmas de Gran Canaria. Her academic background encompasses a comprehensive study of fashion design and a master's in marketing and international trade. Additionally, she has received specialized training in urban commerce management, complemented by a range of courses in innovation and digitalization. Her research intends to focus on Marketing and Fashion Management while also gaining proficiency in Digital Marketing and Videogame Management.

Nuno Tiago Baptista holds a PhD in Marketing and Strategy. He is an Assistant Professor at the Escola Superior de Comunicação Social from Instituto Politécnico de Lisboa, Assistant Professor at Universidade Lusíada, and an integrated researcher at COMEGI. He has publications in leading academic journals, and has been awarded several awards of scientific merit. His main research interests include social marketing, tourism marketing, digital marketing and business strategy.

Anna Carolina Boechat completed her PhD in Strategic Communication with the highest grade at University NOVA of Lisbon, and has worked as an Assistant Professor at prestigious Portuguese institutions such as IADE, University NOVA of Lisbon, Lusíada University of Lisbon, and the Portuguese Catholic University. She is also Marketing & Communication Scientific and Pedagogical Coordinator at IADE, Academic Supervisor, and participates in national and international scientific events as a speaker/ conferencist. She develops Business Consulting projects in the areas of Marketing and Strategic Communication and is specialized in the following topics: Marketing, Strategic Marketing, Sports Marketing, Advertising, Communication, Strategic Communication, Project Management, Consumer Psychology, Market Research, Brand Management, and Corporate Social Responsibility. As an Integrated Researcher at UNIDCOM/IADE, Anna Carolina Boechat has been developing projects and publications in the areas of Strategic Communication, Marketing, Brands, Consumer Behavior, Corporate Social Responsibility, Sustainability, and Metaverse. Complementing the academic spectrum, she has over 10 years of exclusive professional experience in Marketing and Communication, having contributed to companies in different markets, assuming various roles over time.

Sol Castellanos Pérez Lasala was born in Buenos Aires, Argentina. She has a degree in Social Communication and is currently finishing her master's in Marketing and International Trade at the University of Las Palmas de Gran Canaria. She has acquired experience and knowledge in multiple areas such as psychology and network metrics. Furthermore, she developed a marketing strategy, alongside some of her classmates at university, for an NGO in Rosario, Argentina, helping it boost its digital capacities and awareness. Her passion for social marketing and the opportunity to work with her master's tutor has made it possible to co-author a chapter for an upcoming social marketing textbook.

Fainos Chokera is a lecturer in the department of information and marketing sciences.

Jamie Coles is an acclaimed transmedia storyteller, with expertise spanning from video production for global entities such as FC Barcelona and MotoGP, to sustainable and inclusive narratives. Recognized with awards like the Royal Television Society award, Jamie's work has been spotlighted at The Seattle Transmedia and Independent Film Festival. Beyond entertainment, he's contributed to sustainability dialogues, notably as a communication advisor for the Global Centre on Adaptation and European Peatlands Initiative, with Bax & Company, as well as research projects into gender inclusion with More Than Equal and digital literacy inclusion with the University of Bolton.

Catarina Delgado, Ph.D., is an assistant professor at the Faculty of Economics, University of Porto (FEP.UP), and a researcher at CEF.UP and LIAAD/ INESC TEC. Her research interests are primarily in the areas of responsible consumers, responsible e-commerce, sustainable and responsible supply chains, ecotourism, ESG/ CSR disclosure, quality management/ kaizen/ lean six sigma, and scientometrics. Her teaching focus is on Operations and Logistics (operations management, supply chain management, operational research), Quality Management and Continuous Improvement (Kaizen, Lean, Six Sigma), and Social Responsibility and Sustainability Reporting. Author of the book "Supply Chain Social Sustainability for Manufacturing" (Springer, 2020), her academic work has been published in several leading international scientific journals, such as Journal of Cleaner Production, International Journal of Production Economics, Sustainability, Journal of Manufacturing Technology Management, JASIST, Informetrics, Scientometrics, and Social Responsibility Journal.

Edna Denga is a graduate student at the American University of Nigeria.

Gonzalo Díaz Meneses (1966) is a devoted and interdisciplinary lecturer of Marketing at Las Palmas of Gran Canaria University (Spain). He earned his PhD degree in Marketing (ULPGC), MSc in Market Research (UNED), MBA (EAE & UB), MSc in Digital Marketing (UOC), diploma in Datamining (UNED), degrees in Politics and Sociology (UCM) and Geography and History (UCM). His research has focused on marketing, having more than 100 scientific publications in the lines of social marketing, consumer behaviour and tourism. He has published in Annals of Tourism Research, International Journal of Contemporary Hospitality Management and Journal of Destination Marketing and Management.

Ida Ercsey is a retired associate professor. She received her university degrees from the Karl Marx University of Economic Sciences (Master's degree in Transportation) and the Budapest University of Economic Sciences (Part-time Postgraduate Master's degree in Marketing). Her PhD research focused on the consumer evaluation in the public utility services. Between 1991 and 2022 she actively participated in the higher education at the Széchenyi István University in Győr. Between 2014 and 2020 she was Head of Department of Marketing and Management at the Széchenyi István University. She works as the Chairman of the Supervisory Board in the Association for Marketing Education and Research. Since 2021, she has also chaired the Public Service and Nonprofit Marketing Committee of the Hungarian Academy of Sciences. She has nearly 150 scientific publications. Her research interests include non-business marketing, co-creation behaviour, consumer value, mobile health applications, transformative services, subjective quality of life.

Gil Gil Inácio is a marketing professional with a Bachelor's degree in Marketing and currently undertaking a Master's in Marketing and Communication. With a keen understanding of consumer behavior, deep appreciation for cutting-edge technology and strategy, is currently involved in a technology transfer project, has a passion for innovation and bridging the gap between research and practical application. When not at work, Gil loves to switch off by enjoying nature, surfing and capturing the moment through photography.

Deeba Hasan is a Dental Surgeon and Doctoral Scholar at IIT Madras in Human Resource Management & Organizational Behavior. Her areas of interest are job-connectedness, sleep quality and emotion regulation. She bagged a gold medal in Orthodontics in dental college, had a CGPA of 10 for her M.Phil dissertation and a CGPA of 9.55 at IIT Madras during her coursework. She has completed online certificate courses from Harvard University, King's College London, Georgetown University, University of Sheffield, and University of Nottingham. She has published journal papers and book chapters during her Ph.D. journey and has also presented papers at prestigious international conferences like The Indian Academy of Management, IISc Conference- COSMAR, and The Oxford Conference Series held at Oxford University, UK, where she also chaired a session. In 2022, she was selected for the Harvard Project for Asian and International Relations from among applicants across sixty countries, which enabled her to participate in an open forum with global leaders like Presidents and Prime Ministers of nations on international issues.

T. J. Kamalanabhan received his M.Phil. (Psychology) in 1983 and Ph.D. (Organizational Psychology) in 1987 from the University of Madras. He has been published extensively in international and national journals and conferences and is a member of the Indian Society for Technical Education, Editorial Board Member for Journal of Psychometry, Member of the Indian Academy of Applied Psychology, and Editorial board member for the Journal of Human Resource Development Review. He was awarded the DAAD Fellowship in 1998, the Fulbright Fellowship in 2002, and the Erasmus Mundus Teaching Fellowship in 2010, His research interests include Industrial Psychology, Human Resource Management, and Organizational Behavior.

Veronika Keller received her PhD in 2010 from the Doctoral School of Regional and Economic Sciences at Széchenyi István University. Since 2006 she has been teaching marketing communication, international marketing and marketing research at the University of Győr, currently as an associate professor at the Department of Corporate Leadership and Marketing. She is a member of the Board of the Association for Marketing Education and Research. She has published more than 120 papers, 36 of which are in English as book chapters, articles and conference papers. Her research interests include health marketing and the challenges of digital marketing.

Márcia Siqueira Costa Marques is an accomplished academic with a PhD in Communication and Semiotics from PUC-SP (Pontifical Catholic University of São Paulo). Her research interests lie in the intersection of media, technology, and design, with a focus on how these fields interact to shape modern communication. She is particularly interested in exploring the ways in which new technologies are changing the way we consume and produce media, to contribute to advance understanding of how these fields are evolving and transforming our world. She is also a co-leader of the Design and Convergence Group at the Belas Artes University Center in São Paulo, where she collaborates with other researchers and designers to explore the latest developments in media and technology.

Ascensão Braga is currenctly professor in Polytechnic of Guarda, he had a PhD in Management from Évora University (from 2005), a Master in Management from Beira Interior University and a degree in Economy from Coimbra University. He research in Information Society, Management; and Marketing.

Hugo Mendes is a Marketing Major, specializing in Marketing and Communication.

Edward Mudzimba is a lecturer in the Department of Information and Marketing Sciences

Teresa Paiva is a Professor in Management and Marketing at Guarda Polytechnic Institute (IPG). Has a PhD in Management, specialising in Marketing (Consumer Behaviour area). Holds a master's degree in Business Sciences, specialising in Strategic Management and Business Development and a degree in Economics, and a post-graduation course in Incubators, accelerators, and entrepreneurial development centres Direction by the University of Salamanca, and is a certified trainer of Management and Entrepreneurship. Develops research in Marketing, Innovation and Entrepreneurship with several scientific and technical publications, develops activity in trends and product innovation, and works as a consultant for product innovation development. Has experience coordinating several scientific and applied research projects, co-financed by national and/or European funds and participates in European co-financed projects. Has been an evaluator of projects that are candidates for funding programs and business plans, as well as a scientific reviewer, tutor and jury of master and doctoral theses.

Darina Rojíková is a researcher at the Research and Innovation Center at the Faculty of Economics with a interest in urban and regional topics. She orients her research on the selected aspects of urban and regional development, territorial development of peripheral areas, strategic planning of territorial development, place branding, democracy and public policy. She is the co-author of several papers, including scientific articles, chapters, monographs. She is involved in solving domestic and foreign research projects and projects for practice.

Fábio Shimabukuro Sandes is an Assistant Professor of Marketing at Universidade Lusófona and he has complete his Ph.D. in 2020 in Marketing at Fundação Getulio Vargas EAESP, a Brazilian leading business school with triple-crown international accreditation (AACSB, EFMD, AMBA). Fabio also holds a MSc in Marketing at the same school. He was a visiting Ph.D. student at Fordham University in New York during his thesis research.He has worked as a Marketing practitioner for 15 years, working in multinational companies like The LYCRA® company and Vicunha Textiles, consolidating an executive career in the fashion industry. He has published papers in international peer-reviewed journals and presented papers in the most relevant international conferences in Marketing, such as EMAC, ACR, SCP, and AMA. He is a consumer behavior researcher and uses both qualitative and quantitative research methods. He is particularly interested in online consumer behavior and sustainable consumption practices. Due to his background in the Fashion industry, Fabio is also working with advancing the knowledge of the role of Marketing in this market.

Ricardo Silva has a Master's in Sales Management and with a degree in Management, both ministered by Faculty of Economics of Porto. Currently doing a Specialization in Hospital Administration at National School of Public Health of Nova Lisbon University. Ricardo's fields of interest are Public Health management, Health administration, Health social media and Health Marketing.

Mariana Torgal has a degree in Public Relations and Corporate Communication and is currently finishing her Masters in Communication Sciences, specializing in advertising and marketing. She works in a public relations communication agency, where she is dedicated to press and digital consultancy.

Anna Vaňová is an author and co-author of more than 140 scientific papers (domestic, foreign, scientific monographs, articles in impact and CC journals), published and presented mainly abroad. She has worked and works as a principal investigator and a deputy researcher or team member in more than 60 domestic and foreign research projects in the various fields of spatial development. She actively develops cooperation with practice at national, regional and local level (cooperation at the creation of strategic documents, consultations for local, regional and national authorities, etc.).

Paulo Vieira, is currenctly professor in Polytechnic of Guarda, he had a PhD in Computer Science from Salamanca University (from 2015), a Master in Maths from Lisbon University and a degree in Pure Mathematics from University of Porto. He researchs in Artificial Intelligence, Reasoning and Knowledge representation.

Katarína Vitálišová is an associate professor at the Department of Public Economics and Regional Development of Faculty of Economics, Matej Bel University (EF UMB). She orients her research on the issue of public and local governance, building and maintaining relationships and partnerships between stakeholders, strategic planning of the spatial development and implementation of new approaches in it, including creative and smart cities, places marketing what is represented by more than 130 publications. She is a member of several international expert networks in the field of regional and local development, management and marketing places.

Index

N

O

P

R

S

T

U

V

W

www.ingramcontent.com/pod-product-compliance
Lightning Source LLC
LaVergne TN
LVHW082052011026
849162LV00019B/1468